INDESIGN® CS2
at Your Fingertips

TED LOCASCIO

San Francisco • London

Publisher: Dan Brodnitz

Acquisitions Editor: Bonnie Bills

Developmental Editor: Pete Gaughan

Production Editor: Rachel Gunn

Technical Editor: Jon McFarland

Copyeditor: Liz Welch

Compositor: Happenstance Type-O-Rama

Proofreaders: Nancy Riddiough, Jim Brook

Indexer: Ted Laux

Book Designer: Franz Baumhackl

Cover Designer: Ted LoCascio

Cover Illustrator/Photographer: Getty Images

Copyright © 2005 SYBEX Inc., 1151 Marina Village Parkway, Alameda, CA 94501. World rights reserved. No part of this publication may be stored in a retrieval system, transmitted, or reproduced in any way, including but not limited to photocopy, photograph, magnetic, or other record, without the prior agreement and written permission of the publisher.

Library of Congress Card Number: 2005924335

ISBN: 0-7821-4420-9

SYBEX and the SYBEX logo are either registered trademarks or trademarks of SYBEX Inc. in the United States and/or other countries.

Screen reproductions produced with FullShot 99.

FullShot 99 © 1991-1999 Inbit Incorporated. All rights reserved.
FullShot is a trademark of Inbit Incorporated.

Screen reproductions produced with Collage Complete. Collage Complete is a trademark of Inner Media Inc.

SYBEX is an independent entity and not affiliated with Adobe Systems Incorporated, the publisher of Adobe ® InDesign ® software. This is an independent Sybex publication, not endorsed or sponsored by Adobe Systems Incorporated. Adobe ® and InDesign ® are trade marks of Adobe Systems Incorporated.

TRADEMARKS: SYBEX has attempted throughout this book to distinguish proprietary trademarks from descriptive terms by following the capitalization style used by the manufacturer.

The author and publisher have made their best efforts to prepare this book, and the content is based upon final release software whenever possible. Portions of the manuscript may be based upon pre-release versions supplied by software manufacturer(s). The author and the publisher make no representation or warranties of any kind with regard to the completeness or accuracy of the contents herein and accept no liability of any kind including but not limited to performance, merchantability, fitness for any particular purpose, or any losses or damages of any kind caused or alleged to be caused directly or indirectly from this book.

Manufactured in the United States of America

10 9 8 7 6 5 4 3 2 1

To my wonderful wife, Jill, for her neverending love and support.

Acknowledgments

First and foremost, I must thank everyone at Sybex for making this book possible. Thanks to publisher Dan Brodnitz and acquisitions editor Bonnie Bills for sharing my vision on this project and for being as genuinely enthusiastic about InDesign as I am. Thanks also to Pete Gaughan for helping me develop this title and paying such close attention to the details, and to Jon McFarland for acting as my technical editor and making sure every shortcut, tip, and task is correct.

Special thanks to my copyeditor, Liz Welch, for making this book read as well as it does. I must also thank my production editor, Rachel Gunn, for working with me on the book's schedule and keeping everything on track.

I am forever grateful to my NAPP buddy Al Ward, for referring me to Sybex in the first place. I would also like to thank my good friend Steve Weiss for all of his helpful publishing insight and advice. Special thanks also to the entire KW Media staff and all of the Photoshop World instructors who inspired me to write and teach. I would not be doing this if it had not been for you.

I must also thank Lynda Weinman, Garo Green, Michael Ninness, and the rest of the wonderful staff at Lynda.com for making me a part of their excellent online instructor team.

Loving thanks to my wife Jill for being so patient while I was busy writing this book. Thanks also to Mom, Dad, and Val for being so supportive. I must also thank the Threads for keeping me in the band even though I cancelled several rehearsals in order to meet chapter deadlines: Ladies and gentlemen… Stan Arthur, Michael Hoag, Brian Merrill, and Sonny John Sundstrom (look for us in your nearest CD store cut-out bin).

Thanks to Jeff and Cheryl Morey, publishers of *Nursery Retailer* magazine, for allowing me to use their layouts as example projects. Thanks also to R50 for the use of their logo.

I would also like to thank my cats—Ito, Chloe, Tobias, Spencer (we miss you buddy), and Clinton—for forcing me to take breaks from my writing in order play with them.

And of course, thanks to Adobe for making such great software to write about.

About the Author

Ted LoCascio is a professional graphic designer and an expert in InDesign, Photoshop, Illustrator, and QuarkXPress. He served as senior designer at KW Media and the National Association of Photoshop Professionals (NAPP) for several years, and has created layouts and designs for many successful software training books, videos, and magazines. He has contributed articles to *Photoshop User* magazine and taught at PhotoshopWorld. Ted is also the online video author of *Adobe InDesign CS2 Essential Learning,* available at Lynda.com.

A graphic designer for over ten years, Ted's designs and illustrations have been featured in several national newsstand and trade magazines such as *Photoshop User, Mac Design,* Nikon's *Capture User,* PDIA's *Great Output, AAA Going Places,* and *Florida Trend.* Since 2001, he has used Adobe InDesign to create layouts for magazines, books, and various advertising and marketing materials, including brochures, product packaging, posters and signs, and interactive PDFs.

A Chicago native (born a hopeless Cubs fan) and Columbia College alumnus, Ted relocated to the Tampa Bay area in 1994. He currently resides in Tarpon Springs, Florida, with his wife Jill, and four cats.

When he's not designing, writing books, feeding cats, or dodging hurricanes, he writes and records music with his current rock and roll band, the Threads. A guitar player for over 20 years, Ted has played and recorded with national acts such as Barely Pink (Big Deal records) and Hangtown (Black Dog records). For more info, visit www.tedlukas.com and www.thethreads.us.

Contents

INTRODUCTION	ix

WORKSPACE	1

CHAPTER 1	**Interface Overview**	1
1.1	The Macintosh Interface	2
1.2	The Windows Interface	3
1.3	The Document Window	4
1.4	Interface Objects	5

CHAPTER 2	**Menus**	11
2.1	Menu Overview	12
2.2	InDesign Menu (Mac Only)	13
2.3	File Menu	14
2.4	Edit Menu	16
2.5	Layout Menu	18
2.6	Type Menu	19
2.7	Object Menu	20
2.8	Table Menu	22
2.9	View Menu	23
2.10	Window Menu	25
2.11	Help Menu	26

CHAPTER 3	**InDesign Tools**	27
3.1	Toolbox	28
3.2	Control Bar	29
3.3	Selection Tool	32
3.4	Direct Selection and Position Tools	33
3.5	Pen Tools	34
3.6	Type Tools	35
3.7	Pencil Tools	38
3.8	Line Tool	39
3.9	Frame Tools	40
3.10	Shape Tools	41
3.11	Rotate Tool	42
3.12	Scale Tool	43
3.13	Shear Tool	44
3.14	Free Transform Tool	45
3.15	Eyedropper Tool	46
3.16	Measure Tool	47
3.17	Gradient Tool	48
3.18	Button Tool	49
3.19	Scissors Tool	50
3.20	Hand Tool	51
3.21	Zoom Tool	52
3.22	Other Toolbox Functions	53

CHAPTER 4	**InDesign Palettes**	55
4.1	Organizing Palettes	56
4.2	Customizing Your Workspace	59
4.3	Attributes Palette	60
4.4	Automation Palettes	61
4.5	Color Palette	63
4.6	Gradient Palette	64
4.7	Info Palette	65
4.8	Interactive Palettes	66
4.9	Layers Palette	69
4.10	Links Palette	70
4.11	Object & Layout Palettes	71
4.12	Object Styles Palette	74
4.13	Output Palettes	75
4.14	PageMaker Toolbar	78
4.15	Pages Palette	80
4.16	Stroke Palette	82
4.17	Swatches Palette	83
4.18	Tags Palette	85
4.19	Text Wrap Palette	86
4.20	Transparency Palette	87
4.21	Type and Tables Palettes	88
4.22	Book and Library Palettes	95

CHAPTER 5	**Preferences and Presets**	97
5.1	General Preferences	98
5.2	Type Preferences	99
5.3	Advanced Type Preferences	101
5.4	Composition Preferences	102
5.5	Units & Increments Preferences	103
5.6	Grids Preferences	104
5.7	Guides & Pasteboard Preferences	105

5.8	Dictionary Preferences	106
5.9	Spelling Preferences	108
5.10	Autocorrect Preferences	109
5.11	Story Editor Display Preferences	110
5.12	Display Performance Preferences	111
5.13	Appearance of Black Preferences	112
5.14	File Handling Preferences	113
5.15	Document Presets	114
5.16	Print Presets	115
5.17	Adobe PDF Presets	116
5.18	Configure Plug-ins	117
5.19	Keyboard Shortcuts	118

PAGE BUILDING 119

CHAPTER 6 Creating and Managing Documents 119

6.1	Starting a New Document	120
6.2	Saving Document Presets	121
6.3	Opening InDesign Documents	122
6.4	Opening PageMaker and QuarkXPress Documents	124
6.5	Save vs. Save As	125
6.6	Saving Backward with INX Export	126
6.7	Saving Files for Use with InCopy	127
6.8	Adding, Arranging, and Deleting Pages	128
6.9	Creating Multipage Spreads and Master Pages	130
6.10	Targeting vs. Selecting Pages	131
6.11	Creating Master Pages	132
6.12	Converting Document Pages to Master Pages	133
6.13	Applying Master Pages	134
6.14	Deleting Master Pages	135
6.15	Creating and Applying Parent/Child Master Pages	136
6.16	Overriding Master Page Items	137
6.17	Adding Page Numbers to Sections	138
6.18	Adjusting Ruler Guides	139
6.19	Adjusting Margin and Column Guides	140
6.20	Aligning to Baseline Grid	141
6.21	Snapping to Document Grid	142

CHAPTER 7 Frames and Shapes 143

7.1	Frame/Shape Overview	144
7.2	Selection Tool vs. Direct Selection Tool	148
7.3	Selecting Multiple Objects	150
7.4	Selecting Type	151
7.5	Drawing Rectangles, Ellipses, and Polygons	152
7.6	Drawing Custom Shapes	153
7.7	Drawing Freeform Shapes	154
7.8	Modifying Paths and Frames	155
7.9	Nesting Objects	157
7.10	Filling with Solid and Transparent Colors	160
7.11	Filling with Gradients	161
7.12	Filling Text	162
7.13	Stroking Frames, Shapes, and Paths	164
7.14	Stroking Text	166
7.15	Aligning Strokes	167
7.16	Applying Stroked Path Start and End Styles	169
7.17	Saving and Applying Custom Strokes	171
7.18	Applying Gap Color to Open Stroke Styles	172
7.19	Applying Corner Effects	174
7.20	Applying and Editing Compound Paths	175
7.21	Creating Custom Shapes with Pathfinder	176

CHAPTER 8 Manipulating Objects 177

8.1	Moving Objects	178
8.2	Resizing Objects	180
8.3	Rotating Objects	182
8.4	Flipping Objects	184
8.5	Shearing Objects	186
8.6	Grouping and Ungrouping Objects	188
8.7	Selecting Objects within a Group	189
8.8	Nesting Grouped Objects	191
8.9	Stacking, Arranging, and Locking Objects	192
8.10	Duplicating Objects	194
8.11	Aligning Objects	196
8.12	Distributing Objects	197
8.13	Saving Objects to a Library	199
8.14	Deleting Objects	201

8.15	Creating and Naming a New Layer	202
8.16	Placing Objects on Layers	203
8.17	Enabling Layout Adjustment	204

TYPOGRAPHY 207

CHAPTER 9 Working with Text 207

9.1	Text Frame Options	208
9.2	Threading and Unthreading Text Frames	212
9.3	Importing Text	214
9.4	Importing Tagged and ASCII Text	216
9.5	Importing XML	218
9.6	Flowing Text	219
9.7	Filling with Placeholder Text	220
9.8	Editing Using the Story Editor	221
9.9	Changing Case	222
9.10	Check Spelling	223
9.11	Editing the Dictionary	225
9.12	Using the Dictionary with Foreign Languages	226
9.13	Font Overview	227
9.14	Find/Replace Missing Fonts	228
9.15	Applying Find/Change	229

CHAPTER 10 Formatting 231

10.1	Kerning and Tracking	232
10.2	Scaling and Skewing Type	234
10.3	Adjusting Leading and Baseline Shift	236
10.4	Underline and Strikethrough	238
10.5	Copy/Paste Text Formatting	240
10.6	Formatting Paragraphs	241
10.7	Creating Drop Caps	245
10.8	Applying Keep Options	246
10.9	Creating Hanging Indents and Punctuation	248
10.10	Change/Apply Hyphenation	251
10.11	Change/Apply Justification	253
10.12	Bullets and Numbering	255
10.13	Setting Tabs	257
10.14	Inserting Special Characters	259
10.15	Inserting Footnotes	261

CHAPTER 11 Styles 263

11.1	Creating and Applying Character Styles	264
11.2	Creating and Applying Paragraph Styles	266
11.3	Creating and Applying Parent/Child Styles	268
11.4	Creating and Applying Nested Styles	269
11.5	Creating and Applying Object Styles	270
11.6	Editing and Deleting Styles	273
11.7	Importing Styles	276

GRAPHICS 277

CHAPTER 12 Placed Images 277

12.1	Importing a Graphic Image	278
12.2	Setting Import Options	280
12.3	Object Layer Options and Placed PSDs	283
12.4	Copying to and from Adobe Illustrator	286
12.5	Resizing Placed Images	288
12.6	Updating Missing and Modified Links	290
12.7	Emdedding Images	291
12.8	Object-Level Display Settings	292
12.9	Applying and Editing a Photoshop Clipping Path	293
12.10	Creating and Editing an InDesign Clipping Path	295

CHAPTER 13 Combining Graphics with Text 297

13.1	Placing and Editing Text Wraps	298
13.2	Converting Text to Outlines	302
13.3	Creating and Editing Type on a Path	303
13.4	Creating Paragraph Rules	306
13.5	Creating a New Table	307
13.6	Making Table Selections	309
13.7	Adding and Deleting Rows and Columns	310
13.8	Merging and Splitting Cells	313
13.9	Adjusting Cell Spacing and Alignment	315
13.10	Resizing Tables	316
13.11	Setting Table Borders, Strokes, and Fills	319
13.12	Creating and Editing Table Headers and Footers	322
13.13	Importing Tables from Microsoft Word or Excel	324

COLOR 325

CHAPTER 14 Color and Transparency 325
- 14.1 Using Color Settings 326
- 14.2 Color-Managing Imported Graphics 327
- 14.3 Using Proof Setup for Soft Proofing 328
- 14.4 Creating and Saving Mixed-Ink Swatches and Groups 329
- 14.5 Accessing Colors Stored in Libraries 331
- 14.6 Converting Spot Colors to Process 332
- 14.7 Importing Colors from Other Documents 333
- 14.8 Changing an Object's Opacity Level 334
- 14.9 Applying Blend Modes 335
- 14.10 Adding Drop Shadows 336
- 14.11 Feathering 338
- 14.12 Importing Transparent TIFFs 339

OUTPUT 341

CHAPTER 15 Preflighting and Packaging 341
- 15.1 Preflighting Fonts 342
- 15.2 Preflighting Links and Images 343
- 15.3 Preflighting Colors and Inks 344
- 15.4 Preflighting Print Settings 345
- 15.5 Packaging 346
- 15.6 Packaging for GoLive 347

CHAPTER 16 Printing 349
- 16.1 Printing a Document 350
- 16.2 Creating Transparency Flattener Presets 359
- 16.3 Creating and Assigning Trap Presets 360

CHAPTER 17 Exporting 361
- 17.1 Exporting as Adobe PDF 362
- 17.2 Embedding PDF Hyperlinks 370
- 17.3 Embedding Movies and Sound in PDFs 372
- 17.4 Exporting as EPS 374
- 17.5 Exporting as JPEG 376
- 17.6 Exporting as XML 377

CHAPTER 18 Books and Other Large Documents 379
- 18.1 Creating a New Book File 380
- 18.2 Synchronizing Book Chapters 381
- 18.3 Page Numbering across Book Documents 382
- 18.4 Building a Table of Contents 383
- 18.5 Creating and Saving a TOC Style 384
- 18.6 Building an Index 385
- 18.7 Preflighting, Printing, and Exporting Books 388

INDEX 389

Introduction

Since the dawn of desktop publishing, the printing industry has come to rely on page layout applications such as QuarkXPress and Adobe PageMaker. When Adobe first introduced InDesign, it didn't take long for everyone in the industry to recognize it as a serious alternative. It soon became apparent that this is not just another page layout program.

Indeed, InDesign is truly a designer's tool. The familiar Adobe interface alone is enough to set it apart from other "page layout" applications and to inspire graphic designers everywhere to expand their print design horizons. Now, with the release of CS2, InDesigners can push their creativity through the roof with all of its added functionality. New features include the ability to save and apply object formatting with Object Styles, as well as the ability to control PSD and PDF layer visibility through Object Layer Options, and the ability to save and reuse page objects with InDesign Snippets. There is also better integration with the other Creative Suite 2 applications through Adobe Bridge.

What also sets InDesign apart is that it is not solely used for print design. Graphic designers have started to grow increasingly dependent on InDesign's interactive PDF features, including the ability to embed hyperlinks, bookmarks, rollover buttons, sound, and video. This isn't page layout—this is cutting-edge new media!

No matter how you are using InDesign CS2, there is one thing you can be sure of: this is by far the coolest "page layout" program in existence.

Who Should Use This Book

If you are reading this, most likely you are standing in a bookstore or a library, surrounded by several other books about InDesign CS2, trying to select the one that will best suit your needs. If you are looking for a complete resource for InDesign CS2— one that will help you learn new skills and improve your existing ones—you have chosen the right book.

When you're faced with a particular job, would you like to be able to find out quickly how to accomplish just that task? Would you like to know the shortcuts and secrets that help you work faster and better in InDesign? If you are a designer from a non-print field, looking for a guidebook to help you learn InDesign, then this is one you need.

This is the book for you if you're a developer who knows InDesign but could use a quick reference to find a particular and specific task, or to polish up on the new features in InDesign CS2.

The concept behind *InDesign CS2 at Your Fingertips* is to provide InDesign users with a well-organized, comprehensive, and visual resource. Regardless of your skill level, this book provides immediate access to all of the program's features.

Beginning If you are new to InDesign, use this book to get acquainted with the InDesign interface and get step-by-step instruction in fundamental tasks so that you can get right to work on your first few layouts.

Intermediate After you master basic InDesign skills, you can use this book to discover shortcuts and more efficient ways of finishing routine tasks. You can use it as a springboard to specialize your skills for particular uses such as designing publications and marketing materials, creating interactive PDFs, and re-creating your layouts for use on the Web.

Advanced InDesign has undergone a lot of changes in the last few years, and staying ahead of the curve is never easy. This book is a comprehensive reference manual, with thorough cross-referencing to help you find the detailed information you need to stay up-to-date and pick up a few tricks and tips that you might not have realized.

How This Book Is Organized: A Task-Based Reference

When you're working in InDesign CS2, you're trying to *do* something. That's why *InDesign CS2 at Your Fingertips* is organized around the many tasks you can perform. Each section is broken down into several common tasks, where we provide you with a simple explanation of how to perform each one.

Workspace Chapters 1–5 introduce you to the InDesign CS2 interface and detail all the different parts you will be using. Here you will find information about the document window, menus, tools, palettes, preferences, and presets.

Page Building Chapters 6–8 provide the skills that every InDesign user needs to master the core document creation tools and techniques. Here you will learn how to create documents, utilize master pages, and work with objects.

Typography Chapters 9–11 deal with the specific issues involved in adding text to your InDesign documents. Here you will find information about importing and formatting text, and using styles.

Graphics Chapters 12 and 13 teach you how to most effectively place, position, and combine graphics with text in your layouts.

Color Chapter 14 reveals specific skills related to adding and editing color in your documents. Utilizing color management, working with spot colors and color libraries, and applying transparency effects are all covered in this section.

Output Chapters 15–18 lay out the processes you'll need to preflight, package, print, and export your InDesign documents, no matter what format or medium you use. Here you will find information about creating transparency flattener presets, trap presets, exporting PDFs, packaging for GoLive, and using InDesign's book features.

InDesign CS2 at Your Fingertips also supplies keyboard shortcuts using both operating systems' conventions. In the margins, you'll see both the Windows and Macintosh versions, on separate lines if they differ. In text, we've run them together a bit but still provide you with both: Command+Option/Ctrl+Alt means the Command and Option keys on a Mac, the Ctrl and Alt keys in Windows.

Using This Book

Each section in this book is organized around the idea of letting you quickly scan the information to find the page that has what you need or send you to another section in the book to look there. Rather than burying cross-references and keyboard shortcuts in the text, we placed these in their own column, along with general tips and warnings relevant to the topic at hand.

In addition, this book makes extensive use of lettered "callout" labels on the figures to help you identify the various parts of the InDesign CS2 interface and how they work. These are generally integrated with step-by-step instructions or bulleted lists, which refer to particular dialogs or palettes, with the callouts explaining how to set the various options.

Numbered section head Each new section in a chapter starts at the top of a page and is numbered for quick reference.

Quick cross-references Each topic points you to other sections that relate to the subject or offer alternative or more detailed information.

Keyboard shortcuts We provide the keyboard commands relevant to the section's subject.

Tips Additional notes and warnings are included about the task or tool presented in the section.

Callouts Hundreds of images in the book provide detailed labeling to eliminate the guesswork of figuring out how the InDesign interface works.

Sidebars You'll find additional information that can be applied to the tasks presented in the chapter.

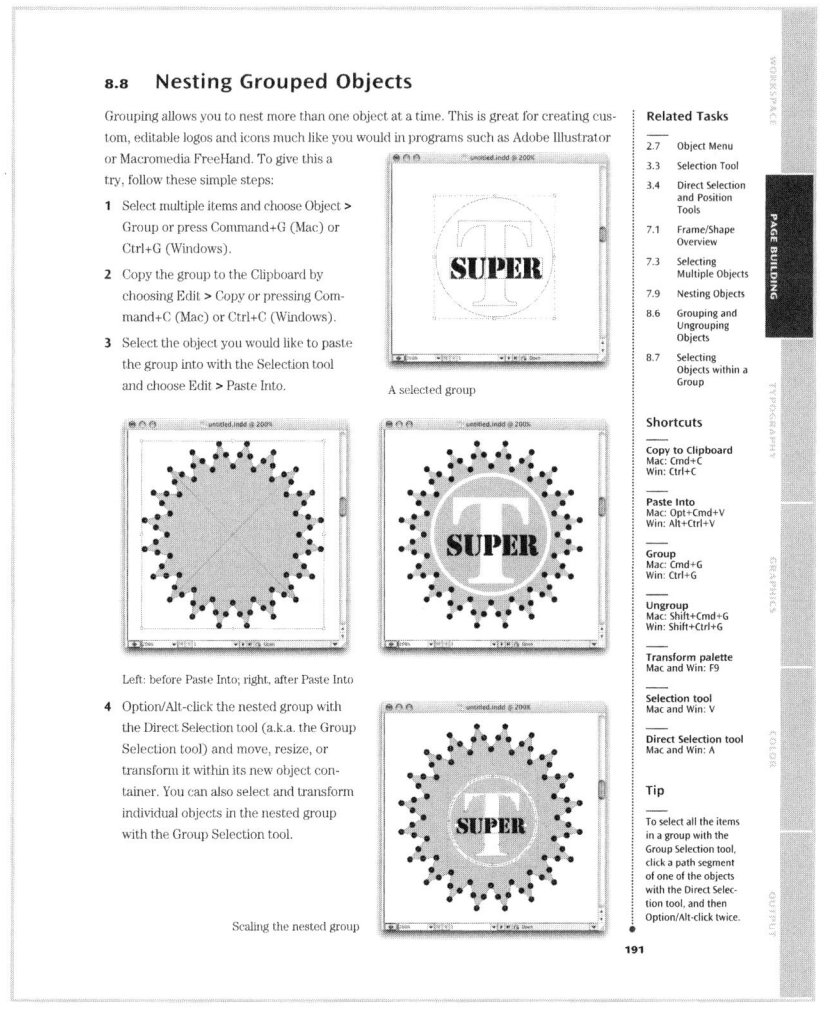

How to Contact the Author

Sybex strives to keep you supplied with the latest tools and information you need for your work. Please check their website at www.sybex.com for additional content and updates that supplement this book. Enter the book's ISBN—4420—in the Search box (or type **indesign and fingertips**), and click Go to get to the book's update page.

Ted LoCascio is always happy to answer any questions that you may have about InDesign CS2. If you can't find the answer in this book, please e-mail your question to indesignquestions@knology.net.

CHAPTER **1**

Interface Overview

GETTING FAMILIAR WITH YOUR new work area (also known as the interface) is the best place to start when learning any new software program. If you're launching InDesign for the first time, you may not know where to start or what to click first. The controls, menus, palettes, and general look of the program are indeed all different from other page layout programs, such as Quark's QuarkXPress or Adobe PageMaker. However, once you become familiar with this new environment, you'll feel right at home with InDesign CS2.

If you're a designer who is familiar with the other programs included in Adobe's Creative Suite, such as Photoshop or Illustrator, then you may already be ahead of the game when it comes to learning InDesign. All three programs share common traits, including interface similarities, keyboard shortcuts, and controls. But even if you've never used Photoshop or Illustrator and you're totally new to the general look and feel of Adobe's software, don't worry; this first chapter will put you in the driver's seat and get you up to speed with InDesign's interface.

- 1.1 **The Macintosh interface**
- 1.2 **The Windows interface**
- 1.3 **The document window**
- 1.4 **Interface objects**

1.1 The Macintosh Interface

Related Tasks

1.3 The Document Window
2.1 Menu Overview
3.1 Toolbox
3.2 Control Bar
4.1 Organizing Palettes

Shortcuts

Minimize window
Mac: Command+M

Show/hide all controls
Mac: Tab

Show/hide all controls except Toolbox and Control bar
Mac: Shift+Tab

Tip

Option-clicking the desktop behind your open document window hides InDesign.

System requirements: Mac OS X version 10.2 or higher; G3 or higher processor; 128 MB of RAM; 1024×768 monitor resolution at 256 colors; 350 MB of free hard drive space; and a CD-ROM drive for installation. You must install QuickTime 6 separately to use InDesign's multimedia features. For Adobe PostScript printing, a PostScript Level 2 or PostScript Language Level 3 printer is required.

Ⓐ Menu bar You can access any of the menu list options by simply clicking any of the word headings in the menu bar.

Ⓑ Application menu (InDesign) This Mac-only menu provides access to InDesign's application-specific options such as Preferences, as well as some Mac OS X system features like Hiding and Showing.

Ⓒ Control bar Options for the tool you currently have selected in the Toolbox always appear here.

Ⓓ Toolbox You can access any of the InDesign tools by clicking one of the icons shown in the Toolbox.

Ⓔ Palettes All of the palettes can be accessed under the Window menu in the menu bar. They are listed alphabetically in the main pull-down, but note that some are grouped into submenus within the list. Once accessed, palettes appear free-floating on your screen, but can also be grouped with other palettes and docked into one of the side tabs.

Ⓕ Document window This window displays the page layout(s) you are currently working on. You can have more than one document window open at a time, but the one you are currently working on always appears in front.

1.2 The Windows Interface

System requirements: Windows 2000 with Service Pack 2, or Windows XP Home or Professional Edition; Intel Pentium II or higher processor; 128 MB of RAM; a video card that supports 1024×768 monitor resolution at 256 colors; 312 MB of free hard drive space; and a CD-ROM drive for installation. You must install QuickTime 6 separately to use InDesign's multimedia features. For Adobe PostScript printing, a PostScript Level 2 or PostScript Language Level 3 printer is required.

Related Tasks

1.3   The Document Window
2.1   Menu Overview
3.1   Toolbox
3.2   Control Bar
4.1   Organizing Palettes

Shortcuts

Minimize all windows
Win: Windows key+M

Show/hide all controls
Win: Tab

Show/hide all controls except Toolbox and Control bar
Win: Shift+Tab

Tip

You can open or close all of the side tabs at once by Alt-clicking any one of the palette names.

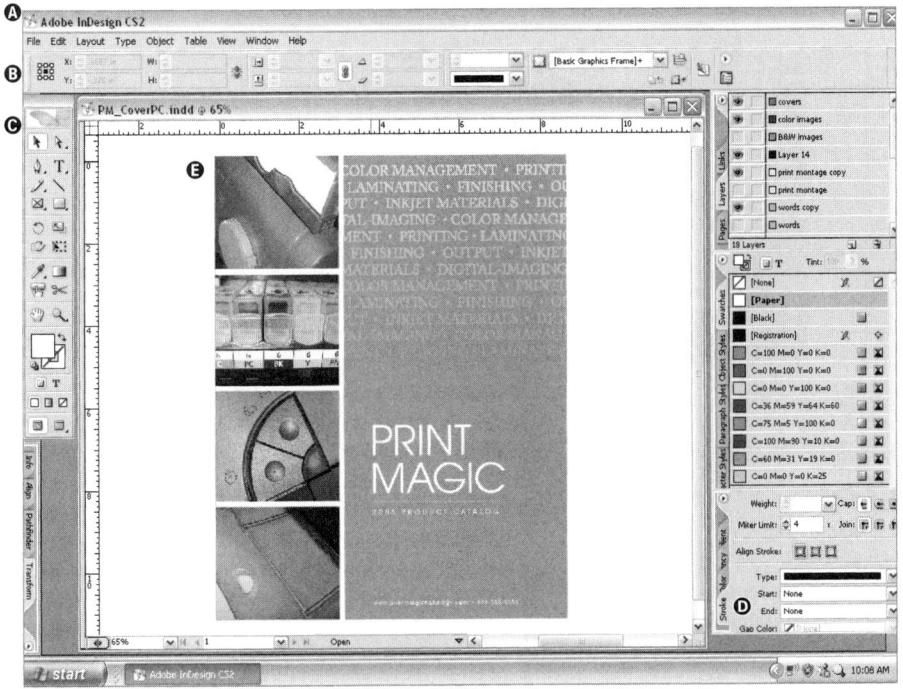

- **Ⓐ Menu bar** You can access any of the menu list options by simply clicking any of the word headings in the menu bar.
- **Ⓑ Control bar** Options for the tool you currently have selected in the Toolbox always appear here.
- **Ⓒ Toolbox** You can access any of the InDesign tools by clicking one of the icons shown in the Toolbox.
- **Ⓓ Palettes** All the palettes can be accessed under the Window menu in the menu bar. They are listed alphabetically in the main pull-down, but note that some are grouped into submenus within the list. Once accessed, palettes appear free-floating on your screen, but can also be grouped with other palettes and docked into one of the side tabs.
- **Ⓔ Document window** This window displays the page layout(s) you are currently working on. You can have more than one document window open at a time, but the one you are currently working on always appears in front.

1.3 The Document Window

Related Tasks

4.2 Customizing Your Workspace

5.1 General Preferences

5.5 Units and Increments Preferences

5.6 Grids Preferences

5.7 Guides and Pasteboard Preferences

5.15 Document Presets

Shortcuts

Close front document window
Mac: Command+W
Win: Ctrl+W

Close all document windows
Mac: Opt+Shift+Cmd+W
Win: Shift+Ctrl+Alt+W

New document
Mac: Command+N
Win: Ctrl+N

Open document
Mac: Command+O
Win: Ctrl+O

Browse for document using Adobe Bridge
Mac: Opt+Cmd+O
Win: Ctrl+Alt+O

Tip

Double-click in the ruler area to add a guide at that exact measurement point on the page.

Any time you open or start a new document in InDesign, it is placed in its own document window. You can view all of the pages in your document within this window.

In both Mac OS X and Windows, controls for view magnification and page access are built right into the document window, located in the bottom-left corner.

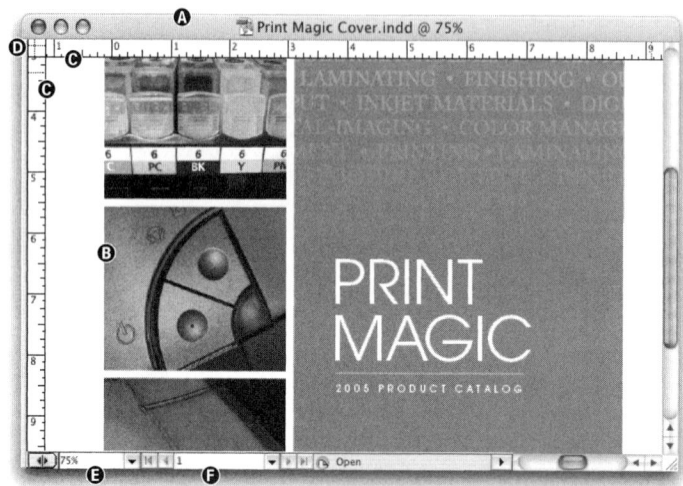

Ⓐ Title bar The filename and view magnification are always displayed here.

Ⓑ Page This is the work area for creating page layouts and designs. It is always surrounded by a thin rule and a hard drop shadow. The white area outside of the page is called the Pasteboard and is not printable. Control-click (Mac) or right-click (Windows) in the Page area to access various control options depending on which tool you currently have selected.

Ⓒ Rulers When made visible, the rulers always surround the top and left sides of your layout in the document window. Units can be chosen in the Preferences dialog. Control-clicking (Mac) or right-clicking (Windows) in the ruler areas allows you to change units and ruler display options. You can also click and drag a guideline from the ruler area to the Page.

Ⓓ Adjust ruler origin Click and drag to change the "zero point" in your document (the point of origin for your rulers). Double-clicking this area resets the zero point to the top-left corner.

Ⓔ Document magnification This number indicates the percentage that your layout is currently being displayed at within the document window. Click the arrow to the right of the number to choose a different percentage preset from the footer menu, or double-click in the text field to type in a value.

Ⓕ Page number access This number indicates which page you are currently viewing in the document window. Click the arrow to the right of it to select a different page from the footer menu, or double-click in the text field to type in the number of the page you'd like to view. A group of arrow buttons for accessing the next, previous, and first or last page of the document is also available.

1.4 Interface Objects

Although they may look slightly different from Mac OS X to Windows, the InDesign interface controls work the same on either platform. All of the controls are labeled with an icon so that you always know what you're adjusting. However, if you're still not sure what a certain control does just by viewing its icon, you can always use tooltips for a brief description.

Label icons and data fields Identifying label icons appear next to their accompanying data fields. The visual markers indicate the control's function. Click the label icon to select the text in the field.

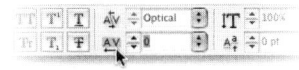

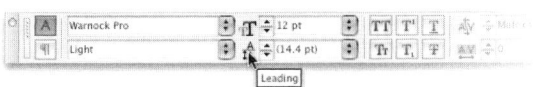

Tooltips These little guys can be really helpful if you're new to InDesign. Some of the visual label icons may be hard to decipher if you're new to the interface, in which case it's tooltips to the rescue! Just hover your mouse over any tool, control, or palette name and in a few seconds, a little yellow box appears with a description.

A few seconds not fast enough for you? Then open the InDesign General Preferences (Command+K on a Mac, Ctrl+K on Windows) and under Tool Tips, choose Fast.

Interface Menus

In addition to the ones found in the menu bar, a series of menus can be accessed at various places within the InDesign interface. Much like Adobe's Photoshop and Illustrator, they are broken down into five categories: palette menus, footer menus, contextual menus, select menus, and drop-downs.

Related Task

5.1 General Preferences

Shortcuts

Show/hide all controls
Mac and Win: Tab

Show/hide all controls except Toolbox and Control bar
Mac and Win: Shift+Tab

Move to next data field (when cursor is in data field)
Mac and Win: Tab

Access contextual menu
Mac: Control-click
Win: Right-click

Tip

Clicking a control's label icon selects the content of its accompanying data field.

5

1.4 Interface Objects *(continued)*

Related Task

4.1 Organizing Palettes

Shortcuts

Open/close side tab
Mac and Win: Click palette name

Show/hide all controls except Toolbox and Control bar
Mac and Win: Shift+Tab

Tip

To show palette menu options in alphabetical order, hold down Shift+Opt+Cmd (Mac) or Shift+Alt+Ctrl (Windows) when you click the arrow.

Palette menu Clicking the circular arrow button opens a palette's flyout menu, where you can choose from several palette-specific options. (See the graphic at the bottom of the previous page.) Shown there are the menu options for the Swatches palette. As you can see, there is quite a bit to choose from. It's always a good idea to click these if you can't find what you're looking for. You might be surprised what you'll find!

Footer menu These work exactly like palette menus but are found at the bottom of the window rather than at the top.

Although there aren't many of these in InDesign, footer menus can be particularly useful. The document window footer menu shown here is a quick and easy way to change view magnification.

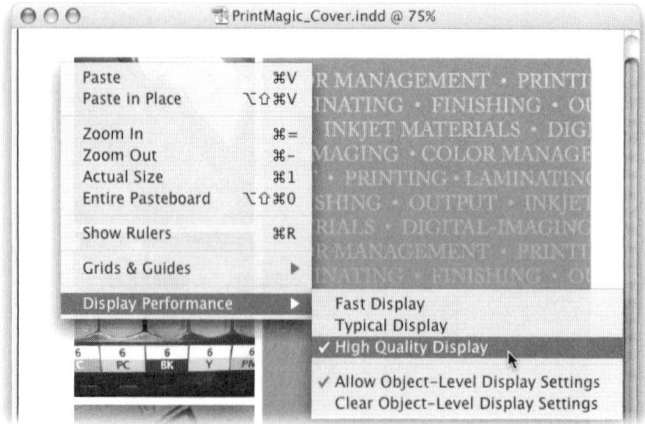

Contextual menu Right-clicking (Windows) or Control-clicking (Mac) in the document window, as well as in certain palettes and dialog windows, gives you quick access to certain item-specific options. These options are determined by which tool you have selected and where you click in the interface. Shown here is the default contextual menu for the Page, accessed by right/Control-clicking with any tool.

1.4 Interface Objects (continued)

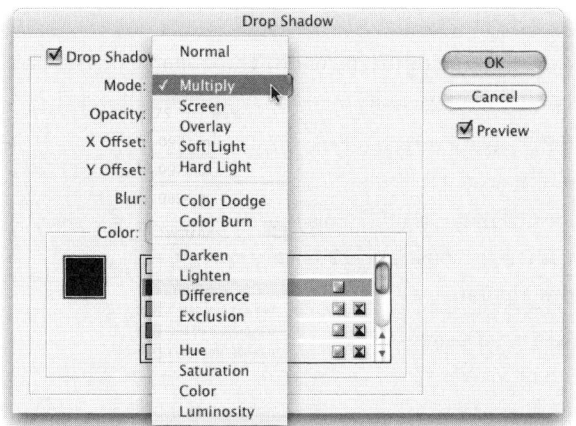

Related Tasks

2   Menus

4.1   Organizing Palettes

Shortcuts

Access Hand tool
Mac and Win: Hold down Spacebar

Access Zoom tool
Mac: Hold down Cmd+Spacebar
Win: Hold down Ctrl+Spacebar

Tip

To access type options quickly, press T to access the Type tool, insert it in a text frame, then right-click (Windows) or Control-click (Mac).

Select menu Some of the dialogs in InDesign contain additional menus embedded within them. From these menus, you can access additional options by clicking the arrow icon.

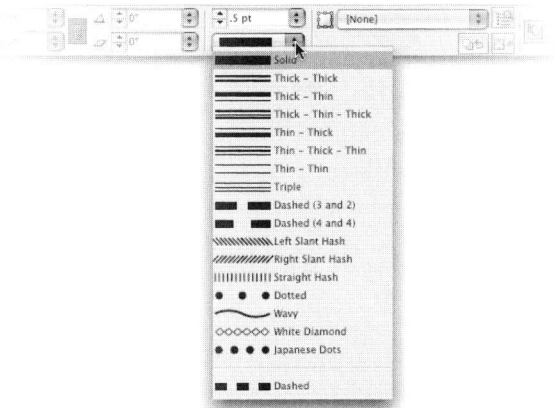

Drop-down The Control bar contains several drop-down menus that provide additional options for specific tools. Shown here are the stroke options available for the Line tool. Click the up/down arrow icon (Mac) or the down arrow icon (Windows) to access these menus.

7

1.4 Interface Objects *(continued)*

Related Tasks

2   Menus

4.1   Organizing Palettes

Shortcuts

Access Hand tool
Mac and Win: Hold down Spacebar

Access Zoom tool
Mac: Hold down Command+Spacebar
Win: Hold down Ctrl+Spacebar

Tip

Want to open or close all of the palettes related to the tool you currently have selected? Try clicking the Toggle button on the far right of the Control bar. But keep in mind that having something selected in your document window may change which palettes are toggled.

Simple On/Off Controls

Some controls in InDesign simply need to be turned on or off. Three simple ways to "hit the switch" for these controls are check boxes, radio buttons, and toggle buttons.

Check box   Certain controls in InDesign are turned on and off by checking boxes. A checked box indicates that the control is on, and an unchecked box indicates that it is off. To place a check in an empty box, click it with your mouse or click once on its accompanying text-field description.

Radio button   Some other controls in InDesign (but not very many) are activated by clicking a radio button. You only encounter these when a control offers multiple choices, in which case you can choose one but never more than one at the same time. Clicking either the empty circle or its accompanying text-field description activates your selection.

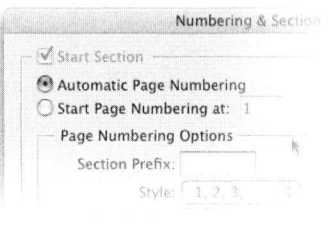

Toggle button   Clicking a toggle button performs a simple, specific task. For instance, clicking the icon shown here in the Control bar launches the Adobe Bridge application. Once Bridge is launched, clicking the toggle button brings Bridge to the front of your open applications.

Data Fields

Data fields are controlled by numerical values that can be typed in. Simply click the label icon or control name to the left of the data field and enter a value. Or click directly in the data field, highlight the current value, and then type.

Certain data fields allow you to adjust values in increments by clicking the up/down arrows to the left of the number.

Some fields are accompanied by drop-down menus, which contain preset values. By clicking the arrow to the right of the data field number, you can access the preset menu.

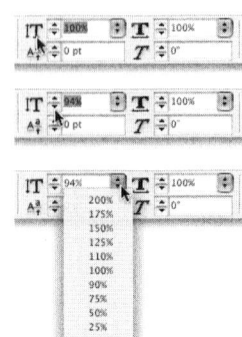

8

1.4 Interface Objects *(continued)*

Also, some data fields contain sliders:

Drop-down slider In addition to letting you select or enter a number, these data fields allow you to adjust a value by using a drop-down slider. Click the arrow to the right of the number to make it visible, and then click and drag the slider arrow to the left or right. You can watch the number change as you click and drag. Lower values are to the left and higher values to the right. You can also click anywhere on the slider line to place the arrow at that exact value.

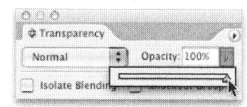

Visible slider Some data fields have a slider control right next to them rather than in a drop-down. These work the same way as drop-down sliders; the only difference is that they are always visible within the palette. Shown here is the slider control for the Color palette.

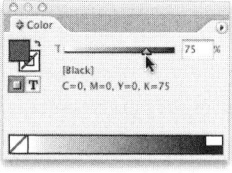

Action button These buttons appear at the bottom of certain palettes. Clicking one performs an action specific to the palette you are working with. Shown here is the New Swatch button for the Swatches palette.

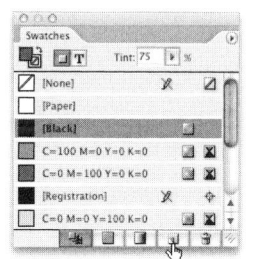

Buttons

Several types of button controls appear throughout the InDesign interface: action buttons, text buttons, and select buttons.

Although they are not labeled, hovering over them with your mouse launches a tooltip description explaining the button's function. To repeat the action, click again.

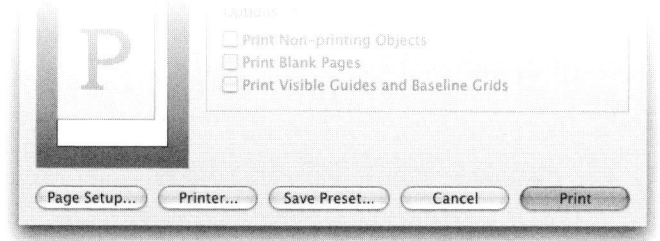

Related Tasks

2   Menus

4.1   Organizing Palettes

Shortcuts

Move to next data field (when cursor is in data field)
Mac and Win: Tab

Show/hide all controls
Mac and Win: Tab

Show/hide all controls except Toolbox and Control bar
Mac and Win: Shift+Tab

Tip

To highlight a data field quickly, click its label icon or text description.

1.4 Interface Objects (continued)

Related Tasks

2   Menus

4.1   Organizing Palettes

Shortcuts

Open/close side tab
Mac and Win: Click palette name

Show/hide all controls
Mac and Win: Tab

Show/hide all controls except Toolbox and Control bar
Mac and Win: Shift+Tab

Move to next data field (when cursor is in data field)
Mac and Win: Tab

Access contextual menu
Mac: Control-click
Win: Right-click

Tips

Not sure what a certain button does? Try hovering your mouse over it until a tooltip description appears.

If your document contains so many layers that you can't see them all in the Layers palette, try selecting Small Palette Rows from the palette's menu.

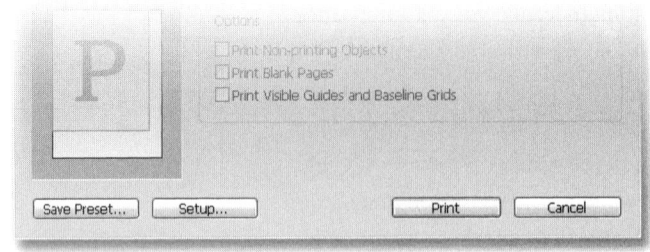

Text button You can find these buttons in specific dialogs (e.g., Print dialog, Package dialog). The button's function is labeled with text rather than an icon. Click the button to perform its specific action. The shaded (Mac OS X) or outlined (Windows) button is InDesign's current choice, which you can also select by pressing Return (Mac OS X) or Enter (Windows).

Select button These buttons are always arranged in related groups, like the text justification buttons shown here in the Paragraph palette. Much like the radio buttons described earlier, you can only select one button at a time from the group. Each button's function is labeled with a descriptive icon, but if you're still not sure what it does, you can always refer to tooltips by hovering over the button with your mouse.

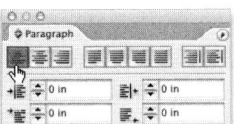

Toggles

Much like Photoshop and Illustrator, InDesign also features toggle controls. An icon appears whenever a toggle control is activated; an empty box appears when it is not. As shown here in the Layers palette, the columns to the left of each layer are used for "toggling" options on or off. The left column toggles the layer's visibility; the right column toggles the layer's lock function.

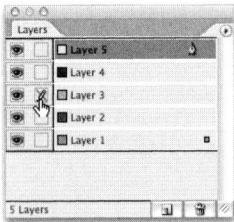

10

CHAPTER 2

Menus

JUST ABOUT EVERY SOFTWARE application contains menus, and InDesign is no exception. So what exactly are menus and what are they used for?

Well, menus exist primarily to help you select the right control for the task at hand. You can access each one by clicking its text label in the menu bar located at the top of your screen (Mac OS X), or at the top of the application window (Windows). Each pull-down list contains subgroups for various tasks, including dialogs, commands, and simple on/off controls. Once you locate a control, you can select it by highlighting and clicking it with your mouse.

This chapter describes in detail where all of the menus are located, what each list contains, and how to use them for every InDesign task.

- 2.1 **Menu overview**
- 2.2 **InDesign menu (Mac only)**
- 2.3 **File menu**
- 2.4 **Edit menu**
- 2.5 **Layout menu**
- 2.6 **Type menu**
- 2.7 **Object menu**
- 2.8 **Table menu**
- 2.9 **View menu**
- 2.10 **Window menu**
- 2.11 **Help menu**

2.1 Menu Overview

Related Tasks

1.1 The Macintosh Interface
1.2 The Windows Interface
1.4 Interface Objects

Shortcuts

Minimize window
Mac: Control+M

Minimize all windows
Win: Windows key+M

Hide all controls
Mac and Win: Tab

Hide all controls except Toolbox and Control bar
Mac and Win: Shift+Tab

Tip

You can also access most of the menu controls by right-clicking (Windows) or Control-clicking (Mac) at various points in the interface.

The menu bar in InDesign CS2 is slightly different on each platform. In Mac OS X, it always appears at the top of the screen. In Windows, it appears at the top of the application window, underneath the application name.

Also, you'll find a menu on the Mac named InDesign, which does not appear in Windows. This menu contains all the application-wide options such as Preferences and Configure Plug-Ins, as well as some OS X features such as hiding the program. In Windows, application-wide options are located in the File, Edit, or Help menu.

InDesign   File   Edit   Layout   Type   Object   Table   View   Window   Help

Top: The menu bar in Mac OS X.

Adobe InDesign CS2
File   Edit   Layout   Type   Object   Table   View   Window   Help

Bottom: The menu bar in Windows.

InDesign includes six different types of menu options. When you click one of the menu text labels in the menu bar, a drop-down list opens that contains some or all of the following:

Submenus A menu option with an arrow icon next to it indicates that you must choose from a submenu of further options. A submenu flyout window appears when you hover over it with your mouse. You can then click a selection from the submenu. Example: File > New opens a submenu of options for creating a new document, book, or library. From the submenu, click which new item you'd like to create.

Commands Clicking a menu command performs an immediate action. Example: Edit > Copy saves the currently selected text or object to memory. Choosing Edit > Paste then places the copied text or object into your document.

Dialogs A menu option with an ellipsis (...) indicates that a dialog will launch when you click it. Example: Object > Text Frame Options opens a dialog where you can enter column and gutter widths, inset spacing amounts, etc.

Show/Hide Several objects within the InDesign interface can be made visible or invisible by selecting Show/Hide menu options. Example: View > Show Rulers makes the document window rulers appear. Once they are visible, the option then reads View > Hide Rulers.

On/off Some options within InDesign can be turned on or off by selecting specific menu options. A checkmark appears next to the item's name in the menu when it is turned on. Example: View > Grids & Guides > Snap To Guides turns the snap function on or off.

Web links The Help menu contains several options that act as hyperlinks to Adobe InDesign's online support, registration, and product updates. If your computer is connected to the Internet, selecting these menu options takes you to a specific webpage.

2.2 InDesign Menu (Mac Only)

In Mac OS X, InDesign CS2 features an application menu located directly next to the Apple in the menu bar. This Mac-specific menu contains all of the application-wide options as well as some additional OS X features.

- **A About InDesign** Selecting this option redisplays the opening splash screen shown at application launch. To close it, click anywhere on the graphic. In Windows, you can find this option under the Help menu.

- **B Configure Plug-ins** Selecting this option displays a dialog that contains several InDesign plug-in management controls. You can find this option under the Help menu in Windows.

- **C Preferences** This option contains a submenu listing of InDesign Preferences. The settings chosen in Preferences control how InDesign looks and behaves on your system. On a Windows machine, Preferences are found under the Edit menu.

- **D Services** The Services option contains a submenu listing of system-wide actions specific to certain, mostly OS X system-based applications (such as the Safari browser, Apple Mail, and TextEdit). If your Mac is connected to the Internet, there is a useful Google-search link and Open URL command. There is also a Speech function that can read selected text back to you.

- **E Hide/Show** This group of options allows you to either hide InDesign, hide all other open applications (except for InDesign), or show (i.e., display) all open applications (including InDesign).

- **F Quit InDesign** This menu command closes the application. In Windows, the quit option is named Exit and can be found under the File menu.

Related Tasks

5   Presets and Preferences

5.18   Configure Plug-ins

Shortcuts

Hide InDesign
Mac: Control+Cmd+H

Quit (or Exit) InDesign
Mac: Cmd+Q
Win: Ctrl+Q

Tip

Want to reset your preferences? Try holding down Shift+Control+Opt+Cmd (Mac) or Shift+Ctrl+Alt (Windows) as you launch InDesign.

TABLES VS. TABS

Using tables instead of tabs can make your life a lot easier when you're setting up a lengthy list of information. Tables are much easier to manipulate than tabs because they allow you to enter and edit text in each individual cell without affecting the positioning of the rest of the text in a frame. Overall, selecting and adjusting table cells is easier than selecting text and resetting tabs.

To disguise a table to appear like a tabbed list, be sure not to set a table border or place any strokes on the rows or columns. When setting up a table this way, keep the frame edges visible so you can continue to see the cells you're working with. To jazz it up a bit, try placing a color tint behind the text on alternating rows or columns.

2.3 File Menu

Related Tasks

5.15 Document Presets
5.16 Print Presets
5.17 Adobe PDF Presets
6.1 Starting a New Document
6.3 Opening InDesign Docs
6.5 Save vs. Save As

Shortcuts

New document
Mac: Cmd+N
Win: Ctrl+N

Open document
Mac: Cmd+O
Win: Ctrl+O

Browse
Mac: Option+Cmd+O
Win: Alt+Ctrl+O

Close document
Mac: Cmd+W
Win: Ctrl+W

Save document
Mac: Cmd+S
Win: Ctrl+S

Save document as
Mac: Shift+Cmd+S
Win: Shift+Ctrl+S

Save a copy
Mac: Opt+Cmd+S
Win: Alt+Ctrl+S

Tip

You can create and save your own InDesign document presets, complete with custom page sizes, column numbers, and margin widths.

The File menu is the place to go for opening, saving, and outputting files in InDesign CS2. You can also access output presets for PDF, print, and other export options; select built-in preflight and packaging options; and even import XML. In Windows, you can also exit InDesign through the File menu.

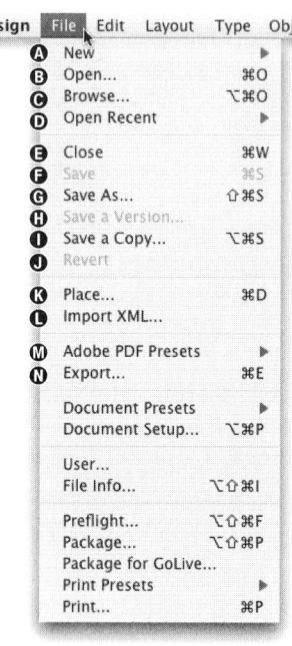

Ⓐ New Contains a submenu of options for creating a new InDesign document, book, or library.

Ⓑ Open Displays a dialog where you can open any recognizable file format from your system.

Ⓒ Browse Launches the Adobe Bridge File Browser, a multiapplication file resource that comes with the Creative Suite 2.

Ⓓ Open Recent Displays a submenu of the last ten opened documents.

Ⓔ Close Closes the currently active open document. A Save prompt appears before closing if you have made any changes to the document since the latest save.

Ⓕ Save Saves the currently active open document. If you are saving the document for the first time, a dialog appears requesting a filename, type, and location. If the document has already been saved once, choosing this option simply updates the file.

Ⓖ Save As Always opens a dialog like the one described for Save, requesting a filename, type, and location, even if the document has already been saved.

Ⓗ Save A Version Works in conjunction with Adobe Version Cue for saving projects to another computer over a local network or via the Internet.

Ⓘ Save A Copy Always opens a dialog but, by default, adds the word "copy" to the existing filename.

Ⓙ Revert Restores the document to its most recent saved state. Because this action cannot be undone, a warning dialog always appears before reverting.

Ⓚ Place Opens a dialog in which you can select a compatible graphic image to place in your document (e.g., TIFF, EPS, AI, PSD).

Ⓛ Import XML Opens a dialog for selecting XML documents to import.

Ⓜ Adobe PDF Presets Displays a submenu of saved PDF export presets. There is also a submenu option for defining a new preset.

Ⓝ Export Opens a dialog with options for outputting a document in a format other than .indd (an InDesign document).

2.3 File Menu *(continued)*

O **Document Presets** Displays a submenu of saved document presets. There is also a submenu option for defining a new preset. The Default preset launches the same dialog as File **>** New **>** Document.

P **Document Setup** Opens a dialog with options for setting up a document, including number of pages, page size, and orientation.

Q **User** Opens a dialog that allows you to choose a username and identifying color associated with the InCopy Notes plug-in.

R **File Info** Opens a dialog that allows you to view and edit saved file information.

S **Preflight** Performs a quick scan of the document resulting in a dialog report that flags possible problem items during output.

T **Package** Performs a preflight check first and then opens a dialog with data fields requesting printing instructions. Clicking Continue opens a second dialog with output collection options.

U **Package for GoLive** Prepares a web-ready version of your document for import into Adobe's GoLive web editor.

V **Print Presets** Displays a submenu of saved print presets. There is also a submenu option for defining a new preset. The Default preset launches the same dialog as File **>** Print.

W **Print** Opens a dialog with options for printing your document.

X **Exit** Closes the application. On the Mac, this option is named Quit InDesign and can be found under the InDesign menu.

Related Tasks

12.1 Importing a Graphic Image
15.5 Packaging
15.6 Packaging for GoLive
16.1 Printing a Document

Shortcuts

Place
Mac: Cmd+D
Win: Ctrl+D

Export
Mac: Cmd+E
Win: Ctrl+E

Document setup
Mac: Opt+Cmd+P
Win: Alt+Ctrl+P

Preflight
Mac: Opt+Shift+Cmd+F
Win: Alt+Shift+Ctrl+F

Package
Mac: Opt+Shift+Cmd+P
Win: Alt+Shift+Ctrl+P

Print
Mac: Cmd+P
Win: Ctrl+P

Tip

You can import XML under the File menu, but it is important to note that XML tags are not the same as InDesign Tagged Text. They are very different ways of importing and exporting InDesign content.

2.4 Edit Menu

Related Tasks

3.3 Selection Tool
3.4 Direct Selection and Position Tools
5.19 Keyboard Shortcuts
7.2 Selection Tool vs. Direct Selection Tool
7.9 Nesting Objects

Shortcuts

Undo
Mac: Cmd+Z
Win: Ctrl+Z

Redo
Mac: Shift+Cmd+Z
Win: Shift+Ctrl+Z

Copy
Mac: Cmd+C
Win: Ctrl+C

Paste
Mac: Cmd+V
Win: Ctrl+V

Paste without formatting
Mac: Shift+Cmd+V
Win: Shift+Ctrl+V

Paste Into
Mac: Opt+Cmd+V
Win: Alt+Ctrl+V

Paste in place
Mac: Opt+Shift+Cmd+V
Win: Alt+Shift+Ctrl+V

Tip

InDesign CS2 allows up to several hundred Undos and Redo's, depending on the amount of RAM installed on your machine and the kinds of actions you have performed.

The Edit menu contains many useful options for working with your layouts, including Undo, Redo, Copy/Paste, and Select All. In addition, the Edit menu contains several options for editing InDesign tools, such as keyboard shortcuts. In Windows, you can also find Preferences under the Edit menu.

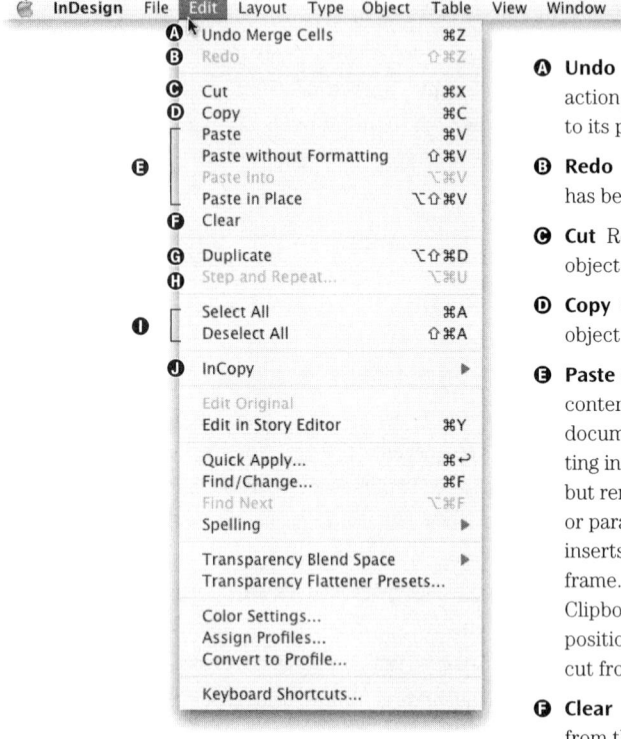

Ⓐ Undo Reverses your most recent action, reverting the document back to its previous state.

Ⓑ Redo Repeats the last action that has been Undone.

Ⓒ Cut Removes any selected text or object and saves it to memory.

Ⓓ Copy Saves any selected text or object to memory.

Ⓔ Paste commands Paste inserts the contents of the Clipboard into your document. Paste Without Formatting inserts the Clipboard material but removes any applied character, or paragraph styles. Paste Into inserts the contents into a selected frame. Paste In Place inserts the Clipboard contents in the same position that they were copied or cut from.

Ⓕ Clear Removes any selected items from the document.

Ⓖ Duplicate Inserts a copy of any selected items using the most recent X and Y coordinates set in the Step and Repeat option (see below).

Ⓗ Step And Repeat Duplicates single or multiple items and places them at different, calculated points on your page. This option always opens a dialog with repeat count and horizontal/vertical offset options.

Ⓘ Select/Deselect All Select All makes a selection of every item on the currently targeted page or spread. When the Type tool is selected, this option selects all of the text within a selected frame. If the Type tool is selected but is not placed within a text frame, this option acts the same as with every other tool by selecting everything on the targeted page. Deselect All releases all currently selected items.

Ⓙ InCopy Displays a submenu of options for preparing InDesign documents and layout items for use with Adobe InCopy.

2.4 Edit Menu *(continued)*

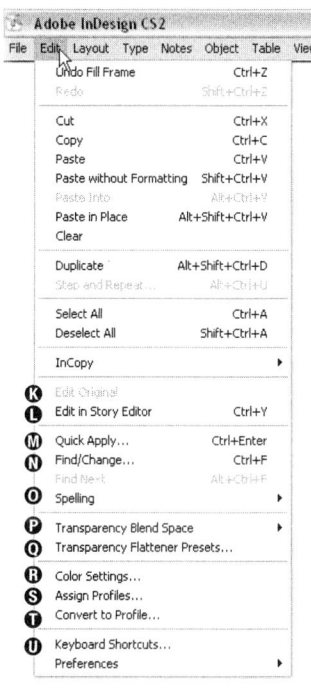

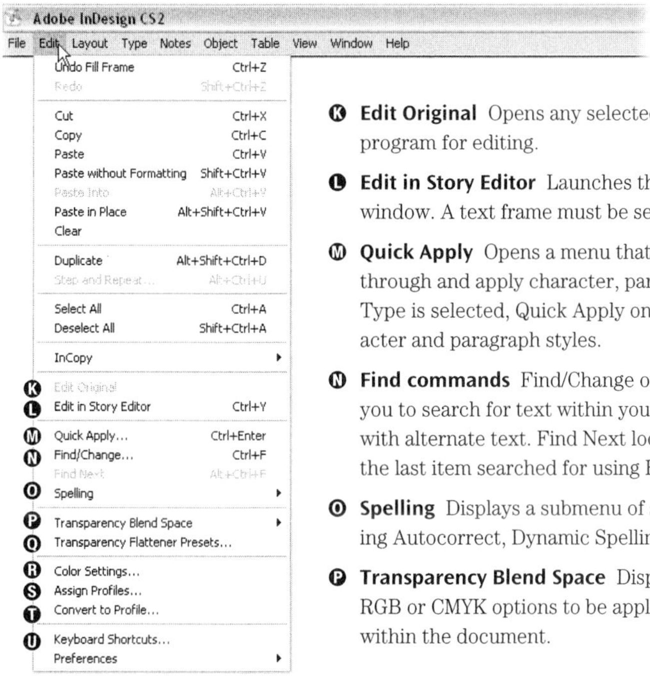

Ⓚ Edit Original Opens any selected, placed item in its native program for editing.

Ⓛ Edit in Story Editor Launches the InDesign Story Editor window. A text frame must be selected to use this option.

Ⓜ Quick Apply Opens a menu that allows you to search through and apply character, paragraph, and object styles. If Type is selected, Quick Apply only allows you to apply character and paragraph styles.

Ⓝ Find commands Find/Change opens a palette that allows you to search for text within your document and replace it with alternate text. Find Next locates the next instance of the last item searched for using Find/Change.

Ⓞ Spelling Displays a submenu of spell-check options, including Autocorrect, Dynamic Spelling, and Dictionary.

Ⓟ Transparency Blend Space Displays a submenu of either RGB or CMYK options to be applied to all transparent items within the document.

Ⓠ Transparency Flattener Presets Opens a dialog that allows you to choose from default Low, Medium, or High resolution presets, as well as options for loading, editing, saving, and deleting custom transparency flattener settings.

Ⓡ Color Settings Opens a dialog that allows you to enable color management and choose specific settings. Color Settings can also be synchronized with the other programs in the Creative Suite 2 via the Adobe Bridge application.

Ⓢ Assign Profiles Opens a dialog that allows you to assign specific RGB and CMYK color management settings to your document.

Ⓣ Convert To Profile Opens a dialog that allows you to convert your document to a specific color management profile.

Ⓤ Keyboard Shortcuts Opens a dialog that allows you to choose from default InDesign, PageMaker 7, and QuarkXPress 3.3 (Mac only) and 4.0 keyboard shortcuts. You can also create, save, edit, and delete your own custom sets.

Related Tasks

9.8 Editing Using the Story Editor
9.10 Check Spelling
9.15 Applying Find/Change
14.1 Using Color Settings

Shortcuts

Duplicate
Mac: Opt+Shift+Cmd+D
Win: Alt+Shift+Ctrl+D

Step and repeat
Mac: Opt+Cmd+U
Win: Alt+Ctrl+U

Select all
Mac: Cmd+A
Win: Ctrl+A

Deselect all
Mac: Shift+Cmd+A
Win: Shift+Ctrl+A

Edit in Story Editor
Mac: Cmd+Y
Win: Ctrl+Y

Quick Apply
Mac: Cmd+Return
Win: Ctrl+Enter

Find/Change
Mac: Cmd+F
Win: Ctrl+F

Find next
Mac: Opt+Cmd+F
Win: Alt+Ctrl+F

Check spelling
Mac: Cmd+I
Win: Ctrl+I

Tip

In InDesign CS2, you can create and save your own custom keyboard shortcuts.

17

2.5 Layout Menu

Related Tasks

4.15 Pages Palette
5.7   Guides and Pasteboard Preferences
6.8   Adding, Arranging, and Deleting Pages
18.4 Building a Table of Contents
18.5 Creating and Saving a TOC Style

Shortcuts

First page
Mac: Shift+Cmd+PageUp
Win: Shift+Ctrl+PageUp

Previous page
Mac and Win: Shift+PageUp

Next page
Mac and Win: Shift+PageDown

Last page
Mac: Shift+Cmd+PageDown
Win: Shift+Ctrl+PageDown

Next spread
Mac: Opt+PageDown
Win: Alt+PageDown

Previous spread
Mac: Opt+PageUp
Win: Alt+PageUp

Tip

Shift+Cmd+P (Mac) or Shift+Ctrl+P (Windows) adds a page to your document without having to access the command from the Layout menu.

The items in the Layout menu are used mainly for setting up pages in an InDesign document. You'll find options for margins, columns, and guides, as well as some navigational commands. The menu also features options for automatic page numbering and creating a table of contents when using InDesign's book feature.

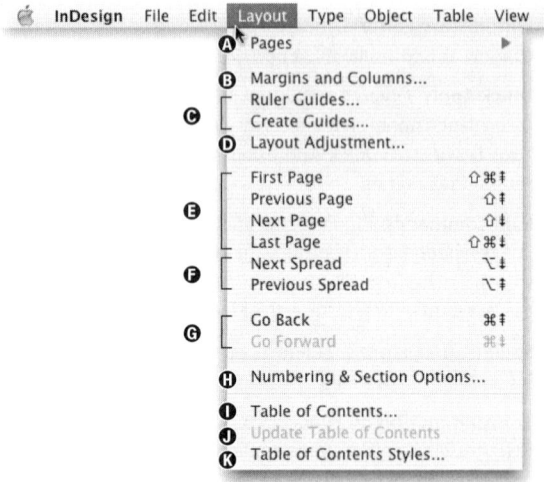

- **Ⓐ Pages** Displays a submenu of options for adding, deleting, duplicating, inserting, and moving pages.
- **Ⓑ Margins And Columns** Opens a dialog requesting specific page coordinates for margins and columns.
- **Ⓒ Guides commands** Ruler Guides opens a dialog with options for view threshold (in percents) and assigned color. Create Guides opens a dialog that allows you to create multiple ruler guides on a page.
- **Ⓓ Layout Adjustment** Opens a dialog that allows you to adjust the distance required for an item to snap to a guide (called Snap Zone), as well as other layout-specific adjustment options.
- **Ⓔ Page navigation** First Page and Last Page display the first or last page of the document. Previous Page and Next Page display the page before or after the one you are currently viewing. If you are viewing the first page, Previous Page and First Page are grayed out; if you are on the last page, Next Page and Last Page are grayed out.
- **Ⓕ Spread navigation** Next Spread displays the spread after the one you are currently viewing. Previous Spread displays the spread before the current one.
- **Ⓖ Go Back/Forward** Go Back returns you to the previously viewed page in the document that falls before the one you are currently viewing. Go Forward returns you to the previously viewed page that falls after the current one.
- **Ⓗ Numbering & Section Options** Opens a dialog that allows you to specify automatic page numbering options based on sections you can create here.
- **Ⓘ Table Of Contents** Opens a dialog with options for creating a TOC style to be used with InDesign's book features.
- **Ⓙ Update Table Of Contents** Updates changes applied to an existing TOC style.
- **Ⓚ Table Of Contents Styles** Opens a dialog that allows you to load, edit, delete, or create a TOC style.

2.6 Type Menu

The Type menu contains options for all text-related items in InDesign. You can access typefaces and sizes, open text-specific palettes, manage fonts, convert text to outlines, change case, and much more. You can even create type on a path!

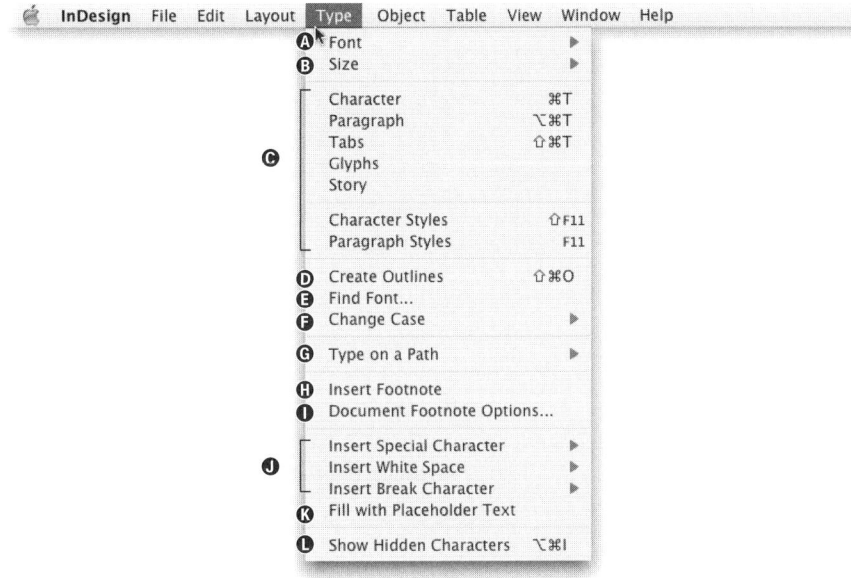

- **A** **Font** Displays a submenu of available fonts loaded into your system.
- **B** **Size** Displays a submenu of default type sizes.
- **C** **Type Palette commands** Each of these options opens the palette by its respective name.
- **D** **Create Outlines** Converts selected, editable text to graphic outlines.
- **E** **Find Font** Opens a dialog that lets you locate and manage any missing fonts within your document.
- **F** **Change Case** Displays a submenu with options for changing selected text to uppercase, title case, sentence case, or lowercase.
- **G** **Type On A Path** Displays a submenu with options specific to the Type on a Path tool.
- **H** **Insert Footnote** Inserts a footnote wherever the Type tool's cursor is placed within the document. You can then enter any pertinent information.
- **I** **Document Footnote Options** Opens a dialog that contains footnote-specific options.
- **J** **Insert commands** Each of these commands displays a submenu of items that can be added into a selected text frame, wherever the Type tool's cursor is placed. Insert Special Character provides special text characters; Insert White Space provides white space items; and Insert Break Character provides break options.
- **K** **Fill With Placeholder Text** Fills the currently selected text frame with fake placeholder text.
- **L** **Show/Hide Hidden Characters** Reveals (or hides) invisible characters in your document, including spaces, returns, and tabs.

Related Tasks

3.6 Type Tools
4.21 Type and Tables Palettes
9.9 Changing Case
9.13 Font Overview
10.13 Inserting Special Characters
10.15 Inserting Footnotes

Shortcuts

Character palette
Mac: Cmd+T
Win: Ctrl+T

Paragraph palette
Mac: Opt+Cmd+T
Win: Ctrl+M

Tabs palette
Mac: Shift+Cmd+T
Win: Shift+Ctrl+T

Character styles
Mac and Win: Shift+F11

Paragraph styles
Mac and Win: F11

Create outlines
Mac: Shift+Cmd+O
Win: Shift+Ctrl+O

Tip

The Fill With Placeholder Text command is InDesign's answer to QuarkXPress's Jabberwocky.

2.7 Object Menu

Related Tasks

3.14 Free Transform Tool

4.11 Object and Layout Palettes

7.20 Applying Corner Effects

7.21 Applying and Editing Compound Paths

Shortcuts

Move
Mac: Shift+Cmd+M
Win: Shift+Ctrl+M

Transform again
Mac: Opt+Cmd+3
Win: Alt+Ctrl+3

Transform sequence again
Mac: Opt+Cmd+4
Win: Alt+Ctrl+4

Bring to front
Mac: Shift+Cmd+]
Win: Shift+Ctrl+]

Bring forward
Mac: Cmd+]
Win: Ctrl+]

Send backward
Mac: Cmd+[
Win: Ctrl+[

Send to back
Mac: Shift+Cmd+[
Win: Shift+Ctrl+[

Text frame options
Mac: Cmd+B
Win: Ctrl+B

Tip

You can't move objects that are locked, but you can still select them (unless they are on a locked layer).

The Object menu contains many options for working with frames and shapes. Here you will find effects such as Drop Shadow and Feather, as well as path options that resemble those in Illustrator. You'll even find interactive options for embedding movies, sound, and rollover buttons in exported pdfs!

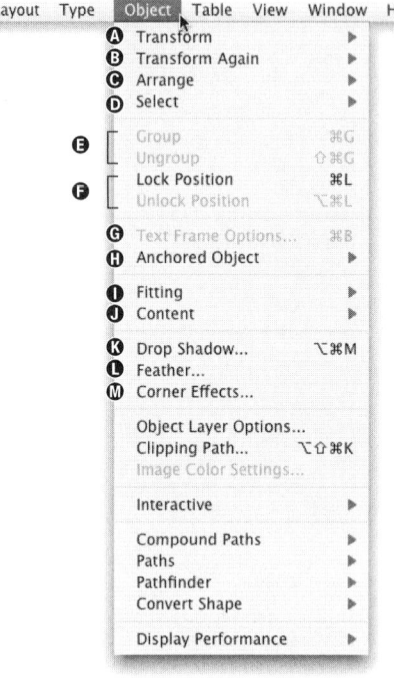

Ⓐ Transform Displays a submenu of options for transforming objects, including Move, Scale, Rotate, and Shear.

Ⓑ Transform Again Displays a submenu of options for repeating a Transform command or sequence of Transform commands.

Ⓒ Arrange Displays a submenu of placement options, including Bring To Front, Bring Forward, Send To Back, and Send Backward.

Ⓓ Select Displays a submenu of options for selecting items in a stack or group.

Ⓔ Group/Ungroup Links two or more selected objects into a group, or separates grouped objects.

Ⓕ Lock/Unlock Position Secures selected objects into their current position so they cannot be moved, or releases selected locked objects.

Ⓖ Text Frame Options Opens a dialog where specific text frame settings can be entered, such as column and gutter widths, inset spacing amounts, etc.

Ⓗ Anchored Object Displays a submenu of options for inserting, releasing, and positioning inline and/or anchored objects.

Ⓘ Fitting Displays a submenu of options for fitting contents into a selected frame.

Ⓙ Content Displays a submenu of options for assigning a selected frame a text, graphic, or unassigned contents holder.

Ⓚ Drop Shadow Opens a dialog with options for placing a graphic drop shadow on a selected frame.

Ⓛ Feather Opens a dialog with options for placing a feathered edge on a selected frame.

Ⓜ Corner Effects Opens a dialog with options for placing corner effects on a selected frame: Rounded, Inset, Inverse Rounded, and more.

2.7 Object Menu (continued)

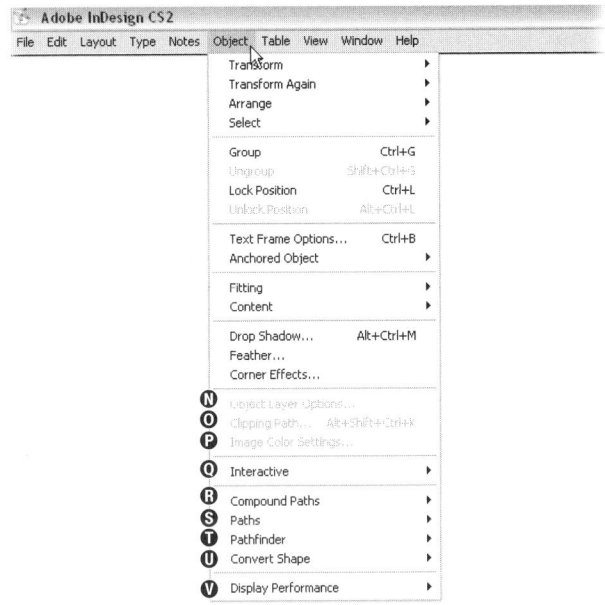

N **Object Layer Options** Opens a dialog with layer visibility options for layered PSD files that have been placed in a document. A frame that contains a layered PSD must be selected in order to access these options.

O **Clipping Path** Opens a dialog that allows you to create a clipping path around a placed graphic selection.

P **Image Color Settings** Opens a dialog that displays your graphic selection's current color settings and allows you to assign it a different profile and/or rendering intent.

Q **Interactive** Displays a submenu of interactive items that can be embedded into an exported PDF of your InDesign document. Options include movies, sound, and web buttons.

R **Compound Paths** Displays a submenu with options to either make a compound path out of two or more selected shapes, or release an existing compound path.

S **Paths** Displays a submenu of options for opening a closed path, closing an open path, or reversing a path's direction.

T **Pathfinder** Displays a submenu of options for combining two or more selected shapes, including Add, Subtract, Intersect, Exclude Overlap, and Minus Back.

U **Convert Shape** Displays a submenu of options for changing the appearance of any shape, line, path, or frame to a rectangle, rounded rectangle, beveled rectangle, inverse rounded rectangle, ellipse, triangle, polygon, line, or orthogonal line.

V **Display Performance** Displays a submenu of display performance options for selected graphics, including Fast, Typical, and High Quality. These options affect the way placed graphics appear on your screen.

Related Tasks

8.1 Moving Objects
8.2 Resizing Objects
8.6 Grouping and Ungrouping Objects
8.9 Stacking, Arranging, and Locking Objects
9.1 Text Frame Options
14.10 Adding Drop Shadows
14.11 Feathering

Shortcuts

Fit content to frame
Mac: Opt+Cmd+E
Win: Alt+Ctrl+E

Fit frame to content
Mac: Opt+Cmd+C
Win: Alt+Ctrl+C

Center content
Mac: Shift+Cmd+E
Win: Shift+Ctrl+E

Fit content proportionately
Mac: Opt+Shift+Cmd+E
Win: Alt+Shift+Ctrl+E

Fill frame proportionately
Mac: Opt+Shift+Cmd+C
Win: Alt+Shift+Ctrl+C

Tip

Turning off a layer's visibility in a placed PSD using Object Layer Options adds an eye icon next to the graphic support's name in the Links palette.

21

2.8 Table Menu

The Table menu goes hand in hand with the Table palette, allowing you to create and edit tables in InDesign CS2. If you've ever used tabs to create tables in a page layout program, you'll really appreciate the Table tools in InDesign—they can make the job a lot easier.

Related Tasks

13.5 Creating a New Table

Shortcuts

Insert table
Mac: Opt+Shift+Cmd+T
Win: Alt+Shift+Ctrl+T

Table setup
Mac: Opt+Shift+Cmd+B
Win: Alt+Shift+Ctrl+B

Tips

You can insert a table inside another table's cell—a process called table "nesting."

You can import tables from Microsoft Word and Excel documents. Choose File > Place, and then select the document containing the table you'd like to import. You can choose to preserve or remove any table styles and formatting in the Import Options dialog.

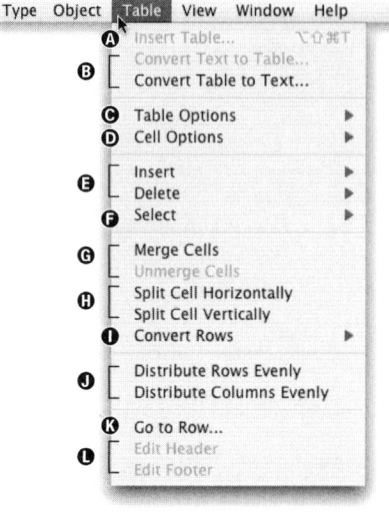

A Insert Table Opens a dialog with options for inserting a table into a selected text frame. The Type tool's cursor must be placed inside a frame in order to insert a table.

B Convert Text To Table/Table To Text Each command opens a dialog with options for converting any text selected with the Type tool into a table, or for converting a table into regular text (to use Table To Text, the Type tool's cursor must be inserted in a table cell).

C Table Options Displays a submenu of options for setting up tables, including borders, spacing, alternating stroke and fill patterns, headers and footers, etc.

D Cell Options Displays a submenu of options for customizing individual cells, including Text, Strokes and Fills, Rows and Columns, and Diagonal Lines. The Type tool's cursor must be placed in a table cell to access these options.

E Insert/Delete Displays submenus with options to add or remove rows or columns or to delete a table. The Type tool's cursor must be inserted in a table cell in order to insert or delete.

F Select Displays a submenu of table selection options including Cells, Rows, Columns, etc. The Type tool's cursor must be placed in a table cell in order to select.

G Merge/Unmerge Cells Merge combines two or more table cells selected with the Type tool. If the Type tool's cursor is in a merged cell, Unmerge redivides the cell.

H Split Cell Horizontally/Vertically Divides any selected table cell(s) in two, in the indicated direction.

I Convert Rows Displays a submenu of conversion options for any table row(s) selected with the Type tool, including To Header, To Body, and To Footer.

J Distribute Rows/Columns Evenly Distributes all selected table rows or columns evenly.

K Go To Row Opens a dialog with row selection options for the currently selected table.

L Edit Header/Footer Select to edit an existing table header or footer.

2.9 View Menu

The View menu includes several options for displaying your work on screen. Proof Setup, Overprint Preview, Screen Mode, and Display Performance are all particularly useful options when you're preparing a document to be printed.

A **Overprint Preview** Displays a simulated preview of overprinting inks in your document.

B **Proof Setup** Displays a submenu of simulated color setting previews. This option refers to your chosen color settings located under the Edit menu, or you can choose a custom proof setup here.

C **Proof Colors** Displays a simulated preview of how the colors used in your document will print, using the settings chosen in Proof Setup (see above). Selecting this option again toggles Proof Colors off.

D **Zoom In/Out** Increases or decreases view magnification percentage. These options always use your current selection as the center point for magnification; however, you don't have to have an object selected to use these commands.

E **Fit view commands** Fit Page In Window, Fit Spread In Window, and Entire Pasteboard automatically adjust view magnification to fit the current page, the current spread, or the Pasteboard proportionately to the edges of the document window. Actual Size sets view magnification at 100%.

F **Screen Mode** Displays a submenu of screen preview modes, including Normal, Preview, Bleed, and Slug.

Related Tasks

5.6 Grids Preferences

5.7 Guides and Pasteboard Preferences

5.12 Display Performance Preferences

Shortcuts

Overprint preview
Mac: Opt+Shift+Cmd+Y
Win: Alt+Shift+Ctrl+Y

Zoom in
Mac: Cmd+=
Win: Ctrl+=

Zoom out
Mac: Cmd+-(minus)
Win: Ctrl+-(minus)

Fit page in window
Mac: Cmd+0
Win: Ctrl+0

Fit spread in window
Mac: Opt+Cmd+0
Win: Alt+Ctrl+0

Actual size
Mac: Cmd+1
Win: Ctrl+1

Entire Pasteboard
Mac: Opt+Shift+Cmd+0
Win: Alt+Shift+Ctrl+0

Tip

You can also access the Display Performance options by right-clicking (Windows) or Control-clicking (Mac) anywhere on the Page or Pasteboard.

2.9 View Menu (continued)

Related Tasks

5.13 Appearance of Black Preferences

6.18 Adjusting Ruler Guides

6.20 Aligning to Baseline Grid

6.21 Snapping to Document Grid

9.5 Importing XML

9.8 Editing Using the Story Editor

14.3 Using Proof Setup for Soft Proofing

Shortcuts

Fast display
Mac: Shift+Cmd+0
Win: Shift+Ctrl+0

Typical display
Mac: Opt+Cmd+Z
Win: Alt+Ctrl+Z

High-quality display
Mac: Opt+Cmd+H
Win: Alt+Ctrl+H

Show structure
Mac: Opt+Cmd+1
Win: Alt+Ctrl+1

Show/hide text threads
Mac: Opt+Cmd+Y
Win: Alt+Ctrl+Y

Show/hide frame edges
Mac: Cmd+H
Win: Ctrl+H

Tip

For a quick to way to show or hide a document's structure, click the left/right arrow button located in the bottom-left corner of the document window.

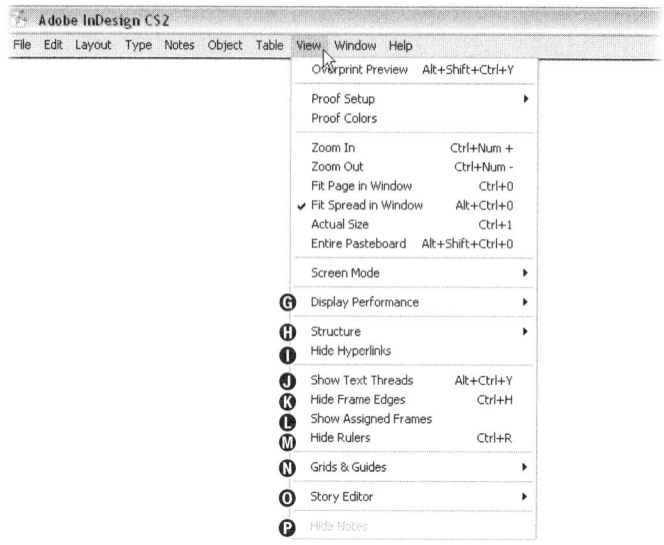

G Display Performance Displays a submenu of overall display performance options, including Fast, Typical, and High Quality. These options affect the way all placed graphic(s) appear on your screen.

H Structure Displays a submenu of Structure view options, including Show/Hide Structure, Show/Hide Tag Markers, and Show/Hide Tagged Frames.

I Show/Hide Hyperlinks Reveals or conceals any existing hyperlinks in the document.

J Show/Hide Text Threads Reveals or conceals any existing text threads in the document. Note that you can only see a thread when a linked text frame is selected with one of the selection tools.

K Show/Hide Frame Edges Reveals or conceals all frame edges in the document.

L Show/Hide Assigned Frames Reveals or conceals any frames assigned to Adobe InCopy users by color-code.

M Show/Hide Rulers Reveals or conceals the document window rulers.

N Grids & Guides Displays a submenu with View, Lock, and Snap options for ruler guides, the baseline grid, and the document grid.

O Story Editor Displays a submenu of Story Editor view options, including Hide Style Name Column, Hide Depth Ruler, and Expand All Footnotes.

P Show/Hide Notes Reveals or conceals any note attachments in the document.

The Display Performance option located under the Object menu controls how individual selected objects are displayed. The Display Performance option located under the View menu controls how the whole document is displayed.

2.10 Window Menu

You can choose which palettes to display on your screen under the Window menu. Select the palettes you want to show or hide, or use the Workspace submenu to save your favorite layouts and restore them as needed.

If you're familiar with the menus in other page layout programs such as QuarkXPress or PageMaker, you may find the Window menu in InDesign much simpler to use. InDesign lists the palettes in alphabetical order, making it easier to find the ones you need.

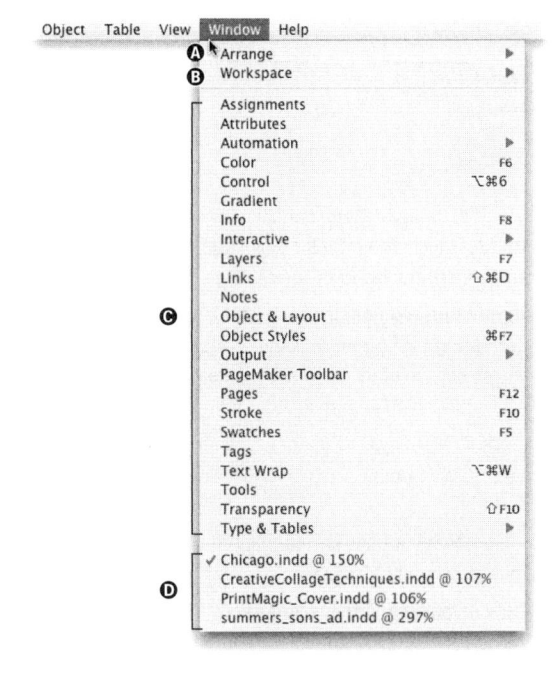

Ⓐ Arrange Here you can choose how you'd like to organize all of the open document windows on your screen. From the submenu options, you can choose New Window, Tile, and Cascade. On the Mac, you can also choose Minimize and Bring All To Front.

Ⓑ Workspace Save the layout of your InDesign Workspace, and then quickly switch between layouts for different needs. Choosing a saved Workspace instantly restores all of the open palettes to their saved position on the screen. How cool is that?

Ⓒ Palette List Choose which palettes you'd like to show or hide from the alphabetical list. Note that some of the items display a submenu of available palettes to choose from. *Example:* Selecting the Object & Layout option displays a submenu of related palettes to choose from, including Align, Navigator, Pathfinder, and Transform.

Ⓓ Open Documents The very bottom of the menu displays a list of all open document windows. A checkmark always appears next to the name of the foreground document.

Related Tasks

4.1 Organizing Palettes

4.2 Customizing Your Workspace

Shortcuts

Color palette
Mac and Win: F6

Control bar
Mac: Opt+Cmd+6
Win: Alt+Ctrl+6

Info palette
Mac and Win: F8

Layers palette
Mac and Win: F7

Links palette
Mac: Opt+Cmd+D
Win: Shift+Ctrl+D

Align palette
Mac and Win: Shift+F7

Transform palette
Mac and Win: F9

Object Styles palette
Mac: Cmd+F7
Win: Ctrl+F7

Separations palette
Mac and Win: Shift+F6

Pages palette
Mac and Win: F12

Stroke palette
Mac and Win: F10

Swatches palette
Mac and Win: F5

Tip

The Window menu lists the available keyboard commands for showing and hiding palettes on the far right, next to each palette's name.

2.11 Help Menu

Related Tasks

3.22 Other Toolbox Functions

Shortcut

InDesign Help
Mac: Help
Win: F1

Tip

If you'd prefer the welcome screen not to appear when you first launch InDesign, simply uncheck the Show This Dialog At Startup box located in the bottom-left corner.

The Help menu is designed to answer any questions you may have about InDesign. In addition, you can access online support and updates, register the software, and visit the InDesign portion of Adobe.com by selecting the link provided here.

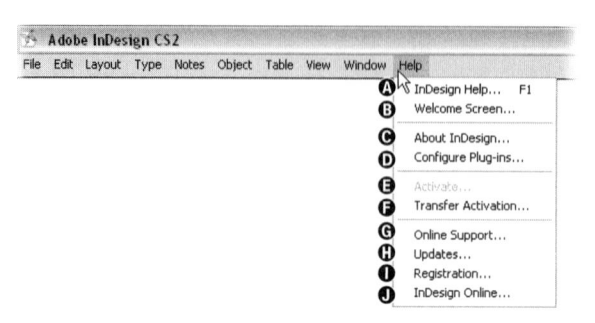

Ⓐ InDesign Help Selecting this option opens an HTML-based Help manual, viewable in your system's default web browser. The actual HTML file is located in the InDesign application folder on your hard drive, so you don't have to be connected to the Internet to use it.

Ⓑ Welcome Screen (Mac OS) or About InDesign (Windows) Relaunches the welcome screen shown when you first start the application. The lines of text in the center of the screen are actually links to online tutorials at Adobe.com. The icons at the bottom of the screen are links you can use to open new or existing documents. The New From Template icon launches the Adobe Bridge application.

Ⓒ About InDesign (Windows)Selecting this option redisplays the opening splash screen shown at application launch. To close it, click anywhere on the graphic.You can find this option under the InDesign menu in Mac OS.

Ⓓ Configure Plug-ins (Windows) Displays a dialog that contains several plug-in management controls. You can find this option under the InDesign menu in Mac OS.

Ⓔ Activate Allows you to activate InDesign CS2 on your primary machine via the Web. In order to continue using the application, you must activate your copy within 30 days of installation. Once it's activated, you can install your purchased copy on one other machine.

Ⓕ Transfer Activation Allows you to transfer activation of your purchased copy of InDesign CS2 to another machine. Once it's transferred, you will not be able to use the application on your original machine.

Ⓖ Online Support Selecting this option takes you to the InDesign support page at Adobe.com. You must have a working Internet connection to access Online Support.

Ⓗ Updates Selecting this option checks for available updates online. You must have a working Internet connection to update InDesign CS2.

Ⓘ Registration Allows you to register your copy of InDesign CS2 via the Internet. You must have a working Internet connection to register.

Ⓙ InDesign Online Selecting this option takes you to the InDesign products page at Adobe.com. You must have a working Internet connection to access Online Support.

CHAPTER 3

InDesign Tools

IT'S IMPOSSIBLE TO CREATE your page layout masterpiece without first learning the tools you have to work with. That's why in this chapter, we're going to take a guided tour through the InDesign Toolbox showing you where each tool is located, what it does, and how best to use it.

The InDesign Toolbox is a lot closer to what you'd see in PageMaker than in QuarkXPress, and almost identical to Illustrator. Although you may not realize it yet, the Toolbox contains quite a few exciting features. Just like any good, overflowing toolbox (you know, like the one in your garage…), digging deeper and deeper into it can reveal some tools you didn't even know you had but could probably put to use right away.

- 3.1 **Toolbox**
- 3.2 **Control Bar**
- 3.3 **Selection Tool**
- 3.4 **Direct Selection and Position Tools**
- 3.5 **Pen Tools**
- 3.6 **Type Tools**
- 3.7 **Pencil Tools**
- 3.8 **Line Tool**
- 3.9 **Frame Tools**
- 3.10 **Shape Tools**
- 3.11 **Rotate Tool**
- 3.12 **Scale Tool**
- 3.13 **Shear Tool**
- 3.14 **Free Transform Tool**
- 3.15 **Eyedropper Tool**
- 3.16 **Measure Tool**
- 3.17 **Gradient Tool**
- 3.18 **Button Tool**
- 3.19 **Scissors Tool**
- 3.20 **Hand Tool**
- 3.21 **Zoom Tool**
- 3.22 **Other Toolbox Functions**

3.1 Toolbox

Related Tasks

3.2 Control Bar
4.2 Customizing Your Workspace
5.1 General Preferences

Shortcuts

Show/hide all controls
Mac and Win: Tab

Show/hide all controls except Toolbox and Control bar
Mac and Win: Shift+Tab

Tip

Double-clicking the tab located at the top of the Toolbox allows you to scroll through the three available display settings: double-column, single-column, or single-row. Just keep double-clicking the top bar until you find the display you like best.

The Toolbox contains all the different tools available to you—each one represented by a descriptive icon. However, if you're still not sure what tool you're viewing, hover your mouse over it in the Toolbox until a small tooltip description appears.

You can activate a tool by clicking its icon, or by typing its assigned keyboard shortcut (which is included in the tooltip). Any icon showing a small arrow in the bottom-right corner indicates an available toolset—more tools are "hidden" under the one shown. Clicking and holding the icon reveals a flyout menu of additional tools.

There are three ways to display the free-floating Toolbox on your screen. The default preference displays it in Adobe's traditional double-column format. But in Preferences > General, you can also change it to display in a single column (like QuarkXPress) or single row.

Each tool or toolset has its own section in this chapter. Nontool items at the bottom of the Toolbox are explained in Section 3.22 at the end of the chapter.

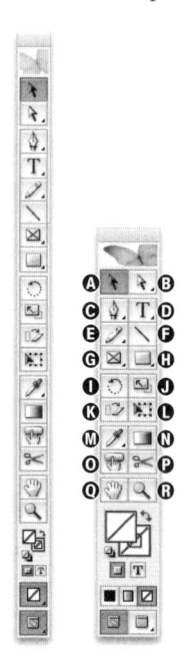

- **Ⓐ** Selection tool (keyboard shortcut V)
- **Ⓑ** Direct Selection (A) and Position (Shift+A) tools
- **Ⓒ** Pen (P), Add Anchor Point (=), Delete Anchor Point (-) and Convert Direction Point (Shift+C) tools
- **Ⓓ** Type (T) and Type on a Path (Shift+T) tools
- **Ⓔ** Pencil tool (N)
- **Ⓕ** Line tool (\)
- **Ⓖ** Rectangle Frame (F), Ellipse Frame, and Polygon Frame tools
- **Ⓗ** Rectangle (M), Ellipse (L), and Polygon tools
- **Ⓘ** Rotate tool (R)
- **Ⓙ** Scale tool (S)
- **Ⓚ** Shear tool (O)
- **Ⓛ** Free Transform tool (E)
- **Ⓜ** Eyedropper (I) and Measure (K) tools
- **Ⓝ** Gradient tool (G)
- **Ⓞ** Button tool (B)
- **Ⓟ** Scissors tool (C)
- **Ⓠ** Hand tool (H)
- **Ⓡ** Zoom tool (Z)

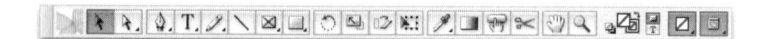

3.2 Control Bar

When you launch InDesign, the Control bar appears docked under the menu bar at the top of your screen. If you prefer, you can drag it to a different location.

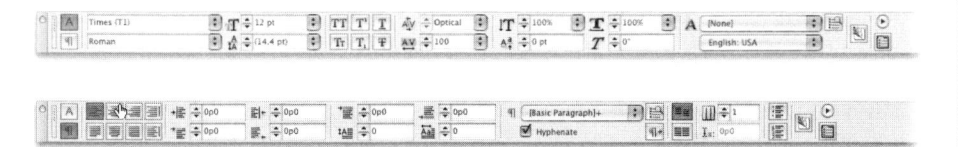

When the Type tool is selected, the Control bar displays either the character (top) or paragraph (bottom) formatting controls; these attributes are explained in the sections covering the Character and Paragraph palettes. Click the icons at the left end of the bar to switch between character and paragraph controls.

Any other tool you choose from the Toolbox displays the controls shown below. When a data field is accompanied by a set of up/down arrows, you can set the value for that attribute by entering a value into the field or by clicking the arrows.

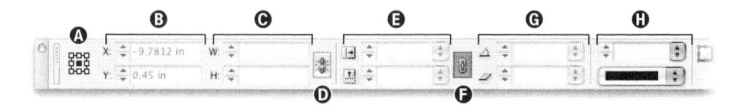

Ⓐ Reference Point Allows you to choose a default axis for making object transformations. Click one of the nine squares to set your preference. Your current position is indicated by a black square; white squares represent available positions.

Ⓑ X and Y Locations Lets you specify the numerical X-axis and Y-axis positions for any currently selected tool or object. Setting one of these repositions the selected object or group of objects along the relevant axis.

Ⓒ Width and Height Allows you to specify the exact width and height measurement for any currently selected object, or any object as it is created with a specific tool.

Ⓓ Constrain Proportions For Width & Height Activates or deactivates the constrain proportions feature when you're drawing objects. A broken-chain icon indicates that the control is off.

Ⓔ Scale X and Y Percentages Lets you specify the X-axis (top) and Y-axis (bottom) percentages for any object you scale. Setting one of these adjusts the scale percentage for a selected object or group of objects.

Ⓕ Constrain Proportions For Scaling Activates or deactivates the constrain proportions feature when scaling objects. A broken-chain icon indicates that the control is off.

Ⓖ Rotation and Shear X Angles The degree of angle for any object you rotate (top) or shear (bottom). Setting one of these adjusts the degree of rotation or shear for a selected object or group of objects.

Ⓗ Stroke Size and Style Allows you to choose a point size (top) and style (bottom) for the stroke on a selected object or group of objects.

Related Tasks

1.4 Interface Objects
3.1 Toolbox
3.6 Type Tools
4.21 Type and Tables Palettes

Shortcuts

Show/hide Control bar
Mac: Opt+Cmd+6
Win: Alt+Ctrl+6

Type tool
Mac and Win: T

Hide all controls except Toolbox and Control bar
Mac and Win: Shift+Tab

Tip

You can minimize the undocked, free-floating Control bar by double-clicking the tab located on the far left.

3.2 Control Bar (continued)

Related Tasks

1.4 Interface Objects
3.1 Toolbox
3.6 Type Tools

Shortcuts

Show/hide Control bar
Mac: Opt+Cmd+6
Win: Alt+Ctrl+6

Type tool
Mac and Win: T

Tip

If you have a text frame selected, Option-clicking (Mac) or Alt-clicking (Windows) the Number Of Columns icon in the Control bar launches the Text Frame Options dialog box.

I Object Style Double-click the icon to create a new object style. Option-click (Mac) or Alt-click (Windows) the icon to edit an existing style. The menu allows you to choose and apply a style to a selected object or group of objects.

J Quick Apply Clicking this toggle opens a palette that allows you to search through and apply character, paragraph, and object styles. If the Type tool is selected, Quick Apply only allows you to apply or edit character and paragraph styles.

K Clear Attributes Not Defined By Style An object must have a style applied to it in order to use this button. Clicking it clears any nondefined attributes from a selected object. After clicking, only styled attributes remain.

L Clear Overrides Click to clear any overridden object style changes made to a selected item.

M Go To Bridge Launches the Adobe Bridge file browser application that comes with the Creative Suite 2.

N Control bar pull-down menu Displays a submenu of options specific to the currently selected object and tool.

O Palette toggle Opens and closes palettes that coincide with the currently selected tool.

InDesign displays different controls at the far right of the Control bar when specific objects are selected with either selection tool. Here are the selections that trigger these changes and the tools that appear.

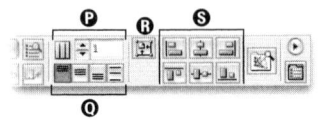

Left, when a single text frame is selected; right, when two or more text frames are selected.

- **P Number of Columns** The number of columns for the selected text frame or group of text frames (you must have a text frame selected for these controls to appear). Option-click (Mac) or Alt-click (Windows) the icon to access the Text Frame Options dialog.
- **Q Text alignment** Selecting a text frame triggers this group of controls to align text within a frame: Align Top, Align Center, Align Bottom, and Justify Vertically.
- **R Fit Frame to Content** Crops the selected frame or frames to fit proportionately around the contents.
- **S Object alignment** Apply specific object alignment to selected text frames: Align Left Edges, Align Horizontal Centers, Align Right Edges, Align Top Edges, Align Vertical Centers, and Align Bottom Edges.

3.2 Control Bar *(continued)*

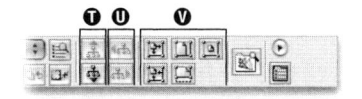

Left, when a single graphic frame is selected; right, when two or more graphic frames are selected

- **① Select Container or Content** Allows you to toggle back and forth between selecting a graphic frame's container (top icon) or its contents (bottom icon)—without having to switch selection tools.
- **① Select Previous or Next Object in a Group** Lets you select the next object (top icon) or previous object (bottom icon) in the stacking order of a group.
- **① Fitting** Allows you to Fit Content To Frame, Fit Frame To Content, Fit Content Proportionately, Fit Frame Proportionately, and Center Content.

Related Tasks

4.21 Type and Tables Palettes

6.16 Overriding Master Page Items

Shortcuts

Hide all controls except Toolbox and Control bar
Mac and Win: Shift+Tab

3.3 Selection Tool

Related Tasks

7.2	Selection Tool vs. Direct Selection Tool
7.3	Selecting Multiple Objects
8.1	Moving Objects
8.2	Resizing Objects
8.6	Grouping and Ungrouping Objects

Shortcuts

Selection tool
Mac and Win: V

Select all
Mac: Cmd+A
Win: Ctrl+A

Deselect all
Mac: Shift+Cmd+A
Win: Shift+Ctrl+A

Tip

You are always able to see your selection whether you're showing or hiding frame edges, or whether you are in normal or preview mode.

The Selection tool is similar to the Item tool in QuarkXPress, and exactly ike the Selection tool in PageMaker and Illustrator. You can use this tool to select items in the document, move them, and/or view or change their settings using the Control bar.

To select an object, just click anywhere on it with the Selection tool. The boundary nodes of the frame or selected group appear, indicating that you now have the item selected. You can then move the selected item(s) by clicking and dragging with your mouse.

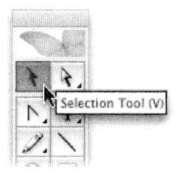

You can access the Selection tool by clicking its icon in the Toolbox or by typing the letter V.

To select more than one item at a time, hold down the Shift key as you click. You can then move the selected items together.

You can also make a selection by dragging with the Selection tool over an area that includes the item(s) you want to select.

Deselecting

To deselect an item or items with the Selection tool, Shift-click the object, or click anywhere else in the document or off the Page.

Click the item you'd like to select. When the object's boundary nodes appear, you'll know it's selected and you can then move the item.

Adjusting Frames

Clicking and dragging one of the boundary nodes of a single selected frame allows you to adjust the frame's dimensions, but not scale the frame's contents. This same rule applies to all frames in a group. To adjust a frame proportionately, be sure that the Constrain Proportions For Width & Height lock is secured in the Control bar. You can also constrain proportions for width and height by holding down the Shift key as you drag a boundary node of a frame. Note that adjusting the frame dimensions can also move the frame's contents.

3.4 Direct Selection and Position Tools

InDesign's Direct Selection tool is designed to work like the one found in Illustrator, but with a few twists. You can use it to select, move, or scale the contents of a graphic frame (such as a placed image) or to select and move points on a drawn path, or to change the shape of a frame by moving any of its corner nodes.

The Direct Selection toolset also includes a dynamic Position tool. This tool is used specifically for cropping placed images inside a graphic frame, not for altering points on a path. However, you can still position placed images with the Direct Selection tool if you prefer.

To crop images with the Position tool, select a graphic frame by clicking one of its edges. You can then select and move any of its corner or side nodes just as you would with the Selection tool. To move an image within a frame, hover the cursor over the image until it dynamically changes into a hand icon, then drag.

To select the contents of a graphic frame, click anywhere on the contents with either tool.

To select and reposition more than one item at a time, hold down the Shift key as you click. However, keep in mind that you are only moving the selected items within the boundaries of each item's container (a.k.a. a frame in InDesign).

You can also make a selection by dragging with the Direct Selection or Position tool over an area that includes the item(s) you want to select.

Deselecting

To deselect an item or items with the Direct Selection Position tool, just click anywhere else in the document or off the Page, or choose Edit > Deselect All

Selecting Points on a Path

The Direct Selection tool also allows you to select and move points on a drawn path.

To reveal the points of a frame, click any frame edge. You can then change the frame's shape by selecting and moving these points.

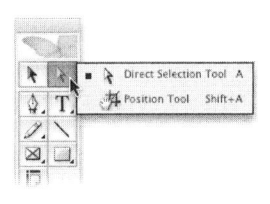

You can access the Direct Selection and Position tools by clicking either icon in the Toolbox or by typing the letter A (Direct Selection tool) or Shift+A (Position tool)

Once selected, the boundary frame of the placed contents appears, indicating that you now have the item selected. You can then reposition the selected item(s) within the frame by clicking and dragging with your mouse.

With the Direct Selection tool, click any drawn path to reveal its points. You can then move the entire path, or click any point and reposition it. To select and/or adjust multiple points on a path, hold down the Shift key as you click.

Related Tasks

7.2 Selection Tool vs. Direct Selection Tool

7.3 Selecting Multiple Objects

8.1 Moving Objects

8.2 Resizing Objects

8.6 Grouping and Ungrouping Objects

Shortcuts

Direct Selection tool
Mac and Win: A

Position tool
Mac and Win: Shift+A

Select all
Mac: Cmd+A
Win: Ctrl+A

Deselect all
Mac: Shift+Cmd+A
Win: Shift+Ctrl+A

Tip

With the Direct Selection or Position tool, you can scale a placed image proportionately within its frame by Shift-clicking and dragging any one of its boundary nodes.

3.5 Pen Tools

Related Tasks

4.11	Object and Layout Palettes
7.1	Frame/Shape Overview
7.2	Selection Tool vs. Direct Selection Tool
7.6	Drawing Custom Shapes
7.8	Modifying Paths and Frames
12.12	Creating a Clipping Path in InDesign
12.13	Editing Clipping Paths

Shortcuts

Pen toolset
Mac and Win: P

Add Anchor Point tool
Mac and Win: =

Delete Anchor Point tool
Mac and Win: -

Convert Direction Point tool
Mac and Win: Shift+C

Tip

You can add or delete points using the Pen tool, without having to switch to the Add Anchor or Delete Anchor tool. To add, just place the Pen tool cursor over a line where there is no point and click. To delete, place the Pen tool cursor over an existing point and click.

The Pen toolset in InDesign mirrors the one found in Illustrator. Although they appear differently in the Illustrator Toolbox, the tools are named the same and work in exactly the same way. This means you can create custom vector drawings right here in InDesign.

Pen Tool

Choose the Pen tool to create a vector path, just as you would in Illustrator or Freehand. Click and drag to create a series of connecting points that result in a custom drawn line or shape. Clicking with the Pen creates a point, and dragging with the mouse creates its curve in relation to the previous point and the next point placed on the path.

Add Anchor Point Tool

This tool adds a point to an existing path, which lets you create intricate curves, corners, and bends to your custom-drawn line or shape. Simply click anywhere along the path to add a new point.

Delete Anchor Point Tool

With this tool, click any existing point to delete it. Keep in mind that deleting points can drastically change the appearance of your custom drawn line or shape.

Convert Direction Point Tool

With this tool you can change the direction of a selected point's curve on an existing path. Click any existing point to reset the curve handles, allowing you to readjust it. Click and drag the handles to change the curve.

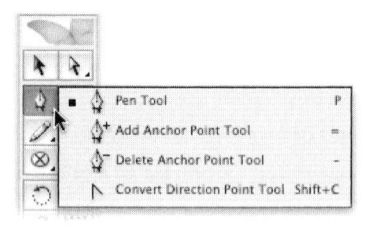

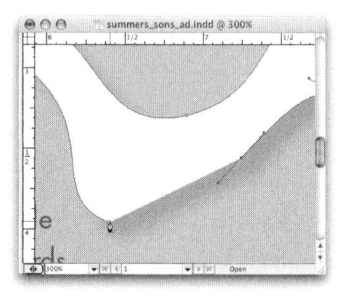

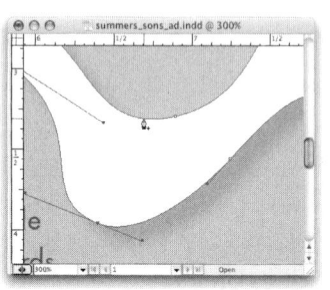

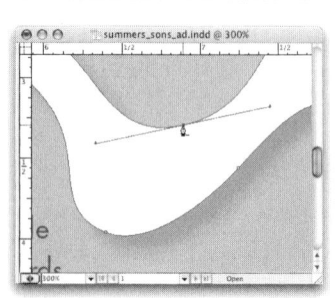

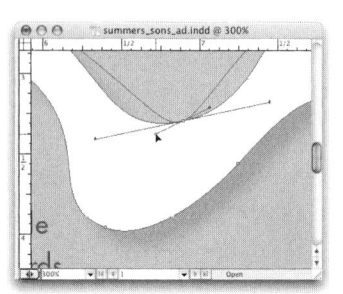

34

3.6 Type Tools

The Type tools in InDesign are very different from those in QuarkXPress. For instance, you can convert any empty frame or shape into a text frame by clicking inside it with the Type tool and entering some text. You can also create type on a path by choosing the Type On A Path tool and clicking the area of the path where you'd like to place some text.

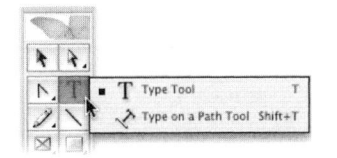

You can access the Type toolset by clicking its icon in the Toolbox or by typing the letter T.

Type Tool

You can set character and paragraph attributes in the Control bar or in the Character and Paragraph palettes. When a data field is accompanied by a set of up/down arrows, you can set the value for that attribute either by entering a value into the field or by clicking the arrows. Arrows to the left of the field provide a list of default standard values; arrows to the right change the value by a fixed increment. Here are the character formatting controls (paragraph formatting controls are illustrated later in this section):

Choose the Type tool when you're ready to add text to your document. Click and drag to create a text frame, or click inside any empty frame or shape and begin typing. Select text by dragging the Type tool cursor over it.

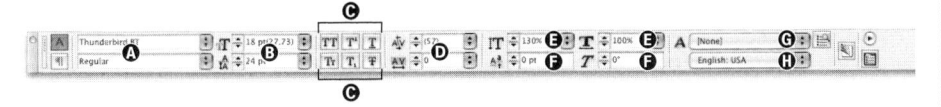

A **Font and Font Style** Let you specify the typeface (top) and typestyle (bottom) of any currently selected text; also allow you to apply a face or style by choosing from lists of those available loaded in your system.

B **Font Size and Leading** Allow you to specify the type size and leading amount of any currently selected text.

C **Type Style buttons** Applies or removes specific styles to selected text, including All Caps, Superscript, Underline, Small Caps, Subscript, and Strikethrough.

D **Kerning and Tracking** Let you specify the kerning (top) and tracking (bottom) amounts in thousandths of an em for any currently selected text.

E **Vertical and Horizontal Scale** Allow you to set the amount of vertical (left) and horizontal (right) scaling for any currently selected text.

F **Baseline Shift and Skew** Let you specify the amount of baseline shift and skew applied to selected text.

G **Character Style controls** Double-click the icon to create a new character style. Option-click (Mac) or Alt-click (Windows) the icon to edit an existing style. Click the menu to choose and apply an existing character style to selected text.

H **Dictionary** Allows you to choose from several language dictionaries available in InDesign.

Related Tasks

4.21	Type and Tables Palettes
5.2	Type Preferences
5.3	Advanced Type Preferences
7.4	Selecting Type
10.1	Kerning and Tracking
10.2	Scaling and Skewing Type
10.3	Adjusting Leading and Baseline Shift
11.1	Creating and Applying Character Styles

Shortcuts

Type tool
Mac and Win: T

Type on a Path tool
Mac and Win: Shift+T

Show/hide Control bar
Mac: Opt+Cmd+6
Win: Alt+Ctrl+6

Tip

You can set your default document type preferences by Deselecting All (Mac: Shift+Cmd+A; Windows: Shift+Ctrl+A), then accessing the Type tool and choosing your preferred attributes in the Control bar or Character/Paragraph palettes.

3.6 Type Tools *(continued)*

Related Tasks

4.21	Type and Tables Palettes
5.2	Type Preferences
5.3	Advanced Type Preferences
7.4	Selecting Type
10.1	Kerning and Tracking
10.2	Scaling and Skewing Type
10.3	Adjusting Leading and Baseline Shift
11.1	Creating and Applying Character Styles
11.2	Creating and Applying Paragraph Styles

Shortcuts

Type tool
Mac and Win: T

Type on a Path tool
Mac and Win: Shift+T

Show/hide Control bar
Mac: Opt+Cmd+6
Win: Alt+Ctrl+6

Tip

To switch between Character and Paragraph formatting controls in the Control bar, access the Type tool and press Opt+Cmd+7 (Mac) or Alt+Ctrl+7 (Windows).

Here are the paragraph formatting controls:

- **Ⓐ Alignment options** Let you apply specific text alignment to selected text frames, including Align Left, Align Center, Align Right, Align Towards Spine, Justify With Last Line Aligned Left, Justify With Last Line Aligned Center, Justify All Lines, Align Away From Spine.

- **Ⓑ Indents** Lets you specify the amounts of paragraph indent for any currently selected text, as follows: top left, left indent; bottom left, first line left indent; top-right, right indent; bottom-right, last-line right indent.

- **Ⓒ Space Before And After** Allows you to set the amount of added space preceding (left) or following (right) any currently selected paragraph.

- **Ⓓ Drop Cap Number Of Lines** Allows you to specify the number of lines an applied drop cap will fall.

- **Ⓔ Drop Cap One Or More Characters** Allows you to specify the number of characters to apply a drop cap to.

- **Ⓕ Paragraph Style controls** Double-click the icon to create a new paragraph style. Option-click (Mac) or Alt-click (Windows) the icon to edit an existing style. Click the menu to choose and apply an existing paragraph style to selected text.

- **Ⓖ Hyphenate** Keeping this box checked allows all paragraphs in your document to hyphenate automatically. To bypass this option, select any paragraphs you don't want hyphenated and uncheck the box, or uncheck it before creating any text frames.

- **Ⓗ Quick Apply** Clicking this opens a palette that allows you to search through and apply character, paragraph, and object styles. If the Type tool is selected, Quick Apply only allows you to apply or edit character and paragraph styles.

- **Ⓘ Clear Overrides In Selection** Selected text must have a style applied to it in order to use this button. Clicking it clears any nondefined attributes from the text; only styled attributes remain.

- **Ⓙ Baseline Grid Alignment controls** Allow you to turn the Snap To Baseline Grid option on or off.

- **Ⓚ Number Of Columns controls** Allow you to change the number of columns for the selected text frame or group of text frames.

- **Ⓛ Horizontal Cursor Position** Lets you specify the current horizontal position of the Type tool's cursor.

- **Ⓜ Bulleted or Numbered List** Clicking one of these toggles applies or removes a bulleted list or numbered list format to any text selected in a frame.

3.6 Type Tools *(continued)*

Type on a Path Tool

You can create type on a path by first accessing the Type On A Path tool (Shift+T), then clicking any existing path, frame, or shape. A special Type On A Path cursor appears once you click, indicating that you can now start typing.

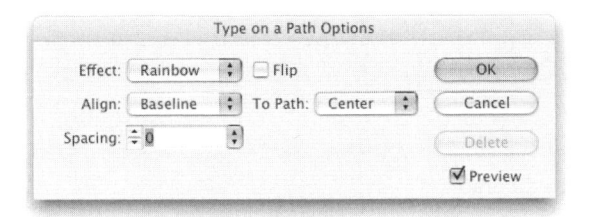

You can open the Type On A Path Options dialog by choosing Type > Type On A Path > Options. This dialog allows you to choose from several styles, including Rainbow, Skew, 3DRibbon, Stair Step, and Gravity. You can also change the spacing, alignment, and justification, and even flip the direction of the type.

It's easy! Just click any path, frame, or shape and start typing!

Related Tasks

4.21	Type and Tables Palettes
5.2	Type Preferences
5.3	Advanced Type Preferences
7.4	Selecting Type
10.1	Kerning and Tracking
10.2	Scaling and Skewing Type
10.3	Adjusting Leading and Baseline Shift
11.2	Creating and Applying Paragraph Styles

Shortcuts

Type tool
Mac and Win: T

Type On A Path tool
Mac and Win: Shift+T

Show/hide Control bar
Mac: Opt+Cmd+6
Win: Alt+Ctrl+6

Tip

You can open the Type On A Path Options dialog by double-clicking the tool's icon in the Toolbox. You can set default Type On A Path options by accessing the dialog with nothing selected, or change options for any currently selected Type On A Path items.

3.7 Pencil Tools

Related Tasks

3.5 Pen Tools
7.7 Drawing Freeform Shapes
7.8 Modifying Paths and Frames

Shortcuts

Pencil tool
Mac and Win: N

Direct Selection tool
Mac and Win: A

Pen tool
Mac and Win: P

Add Anchor Point tool
Mac and Win: =

Delete Anchor Point tool
Mac and Win: -

Convert Direction Point tool
Mac and Win: Shift+C

Tip

You can modify the shape of any text or image frame with the Pencil tool. Select the frame first, then access the Pencil tool and begin drawing.

If trying to manipulate tiny little points and Bezier curves with the Pen toolset drives you nuts, you may want to try using the Pencil toolset instead. These tools allow you to draw freeform just as you would with a real pencil set. And if you use them along with a graphics pen and tablet, you can get a good feel for freeform drawing in InDesign.

Pencil Tool

To create a freeform shape using the Pencil tool, just choose it from the Toolbox and begin drawing. As you draw, InDesign calculates where the points fall on the path and places them for you. You can then switch to the Pen toolset and manipulate the placed points, or you can try using the Smooth and Erase tools.

Smooth Tool

If your drawing winds up a little too freeform, you can always clean it up by clicking and dragging over your points with the Smooth tool. Doing so removes any extraneous anchor points while maintaining the overall shape of the drawing. This is a great tool for "smoothing" out any harsh, jagged edges. I'm sure that after trying this a few times, you'll agree that it's a lot easier doing cleanup work with the Smooth tool than with the Pen tools.

Erase Tool

Sometimes it may just be easier to erase part of your drawing and redraw it. Just choose the Erase tool from the Toolbox and click and drag over any points you want to get rid of. Now you can redraw with the Pencil or Pen tools.

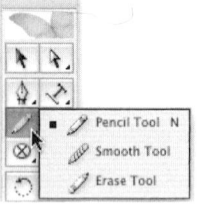

You can access the Pencil toolset by clicking its icon in the Toolbox or by typing the letter N.

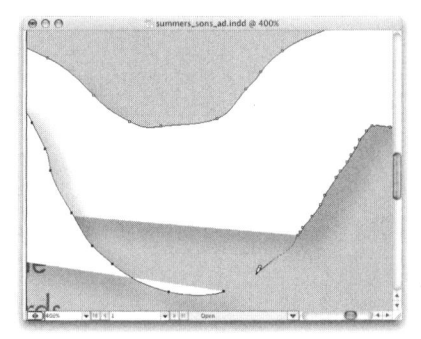

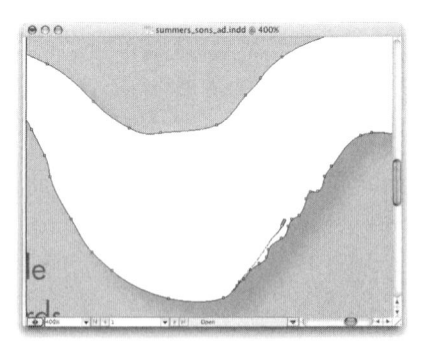

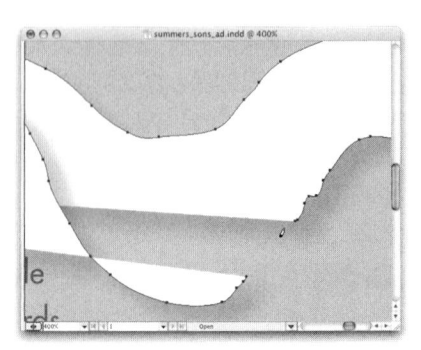

3.8 Line Tool

Drawing with the Pen and Pencil tools is great, but what if you just want to draw a simple line? Well, you can do that in InDesign too.

Unlike with QuarkXPress and PageMaker, you can draw diagonal, vertical or horizontal lines in InDesign with just one Line tool. To constrain the tool to vertical, horizontal, or 45° increments, hold down the Shift key as you draw. For lines at other angles, just click and drag in any direction you like. You can also draw as many lines as you want without the application automatically switching to a selection tool as it does in Quark.

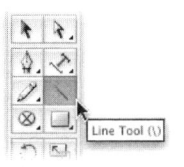

You can access the Line tool by clicking its icon in the Toolbox or by pressing the forward slash key (\).

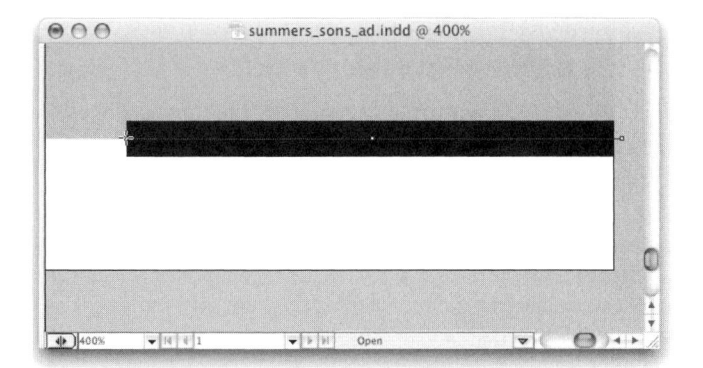

Related Tasks

3.3	Selection Tool
3.4	Direct Selection and Position Tools
3.5	Pen Tools
3.7	Pencil Tools
7.13	Stroking Frames, Shapes, and Paths
7.16	Applying Stroked Path Start and End Styles
7.17	Saving and Applying Custom Strokes
7.18	Applying Gap Color to Open Stroke Styles

Shortcuts

Line tool
Mac and Win: \

Direct Selection tool
Mac and Win: A

Selection tool
Mac and Win: V

Tip

To create vertical, horizontal, or 45° lines with the Line tool, hold down the Shift key to constrain as you draw.

Adjusting the Default Stroke Settings

The default stroke setting for all drawn lines (Pen and Pencil tool included) is 1 pt., solid black. To change the application default setting, close all documents and adjust the point size and stroke style in either the Stroke palette or Control bar. All the lines you draw will then take on these characteristics.

Line Flexibility

Lines drawn with the Line tool are easy to work with in that they have only two points (one on each end) that can be adjusted by selecting either one with the Direct Selection tool and repositioning it. You can also add points to a line using either the Pen or Pencil tools.

In addition, you can move lines with the Selection tool, rotate them with the Rotate tool, and scale them with—yes, you guessed it—the Scale tool.

3.9 Frame Tools

Related Tasks

6.11 Creating Master Pages
6.21 Snapping to Document Grid
7.1 Frame/Shape Overview
7.8 Modifying Paths and Frames
7.9 Nesting Objects
7.13 Stroking Frames, Shapes, and Paths
7.19 Applying Corner Effects
8.1 Moving Objects
11.5 Creating and Applying Object Styles

Shortcuts

Rectangle Frame tool
Mac and Win: F

Move
Mac: Shift+Cmd+M
Win: Shift+Ctrl+M

Lock position
Mac: Cmd+L
Win: Ctrl+L

Unlock position
Mac: Opt+Cmd+L
Win: Ctrl+Alt+L

Place
Mac: Cmd+D
Win: Ctrl+D

Tip

You can convert any empty frame, shape, or path into a text frame. All you have to do is click it with the Type tool.

Frames are the basic building blocks for creating page layouts in InDesign. All text and graphic images must be placed inside a frame. In fact, you can even place a frame inside a frame! QuarkXPress users may find it confusing that you do not always have to create a frame first before placing any text or graphics—but you can if you want to.

To create a frame, choose one of the tools and click and drag. Holding down the Shift key as you click and drag constrains your shape to its original proportions, making a rectangle a perfect square and an ellipse a perfect circle rather than an oval. Holding down the Alt or Option key draws from the center. You can also create a rectangle or ellipse frameby clicking once on the Pasteboard with either tool selected. Enter the preferred width and height settings and click OK for the frame to appear in the same spot as you clicked with the tool.

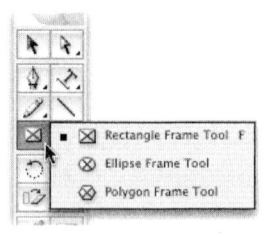

You can access the Frame toolset by clicking and holding on its icon in the Toolbox or by typing the letter F.

Press Cmd+H (Mac) or Ctrl+H (Windows) to show your frame edges if they're not already visible, and you will notice a large X positioned in the center of the rectangle. This indicates that you now have an empty frame on your page waiting for contents. Once you place some contents into the frame, the X disappears. You may find it helpful to use these "X" frames as visible placeholders in a mechanical layout or master page.

You can access the Polygon Settings dialog by double-clicking the Polygon Frame tool icon in the Toolbox; or access the Polygon dialog containing additional width and height settings by clicking once on the Page with the Polygon Frame tool selected. In the dialog choose the number of sides for your polygon and also the percentage of inset for creating a star-shaped frame.

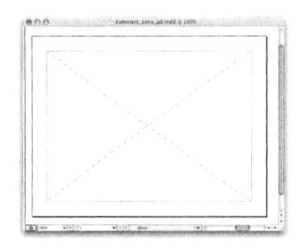

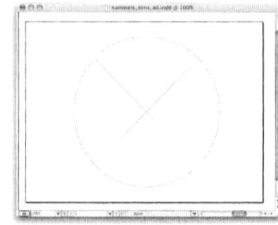

A rectangle frame

An ellipse frame

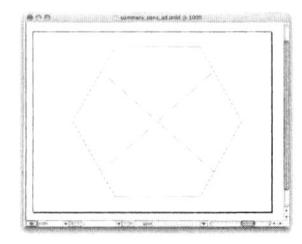

A polygon frame

3.10 Shape Tools

With the Shape tools, you can create rectangles, ellipses, and polygons; but what most people don't realize *is that shapes can also be frames!* That's right—you can place images and text into any shapes you create. With InDesign, just about any object can be turned into a frame.

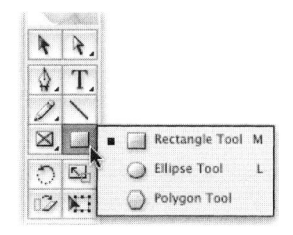

To create a shape, choose the tool and click and drag. Holding down the Shift key as you click and drag constrains your shape to its original proportions, making a rectangle a perfect square and an ellipse a perfect circle rather than an oval. Holding down the Alt or Option key as you click and drag draws from the center.

InDesign applied default stroke settings to your shape, but you can adjust them in either the Stroke palette or in the Control bar. You can also add a fill, place a graphic, add some text, or merge with other shapes.

You can access the Polygon Settings dialog by double-clicking the Polygon Shape tool icon in the Toolbox, or access the Polygon dialog (containing additional width and height settings) by clicking once on the Page with the Polygon Shape tool. The dialog lets you choose the number of sides for your shape and also the percentage of inset to create a star shape.

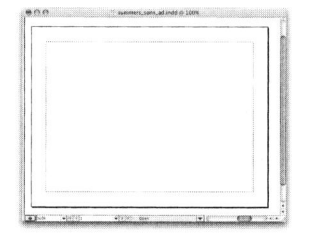

You can access the Rectangle tool by clicking its icon in the Toolbox or by typing the letter M. The shortcut key for the Ellipse tool is L. The poor Polygon tool has no default keyboard shortcut, but you can create one for it by choosing Edit > Keyboard Shortcuts.

A rectangle shape

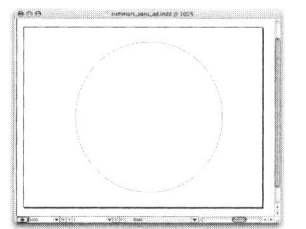

An ellipse shape

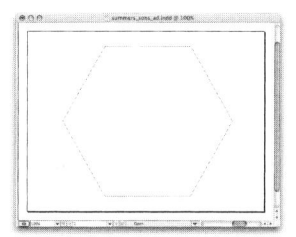

A polygon shape

Related Tasks

6.11	Creating Master Pages
6.21	Snapping to Document Grid
7.1	Frame/Shape Overview
7.8	Modifying Paths and Frames
7.9	Nesting Objects
7.13	Stroking Frames, Shapes, and Paths
7.19	Applying Corner Effects
7.21	Creating Custom Shapes with Pathfinder
8.1	Moving Objects
11.5	Creating and Applying Object Styles

Shortcuts

Rectangle tool
Mac and Win: M

Ellipse tool
Mac and Win: L

Lock position
Mac: Cmd+L
Win: Ctrl+L

Unlock position
Mac: Opt+Cmd+L
Win: Ctrl+Alt+L

Place
Mac: Cmd+D
Win: Ctrl+D

Tip

You can merge selected shapes together using the Pathfinder palette.

3.11 Rotate Tool

Related Tasks

3.14 Free Transform Tool

8.3 Rotating Objects

Shortcuts

Rotate tool
Mac and Win: R

Selection tool
Mac and Win: V

Direct Selection tool
Mac and Win: A

Tip

Holding down the Shift key as you rotate snaps each turn to 45° increments.

If you're familiar with the Rotate tool in Illustrator, you won't find any surprises here—it is exactly the same in InDesign. In comparison to QuarkXPress, InDesign's Rotate tool is slightly different in that it keeps its selection after rotating. You may find it a little easier to maneuver in InDesign.

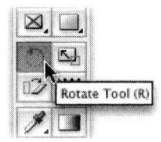

To rotate, access the Rotate tool, select an object, and then click and drag.

The crosshair target that appears in the center of your selected object indicates where the tool is rotating from. The default rotation point is in the absolute center point of the object; however, you can reposition it anywhere in the document window, on or off the Page. Just click the crosshair target and move it to the desired position.

Rotating a Frame's Contents

You can also rotate a placed graphic within its bounding frame. To do so, you must first select a placed graphic with the Direct Selection tool and then switch to the Rotate tool. You can then rotate the image within the frame and reposition the rotation point, just like with any other object.

Rotating a Frame but Not Its Contents

To take it even one step further, you can rotate a frame without rotating its contents! Just make your selection and then double-click the Rotate tool icon in the Toolbox to bring up the Rotate dialog. Uncheck the Rotate Content box and enter a value in the Angle field. Click the Preview check box to see the effect, and if you like what you see, click OK to apply.

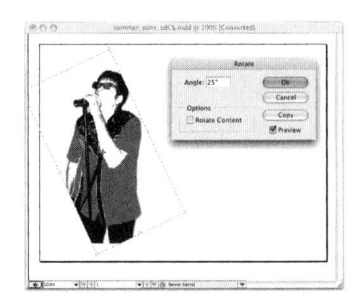

You can access the Rotate tool by clicking its icon in the Toolbox or by typing the letter R.

Rotating a graphics frame. Text frames, shapes, paths, lines, tables, and grouped objects can also be rotated; the tool works the same with every item.

Rotating a placed image within a graphics frame.

Rotating a frame but not its contents

3.12 Scale Tool

Although you can scale objects using the selection tools and various key combinations, it may be easier for you to try scaling in InDesign using the Scale tool. It works just like the Rotate tool, only with scaling rather than rotating.

To scale, access the Scale tool, select an object, and then click and drag. Clicking a corner node and holding down the Shift key as you scale constrains the shape to its original proportions.

The crosshair target that appears in the center of your selected object indicates where the tool is scaling from. The default scale-from point is in the absolute center of the object; however, you can reposition it anywhere in the document window, on or off the Page. Just click the crosshair target and move it to the desired position.

Scaling a Frame's Contents

You can also scale a placed graphic within its bounding frame. To do so, you must first select a placed graphic with the Direct Selection tool and then switch to the Scale tool. You can then scale the image within the frame. You can also reposition the scale-from point, just like with any other object.

Scaling a Frame but Not Its Contents

Just as you can with the Rotate tool, you can also scale a frame without scaling its contents. Make your selection and then double-click the Scale tool's icon in the Toolbox to bring up the Scale dialog. Uncheck the Scale Content box and enter values in the appropriate data fields. Click the Preview check box to see the effect, and if you like what you see, click OK to apply.

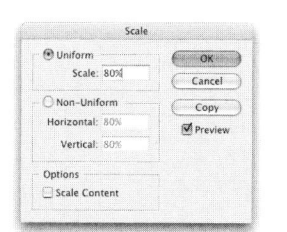

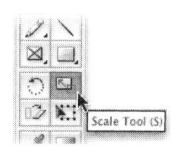

You can access the Scale tool by clicking its icon in the Toolbox or by typing the letter S.

Scaling a graphics frame. Text frames, shapes, paths, lines, tables, and grouped objects can also be scaled; the tool works the same with every item.

Scaling a placed image within a graphics frame

Scaling a frame, but not its content

Related Tasks

8.2   Resizing Objects
10.2 Scaling and Skewing Type
12.6 Resizing Placed Images
13.10 Resizing Tables

Shortcuts

Scale tool
Mac and Win: S

Selection tool
Mac and Win: V

Direct Selection tool
Mac and Win: A

Tip

With grouped items, it is not possible to scale frames alone without also scaling their contents.

3.13 Shear Tool

Related Tasks

8.5 Shearing Objects
10.2 Scaling and Skewing Type

Shortcuts

Shear tool
Mac and Win: O

Selection tool
Mac and Win: V

Direct Selection tool
Mac and Win: A

Tip

You can shear a table and all of its contents at once using the Shear tool.

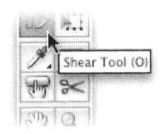

The Shear tool allows you to shear any frame and its contents. Text frames, graphic frames, shapes, paths, lines, tables, and grouped objects can all be sheared with the Shear tool. Access this tool by clicking its icon in the Toolbox or by typing the letter O.

To shear, access the Shear tool, select an object, and then click and drag. Holding down the Shift key constrains along the X-axis as you shear.

The crosshair target that appears in the center of the selected object indicates where the tool is shearing from. The default shear-from point is in the absolute center of the object; however, you can reposition it anywhere in the document window, on or off the Page. Just click the crosshair target and move it to the desired position.

Shearing a graphics frame

Shearing a Frame's Contents

You can also shear a placed graphic within its bounding frame, as shown here. To do so, you must first select a placed graphic with the Direct Selection tool, and then switch to the Shear tool. You can then shear the image within the frame. You can also reposition the shear-from point, just like with any other object.

Shearing a placed image within a graphics frame

Shearing a Frame but Not Its Contents

And yes, as with the Scale and Rotate tools, you can shear a frame without shearing its contents. Just make your selection and then double-click the tool's icon in the Toolbox to bring up the Shear dialog. Uncheck the Shear Content box and enter a value in one of the Angle data fields (overall shear angle or horizontal/vertical only). Click the Preview check box to see the effect, and if you like what you see, click OK to apply.

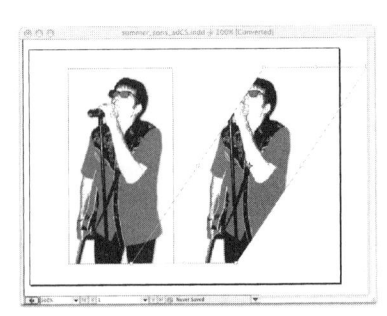

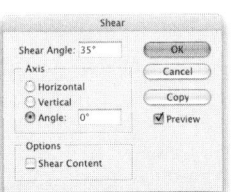

Shearing a frame, but not its contents

3.14 Free Transform Tool

With the Free Transform tool you can move, rotate, and scale objects all at once. Brilliant! Activate the Free Transform tool, then select an object. To scale, click and drag any node. Clicking and dragging one of the corner nodes while holding down the Shift key constrains proportions in the direction that you scale. Clicking and dragging one of the side nodes while holding down the Opt/Alt key constrains in both the direction that you scale and the opposite direction. To rotate, place your mouse over any corner of the selection until the cursor changes to a curved double-sided arrow, indicating that you can click and drag to rotate the object. To move an object, click and drag as you would with the Selection tool.

Notice that a crosshair target does not appear indicating where the rotation or scale-from point is located. The default rotation/scale-from point is always in the absolute center of the object, and you cannot reposition it as you can with the Rotate, Scale, and Shear tools.

You can access this tool by clicking its icon in the Toolbox or by typing the letter E.

You can scale (left) and rotate (right) a graphics frame with the Free Transform tool.

Free Transforming a Frame's Contents

You can also use the Free Transform tool on a placed graphic within its bounding frame, as shown here. To do so, you must first select a placed graphic with the Direct Selection tool, and then switch to the Free Transform tool. You can then scale, move, or rotate the image within the frame.

You can scale (left) and rotate (right) a placed image within a graphics frame using the Free Transform tool.

Free Transforming Text Frames

Yep! You guessed it. The Free Transform tool works on text frames too. Just click any text frame with the Free Transform tool and use it the same way as you would on a graphics frame. And the best part is—you can still edit the text after it has been transformed!

You can scale (left) and rotate (right) a text frame with the Free Transform tool.

Related Tasks

8.2 Resizing Objects
8.3 Rotating Objects
10.2 Scaling and Skewing Type
12.6 Resizing Placed Images
13.10 Resizing Tables

Shortcuts

Free Transform tool
Mac and Win: E

Selection tool
Mac and Win: V

Direct Selection tool
Mac and Win: A

Tip

You can also Free Transform grouped objects.

3.15 Eyedropper Tool

Related Tasks

4.5 Color Palette
4.17 Swatches Palette
7.10 Filling with Solid and Transparent Colors
7.12 Filling Text
10.5 Copy/Paste Type Formatting

Shortcuts

Eyedropper tool
Mac and Win: I

Swatches palette
Mac and Win: F5

Tip

You can also copy/paste InDesign drop shadow settings with the Eyedropper tool.

The Eyedropper tool allows you to sample colors from anywhere in your open InDesign documents (yes, even from placed images!). You can add a sampled color to the Swatches palette and then apply it to the fill or stroke of any frame, shape, path, line, or table. You can also colorize text this way. You can also copy/paste text and object formatting with this tool.

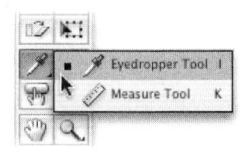

You can access the Eyedropper by clicking its icon in the Toolbox or by typing the letter I.

Sampling Colors

Activate the tool, then click the color you'd like to sample. The Eyedropper icon fills with black, indicating that you now have a sampled color ready to apply. The color also appears in the Fill or Stroke color swatch (whichever is placed in front) in the Toolbox and in the Swatches and Color palettes. You can then add the color to your swatches by clicking the swatch in any of the three locations and dragging it into the Swatches palette list. You can sample and apply colors from placed graphics, as well as from other open InDesign documents.

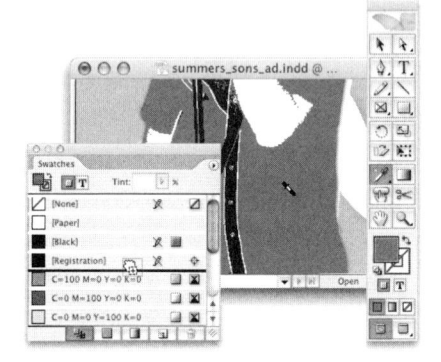

Sampling Styles

You can also use the Eyedropper tool to copy/paste formatting (including character, paragraph, and object styles). Click any text or object containing a style or formatting you'd like to sample with the Eyedropper tool, and notice the cursor icon that shows up next to the full Eyedropper icon. This indicates that you can now apply the sampled style and/or formatting to any text characters you highlight or objects you click with the Eyedropper.

When you're in a hurry this is a great quick and easy way to format a layout without having to set up any styles, especially because you can continue applying the sampled format/styles without having to resample.

You can copy text formatting and styles by clicking text with the Eyedropper.

Paste the sampled formatting and styles by highlighting text with the full Eyedropper icon.

3.16 Measure Tool

The Measure tool goes hand in hand with the Info palette. Use this tool to calculate the size of a placed graphic or the angle of a drawn path to match sizes or angles among objects in a document layout.

Activate the Measure tool, then click and drag along the area you want to measure. The Info palette opens automatically, providing you with specific measurements, including X and Y coordinates, width, height, and angle.

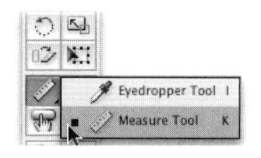

You can access the Measure tool by clicking its icon in the Toolbox or by typing the letter K.

Related Tasks

3.11   Rotate Tool
4.7   Info Palette

Shortcuts

Measure tool
Mac and Win: K

Rotate tool
Mac and Win: R

Info palette
Mac and Win: F8

Tip

Holding down the Shift key as you click and drag constrains the tool to 45-degree angles.

3.17 Gradient Tool

Related Tasks

4.6	Gradient Palette
4.17	Swatches Palette
7.11	Filling with Gradients
7.12	Filling Text
7.14	Stroking Text
13.11	Setting Table Borders, Strokes, and Fills

Shortcuts

Gradient tool
Mac and Win: G

Type tool
Mac and Win: T

Selection tool
Mac and Win: V

Swatches palette
Mac and Win: F5

Tip

A single gradient can also be applied to multiple objects and grouped objects with the Gradient tool.

The Gradient tool allows you to apply various gradient styles to selected items within your layout. This tool works closely with the Gradient and Swatches palettes, allowing you to apply gradients to both fills and strokes on selected frames, shapes, paths, and text.

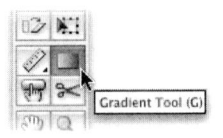

You can access the Gradient tool by clicking its icon in the Toolbox or by typing the letter G.

To apply a gradient, first select an object with the Selection tool or select some text with the Type tool (frames, shapes, paths, and text all work with the Gradient tool). Then activate the Gradient tool and click and drag in any direction to apply a gradient you've created in the Gradient palette or a gradient swatch that has been saved in the Swatches palette. To constrain the gradient in a certain direction, hold down the Shift key as you click and drag.

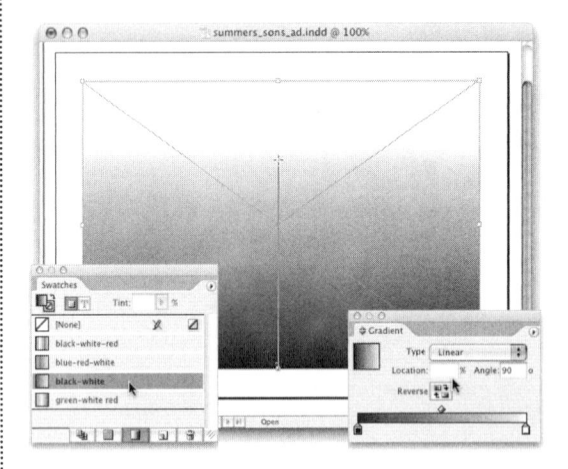

You can apply a gradient to editable text with the Gradient tool.

3.18 Button Tool

The Button tool is used for creating interactive behaviors that you can embed in an exported PDF document. Some of the behaviors you can attach to a button are Go To URL, Go To Anchor, Go To Page, Play Sound, and Play Movie.

Activate the Button tool, then click and drag over the area where you'd like to create an interactive button. Or you can also click once at the upper-left corner of the interactive area and enter the width and height amount for the button in the dialog that appears.

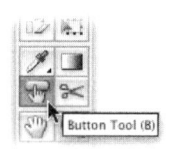

You can access the Button tool by clicking its icon in the Toolbox or by typing the letter B.

Setting Button Options

You can then specify the General and Behaviors options for a selected button by choosing Object > Interactive > Button Options. Choose the Event (Mouse Up, Mouse Down, etc.) and the Behavior (Go To Anchor, Go To Page, Play Sound, etc.) settings for your new button, and click OK.

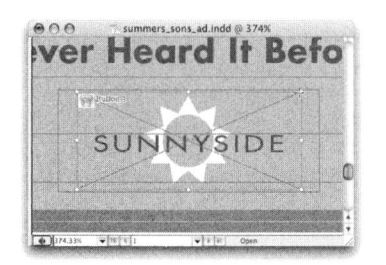

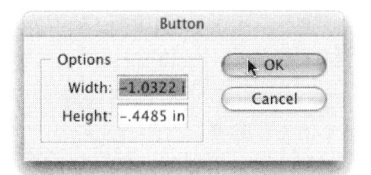

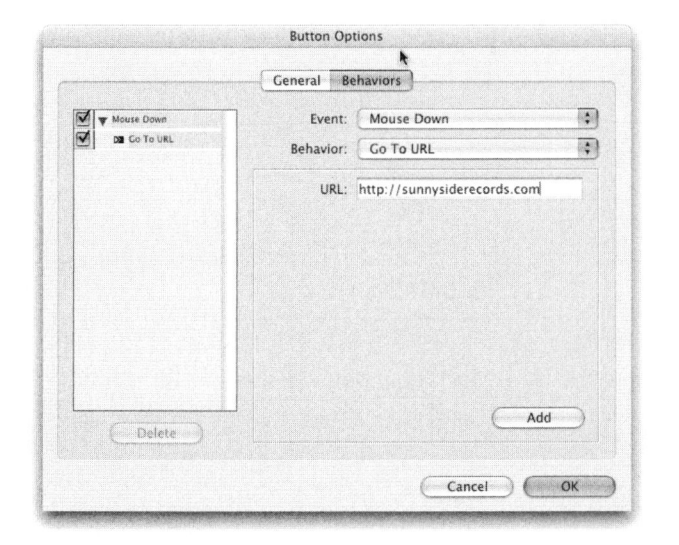

Related Tasks

4.8 Interactive Palettes

17.1 Exporting as PDF

17.3 Embedding Movies and Sound in PDFs

Shortcuts

Button tool
Mac and Win: B

Export
Mac: Cmd+E
Win: Ctrl+E

Tip

You can also embed Rollover buttons in exported InDesign pdfs.

49

3.19 Scissors Tool

Related Tasks

3.5   Pen Tools
3.10 Shape Tools
4.11 Object and Layout Palettes
7.2   Selection Tool vs. Direct Selection Tool
7.6   Drawing Custom Shapes
7.7   Drawing Freeform Shapes
7.8   Modifying Paths and Frames

Shortcuts

Scissors tool
Mac and Win: C

Rectangle tool
Mac and Win: M

Ellipse tool
Mac and Win: L

Direct Selection tool
Mac and Win: A

Selection tool
Mac and Win: V

Make compound path
Mac: Cmd+8
Win: Ctrl+8

Tip

Holding down the Option key (Mac) or Alt key (Windows) with the Scissors tool selected changes it to the Add Anchor Point tool.

InDesign's Scissors tool is used for cutting points and lines on a path. You can divide symmetrical shapes, such as half-circles or diamonds, or remove pieces of a path to create interesting logo effects and design elements.

You can access the Scissors tool by clicking its icon in the Toolbox or by typing the letter C.

Cutting Points on a Path

To cut points on a path, you must first select a shape with the Direct Selection tool, then switch to the Scissors tool. Hover your mouse over a specific point on the path until you see the cursor change to a target symbol. Click to cut the path. Continue clicking points until you've divided the shape the way you like. You can then separate the pieces with the Selection tool.

Cutting Lines on a Path

With the Scissors tool, you don't necessarily have to cut points on a path—you can also cut the connecting lines between points. Select a shape with the Direct Selection tool, then switch to the Scissors tool. Hover your mouse over a line on the path until you see the cursor change to a target symbol, then click to cut it. You'll see a new point added to the line. Keep clicking lines until you've divided the shape to your preference, then separate the pieces with the Selection tool.

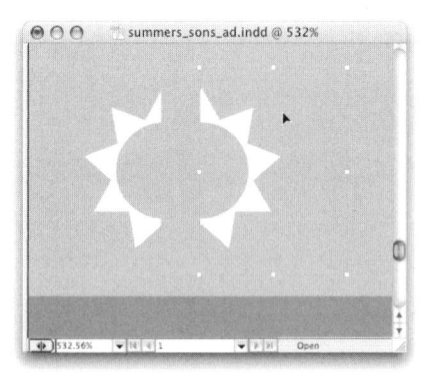

3.20 Hand Tool

The Hand tool allows you to scroll through the pages of your document by clicking and dragging. Need to get somewhere quick? Try using the Hand tool rather than those pesky zoom commands and scroll bars.

Activate the Hand tool, then click and drag with your mouse anywhere in the document. The little hand icon grabs your page as you drag in any direction. You can move pages around in your document window this way, allowing you to access a certain point in the layout quickly and easily. It's sometimes helpful to use the Hand tool along with the Zoom tool and zoom commands to maneuver around a document.

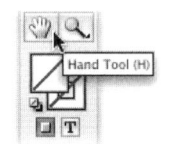

You can access this tool by clicking its icon in the Toolbox or by typing the letter H.

Related Tasks

2.9 View Menu
3.21 Zoom Tool

Shortcuts

Hand tool
Mac and Win: H

Zoom tool
Mac and Win: Z

Zoom in
Mac: Cmd+=
Win: Ctrl+=

Zoom out
Mac: Cmd+-
Win: Ctrl+-

Tip

With any tool selected, you can switch temporarily to the Hand tool by pressing and holding down Opt+Spacebar (Mac) or Alt+Spacebar (Windows).

3.21 Zoom Tool

Related Tasks

2.9   View Menu
3.20 Hand Tool

Shortcuts

Zoom tool
Mac and Win: Z

Hand tool
Mac and Win: H

Zoom in
Mac: Cmd+=
Win: Ctrl+=

Zoom out
Mac: Cmd+-
Win: Ctrl+-

Tip

Holding down Cmd+Spacebar (Mac) or Ctrl+Spacebar (Windows) allows you to switch temporarily to the Zoom tool.

The Zoom tool allows you to increase or decrease view magnification of any selected area of the document.

Zooming with the Zoom tool is easy. Activate the tool, then either click once at the point you'd like to zoom in on, or click and drag over an area to enlarge (a process that is also referred to as "marqueeing"). Clicking in the document zooms in intervals using default percentage amounts, and drawing a marquee over an area zooms in based on your selection size.

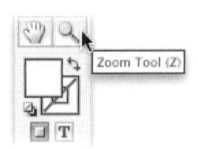

You can access this tool by clicking the icon in the Toolbox or by typing the letter Z.

To zoom out, hold down the Option key (Mac) or the Alt key (Windows) and either click or drag. You'll notice that the Zoom icon changes its appearance, replacing the + sign shown in the magnifying glass with a – sign. You can switch between the two using the Option/Alt key.

You can marquee over the area you'd like to zoom into.

The Zoom tool changes the magnification preview displayed in your document window.

3.22 Other Toolbox Functions

InDesign's Toolbox contains various other controls, including a link to the Adobe website, access to the Color Picker, Fill and Stroke formatting, and available screen modes.

Adobe Online

You can access the InDesign portion of the Adobe website by clicking the colorful icon found just above the Toolbox. You must have a working Internet connection to use this link.

Color Picker

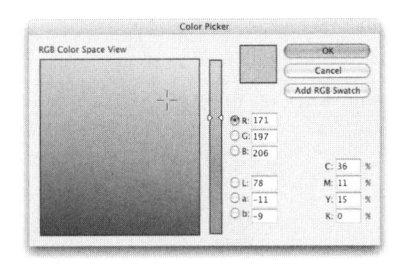

InDesign now features a Color Picker, similar to the one found in Photoshop or Illustrator. To open the Color Picker, double-click the Stroke or Fill swatches located at the bottom of the Toolbox. When the dialog opens, you can click anywhere in the color field to locate a specific RGB, CMYK, or LAB build. Click the Add RGB Swatch button to add the chosen color to the Swatches palette. Click OK and the color appears at the bottom of the Toolbox in the Fill or Stroke swatch (whichever is placed in front), and also at the top of the Swatches palette and in the Color palette.

Fill and Stroke

The Fill and Stroke swatches, located at the bottom of the Toolbox, display either the default Fill and Stroke colors, or the colors of any currently selected object in your document. The forefront swatch, either Fill or Stroke, is the active control. All colors in InDesign are applied according to the active control, which is also found at the top of the Swatches palette.

You can switch between the Fill and Stroke controls by clicking either swatch, or by clicking the swap arrows located at the upper right. You can reset the default Fill and Stroke colors by clicking the Default Fill and Stroke button at the lower left, or just press D on your keyboard.

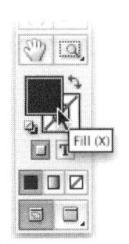

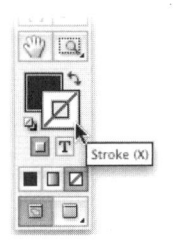

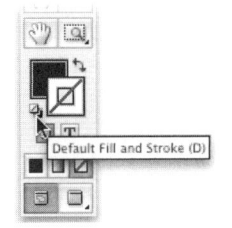

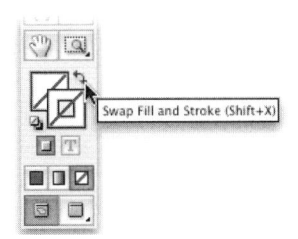

Related Tasks

2.9 View Menu
2.11 Help Menu
3.15 Eyedropper Tool
4.5 Color Palette
4.6 Gradient Palette
4.17 Swatches Palette
7.10 Filling with Solid and Transparent Colors
7.11 Filling with Gradients

Shortcuts

Toggle between fill and stroke
Mac and Win: X

Default fill and stroke
Mac and Win: D

Swap fill and stroke color
Mac and Win: Shift+X

Tip

Double-clicking the Fill or Stroke swatches at the bottom of the Toolbox opens the Color Picker.

3.22 Other Toolbox Functions *(continued)*

Related Tasks

7.12　Filling Text

7.13　Stroking Frames, Shapes, and Paths

7.14　Stroking Text

Shortcuts

Toggle between Normal and Preview modes
Mac and Win: W

Apply None
Mac and Win: / and Num

Apply gradient
Mac and Win: . (period)

Apply color
Mac and Win: , (comma)

Tip

When displaying the Toolbox in a single column or single row, all the Apply controls are gathered in one button that contains a submenu. Screen mode controls are contained this way as well.

Formatting Buttons

The formatting buttons located underneath the Toolbox Fill and Stroke swatches allow you to apply colors to either a text frame or the text itself.

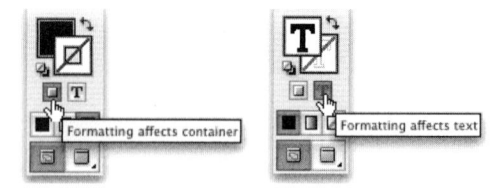

Apply Buttons

The Apply buttons found at the bottom of the Toolbox work hand in hand with the Fill and Stroke controls, allowing you to apply the most recent color or gradient selected (displayed in the button), or apply None to any selected object(s) in the document.

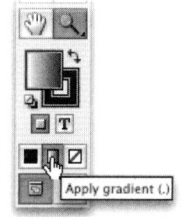

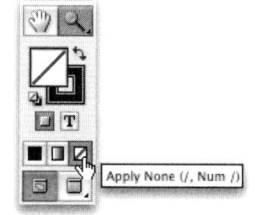

Screen Modes

InDesign also features several screen modes in which you can view your document layout. Normal mode is the default, which allows you to see all your guides, frame edges, and any items positioned off the Page. Preview mode hides all guides and frame edges and fills the entire area surrounding the Page with gray. Bleed mode also hides all guides and frame edges, but reveals any added bleed areas while filling the rest of the area surrounding the Page with gray. Slug mode previews your document in the same way as Bleed mode, but also allows you to view any additional slug areas.

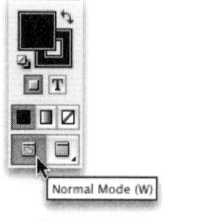

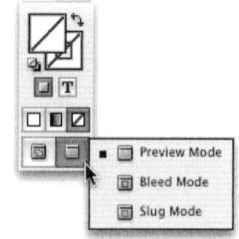

CHAPTER **4**

InDesign Palettes

THERE IS NO SHORTAGE of palettes to work with in InDesign (42 in all!). Much like the Adobe Creative Suite 2 companion applications, Photoshop and Illustrator, a palette is available for practically every task. In fact, if you're unsure of where to locate the controls for a specific task, it is safe to assume that InDesign has a palette dedicated to that function.

As you might have guessed, working with this many palettes can be extremely cumbersome, especially on a small screen. But thankfully, InDesign has included a side-tab option that allows you to dock, show, and hide the large amount of palettes you'll be working with. In addition, you can save your favorite open palette combinations as a custom workspace to be used over and over again. You can take advantage of this feature by saving a different workspace for each project you work on, whether it's a brochure, magazine spread, newsletter, advertisement, or even a whole book. InDesign lets you decide how you want fill up your screen real estate.

The palettes described in this chapter are grouped just as they appear under the Window menu. For example, the Align and Pathfinder palettes are part of the Object & Layout subgroup; therefore, the Align and Pathfinder palette descriptions can be found under the "Object & Layout Palettes" section.

- 4.1 **Organizing Palettes**
- 4.2 **Customizing Your Workspace**
- 4.3 **Attributes Palette**
- 4.4 **Automation Palettes**
- 4.5 **Color Palette**
- 4.6 **Gradient Palette**
- 4.7 **Info Palette**
- 4.8 **Interactive Palettes**
- 4.9 **Layers Palette**
- 4.10 **Links Palette**
- 4.11 **Object & Layout Palettes**
- 4.12 **Object Styles Palette**
- 4.13 **Output Palettes**
- 4.14 **PageMaker Toolbar**
- 4.15 **Pages Palette**
- 4.16 **Stroke Palette**
- 4.17 **Swatches Palette**
- 4.18 **Tags Palette**
- 4.19 **Text Wrap Palette**
- 4.20 **Transparency Palette**
- 4.21 **Type and Tables Palettes**
- 4.22 **Book and Library Palettes**

4.1 Organizing Palettes

Related Tasks

2.10 Window Menu
3.2 Control Bar
4.2 Customizing Your Workspace
5.1 General Preferences

Shortcuts

Show/hide all controls
Mac and Win: Tab

Show/hide all controls except Toolbox and Control bar
Mac and Win: Shift+Tab

Tip

The Palette Toggle button is always available at the far right of the Control bar, no matter what tool you have selected in the Toolbox.

When you're in a creative mind-set, it's tough to stay organized. No one wants to stop work on a killer layout to create more design room on screen. Thankfully, InDesign understands that your creativity should always come first.

To help save screen real estate, you can dock together individual palettes as well as palette windows. And certain palettes can collapse vertically, allowing you to show or hide specific options. If that's not enough to help you stay organized, you can also store individual and docked palettes into the scrollable side tabs.

Here's a breakdown of controls found in all InDesign palettes:

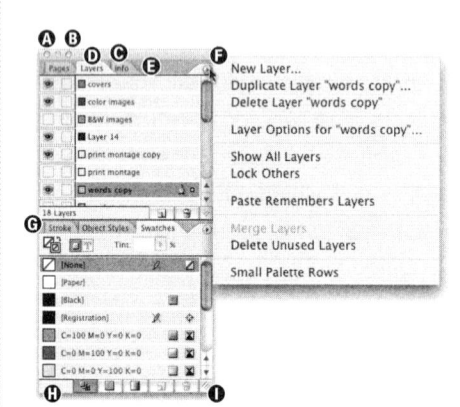

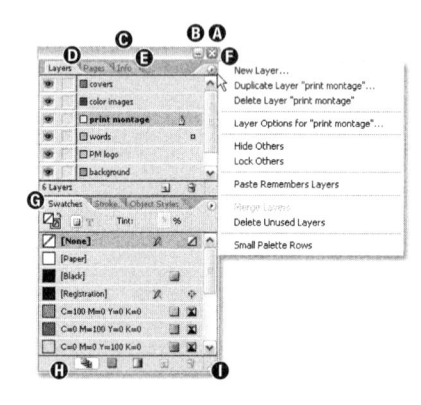

Typical palettes in Mac OS X (left) and Windows XP (right)

- **A** **Close Palette Window** Click this button to close the palette window and all palettes docked inside.
- **B** **Minimize/Maximize Palette Window** Click this button to shrink the palette window, leaving only docked palette tabs visible.
- **C** **Title bar** Click and drag the title bar to reposition the palette window on your screen. Double-click the title bar to collapse the window.
- **D** **Palette tab** Click and drag to dock the palette in another window or side tab. Single-click the tab to bring a docked palette to the front of a group. Double-click the tab to collapse the palette.
- **E** **Docked palettes** Every palette window contains a well to dock other palettes in. Palette tabs are positioned side by side in the well for easy access.
- **F** **Palette menu** Click to access specific palette options. The menu button always appears at the top of the window when the palette is side-tabbed to the right and at the bottom when side-tabbed to the left.
- **G** **Docked palette windows** Palette windows (with multiple palettes docked inside them) can also be connected in a vertical column, as shown here.
- **H** **Footer controls** Various palette-specific action buttons are located at the bottom of the palette window.
- **I** **Resize Palette** Not all palettes feature this option, but for those that do, simply click and drag the icon in the bottom-right corner to resize the palette window.

4.1 Organizing Palettes (continued)

Docking Palettes

To dock palettes together, simply click the tab of one palette and drag it into another. Hold the mouse button down until a thick black outline appears around the palette window you are dragging into, then release. The palettes are now docked together inside the same window.

Clicking a docked palette's tab brings it to the front of the group and grays out all other docked palettes behind it.

To undock a palette, click the tab, hold the mouse button down, and drag it out of the well. Release the mouse button to place the free-floating palette somewhere else on your screen, or dock it into another window or side tab.

Docking Palette Windows

To dock palette windows together, click the tab of one palette, hold the mouse button down, and drag it over the bottom edge of another. Release the mouse button when a thick black line appears at the bottom edge of the window you're docking to. The palette windows dock together in a vertical column.

Click and drag the title bar of the top palette window to reposition the docked group on your screen. Double-click the title bar to collapse the docked windows, leaving only the tabs visible.

Collapsing Palette Windows

InDesign offers four ways to collapse palette windows: double-click the title bar; double-click the palette tab; click the Collapse Window button; or click the up/down arrows located next to the palette name (note: only certain palettes contain these arrows).

Windows with multiple palettes docked inside them can be docked together and collapsed to save space.

One click on the up/down arrows (or one double-click on the tab) collapses the window to reveal only basic options.

Two clicks on the up/down arrows (or two double-clicks on the tab) fully collapses the window.

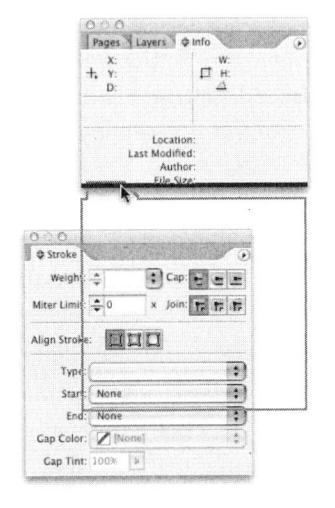

Related Tasks

2.10 Window Menu
3.2 Control Bar
4.2 Customizing Your Workspace
5.1 General Preferences

Shortcuts

Show/hide all controls
Mac and Win: Tab

Show/hide all controls except Toolbox and Control bar
Mac and Win: Shift+Tab

Tip

To show or hide all palettes, Deselect All (Mac: Shift+Cmd+A; Windows: Shift+Ctrl+A), and then click the Palette Toggle button located at the far right of the Control bar.

4.1 Organizing Palettes *(continued)*

Related Tasks

2.10 Window Menu
3.2   Control Bar
4.2   Customizing Your Workspace
5.1   General Preferences

Shortcuts

Show/hide all controls
Mac and Win: Tab

Show/hide all controls except Toolbox and Control bar
Mac and Win: Shift+Tab

Tip

Palettes can only be side-tabbed on the left or right sides of your screen, *not the top or bottom*. Only the Control bar and PageMaker toolbar can be docked at the top and/or bottom of your screen.

Click multiple times on the up/down arrows or the palette tab to incrementally collapse or expand palettes that contain extra options or extensive item lists (e.g., Layers, Styles, Swatches).

Docking Individual Palettes to the Side Tabs

To side-tab a palette, click the palette tab and drag it to either side of your screen. Hold the mouse button down until the horizontal palette outline changes to a vertical outline, then release for the palette window to snap into place. You can then add more palettes to the window if you want.

You can then add more palettes to the side-tabbed window.

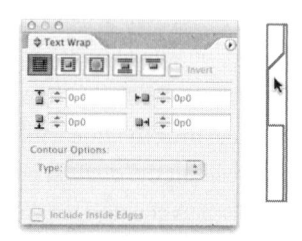

When you side-tab a palette window, it appears collapsed on the side of your screen. Click once on the palette tab to expand the window. You can reposition the side tab by clicking in the gray palette well area and dragging up or down.

You can also expand the side tab vertically. First hover your mouse over the top (Windows only) or bottom edge (Mac and Windows) until the up/down arrow icon appears. Click and drag in either direction to lengthen the palette.

Docking Palette Windows to the Side Tabs

To side-tab a palette window that contains several docked palettes, Opt-click (Mac) or Alt-click (Windows) on any of the docked palette tabs and drag to either side of your screen. Hold the mouse button down until the horizontal palette outline changes to a vertical outline, then release. The palette window will snap into place. You can then add more palettes to the window.

Click and drag the palette tab to the side of your screen.

4.2 Customizing Your Workspace

InDesign allows you to save your workspace environment so that you don't have to spend time repositioning palettes on the screen every time you launch the application. You can create and save a custom workspace for every type of layout work you do. For instance, a production-oriented job might require a totally different set of palettes than a design-oriented one. No problem! InDesign lets you save a workspace for each.

Saving a Workspace

To save your preferred work environment, choose Window > Workspace > Save Workspace. When the dialog appears, enter a name for it and click OK. You can now restore your workspace whenever you like by selecting it under the Window > Workspace submenu.

To save changes made to your custom environment, choose Window > Workspace > Save Workspace, and enter the name of the workspace you want to update. Click OK when the dialog asks you if you want to replace the workspace.

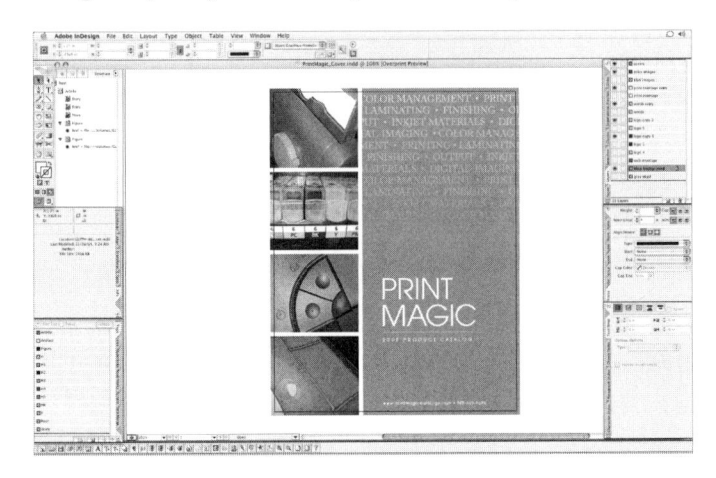

An example of a fully loaded InDesign workspace

Deleting a Workspace

Say you like this feature so much that you've saved dozens of custom workspaces. Weeks go by and you finally admit to yourself that you only use a handful of them. Don't beat yourself up over it. You can always delete a saved workspace by choosing Window > Workspace > Delete Workspace. When the dialog appears, select the one you want to delete from the menu (sorry, you can only delete one at a time). When you're ready to let go, just click Delete and it's gone forever. See? No need to feel guilty.

Restoring the Default Workspace

Maybe the default workspace is perfect for your design needs and you just want to return to that palette arrangement. Well, pat yourself on the back for being exceptionally low-maintenance and then choose Window > Workspace > [Default].

Related Tasks

2.10	Window Menu
3.2	Control Bar
4.2	Customizing Your Workspace
5.1	General Preferences

Shortcuts

Show/hide all controls
Mac and Win: Tab

Show/hide all controls except Toolbox and Control bar
Mac and Win: Shift+Tab

Tip

At application launch, InDesign always displays the last workspace used.

4.3 Attributes Palette

Related Tasks

2.9	View Menu
2.10	Window Menu
4.13	Output Palettes
4.16	Stroke Palette
5.13	Appearance of Black Preferences
5.16	Print Presets
16.1	Printing a Document
16.3	Creating and Assigning Trap Presets

Shortcuts

Show/hide all controls
Mac and Win: Tab

Show/hide all controls except Toolbox and Control bar
Mac and Win: Shift+Tab

Separations Preview palette
Mac and Win: Shift+F6

Tip

To suppress printing for all objects on a layer, you must first select everything on the layer by Opt-clicking (Mac) or Alt-clicking (Windows) on the layer in the Layers palette; then check the Nonprinting check box in the Attributes palette.

The Attributes palette is used to set overprint options that affect the color separation and output of your document. InDesign automatically overprints any solid black items by default; however, all other colors are set to automatically knock out (or replace all underlying inks). You can use the Attributes palette to overprint any colors instead by applying this option to the fills and strokes of any individual frames in your layout.

You can build manual traps with overprinting, or create some cool ink mixing effects, but both can be very tricky to set up. It may be easier to first try using InDesign's built-in trapping feature. For ink effects, try experimenting with Transparency and Blend modes.

The Attributes palette also contains one other hidden feature: the ability to make selected items within your document or master pages nonprintable. This is particularly useful when you are in the early stages of a design and many of your page items are still FPO (for placement only). InDesign allows you to suppress printing of any individual placeholder items or extraneous screen notations.

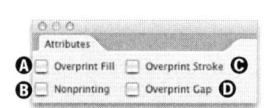

Ⓐ Overprint Fill Check this option to allow a single, selected frame's fill to overprint (rather than knockout, or replace all underlying inks) when outputting color separations.

Ⓑ Nonprinting Check this option to make any selected objects in your document layout or master pages nonprintable.

Ⓒ Overprint Stroke Check this option to allow strokes applied to selected objects to overprint.

Ⓓ Overprint Gap Check this option to allow a single, selected frame's stroke gap color to overprint.

4.4 Automation Palettes

The three palettes found in the Window > Automation submenu greatly expand InDesign's functionality and can help speed up your workflow. The Data Merge palette allows you to create standardized documents based on a data file (e.g., a form letter that you mail to a large list of clients). The Scripts palette and Script Label palette allow you to automate repetitive production tasks such as replacing images or fixing text errors. In many ways, using these palettes is like hiring an assistant to help you do all the grunt work—but without the added expense!

Data Merge Palette

To use the Data Merge palette, you must have a data file prepared to apply to an existing InDesign document. You can merge a .csv file (comma-separated value), or a simple .txt file with all the information separated by either commas or tabs (but not both). The first line of your data file must contain category names separated by either commas or tabs.

To merge, click the menu button and choose Select Data Source. Browse to the .csv or .txt file, make sure Show Import Options is checked at the bottom of the dialog, then click Open. When the dialog opens, choose either Comma Separated or Tab Delimited, depending on which type of data file you are merging, and click OK.

The named categories from the first line of your data file appear in the Data Merge palette and can then be applied to various text items in your InDesign document. Select the text you want the data applied to, and then click the appropriate category name in the Data Merge palette.

The Preview check box displays the data in the applied areas and the Create Merged Document button allows you to generate InDesign pages based on the applied data.

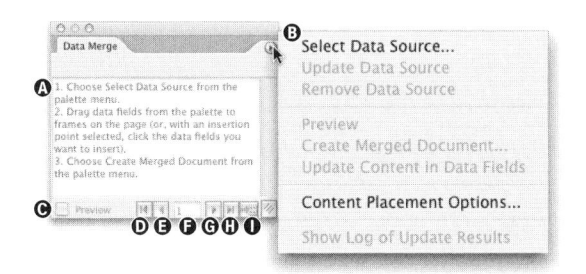

Related Tasks

2.10	Window Menu
3.2	Control Bar
4.2	Customizing Your Workspace
5.1	General Preferences

Shortcuts

Show/hide all controls
Mac and Win: Tab

Show/hide all controls except Toolbox and Control bar
Mac and Win: Shift+Tab

Tip

You can download free InDesign scripts at http://share.studio.adobe.com/.

A **Data Category List** Displays imported data categories. If no data is imported, a set of data merge instructions is displayed instead.

B **Palette menu** Click to access several data merge options. Most of these options are also accessible via the footer controls.

C **Preview** Check this box to display the merged data in the applied fields of your InDesign document.

D **Preview First Record** Click this button to preview the first application of merged data.

E **Preview Previous Record** Click this button to preview the previous application of merged data.

F **Page Number** Displays the number of the page being previewed.

G **Preview Next Record** Click this button to preview the next application of merged data.

H **Preview Last Record** Click this button to preview the last application of merged data.

I **Create Merged Document** Click this button to generate InDesign pages based on the merged data.

4.4 Automation Palettes *(continued)*

Related Tasks

2.10 Window Menu
3.2   Control Bar
4.2   Customizing Your Workspace
5.1   General Preferences

Shortcuts

Show/hide all controls
Mac and Win: Tab

Show/hide all controls except Toolbox and Control bar
Mac and Win: Shift+Tab

Tip

You can download free InDesign scripts at http://share.studio.adobe.com/.

Scripts Palette

Wouldn't it be great if you could automate InDesign to do all the repetitive grunt work for you? Well, you can with scripting. And the best part is—*you don't have to know how to write scripts to use them.*

To run a script just place the script file in the \Presets\Scripts folder located in the InDesign application folder. InDesign can run scripts written in Extend-Script (a cross-platform version of JavaScript), AppleScript (Mac only), or for Windows only: Virtual Basic Script, Virtual Basic for Applications, and Visual Basic.

To learn more about scripting in InDesign, or to try out some example scripts, check out the Adobe InDesign CS2 Scripting Guide found on the installer CD.

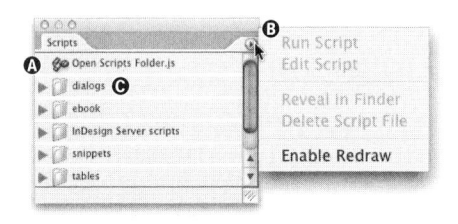

Ⓐ Script Double-click the script name to run the script. Hold down the Option (Mac) or Alt key (Windows) as you double-click to open in a script editor. Hold down the Shift key and double-click the script name to open in the JavaScript debugger.

Ⓑ Palette menu Click to access the Scripts palette options.

Ⓒ Script folder Click the toggle arrow to open the folder and view available InDesign scripts.

Script Label Palette

The Script Label palette allows you to attach a label property to an object in your document. This label helps a script identify an object correctly when performing an automated action.

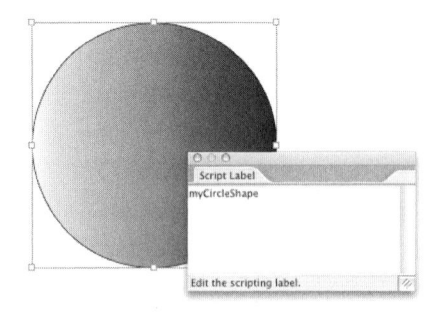

To attach a label, select an object and then type in a label name using the Script Label palette. Adding a label does not change the object's appearance. Using a script editor, you can then refer to the label in an applicable script.

4.5 Color Palette

The Color Palette displays either the default Fill and Stroke colors, or the colors of any currently selected object in your document. The forefront swatch, either Fill or Stroke, is the active control. All colors in InDesign are applied according to the active control, which is also found at the top of the Swatches palette and at the bottom of the Toolbox.

You can switch between the Fill and Stroke controls by clicking either swatch, or by clicking the swap arrows located to the upper right of the swatch icons. The formatting buttons located underneath the Fill and Stroke swatches allow you to apply colors to either the container or its contents.

The buttons, slider, and ramp at the bottom of the Color palette work hand in hand with the Fill and Stroke controls. These allow you to do the following to any selected object(s) in your document: apply None (that is, no stroke or fill); apply the last color selected; or apply a tint of the currently selected color in the Swatches palette or last color selected.

You can also edit a color using the Color palette. Click the menu button and choose a Lab, CMYK, or RGB color space to access the appropriate sliders and edit the color. Save any colors you create by clicking and dragging the swatch directly into the Swatches palette list.

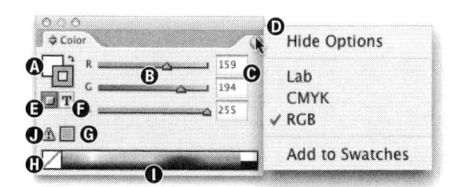

Ⓐ Fill And Stroke Displays either the default Fill and Stroke colors, or the colors of any currently selected object in your document.

Ⓑ Tint slider Drag the slider left or right to create a tint of the currently selected fill or stroke color.

Ⓒ Tint Percentage Displays the tint percentage of the currently selected color.

Ⓓ Palette menu Click to access the Color palette options, particularly the preferred color space for editing colors (LAB, CMYK, or RGB).

Ⓔ Formatting Affects Container Click to apply a color to a selected frame.

Ⓕ Formatting Affects Text Click to apply a color to all editable text in a selected frame.

Ⓖ Apply Last Color Click to apply the last color used.

Ⓗ Apply None Click to apply no color to a fill or stroke.

Ⓘ Color spectrum When editing a color using the Lab, CMYK, or RGB sliders, the ramp will change to a color spectrum. Click anywhere in the spectrum to choose and apply/edit a color. On the far right of the spectrum you'll also find a small white swatch and a small black swatch. Click the white swatch to apply pure white and the black swatch to apply pure black.

Ⓙ Out Of Gamut Warning Indicates that the RGB color build will not print or display properly. Click the alert icon to automatically adjust the color values to fall within the default CMYK profile gamut.

Related Tasks

Color Section
2.10 Window Menu
3.15 Eyedropper Tool
3.22 Other Toolbox Functions
7.10 Filling with Solid and Transparent Colors
7.12 Filling Text
7.13 Stroking Frames, Shapes, and Paths
7.14 Stroking Text
13.11 Setting Table Borders, Strokes and Fills

Shortcuts

Show/hide all controls
Mac and Win: Tab

Show/hide all controls except Toolbox and Control bar
Mac and Win: Shift+Tab

Eyedropper tool
Mac and Win: I

Color palette
Mac and Win: F6

Default fill and stroke colors
Mac and Win: D

Switch between fill and stroke
Mac and Win: X

Tip

To change the application default colors using the Color palette, simply apply your preferred fill and stroke colors with no documents open.

4.6 Gradient Palette

Related Tasks

2.10 Window Menu
3.15 Eyedropper Tool
3.17 Gradient Tool
3.22 Other Toolbox Functions
7.11 Filling with Gradients
13.11 Setting Table Borders, Strokes and Fills

Shortcuts

Show/hide all controls
Mac and Win: Tab

Show/hide all controls except Toolbox and Control bar
Mac and Win: Shift+Tab

Gradient tool
Mac and Win: G

Eyedropper tool
Mac and Win: I

Tip

You can apply a gradient fill and stroke to editable text in InDesign.

The Gradient palette lets you apply various gradient styles to selected items within your layout. This palette works closely with the Gradient tool and Swatches palette, allowing you to apply gradients to both fills and strokes on selected frames, shapes, paths, and even editable text.

You can also create or edit a gradient using the Gradient palette. Click one of the color sliders found at the bottom of the palette. Then drag directly on top of it a color from one of these locations: from the Swatches palette list, from either swatch at the bottom of the Toolbox, or from either swatch at the top of the Swatches palette. Alternatively, you can also drag and drop a swatch anywhere on the gradient line to add a slider. Drag the gradient and color sliders left or right to alter the gradient blend. You can delete a color from the gradient by dragging its slider off the palette; however, you must always have at least two colors present.

You can save any gradients you create by dragging the gradient palette swatch directly into the Swatches palette list.

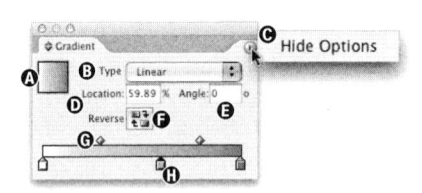

A Gradient Swatch Displays the gradient applied to a selected object, or the gradient you are currently creating or editing.

B Gradient Type Choose either Linear or Radial.

C Palette menu Click to access the palette options.

D Location Displays the gradient bar location percentage of the currently selected color slider.

E Angle Displays the gradient angle measurement in degrees.

F Reverse Click to reverse the direction of the gradient.

G Gradient Slider Click and drag left or right to adjust the balance of gradation between colors.

H Color Slider Click and drag left or right to adjust the location of the currently selected color within the gradient.

4.7 Info Palette

The items displayed in the Info palette vary depending on what you have selected and with what tool. You can use the Info palette to determine a placed object's color space and file size, or the color build of a specific fill or stroke. You can also access valuable information about text items that are selected with the Type tool, such as word and character count.

The Info palette also goes hand in hand with the Measure tool, allowing you to match the size and/or angle of different objects in a document layout.

Ⓐ Cursor coordinates Tracks the exact X and Y coordinates of the cursor as you move around the document. The D value is the distance an object or tool has moved relative to its starting position. Click the small arrow next to the + symbol to change the units of measurement.

Ⓑ Width/Height/Angle Displays the width and height measurement of a selected object. Also displays the rotation angle, but only when you are using the Rotate tool.

Ⓒ Palette menu Click to access the Info palette options. You can also view the metadata of a placed object by choosing File > File Info.

Ⓓ Fill Info Displays the swatch name or color space build of a selected object's fill. Click the small arrow next to the fill icon to switch between Color Space and Swatch Name views.

Ⓔ Stroke Info Displays the swatch name or color space build of a selected object's stroke. Click the small arrow next to the stroke icon to switch between Color Space and Swatch Name views.

Ⓕ Link Info Displays the file info for a placed link.

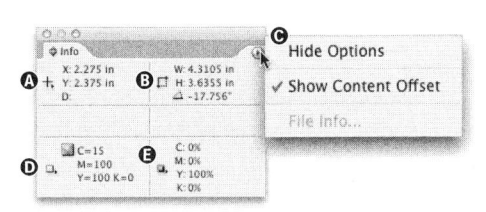

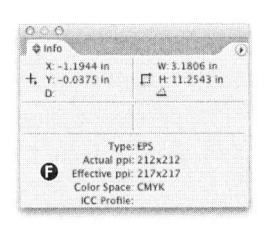

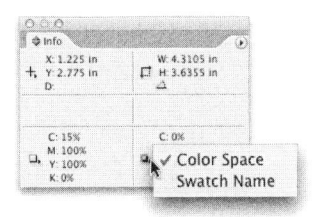

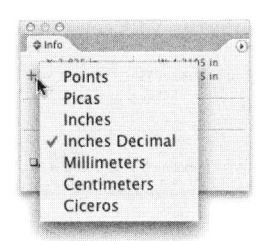

Related Tasks

2.10 Window Menu
3.3   Selection Tool
3.4   Direct Selection and Position Tools
3.16 Measure Tool
12.1 Importing a Graphic Image

Shortcuts

Show/hide all controls
Mac and Win: Tab

Show/hide all controls except Toolbox and Control bar
Mac and Win: Shift+Tab

Selection tool
Mac and Win: V

Direct Selection tool
Mac and Win: A

Measure tool
Mac and Win: K

Info palette
Mac and Win: F8

Tip

To determine the color space of a placed graphic (RGB, CMYK, Grayscale, or Lab), select it with the Selection tool (V) or Direct Selection tool (A), and refer to the Info palette.

4.8 Interactive Palettes

Related Tasks

2.7	Object Menu
2.10	Window Menu
3.18	Button Tool
5.17	Adobe PDF Presets
17.1	Exploring as Adobe PDF

Tip

Hyperlinks created in Microsoft Word documents remain active once imported into InDesign.

Now you can jazz up your PDF documents by including interactive elements. That's right—the Window > Interactive palettes allow you to embed bookmarks, hyperlinks, and even button rollovers into PDFs exported from InDesign.

Bookmarks Palette

The Bookmarks palette allows you to create links to specific pages within your document. This is especially useful when you are creating a layout intended for PDF output. The links appear in the Bookmarks tab when you are viewing in Acrobat and let you navigate a large document much more easily.

To create a page bookmark, double-click a page in the Pages palette and click the Create New Bookmark icon at the bottom of the Bookmarks palette. To create a text bookmark, highlight some text with the Type tool or click an insertion point and click the New Bookmark icon. You can nest text bookmarks within page bookmarks to help keep them organized in the palette. Rearrange bookmarks in the palette by clicking and dragging them anywhere in the list, or choose Sort Bookmarks from the palette menu.

Double-click a bookmark in the palette to go to the link. To rename a bookmark, click once and wait for the data field to appear, or choose Rename Bookmark from the palette fly-out menu. To delete a bookmark, select it, then click the trash icon at the bottom of the palette.

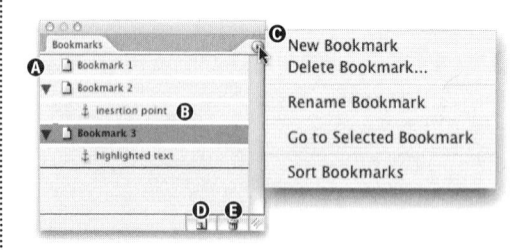

A Bookmark Bookmarks are displayed vertically in the palette. Double-click to go to the link. To rename, single-click and wait for the data field to appear. To select multiple bookmarks at once, hold down the Command/Ctrl key and click. To select a list, press the Shift key and click the first and last items.

B Nested bookmark Bookmarks can be grouped or "nested" within the palette.

C Palette menu Click to access palette options the Sort Bookmarks option.

D Create New Bookmark To create a new bookmark, select an object and click this button (or double-click a page icon in the Pages palette).

E Delete Selected Bookmarks Select a bookmark from the palette and click the trash icon to delete it. You can also delete a bookmark by dragging it directly over the trashcan.

Hyperlinks Palette

Using the Hyperlinks palette, you can add interactive web and e-mail links to your InDesign documents and exported PDFs. To create a basic URL link, highlight the URL from the document with the Type tool and choose New Hyperlink From URL from the Hyperlinks palette menu.

4.8 Interactive Palettes *(continued)*

To create all other types of hyperlinks, select a graphic or text item and click the Create New Hyperlink button at the bottom of the palette. When the dialog appears, choose a name, destination document and type, and appearance setting.

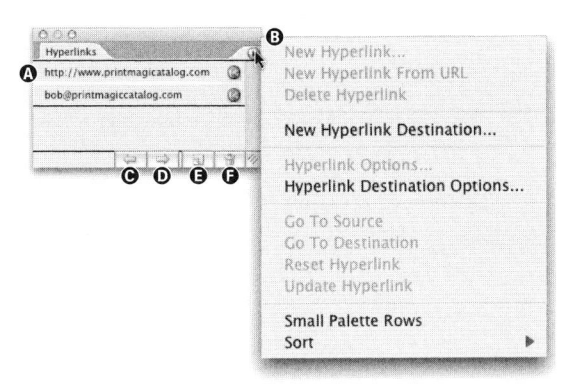

Ⓐ Hyperlink Hyperlinks are displayed vertically in the palette. Double-click to open the options dialog. To select multiple hyperlinks at a time, hold down the Command/Ctrl key and click. To select a list, press the Shift key and click the first and last items.

Ⓑ Palette menu Click to access palette options. If your palette is filling up with lots of hyperlinks, you can change the palette view to Small Palette Rows and also sort hyperlinks from this menu.

Ⓒ Go To Hyperlink Source Click this button to go directly to the hyperlink source in the document.

Ⓓ Go To Hyperlink Destination Click this button to go directly to the hyperlink destination. If the link is to a URL, clicking this button opens the web page in your default browser.

Ⓔ Create New Hyperlink Click this button to apply a new hyperlink to a selected graphic or text item.

Ⓕ Delete Selected Hyperlinks Select a hyperlink from the palette and click the trash icon to delete it. You can also delete a hyperlink by clicking and dragging it directly over the trashcan.

States Palette

The States palette allows you to apply different rollover states to an existing graphic button. Placed graphics can be converted into buttons containing Up, Rollover, and Down states. You can then export a PDF of your document, containing rollover buttons that work the same way as they would in a web browser.

You can apply preset or custom states to your buttons. Select a button and choose a preset from the menu; or to create a custom rollover, click the New State button at the bottom of the palette to create a Rollover state, and once more to create a Down state. By default, all newly created InDesign buttons contain an Up state.

Related Tasks

17.2 Embedding PDF Hyperlinks

17.3 Embedding Movies and Sound in PDFs

Shortcuts

Show/hide all controls
Mac and Win: Tab

Show/hide all controls except Toolbox and Control bar
Mac and Win: Shift+Tab

Button tool
Mac and Win: B

4.8 Interactive Palettes *(continued)*

Related Tasks

2.7	Object Menu
2.10	Window Menu
3.18	Button Tool
5.17	Adobe PDF Presets
17.1	Exporting as Adobe PDF
17.2	Embedding PDF Hyperlinks
17.3	Embedding Movies and Sound in PDFs

Shortcuts

Show/hide all controls
Mac and Win: Tab

Show/hide all controls except Toolbox and Control bar
Mac and Win: Shift+Tab

Button tool
Mac and Win: B

Tip

To quickly access Hyperlink commands, try using contextual menus (Windows: right-click, Mac: Control-click).

With the button still selected, click a state in the palette to make a change to its appearance. You can switch out a placed graphic, edit text, and change the fill and stroke appearance of a button when creating custom states.

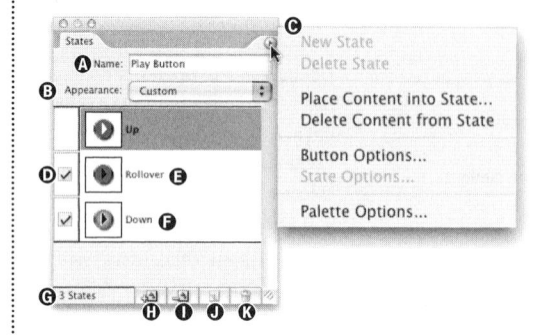

A **Name** Click in the data field to type in a name for the button.

B **Appearance** You can access preset appearances from this menu, or choose Custom to create your own.

C **Palette menu** Click to access palette options. Some options are also accessible in the palette footer controls.

D **Enable/Disable Optional State In Exported PDF** Check this box to enable the state in an exported PDF. Uncheck to disable.

E **Rollover State** When enabled, activates when the user rolls the mouse over the interactive button.

F **Down State** When enabled, activates when user clicks the mouse on the interactive button.

G **Number of States** Displays the current number of states applied to a selected button.

H **Place Content Into Selected State** Select Up, Rollover, or Down from the palette list and click this button to place a new graphic for that state.

I **Delete Content Of Selected State** Select a state from the palette list and click this button to delete its contents.

J **Create New Optional State** Click this button to add a new optional state to the rollover. Buttons can have three states: Up, Rollover, or Down.

K **Delete Optional State And Its Content** Click this button to delete an optional state and its contents from the rollover.

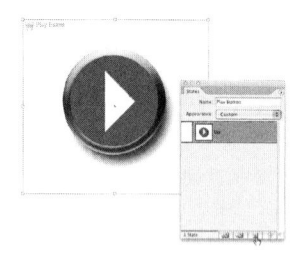

Select a placed graphic and choose Object > Interactive > Convert To Button.

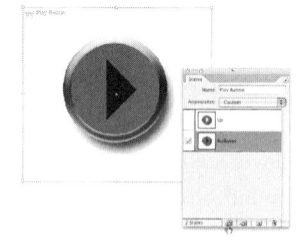

Click the New State Button to create the Rollover state. Then click the Place Content Into Selected State button, select the replacement graphic, and click OK.

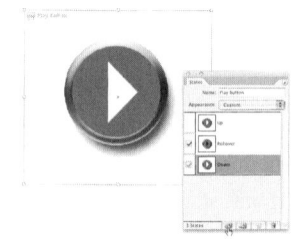

Click the New State Button again to create the Down state. Then click the Place Content Into Selected State button, select the replacement graphic, and click OK.

68

4.9 Layers Palette

The Layers palette allows you to separate various objects in your layout by placing them on different layers. This makes it easy to place multiple versions of a design all in one document with very few pages involved. Just place the different design elements on their own layers and toggle them on or off. Now if only we could convince the Adobe programmers to add a Layer Comps palette like in Photoshop…

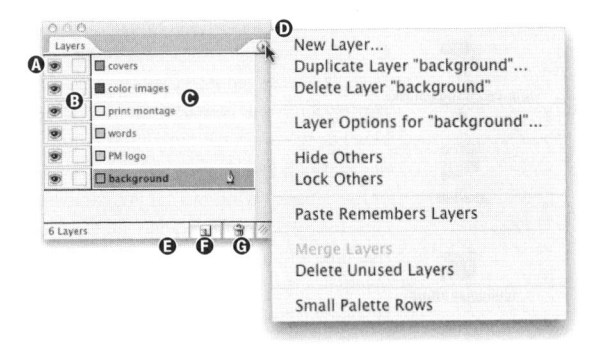

Ⓐ Toggle Visibility Click the eye icon to hide or show the items placed on a layer.

Ⓑ Toggle Lock (editable when blank) Click the icon to lock positioning of all items on a layer.

Ⓒ Layer Click the layer to make it active. Double-click to access layer options. Click and drag to rearrange layer positioning. Option-click (Mac) or Alt-click (Windows) to select all objects on the layer.

Ⓓ Palette menu Click to access palette options. Some options are also accessible in the palette footer controls and Layer Options dialog. You can condense the palette view by selecting Small Palette Rows from the menu.

Ⓔ Number Of Layers Displays the total number of layers in the document.

Ⓕ Create New Layer Click to add a new layer. (Note: New layers always appear at the top of the Layers palette list.)

Ⓖ Delete Selected Layers Click to delete selected layers and their contents.

Related Tasks

2.10 Window Menu
8.16 Placing Objects on Layers

Shortcuts

Show/hide all controls
Mac and Win: Tab

Show/hide all controls except Toolbox and Control bar
Mac and Win: Shift+Tab

Layers palette
Mac and Win: F7

Tip

To lock an Item and also make it nonselectable (like in Adobe Illustrator), place it on its own layer and lock the layer.

69

4.10 Links Palette

The Links palette displays a list of all placed items in the document. Similar to using the Picture Usage feature in QuarkXPress, you can use this palette to update modified links, relink missing items, and embed small graphics. You can also open a link to be edited in its native application (such as Photoshop or Illustrator).

Related Tasks

- 2.3 File Menu
- 2.10 Window Menu
- 12.1 Importing a Graphic Image
- 12.2 Setting Import Options
- 12.4 Object Layer Options and Placed PSDs
- 12.7 Updating Missing and Modified Links
- 12.8 Embedding and Unembedding Images

Shortcuts

Show/hide all controls
Mac and Win: Tab

Show/hide all controls except Toolbox and Control bar
Mac and Win: Shift+Tab

Links palette
Mac: Shift+Cmd+D
Win: Shift+Ctrl+D

Place
Mac: Cmd+D
Win: Ctrl+D

Tip

Using the Links palette, you can update all of your modified links at once by Shift-clicking the first and last items in the list and then clicking the Update Link action button located at the bottom (it's the one that looks like a floppy disk).

A **Link** Displays the filename of the placed item. Selected links appear highlighted in the list. You can sort the list by Name, Page, or Status (choose the preferred display option from the palette menu). Double-click to access the Link Information dialog. Hold down the Option key (Mac) or the Alt key (Windows) as you double-click to select it in the document. Note that links hidden in an interactive button's inactive state cannot be selected this way. Hold down the Command key (Mac) or the Ctrl key (Windows) as you double-click to select all links in the palette.

B **Page Number** Displays the page number where the link is placed in the document.

C **Palette menu** Click to access palette options. Some options are also accessible in the palette footer controls.

D **Relink** Click to relink a missing graphic. When the dialog opens, locate the link on your drive and click OK.

E **Go To Link** Select a link from the palette list and click this button to go directly to the page it is placed on in the document.

F **Update Link** Click to update a modified link. You can update multiple modified links at once by selecting them all first and then clicking the Update button.

G **Edit Original** Select a link from the palette list and click this button to open it in a native editing or viewing application (such as Photoshop or Preview).

H **Missing Link** Indicates that the link has been moved from its previous location on your system.

I **Modified Link** Indicates that the link has been edited outside of InDesign and must be updated.

4.11 Object & Layout Palettes

The Window > Object & Layout group of palettes provide several options for moving, aligning, transforming, combining, and viewing objects in a document.

Align Palette

The Align palette lets you position and distribute selected objects in a document. Simply select two or more objects and click one of the preset buttons in the palette.

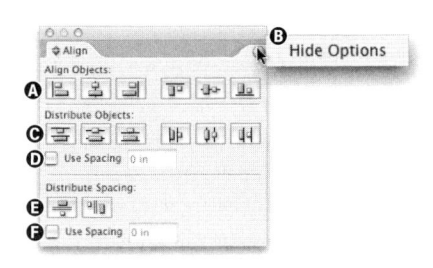

Ⓐ Align Objects Select two or more objects on a page and click one of the Align preset buttons to automatically position them. From left to right: Align Left Edges, Align Horizontal Centers, Align Right Edges, Align Top Edges, Align Vertical Centers, Align Bottom Edges.

Ⓑ Palette menu Click to access palette options. Some options are also accessible in the Control bar.

Ⓒ Distribute Objects Check the Use Spacing check box and enter a value in the data field. Select two or more objects on a page and click one of the Distribute preset buttons to automatically position them accordingly. From left to right: Distribute Top Edges, Distribute Vertical Centers, Distribute Bottom Edges, Distribute Left Edges, Distribute Horizontal Centers, Distribute Right Edges

Ⓓ Use Spacing For Distribute Objects Check the box to apply spacing to the palette's uniform distribution presets. Enter a specific spacing amount in the neighboring data field.

Ⓔ Distribute Spacing Check the Use Spacing check box and enter a value in the data field. Select two or more objects on a page and click one of the Distribute Spacing preset buttons to position them accordingly. From left to right: Distribute Vertical Space, Distribute Horizontal Space.

Ⓕ Use Spacing For Distribute Spacing Check the box to apply spacing to the palette's uniform distribution spacing presets. Enter a specific spacing amount in the neighboring data field.

Related Tasks

2.7	Object Menu
2.10	Window Menu
3.2	Control Bar
3.10	Shape Tools
7.8	Modifying Paths and Frames

Shortcuts

Show/hide all controls
Mac and Win: Tab

Show/hide all controls except Toolbox and Control bar
Mac and Win: Shift+Tab

Align palette
Mac and Win: Shift+F7

Transform palette
Mac and Win: F9

4.11 Object & Layout Palettes *(continued)*

Related Tasks

8.1	Moving Objects
8.2	Resizing Objects
8.10	Duplicating Objects
8.11	Aligning Objects
12.6	Resizing Placed Images

Shortcuts

Transform Again
Mac: Opt+Cmd+3
Win: Alt+Ctrl+3

Transform Sequence Again
Mac: Opt+Cmd+4
Win: Alt+Ctrl+4

Move
Mac: Shift+Cmd+M
Win: Shift+Ctrl+M

Tip

To change the outline color of the Navigator view box, choose Palette Options from the Navigator palette menu.

Navigator Palette

The Navigator palette provides another way to zoom in and out of your documents. Position the red outline in the palette over the area you'd like to zoom in/out of, and then use the zoom slider or buttons to increase/decrease view magnification over the selected area. You can also expand the palette to increase the size of the thumbnail.

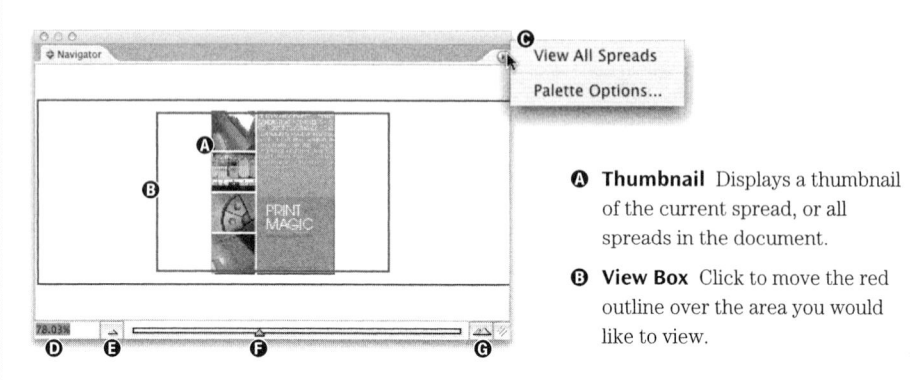

Ⓐ Thumbnail Displays a thumbnail of the current spread, or all spreads in the document.

Ⓑ View Box Click to move the red outline over the area you would like to view.

Ⓒ Palette menu Click to Navigator Palette Options or to View All Spreads in the thumbnail.

Ⓓ Zoom Edit Box Displays the current view magnification percentage. Click in the data field to enter a specific zoom amount.

Ⓔ Zoom Out Click to zoom out of the area selected in the view box using default interval amounts.

Ⓕ Zoom Slider Drag left or right to adjust view magnification of the area selected in the view box.

Ⓖ Zoom In Click to zoom in on the area selected in the view box using default interval amounts.

Pathfinder Palette

Similar to the Pathfinder palette in Adobe Illustrator, InDesign's Pathfinder allows you to combine shapes quickly and easily. Select two or more shapes and then click one of the Pathfinder buttons to combine them in various ways. This can be especially useful when creating compound paths.

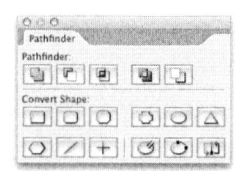

Pathfinder Options

CLICK	ACTION	RESULT
	Original shapes	
	Add	
	Subtract front from back	
	Intersect	
	Exclude Overlap	
	Minus Back	

4.11 Object & Layout Palettes (continued)

You can also convert shapes using the Pathfinder palette. Select any shape, line, path, or even text frame, and click one of the Convert Shape buttons to change its appearance. Convert Shape also allows you to open, close, or reverse the direction of a path.

Convert Shape Options

CLICK	ACTION	CLICK	ACTION
▭	Converts shape to a rectangle	◯	Converts shape to a polygon
▢	Converts shape to a rounded rectangle	╱	Converts shape to a line
▢	Converts shape to a beveled rectangle	+	Converts shape to a vertical or horizontal line
▢	Converts shape to an inverse rounded rectangle		Opens path
◯	Converts shape to an ellipse	↺	Closes path
△	Converts shape to a triangle		Reverses path

Transform Palette

The Transform palette allows you to rotate, flip, skew, scale, and distort objects. Select the item(s) you want to transform and enter the appropriate settings in the various data fields (also found in the Control bar), or choose a preset option from the palette menu.

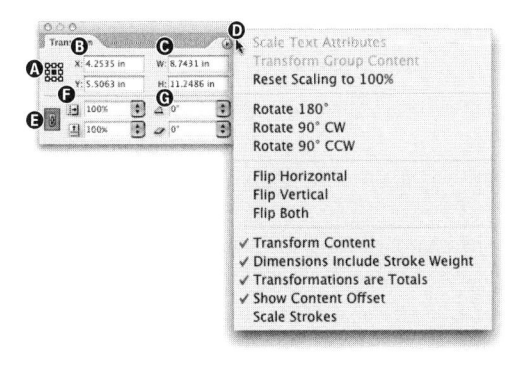

Ⓐ Reference Point Allows you to choose a default base point for transformation. Click one of the nine squares to set your preference. Your current position is indicated by a black square, available positions by white squares.

Ⓑ X and Y Locations Displays the numerical X- and Y-axis positions for the selected reference point.

Ⓒ Width and Height Displays the exact width and height measurement for any currently selected object, or any object as it is created with a specific tool.

Ⓓ Palette menu Click to access palette options. Choose from default rotation and flip options, as well as more specific on/off transform settings such as Scale Strokes.

Ⓔ Constrain Proportions For Scaling Activates or deactivates the constrain proportions feature when scaling objects. A broken chain link icon indicates that the control is off.

Ⓕ Scale X/Scale Y Percentage Display the horizontal and vertical percentage for any object you scale.

Ⓖ Rotation or Shear X Angle Display the degree of angle for any object you rotate or shear.

Related Tasks

2.7	Object Menu
2.10	Window Menu
3.2	Control Bar
3.10	Shape Tools
7.8	Modifying Paths and Frames
8.1	Moving Objects
8.2	Resizing Objects
8.3	Rotating Objects
8.4	Flipping Objects
8.5	Shearing Objects
12.6	Resizing Placed Images

Shortcuts

Transform palette
Mac and Win: F9

Transform Again
Mac: Opt+Cmd+3
Win: Alt+Ctrl+3

Transform Sequence Again
Mac: Opt+Cmd+4
Win: Alt+Ctrl+4

Move
Mac: Shift+Cmd+M
Win: Shift+Ctrl+M

Show/hide all controls
Mac and Win: Tab

Show/hide all controls except Toolbox and Control bar
Mac and Win: Shift+Tab

Align palette
Mac and Win: Shift+F7

Tip

You can quickly close an open path by first selecting it and then clicking the Close Path button located under Convert Shapes in the Pathfinder palette.

4.12 Object Styles Palette

The object styles in InDesign are similar to the graphic styles in Adobe Illustrator. The idea here is to save your favorite combination of characteristics, such as stroke, fill, feather, drop shadow, and corner effect, and apply them to various objects again and again. You can also create, save, and apply object styles to text frames. (You can also apply styles from the Control bar Object Style menu or by using Quick Apply.)

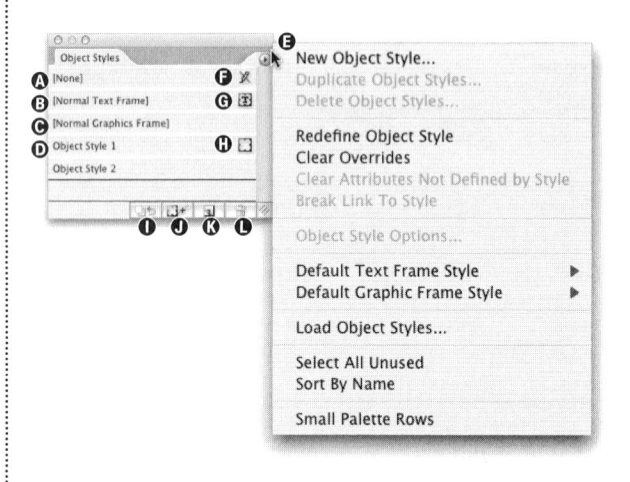

Ⓐ None Applied Click to remove all object styles from a selected item or items.

Ⓑ Basic Text Frame Defaults Double-click to open the Object Style Options dialog and choose your preferred Basic Text Frame settings. Apply these settings to newly drawn text frames by clicking the Basic Text Frame style in the Object Styles palette.

Ⓒ Basic Graphics Frame Defaults Double-click to open the Object Style Options dialog and choose your preferred Basic Graphics Frame settings. Apply these settings to newly drawn graphics frames by clicking the Basic Graphics Frame Style in the Object Styles palette.

Ⓓ Object Style Click the object style name to apply to a selected object or objects.

Ⓔ Palette menu Click to access the palette options, some of which are also accessible in the palette footer controls.

Ⓕ Style Cannot Be Removed Or Edited Indicates that the currently selected object style cannot be edited in the Object Style Options dialog.

Ⓖ Style Applied To New Text Frames Indicates that the object style containing this icon is the current text frame default. Click and drag the icon to a new style to change the default.

Ⓗ Style Applied To New Graphic Objects Indicates that the object style containing this icon is the current graphics frame default. Click and drag the icon to a new style to change the default.

Ⓘ Clear Attributes Not Defined By Style Click to remove any added attributes that are not part of the applied object style.

Ⓙ Clear Overrides Click to clear any overridden object style changes made to a selected frame.

Ⓚ Create New Style Click to create a new object style. Clicking this button with nothing selected creates a new style based on the last one selected in the palette or in the Control bar Object Style menu. Clicking this button with an object selected adopts all object style properties applied to it and applies them to the new style.

Ⓛ Delete Selected Style Click to delete a selected object style (or styles) from the palette list.

Related Tasks

2.4	Edit Menu
2.7	Object Menu
2.10	Window Menu
3.15	Eyedropper Tool
3.22	Other Toolbox Functions
4.5	Color Palette
4.16	Stroke Palette
4.17	Swatches Palette
7.10	Filling with Solid and Transparent Colors
7.11	Filling with Gradients
7.19	Applying Corner Effects
11.5	Creating and Applying Object Styles

Shortcuts

Show/hide all controls
Mac and Win: Tab

Show/hide all controls except Toolbox and Control bar
Mac and Win: Shift+Tab

Quick Apply
Mac: Cmd+Return
Win: Ctrl+Enter

Object Styles palette
Mac: Cmd+F7
Win: Ctrl+F7

Eyedropper tool
Mac and Win: I

Tip

You can copy and paste object styles using the Eyedropper tool.

4.13 Output Palettes

The Window > Output palettes can assist you in troubleshooting any potential printing and exporting problems you might encounter with your InDesign documents. Being able to preview your color separations and flattened transparencies on screen is certainly not a bad thing; neither is the ability to create and save custom trap presets. We're talking about virtual prepress Nirvana here. (No, not the alternative grunge-rock band. I'm referring to the state of enlightenment… oh, never mind!)

Flattener Preview Palette

The Flattener Preview palette allows you to highlight areas in a document that are affected by transparency flattening during output and also apply the proper flattener preset. Translation: *The blend mode you used on that type may not print right. Use this palette to avoid problems when printing.*

You can apply different transparency flattener presets to all transparent items in your document when printing or exporting to PDF, SVG, or EPS. Choose from default Low, Medium, or High presets, or select a saved custom preset. You can create, save, and apply your own custom presets in the Transparency Flattener Presets dialog accessible through the Flattener Preview palette menu. InDesign Help also contains a thorough list of output guidelines that you can refer to when creating or editing flattener presets.

Note: Use the Flattener Preview palette along with Overprint Preview (Mac: Opt+Shift+Cmd+Y, Windows: Alt+Shift+Ctrl+Y) for accurate on-screen previewing of all transparencies, spot colors, blend modes, and overprints in a document.

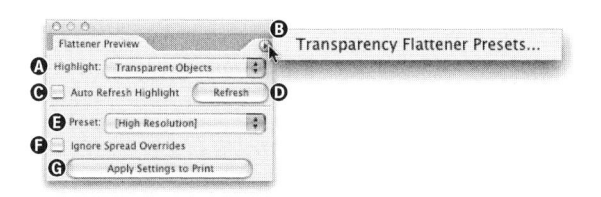

Related Tasks

2.9 View Menu
2.10 Window Menu
4.16 Stroke Palette

Shortcuts

Show/hide all controls
Mac and Win: Tab

Show/hide all controls except Toolbox and Control bar
Mac and Win: Shift+Tab

Tip

If the default transparency flattener presets aren't working well enough with your inkjet or laser printer, you can create and save your own custom settings. To access the options dialog, choose Edit > Transparency Flattener Presets and click the New button.

Ⓐ Highlight Choose from the default list of potential transparent items to highlight in the document. Be sure to set the menu selection back to None when you've finished previewing.

Ⓑ Palette menu Click to access the Transparency Flattener Presets dialog.

Ⓒ Auto Refresh Highlight Check this box to automatically update the highlighted preview when changes to the document have been made.

Ⓓ Refresh Click this button to update the preview manually.

Ⓔ Preset Choose a transparency flattener preset from the menu.

Ⓕ Ignore Spread Overrides Checking Ignore Spread Overrides applies the selected preset to the entire document, and ignores any overridden flattener presets applied to individual spreads.

Ⓖ Apply Settings to Print Click to allow the chosen flattener setting to automatically appear in the Print dialog.

4.13 Output Palettes (continued)

Related Tasks

5.13 Appearance of Black Preferences

5.16 Print Presets

16.1 Printing a Document

Shortcuts

Separations palette
Mac and Win: Shift+F6

Overprint Preview
Mac: Opt+Shift+Cmd+Y
Win: Alt+Shift+Ctrl+Y

Separations Preview Palette

The Separations Preview palette allows you to preview CMYK process plates individually on screen, before outputting. You can use the separations preview to check rich black builds, total ink coverage (to make sure it does not exceed press limitations), and overprinting (including transparency and blends). You can also use it to preview transparent varnishes and coatings on screen as black.

Click a single process plate in the palette (C, M, Y, or K) to preview that separation. By default, the individual separations appear on screen as black. However, you can change the preview setting to reflect actual plate colors by disabling the Show Single Plates In Black option in the palette menu.

A **View** Choose Separations or Ink Limit from the menu. Choosing Separations allows you to preview CMYK process plates individually. Choosing Ink Limit allows you to enter an ink limit percentage (you should get this number from your printer) and displays any excessive ink coverage in red.

B **Ink Limit Percentage** Choose a number from the default list or enter a value in the data field.

C **Palette menu** Click to access the Separations Preview options.

D **Toggle Visibility** Click the eye icon to hide or show a color plate.

E **View All Colors** Click to preview all four color plates together.

F **Color Separations** Click a color plate to preview. To preview more than one plate at a time (but not all), use the visibility toggles.

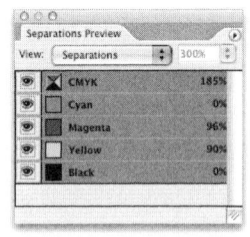

Hover your mouse over any area in the document to view the CMYK numerical build for a specific color. The percentage numbers appear next to each plate color, and change as you move your mouse around the document.

4.13 Output Palettes *(continued)*

Trap Presets Palette

The Trap Presets palette can assist you in creating, saving, loading, and applying trap presets. You can apply the default preset, no preset, or a custom preset to any or all the pages in a document. You can also load trap presets from other InDesign documents.

To assign a saved trap preset, the default trap preset, or no trap preset at all to the document or to a page range, click the desired option and select Assign Trap Preset from the palette menu. If a Trap Preset is not applied manually to a page range using the Trap Presets palette, InDesign uses the Default setting.

Ⓐ No Trap Preset Click this option and select Assign Trap Preset from the palette menu to remove any trap preset from the document or from a page range.

Ⓑ Default To edit the default settings, double-click to access the Modify Trap Preset Options dialog. Make your changes and click OK to save.

Ⓒ Trap preset Double-click to edit in the Modify Trap Preset Options dialog.

Ⓓ Palette menu Click to access the palette options, some of which are also available in the footer controls.

Ⓔ Create New Trap Preset Click to create a new trap preset. Double-click the new preset in the palette list to enter settings in the Modify Trap Preset Options dialog. Click OK when ready to save.

Ⓕ Delete Selected Preset Click to delete a selected trap preset (or presets) from the palette list.

Related Tasks

16.1 Printing a Document

16.3 Creating and Assigning Trap Presets

4.14 PageMaker Toolbar

Related Tasks

2.10   Window Menu

4.2   Customizing Your Workspace

6.4   Opening PageMaker and QuarkXPress Documents

Shortcuts

Show/hide all controls
Mac and Win: Tab

Show/hide all controls except Toolbox and Control bar
Mac and Win: Shift+Tab

Tip

Double-click the tab on the far left of the PageMaker toolbar (where the close button is located) to minimize it.

The PageMaker toolbar used to be available only to InDesign users as part of the PageMaker Plug-in Pack. Luckily, it is now part of the InDesign interface and installs with the application. This handy little palette contains 31 different one-click controls that can save you several trips to the menu bar.

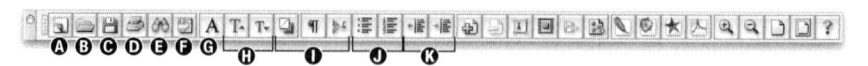

Ⓐ New Document Click to access the New Document dialog.

Ⓑ Open Document Click to access the Open A File dialog.

Ⓒ Save Click to apply the Save command.

Ⓓ Print Click to access the Print dialog.

Ⓔ Find/Change Click to access the Find/Change dialog.

Ⓕ Check Spelling Click to access the Check Spelling dialog.

Ⓖ Character Palette Click to open or close the Character palette.

Ⓗ Increase/Decrease Font Size Click to increase/decrease the font size of text highlighted with the Type tool in 2-point increments.

Ⓘ Palette toggles Click to open or close the Swatches, Paragraph, or Tabs palette.

Ⓙ Bulleted or Numbered Lists Click to apply a bulleted or numbered list to the text of a selected frame. Select multiple text frames to apply a list format to all text items at once. Click again to undo. Option-click (Mac) or Alt-click (Windows) to access the Bullets And Numbering options dialog.

Ⓚ Decrease/Increase Left Indent Click to increase/decrease the left indent of a text frame in 0.5-inch increments.

4.14 PageMaker Toolbar (continued)

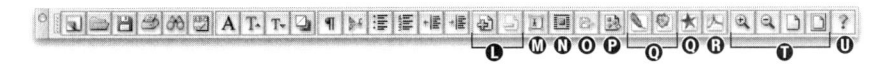

Related Tasks

2.10 Window Menu

4.2 Customizing Your Workspace

6.4 Opening PageMaker and QuarkXPress Documents

- **L Insert/Remove Pages** Click to access the Insert Pages or Remove Pages dialog.
- **M Text Frame Options** Click to access the Text Frame Options dialog.
- **N Text Wrap Palette** Click to open or close the Text Wrap palette.
- **O Update Link** Click to update a selected, modified link.
- **P Place** Click to open the Place dialog and place an item in a document.
- **Q Photoshop/Illustrator** Click to launch Adobe Photoshop or Adobe Illustrator (application must already be installed on your system). If the program is already open, click to bring it to the front of your open applications.
- **R Package for GoLive** Click to package a web version of an InDesign document to be opened in Adobe GoLive.
- **S Export Adobe PDF** Click to export a document as a PDF.
- **T Zoom/View commands** Click to zoom in or out of a document using default interval amounts, to display the document at 100% view magnification in the document window, or to display the entire spread you are currently working on in the document window.
- **U Help** Click to launch the Adobe Help Center.

Shortcuts

Show/hide all controls
Mac and Win: Tab

Show/hide all controls except Toolbox and Control bar
Mac and Win: Shift+Tab

Tip

Double-click the tab on the far left of the Page-Maker toolbar (where the close button is located) to minimize it.

4.15 Pages Palette

Related Tasks

2.10 Window Menu
5.15 Document Presets
6.1 Starting a New Document
6.2 Saving Document Presets
6.8 Adding, Arranging, and Deleting Pages
6.9 Creating Multipage Spreads and Master Pages
6.10 Targeting vs. Selecting Pages

Shortcuts

Show/hide all controls
Mac and Win: Tab

Show/hide all controls except Toolbox and Control bar
Mac and Win: Shift+Tab

Pages palette
Mac and Win: F12
Win: Alt+Shift+Ctrl+L

The Pages palette allows you to insert, manage, and delete both master and document pages. Like the Page Layout palette in QuarkXPress, the top portion of InDesign's Pages palette displays any saved master spreads, and the bottom displays all document spreads (although, unlike XPress, this palette layout can be reversed in the Palette Options dialog). Click a thumbnail to target a page and double-click to display it in the document window.

You can apply master pages by clicking and dragging master page thumbnails over document page thumbnails in the palette. In addition, a document page can be converted to a master page by clicking and dragging a document thumbnail into the master pages portion of the palette.

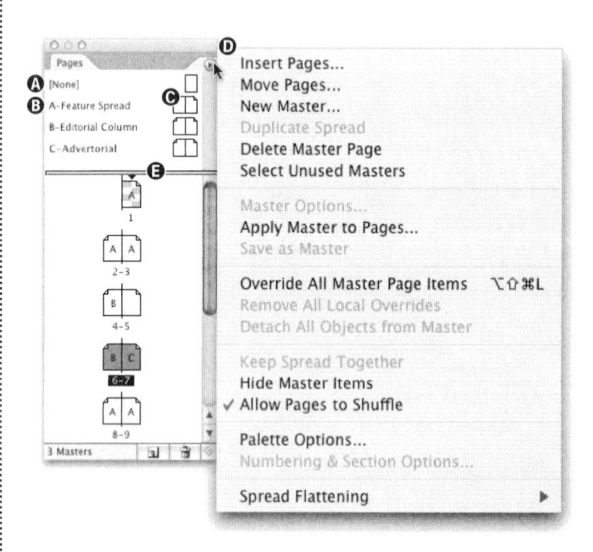

- **Ⓐ None** Click and drag over a document thumbnail to apply the default None master style to a document page. The None master cannot be edited.
- **Ⓑ Master Page Name** Displays the assigned prefix and master page name. To edit, Option-click (Mac) or Alt-click (Windows) to access the Master Options dialog.
- **Ⓒ Master Page icon** Click and drag over a document thumbnail to apply the saved master page style to a document page. With a document page targeted in the document portion of the palette, Option-click (Mac) or Alt-click (Windows) to apply the master page to the selection. You can also add document pages with a master style applied to them by clicking and dragging a master page/spread icon into the document page portion of the Pages palette. Double-click to edit the master page in the document window.
- **Ⓓ Palette menu** Click to access palette options. Some of these options are also available in the palette footer controls and under the Layout > Pages submenu.
- **Ⓔ Pages Palette divider** Divides the master and document portions of the palette. Click and drag up or down to reposition.

4.15 Pages Palette

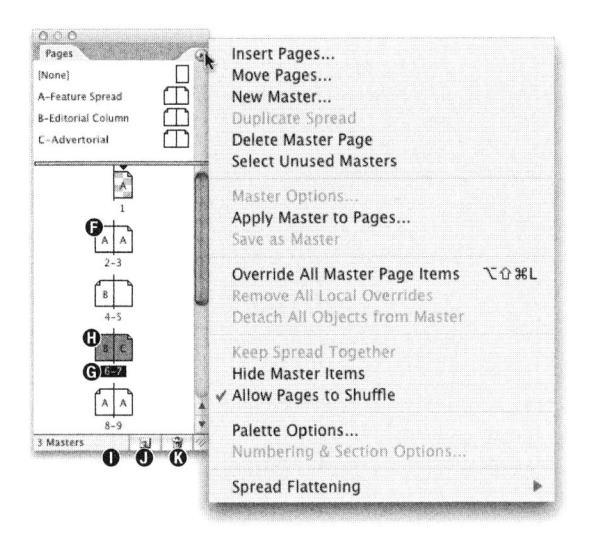

Related Tasks

- 6.11 Creating Master Pages
- 6.12 Converting Document Pages to Master Pages
- 6.13 Applying Master Pages
- 6.14 Deleting Master Pages
- 6.15 Creating and Applying Parent/Child Master Pages
- 6.16 Overriding Master Page Items
- 6.17 Adding Page Numbers to Sections

Shortcuts

New document
Mac: Cmd+N
Win: Ctrl+N

Document setup
Mac: Opt+Cmd+P
Win: Alt+Ctrl+P

Add page
Mac: Shift+Cmd+P
Win: Shift+Ctrl+P

Override all master page items
Mac: Opt+Shift+Cmd+L

Tip

You can copy master page spreads from one open InDesign document to another. Select the spreads you want to copy by clicking them in the Master Pages portion of the Pages palette, then drag them into another open document.

F Document Page icons Click a thumbnail to target a page; double-click to display it in the document window. To convert a document page into a master, click and drag the icon into the master pages portion of the palette. To target multiple pages or spreads at a time, hold down the Shift key as you click.

G Targeted Page/Spread Targeted pages or spreads always appear with a black highlight over the page number in the Pages palette. Targeted pages or spreads are not always displayed in the document window, especially when hand scrolling through the document

H Selected Spread Currently selected pages or spreads always appear with a highlighted page icon (not page number) in the Pages palette.

I Number Of Document Or Master Pages/Spreads Displays the total number of document or master pages and spreads existing in the document. Master or document display reflects the portion of the palette you currently have a page selected from.

J Create New Page Click to add a page immediately following the currently selected page in the document. The new page inherits the master style applied to the previous page.

K Delete Selected Pages Click to delete any selected pages or spreads and their contents from the document.

4.16 Stroke Palette

Related Tasks

7.13 Stroking Frames, Shapes, and Paths

7.14 Stroking Text

7.15 Aligning Strokes

7.16 Applying Stroked Path Start and End Styles

7.17 Saving and Applying Custom Strokes

7.18 Applying Gap Color to Open Stroke Styles

11.5 Creating and Applying Object Styles

Shortcuts

Stroke palette
Mac and Win: F10

Object Styles palette
Mac: Cmd+F7
Win: Ctrl+F7

Eyedropper tool
Mac and Win: I

Tip

To create and save your own stroke styles, click the palette menu button and choose Stroke Styles. When the dialog opens, click the New button to access the New Stroke Style options.

You can apply a gradient to a stroke style.

The Stroke palette allows you to define a stroke style and apply it to a selected object or objects. You can also save your favorite custom stroke styles or load them from other InDesign documents.

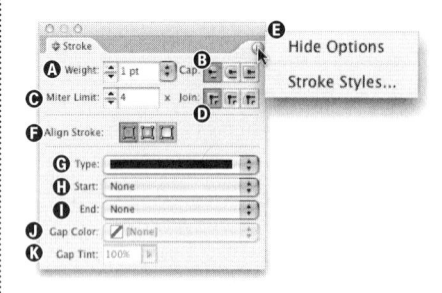

A **Weight** Allows you to choose a specific stroke size to apply to a selected object or group of objects. Select a default stroke weight from the menu or click in the data field to enter a value. A selected object's stroke weight can also be adjusted in increments by clicking the up/down arrows located next to the data field.

B **Cap Style** Click Butt, Round, or Projecting to define how the stroke ends of an open path or line appear.

C **Join Style** Click Miter, Round, or Bevel to define how the corners of a stroke appear.

D **Miter Limit** This control is available only when using the Miter Join Style. This sets the distance the corner of a stroke can extend before automatically applying a bevel. Click in the data field to enter a miter limit amount.

E **Palette menu** Click to show/hide the palette options or to access the Stroke Styles dialog.

F **Align Stroke** Click to align a stroke to the center of an object, the inside, or the outside.

G **Type** Click the menu to choose from a list of stroke styles to apply to a selected object or group of objects.

H **Start** Click the menu to choose from a list of stroke start styles.

I **End** Click the menu to choose from a list of stroke end styles.

J **Gap Color** This control is available only when using an open stroke type. Click the menu to choose from a list of available colors in the Swatches palette.

K **Gap Tint** This control is available only when you apply Gap Color to an open stroke. Click the arrow button to access the drop-down slider, or click in the data field to enter a tint percentage.

4.17 Swatches Palette

The Swatches palette acts as the central hub for applying and editing color when working in InDesign. You can easily drag and drop swatches from the Toolbox, Color palette, and Gradient palette into the Swatches palette for future use. You can store your favorite color and gradient swatches, load colors from other documents (InDesign, QuarkXPress, and PageMaker included), and add colors from various libraries.

A **Fill/Stroke** Displays either the default fill and stroke colors, or the colors of any currently selected object in the document. Switch between fill and stroke controls by clicking either swatch. You can also swap applied fill and stroke colors by clicking the arrows located to the upper right of the swatch icons.

B **Formatting Affects Container** Click to apply a color to a selected frame.

C **Formatting Affects Text** Click to apply a color to all editable text in a selected frame.

D **Tint** Click the arrow button to access the drop-down slider, or click in the data field to enter a tint percentage to apply to a selected swatch.

E **Palette menu** Click to access the palette options. Some of these options are also available in the palette footer controls.

F **None** Click to apply no color to a fill or stroke of a selected object or objects.

G **Paper** Click to apply the chosen Paper color to the fill or stroke of a selected object or objects. The default Paper color is 100% white but can be edited.

H **Black** Click to apply a 100% black fill or stroke to a selected object or objects.

I **Registration** Click to allow the fill or stroke to appear on all color plates.

J **Selected Color** Click to apply the saved color to a fill or stroke of a selected object or objects. Double-click to edit the swatch.

Related Tasks

3.15 Eyedropper Tool
3.17 Gradient Tool
3.22 Other Toolbox Functions
4.5 Color Palette
4.16 Stroke Palette
7.10 Filling with Solid and Transparent Colors
7.11 Filling with Gradients
7.12 Filling Text
7.13 Stroking Frames, Shapes, and Paths
7.14 Stroking Text

Shortcuts

Show/hide all controls
Mac and Win: Tab

Show/hide all controls except Toolbox and Control bar
Mac and Win: Shift+Tab

Swatches palette
Mac and Win: F5

Object Styles palette
Mac: Cmd+F7
Win: Ctrl+F7

Eyedropper tool
Mac and Win: I

Gradient tool
Mac and Win: G

Tip

You can create a two-color spot job that prints like four-color process by taking advantage of Mixed Ink Groups.

4.17 Swatches Palette (continued)

Related Tasks

11.5 Creating and Applying Object Styles

14.4 Creating and Saving Mixed Ink Swatches and Groups

14.5 Accessing Colors Stored in Libraries

14.6 Converting Spot Colors to Process

14.7 Importing Colors from Other Documents

Shortcuts

Show/hide all controls
Mac and Win: Tab

Show/hide all controls except Toolbox and Control bar
Mac and Win: Shift+Tab

Swatches palette
Mac and Win: F5

Object Styles palette
Mac: Cmd+F7
Win: Ctrl+F7

Eyedropper tool
Mac and Win: I

Gradient tool
Mac and Win: G

Tip

You can change the application default color swatch list by first closing all open documents, then adding or deleting colors in the Swatches palette.

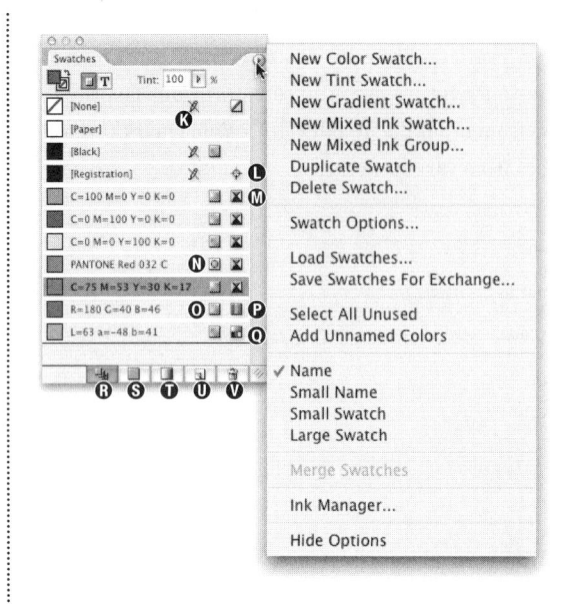

Ⓚ Color Cannot Be Edited Indicates that the currently selected color cannot be edited in the Swatch Options dialog.

Ⓛ Prints On All Plates Indicates that the currently selected swatch appears on all color plates when applied.

Ⓜ CMYK icon Indicates that the color mode of the currently selected swatch is set to CMYK.

Ⓝ Spot Color icon Indicates that the color type of the currently selected swatch is set to Spot.

Ⓞ Process Color icon Indicates that the color type of the currently selected swatch is set to Process.

Ⓟ RGB icon Indicates that the color mode of the currently selected swatch is set to RGB.

Ⓠ LAB icon Indicates that the color mode of the currently selected swatch is set to Lab.

Ⓡ Show All Swatches Click the button to show all swatches (Color and Gradient) in the palette.

Ⓢ Show Color Swatches Click the button to show only saved Color swatches in the palette.

Ⓣ Show Gradient Swatches Click the button to show only saved Gradient swatches in the palette.

Ⓤ New Swatch Click the button to duplicate the currently selected or last selected swatch in the palette. Double-click the new swatch to edit.

Ⓥ Delete Swatch Click the button to delete a selected swatch or group of swatches from the palette.

4.18 Tags Palette

Okay, I know what you're thinking. What the heck are tags, right? Tags provide a way to map objects in your InDesign document with elements in its XML structure. The Tags palette helps you create, manage, and apply tags to elements.

So why would you want to do this? Well, because importing and exporting XML structures in InDesign allows you to set up document templates for a repeated workflow schedule (newsletters, databases, etc.). You can also use XML to apply a document's structure to a web version of the layout.

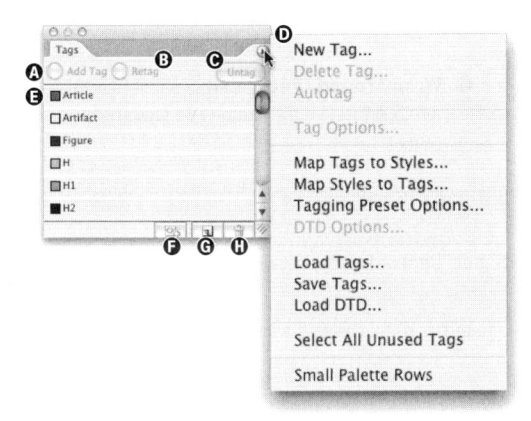

Ⓐ Add Tag Selecting an untagged text item with the Type tool activates the Add Tag radio button. Click a tag from the palette to assign it.

Ⓑ Retag Selecting a tagged text item with the Type tool activates the Retag radio button. Click a different tag from the palette to assign it.

Ⓒ Untag Click to remove a tag from a selected element in the structure view.

Ⓓ Palette menu Click to access the palette options. Some of these options are also available in the palette footer controls.

Ⓔ Tag Displays the tag name and its identifying color. Double-click to access the Tag Options dialog and assign a new name and/or color.

Ⓕ Autotag Select an untagged text item with the Type tool and click the Autotag button for InDesign to apply a related tag to the element.

Ⓖ New Tag Click the button to create a new tag. Double-click the new tag to edit.

Ⓗ Delete Tag Click to delete a selected tag or group of tags from the palette.

Related Tasks

2.10 Window Menu
9.5 Importing XML
15.6 Packaging for GoLive
17.1 Exporting as Adobe PDF
17.6 Exporting as XML

Shortcuts

Show/hide all controls
Mac and Win: Tab

Show/hide all controls except Toolbox and Control bar
Mac and Win: Shift+Tab

Show Structure
Mac: Opt+Cmd+1
Win: Alt+Ctrl+1

Tip

You can apply structure tags to a document for PDF Export. This can greatly expand PDF usability and accessibility.

4.19 Text Wrap Palette

Related Tasks

2.7 Object Menu
2.10 Window Menu
3.4 Direct Selection and Position Tools
3.5 Pen Tools
12.11 Altering an Embedded Photoshop Path
12.12 Creating a Clipping Path in InDesign
13.1 Placing and Editing Text Wraps

Shortcuts

Text Wrap palette
Mac: Opt+Cmd+W
Win: Alt+Ctrl+W

Direct Selection tool
Mac and Win: A

Pen tool
Mac and Win: P

Tip

A graphic text wrap can be turned off when the layer containing it is hidden. Just place the graphic with the text wrap applied to it on its own layer, and then double-click the layer in the Layers palette. When the Layer Options dialog appears, check the Suppress Text Wrap When Layer Is Hidden box and click OK. You can then hide the layer to turn off the text wrap.

InDesign takes the concept of text wraps to a whole new level of creativity. The Text Wrap palette is your master control for creating, editing, and applying this popular effect. The various options available in this palette are so simple to use that they just beg for you to experiment and discover new and exciting ways to wrap text in a layout.

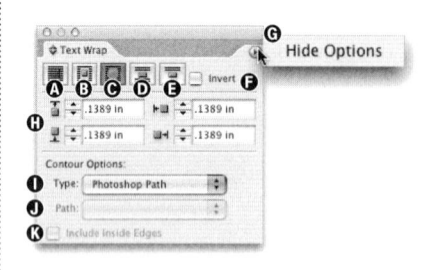

A **No Text Wrap** Click to apply no text wrap to a selected object or objects.

B **Wrap Around Bounding Box** Click to apply a text wrap around the bounding box of a selected object (not the contents).

C **Wrap Around Object Shape** Click to apply a text wrap evenly around the shape of an object.

D **Jump Object** Click to apply a wrap that "jumps" text over an object, resulting in text above and below the offset, but not to the left or right.

E **Jump To Next Column** Click to apply a wrap that "jumps" text to the next column, stopping the text at the top of the offset.

F **Invert** Click to create an "inside-out" wrap. This feature works well with the Object Shape wrap option.

G **Palette menu** Click to show/hide palette options.

H **Top/Bottom/Left/Right Offset** Allows you to choose a specific offset amount to apply to a selected object or group of objects. Click in the data field to enter a value, or adjust the value in default increments by clicking the up/down arrows located next to the data field.

I **Contour Options Type** Only accessible when applying a text wrap to a clipping path on a placed graphic. Choose one of the following:

Bounding Box Applies a text wrap to the outer edge of the placed graphic (this includes all areas cropped by a graphic frame).

Detect Edges Applies a text wrap based on edges detected by any white areas in the placed graphic.

Alpha Channel or Photoshop Path Applies a text wrap to a placed graphic that contains an embedded path or channel.

Graphic Frame Applies a text wrap to the container.

Same as Clipping Applies a text wrap to a clipping path that is created in InDesign.

J **Path** Only accessible when applying a text wrap to a placed graphic containing embedded Photoshop paths or alpha channels. InDesign recognizes all saved paths and channels in the placed file. If the placed graphic contains more than one path or channel, you can choose which one to apply the text wrap to from the Path menu.

K **Include Inside Edges** Only accessible when applying a text wrap to a placed graphic using Detect Edges. Check this box to make areas inside a clipping path transparent.

4.20 Transparency Palette

With the Transparency palette, InDesign allows you to adjust opacity levels and apply blend modes to selected fills and strokes, placed graphics, and editable text. Applied transparency and blend modes affect the entire object (fill and stroke), as well as all frame contents (placed graphic or text). It is not possible to apply different transparency effects or values to the fill and stroke of an object or to individual text characters or layers.

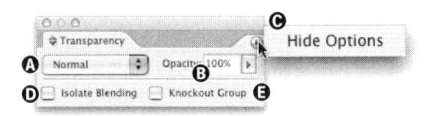

A **Blend Mode** Click to apply one of 16 blend modes to an object or object group.

B **Opacity** Click the arrow button to access the drop-down slider, or click in the data field to enter an opacity amount to apply to a selected object or object group.

C **Palette menu** Click to show/hide palette options.

D **Isolate Blending** Check this box to allow items in a selected group with blend modes applied to them to affect only objects in the group.

E **Knockout Group** Check this box to allow transparent items in a selected group to block each other out visually.

Related Tasks

2.10 Window Menu
4.5 Color Palette
4.6 Gradient Palette
4.12 Object Styles Palette
4.16 Stroke Palette
7.10 Filling with Solid and Transparent Colors
14.9 Applying Blend Modes

Shortcuts

Show/hide all controls
Mac and Win: Tab

Show/hide all controls except Toolbox and Control bar
Mac and Win: Shift+Tab

Transparency palette
Mac and Win: Shift+F10

Tip

InDesign flags any pages containing transparent items in the Pages palette by displaying a checkerboard pattern on the thumbnail icon.

VIEWING TAGS

You can choose to show/hide tag markers and tagged frames under the View > Structure submenu. A tagged frame is highlighted with its corresponding tag color as shown in the Tags palette.

You can also locate tagged items by viewing the document structure. To reveal the structure, click the left/right arrows at the very bottom left corner of the document window or press Opt+Cmd+1 (Mac) or Alt+Ctrl+1 (Windows). Click an element from the structure and then choose Go To Item from the structure panel fly-out menu for InDesign to highlight the item in the document.

4.21 Type and Tables Palettes

Related Tasks

2.10 Window Menu
3.2 Control Bar
3.6 Type Tools
5.2 Type Preferences
5.3 Advanced Type Preferences

Tip

To apply a keyboard shortcut to a character style in the Character Style Options dialog, make sure your keyboard Num Lock is turned on. Then choose any combination of Shift, Option (Mac), Alt (Window), Ctrl (Windows), or Command (Mac) and a number from the numeric keypad. Letters and non-keypad numbers are not applicable.

The Window > Type & Tables submenu contains nine palettes pertaining to text and table formatting in InDesign. Here you will find palettes for character and paragraph attributes and styles, as well as for glyphs, tabs, tables, and index settings. A Story palette for adjusting optical margin alignment is also available.

Character Palette

With the Type tool selected, every control in the Character palette also appears in the Control bar; however, some users prefer to set attributes using the Character palette. For many options, you can adjust the value by clicking the up/down arrows, choosing from the default menu, or entering a value in the data field

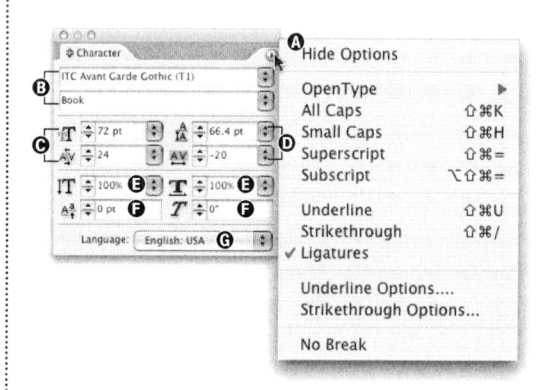

Ⓐ Palette menu Click to access palette options. Some options are also available in the Control bar.

Ⓑ Font and Style Display the typeface and style of any currently selected text.

Ⓒ Font Size and Leading Display (left) the type size and (right) leading amount for any currently selected text.

Ⓓ Kerning and Tracking Display the (left) kerning amount and (right) tracking amount, in thousandths of an em, for any currently selected text.

Ⓔ Vertical/Horizontal Scale Display the amount of (left) vertical and (right) horizontal scaling for any currently selected text.

Ⓕ Baseline Shift and Skew Display (left) the amount of baseline shift and (right) degree of skew for selected text.

Ⓖ Language Allows you to choose from several language dictionaries available in InDesign.

Character Styles Palette

You can save and apply your favorite character attributes using the Character Styles palette. Select some text or click an insertion point with the Type tool to highlight any currently applied styles in the palette. If multiple styles are applied to selected text, the palette does not highlight anything.

4.21 Type and Tables Palettes *(continued)*

From the palette menu, you can also load character styles from other InDesign documents.

A **None** Click to remove any character style from a selected text item or items.

B **Character Style** Click the character style name to apply it to a selected text item or items. You can also apply the style from the Control bar Character Style menu or by using Quick Apply. Double-click to edit in the Character Style Options dialog.

C **Palette menu** Click to access the palette options. Some options are also available in the palette footer controls.

D **Create New Style** Click to create a new character style. Clicking this button creates a new style based on the style currently selected in the palette.

E **Delete Selected Styles** Deletes the selected character style (or styles) from the palette list.

Glyphs Palette

Certain fonts (such as OpenType fonts) contain extra characters that are easily accessible in InDesign via the Glyphs palette. You can also create and save glyph sets to refer to again and again.

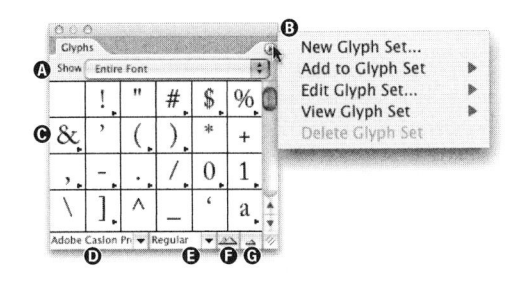

A **Show** Click to choose Glyphs palette display options for a selected font in a document.

B **Palette menu** Click to access the glyph set options.

C **Glyph** Displays various glyph characters available for a selected font. Double-click to replace any text characters highlighted with the Type tool or to add a glyph anywhere a text insertion point is placed with the Type cursor.

D **Font** Displays the currently selected font. Click the arrow button to choose a different font from the menu.

E **Style** Displays the currently selected type style. Click the arrow button to choose a different style from the menu.

F **Zoom In** Click to make the glyph preview characters appear larger in the palette.

G **Zoom Out** Click to make the glyph preview characters appear smaller in the palette.

Related Tasks

2.10 Window Menu
3.6   Type Tools
5.2   Text Preferences
10.1 Kerning and Tracking
11.1 Creating and Applying Character Styles
11.6 Editing and Deleting Styles
11.7 Importing Styles

Shortcuts

Type tool
Mac and Win: T

Character palette
Mac: Cmd+T
Win: Ctrl+T

Character Styles palette
Mac and Win: Shift+F11

Type tool
Mac and Win: T

Index palette
Mac and Win: Shift+F8

Tip

OpenType fonts often contain multiple glyphs for standard characters.

4.21 Type and Tables Palettes (continued)

Related Tasks

5.3 Advanced Type Preferences

10.14 Inserting Special Characters

18.6 Building an Index

Index Palette

The Index palette allows you to create, edit, and preview an index for a large document or book. You can preview the index in the palette using either Reference mode (displays all index entries) or Topic mode (displays only topics—not page numbers or cross-references). Index entries are listed alphabetically when previewing in Reference mode. Click the triangles to show/hide index subentries, page numbers, and cross references.

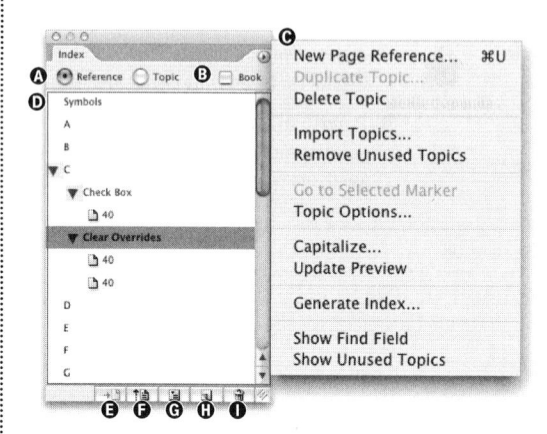

Ⓐ Reference/Topic Click either radio button to specify the palette preview mode.

Ⓑ Book Check this box to include book index entries, cross references, and topics.

Ⓒ Palette menu Click to access the palette options. Some options are also found in the palette footer controls.

Ⓓ Index Entry Entries are listed according to the chosen preview mode (Reference or Topic). Click the triangles to view subentries, page numbers, and cross references. Double-click an entry to edit its properties.

Ⓔ Go To Selected Marker Click to display a selected index entry item in the document window.

Ⓕ Update Preview Click to refresh the index palette preview after changes have been made to the document.

Ⓖ Generate Index Click to access the Generate Index dialog.

Ⓗ Create A New Index Entry Select an object in the document and click this button to create a new page reference or cross-reference.

Ⓘ Delete Selected Entry Click to delete a selected index entry.

4.21 Type and Tables Palettes *(continued)*

Paragraph Palette

Just as in the Character palette, every control in the Paragraph palette also appears in the Control bar when the Type tool is selected. Again, some users prefer to use the Paragraph palette for setting attributes.

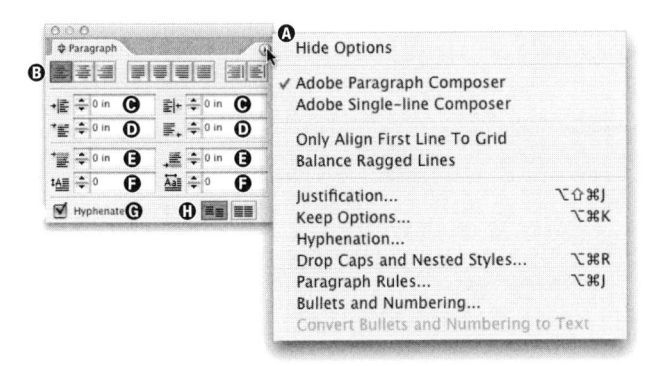

A **Palette menu** Click to access palette options. Some options are also available in the Control bar.

B **Alignment/Justification** Applies specific text alignment options to selected text frames: Align Left, Align Center, Align Right, Justify With Last Line Aligned Left, Justify With Last Line Aligned Center, Justify With Last Line Aligned Right, Justify All Lines, Align Towards Spine, Align Away From Spine.

C **Left/Right Indent** Display the amount of paragraph left indent and right indent for any currently selected text.

D **First Line Left and Last Line Right Indent** Display the amount of first line left indent and last line right indent for any currently selected text.

E **Space Before/After** Display the amount of added space above and below any currently selected paragraph.

F **Drop Cap Number Of Lines and Characters** Allow you to specify the number of lines an applied drop cap will fall and the number of characters to apply a drop cap to.

G **Hyphenate** Keeping this box checked allows all paragraphs in your document to hyphenate automatically. To bypass this option, select any paragraphs you don't want hyphenated and uncheck the box, or uncheck it before creating any text frames.

H **Align To Baseline Grid** Toggles this alignment on or off.

Related Tasks

5.4 Composition Preferences

10.1 Kerning and Tracking

10.11 Change/Apply Justification

10.13 Setting Tabs

Tip

As with master pages, you can create paragraph styles that have "parent-child" relationships. This means that you can base several paragraph styles on a master "parent" style. When you make a change to the master "parent" style, it then ripples down through all of its "children."

4.21 Type and Tables Palettes *(continued)*

Related Tasks

11.1 Creating and Applying Character Styles

11.2 Creating and Applying Paragraph Styles

11.6 Editing and Deleting Styles

11.7 Importing Styles

Shortcuts

Paragraph palette
Mac: Opt+Cmd+T
Win: Alt+Ctrl+T

Paragraph Styles palette
Mac and Win: F11

Character palette
Mac: Cmd+T
Win: Ctrl+T

Character Styles palette
Mac and Win: Shift+F11

Paragraph Styles Palette

You can save and apply your favorite paragraph attributes using the Paragraph Styles palette. Select some text or click an insertion point with the Type Tool to highlight any currently applied styles in the palette. If multiple styles are applied to selected text, the palette does not highlight anything.

From the palette menu, you can also load paragraph styles from other InDesign documents.

Ⓐ Paragraph Style Click the paragraph style name to apply it to a selected text item or items. You can also apply the style from the Control bar's Paragraph Style menu or by using Quick Apply. To edit, double-click the style name in the palette to access the Paragraph Style Options dialog.

Ⓑ Palette menu Click to access palette options. Some options are also available in the palette footer controls.

Ⓒ Normal Click to apply the default Normal paragraph style to a selected text item or items. Double-click to edit the Normal style.

Ⓓ Style Indicator Indicates when No Style or Mixed Styles is applied to selected text items in the document.

Ⓔ Clear Overrides in Selection Click to clear any attributes applied to a paragraph style of a selected text item or items and revert to the style's last saved state.

Ⓕ Create New Style Click to create a new paragraph style. Clicking this button with nothing selected creates a new style based on the last one chosen from the Paragraph Styles palette or Control bar's Paragraph Style menu.

Ⓖ Delete Selected Styles Click to delete a selected paragraph style (or styles) from the palette list.

4.21 Type and Tables Palettes *(continued)*

Story Palette

The Story palette lets you adjust the optical margin alignment for selected text frames in a document. Enabling this option helps display large amounts of body text in an easy-to-read format by positioning punctuation marks (such as quotation marks) and other specific characters outside the column.

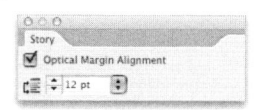

Check the Optical Margin Alignment box to apply that alignment to selected text frames in the document. The second row (Align Based On Size) displays the amount of optical margin alignment for any currently selected text.

Table Palette

The Table palette allows you to adjust an inserted table's number of rows and columns, as well as its row and column height/width measurements. You can also adjust an individual table cell's text alignment, justification, rotation, and inset.

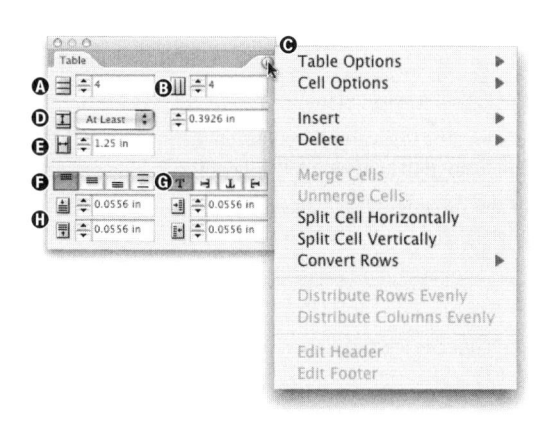

A **Number Of Rows** Displays the number of rows for a currently selected table.

B **Number Of Columns** Displays the number of columns for a currently selected table.

C **Palette menu** Click to access palette options. Some options are also available under the Table menu.

D **Row Height** Displays the amount of row height for a currently selected table. Choose At Least or Exactly from the menu to specify measurement application.

E **Column Width** Displays the amount of column width for a currently selected table.

F **Cell Text Alignment/Justification** Select a table cell (or cells) with the Type tool, then click a button to Align Top, Align Center, Align Bottom, or Justify Vertical.

G **Cell Text Rotation** Select a table cell (or cells) with the Type tool, then click a button to rotate by 0°, 90°, 180°, or 270°.

H **Top/Bottom/Left/Right Cell Inset** Displays the amount of text inset for a currently selected table cell.

Related Tasks

10.13 Setting Tabs

11.2 Creating and Applying Paragraph Styles

13.5 Creating a New Table

Shortcuts

Table palette
Mac and Win: Shift+F9

Tabs palette
Mac: Shift+Cmd+T
Win: Shift+Ctrl+T

4.21 Type and Tables Palettes *(continued)*

Related Tasks

13.6 Making Table Selections

13.7 Adding and Deleting Rows and Columns

Tip

To change an inserted tab's justification, select it in the Tabs palette and Option-click (Mac) or Alt-click (Windows).

Tabs Palette

You can set tabs and paragraph indents with the Tabs palette. To apply tabs and indents to all of the text in a selected frame, you must first highlight all of the text with the Type tool. Tabs can also be saved as part of a paragraph style.

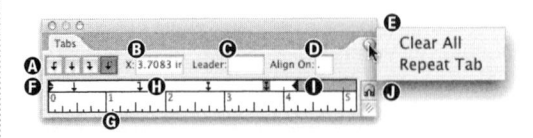

Ⓐ Tab Justification Click to specify justification for inserted tabs. Choose Left, Center, Right, or Align To Decimal.

Ⓑ X Location Displays the current x-axis coordinate for inserted tabs. To adjust, enter a specific coordinate in the data field, or simply reposition the tab icon above the ruler.

Ⓒ Leader Displays the current leader character to be placed before an inserted tab's x-location (e.g., a period or bullet). Enter a new leader character by entering one in the data field.

Ⓓ Align On Displays the current character to align a specified character tab to. Enter a new character by typing one in the data field.

Ⓔ Palette menu Click to either clear all tabs or repeat a selected tab.

Ⓕ Left Indent/First Line Left Indent Click and drag the top arrow to reposition the first line left indent. Click and drag the bottom arrow to reposition the paragraph left indent.

Ⓖ Ruler Displays the chosen unit of measurement directly above a selected text frame. Click and drag left or right to reposition within the Tabs palette.

Ⓗ Tab Click anywhere above the ruler to set a tab. Click and drag a tab left or right to reposition. Click and drag off the palette to delete.

Ⓘ Area Outside Of Text Frame All areas located outside a selected text frame are displayed as gray in the palette.

Ⓙ Position Palette Above Text Frame Click the magnet icon to position the Tabs palette directly above a selected text frame.

4.22 Book and Library Palettes

InDesign also features two other palettes that are not accessible under the Window menu. To open either of these palettes, you must first create a new book or library document under File > New. The palettes automatically open once you create or open a saved InDesign book or library document.

Book Palette

The Book palette allows you to synchronize all of the documents that make up a book or large document. You can choose a master document as the style source to apply to all the documents in the palette. You can also control auto page numbering across all documents in the book, export the entire book to PDF, and print all the documents at once.

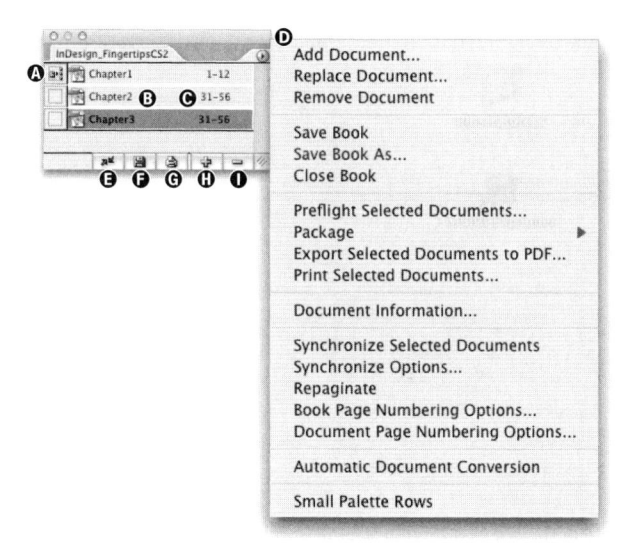

Related Tasks

8.13 Saving Objects to a Library

18.1 Creating a New Book File

18.2 Synchronizing Book Chapters

18.3 Page Numbering Across Book Documents

Tip

Both the Book and Library palettes can be docked and side-tabbed.

- **A Style Source** Click the area next to a document's name to select it as the master style source for the book.
- **B Document Name** Displays the names of all documents included in the book. Double-click to open.
- **C Page Range** Displays the page numbers assigned to a document.
- **D Palette menu** Click to access palette options.
- **E Synchronize Styles And Swatches With The Style Source** Click to synchronize all documents or selected documents in the palette to the style source.
- **F Save The Book** Click to save the book document.
- **G Print The Book** Click to print all documents (or selected documents) in the book.
- **H Add Documents** Click to add a document to the book.
- **I Remove Documents** Click to remove a selected document (or documents) from the book.

4.22 Book and Library Palettes (continued)

Related Tasks

18.7 Preflighting, Printing, and Exporting Books

Shortcuts

Open
Mac: Cmd+O
Win: Ctrl+O

Save
Mac: Cmd+S
Win: Ctrl+S

Index palette
Mac and Win: Shift+F8

Library Palette

The Library palette displays all objects stored in a saved library. You can save and open as many libraries as you like, which makes it possible to have more than one Library palette open at a time.

A saved library can contain shapes, frames, text items, and even placed graphics to include in your layouts. Placed graphics appear as links when dragged into a document from a library, and editable text items require that all fonts be loaded on your system.

You can add as many objects as you want to a library by simply dragging them into the palette. To change an object's name, specify an object type, or add an item description, double-click the object in the library list to access the Item Information dialog. You can also search for objects in the library by name, date added, object type, or description.

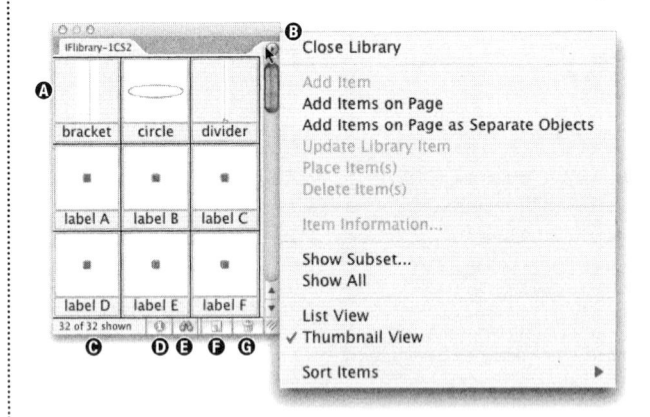

- **A** **Library Item** Displays a thumbnail of the object stored in the library and its name. To apply the object to your layout, click and drag it into the document. Double-click the object thumbnail to access the item's information or to rename it.
- **B** **Palette menu** Click to access palette options.
- **C** **Number Of Library Items** Displays the current number of items available in the library.
- **D** **Library Item Information** Select an object from the palette and click here to access the Item Information dialog.
- **E** **Show Library Subset** Click to search for an item in the library by name, creation date, object type, or description.
- **F** **New Library Item** Select an object in the document and click here to add it to the list.
- **G** **Delete Library Item** Click to remove a selected object (or objects) from the library.

CHAPTER **5**

Preferences and Presets

INDESIGN IS ALL ABOUT options. In fact, it has so many options you might feel overwhelmed. Even still, these options are worth exploring. Once you get to know them all, you'll discover that some are major time-savers, while others are simply a matter of, well… *preference!*

The Preferences dialog contains some of the most powerful options in InDesign. You can access the dialog under the InDesign menu (Mac) or the Edit menu (Windows). In the preferences listing on the left of the dialog are various options for screen display, measurement units, text handling, spell-check options, display performance, and much more. This chapter examines all the controls in each preference panel so that you can start applying them to your InDesign workflow.

To use the Preferences dialog, click one of the listings to open a specific panel and then choose your preferred settings. As soon as you click OK, your new settings are implemented.

Once you have your preferences set and start working in InDesign, you may grow frustrated with having to repeat some of the same tasks over and over again. Not to worry—to save time, you can save these tasks as presets. Learn to use presets correctly and you'll never have to set up a print dialog to handle spreads more than once.

- 5.1 **General Preferences**
- 5.2 **Type Preferences**
- 5.3 **Advanced Type Preferences**
- 5.4 **Composition Preferences**
- 5.5 **Units & Increments Preferences**
- 5.6 **Grids Preferences**
- 5.7 **Guides & Pasteboard Preferences**
- 5.8 **Dictionary Preferences**
- 5.9 **Spelling Preferences**
- 5.10 **Autocorrect Preferences**
- 5.11 **Story Editor Display Preferences**
- 5.12 **Display Performance Preferences**
- 5.13 **Appearance of Black Preferences**
- 5.14 **File Handling Preferences**
- 5.15 **Document Presets**
- 5.16 **Print Presets**
- 5.17 **Adobe PDF Presets**
- 5.18 **Configure Plug-ins**
- 5.19 **Keyboard Shortcuts**

5.1 General Preferences

Related Tasks

1.4	Interface Objects
2.5	Layout Menu
3.1	Toolbox
4.15	Pages Palette
4.21	Type and Tables Palettes
6.17	Adding Page Numbers to Sections
10.14	Inserting Special Characters

Shortcuts

General Preferences
Mac: Cmd+K
Win: Ctrl+K

Pages palette
Mac and Win: F12

Show/hide all controls
Mac and Win: Tab

Show/hide all controls except Toolbox and Control bar
Mac and Win: Shift+Tab

Tip

You can scroll through preferences in the dialog by using the up/down arrow keys.

The General Preferences panel is the first to display when you access the Preferences dialog from the menu. It contains options for displaying document page numbering, tooltips, and the Tools palette, as well as options for font downloading and embedding. It also contains a warning dialog reset button.

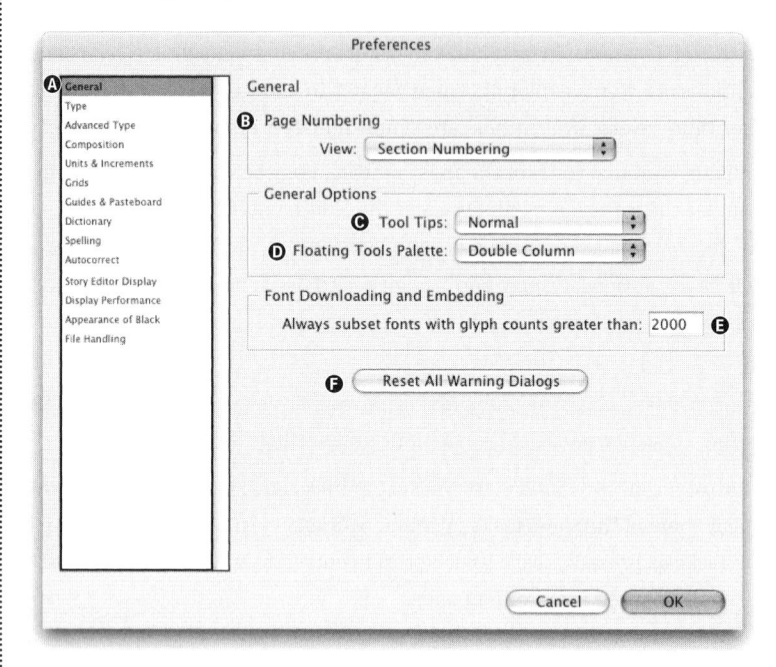

- **A General** Click to access the General Preferences panel.
- **B Page Numbering View** Choose either Section Numbering (defined in the Numbering & Section Options dialog located under the Layout menu) or Absolute Numbering (consecutive numbering starting with the first page of the document).
- **C Tool Tips** Choose Normal or Fast display speed, or turn off tooltip display by choosing None.
- **D Floating Tools Palette** Choose Double Column, Single Column, or Single Row Tools palette display.
- **E Font Downloading And Embedding** Enter a number of glyph characters to trigger font subsetting when printing or exporting.
- **F Reset All Warning Dialogs** Click to allow all warning dialogs that have been turned off to reappear. Note: Specific warning dialogs can be individually turned off by checking the box in the lower left, labeled "Do not display this dialog again."

5.2 Type Preferences

The Type Preferences panel contains various options for working with type, editing text with drag and drop, and importing text as links. Also included is a preference for pasting text and tables from other applications such as Microsoft Word or Excel.

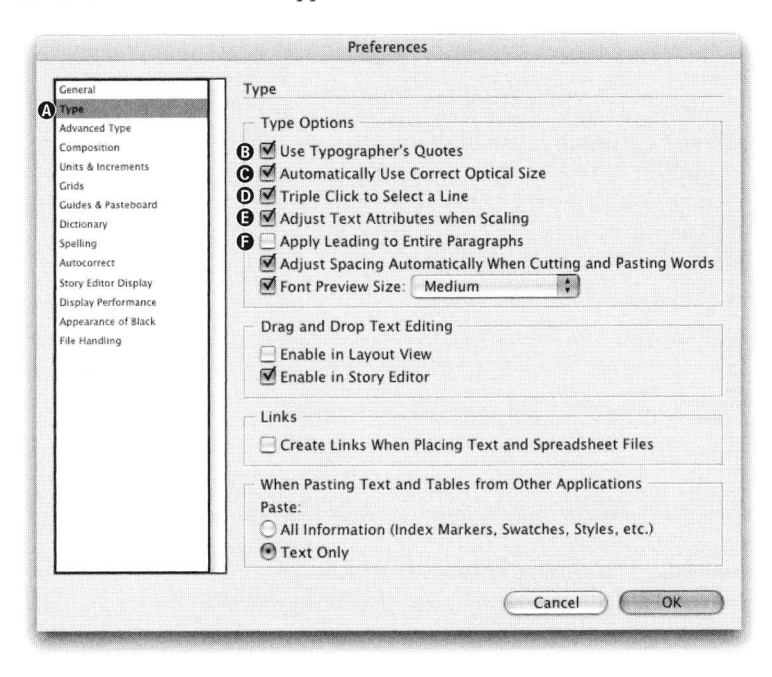

Related Tasks

2.6 Type Menu
3.6 Type Tools
4.21 Type and Tables Palettes
9.3 Importing Text

Shortcuts

Type tool
Mac and Win: T

Scale tool
Mac and Win: S

Free Transform tool
Mac and Win: E

Tip

When the option is enabled, you can use drag-and-drop text editing between frames, views, layout windows, and Story Editor windows and documents. You can also drag and drop text into the Find/Change dialog.

A **Type** Click to access the Type Preferences panel.

B **Use Typographer's Quotes** Check this box to allow quotes to display as typographer's quotation marks (curled), as opposed to displaying as inch marks (straight).

C **Automatically Use Correct Optical Size** Check this box to allow InDesign to automatically use the correct optical size when displaying multiple master fonts that contain a defined optical size axis. Enabling this option can improve the overall appearance of these types of multiple master fonts by matching the optical size axis to the point size of the text. When this option is disabled, InDesign uses the defined optical size axis, which may not display as well.

D **Triple Click To Select A Line** Check this box to allow a triple mouse click with the Type tool to select a whole line of text rather than the whole paragraph.

E **Adjust Text Attributes When Scaling** Check this box to display the values shown in the Control bar, Character, and Transform palettes a certain way when scaling text. Example: With this option enabled, if you scale 10-point text to triple its size, the Character palette and Control bar display at 30 points and the Transform palette displays at 100%. With this option disabled, if you scale 10-point text to triple its size, the Character palette and Control bar display at 10 points (30), and the Transform palette displays at 300%.

F **Apply Leading To Entire Paragraphs** Check this box to allow leading values to apply to an entire paragraph rather than to text within a paragraph. Note: Unlike QuarkXPress, InDesign treats leading as a default character attribute. Therefore, when this option is disabled, you can apply more than one leading value within a paragraph.

5.2 Type Preferences *(continued)*

Related Tasks

9.8 Editing Using the Story Editor
9.13 Font Overview
10.2 Scaling and Skewing Type
13.13 Importing Tables from Microsoft Word or Excel

Shortcuts

Story Editor
Mac: Cmd+Y
Win: Ctrl+Y

Links palette
Mac: Shift+Cmd+D
Win: Shift+Ctrl+D

Paste
Mac: Cmd+V
Win: Ctrl+V

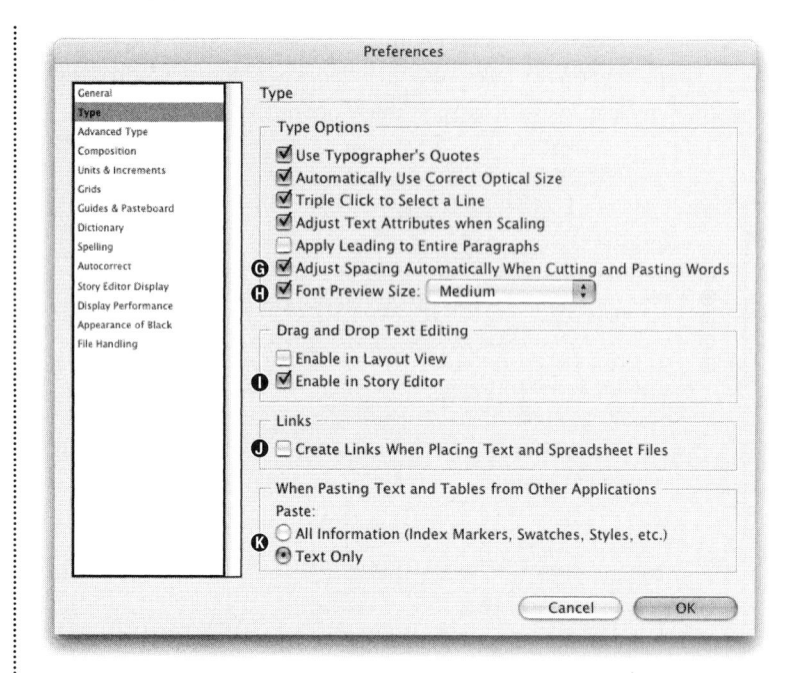

G **Adjust Spacing Automatically When Cutting and Pasting Words** Check this box to automatically add or remove appropriate word spacing when cutting, pasting, deleting, or replacing text.

H **Font Preview Size** Check this box to allow the Type > Font submenu to preview at the size you choose. Choose Small, Medium, or Large.

I **Drag And Drop Text Editing—Enable In Layout View/Story Editor** Check either box to turn on the drag-and-drop text edit feature in Layout View and/or the Story Editor. With this option enabled, you can copy/paste text by highlighting it with the Type tool and dragging it to another place in the story—no need to use key commands!

J **Create Links When Placing Text And Spreadsheet Files** Check this box to allow placed text and spreadsheet documents (e.g., Word and Excel files) to be treated as links.

K **When Pasting Text and Tables from Other Applications** Click the All Information or Text Only radio button when importing text and tables from other applications (e.g., Word and Excel files).

5.3 Advanced Type Preferences

The Advanced Type Preferences panel provides character settings for Superscript, Subscript, and Small Caps. It also contains an inline input option for Non-Latin text.

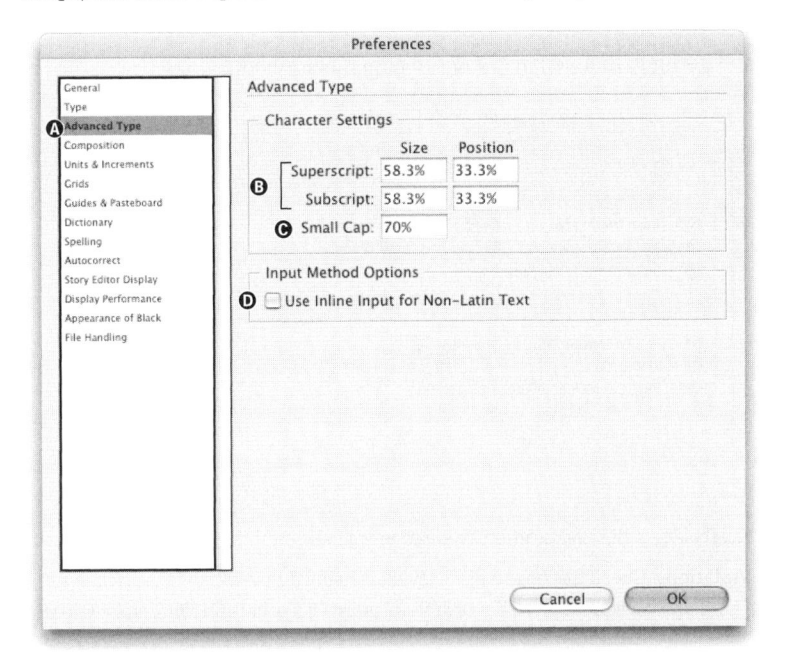

Related Tasks

3.2 Control Bar
3.6 Type Tools
4.21 Type and Tables Palettes

Shortcuts

Type tool
Mac and Win: T

Superscript
Mac: Shift+Cmd+=
Win: Shift+Ctrl+=

Subscript
Mac: Opt+Shift+Cmd+=
Win: Alt+Shift+Ctrl+=

Small caps
Mac: Shift+Cmd+H
Win: Shift+Ctrl+H

Tip

To open the Advanced Type Preferences dialog, Option-click (Mac) or Alt-click (Windows) on the Superscript, Subscript, or Small Caps control buttons in the Control bar.

Ⓐ Advanced Type Click to access the Advanced Type Preferences panel.

Ⓑ Superscript/subscript character settings Enter default size and position values to be used for superscript and subscript type styles. Chosen percentages are applied based on current font size and leading.

Ⓒ Small cap character setting Enter a default percentage to be used for the small cap type style. The chosen setting is applied based on current font size.

Ⓓ Use Inline Input For Non-Latin Text Check this box to allow system input (if available), for 2-byte and 4-byte non-Latin characters.

5.4 Composition Preferences

Related Tasks

3.2	Control Bar
3.6	Type Tools
4.21	Type and Tables Palettes
9.3	Importing Text
9.13	Font Overview
10.1	Kerning and Tracking
10.14	Inserting Special Characters
13.1	Placing and Editing Text Wraps

Shortcuts

Type tool
Mac and Win: T

Text Wrap palette
Mac: Opt+Cmd+W
Win: Alt+Ctrl+W

Adjust kerning/ tracking of selected text
Mac: Opt+Right/ Left Arrow
Win: Alt+Right/ Left Arrow

Tip

To allow a text frame to ignore a text wrap by bringing it to the front of the stacking order (as you would in QuarkXPress), turn on the Text Wrap Only Affects Text Beneath option in Composition Preferences.

The Composition Preferences panel contains various highlight and text wrap options. InDesign places assigned colored boxes over the items you choose in the Highlight section. This is a great way to flag subtle items in a document, such as paragraph breaks and custom tracking and kerning, that you may want to adjust before outputting.

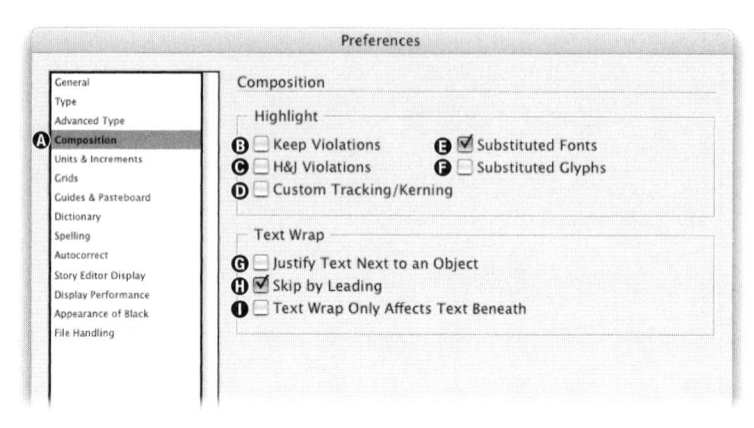

Ⓐ Composition Click to access the Composition Preferences panel.

Ⓑ Highlight Keep Violations Check this box to place a yellow highlight over items that violate settings in the Keep Options dialog. To access Keep Options press Opt+Cmd+K (Mac) or Alt+Ctrl+K (Windows).

Ⓒ Highlight H&J Violations Check this box to place a yellow highlight over items that violate settings chosen in the Hyphenation Settings and Justification dialogs (both accessible via the Paragraph palette menu). The darkest of three shades highlights the most serious violations.

Ⓓ Highlight Custom Tracking/Kerning Check this box to place a green highlight over items that have been manually kerned or tracked.

Ⓔ Highlight Substituted Fonts Check this box to place a pink highlight over any missing fonts.

Ⓕ Highlight Substituted Glyphs Check this box to place a yellow highlight over any alternate glyphs used in a document.

Ⓖ Text Wrap Justify Text Next To An Object Check this box to justify any text placed next to an object that has a text wrap applied to it.

Ⓗ Text Wrap Skip By Leading Check this box to force any wrapped text to apply the next available leading increment below a text-wrapped object, allowing the lines of text to line up evenly. Keeping this option off may cause lines of text to jump down below a wrapped object and not line up with neighboring columns or text frames.

Ⓘ Text Wrap Only Affects Text Beneath Check this box to allow a text frame to ignore a text wrap by bringing it to the front of the stacking order.

5.5 Units & Increments Preferences

The Units & Increment Preferences panel contains various options for ruler units, point/pica size, and keyboard increments. You can apply different measurement units to the horizontal and vertical rulers, specify a ruler origin point, apply PostScript or traditional points per inch, and choose default increments for keyboard shortcuts.

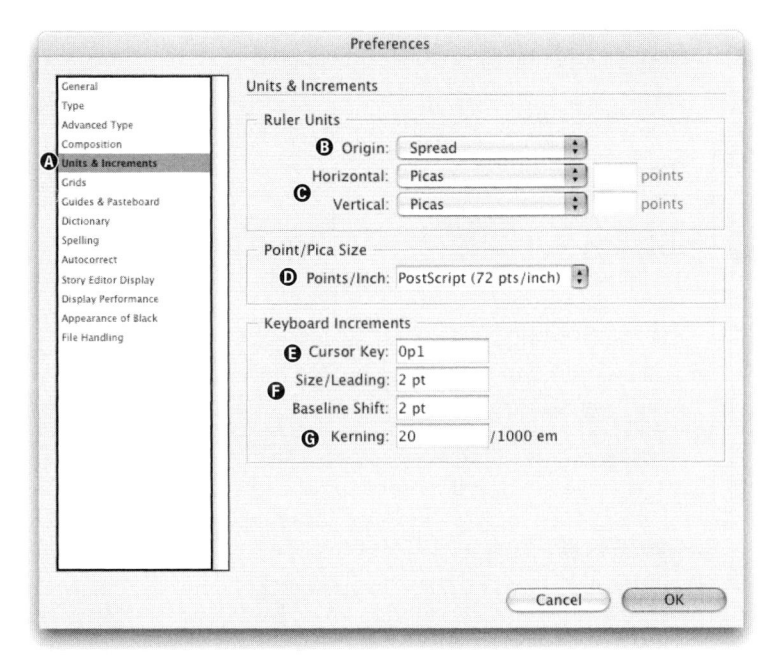

Related Tasks

- 1.3 Document Window
- 3.2 Control Bar
- 3.6 Type Tools
- 4.21 Type and Tables Palettes
- 10.1 Kerning and Tracking
- 10.3 Adjusting Leading and Baseline Shift

A **Units & Increments** Click to access the Units & Increments Preferences panel.

B **Ruler units origin** Choose an origin point for the document rulers: Spread, Page, or Spine.

C **Horizontal/vertical ruler units** Choose preferred measurement units for horizontal and vertical rulers. When choosing Custom, enter a point value in the respective data field to indicate where large tick marks should be placed.

D **Points/Inch** Choose whether to use PostScript points (72 points/inch), traditional printer points (72.27 points/inch), or two other values: 72.23 and 72.3.

E **Cursor Key increment** Enter a default distance amount to use when nudging selected objects with the arrow keys.

F **Size/Leading and Baseline Shift increments** Enter a default value for increasing/decreasing text size, leading, and baseline shift with keyboard shortcuts.

G **Kerning increment** Enter a default value (in thousandths of an em) to use when manually kerning with keyboard shortcuts.

Shortcuts

Show/hide rulers
Mac: Cmd+R
Win: Ctrl+R

Type tool
Mac and Win: T

Adjust kerning/tracking
Mac: Opt+Right/Left Arrow
Win: Alt+Right/Left Arrow

Increase type size
Mac: Cmd+Shift+>
Win: Ctrl+Shift+>

Decrease type size
Mac: Cmd+Shift+<
Win: Ctrl+Shift+<

Adjust leading
Mac: Opt+Up/Down Arrow
Win: Alt+Up/Down Arrow

Adjust baseline shift
Mac: Shift+Opt+Up/Down Arrow
Win: Shift+Alt+Up/Down Arrow

Tip

To open the Units & Increments Preferences dialog, Option-click (Mac) or Alt-click (Windows) the Kerning control icon in the Control bar.

5.6 Grids Preferences

Related Tasks

6.20 Aligning to Baseline Grid

6.21 Snapping to Document Grid

Shortcuts

Show/hide baseline grid
Mac: Opt+Cmd+'
Win: Alt+Ctrl+'

Show/hide document grid
Mac: Cmd+'
Win: Ctrl+'

Snap to document grid
Mac: Shift+Cmd+'
Win: Shift+Ctrl+'

Tip

You can also access the Grids In Back option through the contextual menu (Mac: Control-click; Windows: right-click).

The Grids Preferences panel provides options for both the baseline and document grids. The baseline grid displays a series of horizontal lines on the page that should reflect the chosen document leading amount. Alternatively, the document grid displays a series of both vertical and horizontal lines on the page, like transparent graph paper over your layout. You can use both grids as a visual guide to line up text columns and images. You can also snap objects to the grids whether they are visible or hidden.

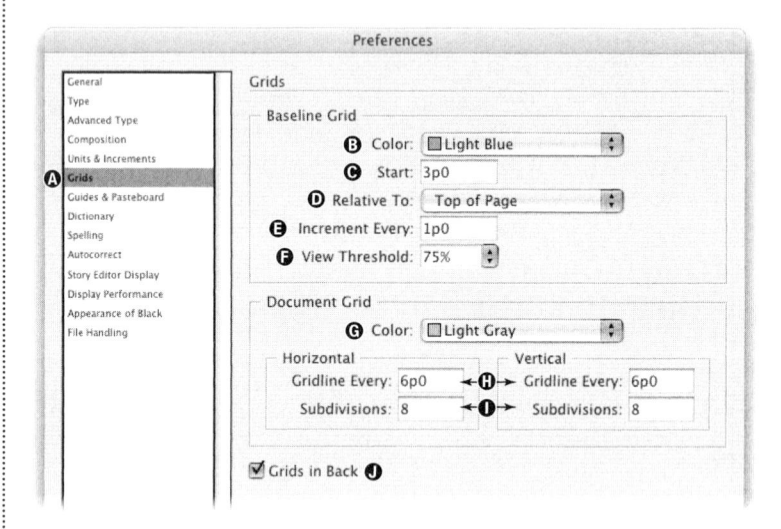

Ⓐ Grids Click to access the Grids Preferences panel.

Ⓑ Color Choose a baseline grid display color. You can also choose Custom (located at the very bottom of the menu list) to create, save, and apply a custom color.

Ⓒ Start Enter a value in the data field indicating the distance the first line of the baseline grid should be placed relative to the top of the page or margin.

Ⓓ Relative To Choose Top Of Page or Top Of Margin for where the grid start measures from.

Ⓔ Increment Every Enter a value in the data field indicating the uniform distance to place between grid lines. Generally, the default document leading amount should be entered here.

Ⓕ View Threshold Enter a value in the data field indicating the necessary view magnification amount for the baseline grid to appear in the document window.

Ⓖ Color Choose a document grid display color. You can also choose Custom (located at the very bottom of the menu list) to create, save, and apply a custom color.

Ⓗ Gridline Every Enter a value in the data field indicating the uniform distance to place between horizontal and vertical document grid lines.

Ⓘ Subdivisions Enter the number of subdivisions to set between each grid line. Enter 1 if you don't want to subdivide the grid.

Ⓙ Grids In Back Check this box to position the grids behind all objects on the page.

5.7 Guides & Pasteboard Preferences

The Guides & Pasteboard Preferences panel allows you to choose display colors for margin and column guides, bleed and slug areas, and the preview background. You can also specify a Snap To Zone distance and a minimum vertical offset amount for the Pasteboard.

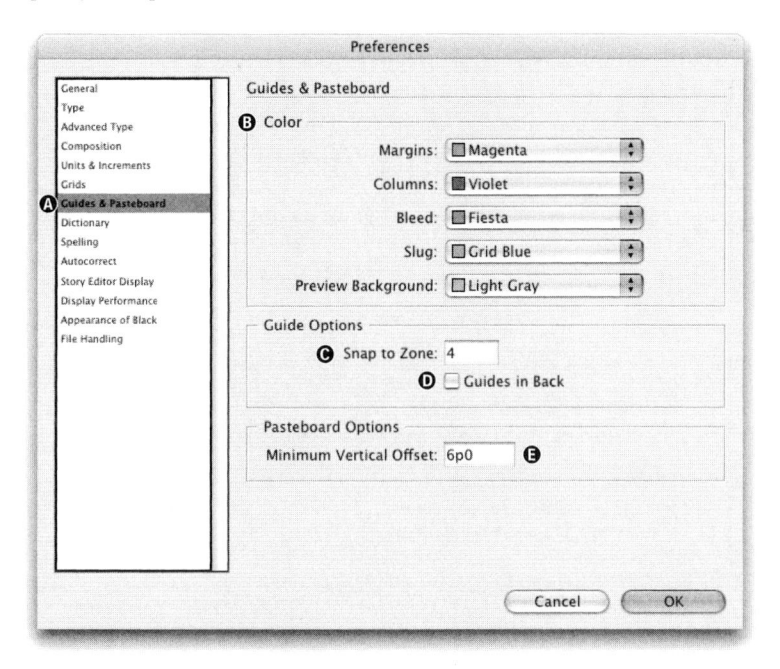

Related Tasks

1.3 Document Window
6.1 Starting a New Document
6.18 Adjusting Ruler Guides
6.19 Adjusting Margin and Column Guides

Shortcuts

Show/hide guides
Mac: Cmd+;
Win: Ctrl+;

Lock guides
Mac: Opt+Cmd+;
Win: Alt+Ctrl+;

Snap to guides
Mac: Shift+Cmd+;
Win: Shift+Ctrl+;

Tip

You can change the view threshold amount for guides via the contextual menu. To access the dialog, Control-click (Mac) or right-click (Windows) a *selected* guide and choose Ruler Guides from the menu.

A **Guides & Pasteboard** Click to access the Guides & Pasteboard Preferences panel.

B **Color** Choose display colors for margin and column guides, bleed and slug areas, and the preview background. You can also choose Custom (located at the very bottom of each menu list) to create, save, and apply a custom color.

C **Guide Options Snap To Zone** Enter a pixel amount in the data field to set as the default distance for objects to snap to guides.

D **Guides In Back** Check this box to position the guides behind all objects on the page.

E **Pasteboard Options—Minimum Vertical Offset** Enter a value to set the distance from the top or bottom of the page to the outer edge of the Pasteboard. Increase the number to heighten the Pasteboard; decrease to shorten.

5.8 Dictionary Preferences

Related Tasks

3.2 Control Bar
4.21 Type and Tables Palettes
9.10 Check Spelling

Shortcuts

Check spelling
Mac: Cmd+I
Win: Ctrl+I

Tip

There are 28 languages to choose from in the built-in user dictionary.

The Dictionary Preferences panel allows you to choose, create, and load user dictionaries from anywhere on your system, and to apply hyphen and spelling exception lists in various ways. In addition, you can choose custom characters to use as double and single quotes.

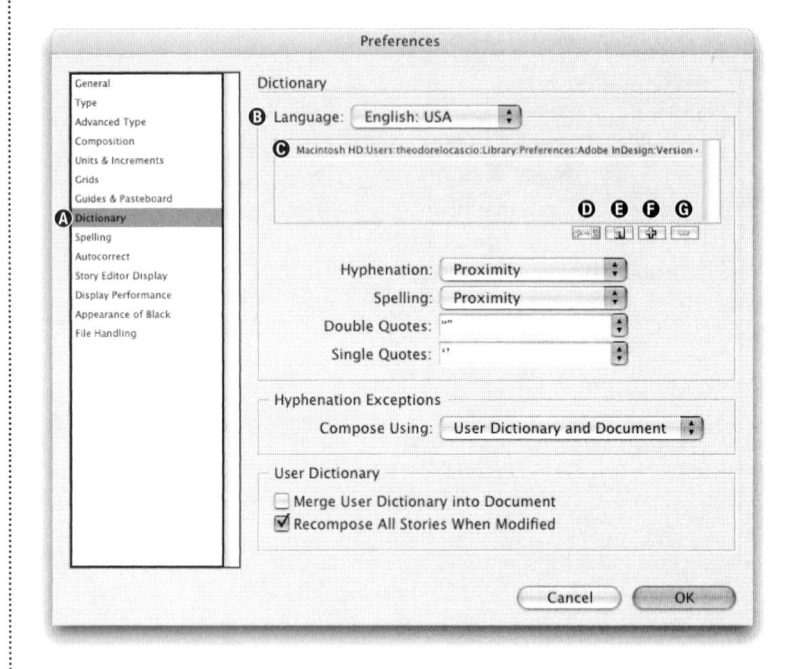

- **A Dictionary** Click to access the Dictionary Preferences panel.
- **B Language** Choose a default language.
- **C Available User Dictionaries** Displays a list of available user dictionaries by system location. Click to select.
- **D Relink User Dictionary** Click to relink a selected user dictionary (.udc file) to its current location on your system.
- **E New User Dictionary** Click to create a new user dictionary. A second dialog will open, prompting you to choose a name and system location for the new .udc file.
- **F Add User Dictionary** Click to load a user dictionary (.udc file) from anywhere on your system.
- **G Remove User Dictionary** Click to remove a selected user dictionary from the list.

5.8 Dictionary Preferences *(continued)*

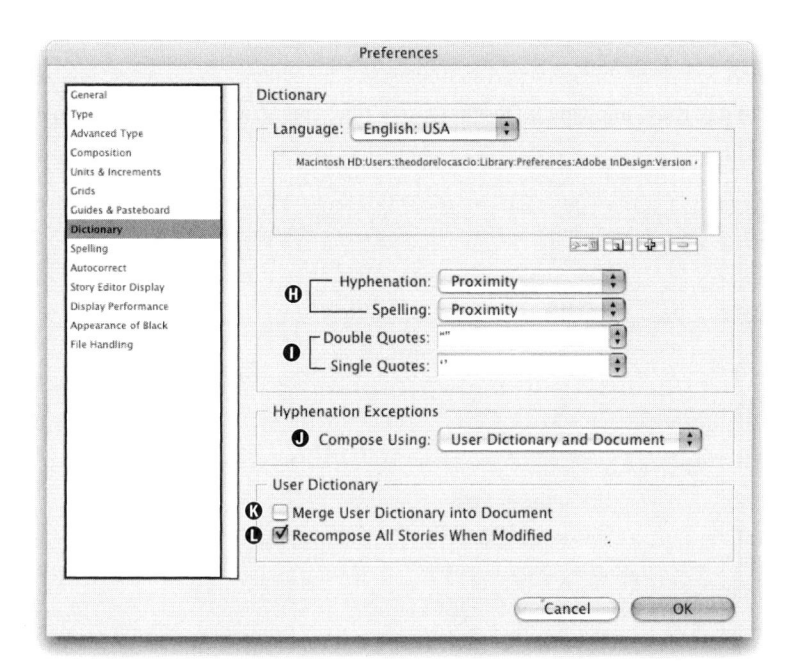

Related Tasks

9.11 Editing the Dictionary

9.12 Using the Dictionary with Foreign Languages

Shortcuts

Story Editor
Mac: Cmd+Y
Win: Ctrl+Y

Find/Change
Mac: Cmd+F
Win: Ctrl+F

H Hyphenation/Spelling The standard version of InDesign CS2 includes only "Proximity" dictionaries. Alternate versions of InDesign and dictionary components created by companies other than Adobe may feature different languages and other hyphenation and spelling options to choose from.

I Double/Single Quotes Enter the characters you'd like to use as double and single quotes, or choose a set from the menu lists.

J Hyphenation Exceptions—Compose Using Choose a list of dictionary "exceptions" to use (i.e., words and hyphenation points added to the dictionary). Choose from the current user dictionary exceptions, the list stored in the document, or both.

K Merge User Dictionary Into Document Check this box to apply the user dictionary list of hyphenation and spelling exceptions to any document you open. Note: Enabling this option can cause problems when you're working with multiple documents that come from various sources. We recommend you leave this option turned off.

L Recompose All Stories When Modified Check this box to recompose all stories (text frames) in a document when the user dictionary or Compose Using option has been changed. This can be a lengthy process depending on how much text a document contains. Therefore, we recommend you turn this option off.

107

5.9 Spelling Preferences

Related Tasks

3.2 Control Bar
4.21 Type and Tables Palettes
9.10 Check Spelling
9.11 Editing the Dictionary
9.12 Using the Dictionary with Foreign Languages

Shortcuts

Check spelling
Mac: Cmd+I
Win: Ctrl+I

Story Editor
Mac: Cmd+Y
Win: Ctrl+Y

Find/Change
Mac: Cmd+F
Win: Ctrl+F

Tip

You can add and remove words to and from a user dictionary under Edit > Spelling > Dictionary.

The Spelling Preferences panel contains options for locating misspelled words, repeated words, uncapitalized words, or uncapitalized sentences in a document. You can also enable the Dynamic Spelling feature, allowing InDesign to underline spell-check errors in assigned colors.

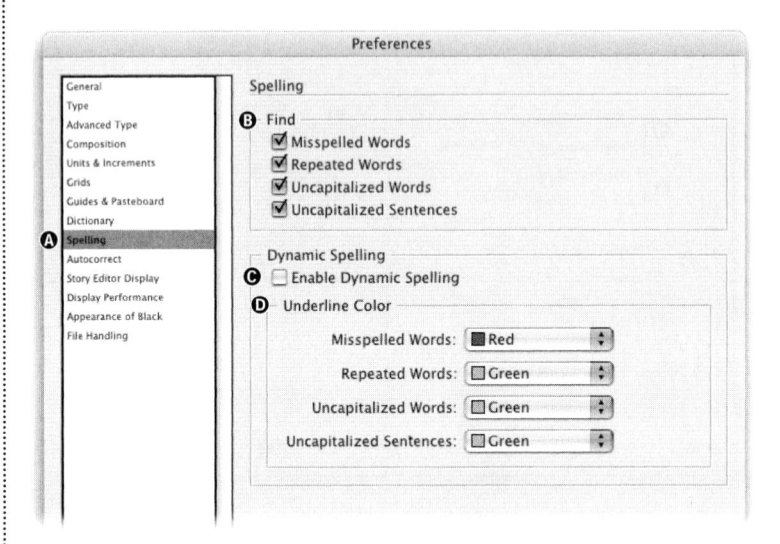

- **Ⓐ Spelling** Click to access the Spelling Preferences panel.
- **Ⓑ Find** Check the corresponding boxes to allow the Spelling feature to locate misspelled words, repeated words, uncapitalized words, or uncapitalized sentences.
- **Ⓒ Enable Dynamic Spelling** Check this box to turn on the Dynamic Spelling feature. Enabling this option allows InDesign to underline spell-check errors in assigned colors.
- **Ⓓ Underline Color** Choose an underline color for dynamic spell-check items. You can also choose Custom (located at the very bottom of each menu list) to create, save, and apply a custom color.

THE HIDDEN RESET BUTTON

Let's say you just got through setting up a bunch of new presets in the Print Presets dialog, and just before clicking OK to save them all, you realize you entered the wrong margin width for all of them. And some of the page sizes are wrong too.

In this case it might be best to start all over. Rather than selecting them all and clicking the Delete button, hold down the Option key (Mac) or Alt key (Win) and notice the Cancel button change to read Reset. Keep holding down the Option or Alt key and click the Reset button to delete all the incorrect new presets and start over. There's also a hidden Reset button in the New Document and Export Adobe PDF dialogs.

5.10 Autocorrect Preferences

When enabled, the Autocorrect feature can fix spell-check errors as you type. The Autocorrect Preferences panel not only lets you to turn on the feature, but it also allows you to indicate which words are to be corrected. Note that Autocorrect only fixes misspelled words that are included in the Autocorrect list.

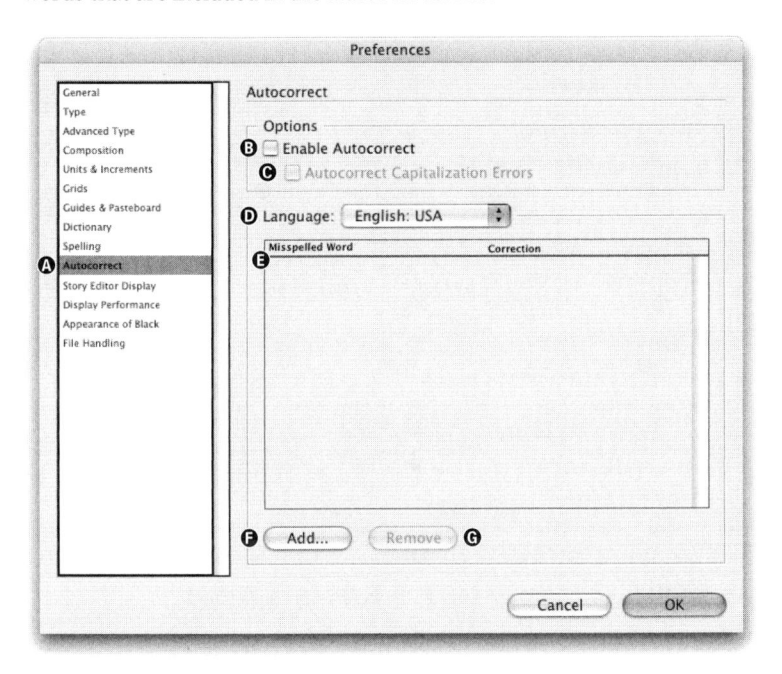

- **Ⓐ Autocorrect** Click to access the Autocorrect Preferences panel.
- **Ⓑ Enable Autocorrect** Check this box to turn on the Autocorrect feature.
- **Ⓒ Autocorrect Capitalization Errors** Check this box to allow Autocorrect to fix capitalization errors as you type.
- **Ⓓ Language** Choose a default language for Autocorrect to use.
- **Ⓔ Misspelled Word/Correction** Displays a list of misspelled words for Autocorrect to identify and fix as you type. You must add these words and their corrections to the preferences list before typing if you are going to rely on Autocorrect to fix them.
- **Ⓕ Add** Click to add a misspelled word and its correction to the Autocorrect list.
- **Ⓖ Remove** Click to remove a misspelled word and its correction from the Autocorrect list.

Related Tasks

3.2	Control Bar
4.21	Type and Tables Palettes
9.10	Check Spelling
9.11	Editing the Dictionary
9.12	Using the Dictionary with Foreign Languages

Shortcuts

Check spelling
Mac: Cmd+I
Win: Ctrl+I

Story Editor
Mac: Cmd+Y
Win: Ctrl+Y

Find/Change
Mac: Cmd+F
Win: Ctrl+F

Tip

You cannot eliminate extra white spaces or tabs as you type them with Autocorrect, but you can eliminate existing ones using Find/Change.

5.11 Story Editor Display Preferences

Related Tasks

3.2 Control Bar
3.6 Type Tools
4.21 Type and Tables Palettes
9.10 Check Spelling
9.11 Editing the Dictionary
9.12 Using the Dictionary with Foreign Languages

Shortcuts

Check spelling
Mac: Cmd+I
Win: Ctrl+I

Story Editor
Mac: Cmd+Y
Win: Ctrl+Y

Find/Change
Mac: Cmd+F
Win: Ctrl+F

Tip

You can turn Dynamic Spelling on or off via the contextual menu (Mac: Control-click; Windows: right-click) in both the Story Editor and the layout.

The Story Editor Display Preferences panel lets you specify various display options, including font, text size, line spacing, text/background color, and cursor type. You can also choose a preset "theme" display, such as Terminal (green text on a black background) or the more traditional Ink On Paper. InDesign also offers a choice of anti-aliasing options for Story Editor Display, including one that is optimized for LCD monitors.

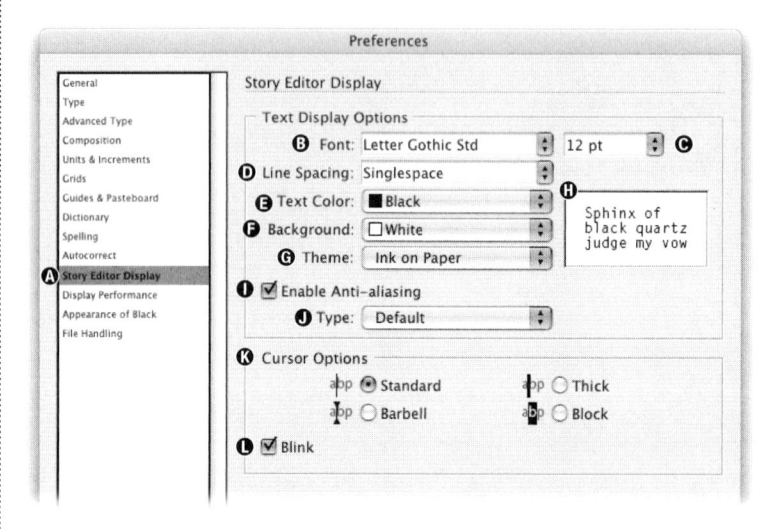

Ⓐ Story Editor Display Click to access the Story Editor Display Preferences panel.

Ⓑ Text Display Font Enter the font you'd like to use in the Story Editor, or choose from the menu.

Ⓒ Text Display Size Enter the type size to use, or choose a size from the menu.

Ⓓ Text Display Line Spacing Enter a preferred line spacing value, or choose one from the menu.

Ⓔ Text Display Color Choose a text display color. Unlike grids, guides, and dynamic spelling underlines, you cannot apply a custom color.

Ⓕ Text Display Background Choose a background color. You cannot apply a custom color.

Ⓖ Text Display Theme Choose a preset Story Editor theme. Available color combinations include Ink On Paper, Amber Monochrome, Classic System, and Terminal. Applying a theme overrides any previously chosen Story Editor text display and background colors.

Ⓗ Text Display Preview Displays a preview of the chosen Story Editor font, text color, and background color, or theme. Font size and line spacing do not preview.

Ⓘ Enable Anti-aliasing Check this box to smooth out text edges in the Story Editor display.

Ⓙ Anti-aliasing Type Choose an anti-aliasing option: Default, LCD Optimized, and Soft.

Ⓚ Cursor Options Click the radio button to choose Standard, Barbell, Thick, or Block cursor display.

Ⓛ Blink Check this box to allow the chosen Story Editor cursor to blink.

5.12 Display Performance Preferences

The Display Performance Preferences panel allows you to choose a default view and adjust the parameters for each view setting. You can decide how you'd like to display raster images, vector graphics, and transparencies in all of your documents.

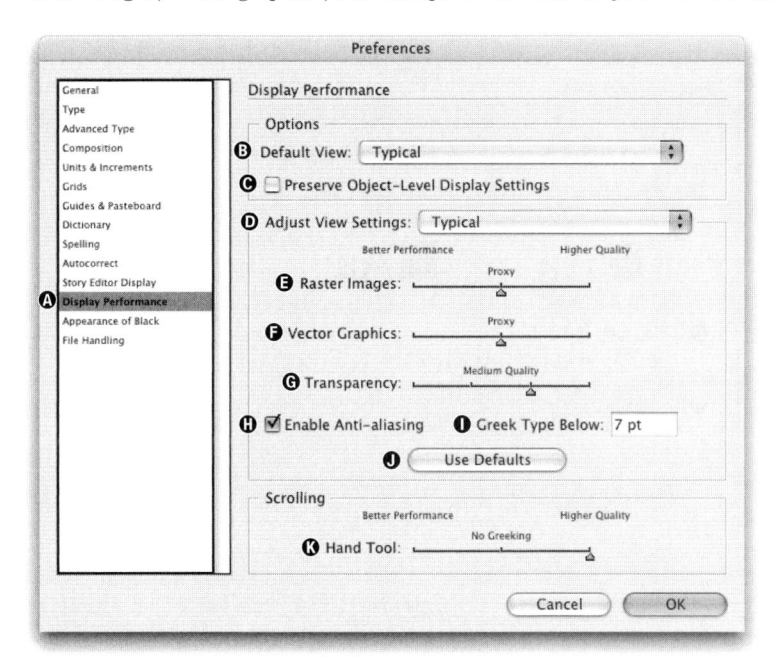

Related Tasks

1.4	Interface Objects
2.9	View Menu
4.20	Transparency Palette
12.9	Object-Level Display Settings

Shortcuts

Fast display
Mac: Shift+Cmd+0
Win: Shift+Ctrl+0

Typical display
Mac: Opt+Cmd+Z
Win: Alt+Ctrl+Z

High Quality display
Mac: Opt+Cmd+H
Win: Alt+Ctrl+H

Tip

In Display Performance Preferences, you can adjust the default View Settings for Typical Display to always preview vector graphics (such as placed Illustrator EPS or AI files) at high resolution.

- **Ⓐ Display Performance** Click to access the Display Performance Preferences panel.
- **Ⓑ Default View** Choose High Quality, Typical, or Fast as the default view.
- **Ⓒ Preserve Object-Level Display Settings** Check this box to save all document display settings when closing and reopening. Note that saving high-quality display settings can slow down the reopening process.
- **Ⓓ Adjust View Settings** Choose the view setting you'd like to adjust (High Quality, Typical, or Fast).
- **Ⓔ Raster Images** Click and drag the slider left or right to adjust the screen display of imported bitmap images (such as TIFF, JPEG, and GIF).
- **Ⓕ Vector Graphics** Click and drag the slider left or right to adjust the screen display of imported vector graphics (such as EPS, DCS, and PDF).
- **Ⓖ Transparency** Click and drag the slider left or right to adjust the screen display of transparent items.
- **Ⓗ Enable Anti-aliasing** Check this box to smooth out object edges.
- **Ⓘ Greek Type Below** Enter a point size to indicate when InDesign can display small, illegible text as a gray bar.
- **Ⓙ Use Defaults** Click to reset the default view settings.
- **Ⓚ Hand Tool Scrolling** Click and drag the slider left or right to adjust how InDesign handles display performance when scrolling with the Hand tool. Lower settings can mean faster scrolling.

5.13 Appearance of Black Preferences

Related Tasks

4.3	Attributes Palette
4.5	Color Palette
4.17	Swatches Palette
5.16	Print Presets
5.17	Adobe PDF Presets
15.3	Preflighting Colors and Inks
16.1	Printing a Document

Shortcuts

Print
Mac: Cmd+P
Win: Ctrl+P

Preflight
Mac: Opt+Shift+Cmd+F
Win: Alt+Shift+Ctrl+F

Export
Mac: Cmd+E
Win: Ctrl+E

Swatches palette
Mac and Win: F5

Color palette
Mac and Win: F6

Tip

Not sure what the Appearance of Black Preferences panel is all about? Try hovering your mouse over any of the option headings and refer to the description at the bottom of the dialog.

The Appearance of Black Preferences panel allows you to choose how you'd like to view, print, and export blacks in a document. You can choose to view, print, and export blacks accurately (100% black) or as rich black (a CMYK build).

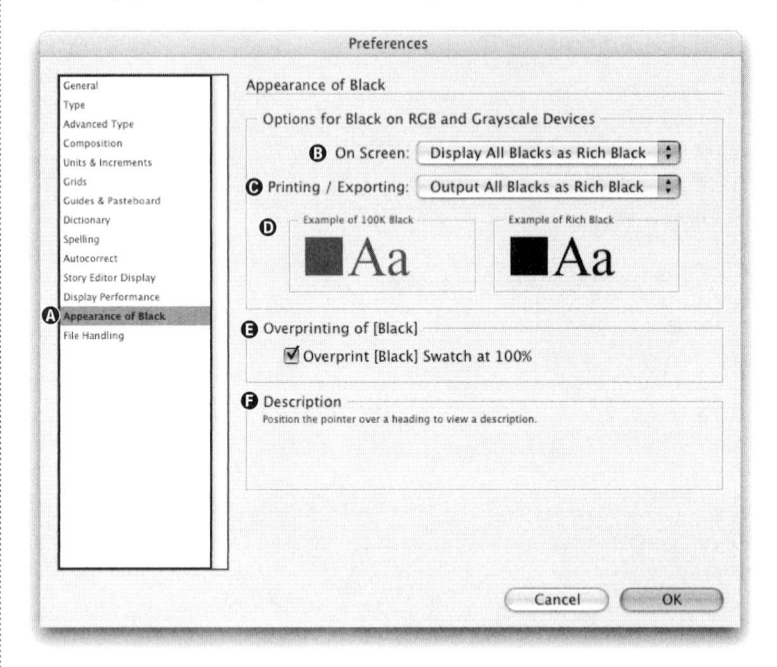

- **Ⓐ Appearance of Black** Click to access the Appearance of Black Preferences panel.
- **Ⓑ On Screen options** Choose whether all blacks in the document should display accurately (100% black) or as rich black (CMYK build).
- **Ⓒ Printing/Exporting options** Choose whether all blacks in the document should print/export accurately (100% black) or as rich black (CMYK build).
- **Ⓓ Example of 100K Black/Rich Black** Display examples of 100K black and rich black.
- **Ⓔ Overprinting of [Black] Swatch at 100%** Check this box to overprint any use of the default [Black] swatch at 100%.
- **Ⓕ Description** Displays a description for each available option in the Appearance of Black Preferences panel. Position the pointer over a heading to view the description.

5.14 File Handling Preferences

The File Handling Preferences panel allows you to choose a document recovery data location and enable Adobe Version Cue (if it's installed on your system). There are also options for saving preview images with documents, and copy/pasting to and from the Clipboard.

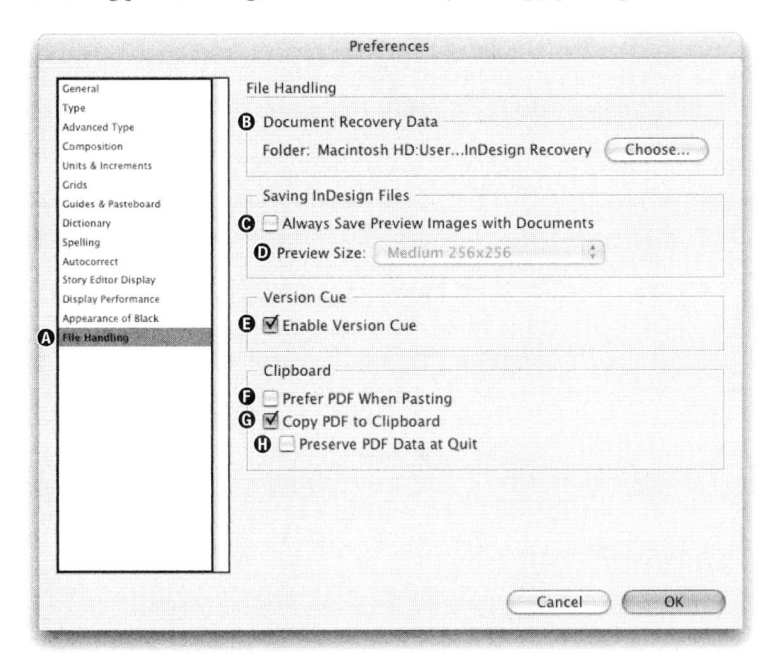

Related Tasks

2.3 File Menu
2.4 Edit Menu
6.5 Save vs. Save As
8.10 Duplicating Objects
12.1 Importing a Graphic Image

Shortcuts

Save
Mac: Cmd+S
Win: Ctrl+S

Save As
Mac: Shift+Cmd+S
Win: Shift+Ctrl+S

Copy
Mac: Cmd+C
Win: Ctrl+C

Paste
Mac: Cmd+V
Win: Ctrl+V

Tip

You can turn the Always Save Preview Images With Documents option on or off in the Save As and Save A Copy dialogs as well as in File Handling Preferences panel.

Ⓐ File Handling Click to access the File Handling Preferences panel.

Ⓑ Document Recovery Data location Displays the current location for InDesign's temporary data files. To save disk space or improve system performance, you can choose a new location (e.g., a faster external drive), by clicking the Choose (Mac) or Browse (Windows) button.

Ⓒ Always Save Preview Images With Documents Check this box to allow a preview image to be saved with a document file. Note that saved previews can slightly increase document file sizes and are also not very accessible.

Ⓓ Preview Size Choose a preferred image size to apply when Always Save Preview Images With Documents is enabled (see above).

Ⓔ Enable Version Cue Check this box to enable Adobe's project management application. Version Cue must already be installed on your system.

Ⓕ Prefer PDF When Pasting Keep this box unchecked to allow copied PDF data (such as editable paths copied from Illustrator) to be pasted into InDesign.

Ⓖ Copy PDF To Clipboard Check this box to copy editable objects as PDF data (such as editable paths created in InDesign).

Ⓗ Preserve PDF Data At Quit Check this box to preserve PDF data that has been copied to the Clipboard even after quitting InDesign.

5.15 Document Presets

Related Tasks

2.3	File Menu
4.15	Pages Palette
6.1	Starting a New Document
6.9	Creating Multipage Spreads and Master Pages

Shortcuts

New document
Mac: Cmd+N
Win: Ctrl+N

Document setup
Mac: Opt+Cmd+P
Win: Alt+Ctrl+P

New document based on last preset used
Mac: Opt+Cmd+N
Win: Alt+Ctrl+N

Tip

To bypass the New Document dialog, hold down the Shift key while selecting from the File > Document Presets submenu.

If you wind up entering the same settings in the New Document dialog every time you start a new project, you should try saving them as a preset. Once you do, you can select the preset from the File > Document Presets submenu and then click OK in the New Document dialog. This way, you don't have to stop to enter any settings.

You can also save, load, and edit document presets, which makes it all that much easier when starting a new project. To access the Document Presets dialog, select File > Document Presets > Define.

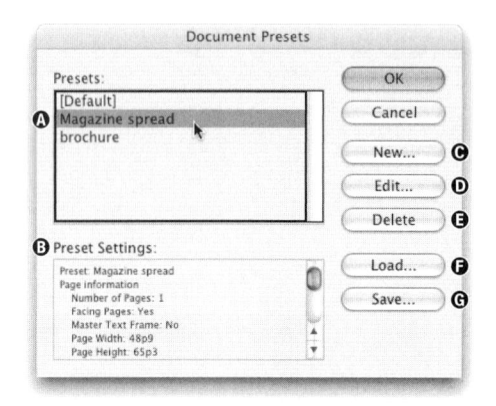

Ⓐ Document Presets Displays a list of saved document presets. Click a preset name to select. Double-click to edit.

Ⓑ Document Preset Settings Displays a summary of New Document dialog settings for the selected preset, including page information, margins and columns, and bleed and slug offsets.

Ⓒ New Click to access the New Document Preset dialog and choose your preferred settings. Click OK to save the preset and add it to the list.

Ⓓ Edit Select a preset from the list and click the Edit button to adjust the settings in the Edit Document Preset dialog. Click OK to save your changes and return to the Document Presets dialog.

Ⓔ Delete Select a preset from the list and click the Delete button to remove it. When the warning dialog appears, click OK to commit (this action cannot be undone).

Ⓕ Load Click to access the Load Document Presets dialog. Locate a document presets file type (.dcst) from your system and then click Open to load.

Ⓖ Save Click to access the Save Document Presets dialog. Choose a system location to save the .dcst file to and then click Save.

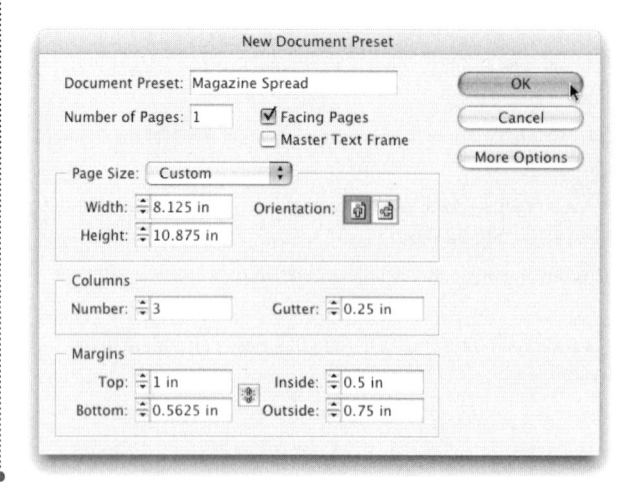

5.16 Print Presets

It is a proven fact that having to set up a complicated print dialog every time you need to output a document can drive you nuts. To save your sanity, try using print presets. Select the preset from the File > Print Presets submenu and click Print when the Print dialog appears—without having to stop and enter any settings.

Also, just as you can with document presets, you can save, load, and edit print presets. In fact, the Document and the Print Preset dialogs work in exactly the same way. To access the Print Presets dialog, select File > Print Presets > Define.

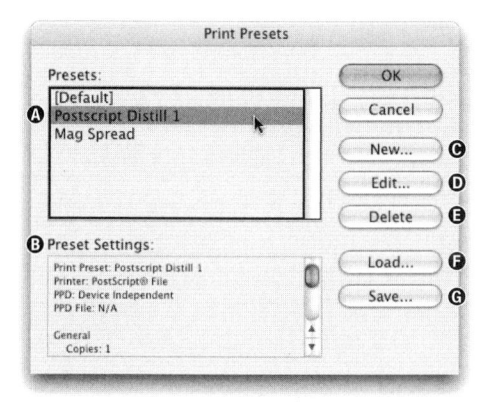

Ⓐ Print Presets Displays a list of saved print presets. Click a preset name to select. Double-click to edit.

Ⓑ Print Preset Settings Displays a summary of print dialog settings for the selected print preset, including setup, marks and bleed, output, graphics, and color management.

Ⓒ New Click to access the New Print Preset dialog and choose your preferred settings. Click OK to save the preset and add it to the list.

Ⓓ Edit Select a preset from the list and click the Edit button to adjust the settings in the Edit Print Preset dialog. Click OK to save your changes and return to the Print Presets dialog.

Ⓔ Delete Select a preset from the list and click the Delete button to remove it. When the warning dialog appears, click OK to commit (this action cannot be undone).

Ⓕ Load Click to access the Load Print Presets dialog. Locate a print presets file type (.prst) from your system and then click Open to load.

Ⓖ Save Click to access the Save Print Presets dialog. Choose a system location to save the .prst file to and then click Save.

Related Tasks

2.3 File Menu
4.3 Attributes Palette
4.13 Output Palettes
16.1 Printing a Document

Shortcuts

Print
Mac: Cmd+P
Win: Ctrl+P

Tip

To bypass the Print dialog, hold down the Shift key while selecting from the File > Print Presets submenu.

5.17 Adobe PDF Presets

Related Tasks

2.3   File Menu
4.13 Output Palettes
17.1 Exporting as Adobe PDF

Shortcuts

Export
Mac: Cmd+E
Win: Ctrl+E

Tip

Ink Manager and Security settings are not included in saved PDF Export Presets.

Adobe PDF Presets make it quick and easy to generate a PDF of your InDesign document. To export a high-quality, press-quality, PDF/X, or screen-optimized PDF, select the appropriate preset from the default list located under File > Adobe PDF Presets.

You can create, save, and load your own PDF presets, and also share them with the other applications in the Adobe Creative Suite 2 via the Bridge application. To access the Adobe PDF Presets dialog, select File > Adobe PDF Presets > Define.

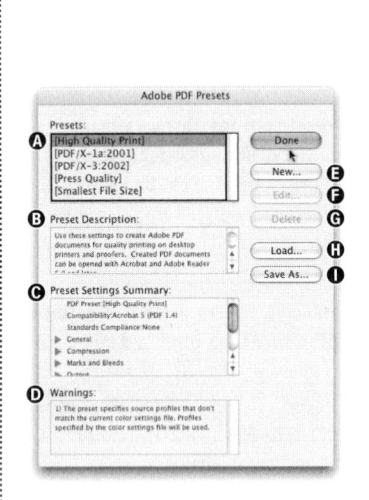

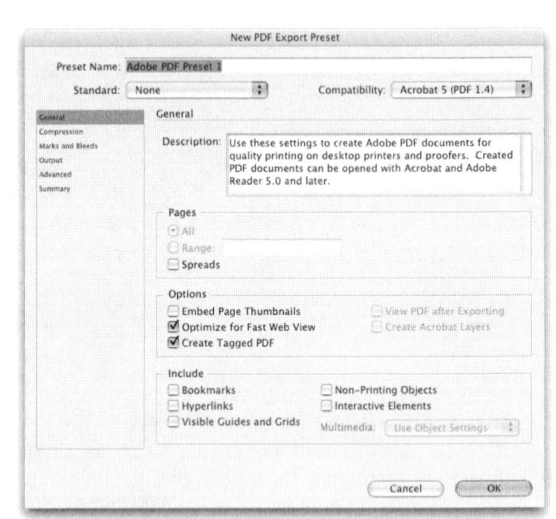

- **Ⓐ PDF Presets** Displays a list of default and saved Adobe PDF presets. Click a preset name to select. Double-click a saved PDF preset name to edit. Default PDF presets appear in brackets (e.g., [High Quality Print]) and cannot be edited or deleted.

- **Ⓑ PDF Preset Description** Displays a detailed description for the selected PDF preset, including its functionality and accessibility.

- **Ⓒ PDF Preset Settings Summary** Displays a summary of PDF export dialog settings for the selected PDF preset, including General, Compression, Marks and Bleeds, Output, and Advanced.

- **Ⓓ Warnings** Displays a list of potential problems that may occur when exporting using the selected PDF preset.

- **Ⓔ New** Click to access the New PDF Export Preset dialog and choose your preferred settings. Click OK to save the preset and add it to the list.

- **Ⓕ Edit** Select a preset from the list and click the Edit button to adjust the settings in the Edit PDF Export Preset dialog. Click OK to save your changes and return to the Adobe PDF Presets dialog.

- **Ⓖ Delete** Select a preset from the list and click the Delete button to remove it. When the warning dialog appears, click OK to commit (this action cannot be undone).

- **Ⓗ Load** Click to access the Load PDF Export Presets dialog. Locate a PDF Export presets file type (.joboptions) from your system and then click Open to load.

- **Ⓘ Save As** Click to access the Save PDF Export Presets dialog. Choose a system location to save the .joboptions file to and then click Save.

5.18 Configure Plug-ins

When you think about it, InDesign is really nothing more than a plug-in manager. Most of the application's various functions are controlled by plug-ins. This means that you have the option to turn off any features you don't use (or don't like!). Doing so can reduce the amount of system memory InDesign consumes.

You can access the Configure Plug-ins dialog under the InDesign menu (Mac) or the Help menu (Windows).

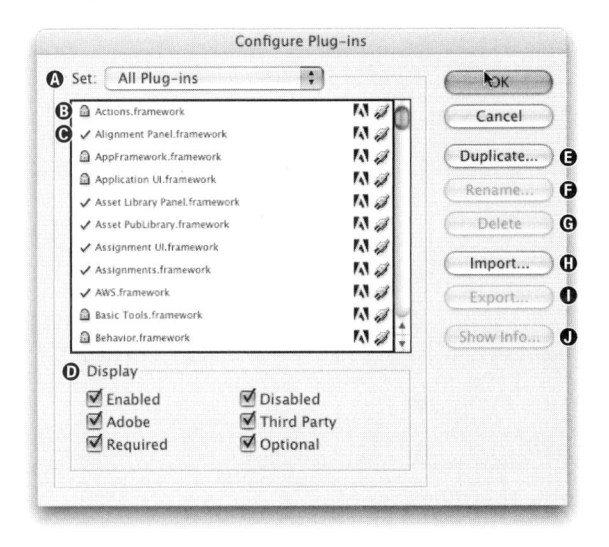

Related Tasks

2.2 InDesign Menu (Mac Only)

2.11 Help Menu

Shortcuts

Quit (Mac)/Exit (Win)
Mac: Cmd+Q
Win: Ctrl+Q

Tip

Always save your current plug-in set, just in case you need to refer back to it later.

- **A** **Plug-in Set** Click to select a plug-in set from the menu.
- **B** **Required Plug-in icon** Indicates that the plug-in is required and cannot be disabled.
- **C** **Enabled Plug-in icon** Indicates that the plug-in is currently installed and in use. Note: Default plug-in sets cannot be modified.
- **D** **Configure Plug-ins Display options** Check the respective boxes for the plug-ins you would like displayed in the dialog list. Options include Enabled, Disabled, Adobe, Third Party, Required, and Optional.
- **E** **Duplicate** Click to duplicate the currently selected plug-in set. A dialog will open prompting you to rename the duplicate. Click OK to save and the duplicate set will then be added to the menu.
- **F** **Rename** Click to rename the currently selected plug-in set. Enter a name in the dialog that opens and click OK to save. The new set name will appear in the menu replacing the old one.
- **G** **Delete** Select a plug-in set from the menu and click the Delete button to remove it. When the warning dialog appears, click OK to commit (this action cannot be undone).
- **H** **Import** Click to locate a plug-in set (.pset file) on your system and then click Open to import it.
- **I** **Export** Click to export a copy of the currently selected plug-in set. Choose a system location to save the .pset file to and then click Save.
- **J** **Show Info** Click a plug-in name to select it and then click the Show Info button to access the Plug-in Information dialog.

5.19 Keyboard Shortcuts

Related Tasks

1.4 Interface Objects
2.4 Edit Menu
5.1 General Preferences

Shortcuts

General Preferences
Mac: Cmd+K
Win: Ctrl+K

Tip

To print out a list of keyboard shortcuts from a chosen set, click the Show Set button in the dialog to open the list in your default text edit application.

InDesign allows you to change any of the default keyboard shortcuts. You can also choose to apply and edit shortcuts from QuarkXPress 4 or PageMaker 7 (Mac and Windows) or QuarkXPress 3.3 (Mac only). Additionally, you can create and save your own custom keyboard shortcut sets by choosing Edit > Keyboard Shortcuts.

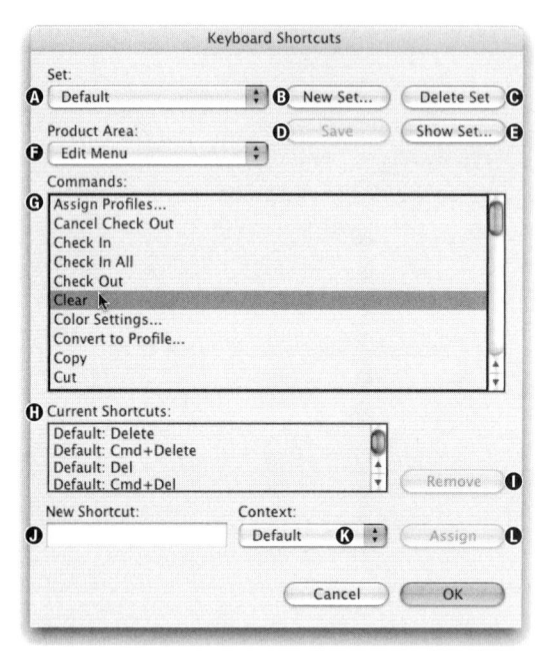

Ⓐ Keyboard Shortcut Set Choose a set to use and/or edit.

Ⓑ New Set Click to create a new set based on one of the defaults. Enter a name for the set in the dialog that opens, and then click OK to add it to the shortcut list. You can then edit and save the shortcuts for the new set. When you're ready, click OK to close the Keyboard Shortcuts dialog and start using them.

Ⓒ Delete Set Click to delete the currently selected set. When the warning dialog appears, click Yes to commit (this action cannot be undone).

Ⓓ Save Click to save any changes made to the currently selected set.

Ⓔ Show Set Click the button to open a list of available commands with and without assigned shortcuts for the currently selected set in your default text edit application.

Ⓕ Product Area Click to select a product area subgroup of commands to display in the window below.

Ⓖ Commands Displays a list of available commands to assign keyboard shortcuts to, or edit existing ones. Click to select a command from the list and display its existing shortcut in the window below. Note that some of the commands may not yet have shortcuts assigned to them.

Ⓗ Current Shortcuts Displays a list of shortcuts assigned to a selected command. Note that a command can have more than one keyboard shortcut assigned to it. Click a shortcut to select it.

Ⓘ Remove Click to remove a selected shortcut from its assigned command.

Ⓙ New Shortcut Enter a new keyboard shortcut into the data field. Any conflicting shortcuts will appear directly below. Click the Assign button to remove the conflicting shortcut (if any) from its former command and apply it to the currently selected command.

Ⓚ Context Click to choose a preferred context for a new shortcut. The assigned context is what appears before the key combination in the Current Shortcuts window (e.g., "Default" is the assigned context for the shortcut labeled Default: Cmd+Delete). Assigning a context allows you to use the same key combination for more than one shortcut. Options include Alerts/Dialogs, Default, Tables, XML Selection, and Text.

Ⓛ Assign Click to assign a new shortcut to a selected command.

CHAPTER **6**

Creating and Managing Documents

NOW THAT YOU'RE COMFORTABLE with the InDesign CS2 workspace, it's time for a crash course in creating and managing documents—and not just InDesign documents either. That's right. You can also open documents created in QuarkXPress and PageMaker.

In this chapter, we'll explore all aspects of document management, including how to create, save, open, and close your projects. In addition, we'll explain how to save files for backward compatibility with previous versions of InDesign. We'll also discuss the various ways of working with document pages, master pages, and the Pages palette.

- 6.1 Starting a New Document
- 6.2 Saving Document Presets
- 6.3 Opening InDesign Documents
- 6.4 Opening PageMaker and QuarkXPress Documents
- 6.5 Save vs. Save As
- 6.6 Saving Backward with INX Export
- 6.7 Saving Files for Use with InCopy
- 6.8 Adding, Arranging, and Deleting Pages
- 6.9 Creating Multipage Spreads and Master Pages
- 6.10 Targeting vs. Selecting Pages
- 6.11 Creating Master Pages
- 6.12 Converting Document Pages to Master Pages
- 6.13 Applying Master Pages
- 6.14 Deleting Master Pages
- 6.15 Creating and Applying Parent/Child Master Pages
- 6.16 Overriding Master Page Items
- 6.17 Adding Page Numbers to Sections
- 6.18 Adjusting Ruler Guides
- 6.19 Adjusting Margin and Column Guides
- 6.20 Aligning to Baseline Grid
- 6.21 Snapping to Document Grid

6.1 Starting a New Document

Related Tasks

2.3	File Menu
4.14	PageMaker Toolbar
4.15	Pages Palette
5.15	Document Presets
6.2	Saving Document Presets
6.8	Adding, Arranging, and Deleting Pages
6.9	Creating Multipage Spreads and Master Pages
6.11	Creating Master Pages
6.18	Adjusting Ruler Guides
6.19	Adjusting Margin and Column Guides

Shortcuts

New document
Mac: Cmd+N
Win: Ctrl+N

Insert Pages dialog
Mac: Opt-click Create New Page button
Win: Alt-click Create New Page button

Add page
Mac: Shift+Cmd+P
Win: Shift+Ctrl+P

Tip

The Master Text Frame option located in the InDesign New Document dialog is similar to the Automatic Text Box option found in the QuarkXPress New Project dialog.

Your first step when starting a new project is to create a new InDesign document. To get started, choose File > New > Document, or press Command+N (Mac) or Ctrl+N (Windows). When the New Document dialog opens, enter the preferred page settings and click OK.

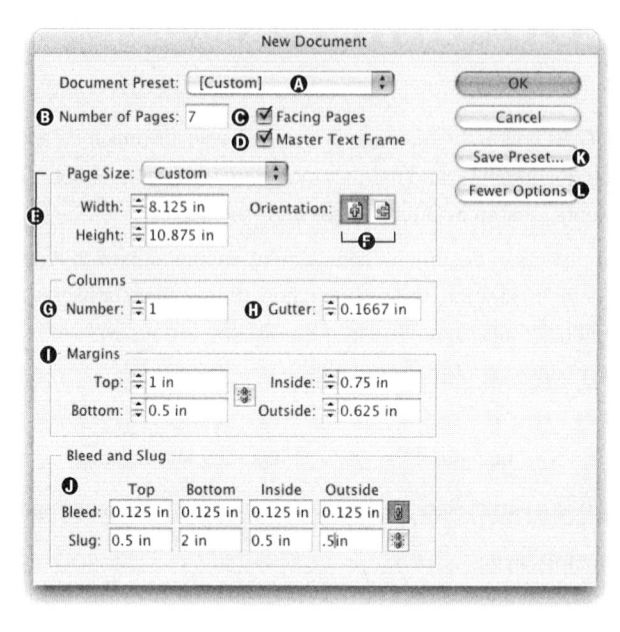

A **Document Preset** Choose from a list of saved document presets. The menu automatically displays [Custom] when entering new settings in the dialog.

B **Number Of Pages** Enter the number of pages you'd like to include in the document.

C **Facing Pages** Check this box to allow document pages to face each other in "reader spreads" (when this is unchecked, Inside/Outside values in the Margin section read Left/Right).

D **Master Text Frame** Check this box to place an automatic text frame on the A-Master page of the new document. All pages in the document automatically have the A-Master applied to them.

E **Page Size** Choose a default page size from the list, or enter custom width and height settings in the corresponding data fields.

F **Orientation** Click either Portrait (left) or Landscape (right) to apply your preference.

G **Number of columns** Enter the preferred number of column guides to apply to the document.

H **Gutter** Enter the preferred amount of gutter width to apply between column guides.

I **Margins** Enter the preferred amount of spacing to apply to top, bottom, inside, and outside margin guides. Margin spacing is applied from the outer edge of the document in. Click the chain icon to link or unlink the data fields. A solid-chain icon indicates that all settings are made the same. A broken-chain icon indicates that you can apply separate settings to each data field.

J **Bleed And Slug** Enter the preferred amount of spacing to apply to top, bottom, inside, and outside bleed and slug areas. Spacing is applied around the outer edges of the page. Click the chain icons to link or unlink the respective Bleed and Slug data fields. A solid-chain icon indicates that all settings are made the same. A broken-chain icon indicates that you can apply separate settings to each data field.

K **Save Preset** Click to preserve your document settings as a preset. The new preset appears in all document preset menus.

L **Fewer/More Options** Click to show or hide the Bleed And Slug settings at the bottom of the dialog.

6.2 Saving Document Presets

If you think you might want to use the settings you've entered in the New Document dialog more than once, you should save them as a document preset. Before clicking OK to close the dialog and start work on your new document, click the Save Preset button. When the Save Preset dialog appears, enter a name for it and click OK. The new preset appears in all document preset menus.

You can also save a preset at any time while working on a document by selecting File > Document Presets > Define. When the Document Presets dialog opens, click the New button to launch the New Document Preset dialog and enter your preferred settings. When you're ready, click OK to add the preset to the menu list.

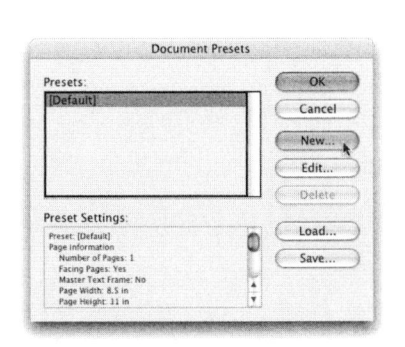

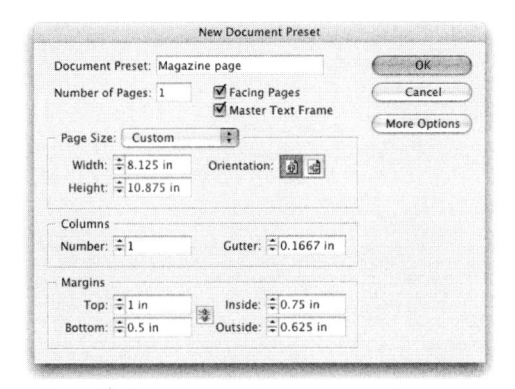

Related Tasks

2.3	File Menu
5.15	Document Presets
6.1	Starting a New Document
6.8	Adding, Arranging, and Deleting Pages
6.9	Creating Multipage Spreads and Master Pages
6.19	Adjusting Margin and Column Guides

Shortcuts

New document
Mac: Cmd+N
Win: Ctrl+N

Document Setup dialog
Mac: Opt+Cmd+P
Win: Alt+Ctrl+P

Tip

You can also load and save document presets for use with other InDesign projects.

6.3 Opening InDesign Documents

Related Tasks

2.3 File Menu
4.14 PageMaker Toolbar
5.4 Composition Preferences
6.4 Opening PageMaker and QuarkXPress Documents

Shortcuts

Open
Mac: Cmd+O
Win: Ctrl+O

Browse
Mac: Opt+Cmd+O
Win: Alt+Ctrl+O

Export
Mac: Cmd+E
Win: Ctrl+E

To open an existing InDesign document or template, choose File > Open, or press Command+O (Mac) or Ctrl+O (Windows). When the dialog appears, browse to a compatible file on your system and click the Open button.

Open and Open As

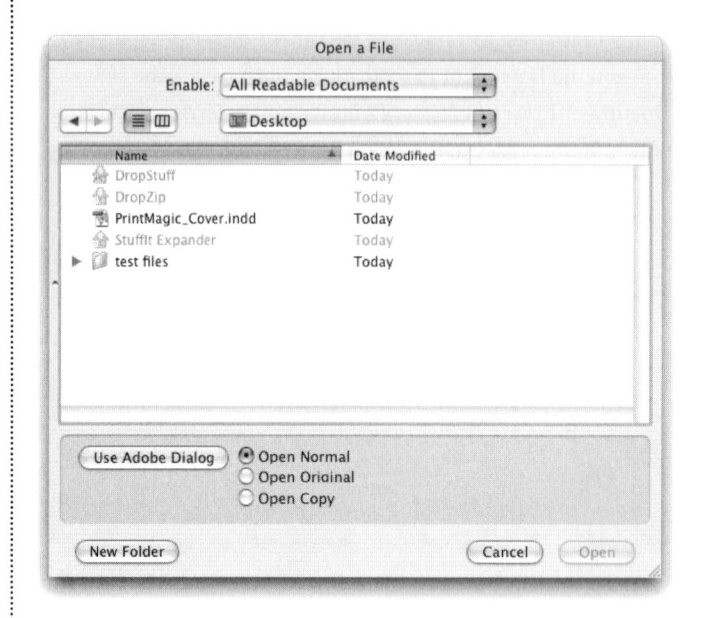

At the bottom of the Open A File dialog, you'll find three radio buttons:

- With Open Normal—the default setting—InDesign opens the document in a new window.
- Choosing Open Original allows you to open and edit documents that have been saved as InDesign templates.
- Open Copy allows you to do just that—open a copy of the selected file.

6.3 Opening InDesign Documents (continued)

Opening InDesign 2 and CS Docs

Both the Mac and Windows versions of InDesign CS2 can open documents created in InDesign 2 or CS. However, don't panic if the Color Settings warning dialog appears. This doesn't mean there is a problem opening your old files.

InDesign CS2 contains enhanced color management features that can be synchronized with the other applications in the Adobe Creative Suite 2, such as Photoshop and Illustrator, via the Adobe Bridge application. Color Settings are enabled by default at application launch.

If the InDesign 2 or CS document you're trying to open does not contain a saved profile that matches the applied Color Settings in CS2, and the Ask When Opening Color Management Policies option is enabled, these warning dialogs may appear. You can disable these warning dialogs and/or color management all together by selecting Edit > Color Settings and making the proper adjustments in the dialog.

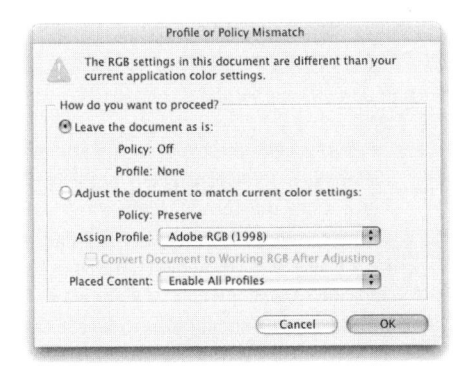

When these warning dialogs appear, if you're not sure how you want to color-manage the document (or if you even want to use color management at all), select the Leave As Is option and click OK. If you've already set up your Color Settings and you know that you want to apply them to the InDesign 2 or CS doc you're opening, then select the Adjust Document To Match option and click OK.

Related Tasks

6.6 Saving Backward with INX Export

14.1 Using Color Settings

14.2 Color Managing Imported Graphics

Tips

You can select and open multiple InDesign documents, books, and libraries as long as they are all located in the same folder on your drive.

Exporting an InDesign CS2 document using the INX interchange format makes it InDesign CS compatible.

123

6.4 Opening PageMaker and QuarkXPress Documents

Related Tasks

2.3 File Menu
4.14 PageMaker Toolbar
5.4 Composition Preferences

Shortcuts

Open
Mac: Cmd+O
Win: Ctrl+O

Save
Mac: Cmd+S
Win: Ctrl+S

Save As
Mac: Shift+Cmd+S
Win: Shift+Ctrl+S

Tip

InDesign CS2 cannot open QuarkXPress book or library documents.

InDesign CS2 can open documents and templates created in QuarkXPress 3.3–4.1 (not Quark 5.x–6.x) and PageMaker 6.5x–7.x. Now, if it just so happens that most of the documents you need to convert are Quark 5 and 6 files, try saving them backward to Quark 4 first before opening them in InDesign CS2. It works!

(Left) The PageMaker 7.x document icon; (right) the QuarkXPress 4.x document icon

Upon opening, InDesign converts these documents to an unsaved .indd format and does not overwrite the original Quark or PageMaker files. You can then save the new InDesign version anywhere on your system.

How well this works depends on the document you are trying to convert. More often than not, you'll find that InDesign does a really good job of converting Quark and PageMaker documents, but there is always something that changes.

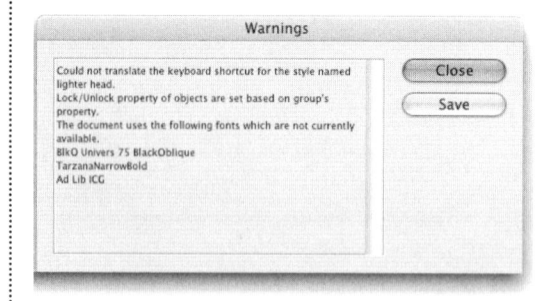

After a successful conversion, a Warnings dialog pops up displaying any problem items. Click the Save button if you'd like to refer to these items later; otherwise click Close. It is recommended that in addition to taking note of everything in this dialog, you should take a close look at the converted InDesign document and compare it to the original Quark or PageMaker file.

Once you make any necessary adjustments to the items that didn't convert quite right, save the document as an InDesign file, and you're good to go. It's a heck of a lot easier than rebuilding pages from scratch, don't you think?

6.5 Save vs. Save As

To save an InDesign document, choose File > Save, or press Command+S (Mac) or Ctrl+S (Windows). If you're saving the document for the first time, the Save As dialog appears. Browse to where you'd like to save the file on your system and click the Save button. To update a previously saved document to include any changes or edits you've made, choose File > Save again, or press Command/Ctrl+S.

To save an alternate version of an open document without saving over the original, choose File > Save As, or press Shift+Cmd+S (Mac) or Shift+Ctrl+S (Windows). Browse to where you'd like to save the file on your system and click Save.

Another way to save an alternate version of an existing document without saving over the original is to create a template to work from. To save a document as a template, choose File > Save As and then choose InDesign CS Template from the Format menu (Mac) or Save As Type menu (Windows).

Clicking the Use Adobe Dialog button changes the interface of the dialog, allowing you to take advantage of Creative Suite 2 project management features available through Bridge and Version Cue.

Related Tasks

2.3 File Menu
4.14 PageMaker Toolbar
5.14 File Handling Preferences

Shortcuts

Save
Mac: Cmd+S
Win: Ctrl+S

Save As
Mac: Shift+Cmd+S
Win: Shift+Ctrl+S

Tip

If you accidentally choose Save instead of Save As and wind up saving over an important document, all is not lost—just don't close the file! Press Command+Z (Mac) or Ctrl+Z (Windows) as many times as necessary until you're back to the original (InDesign CS2 allows up to several hundred Undos and Redo's, depending on the amount of RAM installed on your machine and the kinds of actions you have performed). Now choose Save As to preserve a copy of the original.

6.6 Saving Backward with INX Export

Related Tasks

2.3 File Menu
6.3 Opening InDesign Documents
6.5 Save vs. Save As

Shortcuts

Export
Mac: Cmd+E
Win: Ctrl+E

When InDesign CS was first introduced, everyone was blown away by all the cool new features—and then we realized that the folks at Adobe forgot to include one really important one: the ability to save files "backward" for use with InDesign 2. Thankfully, they remembered to include it with CS2.

You can now save CS2 files "backward" for use with InDesign CS via the INX export feature. Open the file you want to save backward, and then choose File > Export, or press Command+E (Mac) or Ctrl+E (Windows). When the Export dialog appears, browse to where you'd like to save the .inx file, and then choose InDesign Interchange from the Format menu (Mac) or Save As Type menu (Windows). You can then open the .inx file in InDesign CS.

Keep in mind that when saving backward, the features added in CS2 are not be available in CS (object styles, anchored objects, etc).

Clicking the Use Adobe Dialog button changes the interface of the dialog, allowing you to take advantage of Creative Suite 2 project management features available through Bridge and Version Cue.

6.7 Saving Files for Use with InCopy

If your production team includes copy editors as well as designers, you may want to consider purchasing and implementing Adobe InCopy into your workflow. InCopy is designed to work hand in hand with InDesign, allowing both editors and designers to work on files at the same time without getting their wires crossed.

With InCopy installed, several new interface items appear in InDesign CS2, including the Assignments and Notes palettes. A Notes menu and Notes tool also appear. The Assignments palettes in both applications allow all users to manage editing duties for specific "stories" (text frames) and graphics in the publication. The Notes features allow users of both applications to communicate with each other right in the document itself—no more e-mails!

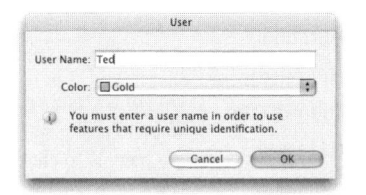

Each InDesign and InCopy user in the production workflow must choose a user name and color, accessible in both applications under File > User. Once chosen, both applications apply this info so that users can identify each other when placing Notes.

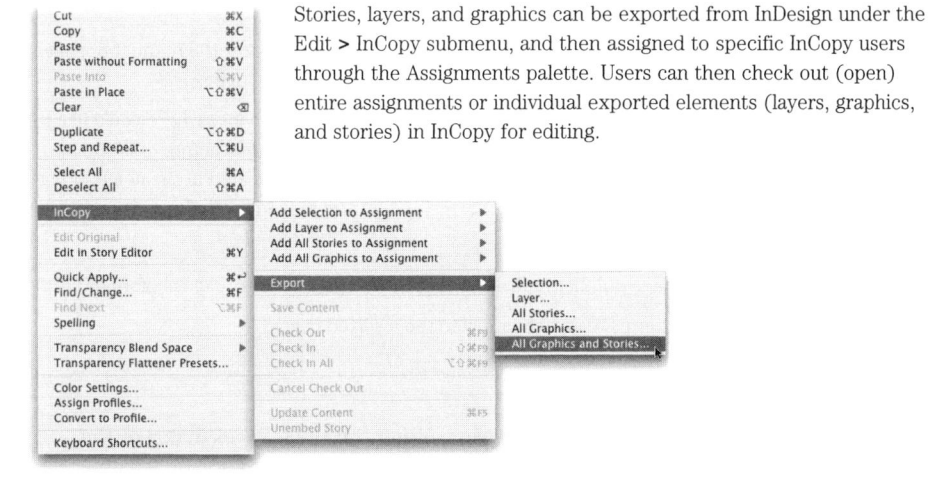

Stories, layers, and graphics can be exported from InDesign under the Edit > InCopy submenu, and then assigned to specific InCopy users through the Assignments palette. Users can then check out (open) entire assignments or individual exported elements (layers, graphics, and stories) in InCopy for editing.

Users in both applications must check assigned stories in and out using the Assignments palette in order to edit them. The palette acts as a content manager, displaying which stories and/or graphics in an assignment have or have not been edited so that both editors and designers can stay up to date.

Related Tasks

2.3 File Menu
2.4 Edit Menu

Shortcuts

Export
Mac: Cmd+E
Win: Ctrl+E

Place
Mac: Cmd+D
Win: Ctrl+D

Tip

Stories created in InCopy and saved in the INX interchange format or as an InCopy document can be placed into an InDesign CS2 document using the Place command.

6.8 Adding, Arranging, and Deleting Pages

Related Tasks

2.5 Layout Menu

4.14 PageMaker Toolbar

Shortcuts

Insert Pages dialog
Mac: Opt-click Create New Page button
Win: Alt-click Create New Page button

Add page
Mac: Shift+Cmd+P
Win: Shift+Ctrl+P

InDesign CS2 offers several ways to add, arrange, and delete pages in a document.

Adding Pages

There are three ways to add a single page after the page you currently have selected in a document: choose Layout > Pages > Add Page; press Shift+Cmd+P (Mac) or Shift+Ctrl+P (Windows); or click the Create New Page footer control located at the bottom of the Pages palette.

By the same token, there are four ways you can access the Insert Pages dialog and add single or multiple pages to a document: choose Layout > Pages > Insert Pages; click the Pages palette menu button and choose Insert Pages; Option-click (Mac) or Alt-click (Windows) the Create New Page footer control located at the bottom of the Pages palette; or click the Insert Pages control located in the PageMaker toolbar.

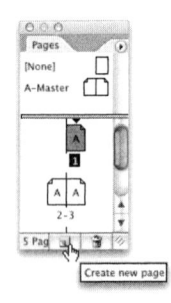

One of the quickest ways to add a single page is to click the Pages palette footer control.

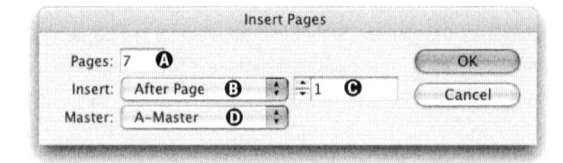

A **Pages** Enter the number of pages you'd like to insert.

B **Insert** Choose where you'd like to insert pages: before or after the page indicated in the neighboring data field, or at the start or end of the document.

C **Page number** Enter the page number indicating where you'd like to insert pages before or after.

D **Master** Choose which master page style to apply to the inserted pages.

Arranging Pages

You can move pages around in a document using either the Move Pages dialog or the Pages palette. To access the dialog, select Move Pages from the Layout > Pages submenu or from the Pages palette menu.

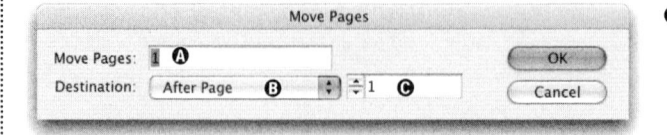

A **Move Pages** Enter the page number(s) currently assigned to the page(s) you'd like to move.

B **Destination** Choose where you'd like to move pages: before or after the page indicated in the neighboring data field, or at the start or end of the document.

C **Page number** Enter the page number indicating where you'd like to move pages before or after.

6.8 Adding, Arranging, and Deleting Pages *(continued)*

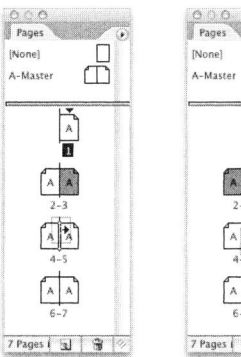

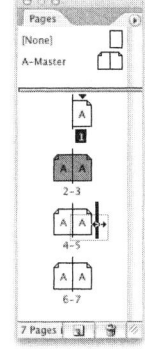

To move a page from within the Pages palette, select it by clicking its icon in the palette, then drag it to another location in the thumbnail layout. The black arrows indicate where the page will be placed once you release the mouse button. You can also Command/Ctrl-click to select and move multiple pages, and Shift-click to select and move a series of pages.

Deleting Pages

You can delete pages from a document by choosing Layout > Pages > Delete Page(s) (or Delete Spread(s) if you have facing pages selected in the Pages palette). You can also access the Delete Page(s) command from the Pages palette menu.

To delete pages with the Remove Pages dialog, click the Remove Pages control in the PageMaker toolbar.

If any of the selected pages contain objects, InDesign displays a warning dialog before deleting them. Click OK if you still want to delete, or Cancel if you think you may have selected the wrong pages. If you do accidentally delete the wrong pages, you can retrieve them with the Undo command (Mac: Command+Z, Windows: Ctrl+Z), as long as you don't close the document first.

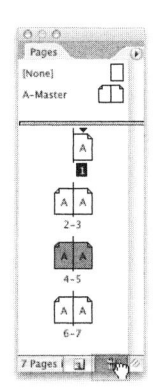

Probably the easiest way to delete pages is to select the ones you want to get rid of (by Shift-clicking their thumbnail icons in the Pages palette), then either clicking the trash icon at the bottom of the palette or dragging the selected pages to the trash.

Related Tasks

4.15 Pages Palette
6.1   Starting a New Document

Shortcuts

Undo
Mac: Cmd+Z
Win: Ctrl+Z

Pages palette
Mac and Win: F12

Tips

You can click and drag pages and spreads from the Pages palette and place them into another open InDesign document.

To bypass the "affected pages contain objects" warning dialog, hold down the Option key (Mac) or Alt key (Windows) as you delete.

6.9 Creating Multipage Spreads and Master Pages

Related Tasks

4.15 Pages Palette
6.1   Starting a New Document
6.2   Saving Document Presets
6.8   Adding, Arranging, and Deleting Pages
6.11 Creating Master Pages

Shortcuts

Insert Pages dialog
Mac: Opt-click Create New Page button
Win: Alt-click Create New Page button

Add page
Mac: Shift+Cmd+P
Win: Shift+Ctrl+P

Pages palette
Mac and Win: F12

Document Setup dialog
Mac: Opt+Cmd+P
Win: Alt+Ctrl+P

Tip

To save a multipage document spread as a master page, click and drag the multipage spread icons into the master pages portion of the Pages palette.

With InDesign, you can create what is known as a "gatefold" spread. Gatefolds contain more than two adjoining pages and are commonly used for large brochure or ad designs that feature multiple folds.

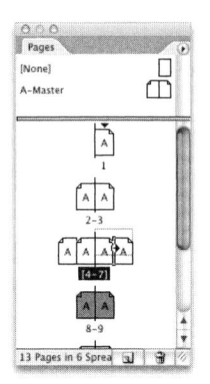

1. Select a page (single-sided document), or a spread (facing pages document), and click the palette menu button. Choose Keep Spread Together and notice the page number(s) for this page or spread appear in brackets in the Pages palette thumbnail display.

2. In the Pages palette, click and drag a document or master page icon into the bracketed spread. Continue to add additional pages to the spread as needed.

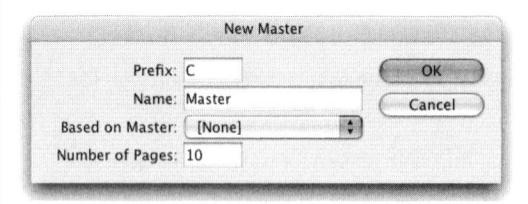

To create a multipage master spread, select New Master from the Pages palette menu. Then enter the number of pages to include in the dialog (between 1 and 10) and click OK.

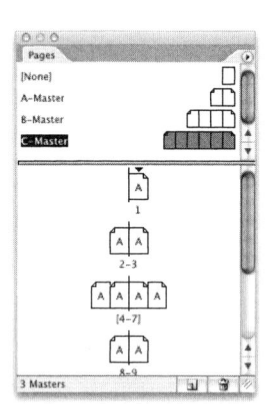

Your new gatefold master appears in the master pages portion of the palette.

6.10 Targeting vs. Selecting Pages

In InDesign, you can target a page and also select one. I know, it sounds like the same thing, but they are actually two totally different actions.

By default, a targeted page or spread is the one you are working on in the document window; however, if you hand-scroll to another page in the document, the original page you were working on remains targeted. So let's say you're working on page 6 and have a text frame selected. Then you decide to hand-scroll to page 4, but can't see the whole page because you were zoomed in to 200%. You press Command/Ctrl+1 to view the page at 100%, and now you're back on page 6! How the heck did that happen?

You can target only one page or spread at a time; therefore, the page that you hand-scrolled to does not become targeted until you actually click somewhere on the page with any tool except the Hand or Zoom tools.

Don't worry—there is a solution. If you're addicted to hand-scrolling and tend to get lost in your own documents (I do this all the time), refer to the Pages palette to identify which page or spread is actually the targeted one. It's the one with the black highlight over the page number.

So what's the difference between a targeted page and a selected page, and more importantly, why should you care? Well, a page is selected when *its page icon* (not its page number) appears highlighted in the Pages palette. You can select a page by clicking its icon in the palette, and then apply specific page editing commands to it (such as adjusting margins and columns, or moving the page), even when another page is targeted and centered in the document window.

You can select and edit multiple pages by Command/Ctrl-clicking the page icons in the Pages palette. To target a selected page, double-click the page icon for it to appear centered in the document window.

Related Tasks

1.3 The Document Window
2.5 Layout Menu
4.15 Pages Palette
6.13 Applying Master Pages

Shortcuts

Select page number in Page box
Mac: Cmd+J
Win: Ctrl+J

Go back/forward to last viewed page
Mac: Cmd+Page Up/Page Down
Win: Ctrl+Page Up/Page Down

Go to previous/next spread
Mac: Opt+Page Up/Page Down
Win: Alt+Page Up/Page Down

Go to first/last page
Mac: Shift+Cmd+Page Up/Page Down
Win: Shift+Ctrl+Page Up/Page Down

Pages palette
Mac and Win: F12

Tip

To select a block of pages in the Pages palette, click the page icon for the first page in the series, then hold down the Shift key and click the last page in the series.

6.11 Creating Master Pages

Related Tasks

- 2.5 Layout Menu
- 4.15 Pages Palette
- 6.9 Creating Multipage Spreads and Master Pages
- 6.12 Converting Document Pages to Master Pages
- 6.13 Applying Master Pages
- 6.14 Deleting Master Pages
- 6.15 Creating and Applying Parent/Child Master Pages

Shortcuts

New Master dialog
Mac: Cmd+Opt-click Create New Page button
Win: Ctrl+Alt-click Create New Page button

Create new master page
Mac: Cmd-click Create New Page button
Win: Ctrl-click Create New Page button

Apply master to selected page
Mac: Opt-click Master Page Icon
Win: Alt-click Master Page Icon

Pages palette
Mac and Win: F12

Tip

You can place more than one group of threaded text frames on a master spread.

Creating a master page allows you to save a layout to apply to other pages in a document—eliminating the need for repetitive page formatting. Items that reoccur in a publication, such as page numbers and folios, are perfect candidates for a master page.

One of the benefits to using master pages is that when they are applied to document pages throughout a document, all the master page items are placed in the same position simultaneously. What a relief not to have to place them all individually on each document page!

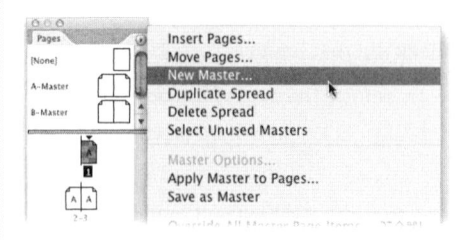

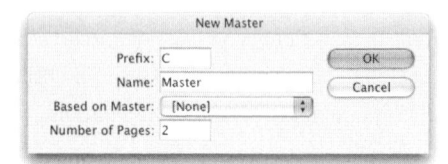

To create a master page, open the Pages palette menu and choose New Master. When the dialog opens, choose a prefix, name, and number of pages to apply. To base the new master on another master (creating a parent/child relationship), choose a master from the Based On Master drop-down menu. Click OK for the master page to appear centered in the document window.

You can then place the objects you'd like to appear on any page the master is applied to.

Duplicating Master Pages

To duplicate an existing master page, select it from the master pages portion of the Pages palette and then choose Pages > Duplicate Master Spread from the Layout menu or from the Pages palette menu. The duplicate master automatically appears in the Pages palette with the word "copy" placed at the end of its name.

To rename, change the prefix, add pages, or base the duplicate on an existing master, choose Master Options from the Pages palette menu and enter the appropriate settings in the dialog.

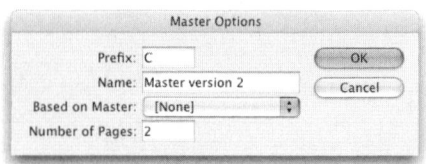

6.12 Converting Document Pages to Master Pages

You created the perfect spread to use as the formatted layout for an entire publication. The only problem is—you forgot to create it on a master page!

No problem. To convert a document page into a master page, select it from the Pages palette and then choose Save As Master from the palette menu (see below left). The converted master automatically appears at the bottom of the master page list with the next available prefix (A, B, C, etc.) applied to its name.

As if that isn't easy enough, there's an even easier way to convert a document page into a master page. Just select the page or spread in the document portion of the Pages palette and drag it into the master pages portion (see below right).

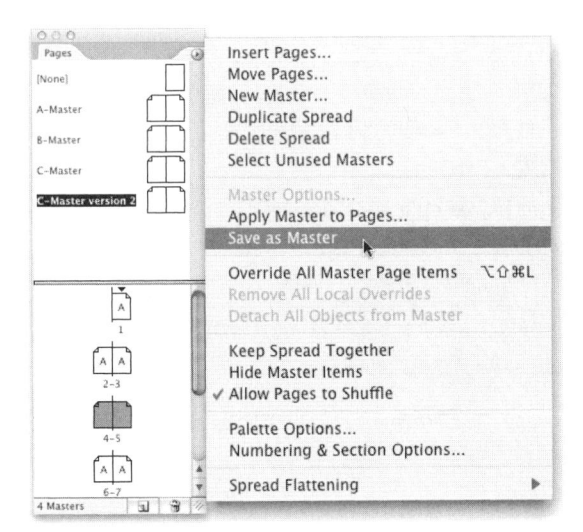

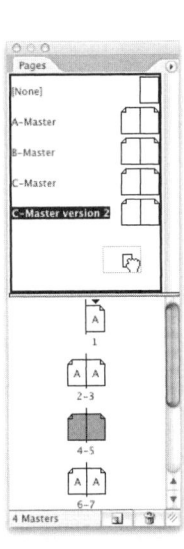

Related Tasks

4.15 Pages Palette
6.9 Creating Multipage Spreads and Master Pages
6.11 Creating Master Pages
6.13 Applying Master Pages
6.15 Creating and Applying Parent/Child Master Pages

Shortcuts

Create master page
Mac: Cmd-click Create New Page button
Win: Ctrl-click Create New Page button

Apply master to selected page
Mac: Opt-click Master
Win: Alt-click Master

Pages palette
Mac and Win: F12

Tips

You can convert a document page that has a master page applied to it into a master page. It automatically becomes a "child" to the "parent" master.

If you have so many master pages applied in your multipage document that you're not sure which items are master page items and which are not, choose Hide Master Items from the Pages palette menu.

133

6.13 Applying Master Pages

Related Tasks

2.5 Layout Menu
4.15 Pages Palette
6.9 Creating Multipage Spreads and Master Pages
6.11 Creating Master Pages
6.15 Creating and Applying Parent/Child Master Pages
6.16 Overriding Master Page Items

Shortcuts

Create master page
Mac: Cmd-click Create New Page button
Win: Ctrl-click Create New Page button

Apply master to selected page
Mac: Opt-click Master
Win: Alt-click Master

Pages palette
Mac and Win: F12

Tip

You can open master pages through the menu found at the bottom of the document window. Click the down arrow located next to the page number data field and choose a master page from the bottom of the list.

To apply a master page, select the document pages you want to apply a master to in the Pages palette. You can do so by Command/Ctrl-clicking page icons in the Pages palette, or Shift-clicking to select contiguous pages. Once the pages are selected, choose Apply Master To Pages from the Layout > Pages submenu or the Pages palette menu.

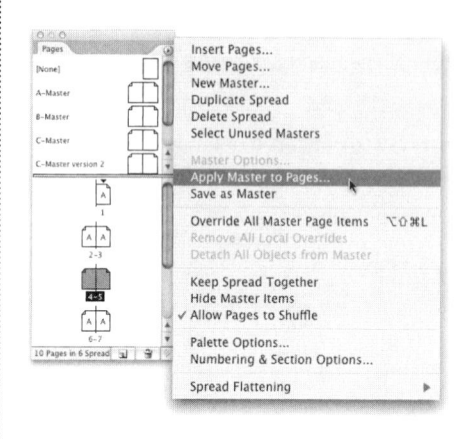

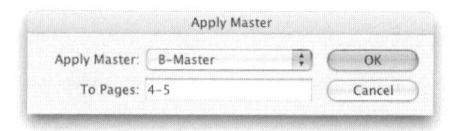

The page numbers automatically appear in the To Pages field of the dialog. If you choose not to select the pages first before opening the dialog, you can also enter the page numbers in the To Pages field, separated by commas. Click OK to apply the master.

Once the master page is applied, all items placed on it are also placed on the document page. To manipulate master page items in the document layout, you must override them by Cmd+Shift-clicking (Mac) or Ctrl+Shift-clicking (Windows) with one of the selection tools.

One other fast way to apply a master style to several pages at once is to select the pages in the Pages palette and Option/Alt-click the Master page icon.

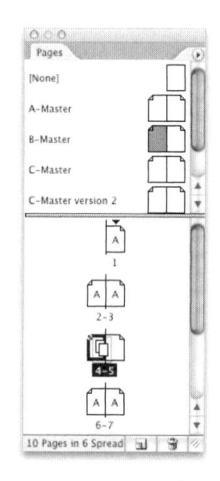

You can also apply a master page by selecting it from the master pages portion of the Pages palette and dragging it over a document page icon—just like in QuarkXPress. By positioning the cursor over the page icons until a thick black line appears around the entire spread, you can apply the master style to all pages in the spread when you release the mouse button.

6.14 Deleting Master Pages

To delete a master page, select the master you want to delete from the master pages list in the Pages palette and choose Delete Master Spread from the Layout > Pages submenu or the Pages palette menu.

You can also delete a master page by selecting it from the master pages list in the Pages palette and dragging it over the trash icon footer control. Or—if you like clicking better than dragging—select the master pages you want to delete and click the trash icon without having to drag the pages down.

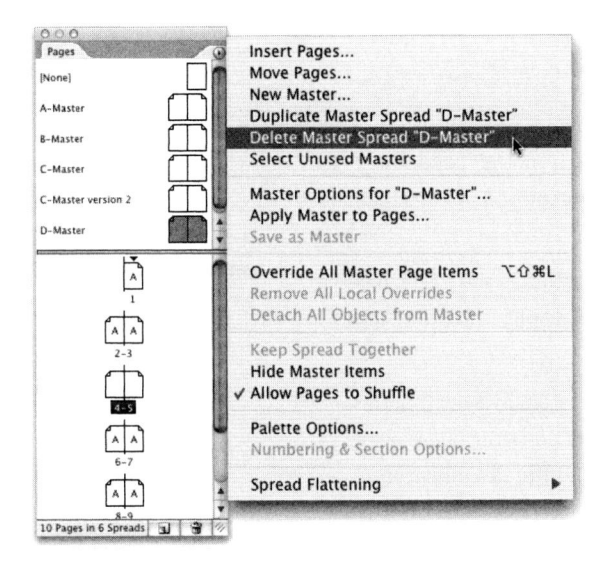

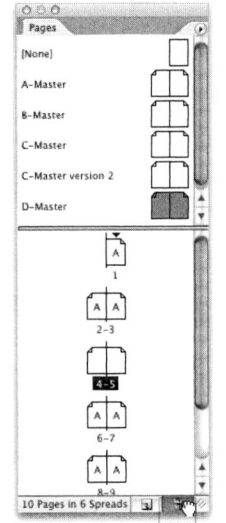

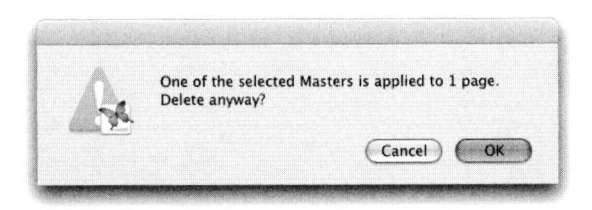

InDesign displays a warning dialog if the master page you are deleting is applied to a page in the document. Click OK if you're sure you still want to delete the master. Upon deleting, all of the page items that were placed on the master no longer appear in the document.

Related Tasks

2.5 Layout Menu
4.15 Pages Palette
6.9 Creating Multipage Spreads and Master Pages
6.11 Creating Master Pages
6.15 Creating and Applying Parent/Child Master Pages
6.16 Overriding Master Page Items

Shortcuts

Create master page
Mac: Cmd-click Create New Page button
Win: Ctrl-click Create New Page button

Apply master to selected page
Mac: Opt-click Master
Win: Alt-click Master

Pages palette
Mac and Win: F12

Tip

To bypass the "selected Master is applied to a page" warning dialog, hold down the Option key (Mac) or Alt key (Windows) as you delete.

135

6.15 Creating and Applying Parent/Child Master Pages

Related Tasks

2.5	Layout Menu
4.15	Pages Palette
6.9	Creating Multipage Spreads and Master Pages
6.11	Creating Master Pages
6.16	Overriding Master Page Items

Shortcuts

Create master page
Mac: Cmd-click Create New Page button
Win: Ctrl-click Create New Page button

Apply master to selected page
Mac: Opt-click Master
Win: Alt-click Master

Pages palette
Mac and Win: F12

Tip

You can also Option-click (Mac) or Alt-click (Windows) the master you want to base another selected master on. This applies all parent master page items to the child master.

InDesign allows you to create master pages that are based on another master page. When you do this, all shared master page items change dynamically when the "parent" master is edited. Just as with document pages, all parent master page items applied to child masters cannot be edited unless overridden.

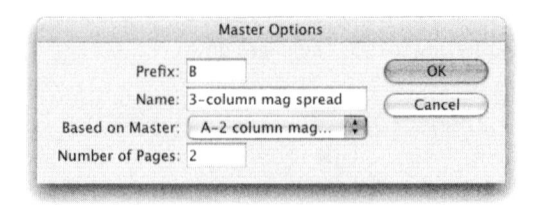

To create a new master that is based on an existing "parent" master, click the menu button on the Pages palette and choose New Master. When the dialog opens, choose a prefix, name, number of pages, and a parent master to base the new child master on from the menu. Click OK for the child master page to appear centered in the document window.

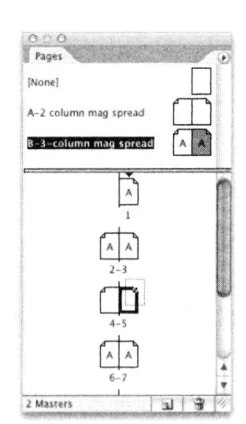

It's easy to identify parent/child masters in the Pages palette; the child master page icons always display the prefix letter of the parent master.

You can also create parent/child masters by selecting the master page icon of a chosen parent and dragging it over the page icon of a chosen child. This applies all parent master page items to the child master.

6.16 Overriding Master Page Items

Master page items that have been applied to a document page cannot be edited unless overridden. To override, press Command+Shift (Mac) or Ctrl+Shift (Windows) and click the item. This allows you to edit the item on the document page only. Any changes made do not affect the original item on the master page.

Note that you do not need to override a master text or graphic frame to place content in it. Clicking the frame with a loaded place icon activates it.

Also note that even though the master page item may be overridden on a document page, it is still linked to the item on the master page. For example, if you were to change the fill color of a master page item on a document page by overriding it, any edits *other than fill color* that are made to the item on the master page are still applied. To unlink an overridden master page item from the original, select it on the document page and choose Detach Selection From Master from the Pages palette menu.

By default, frame contents (text or graphics) are always detached from the master page when overridden.

To override all master page items for a selected page or spread, choose Override All Master Page Items from the Pages palette menu, or press Cmd+Opt+Shift+L (Mac) or Ctrl+Alt+Shift+L (Windows).

To undo any overrides made to selected master page items on a page or spread, choose Remove All Local Overrides from the Pages palette menu.

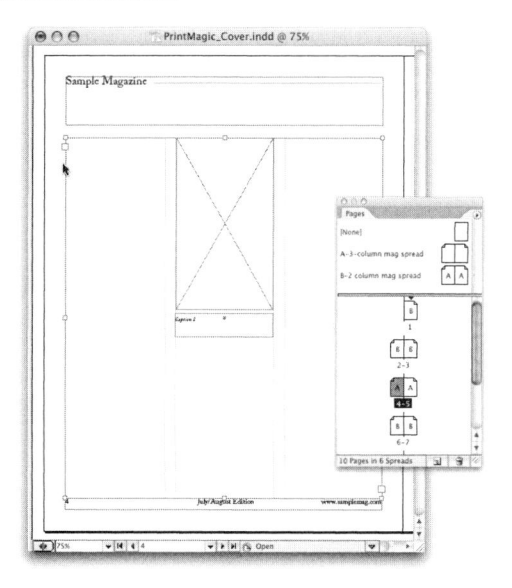

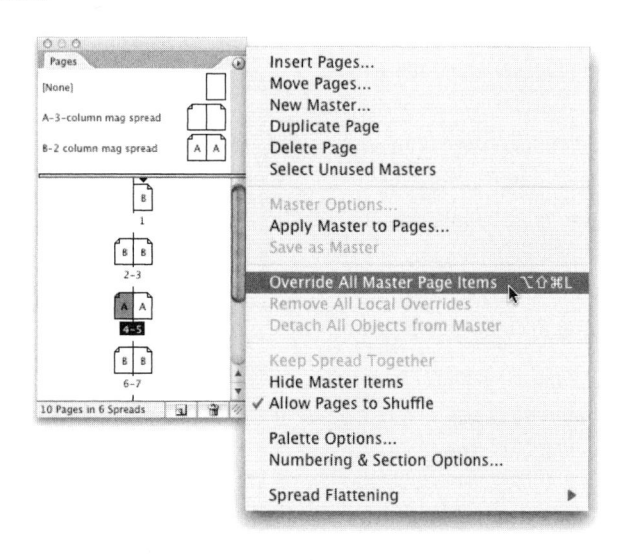

Related Tasks

4.15 Pages Palette
6.9 Creating Multipage Spreads and Master Pages
6.11 Creating Master Pages
6.12 Converting Document Pages to Master Pages
6.13 Applying Master Pages

Shortcuts

Override all master page items for selected spread
Mac: Cmd+Opt+Shift+L
Win: Ctrl+Alt+Shift+L

Create master page
Mac: Cmd-click Create New Page button
Win: Ctrl-click Create New Page button

Apply master to selected page
Mac: Opt-click Master
Win: Alt-click Master

Pages palette
Mac and Win: F12

Tip

To detach all overridden objects on a document page, choose Detach All Objects From Master from the Pages palette menu.

137

6.17 Adding Page Numbers to Sections

Related Tasks

2.5 Layout Menu
4.15 Pages Palette
4.22 Book and Library Palettes
5.1 General Preferences
18.3 Page Numbering Across Book Documents

Shortcuts

Insert Auto Page Numbering character
Mac: Opt+Shift+Cmd+N
Win: Alt+Shift+Ctrl+N

Pages palette
Mac and Win: F12

Tip

An InDesign document can include more than one numbered section.

With InDesign, you can apply auto page numbering and also create more than one numbered section in a document.

When you insert the special Auto Page Number character on applied master pages, the folios automatically number themselves. Learn to use this feature, and you'll never have to correct any page numbering when adding, deleting, and moving pages in a document.

On your master page or spread, create a text frame where you'd like the page numbers to appear and then choose Type > Insert Special Character > Auto Page Number, or press Opt+Shift+Cmd+N (Mac) or Alt+Shift+Ctrl+N (Windows). Apply the master to your document and watch the pages number themselves. It's like magic!

To start a new numbered section within a document, select a page in the Pages palette where you'd like it to start, and then choose Numbering & Section Options from the Layout menu or the Pages palette menu. Click the radio button for Start Page Numbering At, and enter a page number in the data field. Once applied, Auto Page Numbering characters recognize any changes made in the Numbering & Section Options dialog.

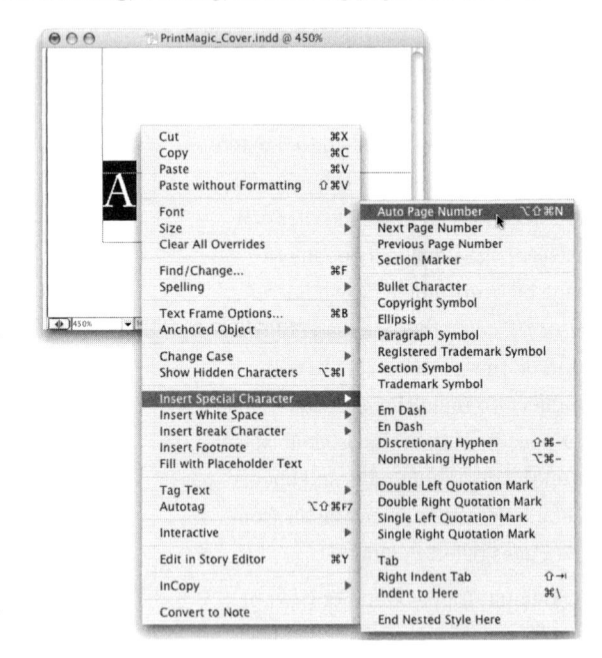

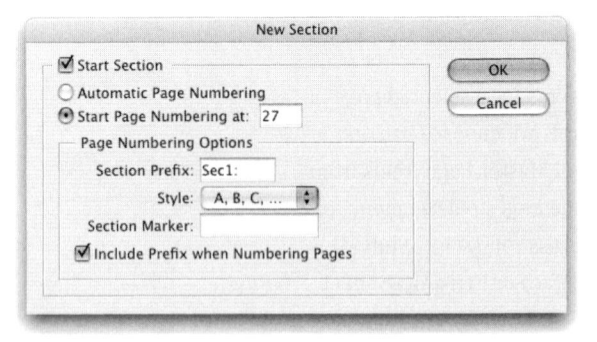

Using this dialog, you can also apply a custom prefix, a numerical style (Arabic, Roman numeral, letters, etc.), or a section marker (section number, chapter name, etc.) to the page numbering scheme.

6.18 Adjusting Ruler Guides

Some designers find ruler guides extremely helpful when setting up page layouts and templates. You can use guides to line up page items evenly and snap them into place. Guides are not printable—they are only available on screen. It is easy to move, lock, snap to, add, or delete guides, and you can even assign them different colors.

You can click and drag a new guide out from the horizontal or vertical rulers and onto the targeted page (or master page) at any time, no matter what tool you are using. Once the guide is placed, you can select it with either selection tool by hovering over it and clicking. To select multiple guides, Shift-click or marquee.

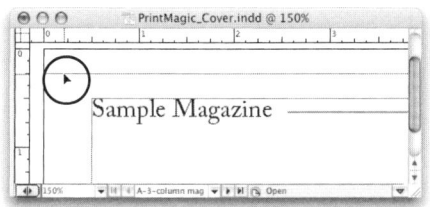

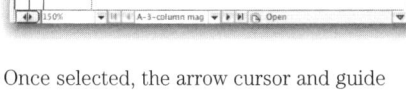

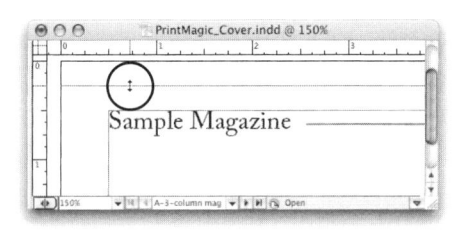

Once selected, the arrow cursor and guide change color.

Click and drag to move the guides vertically or horizontally.

You can also choose to Hide/Show, Lock/Unlock, or Snap To guides under the View > Grids & Guides submenu, or in the context menu (Control-clicking/right-clicking anywhere on the Pasteboard). To access the Ruler Guides dialog, choose Layout > Ruler Guides, or select a guide and choose it from the context menu.

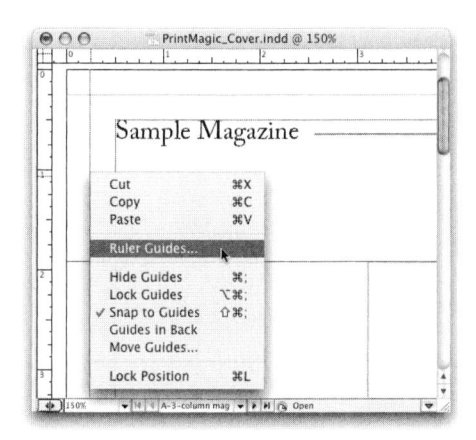

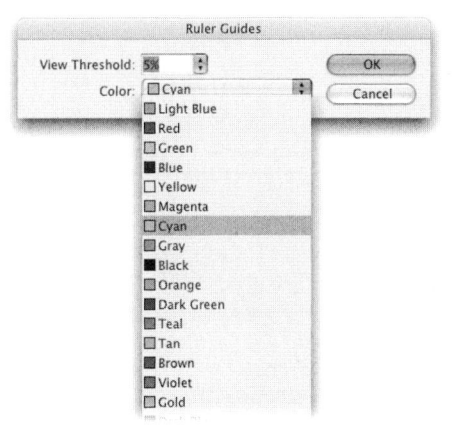

Different colors can be applied to selected guides by accessing the Ruler Guides dialog and choosing an alternate color from the menu. You can also set a View Threshold amount in this dialog.

To delete guides, select the ones you want to remove and press Delete (Mac) or Backspace (Windows).

Related Tasks

1.3 The Document Window
2.5 Layout Menu
5.7 Guides & Pasteboard Preferences
6.19 Adjusting Margin and Column Guides

Shortcuts

Show/hide guides
Mac: Cmd+;
Win: Ctrl+;

Show/hide rulers
Mac: Cmd+R
Win: Ctrl+R

Lock guides
Mac: Opt+Cmd+;
Win: Alt+Ctrl+;

Snap to guides
Mac: Shift+Cmd+;
Win: Shift+Ctrl+;

Select all guides on a page or spread
Mac: Opt+Cmd+G
Win: Alt+Ctrl+G

Tip

Try assigning specific sets of ruler guides to their own layers for more control over their visibility.

139

6.19 Adjusting Margin and Column Guides

Related Tasks

2.3	File Menu
2.5	Layout Menu
5.7	Guides & Pasteboard Preferences
6.1	Starting a New Document
6.2	Saving Document Presets
6.18	Adjusting Ruler Guides

Shortcuts

Show/hide guides
Mac: Cmd+;
Win: Ctrl+;

New document
Mac: Cmd+N
Win: Ctrl+N

Tip

To allow InDesign to resize or reposition any object that is aligned to a margin, column, or ruler guide, enable the Layout Adjustment feature located under the Layout menu.

You can set margin and column guides in the New Document dialog when starting a new project. However, you can edit them at any time while working in the document. To edit, choose Layout **>** Margins and Columns.

Unlike in QuarkXPress, you can edit the margin and column settings for individual document pages—not just master pages. Margin and column guides are applied just like any other master page item, but they can also be edited in the document page using the Margin And Columns dialog.

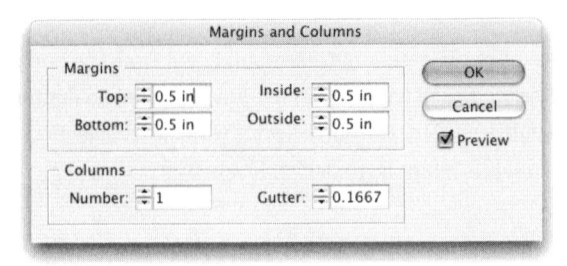

KEEP IT EVEN

Moving, adding, and deleting pages can sometimes cause problems in a publication that is set up using reader spreads, especially if it contains specific left and right page margins. Always be careful when adding, deleting, or moving pages in a document containing facing pages, as doing so may require that you reapply left/right master page styles to any pages that shift (which can result in a mess of duplicated master page items). It is best to only add or remove an even number of pages at a time.

6.20 Aligning to Baseline Grid

Aligning multiple columns of body text to the baseline grid can greatly improve the overall appearance of a document. To display the baseline grid, choose View > Grids & Guides > Show Baseline Grid or press Opt+Cmd+' (Mac) or Alt+Ctrl+' (Windows).

In Grids Preferences, enter the leading amount you're using for body text in the Increment Every data field, and click OK. Select the text frame and click the Align To Baseline Grid control in either the Paragraph palette or the Control bar.

To align just the first line of each paragraph to the baseline grid, select the text frame and choose Only Align First Line To Grid from the Paragraph palette menu.

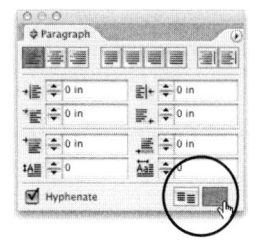

An example of how snapping the baselines of paragraph text to a "leading grid" can improve the look of your page

Related Tasks

2.9 View Menu
3.2 Control Bar
4.21 Type and Tables Palettes
5.6 Grids Preferences

Shortcuts

Show/hide baseline grid
Mac: Opt+Cmd+'
Win: Alt+Ctrl+'

Show/hide Control bar
Mac: Opt+Cmd+6
Win: Alt+Ctrl+6

Paragraph palette
Mac: Opt+Cmd+T
Win: Alt+Ctrl+T

Tip

You can adjust the View Threshold For The Baseline Grid setting in Grids Preferences.

6.21 Snapping to Document Grid

Related Tasks

2.9 View Menu
5.6 Grids Preferences
6.20 Aligning to Baseline Grid

Shortcuts

Show/hide document grid
Mac: Cmd+'
Win: Ctrl+'

Snap to document grid
Mac: Shift+Cmd+'
Win: Shift+Ctrl+'

Tip

You can apply a custom color to the document grid in Grids Preferences.

You can align objects evenly on the page by snapping to the document grid. When made visible, the grid can be very distracting to work with—even when placed in back with a lighter color applied to it. Thankfully, you can still snap to the document grid even when it is hidden.

Document Grid color settings and gridline options are accessible in Grids Preferences. To align graphic frames and other objects to the top and bottom lines of paragraph text, enter gridline subdivision values that coincide with the baseline grid.

Select View > Grids & Guides > Snap To Document Grid, or Control/right-click anywhere on the Pasteboard and select it from the context menu.

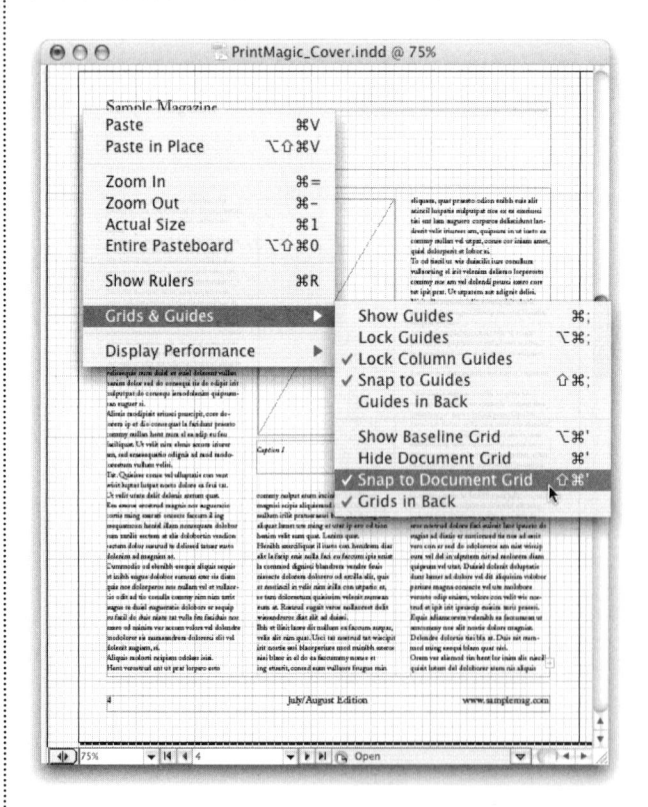

142

CHAPTER **7**

Frames and Shapes

ALL PAGE LAYOUTS IN InDesign are made up of frames and shapes, but what exactly are they? And what is the difference between the two? Well, frames are basically containers that are used for displaying placed images and bodies of text (also known as stories). Shapes (or paths) can be drawn and used as design elements, or converted into graphic or text frames.

It's fun to experiment with the flexibility of frames and shapes in InDesign. Placing graphics and text into custom shapes can certainly jazz up a layout. It's also possible to allow frames and shapes to contain *even more frames and shapes* through a process called "nesting."

Combining the versatility of frames and shapes with applied fills, stroke styles, corner effects, and transparency can take your designs to a whole new level of creativity.

- 7.1 Frame/Shape Overview
- 7.2 Selection Tool vs. Direct Selection Tool
- 7.3 Selecting Multiple Objects
- 7.4 Selecting Type
- 7.5 Drawing Rectangles, Ellipses, and Polygons
- 7.6 Drawing Custom Shapes
- 7.7 Drawing Freeform Shapes
- 7.8 Modifying Paths and Frames
- 7.9 Nesting Objects
- 7.10 Filling with Solid and Transparent Colors
- 7.11 Filling with Gradients
- 7.12 Filling Text
- 7.13 Stroking Frames, Shapes, and Paths
- 7.14 Stroking Text
- 7.15 Aligning Strokes
- 7.16 Applying Stroked Path Start and End Styles
- 7.17 Saving and Applying Custom Strokes
- 7.18 Applying Gap Color to Open Stroke Styles
- 7.19 Applying Corner Effects
- 7.20 Applying and Editing Compound Paths
- 7.21 Creating Custom Shapes with Pathfinder

7.1 Frame/Shape Overview

Related Tasks

2.7 Object Menu
2.9 View Menu
3.2 Control Bar
3.5 Pen Tools

Shortcuts

Rectangle Frame tool
Mac and Win: F

Rectangle tool
Mac and Win: M

The frame/shape relationship can be confusing to new users coming over from QuarkXPress. I can't tell you how many times I've been asked, "Why does the Toolbox have two rectangles? Which one is for text and which one is for graphics? How do I draw a text box?"

By definition, a frame is a container that holds either an image or a body of text. A shape is not intended to be a text or image container, but can be converted into one.

In Quark language, this means that the "box tool" with the "X" in it (the Rectangle Frame tool) is used to draw picture boxes. The box without the "X" (the Rectangle tool) is used for drawing shapes. Finally, "text boxes" can be drawn with the Type tool.

In InDesign, both rectangle tools can be used to draw a "picture box" or a "text box." You see, InDesign is extremely liberal. Frames can be shapes and shapes can be frames, and you do not have to draw a "box" first before placing an image! However, you should be aware of some differences between frames and shapes.

Frames

A frame is a container that holds either an image or a body of text. If you prefer to draw frames first before placing content in them, you can do so using the Rectangle, Ellipse, or Polygon Frame tool. A newly drawn, empty frame can be assigned as a text or a graphic placeholder using object styles, accessible in both the Control bar and Object Styles palette. Note: An object style can only be applied to an existing frame, not selected beforehand and applied as it is drawn.

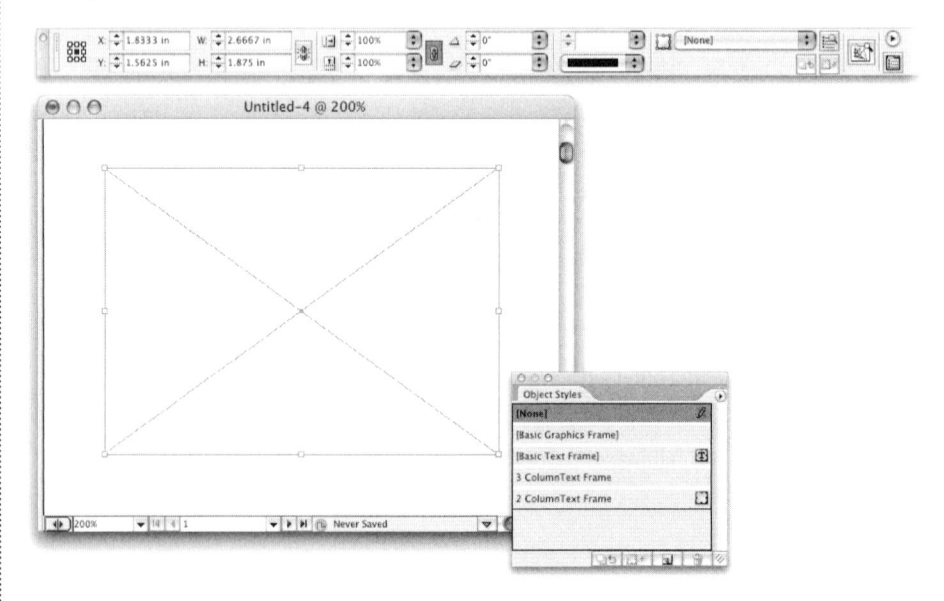

A selected Rectangle frame with the default, noneditable None object style (neither graphic nor text frame) applied to it.

7.1 Frame/Shape Overview *(continued)*

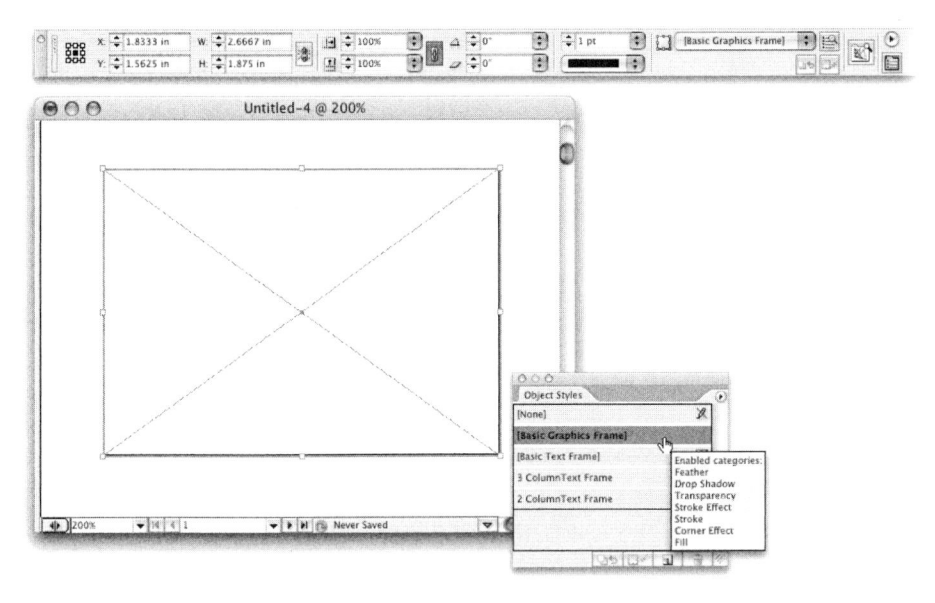

A selected Rectangle frame with the editable, default Basic Graphics Frame object style applied to it. Notice the tooltip description of its applied attributes.

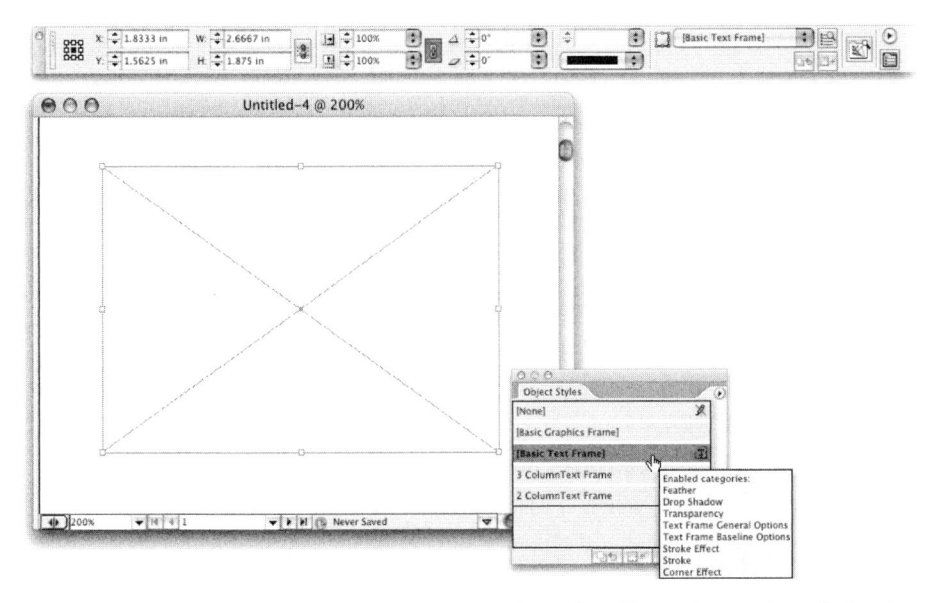

A selected Rectangle frame with the editable, default Basic Text Frame object style applied to it. Note the placeholder "X" that is still displayed, despite the text frame conversion.

Related Tasks

3.6 Type Tools
3.7 Pencil Tools
3.9 Frame Tools
3.10 Shape Tools

Shortcuts

Ellipse tool
Mac and Win: L

Selection tool
Mac and Win: V

145

7.1 Frame/Shape Overview (continued)

Related Tasks

4.10 Links Palette
4.11 Object and Layout Palettes
4.12 Object Styles Palette
4.16 Stroke Palette

Shortcut

Direct Selection tool
Mac and Win: A

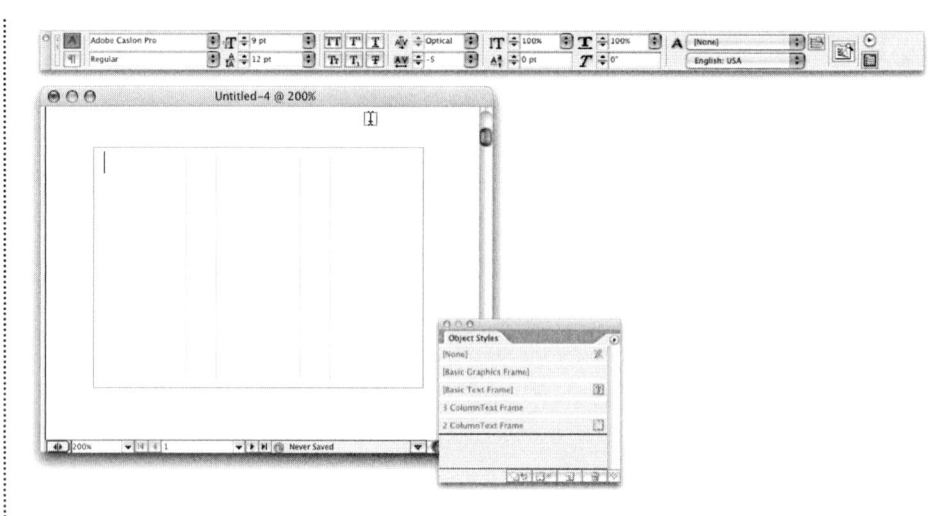

Clicking the Type tool cursor inside the assigned text frame changes its appearance accordingly.

If you prefer to paste content first and resize frames later, you can place graphics (or text) using the Place command (Mac: Command+D; Windows: Ctrl+D). A frame is automatically drawn for you when you click the loaded cursor anywhere on the Page.

Left, the loaded graphics cursor; right, the loaded text cursor

A text frame can also contain a "nested" graphic or text frame. "Nesting" allows a text frame to contain an anchored object.

Shapes

Shapes are drawn using the Rectangle, Ellipse, or Polygon tools. Custom shapes can be drawn using the Pen toolset, and freeform shapes can be drawn using the Pencil toolset. Assigned shape attributes can be saved as object styles and later applied to other shapes or frames (empty or with content).

Two or more shapes can be combined in various ways using the Pathfinder palette controls. You can also change a selected shape's appearance by selecting the Convert Shape commands found under the Object menu, or by clicking the Convert Shape controls located in the Pathfinder palette.

To convert a shape or path into a text frame, click inside it with the Type tool. The shape retains any applied object style attributes even after adding text.

7.1 Frame/Shape Overview (continued)

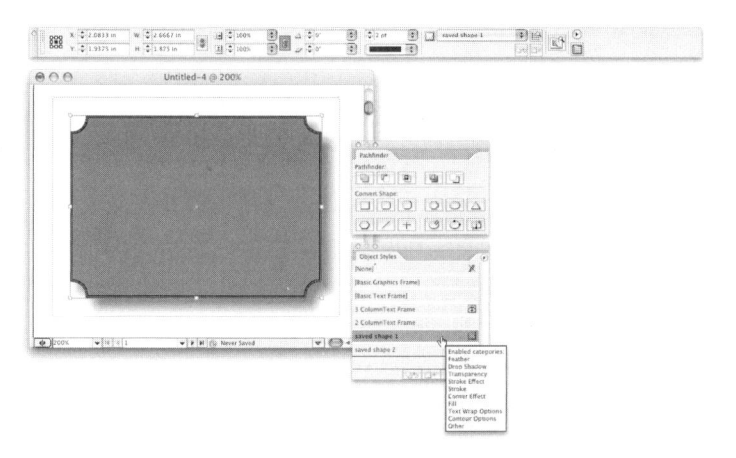

A selected rectangle with a saved object style applied to it. Notice the tooltip description of applied attributes.

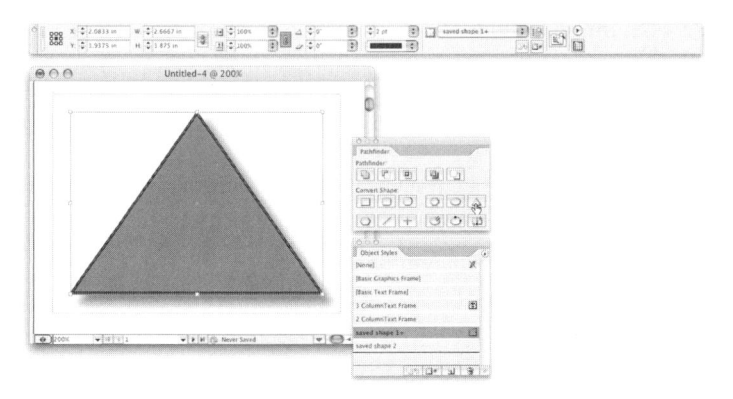

The same rectangle converted into a triangle using the Convert Shape control located in the Pathfinder palette. Whenever possible, shapes retain any applied object style attributes after conversion.

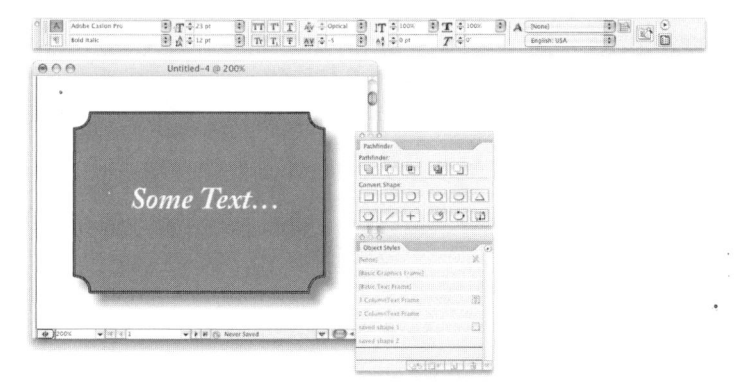

The original rectangle with an object style applied and some text added

Related Tasks

7.13 Stroking Frames, Shapes, and Paths

7.19 Applying Corner Effects

13.1 Placing and Editing Text Wraps

Shortcut

Position tool
Mac and Win: Shift+A

Tips

You can reshape any frame using the Pencil tool.

Text that is converted to outlines can be used as a graphic frame.

7.2 Selection Tool vs. Direct Selection Tool

Related Tasks

2.4	Edit Menu
2.7	Object Menu
3.3	Selection Tool
3.4	Direct Selection and Position Tools
3.9	Frame Tools
3.10	Shape Tools
4.10	Links Palette
4.11	Object and Layout Palettes
7.1	Frame/Shape Overview
7.3	Selecting Multiple Objects

Shortcuts

Selection tool
Mac and Win: V

Direct Selection tool
Mac and Win: A

Place command
Mac: Cmd+D
Win: Ctrl+D

Select All
Mac: Cmd+A
Win: Ctrl+A

The selection tools in InDesign work very much like the ones found in Adobe Illustrator. The Selection tool allows you to select, move, and resize an entire path, while the Direct Selection tool lets you select, move, and resize individual points on a path. Differences also exist in the way the tools are used to select, move, and resize frames and placed images.

Placing

Both tools can be used to place images using the Place command. You can either place an image into a selected frame or click the loaded place icon anywhere on the Page. When you click, a frame is automatically created to fit the image at 100% of its actual size.

Selecting

Click any frame (text or graphic) with the Selection tool to select it. Hold down the Shift key as you click to select multiple items.

Like with the Selection tool, you can use the Direct Selection tool to select a text frame by clicking anywhere on the text. However, unlike the Selection Tool, the Direct Selection tool also lets you select a single frame edge or corner node of any text or graphic frame. So be careful where you click with the Direct Selection tool!

Here's one other thing the Direct Selection tool lets you do that the Selection tool does not: select the contents of a graphic frame, separate from its container. Hovering your mouse directly over a placed image changes the Direct Selection tool's icon to display a hand. This indicates that you can now move the image around within the confines of the graphic frame.

Moving

Which selection tool should you use to move an image? Well, that depends on how you'd like to move it—with the frame, or inside the frame?

Click and drag with the Selection tool to move both the frame and the image.

Click and drag with the Direct Selection tool to move the image inside the frame.

7.2 Selection Tool vs. Direct Selection Tool *(continued)*

Resizing

So which selection tool should you use to scale an image? Again, it depends on how you would like it resized.

Use the Selection tool to resize the frame (and not the image) by clicking and dragging one of the frame nodes. Hold down the Shift key to constrain proportions as you drag.

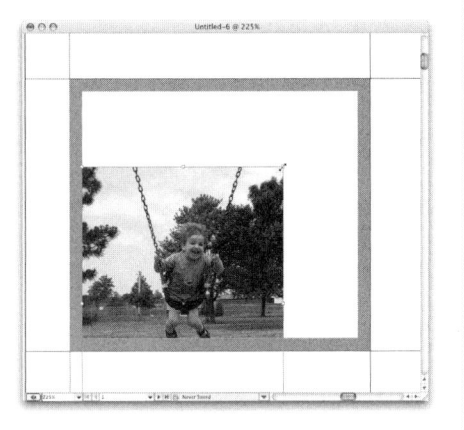

Use the Direct Selection tool to resize the image inside the frame. Click directly on the image itself and then click and drag one of the frame nodes. Hold down the Shift key to constrain proportions as you drag.

Use the Selection tool to resize the frame and image together by pressing the Command key (Mac) or Ctrl key (Windows) and clicking and dragging one of the frame nodes. Hold down the Shift key to constrain proportions as you drag.

Use the Direct Selection tool to select, reposition, or even delete the nodes of a frame. Click directly on the frame edge and then click and drag one of the nodes to reposition it. Press Delete (Mac) or Delete/Backspace (Windows) to remove a node from the frame and create an open path.

Related Tasks

- 8.1 Moving Objects
- 8.2 Resizing Objects
- 8.3 Rotating Objects
- 8.7 Selecting Objects within a Group
- 8.10 Duplicating Objects
- 12.6 Resizing Placed Images
- 12.11 Altering an Embedded Photoshop Path
- 12.12 Creating a Clipping Path in InDesign
- 13.1 Placing and Editing Text Wraps

Shortcuts

Deselect All
Mac: Shift+Cmd+A
Win: Shift+Ctrl+A

Group objects
Mac: Cmd+G
Win: Ctrl+G

Ungroup objects
Mac: Shift+Cmd+G
Win: Shift+Ctrl+G

Tip

To temporarily access the Selection or Direct Selection tool (whichever was last used), press the Command key (Mac) or Ctrl key (Windows).

7.3 Selecting Multiple Objects

Related Tasks

2.4 Edit Menu
2.7 Object Menu
3.3 Selection Tool
3.4 Direct Selection and Position Tools
8.6 Grouping and Ungrouping Objects
8.7 Selecting Objects within a Group
8.8 Nesting Grouped Objects
8.9 Stacking, Arranging, and Locking Objects

Shortcuts

Selection tool
Mac and Win: V

Direct Selection tool
Mac and Win: A

Select All
Mac: Cmd+A
Win: Ctrl+A

Deselect All
Mac: Shift+Cmd+A
Win: Shift+Ctrl+A

Group objects
Mac: Cmd+G
Win: Ctrl+G

Ungroup objects
Mac: Shift+Cmd+G
Win: Shift+Ctrl+G

Tip

To select more than one object in a group, hold down the Shift key and click each item with the Direct Selection tool. Click again to deselect.

To select multiple objects, access either of the selection tools and Shift-click the items on the page, or hold down the Shift key and marquee over an area that includes the objects you would like to select. You can tell that the objects are selected when the boundary nodes of the frame or shape appear. Shift-click again to deselect.

You can select the contents of multiple frames by Shift-clicking with the Direct Selection tool. You can also add other objects to a selection, such as text frames, shapes, and lines, by continuing to hold down Shift as you click.

Once selected, multiple objects (including points on a path) can be moved simultaneously by dragging the mouse or pressing the arrow keys. To resize the selected objects, press S to switch to the Scale tool, then click and drag. You can also rotate, shear, and free transform multiple selected objects.

Scaling editable text with the Selection tool is a tricky thing to do, but it is possible. With the Selection tool accessed, click and drag a text frame node while holding down the Cmd key (Mac) or the Ctrl key (Windows). You can also scale editable text using the Scale and Free Transform tools.

Multiple objects selected with the Selection tool

Multiple objects selected with the Direct Selection tool and moved simultaneously

7.4 Selecting Type

To select editable type characters, you must use the Type tool. Click an insertion point in any text frame with the cursor, and then highlight the characters by clicking and dragging over them.

You can also select editable text by clicking with the mouse:

- Double-clicking selects a single word.
- Triple-clicking selects a line if the Triple Click To Select A Line option is enabled in Type Preferences; otherwise it selects the entire paragraph.
- Clicking four times selects the entire paragraph if the Triple Click To Select A Line option is enabled; otherwise it selects the entire story.
- Clicking five times selects the entire story when the Triple Click To Select A Line option is enabled in Type Preferences.

Click and drag over the text with the Type tool to select it.

To select all of the text in a story, click an insertion point with the Type tool cursor and then click five times, or press Command+A (Mac) or Ctrl+A (Windows).

Related Tasks

2.4 Edit Menu
3.6 Type Tools
5.2 Type Preferences
10.5 Copy/Paste Text Formatting

Shortcuts

Select a single character right or left
Mac and Win: Shift+Right arrow/Left arrow

Select one line above or below
Mac and Win: Shift+Up arrow/Down arrow

Select to start or end of Line
Mac and Win: Shift+Home/End

Select paragraph before or after
Mac: Shift+Cmd+Up arrow/Down arrow
Win: Shift+Ctrl+Up arrow/Down arrow

Select current line
Mac: Shift+Cmd+\
Win: Shift+Ctrl+\

Select to start or end of story
Mac: Shift+Cmd+Home/End
Win: Shift+Ctrl+Home/End

Tip

You can select editable text by clicking with the mouse in both layout and story editor views.

151

7.5 Drawing Rectangles, Ellipses, and Polygons

Related Tasks

3.9 Frame Tools
3.10 Shape Tools
4.11 Object and Layout Palettes
7.1 Frame/Shape Overview
7.6 Drawing Custom Shapes
7.7 Drawing Freeform Shapes
7.8 Modifying Paths and Frames

Shortcuts

Rectangle Frame tool
Mac and Win: F

Rectangle tool
Mac and Win: M

Ellipse tool
Mac and Win: L

Tip

When drawing a polygon shape, press the Up/Down arrow keys as you click and drag to increase/decrease the number of sides.

There are two ways to create rectangles, ellipses, and polygons with the shape and frame tools—by drawing them, or by entering settings into the tool's dialog.

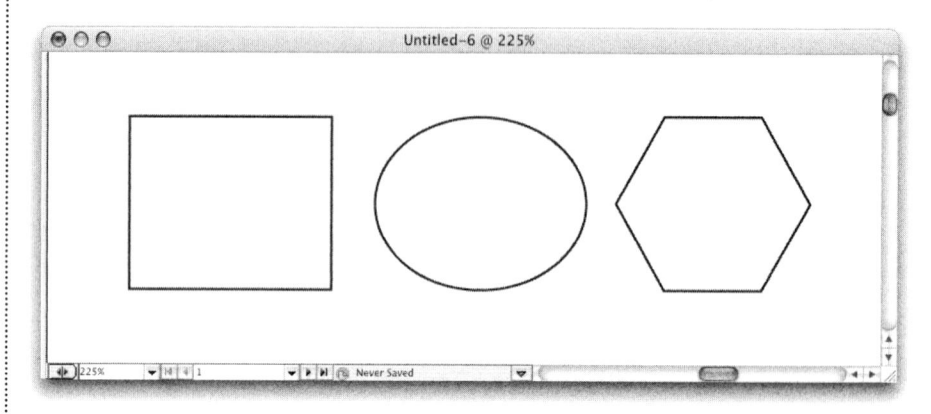

To draw a rectangle, ellipse, or polygon, choose the appropriate frame or shape tool and click and drag. If you hold down the Shift key as you draw, it constrains proportions, making a rectangle a perfect square and an ellipse a perfect circle (rather than an oval). Holding down the Alt or Option key allows you to draw from the center.

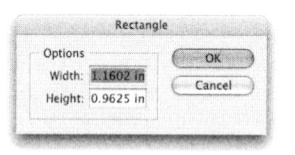

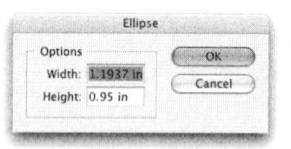

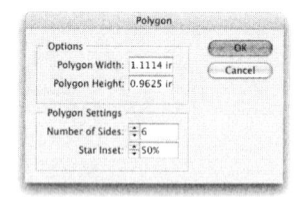

You can also create a rectangle, ellipse, or polygon frame or shape by clicking once on the Page with the tool and entering Width and Height settings in a dialog. Then, click OK for the shape to appear in the same spot as you clicked with the tool.

The Polygon dialog contains additional settings for Number Of Sides and Star Inset. Enter a number of sides and a percentage of inset for creating a star shape. You can access these default settings by double-clicking the tool icon in the Toolbox. (The shape dialogs are used to set parameters for a newly drawn shape, not for adjusting a selected shape.)

InDesign automatically applies default stroke settings to your shape, but you can always adjust them in either the Stroke palette or the Control bar. You can also add a fill, place a graphic, add some text, apply an object style, or use the Pathfinder controls to merge with other shapes. To change your shape entirely without having to redraw it, use the Convert Shape commands located under the Object menu or in the Pathfinder palette.

7.6 Drawing Custom Shapes

Using the Pen toolset, you can create custom drawn shapes just as you would in applications such as Adobe Illustrator or Macromedia FreeHand.

To start, press P to access the Pen tool, then click and drag to create a series of connecting points that result in a custom-drawn shape. Clicking with the Pen creates a point, and dragging with your mouse creates its curve in relation to the previous and next points placed on the path. Every curve contains its own set of control handles that can also be adjusted. Points, segments, and control handles can also be moved and modified using the Direct Selection tool.

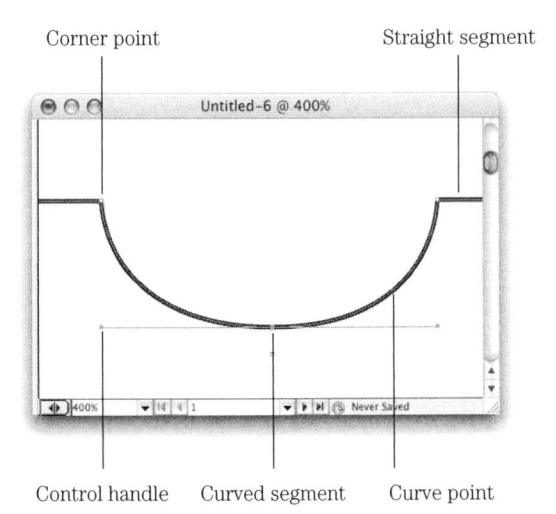

Corner point — Straight segment

You can create a corner point by clicking on an anchor point of a curved path with the Pen tool immediately after drawing it. Then press the Option/Alt key and drag to create a new control handle that is facing in a different direction. Click and drag again to create the next curved segment of the path.

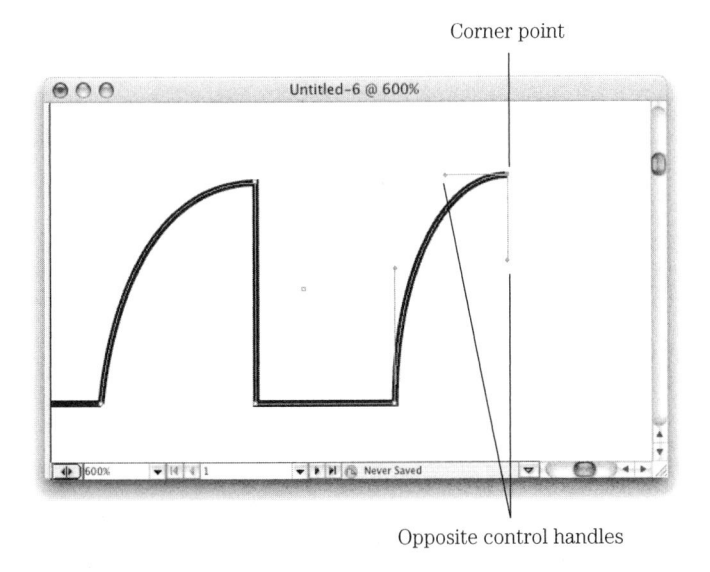

Control handle — Curved segment — Curve point

Corner point

Opposite control handles

Related Tasks

3.5 Pen Tools
7.7 Drawing Freeform Shapes
7.8 Modifying Paths and Frames

Shortcuts

Pen tool
Mac and Win: P

Add Anchor Point tool
Mac and Win: =

Delete Anchor Point tool
Mac and Win: -

Convert Direction Point tool
Mac and Win: Shift+C

Direct Selection tool
Mac and Win: A

Temporarily select Convert Direction Point tool
Mac: Pen tool+Opt, or Direct Selection tool+Opt+Cmd
Win: Pen tool+Alt, or Direct Selection tool+Alt+Ctrl

Temporarily switch between Add/Delete Anchor Point tools
Mac: Opt
Win: Alt

Tip

You can move an anchor point and its handles when drawing with the Pen tool. To do so, click to create a new point, hold the mouse button down, and then press the spacebar to move it.

7.7 Drawing Freeform Shapes

Related Tasks

3.4 Direct Selection and Position Tools
3.5 Pen Tools
3.7 Pencil Tools
3.8 Line Tool

Shortcuts

Pencil tool
Mac and Win: N

Pen tool
Mac and Win: P

Add Anchor Point tool
Mac and Win: =

Delete Anchor Point tool
Mac and Win: -

Convert Direction Point tool
Mac and Win: Shift+C

Line tool
Mac and Win: \

Direct Selection tool
Mac and Win: A

Tip

When drawing with the Pencil tool, press the Option/Alt key to temporarily access the Smooth tool.

To create a freeform shape using the Pencil tool, press N to access it from the Toolbox and begin drawing. As you draw, InDesign calculates where the points fall on the path and places them for you. You can then switch to the Pen toolset and adjust the placed points, or use the Smooth and Erase tools to edit.

Entering specific settings in the Pencil Tool Preferences dialog before you begin drawing can eliminate the need for editing and smoothing of points later. To access the dialog, double-click the Pencil tool icon in the Toolbox.

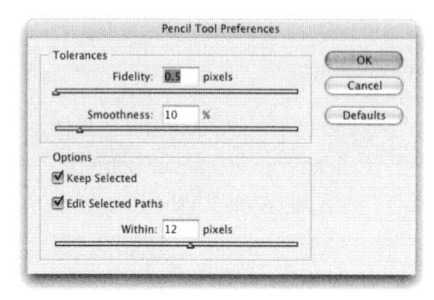

Lower Fidelity and Smoothness values result in jagged paths.

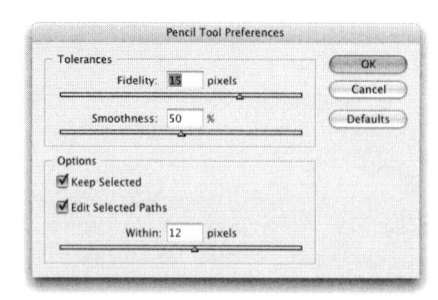

Higher Fidelity and Smoothness values result in cleaner paths.

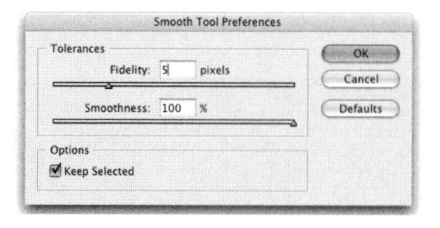

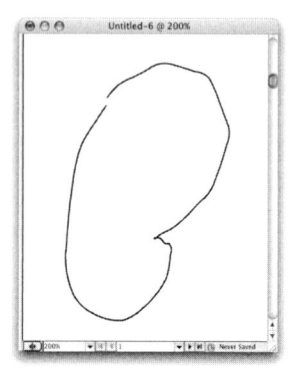

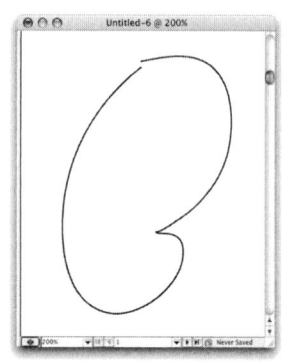

The Smooth tool has a similar set of preferences that you can access by double-clicking the Smooth tool icon in the Toolbox.

Drawing with the Pencil tool often results in open path shapes. To close a path quickly, select it and choose Object > Paths > Close Path, or click the Pathfinder Palette Close Path control.

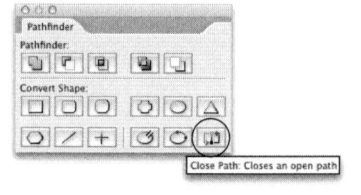

154

7.8 Modifying Paths and Frames

The cursors for the Direct Selection and Pen tools change as you position them over different points and segments of a path:

	Start a new path		Convert a direction point
	Create a corner point		Snap point to a guide
	Add an anchor point		Move or modify a point
	Close a path		Move or modify a segment
	Delete an anchor point		Move or extend a control handle

Adding and Deleting Points

You can add points to a path or frame using the Add Anchor Point tool. Doing so allows you to add intricate curves, corners, and bends to your shape or frame. Click anywhere along the path to add a new point.

You can delete points using the Delete Anchor Point tool. To do so, just click any existing point. But keep in mind that deleting points can drastically change the appearance of a shape or frame.

It is also possible to delete an anchor point by selecting it with the Direct Selection tool and pressing the Delete/Backspace key. Doing so results in an open path, whereas using the Delete Anchor Point tool does not.

Converting Point Direction

Use the Convert Direction Point tool to change the direction of a selected point's curve on an existing path. Click any existing point to reset the curve handles. Click and drag the handles to change the curve.

Cutting, Joining, and Closing Paths

Use the Scissors tool to cut points and lines on a path. You can create open paths, divide symmetrical shapes such as half-circles or diamonds, or remove pieces of a path or frame to create interesting logo effects and design elements.

Related Tasks

3.4 Direct Selection and Position Tools
3.5 Pen Tools
3.7 Pencil Tools
3.9 Frame Tools
3.10 Shape Tools
3.19 Scissors Tool
4.11 Object and Layout Palettes

Shortcuts

Direct Selection tool
Mac and Win: A

Pencil tool
Mac and Win: N

Pen tool
Mac and Win: P

Add Anchor Point tool
Mac and Win: =

7.8 Modifying Paths and Frames (continued)

Related Tasks

7.1 Frame/Shape Overview

7.2 Selection Tool vs. Direct Selection Tool

7.5 Drawing Rectangles, Ellipses, and Polygons

7.6 Drawing Custom Shapes

7.7 Drawing Freeform Shapes

7.20 Applying and Editing Compound Paths

7.21 Creating Custom Shapes with Pathfinder

Shortcuts

Delete Anchor Point tool
Mac and Win: -

Convert Direction Point tool
Mac and Win: Shift+C

Scissors tool
Mac and Win: C

Tip

When working with the Scissors Tool, press the Option (Mac) or Alt (Windows) key to temporarily access the Add Anchor Point tool.

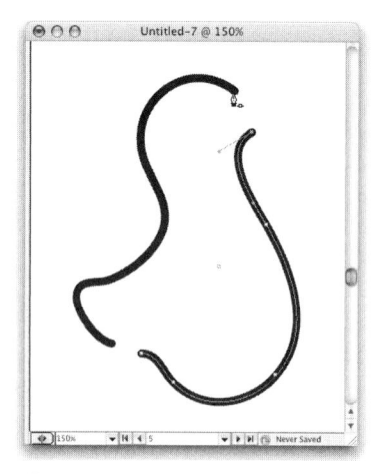

To join two line segments or open paths, select one with the Direct Selection tool, press P to switch to the Pen tool, and then click the endpoint you would like to merge.

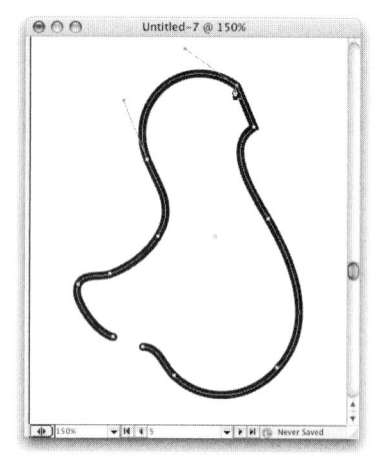

Hover the Pen tool cursor over the endpoint of another path until you see the Join Two Paths cursor appear and then click. The two paths are now joined!

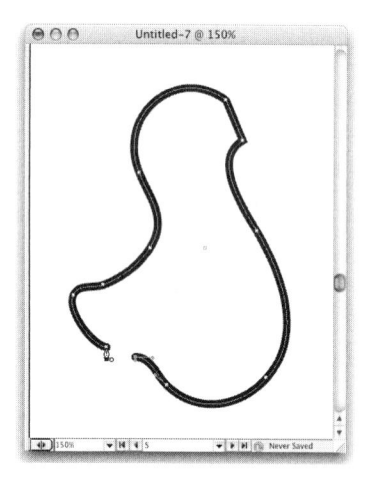

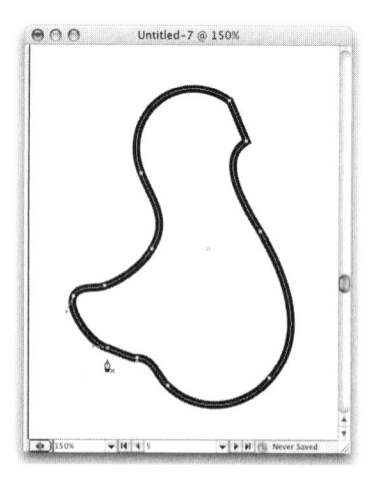

To close the open path, click one of the remaining two endpoints with the Pen tool. Hover the Pen tool cursor over the other endpoint until you see the Close A Path cursor appear and click.

To further enhance a shape or frame, you can add, smooth, or erase points using the Pencil toolset, as well as add a fill, place a graphic, add some text, apply or save an object style, or use the Pathfinder controls to merge with other shapes. You can also change the shape entirely by applying one of the Convert Shape commands/controls located under the Object menu or in the Pathfinder palette.

156

7.9 Nesting Objects

Objects can be nested inside one another to create interesting design and logo effects. Nested objects placed in a text frame are also referred to as anchored objects. Objects can be nested as deep as you like (an object placed inside an object, placed inside an object, etc.), but multiple objects cannot be nested without grouping them first.

Nested Objects

You can create a nested object by copy/pasting a graphic frame, text frame, or path *into* another graphic frame, text frame, or path. Select an object with the Selection tool (graphic frame, text frame, or path) and copy or cut it to the Clipboard. Then select another object and choose Edit > Paste Into for the object to appear nested inside the frame or path.

Two separate objects: a body of editable text with a gradient applied to it and some bold characters that have been converted to outlines, made into a compound path, and filled with black

To select an object after it has been pasted into another frame or path, click the nested object's frame edge with the Direct Selection tool and then press V to switch to the Selection tool. You can then resize the frame, move it, or nudge it with the arrow keys. Switch back to the Direct Selection tool to resize, move, or nudge the nested components. Switch to the Type tool to select and edit nested text.

The gradient text frame nested inside the compound character path

Related Tasks

2.4 Edit Menu
3.3 Selection Tool
3.4 Direct Selection and Position Tools

Shortcuts

Copy to Clipboard
Mac: Cmd+C
Win: Ctrl+C

Paste Into
Mac: Opt+Cmd+V
Win: Alt+Ctrl+V

Cut to Clipboard
Mac: Cmd+X
Win: Ctrl+X

7.9 Nesting Objects *(continued)*

Related Tasks

3.9 Frame Tools
3.10 Shape Tools
7.1 Frame/Shape Overview

Shortcuts

Rectangle Frame tool
Mac and Win: F

Rectangle tool
Mac and Win: M

Anchored Objects

To place an anchored object into a body of text:

1 Select a graphic frame, text frame, or path with the Selection tool and copy or cut it to the Clipboard.

2 Press T to switch to the Type tool and click an insertion point.

3 Choose Edit **>** Paste to anchor the object in the line of text.

Another way to create an anchored object is through the Insert command located under the Anchored Object submenu. Inserting this way provides many additional options, such as the ability to place an anchored object above or beside a text column.

Select the empty frame and place some contents into it using the Place or Paste Into command, or add text to it with the Type tool.

You can select an anchored object by clicking the frame with either selection tool. It is possible to resize an anchored frame, but you can only move it up or down. You can resize and reposition an anchored frame's contents (graphic or text) however you like.

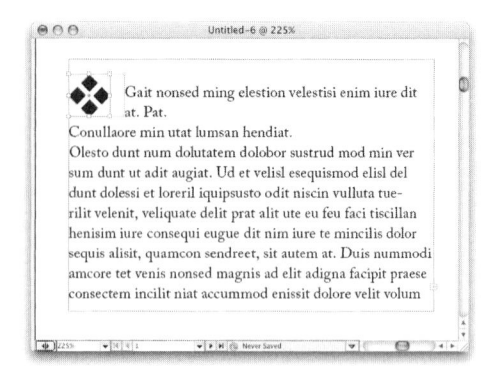

A small graphic object pasted into a body of placeholder text

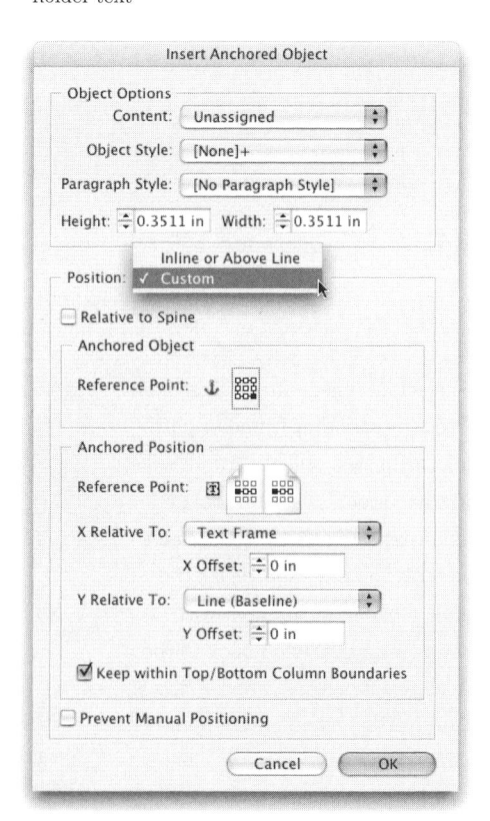

Place the Type tool cursor inside of a text frame and choose Object **>** Anchored Object **>** Insert. When the dialog appears, choose the preferred settings and click OK.

7.9 Nesting Objects *(continued)*

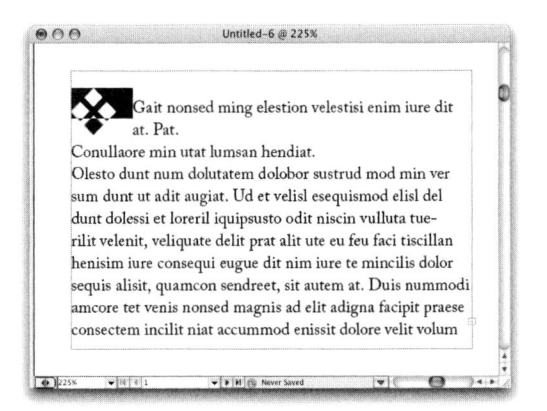

By highlighting an anchored object with the Type tool, you can apply text attributes such as kerning and baseline shift. Click and drag with the Type tool to select an anchored object and adjust it just as you would any other editable text character.

To make adjustments to an existing anchored object using the Anchored Object Options dialog, select it with either selection tool or the Type tool and choose Object >Anchored Object > Options. Enter the preferred settings in the dialog and click OK to apply.

Related Tasks

7.2 Selection Tool vs. Direct Selection Tool

8.8 Nesting Grouped Objects

Shortcuts

Ellipse tool
Mac and Win: L

Selection tool
Mac and Win: V

Direct Selection tool
Mac and Win: A

Tip

You can apply a text wrap to an anchored object.

159

7.10 Filling with Solid and Transparent Colors

Related Tasks

4.5 Color Palette
4.17 Swatches Palette
4.20 Transparency Palette
7.12 Filling Text
14.5 Accessing Colors Stored in Libraries
14.6 Converting Spot Colors to Process
14.7 Importing Colors from Other Documents

Shortcuts

Color palette
Mac and Win: F6

Swatches palette
Mac and Win: F5

Transparency palette
Mac and Win: Shift+F10

Color Picker
Mac and Win: Double-click Fill/Stroke swatch in Color palette or Toolbox

Switch to default colors
Mac and Win: D

Swap Fill/Stroke colors
Mac and Win: X

Switch color modes (CMYK, RGB, Lab)
Mac and Win: Shift-click Tint Ramp/Spectrum in Color palette

Tips

Shift-drag to move the color sliders in the Color palette or Swatch Options dialog in tandem.

There are five methods for applying fill color. To start, bring the Fill swatch to the forefront by clicking it in one of three places: at the bottom of the Toolbox, at the top of the Swatches palette, or in the Color palette. Then with either selection tool, proceed to select any frame, shape, or path (or any combination thereof) and apply the fill color using any one of the five following methods:

- Click directly on a swatch name in the Swatches palette.
- Create a color using the Color palette.
- Choose a color using the Color Picker and click OK.
- Choose and apply a sampled color with the Eyedropper tool (this also samples and applies all other object style attributes).
- Click the Apply (Last Used) Color button located at the bottom of the Toolbox, or press the comma key.

In every instance, the chosen Fill color is applied to all selected objects. Note: Applying a fill color *does not* automatically add the chosen color to the Swatches palette.

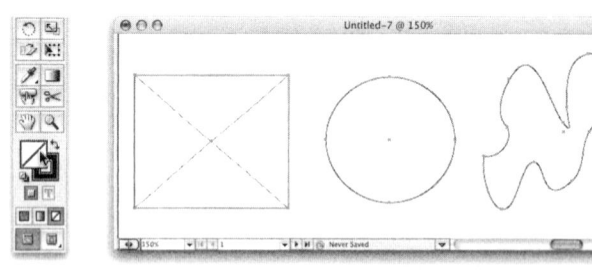

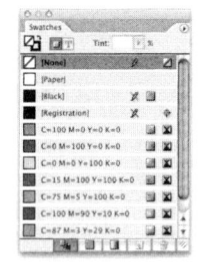

A selected frame, shape, and path—each with a Fill color of None

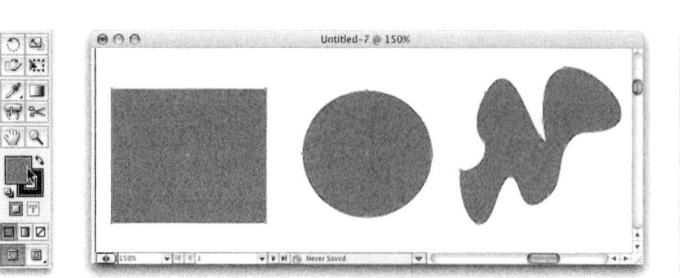

The same objects with Fill color applied using any of the five methods described above

7.11 Filling with Gradients

There are five methods for applying a gradient fill. As with solid color and transparent fills, you must bring the Fill swatch to the forefront by clicking it in one of three places: at the bottom of the Toolbox, at the top of the Swatches palette, or in the Color palette. Then with either selection tool, proceed to select any frame, shape, or path (or any combination thereof), and apply the gradient fill using any one of the following methods:

- Click directly on a gradient swatch name in the Swatches palette.
- Create a gradient using the Gradient palette.
- Choose and apply a sampled gradient with the Eyedropper tool (this also samples and applies all other object style attributes).
- Click the Apply (Last Used) Gradient button located at the bottom of the Toolbox, or press the period key.
- Apply a gradient chosen from the Swatches palette or created in the Gradient palette by clicking and dragging with the Gradient tool.

In every instance except the last, the chosen gradient fill is applied to all selected objects separately. To apply the same gradient across multiple selected objects, use the Gradient tool method described in the last bullet. Note: Applying a gradient fill *does not* automatically add the sampled or created gradient to the Swatches palette. Gradient fills can also be applied to editable text.

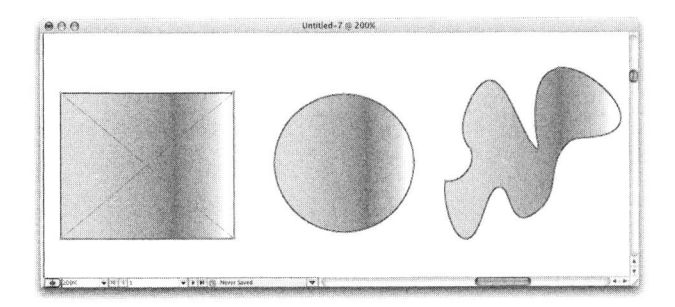

A frame, shape, and path each with a gradient fill color applied using the first four methods described above

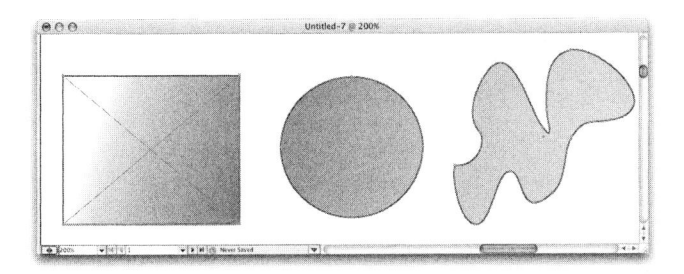

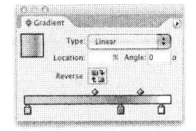

Applying the same gradient across multiple selected objects using the Gradient tool method

Related Tasks

3.3	Selection Tool
3.4	Direct Selection and Position Tools
3.9	Frame Tools
3.10	Shape Tools
3.17	Gradient Tool
3.22	Other Toolbox Functions
4.6	Gradient Palette
4.17	Swatches Palette

Shortcuts

Swatches palette
Mac and Win: F5

Object Styles palette
Mac: Cmd+F7
Win: Ctrl+F7

Color Picker
Mac and Win: Double-click Fill/Stroke Swatch in Color palette or Toolbox

Switch to default colors
Mac and Win: D

Swap fill/stroke colors
Mac and Win: X

Switch color modes (CMYK, RGB, LAB)
Mac and Win: Shift-click Tint Ramp/Spectrum in Color palette

Tip

To view a list of only the document gradient swatches (not solid colors or tints), click the Show Gradient Swatches footer control located at the bottom of the Swatches palette.

7.12 Filling Text

Related Tasks

3.3	Selection Tool
3.4	Direct Selection and Position Tools
3.6	Type Tools
3.17	Gradient Tool
3.22	Other Toolbox Functions
4.5	Color Palette

Shortcuts

Swatches palette
Mac and Win: F5

Color Picker
Mac and Win: Double-click Fill/Stroke Swatch in Color palette or Toolbox

Switch to default colors
Mac and Win: D

There are five methods for applying a fill color or gradient to editable text. To start, bring the Fill swatch to the forefront by clicking it in one of three places: at the bottom of the Toolbox, at the top of the Swatches palette, or in the Color palette.

How the color is applied depends on how the text is selected. To apply a fill color or gradient to all editable text in the story, select any text frame (or frames) with either selection tool, and click the Formatting Affects Text button located at the bottom of the Toolbox, at the top of the Swatches palette, or in the Color palette. To apply a fill color to specific characters within a story, highlight them with the Type tool cursor.

Once the characters are selected, use any one of the five following methods to apply a fill color:

- Click directly on a color or gradient swatch name in the Swatches palette.
- Create a color or gradient using their respective palettes.
- Choose a color using the Color Picker and click OK.
- Choose and apply a sampled color or gradient fill with the Eyedropper tool (this also samples and applies all other object style attributes).
- Click the Apply (Last Used) Color or Gradient button located at the bottom of the Toolbox, or press the comma key (color) or period key (gradient).

In every instance, the chosen fill color or gradient is applied to all selected type characters. Note: Applying a fill color or gradient *does not* automatically add the chosen color or gradient to the Swatches palette.

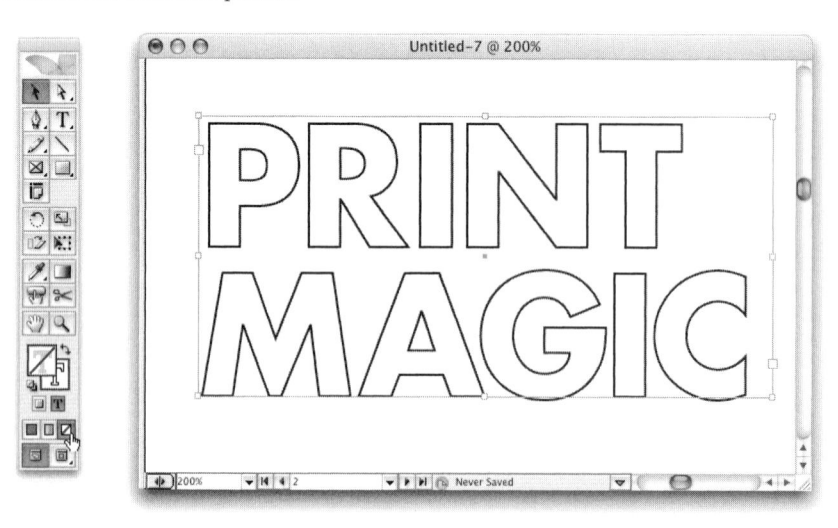

A selected text frame with a fill color of None and a 1-point black stroke applied to all of its characters

162

7.12 Filling Text *(continued)*

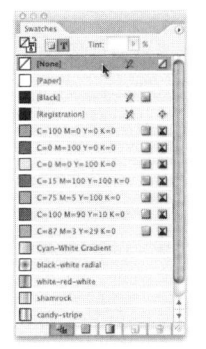

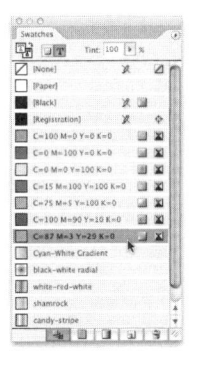

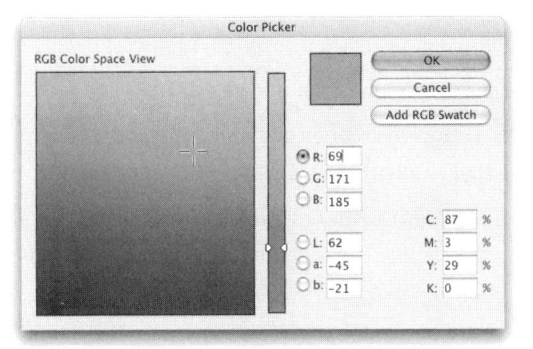

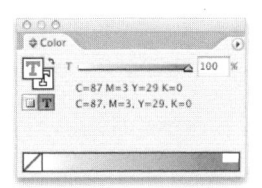

The same text frame with a fill color applied to all the characters

Related Tasks

4.6 Gradient Palette

4.17 Swatches Palette

7.10 Filling with Solid and Transparent Colors

7.11 Filling with Gradients

11.1 Creating and Applying Character Styles

11.2 Creating and Applying Paragraph Styles

Shortcuts

Swap fill/stroke colors
Mac and Win: X

Switch color modes (CMYK, RGB, LAB)
Mac and Win: Shift-click Tint Ramp/Spectrum in Color palette

Eyedropper tool
Mac and Win: I

Type tool
Mac and Win: T

Tip

To create a new swatch based on the one currently selected in the Swatches palette, Option/Alt-click the New Swatch button located at the bottom of the Swatches palette.

TINT VS. TRANSPARENCY

The Fill color of a selected object (or objects) can be made transparent by adjusting the Opacity control located in the Transparency palette. This is not to be confused with the Tint control located in the Swatches palette. Although both controls can appear to lighten a selected fill color, lowering the Opacity value also allows you to see through the object—something the Tint control does not do. For visual examples of these differences, please refer to the color section.

163

7.13 Stroking Frames, Shapes, and Paths

Related Tasks

3.3	Selection Tool
3.4	Direct Selection and Position Tools
3.5	Pen Tools
3.7	Pencil Tools
3.9	Frame Tools
3.10	Shape Tools
3.22	Other Toolbox Functions
4.5	Color Palette
4.6	Gradient Palette

Shortcuts

Stroke palette
Mac and Win: F10

Swatches palette
Mac and Win: F5

Color palette
Mac and Win: F6

Object Styles palette
Mac: Cmd+F7
Win: Ctrl+F7

Color Picker
Mac and Win: Double-click Fill/Stroke Swatch in Color palette or toolbox

To apply a color or gradient stroke to a selected frame, shape, or path, bring the Stroke swatch to the forefront by clicking it in one of three places: at the bottom of the Toolbox, at the top of the Swatches palette, or in the Color palette.

Choose a stroke style and weight in either the Control bar or the Stroke palette. Other stroke options, including alignment, start/end styles, and gap color, can be set in the Stroke palette.

With either selection tool, proceed to select any frame, shape, or path (or any combination thereof) and apply a color or gradient to the stroke using any one of the five following methods:

- Click directly on a color or gradient swatch name in the Swatches palette.
- Create a color or gradient using their respective palettes.
- Choose a color using the Color Picker and click OK.
- Choose and apply a sampled color or gradient stroke with the Eyedropper tool (this also samples and applies all other object style attributes).
- Click the Apply (Last Used) Color or Gradient button located at the bottom of the Toolbox, or press the comma key (color) or period key (gradient).

7.13 Stroking Frames, Shapes, and Paths *(continued)*

In every instance, the chosen color or gradient is applied to the stroke of all selected objects. Note: Applying a stroke color or gradient *does not* automatically add the chosen color or gradient to the Swatches palette.

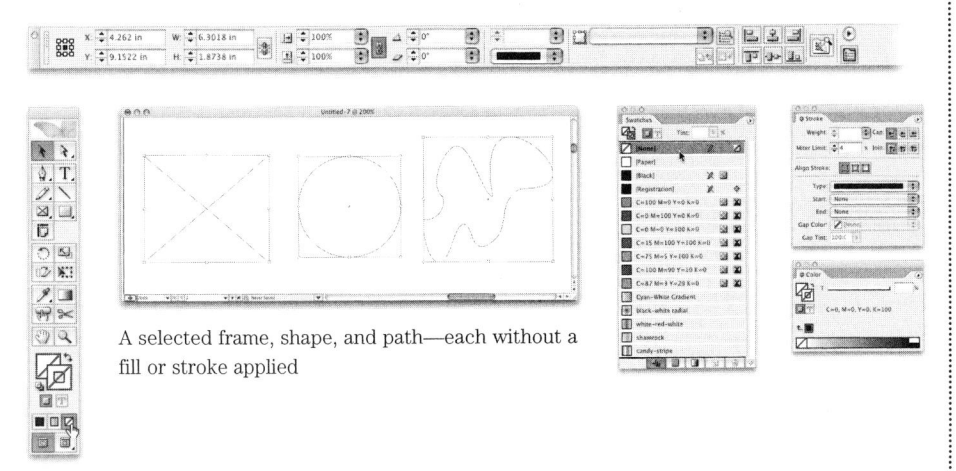

A selected frame, shape, and path—each without a fill or stroke applied

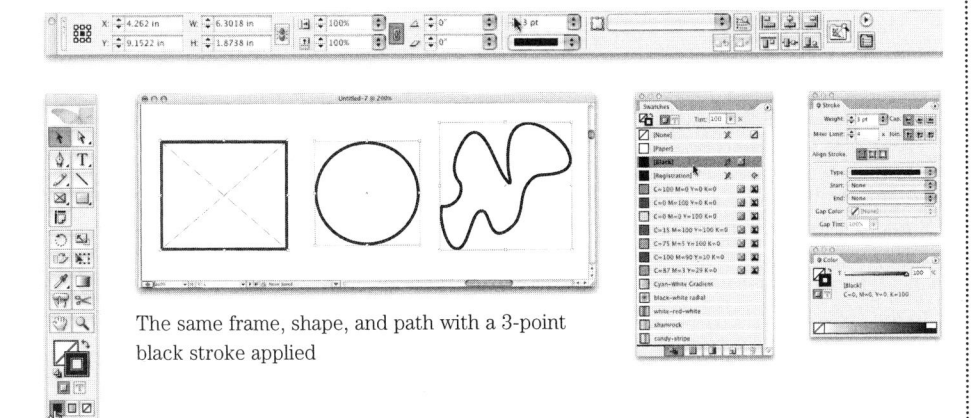

The same frame, shape, and path with a 3-point black stroke applied

Related Tasks

4.16 Stroke Palette
4.17 Swatches Palette
7.13 Stroking Frames, Shapes, and Paths
7.14 Stroking Text
7.15 Aligning Strokes
7.16 Applying Stroked Path Start and End Styles
7.17 Saving and Applying Custom Strokes
7.18 Applying Gap Color to Open Stroke Styles
11.5 Creating and Applying Object Styles

Shortcuts

Switch to default colors
Mac and Win: D

Swap fill/stroke colors
Mac and Win: X

Switch color modes (CMYK, RGB, LAB)
Mac and Win: Shift-click Tint Ramp/Spectrum in Color palette

Eyedropper tool
Mac and Win: I

Tip

Stroke styles can be copied and applied using the Eyedropper tool.

165

7.14 Stroking Text

Related Tasks

4.16 Stroke Palette
4.17 Swatches Palette
7.13 Stroking Frames, Shapes, and Paths
7.15 Aligning Strokes
7.17 Saving and Applying Custom Strokes
7.18 Applying Gap Color to Open Stroke Styles

Shortcuts

Stroke palette
Mac and Win: F10

Swatches palette
Mac and Win: F5

Color palette
Mac and Win: F6

Color Picker
Mac and Win: Double-click Fill/Stroke Swatch in Color palette or toolbox

Switch to default colors
Mac and Win: D

Swap fill/stroke colors
Mac and Win: X

Switch color modes (CMYK, RGB, LAB)
Mac and Win: Shift-click Tint Ramp/Spectrum in Color palette

Type tool
Mac and Win: T

Tip

You cannot apply a tint value to strokes placed on editable text characters.

To apply a color or gradient stroke to editable text, bring the Stroke swatch to the forefront by clicking on it in one of three places: at the bottom of the Toolbox, at the top of the Swatches palette, or in the Color palette. Enter a stroke weight in either the Control bar or the Stroke palette.

How the color or gradient is applied to the stroke depends on how the text is selected. To apply a color or gradient stroke to all editable text in a story, select any text frame (or frames) with either selection tool, and click the Formatting Affects Text button located at the bottom of the Toolbox, at the top of the Swatches palette, or in the Color palette. To apply a stroke to specific characters within a story, highlight them with the Type tool cursor.

Once the characters are selected, use any one of the five following methods to apply a color or gradient to the stroke:

- Click directly on a color or gradient swatch name in the Swatches palette.
- Create a color or gradient using their respective palettes.
- Choose a color using the Color Picker and click OK.
- Choose and apply a sampled color or gradient stroke with the Eyedropper tool (this also samples all other object style attributes applied).
- Click the Apply (Last Used) Color or Gradient button located at the bottom of the Toolbox, or press the comma key (color) or period key (gradient).

In every instance, the chosen color or gradient is applied to the stroke of all selected type characters. Note: Applying a stroke color or gradient *does not* automatically add the chosen color or gradient to the Swatches palette.

A 1-point black stroke applied to all the characters in a text frame

166

7.15 Aligning Strokes

You can choose a specific alignment when applying a stroke to a frame, shape, or path, but not when applying a stroke to editable text. To align a stroke to the center, inside, or outside a selected object, click one of the three alignment buttons located in the Stroke palette.

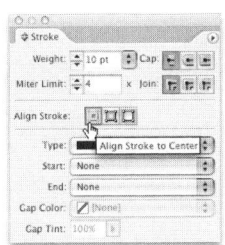

A 10-point stroke aligned to the center

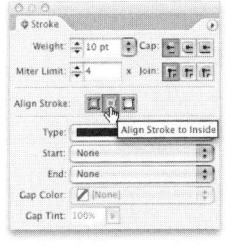

A 10-point stroke aligned to the inside

Related Tasks

3.3 Selection Tool

3.4 Direct Selection and Position Tools

3.5 Pen Tools

3.7 Pencil Tools

3.8 Line Tool

Shortcuts

Stroke palette
Mac and Win: F10

Object Styles palette
Mac: Cmd+F7
Win: Ctrl+F7

Rectangle Frame tool
Mac and Win: F

Rectangle tool
Mac and Win: M

Ellipse tool
Mac and Win: L

7.15 Aligning Strokes *(continued)*

Related Tasks

4.16   Stroke Palette

4.17   Swatches Palette

7.17   Saving and Applying Custom Strokes

7.18   Applying Gap Color to Open Stroke Styles

11.5   Creating and Applying Object Styles

Shortcuts

Selection tool
Mac and Win: V

Direct Selection tool
Mac and Win: A

Eyedropper tool
Mac and Win: I

Pen tool
Mac and Win: P

Pencil tool
Mac and Win: N

Tip

To maintain legibility, it's usually best to align thick strokes to the outside of any text that has been converted to outlines.

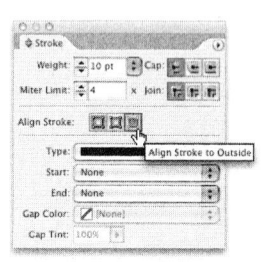

A 10-point stroke aligned to the outside

TEXT GLOW EFFECT

To create an interesting text glow effect in InDesign, try duplicating a text frame that contains some large, headline style text. Then, on the original text frame (behind the duplicate), place a thick color stroke and a None fill. Choose Object > Feather and soften the edges of the stroked text using the controls in the Feather dialog. When you're ready, click OK to apply the feather. If you like, nudge the feathered text frame using the arrow keys until it is slightly offset behind the duplicate text layer.

7.16 Applying Stroked Path Start and End Styles

To apply a stroke start and end style to a selected line or path, open the Stroke palette and choose from the Start and End menu lists. The chosen style is immediately applied. You can apply a start style without an end style and vice versa—or apply both—so have fun experimenting with different combinations.

Start and end styles can be applied with any chosen stroke type, but cannot be saved as part of a Stroke Style. However, to make up for it, they can be saved as part of an object style.

Keep in mind that stroked path start and end styles can be applied to any open custom and freeform drawn paths and lines, which makes it possible to get really creative with your design elements.

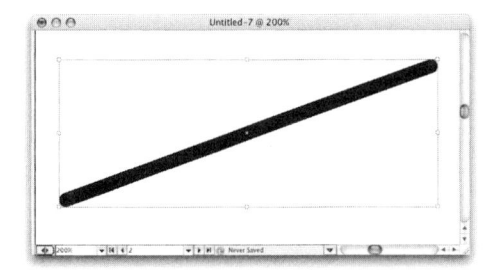

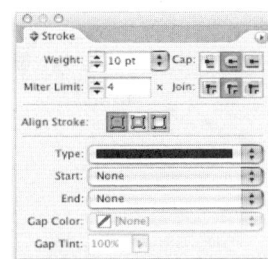

Related Tasks

3.3 Selection Tool
3.4 Direct Selection and Position Tools
3.5 Pen Tools
3.7 Pencil Tools
3.8 Line Tool

Shortcuts

Stroke palette
Mac and Win: F10

Object Styles palette
Mac: Cmd+F7
Win: Ctrl+F7

Rectangle Frame tool
Mac and Win: F

Rectangle tool
Mac and Win: M

Ellipse tool
Mac and Win: L

A diagonal line with a 10-point black stroke and Round Caps applied

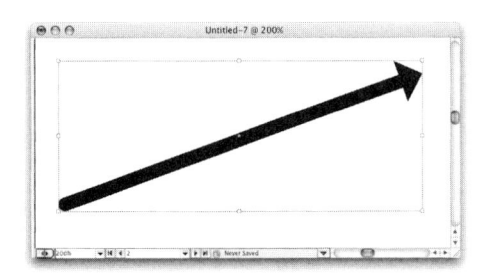

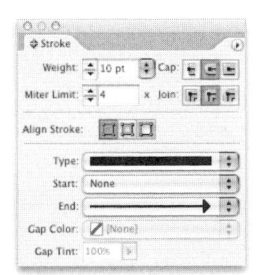

The same line with the TriangleWide end style applied

7.16 Applying Stroked Path Start and End Styles *(continued)*

Related Tasks

4.16 Stroke Palette

4.17 Swatches Palette

7.17 Saving and Applying Custom Strokes

7.18 Applying Gap Color to Open Stroke Styles

11.5 Creating and Applying Object Styles

Shortcuts

Selection tool
Mac and Win: V

Direct Selection tool
Mac and Win: A

Eyedropper tool
Mac and Win: I

Pen tool
Mac and Win: P

Pencil tool
Mac and Win: N

Tip

Start and end styles can only be applied to lines and open paths—not closed paths, frames, and shapes.

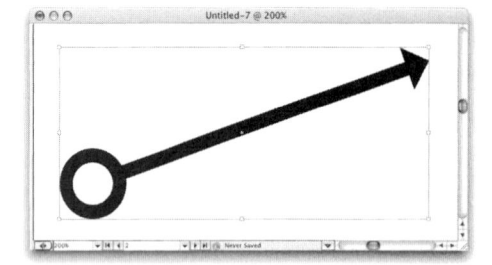

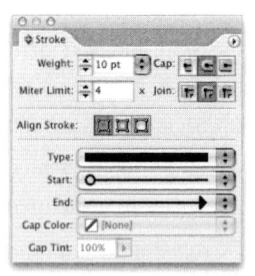

Our new design element after applying the Circle start style

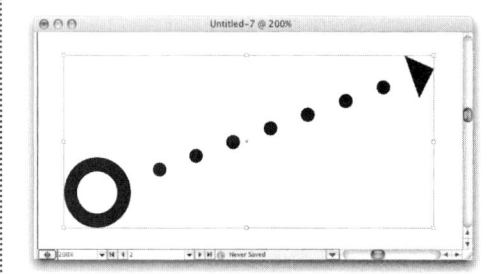

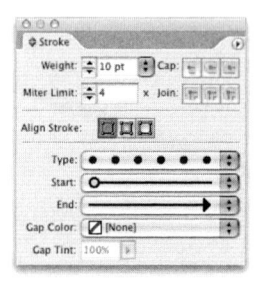

Taking it one step further by changing the stroke Type to Dotted

7.17 Saving and Applying Custom Strokes

One of the hidden features of InDesign is the ability to create, save, and apply custom stroke styles.

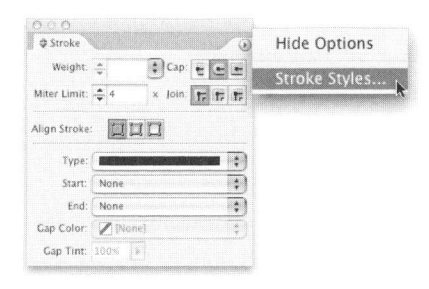

To create a custom stripe, dash, or dotted stroke, click the menu button on the Stroke palette and choose Stroke Styles. The Stroke Styles dialog appears and displays a list of noneditable default stroke styles. Click the New button to create a whole new stroke style.

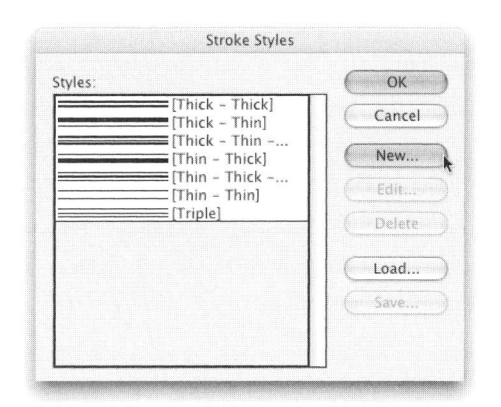

When the New Stroke Style dialog opens, click the stroke Type menu and choose Stripe, Dash, or Dotted. Each one has its own set of controls that displays in the dialog once selected.

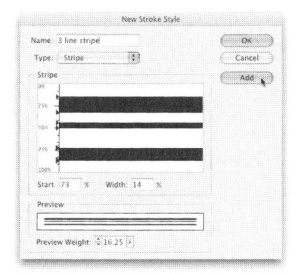

A custom, three-line stripe stroke style

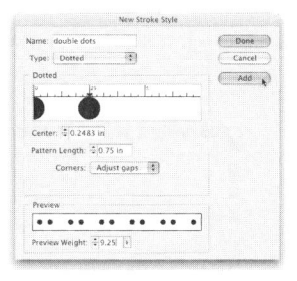

A custom, double dotted style

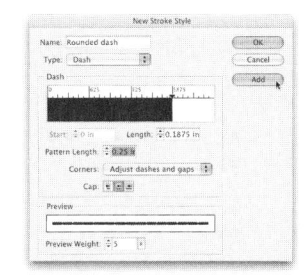

A custom, rounded dash style

The Type and Preview sections of the dialog change when a selection is made from the stroke Type menu. Enter the preferred settings and refer to the window below for a preview of how the stroke will look once applied. When you're ready to save your style, enter a name for it and click the Add button.

InDesign displays your new styles at the bottom of the Stroke Styles dialog Styles list. When you've finished creating and editing, click OK.

To apply your new stroke style, select any frame, shape, or path with either selection tool and choose it from the Stroke palette Type list.

Related Tasks

- 3.5 Pen Tools
- 3.7 Pencil Tools
- 3.8 Line Tool
- 4.16 Stroke Palette
- 4.17 Swatches Palette
- 7.13 Stroking Frames, Shapes, and Paths
- 7.14 Stroking Text
- 7.15 Aligning Strokes
- 7.16 Applying Stroked Path Start and End Styles
- 7.18 Applying Gap Color to Open Stroke Styles

Shortcuts

Stroke palette
Mac and Win: F10

Pen tool
Mac and Win: P

Pencil tool
Mac and Win: N

Tips

You can assign a keyboard shortcut for accessing the Stroke Styles dialog under Edit > Keyboard Shortcuts. In the dialog, select Palette Menus from the Product Area menu, and Stroke: Stroke Styles from the Commands list. Enter your shortcut in the New Shortcut field and click OK.

You can save and load custom stroke styles to be used with other InDesign documents.

Related Tasks

3.3 Selection Tool
3.4 Direct Selection and Position Tools
3.5 Pen Tools
3.7 Pencil Tools
3.8 Line Tool
3.15 Eyedropper Tool
4.16 Stroke Palette
4.17 Swatches Palette

Shortcuts

Stroke palette
Mac and Win: F10

Object Styles palette
Mac: Cmd+F7
Win: Ctrl+F7

Rectangle Frame tool
Mac and Win: F

Rectangle tool
Mac and Win: M

Ellipse tool
Mac and Win: L

7.18 Applying Gap Color to Open Stroke Styles

Open stroke styles contain gaps between stripes, dashes, or dots. These gaps can be filled with solid colors, tints, or gradients. Try experimenting with this some and you'll find that combining gap color with stroke color can create some interesting effects.

To apply gap color to an open stroke style, select the stroked object with either selection tool and choose a color or gradient from the Gap Color menu located in the Stroke palette. The Gap Color menu contains the same colors and gradients as the Swatches palette.

To apply a tint to a chosen gap color, enter a value in the Gap Tint field located at the bottom of the Stroke palette or use the slider control. A tint can only be applied to solid colors and not gradients.

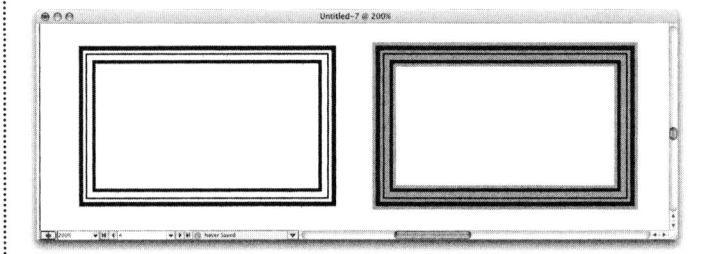

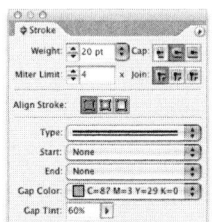

A rectangle frame before (left) and after (right) applying a tinted gap color

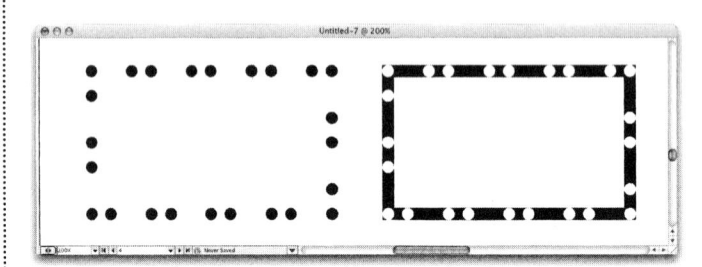

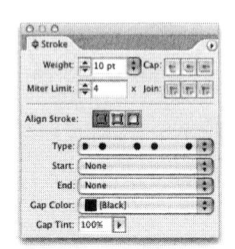

A rectangle frame before and after applying gap color to a custom, dotted stroke style. In this example, gap color is set to 100% black and stroke color to 100% white.

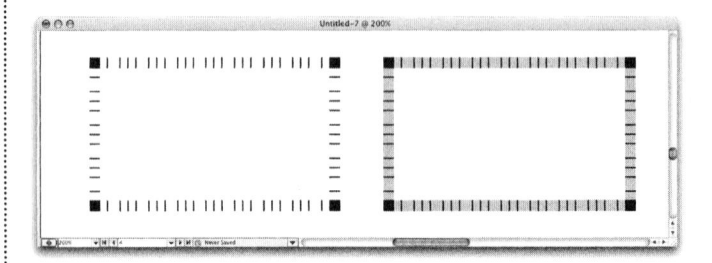

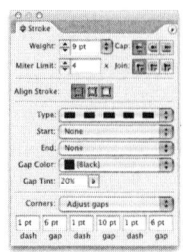

A rectangle frame before and after applying a tinted gap color to a custom, dashed stroke style. Gap color is set to 20% opaque black and stroke color to 100% black. Notice the custom dash and gap settings located at the bottom of the Stroke palette.

7.18 Applying Gap Color to Open Stroke Styles *(continued)*

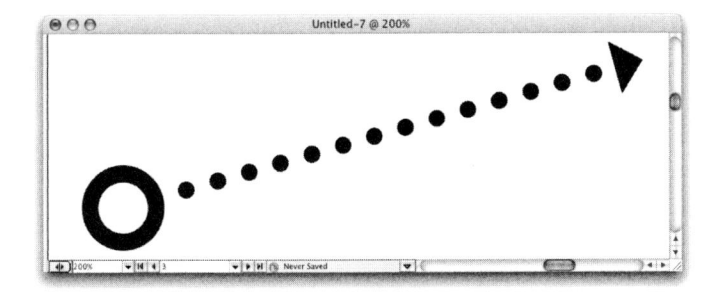

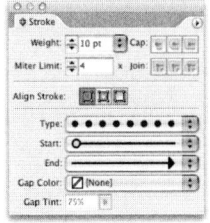

A 100% solid black diagonal line with a 10-point dotted stroke style and two different start and end styles applied

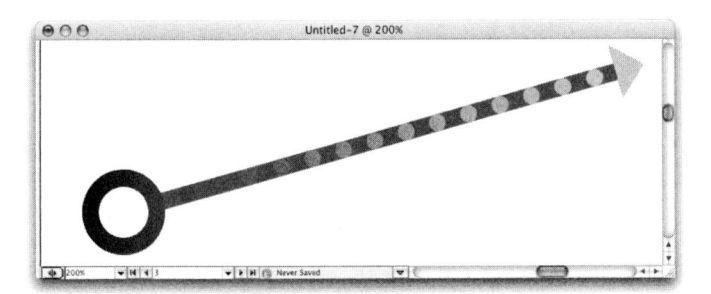

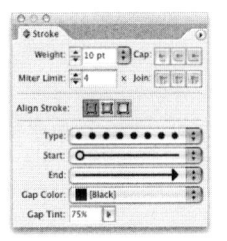

The same design element with a linear gradient chosen as the stroke color and a tinted gap color of 75% opaque black applied

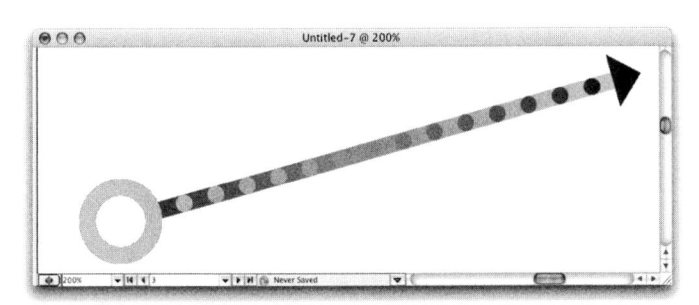

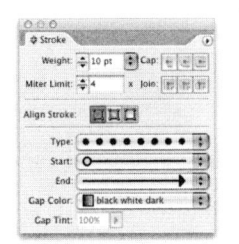

Once more with two reversed gradients applied as stroke and gap color

Related Tasks

7.13 Stroking Frames, Shapes, and Paths

7.14 Stroking Text

7.15 Aligning Strokes

7.16 Applying Stroked Path Start and End Styles

7.18 Applying Gap Color to Open Stroke Styles

11.5 Creating and Applying Object Styles

Shortcuts

Selection tool
Mac and Win: V

Direct Selection tool
Mac and Win: A

Eyedropper tool
Mac and Win: I

Pen tool
Mac and Win: P

Pencil tool
Mac and Win: N

Tip

You can apply a gradient swatch to a stroke's gap color.

7.19 Applying Corner Effects

Related Tasks

4.16 Stroke Palette
4.17 Swatches Palette
7.13 Stroking Frames, Shapes, and Paths
7.14 Stroking Text
7.15 Aligning Strokes
7.18 Applying Gap Color to Open Stroke Styles
11.5 Creating and Applying Object Styles

Shortcuts

Stroke palette
Mac and Win: F10

Object Styles palette
Mac: Cmd+F7
Win: Ctrl+F7

Rectangle Frame tool
Mac and Win: F

Rectangle tool
Mac and Win: M

Selection tool
Mac and Win: V

Direct Selection tool
Mac and Win: A

Eyedropper tool
Mac and Win: I

Pen tool
Mac and Win: P

Tip

A placed photo does not require that its frame container have a stroke placed on it in order to apply corner effects.

You can apply any one of the six default corner effects to any selected frame, shape, or path. To access the dialog, select the object with either selection tool and choose Object > Corner Effects. When the dialog opens, choose Fancy, Bevel, Inset, Inverse Rounded, or Rounded from the Effect menu. Enter an amount for Size and check the Preview box to see the effect before applying. When you're ready, click OK to apply the corner effect.

Applying corner effects does not permanently change an object. You can change the size, try a different effect, or turn them off at any time. To turn off corner effects for a selected object, select None from the Corner Effects dialog's Effect menu.

Corner effects generally work best with rectangle frames and shapes. But if you're feeling extra creative, try applying any of these effects to a triangle or polygon shape.

7.20 Applying and Editing Compound Paths

A compound path is created when two objects are placed on top of each other and merged together, allowing any overlapping areas to become transparent. In basic terms, this means that two overlapping shapes with separate fills can be converted into one shape with a hole in it. When the compound path is placed in front, you can see any underlying objects through the transparent hole.

To create a compound path, select two overlapping frames, shapes, or paths and choose Object > Compound Paths > Make, or press Command+8 (Mac) or Ctrl+8 (Windows).

Compound paths can be edited just like any other object. The entire shape can be transformed (moved, scaled, sheared, or rotated) when selected with the Selection tool. In addition, individual points can be selected with the Direct Selection tool and repositioned or deleted.

To revert a compound path, select it and choose Object > Compound Paths > Release or press Option+Command+8 (Mac) or Alt+Ctrl+8 (Windows). Doing so reverts the shapes back into separate objects but may not include all previously applied attributes (fill color, stroke, etc.).

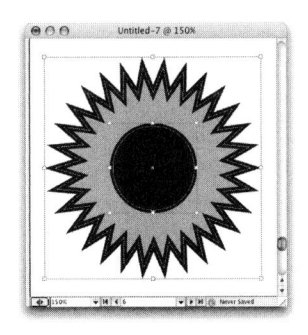

Two selected shapes—each with different fills—placed on top of each other

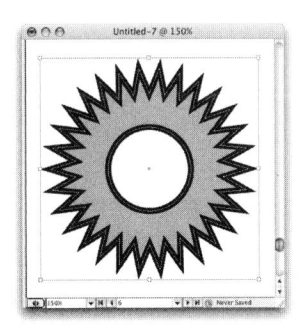

Both shapes combined into a single compound path

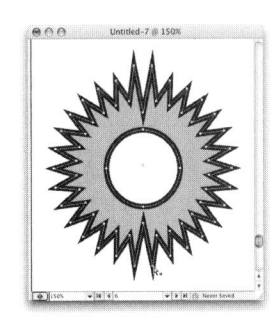

The individual points of a compound path can be moved by selecting them with the Direct Selection tool and nudging them with the arrow keys.

Related Tasks

3.3	Selection Tool
3.5	Pen Tools
3.7	Pencil Tools
3.8	Line Tool
4.11	Object and Layout Palettes
4.16	Stroke Palette
4.17	Swatches Palette
7.3	Selecting Multiple Objects
7.5	Drawing Rectangles, Ellipses, and Polygons
7.6	Drawing Custom Shapes
7.7	Drawing Freeform Shapes
7.13	Stroking Frames, Shapes, and Paths
7.21	Creating Custom Shapes with Pathfinder
8.6	Grouping and Ungrouping Objects

Shortcuts

Make compound path
Mac: Cmd+8
Win: Ctrl+8

Release compound path
Mac: Opt+Cmd+8
Win: Alt+Ctrl+8

Pen tool
Mac and Win: P

Tip

Compound paths can contain placed images.

175

7.21 Creating Custom Shapes with Pathfinder

Related Tasks

7.3 Selecting Multiple Objects

7.5 Drawing Rectangles, Ellipses, and Polygons

7.6 Drawing Custom Shapes

7.7 Drawing Freeform Shapes

Shortcuts

Rectangle Frame tool
Mac and Win: F

Rectangle tool
Mac and Win: M

Ellipse tool
Mac and Win: L

Selection tool
Mac and Win: V

Pen tool
Mac and Win: P

Pencil tool
Mac and Win: N

Tip

To allow a self-intersecting path to fill using the "Even-Odd Rule," as it would in drawing programs such as Illustrator or FreeHand, copy the path and paste it in place. Then select both paths and click the Add button in the Pathfinder palette. A compound path is created allowing self-intersecting points to become transparent.

InDesign enters into Illustrator territory here by allowing you to combine selected frames, shapes, and paths using a Pathfinder palette. Although the Pathfinder palette in InDesign does not contain all of the same functions as the one found in Illustrator, the basics are all here.

Combining objects with Pathfinder is a quick and easy way to create icons or design elements for use in your layouts. All you need to do is select two or more overlapping shapes, frames, or paths and click one of the Pathfinder controls in the palette.

Note: Pathfinder commands are permanent and can only be undone using the Undo command (Command/Ctrl+Z).

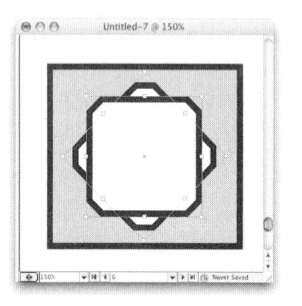

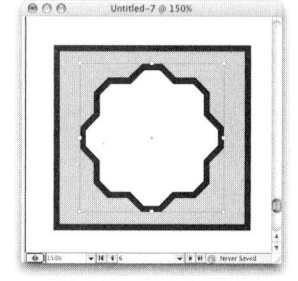

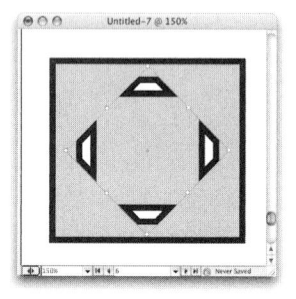

Original two shapes

Add

Subtract

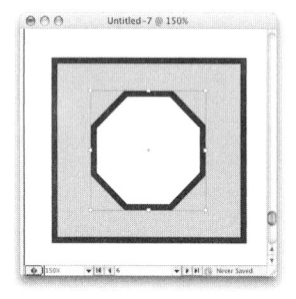

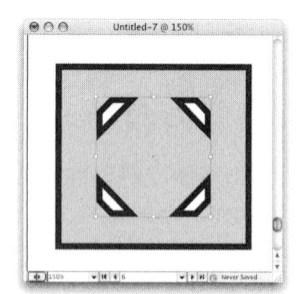

Intersect

Exclude Overlap

Minus Back

CHAPTER **8**

Manipulating Objects

MOST DESIGNERS SPEND QUITE a bit of time maneuvering objects around the page before they come up with a design they're satisfied with. If you're one of those designers, you might also want to learn the various ways of manipulating page objects in InDesign—it may save you time in the long run.

In this chapter we'll cover how to transform, group, arrange, lock, duplicate, align, and distribute objects. We'll also explain how to use layers and save objects into a library.

- 8.1 **Moving Objects**
- 8.2 **Resizing Objects**
- 8.3 **Rotating Objects**
- 8.4 **Flipping Objects**
- 8.5 **Shearing Objects**
- 8.6 **Grouping and Ungrouping Objects**
- 8.7 **Selecting Objects within a Group**
- 8.8 **Nesting Grouped Objects**
- 8.9 **Stacking, Arranging, and Locking Objects**
- 8.10 **Duplicating Objects**
- 8.11 **Aligning Objects**
- 8.12 **Distributing Objects**
- 8.13 **Saving Objects to a Library**
- 8.14 **Deleting Objects**
- 8.15 **Creating and Naming a New Layer**
- 8.16 **Placing Objects on Layers**
- 8.17 **Enabling Layout Adjustment**

8.1 Moving Objects

Related Tasks

2.7	Object Menu
3.2	Control Bar
3.3	Selection Tool
3.4	Direct Selection and Position Tools
3.14	Free Transform Tool
4.11	Object & Layout Palettes

Shortcuts

Move
Mac: Shift+Cmd+M
Win: Shift+Ctrl+M

Move selection by 10 times the Cursor Key distance
Mac and Win:
Shift+Arrow keys

Apply Transform palette values and copy selected object
Mac: Opt+Return
Win: Alt+Enter

Duplicate and offset selection
Mac: Opt+Arrow keys
Win: Alt+Arrow keys

To move an object, you must first select it with the Selection tool (by clicking anywhere on it) or with the Direct Selection tool (by clicking its center point). You can then use any one of these methods to reposition it on the page:

- Drag the selected object to a new location.

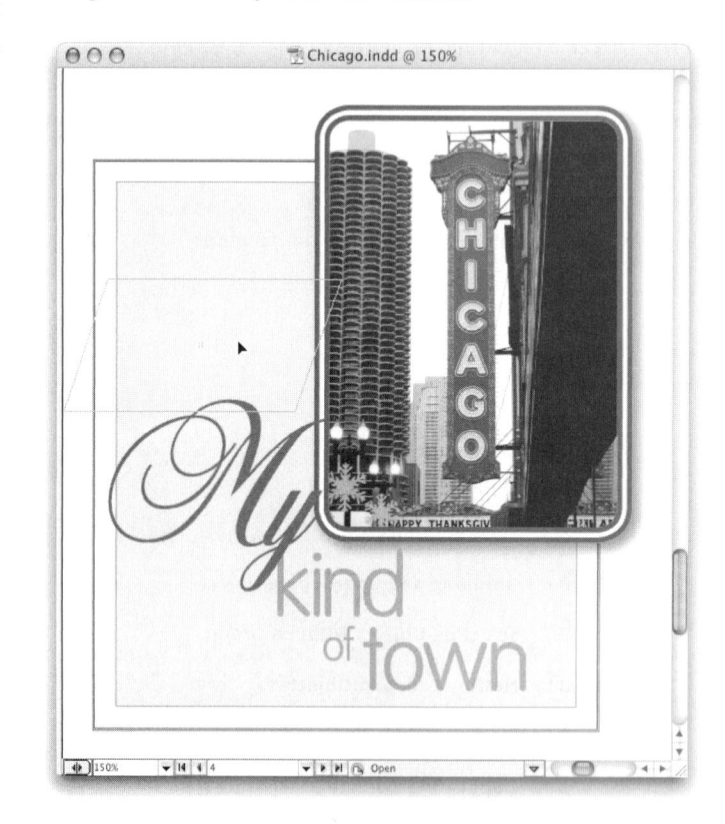

- Enter new X and Y coordinates in either the Transform palette or Control bar.

178

8.1 Moving Objects *(continued)*

- Access the Move dialog (Object > Transform > Move). Enter values for Position, Distance, and Angle, and click OK.

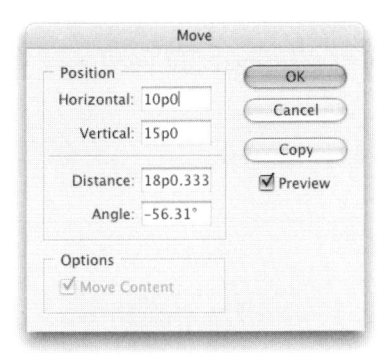

- Nudge the object using the arrow keys. Note: The arrow keys use the Cursor Key distance amount entered in the Units & Increments Preferences.

Related Tasks

5.5 Units & Increments Preferences

5.6 Grids Preferences

5.7 Guides & Pasteboard Preferences

6.21 Snapping to Document Grid

8.3 Rotating Objects

8.17 Enabling Layout Adjustment

Shortcuts

Duplicate and offset selection by 10 times
Mac: Opt+Shift+ Arrow keys
Win: Alt+Shift+Arrow keys

Transform palette
Mac and Win: F9

Selection tool
Mac and Win: V

Direct Selection tool
Mac and Win: A

Tip

You can access the Move dialog by selecting an object and Option/Alt-clicking the X or Y icons located in the Control bar.

8.2 Resizing Objects

Related Tasks

2.7 Object Menu
3.2 Control Bar
3.3 Selection Tool
3.4 Direct Selection and Position Tools
3.12 Scale Tool
3.14 Free Transform Tool
4.11 Object and Layout Palettes
5.6 Grids Preferences

Shortcuts

Increase/decrease size of selected object by 1%
Mac: Cmd+> (increase) / Cmd+< (decrease)
Win: Ctrl+> (increase) / Ctrl+< (decrease)

Increase/decrease size of selected object by 5%
Mac: Opt+Cmd+> (increase) / Opt+Cmd+< (decrease)
Win: Alt+Ctrl+> (increase) / Alt+Ctrl+< (decrease)

Resize container and contents
Mac: Selection tool+Cmd-drag
Win: Selection tool+Ctrl-drag

Resize container and contents proportionately
Mac: Selection tool+Shift+Cmd-drag
Win: Selection tool+Shift+Ctrl-drag

To resize an object, you must first select it with the Selection tool, and then perform any one of the following actions:

- Drag one of the object's frame nodes with the Selection tool. Press the Shift key to constrain proportions as you drag. To scale an object's contents at the same time, press Command (Mac) or Ctrl (Windows) as you drag.

Resizing the container    Resizing the containers and its contents

- To scale a container and its contents, enter new scale X and Y percentages or new width and height values in either the Transform palette or Control bar.

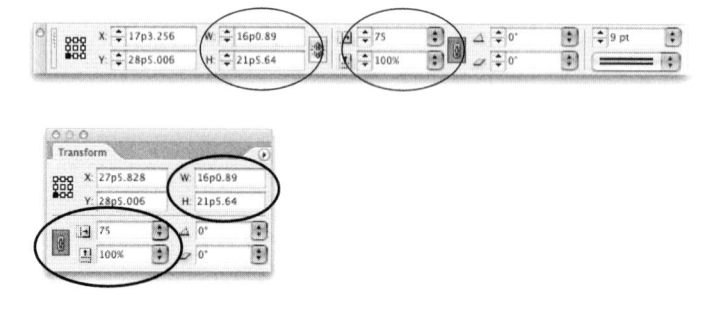

180

8.2 Resizing Objects *(continued)*

- Press S to access the Scale tool, then click and drag. Press the Shift key to constrain proportions or limit the scale to one axis.

- Access the Scale dialog by choosing Object > Transform > Scale. Enter values for Uniform or Non-Uniform scaling and click OK. Note: To resize the container without its contents, uncheck the Scale Content option in the dialog before clicking OK.

- Press E to access the Free Transform tool and click and drag. Press the Shift key to constrain proportions.

Related Tasks

5.7	Guides & Pasteboard Preferences
6.21	Snapping to Document Grid
7.1	Frame/Shape Overview
7.2	Selection Tool vs. Direct Selection Tool
8.3	Rotating Objects
8.17	Enabling Layout Adjustment
12.6	Resizing Placed Images
13.10	Resizing Tables

Shortcuts

Transform palette
Mac and Win: F9

Selection tool
Mac and Win: V

Direct Selection tool
Mac and Win: A

Scale tool
Mac and Win: S

Free Transform tool
Mac and Win: E

Tip

You can access the Scale dialog by selecting an object and double-clicking the Scale tool icon in the Toolbox.

8.3 Rotating Objects

Related Tasks

- 2.7 Object Menu
- 3.2 Control Bar
- 3.3 Selection Tool
- 3.4 Direct Selection and Position Tools
- 3.11 Rotate Tool
- 3.14 Free Transform Tool
- 4.11 Object and Layout Palettes
- 5.6 Grids Preferences
- 5.7 Guides & Pasteboard Preferences

Shortcuts

Apply Transform palette values and copy selected object
Mac: Opt+Return
Win: Alt+Enter

Apply Transform palette width, height, or scale percentage values proportionately
Mac: Cmd+Return
Win: Ctrl+Enter

Transform palette
Mac and Win: F9

There are several ways to rotate objects in InDesign. All of the methods described here rotate from the reference point selected in the reference point icon in the Control bar and Transform palette. The default reference point is the absolute center of the object; however, you can reposition it by clicking a different square in the reference point icon.

To rotate an object, perform any one of the following actions:

- Select the object you would like to rotate by clicking its frame or shape edge with the Rotate tool, then click and drag. Press the Shift key as you drag to constrain rotation angles to 45° increments.

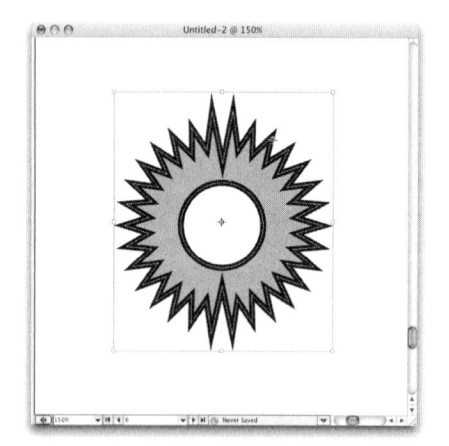

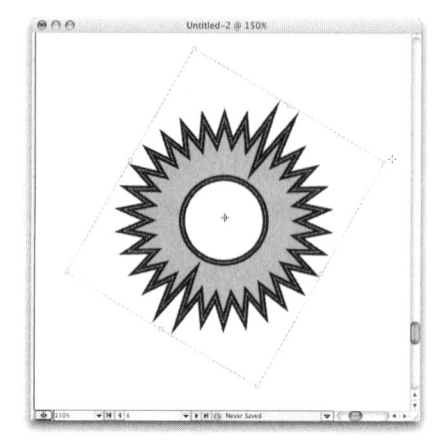

- The crosshair target that appears in the center of the selected object indicates the reference point for rotation. You can reposition it anywhere in the document window by clicking and dragging.

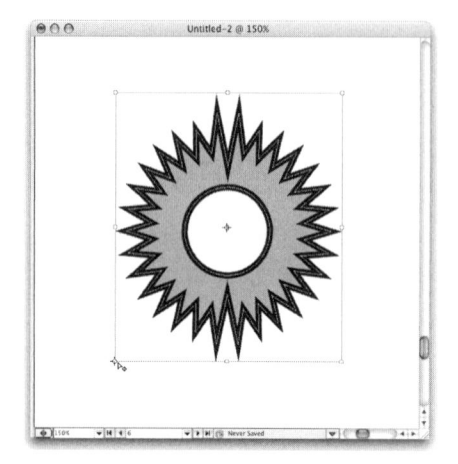

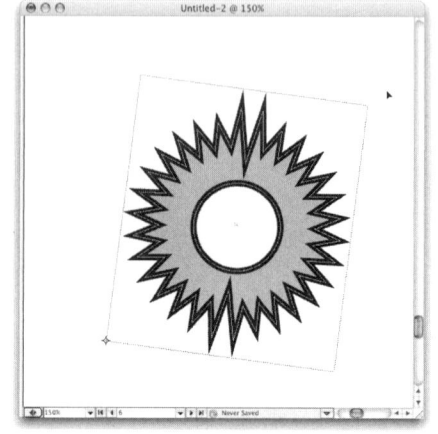

8.3 Rotating Objects *(continued)*

- Select the object you would like to rotate with the Selection tool. Enter a value in the Rotation Angle field located in the Transform palette or Control bar. You can also select a preset value from the pop-up menu or from the Transform palette menu.

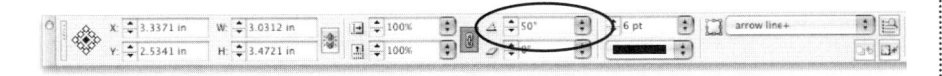

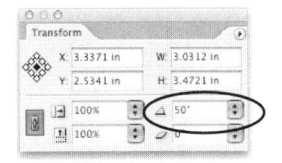

- Access the Rotate dialog by choosing Object > Transform > Rotate. Enter an Angle value and click OK.

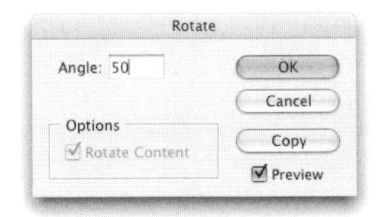

- Select the object you would like to rotate by clicking its frame or shape edge with the Free Transform tool. Hover your mouse over one of the corner nodes. When the left/right arrow icon appears, click and drag. Press the Shift key as you drag to constrain rotation angles to 45° increments.

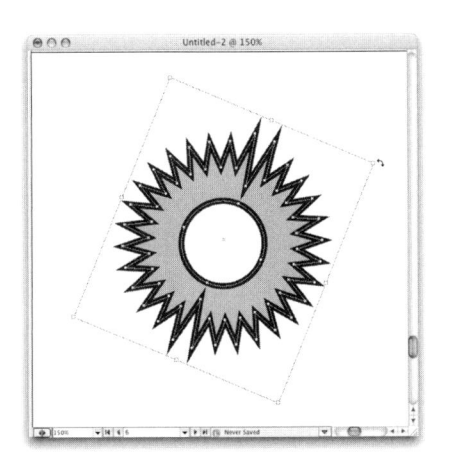

Related Tasks

6.21	Snapping to Document Grid
7.1	Frame/Shape Overview
7.2	Selection Tool vs. Direct Selection Tool
8.1	Moving Objects
8.2	Resizing Objects
8.17	Enabling Layout Adjustment
10.2	Scaling and Skewing Type
12.6	Resizing Placed Images

Shortcuts

Selection tool
Mac and Win: V

Direct Selection tool
Mac and Win: A

Rotate tool
Mac and Win: R
Mac and Win: O

Free Transform tool
Mac and Win: E

Tip

To apply a transformation to an object and its contents, make sure that the Transform Content option is checked in the Transform palette fly-out menu.

183

8.4 Flipping Objects

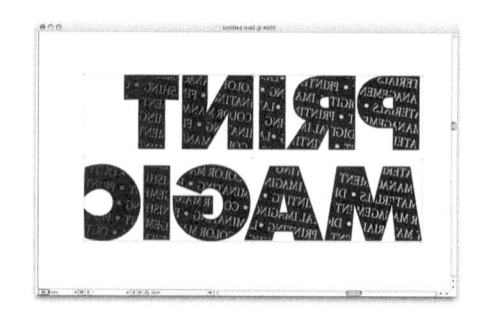

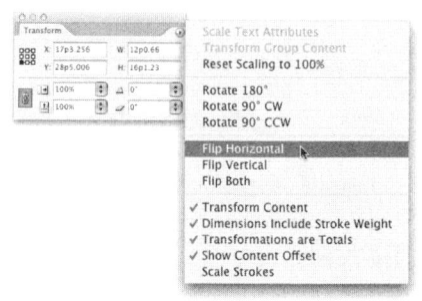

Related Tasks

2.7	Object Menu
3.2	Control Bar
3.3	Selection Tool
3.4	Direct Selection and Position Tools
3.14	Free Transform Tool
4.11	Object and Layout Palettes
5.6	Grids Preferences
5.7	Guides & Pasteboard Preferences

Shortcuts

Apply Transform palette values and copy selected object
Mac: Opt+Return
Win: Alt+Enter

Apply Transform palette width, height, or scale percentage values proportionately
Mac: Cmd+Return
Win: Ctrl+Enter

Transform palette
Mac and Win: F9

There are several ways to flip objects in InDesign. All of the methods described here flip objects using the point selected in the reference point icon in the Control bar and Transform palette. The default reference point is the absolute center of the object; however, you can reposition it by clicking a different square in the reference point icon.

To flip an object, perform any one of the following actions:

- Click the Transform palette menu button and choose Flip Horizontal, Flip Vertical, or Flip Both.

184

8.4 Flipping Objects *(continued)*

- Enter a negative Scale X or Scale Y Percentage value in the Transform palette or Control bar.

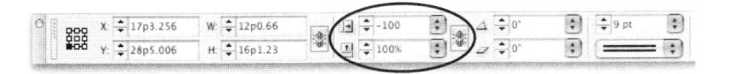

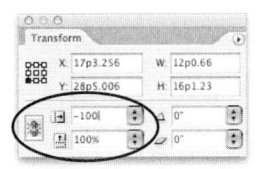

- Select one of the object's frame nodes with the Selection tool and drag it past the opposite side.

- Press A to switch to the Direct Selection tool and drag one of the object's line segments past the opposite side.

- Select the object you would like to flip by clicking its frame or shape edge with the Free Transform tool. Drag one of the object's frame nodes past the opposite side.

Related Tasks

6.21 Snapping to Document Grid

7.1 Frame/Shape Overview

7.2 Selection Tool vs. Direct Selection Tool

8.1 Moving Objects

8.2 Resizing Objects

8.17 Enabling Layout Adjustment

10.2 Scaling and Skewing Type

12.6 Resizing Placed Images

Shortcuts

Selection tool
Mac and Win: V

Direct Selection tool
Mac and Win: A

Free Transform tool
Mac and Win: E

Tip

To apply a transformation to an object and its contents, make sure that the Transform Content option is checked in the Transform palette fly-out menu.

8.5 Shearing Objects

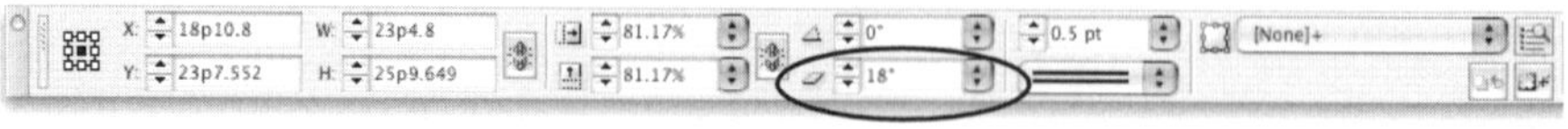

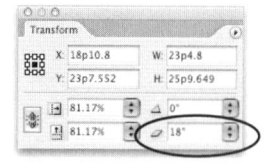

Related Tasks

2.7	Object Menu
3.2	Control Bar
3.3	Selection Tool
3.4	Direct Selection and Position Tools
3.13	Shear Tool
3.14	Free Transform Tool
4.11	Object and Layout Palettes
5.6	Grids Preferences

Shortcuts

Apply Transform palette values and copy selected object
Mac: Opt+Return
Win: Alt+Enter

Apply Transform palette width, height, or scale percentage values proportionately
Mac: Cmd+Return
Win: Ctrl+Enter

Transform palette
Mac and Win: F9

InDesign provides several ways to shear objects. All of the methods described here do so from the reference point selected in the reference point icon in the Control bar and Transform palette. The default reference point is the absolute center of the object; however, you can reposition it by clicking a different square in the reference point icon.

To shear an object, perform any one of the following actions:

- Select the object you would like to shear by clicking its frame or shape edge with the Shear tool and click and drag. Press the Shift key as you drag to constrain along the horizontal axis.

- Select the object you would like to shear with the Selection tool, and enter a value in the shear X angle field located in the Transform palette or Control bar. You can also select a preset value from the pop-up menu.

8.5 Shearing Objects (continued)

- Select the object you would like to shear with the Selection tool. Access the Shear dialog by choosing Object **>** Transform **>** Shear and enter a value for Shear Angle. Choose an axis (Horizontal, Vertical, or specified Angle) and click OK.

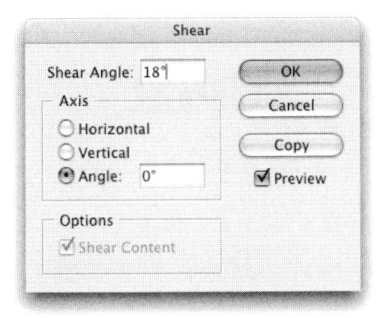

- Select the object you would like to shear by clicking its frame or shape edge with the Free Transform tool. As you begin to click and drag a side node, hold down the Option+Command key (Mac) or the Ctrl+Alt key (Windows). Press the Shift key as you drag to constrain vertically or horizontally.

Related Tasks

5.7 Guides & Pasteboard Preferences
6.21 Snapping to Document Grid
7.1 Frame/Shape Overview
7.2 Selection Tool vs. Direct Selection Tool
8.1 Moving Objects
8.2 Resizing Objects
8.17 Enabling Layout Adjustment
10.2 Scaling and Skewing Type
12.6 Resizing Placed Images

Shortcuts

Selection tool
Mac and Win: V

Direct Selection tool
Mac and Win: A

Shear tool
Mac and Win: O

Free Transform tool
Mac and Win: E

Tips

You can access the Shear dialog by selecting an object and double-clicking the Shear tool icon in the Toolbox.

To apply a transformation to an object and its contents, make sure that the Transform Content option is checked in the Transform palette fly-out menu.

8.6 Grouping and Ungrouping Objects

Related Tasks

2.7	Object Menu
3.3	Selection Tool
3.4	Direct Selection and Position Tools
7.3	Selecting Multiple Objects
8.1	Moving Objects
8.2	Resizing Objects
8.3	Rotating Objects
8.7	Selecting Objects within a Group
8.8	Nesting Grouped Objects

Shortcuts

Group
Mac: Cmd+G
Win: Ctrl+G

Ungroup
Mac: Shift+Cmd+G
Win: Shift+Ctrl+G

Temporarily select Group Selection tool
Mac: Direct Selection tool+Opt
Win: Direct Selection tool+Alt

Transform palette
Mac and Win: F9

Selection tool
Mac and Win: V

Direct Selection tool
Mac and Win: A

Tip

It is possible to select multiple groups and group them, creating a group of groups!

At some point you may want to move, resize, or transform multiple items at once. The best thing to do in this instance is group the items first and then apply the action.

To group in InDesign, select multiple objects with either selection tool and choose Object > Group or press Command+G (Mac) or Ctrl+G (Windows). A dotted rectangle appears around the objects indicating that they are now grouped. You can then apply an action to all the objects at once.

To ungroup, select the group with the Selection tool and choose Object > Ungroup or press Shift+Cmd+G (Mac) or Shift+Ctrl+G (Windows). The dotted rectangle disappears!

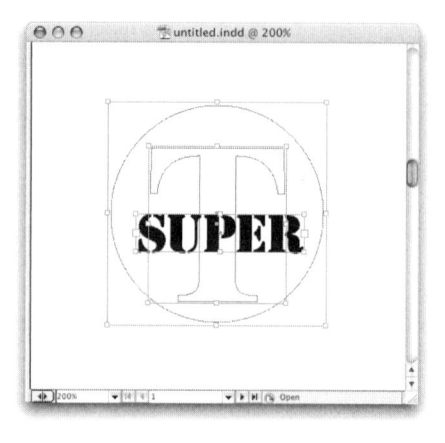

Selected objects

Grouped objects

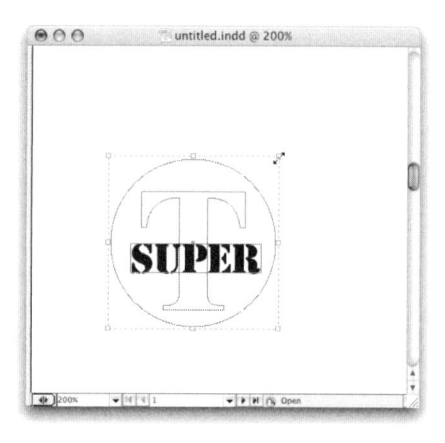

Grouped objects scaled

8.7 Selecting Objects within a Group

Grouping multiple objects is easy, but what if you want to select and transform an object within a group?

To select an object that is part of a group, click directly on a path segment with the Direct Selection tool. Shift-click to select multiple objects in the group.

To move, resize, or transform the object, you must select the entire path by clicking directly on its center point or Option/Alt-clicking on a path segment with the Direct Selection tool (also referred to as the Group Selection tool). You will know that the entire path is selected when all of the points of the path appear solid rather than hollow.

Related Tasks

2.7	Object Menu
3.3	Selection Tool
3.4	Direct Selection and Position Tools
3.11	Rotate Tool
3.12	Scale Tool
3.13	Shear Tool
3.14	Free Transform Tool

Shortcuts

Group
Mac: Cmd+G
Win: Ctrl+G

Ungroup
Mac: Shift+Cmd+G
Win: Shift+Ctrl+G

Temporarily select Group Selection tool
Mac: Direct Selection tool+Opt
Win: Direct Selection tool+Alt

8.7 Selecting Objects within a Group *(continued)*

Related Tasks

4.11 Object and Layout Palettes

7.3 Selecting Multiple Objects

8.1 Moving Objects

8.2 Resizing Objects

8.3 Rotating Objects

8.6 Grouping and Ungrouping Objects

8.8 Nesting Grouped Objects

Shortcuts

Transform palette
Mac and Win: F9

Selection tool
Mac and Win: V

Direct Selection tool
Mac and Win: A

Tip

You can reset a grouped transformation value (such as a 20˚ shear back to 0˚) by choosing Transform Group Content from the Transform palette menu. This makes the formerly transformed amount (20˚) the new starting point for future transformations (0˚).

Once an object in a group is selected with the Direct Selection tool, press V to select it with the Selection tool and change its shape by dragging any of its nodes. You can move the grouped object with the Selection tool by clicking its center point and dragging.

Left: An object selected within a group and resized with the Selection tool. Right: An object selected within a group and moved by clicking its center point and dragging with the Selection tool.

To place a graphic into a grouped object, select it with the Direct Selection tool and choose File > Place, or press Command+D (Mac) or Ctrl+D (Windows). You can select the contents of a grouped object by clicking directly on it with the Direct Selection tool.

8.8 Nesting Grouped Objects

Grouping allows you to nest more than one object at a time. This is great for creating custom, editable logos and icons much like you would in programs such as Adobe Illustrator or Macromedia FreeHand. To give this a try, follow these simple steps:

1. Select multiple items and choose Object > Group or press Command+G (Mac) or Ctrl+G (Windows).

2. Copy the group to the Clipboard by choosing Edit > Copy or pressing Command+C (Mac) or Ctrl+C (Windows).

3. Select the object you would like to paste the group into with the Selection tool and choose Edit > Paste Into.

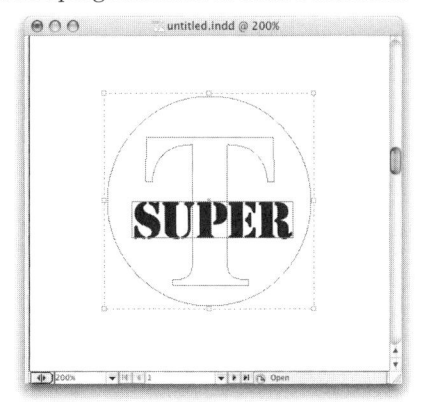

A selected group

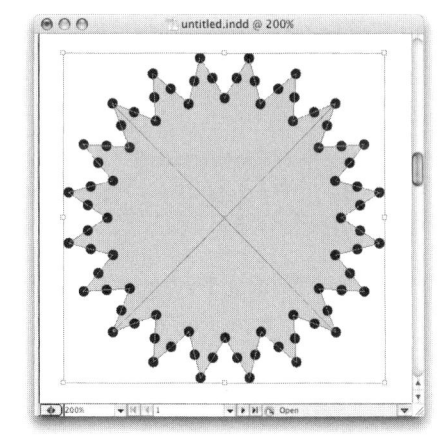

Left: before Paste Into; right, after Paste Into

4. Option/Alt-click the nested group with the Direct Selection tool (a.k.a. the Group Selection tool) and move, resize, or transform it within its new object container. You can also select and transform individual objects in the nested group with the Group Selection tool.

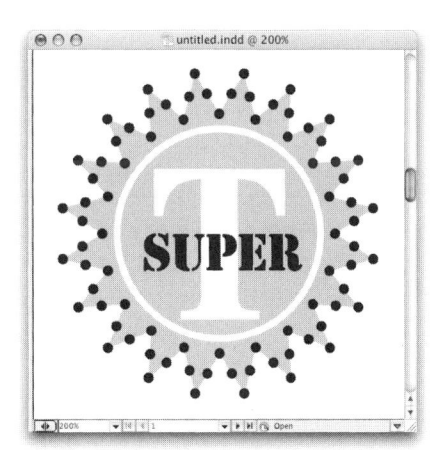

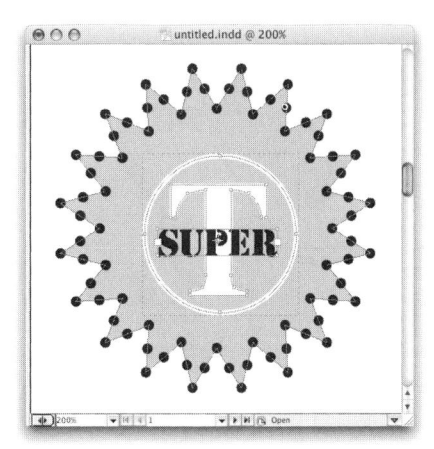

Scaling the nested group

Related Tasks

- 2.7 Object Menu
- 3.3 Selection Tool
- 3.4 Direct Selection and Position Tools
- 7.1 Frame/Shape Overview
- 7.3 Selecting Multiple Objects
- 7.9 Nesting Objects
- 8.6 Grouping and Ungrouping Objects
- 8.7 Selecting Objects within a Group

Shortcuts

Copy to Clipboard
Mac: Cmd+C
Win: Ctrl+C

Paste Into
Mac: Opt+Cmd+V
Win: Alt+Ctrl+V

Group
Mac: Cmd+G
Win: Ctrl+G

Ungroup
Mac: Shift+Cmd+G
Win: Shift+Ctrl+G

Transform palette
Mac and Win: F9

Selection tool
Mac and Win: V

Direct Selection tool
Mac and Win: A

Tip

To select all the items in a group with the Group Selection tool, click a path segment of one of the objects with the Direct Selection tool, and then Option/Alt-click twice.

8.9 Stacking, Arranging, and Locking Objects

Related Tasks

2.7 Object Menu

3.3 Selection Tool

3.4 Direct Selection and Position Tools

4.11 Object and Layout Palettes

7.1 Frame/Shape Overview

7.3 Selecting Multiple Objects

Shortcuts

Bring Forward
Mac: Cmd+]
Win: Ctrl+]

Bring to Front
Mac: Shift+Cmd+]
Win: Shift+Ctrl+]

Send Backward
Mac: Cmd+[
Win: Ctrl+[

Send To Back
Mac: Shift+Cmd+[
Win: Shift+Ctrl+[

Select first object above
Mac: Opt+Shift+Cmd+]
Win: Alt+Shift+Ctrl+]

When placing objects on top of one another (called *stacking*), you may find it challenging to try and individually select the objects positioned in the lower layers of the stacking order and rearrange them—especially if you are using transparency and can see right through all the objects in the stack! An object may appear to be in front when it is actually in back.

To select through the stacking order, press the Command key (Mac) or Ctrl key (Windows) and click. The first click selects the topmost object and every click afterward selects the next object below. Keep clicking until you get to the object you're trying to select.

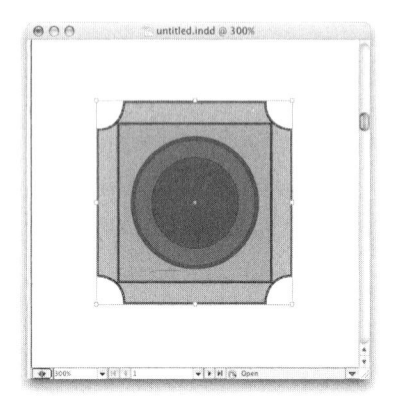

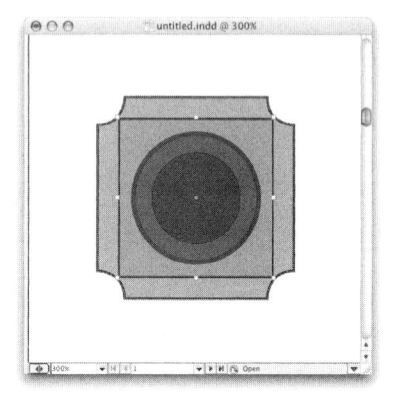

Left: Click once to select the topmost object in the stack. Right: Cmd/Ctrl-click to select the next object below.

You can rearrange the order of stacked objects by selecting them and choosing one of the four commands located under the Object > Arrange submenu: Bring To Front, Bring Forward, Send Backward, and Send To Back. Or you can use any of the assigned keyboard shortcuts for arranging (see the list under Shortcuts), or access the commands through the contextual menu (Mac: Control-click; Windows: right-click).

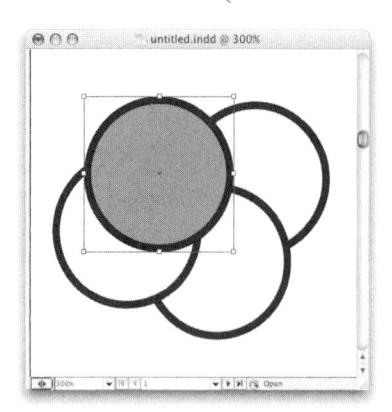

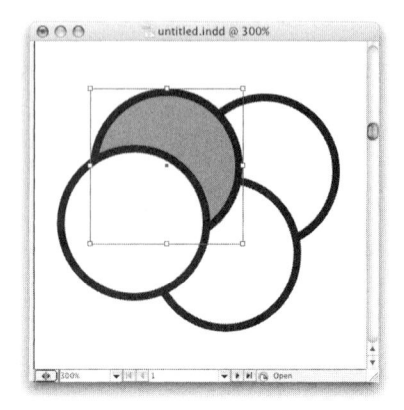

Bring To Front   Send Backward

8.9 Stacking, Arranging, and Locking Objects *(continued)*

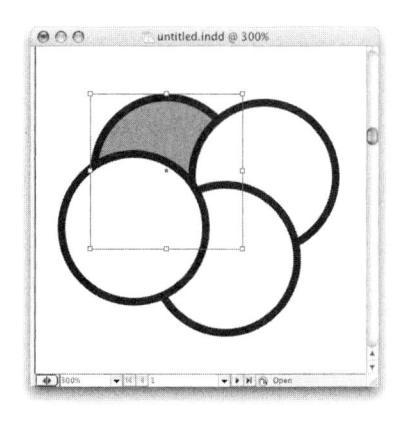

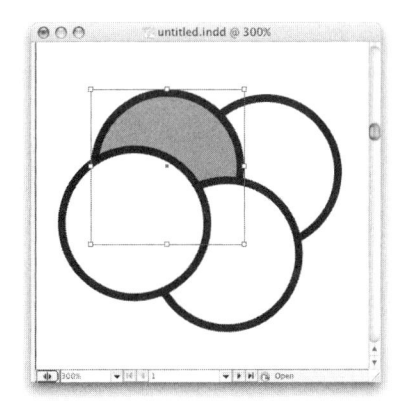

Send To Back Bring Forward

To lock an object, select it with either selection tool and choose Object > Lock Position, or press Command+L (Mac) or Ctrl+L (Windows). Locking an object prevents you from deleting or transforming it in any way, although you can still select it and edit any text or formatting attributes (stroke, fill color, corner effects, apply object styles, etc). To lock an object even more securely (so that it cannot be selected or edited at all), place it on its own layer and click the lock toggle icon in the Layers palette.

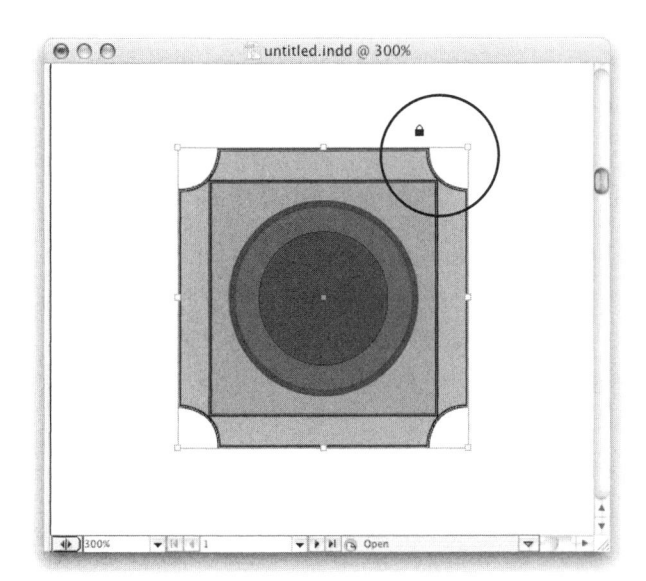

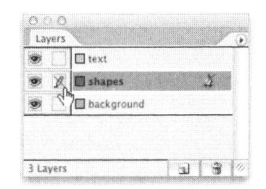

Left, a locked object; right, a locked layer

To unlock an object, select it with either selection tool and choose Object > Unlock Position or press Opt+Cmd+L (Mac) or Alt+Ctrl+L (Win).

Related Tasks

8.6 Grouping and Ungrouping Objects

8.7 Selecting Objects within a Group

8.11 Aligning Objects

8.12 Distributing Objects

8.16 Placing Objects on Layers

Shortcuts

Select last object below
Mac: Opt+Shift+Cmd+[
Win: Alt+Shift+Ctrl+[

Select next object above
Mac: Opt+Cmd+]
Win: Alt+Ctrl+]

Select next object below
Mac: Opt+Cmd+[
Win: Alt+Ctrl+[

Lock position
Mac: Cmd+L
Win: Ctrl+L

Unlock position
Mac: Opt+Cmd+L
Win: Alt+Ctrl+L

Tip

Warning! The keyboard commands for selecting stacked objects refer to the placed order of all items on the page, and not their visual order. Therefore when using these shortcuts, do not panic if you wind up selecting various page items that are not at all related to the stack you are focusing on. This is not a bug in the application—it is just one of those little InDesign quirks!

8.10 Duplicating Objects

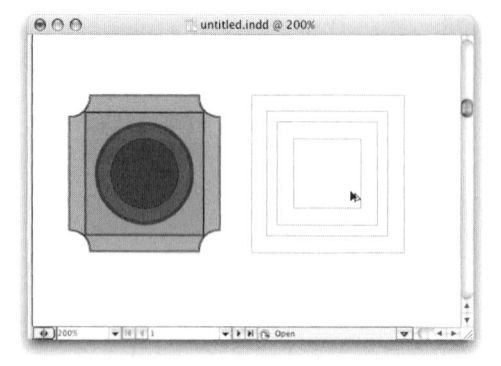

Related Tasks

2.4 Edit Menu
3.3 Selection Tool
3.4 Direct Selection and Position Tools

Shortcuts

Copy to Clipboard
Mac: Cmd+C
Win: Ctrl+C

Paste
Mac: Cmd+V
Win: Ctrl+V

Paste Into
Mac: Opt+Cmd+V
Win: Alt+Ctrl+V

Paste without formatting
Mac: Shift+Cmd+V
Win: Shift+Ctrl+V

Paste in place
Mac: Opt+Shift+Cmd+V
Win: Alt+Shift+Ctrl+V

Duplicate
Mac: Opt+Shift+Cmd+D
Win: Alt+Shift+Ctrl+D

Step and repeat
Mac: Opt+Cmd+U
Win: Alt+Ctrl+U

To duplicate an object, you must first select it with either selection tool, and then perform any one of the following actions:

- Copy the selected item to the Clipboard by choosing Edit > Copy or pressing Command+C (Mac) or Ctrl+C (Windows). You can then paste the object by choosing Edit > Paste or pressing Command+V (Mac) or Ctrl+V (Windows). By default the object is placed in the center of the page, unless you choose Edit > Paste In Place, which places the copy directly in front of the original.

- Choose Edit > Duplicate to copy/paste a selected object all in one step. For placement, the Duplicate command uses the current Horizontal Offset and Vertical Offset values set in the Step And Repeat dialog. Note: As an alternative method of pasting in place, try setting the Horizontal/Vertical Offset amounts to 0 in the Step And Repeat dialog. This allows you to paste the duplicated object directly in front of the original when using the Duplicate command.

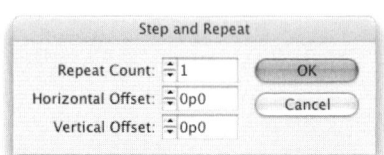

- To duplicate and distribute several copies of a selected object, choose Edit > Step And Repeat. When the dialog opens, enter settings for Repeat Count and Horizontal/Vertical Offset. Click OK to duplicate and distribute.

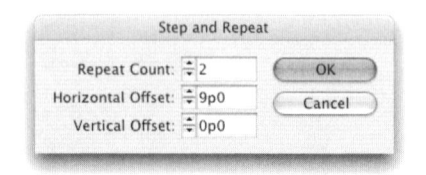

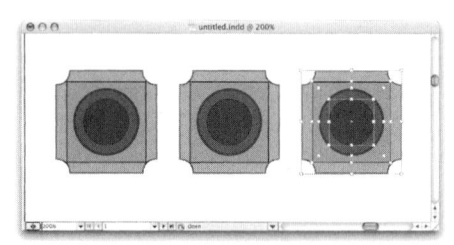

- Hold down the Option/Alt key and drag. It doesn't get any easier than this!

8.10 Duplicating Objects *(continued)*

- Enter a transformation value in one of the move, scale, shear, or rotation fields located in the Transform palette or Control bar and press Option+Return (Mac) or Alt+Enter (Windows). This transforms a copy of the original.

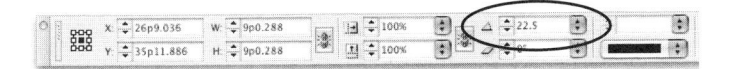

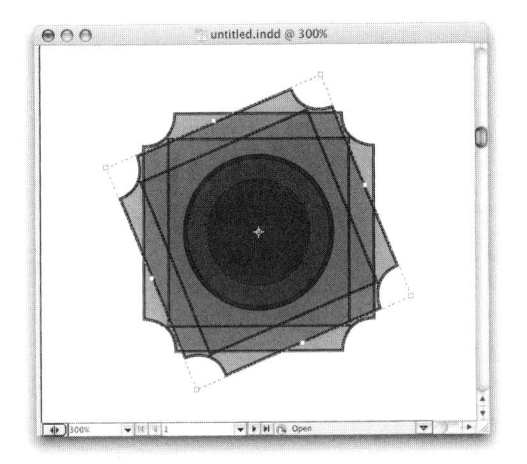

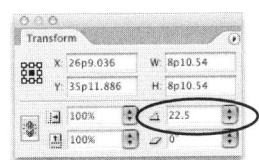

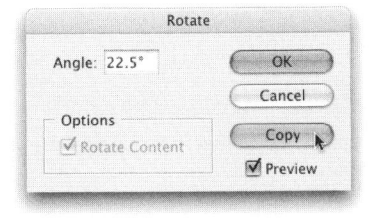

You can also transform and copy through the Move, Scale, Shear, or Rotate dialogs. Access the dialog and enter your preferred settings, then click the Copy button.

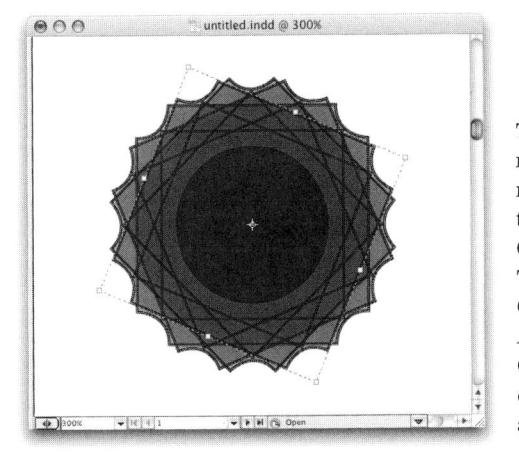

To transform and copy multiple times sequentially, make your initial transformation, and then choose Object > Transform Again > Transform Again or press Opt+Cmd+3 (Mac) or Alt+Ctrl+3 (Windows). Continue to apply the command as many times as needed.

Related Tasks

4.11 Object and Layout Palettes

12.5 Copying to and from Adobe Illustrator

Shortcuts

Apply Transform palette values and copy selected object
Mac: Opt+Return
Win: Alt+Enter

Transform Again
Mac: Opt+Cmd+3
Win: Alt+Ctrl+3

Duplicate and offset selection
Mac: Opt+Arrow keys
Win: Alt+Arrow keys

Duplicate and offset selection by 10 times the Cursor Key distance
Mac: Opt+Shift+Arrow keys
Win: Alt+Shift+Arrow keys

Transform palette
Mac and Win: F9

Selection tool
Mac and Win: V

Direct Selection tool
Mac and Win: A

Tip

With an object selected, you can access the Scale, Rotate, and Shear dialogs by Option/Alt-clicking their respective icons in the Transform palette. Option/Alt-click the X or Y location icons to access the Move dialog.

195

8.11 Aligning Objects

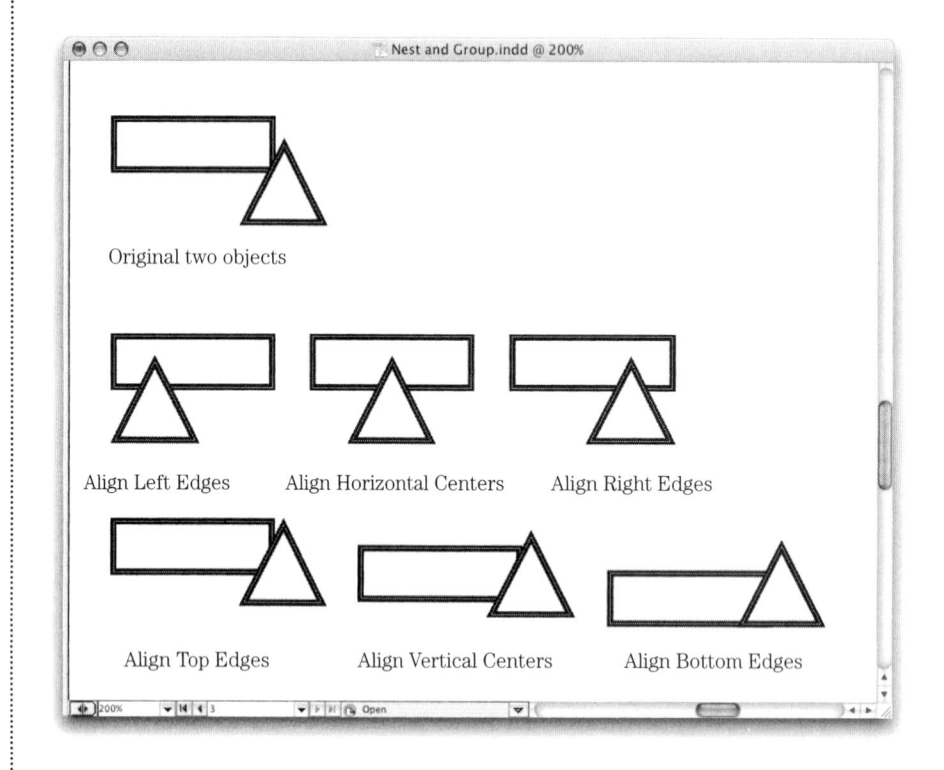

Related Tasks

3.3 Selection Tool

3.4 Direct Selection and Position Tools

4.11 Object and Layout Palettes

8.1 Moving Objects

8.3 Rotating Objects

8.9 Stacking, Arranging, and Locking Objects

8.12 Distributing Objects

Shortcuts

Align palette
Mac and Win: Shift+F7

Transform palette
Mac and Win: F9

Apply Transform palette values and copy selected object
Mac: Opt+Return
Win: Alt+Enter

Duplicate and offset selection
Mac: Opt+Arrow keys
Win: Alt+Arrow keys

Duplicate and offset selection by 10 times the Cursor Key distance
Mac: Opt+Shift+ Arrow keys
Win: Alt+Shift+ Arrow keys

Selection tool
Mac and Win: V

Direct Selection tool
Mac and Win: A

Tip

You can select and align objects that are placed on different layers.

You can position multiple selected objects in a document precisely using the Align palette. Simply select two or more objects and click one of the preset buttons located at the top of the palette.

Original two objects

Align Left Edges   Align Horizontal Centers   Align Right Edges

Align Top Edges   Align Vertical Centers   Align Bottom Edges

196

8.12 Distributing Objects

In addition to the alignment controls, the Align palette allows you to precisely distribute multiple selected objects and their spacing both vertically and horizontally. Choose Show Options from the palette menu to access the Distribute Spacing controls.

To distribute, select two or more objects and click one of the preset buttons located in the palette.

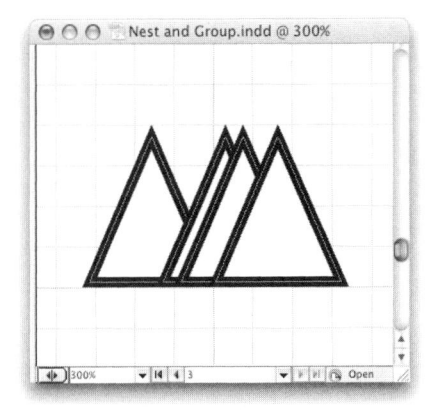

Original objects

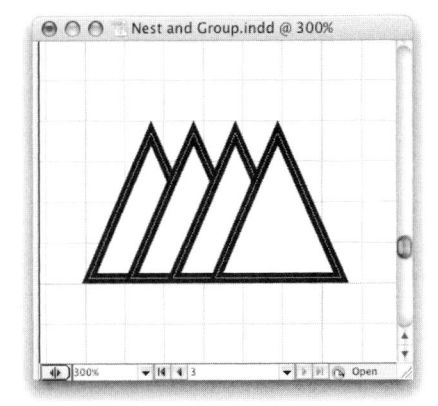

Objects distributed horizontally within the boundaries of the selection

Related Tasks

3.3 Selection Tool
3.4 Direct Selection and Position Tools
4.11 Object and Layout Palettes
8.1 Moving Objects

Shortcuts

Align palette
Mac and Win: Shift+F7

Transform palette
Mac and Win: F9

Apply Transform palette values and copy selected object
Mac: Opt+Return
Win: Alt+Enter

Duplicate and offset selection
Mac: Opt+Arrow keys
Win: Alt+Arrow keys

197

8.12 Distributing Objects *(continued)*

Related Tasks

8.3 Rotating Objects

8.9 Stacking, Arranging, and Locking Objects

8.11 Aligning Objects

Shortcuts

Duplicate and offset selection by 10 times the Cursor Key distance
Mac: Opt+Shift+Arrow keys
Win: Alt+Shift+Arrow keys

Selection tool
Mac and Win: V

Direct Selection tool
Mac and Win: A

Tip

You can select and distribute objects that are placed on different layers.

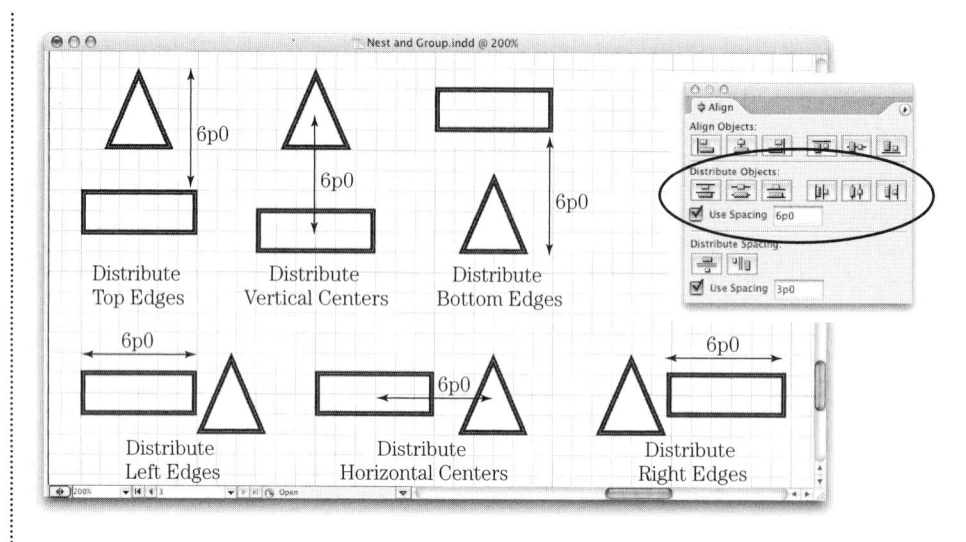

The Use Spacing option as applied to each Distribute Objects control

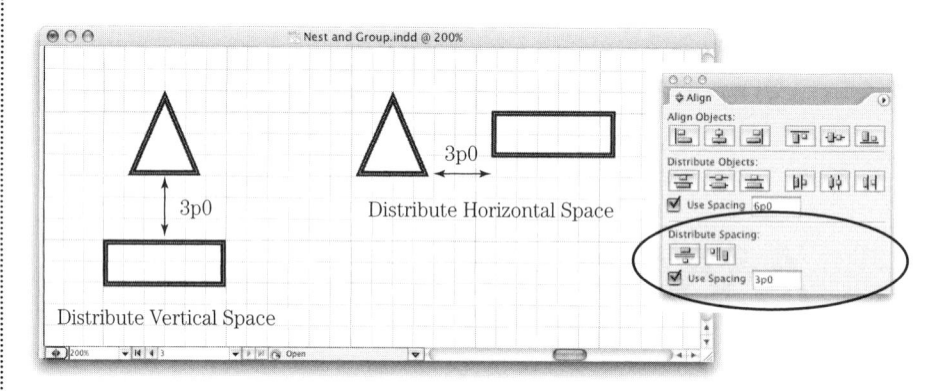

The Use Spacing option as applied to each Distribute Spacing control

198

8.13 Saving Objects to a Library

Libraries are great for storing objects that you know you will use repeatedly in your layouts. Common items such as logos, end marks, icons, formatted tables, and even style samples are all perfect candidates for storing in a library. Once the objects are saved in the library, you can place them into your layouts by dragging them from the Library palette.

To save objects into a library, you must first create one by choosing File **>** New **>** Library. Enter a name in the File Name field and then click the Save button. A new Library palette appears on your screen.

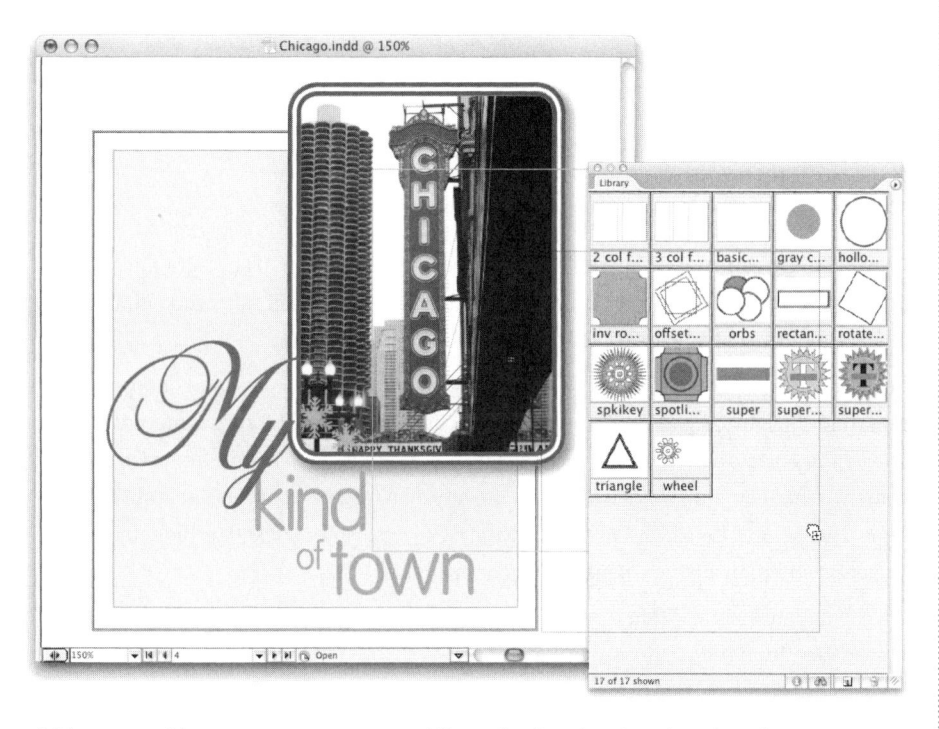

Add as many objects as you want to a saved library by dragging them into the palette.

You can change an item's name, specify an object type, or add an item description in the Item Information dialog. Access it by double-clicking the object in the library list or clicking the library item information button located at the bottom of the Library palette.

Related Tasks

2.3   File Menu
3.3   Selection Tool

Shortcuts

Open
Mac: Cmd+O
Win: Ctrl+O

Selection tool
Mac and Win: V

Direct Selection tool
Mac and Win: A

8.13 Saving Objects to a Library *(continued)*

Related Tasks

3.4 Direct Selection and Position Tools

4.22 Book and Library Palettes

Tip

You can only open the Library palette by creating or opening a saved library under the File menu—it is not listed under the Window menu.

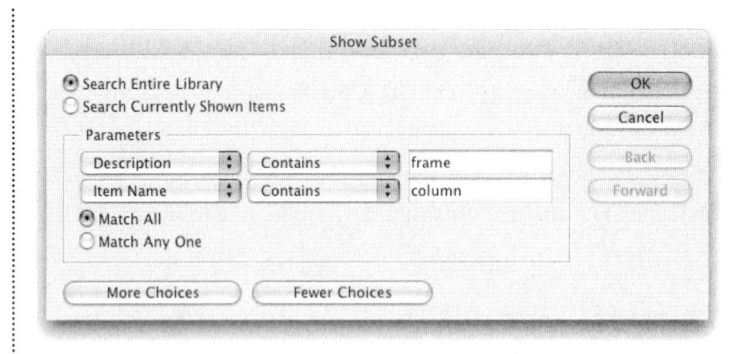

To search for objects in the library by item name, creation date, object type, or description, click the Show Library Subset button located at the bottom of the Library palette. When the dialog opens, enter your search parameters and click OK. Any found items appear in the Library palette by themselves.

A saved library can contain shapes, frames, text items, and even placed graphics. Placed graphics appear as links when dragged into a document from a library, and editable text items require that all necessary fonts be loaded on your system.

You can also add items to a library by selecting an object on the page and choosing Add Item from the Library palette fly-out menu or clicking the New Library Item button. To save all the objects on a targeted page as one library item, choose Add Items On Page from the palette menu. To save all of the objects on a targeted page as separate library items, choose Add Items On Page As Separate Objects. Note: Locked or hidden objects cannot be stored in a library using these commands.

You can update a library item that has been modified in the document by choosing Update Library Item from the palette fly-out menu.

To close the library, click the Close Palette Window button (Mac) or the Close button (Windows) or choose Close Library from the palette menu. You can reopen it later by choosing File > Open and browsing to the library's stored location on your system.

8.14 Deleting Objects

In the heat of what I call "design mode" you may find yourself surrounded by the remains of abandoned layout ideas. When this happens, it's time to win back control of your creative mess... um, I mean kingdom... and start deleting unused objects.

To delete objects from your InDesign layouts, first use either selection tool to select the object(s) you want to delete, then do one of the following:

- Press the Delete or Backspace key.
- Choose Edit > Clear.
- Drag the selected object(s) to the Trash icon in the dock (Mac OS X only).

Note: Deleting master pages and layers also deletes all objects placed on them—and some of them may still be applied to your document pages. However, any time you are about delete a master page or layer containing applied objects, a warning dialog appears. Click Yes if you are sure you want to delete and No if you have a sudden change of heart.

Related Tasks

2.4 Edit Menu
3.3 Selection Tool
3.4 Direct Selection and Position Tools
4.9 Layers Palette
6.14 Deleting Master Pages
8.16 Placing Objects on Layers

Shortcuts

Clear
Mac: Delete
Win: Backspace

Selection tool
Mac and Win: V

Direct Selection tool
Mac and Win: A

Tip

Ruler guides can also be selected and deleted.

201

8.15 Creating and Naming a New Layer

Related Tasks

4.9 Layers Palette
8.16 Placing Objects on Layers

Shortcuts

Layers palette
Mac and Win: F7

Select all objects on layer
Mac: Opt-click layer
Win: Alt-click the layer name

Copy selection to new layer
Mac: Opt-drag square icon to new layer in the palette
Win: Alt-drag square icon to new layer in the palette

Tips

To access the New Layer dialog, Option/Alt-click the Create New Layer icon located at the bottom of the Layers palette.

For organizational purposes, it's always a good idea to name your layers.

The great thing about using layers in InDesign is that you can place multiple versions of a design all in one document with very few pages involved. The Layers palette allows you to separate various objects in a layout by placing them on different layers. By toggling layer visibility on or off, you can view different design compositions and create PDFs of them for your client.

Before you can place objects on layers, you first need to create them. By default, all new documents start with one layer. Use either one of the following methods to create additional layers:

- Click the Create New Layer button located at the bottom of the Layers palette. When the new layer appears at the top of the palette list, double-click it and enter a name in the Layer Options dialog.

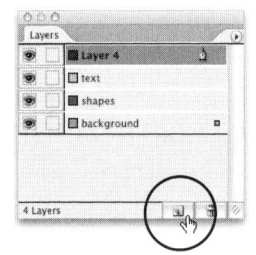

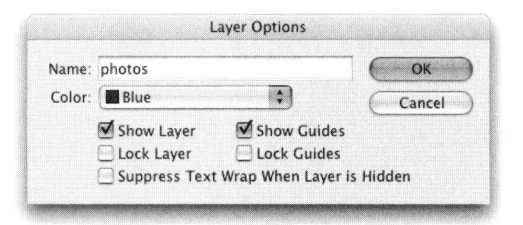

- Choose New Layer from the Layers palette fly-out menu. When the Layer Options dialog appears, enter a name for it and click OK. New layers appear at the top of the palette list.

NEW LAYERS: FROM TOP TO BOTTOM

By default, new layers always appear at the top of the list in the Layers palette. However, if you'd like to create a new layer directly underneath the layer you currently have selected, press Command+Option (Mac) or Ctrl+Alt (Windows) and click the Create New Layer button or choose New Layer Below from the palette fly-out menu. To create a new layer directly above the one you currently have selected, press Command (Mac) or Ctrl (Windows).

8.16 Placing Objects on Layers

Once you've created a new layer, select the original layer in the Layers palette. Then select the items you'd like to place on the new layer. Once you do, a small square appears to the far right of the original layer's name in the Layers palette. Click the square and drag it to the new layer. That's all there is to it! The objects are now on separate layers.

Notice that the outline frames of your selection have changed color. Every layer you create has an assigned color. These colors are applied to the outline frames of all your selections to indicate which layers the objects are placed on.

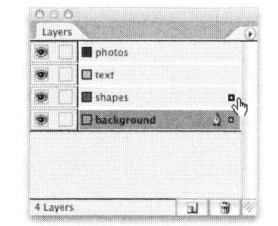

If you know ahead of time which layer you'd like to place an object on before it is created or dragged in from a library, select it from the Layers palette first.

Related Tasks

4.9 Layers Palette

8.16 Placing Objects on Layers

Shortcuts

Layers palette
Mac and Win: F7

Select all objects on layer
Mac: Opt-click layer
Win: Alt-click layer

Copy selection to new layer
Mac: Opt-drag square icon to new layer in the palette
Win: Alt-drag square icon to new layer in the palette

Tip

Unlike with Adobe Photoshop, you do not have to select the layer that an object is placed on in order to select it in the document.

To view a single layer and no others, Option/Alt-click the layer's Eye icon in the Layers palette.

8.17 Enabling Layout Adjustment

Related Tasks

1.3	The Document Window
2.3	File Menu
2.5	Layout Menu
4.15	Pages Palette
5.6	Grids Preferences
5.7	Guides & Pasteboard Preferences
6.8	Adding, Arranging, and Deleting Pages

Shortcuts

New Master dialog
Mac: Cmd+Opt-Click Create New Page button
Win: Ctrl+Alt-click Create New Page button

Create New Master Spread
Mac: Cmd-click Create New Page button
Win: Ctrl-click Create New Page button

Apply master to selected page
Mac: Opt-click Master
Win: Alt-click Master

Unfortunately in the design world, last-minute changes happen more frequently than not. Having to rework a complicated layout to compensate for changes is always a stress nightmare, especially when it happens on a tight deadline.

I recommend preparing ahead of time for impending disaster and enabling the Layout Adjustment option. It's the best way to protect yourself from having to perform hours of unnecessary extra work. With this option enabled, you can resize a document, apply new margin and column settings, apply totally different master pages, and even change page orientation without reworking anything—InDesign adjusts the page items for you!

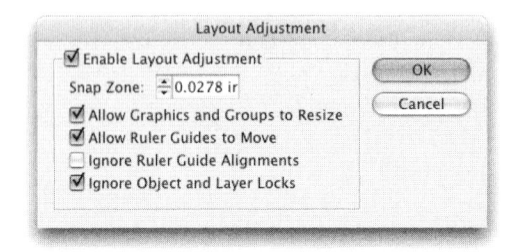

You can turn this option on in the Layout Adjustment dialog. Choose Layout > Layout Adjustment and click the Enable Layout Adjustment check box. The other settings in the dialog determine which items in the document InDesign is allowed to automatically adjust: graphics and groups, ruler guides, and/or locked objects and layers.

Layout Adjustment relies on proper guide placement, since it uses margin, column, and ruler guides to calculate how page items are resized and repositioned.

The Snap Zone amount entered in the dialog indicates how close page items need be to the document guides in order for auto adjustment to occur. Layout Adjustment also works better if you keep the Ignore Ruler Guide Alignments option turned off. By doing so, you are telling InDesign to use ruler guides in addition to page edges and margin/column guides to recalculate.

The next step is to set up your master pages properly. Make sure all of your master page guides are in position for added document page items to snap to. You can turn the snap function on by choosing View > Grids & Guides > Snap To Guides.

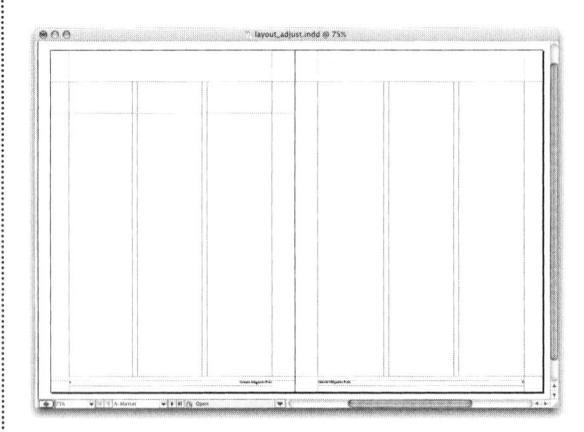

Master Page A

8.17 Enabling Layout Adjustment *(continued)*

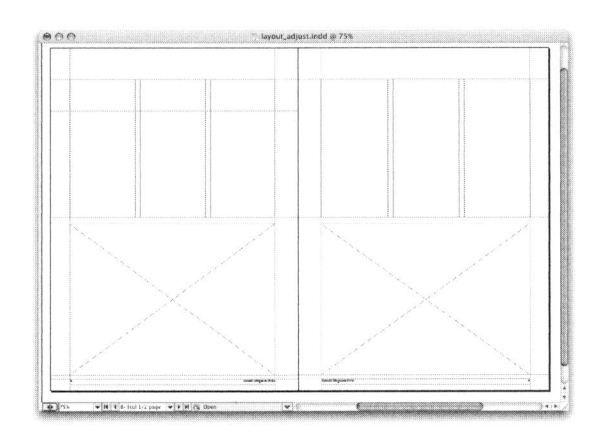

Master Page B—notice the difference in margin/column and ruler guides.

Now it's time to set up a document layout using these master pages.

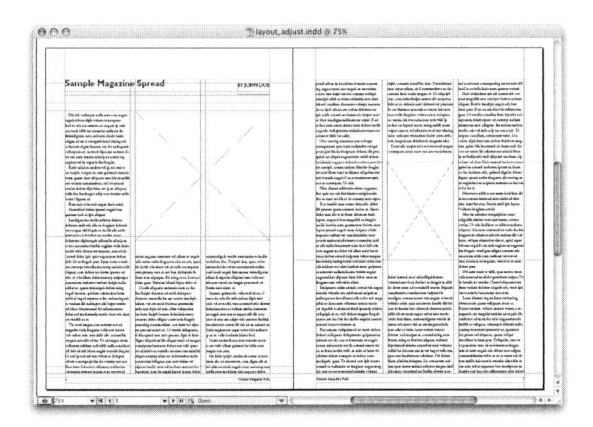

A basic layout with Master Page A applied.

As you're designing, be sure to add ruler guides for your page items to snap to. You can also use the margin and column guides.

Related Tasks

6.9 Creating Multipage Spreads and Master Pages

6.10 Targeting vs. Selecting Pages

6.11 Creating Master Pages

6.13 Applying Master Pages

6.15 Creating and Applying Parent/Child Master Pages

6.16 Overriding Master Page Items

Shortcuts

Override all master page items for selected spread
Mac: Cmd+Opt+Shift+L
Win: Ctrl+Alt+Shift+L

Show/hide guides
Mac: Cmd+;
Win: Ctrl+;

Show/hide rulers
Mac: Cmd+R
Win: Ctrl+R

205

8.17 Enabling Layout Adjustment *(continued)*

Related Tasks

6.18 Adjusting Ruler Guides

6.19 Adjusting Margin and Column Guides

6.20 Aligning to Baseline Grid

8.1 Moving Objects

8.2 Resizing Objects

9.2 Threading and Unthreading Text Frames

Shortcuts

Lock guides
Mac: Opt+Cmd+;
Win: Alt+Ctrl+;

Snap to guides
Mac: Shift+Cmd+;
Win: Shift+Ctrl+;

Select all guides on a page or spread
Mac: Opt+Cmd+G
Win: Alt+Ctrl+G

Pages palette
Mac and Win: F12

Tip

When applied, Layout Adjustment never scales editable text in a text frame.

As a test, let's apply Master Page B to one of the pages of our spread and see what happens. In the Pages palette, click and drag Master Page B on top of the second page of the document spread.

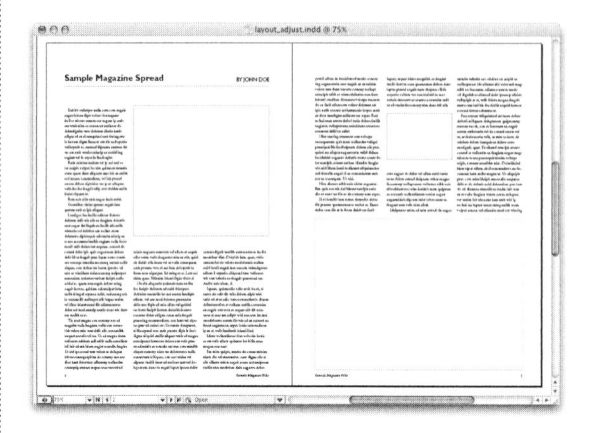

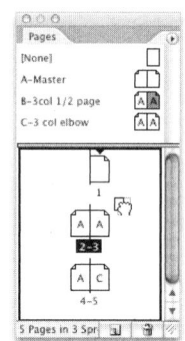

It works! All of the page items have been resized and repositioned to fit the newly applied master style.

Now let's try applying a much more drastic change. Under the File menu, choose Document Setup. When the dialog opens, change the Orientation setting from Portrait to Landscape and click OK.

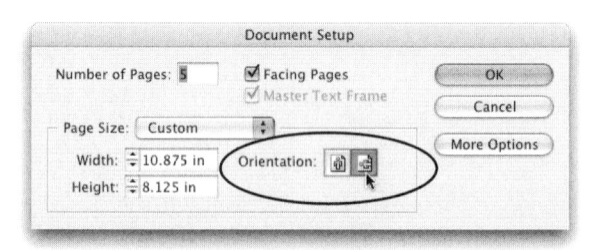

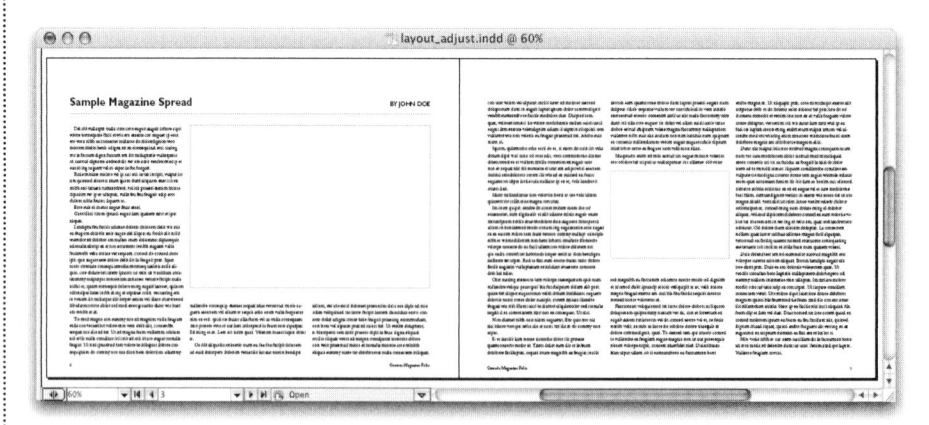

By setting up your documents properly ahead of time and enabling Layout Adjustment, you can make last-minute changes *a lot* less painful.

CHAPTER **9**

Working with Text

IN MANY WAYS, TEXT is the most important part of a layout. Colorful graphics and images can certainly attract a reader's attention, but the *text* is what actually communicates the message. Therefore, it is essential to learn and understand the many ways of working with text in InDesign.

In this chapter we will explore the various methods of importing, flowing, viewing, and editing text. We will cover how to use the Story Editor, the Check Spelling palette, Find/Change, Find Font, and all of the dialogs for importing text from Word documents, RTF files, InDesign tagged text, and XML.

- 9.1 **Text Frame Options**
- 9.2 **Threading and Unthreading Text Frames**
- 9.3 **Importing Text**
- 9.4 **Importing Tagged and ASCII Text**
- 9.5 **Importing XML**
- 9.6 **Flowing Text**
- 9.7 **Filling with Placeholder Text**
- 9.8 **Editing Using the Story Editor**
- 9.9 **Changing Case**
- 9.10 **Check Spelling**
- 9.11 **Editing the Dictionary**
- 9.12 **Using the Dictionary with Foreign Languages**
- 9.13 **Font Overview**
- 9.14 **Find/Replace Missing Fonts**
- 9.15 **Applying Find/Change**

9.1 Text Frame Options

Related Tasks

2.7 Object Menu
3.2 Control Bar
3.3 Selection Tool

Shortcuts

Type tool
Mac and Win: T

Selection tool
Mac and Win: V

Every text frame that you create has its own set of options that can affect the way text is displayed in a document. To access these options, select a text frame with either selection tool (or click it with the Type tool), then choose Object **>** Text Frame Options or press Command+B (Mac) or Ctrl+B (Windows).

Click the General tab at the top of the dialog to access the following options:

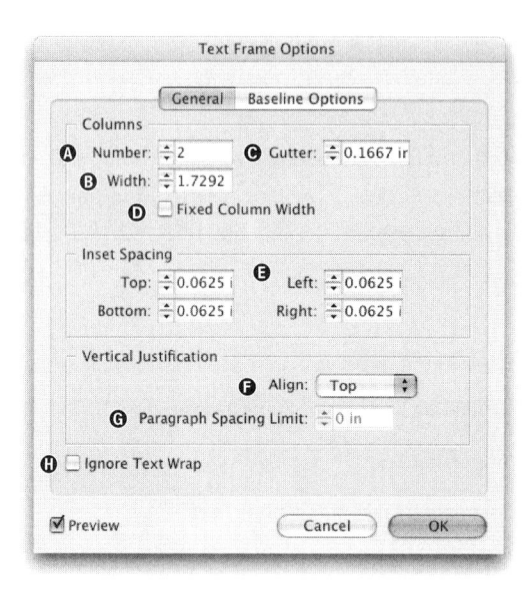

A **Number of Columns** Set the number of columns for a new or selected text frame or group of text frames.

B **Column Width** Apply a specific text frame column width.

C **Gutter** Apply a specific amount of space between columns.

D **Fixed Column Width** Check this box to maintain specified column and gutter width settings when the frame is scaled, or made wider or narrower.

E **Inset Spacing** Apply a specific amount of inset spacing at the top, bottom, left, or right of each column in the text frame.

F **Vertical Justification Align** Click the menu to apply Top, Center, Bottom, or Justified vertical text alignment in the frame.

G **Paragraph Spacing Limit** Apply a limit for paragraph spacing when applying Justified vertical alignment. This value sets the maximum amount of space allowed between paragraphs in the text frame when justified. InDesign adjusts the leading of each line to up to the amount entered. Enter higher values to prevent a change in leading.

H **Ignore Text Wrap** Check this box to allow a text frame not to be affected by surrounding text wraps.

208

9.1 Text Frame Options *(continued)*

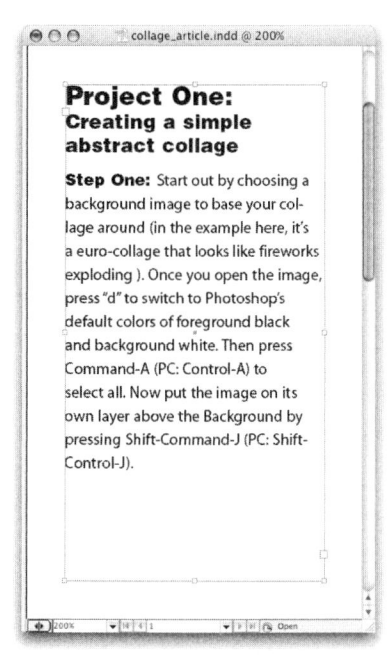

Vertical Text Alignment set to Top

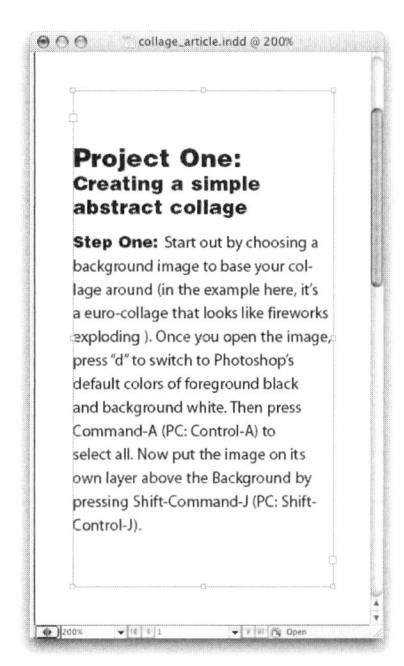

Vertical Text Alignment set to Center

Vertical Text Alignment set to Bottom

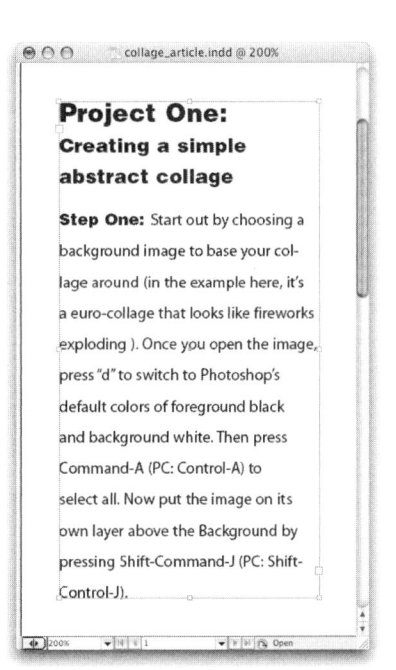

Vertical Text Alignment set to Justify with a Paragraph Spacing Limit of 0

Related Tasks

3.4 Direct Selection and Position Tools

3.6 Type Tools

4.21 Type and Tables Palettes

Shortcuts

Text frame options
Mac: Cmd+B
Win: Ctrl+B

Place
Mac: Cmd+D
Win: Ctrl+D

9.1 Text Frame Options *(continued)*

Related Tasks

5.6	Grids Preferences	
7.1	Frame/Shape Overview	
9.2	Threading and Unthreading Text Frames	

Shortcuts

Direct Selection tool
Mac and Win: A

Rectangle Frame tool
Mac and Win: F

Baseline Options

Click the Baseline Options tab at the top of the dialog to apply custom grid and first baseline settings to a selected frame(s).

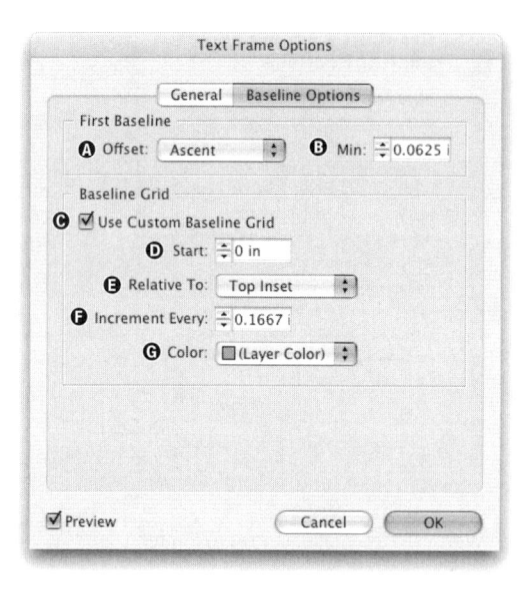

Ⓐ First Baseline Offset Apply Ascent, Cap Height, Leading, X Height, or Fixed First Baseline Offset to the frame. Note: Vertical Text Alignment settings can affect the appearance of First Baseline Offset. The examples shown on the next page have the Vertical Text Alignment set to Top.

Ⓑ Minimum offset amount Apply a minimum distance amount for use with the Fixed First Baseline Offset option.

Ⓒ Use Custom Baseline Grid Check this box to enable Custom Baseline Grid options.

Ⓓ Start Indicate the distance the first line of the baseline grid should be placed relative to the top of the page, margin, frame, or inset.

Ⓔ Relative To Choose Top of Page, Top Margin, Top of Frame, or Top Inset. The Relative To option affects where the grid line Start point falls (see above).

Ⓕ Increment Every Indicate the uniform distance to place between grid lines. Generally, the chosen document leading amount should be entered here.

Ⓖ Color Choose a baseline grid display color. To apply the color currently assigned to the selected layer, choose Layer Color (located at the very top of the menu list).

9.1 Text Frame Options *(continued)*

When the First Baseline Offset option is set to Ascent, the tops of the uppercase characters almost touch the top of the frame or the frame's inset (as shown here).

When the First Baseline Offset option is set to Cap Height, the tops of the uppercase characters touch the top of the frame or inset exactly.

When the First Baseline Offset option is set to Leading, the characters (of any size or inline graphic height) are placed one leading increment away from the top of the frame or inset.

When the First Baseline Offset option is set to X Height, the tops of the lowercase characters touch the top of the frame or inset exactly, while the uppercase characters extend above.

When the First Baseline Offset option is set to Fixed, InDesign uses the Min setting entered to determine how far the characters are placed from the top of the frame or inset. The example shown here uses a Min setting of .0625˝.

Related Tasks

9.3 Importing Text
9.7 Filling with Placeholder Text
13.1 Placing and Editing Text Wraps

Shortcuts

Rectangle tool
Mac and Win: M

Show/hide baseline grid
Mac: Opt+Cmd+'
Win: Alt+Ctrl+'

Tip

To set default text frame options, enter settings in the dialog without any frames selected.

211

9.2 Threading and Unthreading Text Frames

Related Tasks

2.9   View Menu
3.3   Selection Tool
3.4   Direct Selection and Position Tools
3.6   Type Tools
3.9   Frame Tools
3.10 Shape Tools

Shortcuts

Type tool
Mac and Win: T

Selection tool
Mac and Win: V

Direct Selection tool
Mac and Win: A

Rectangle Frame tool
Mac and Win: F

In QuarkXPress this particular task is called "linking and unlinking text boxes." However, in InDesign it is referred to as "threading and unthreading text frames"—same task, different name.

XPress requires that you use a special "linking or unlinking" tool to perform this task, but InDesign provides no special tools for "threading and unthreading." Instead, you must click the in or out "port" of a selected text frame with the Selection or Direct Selection tool.

The in port is located at the upper left of the text frame and the out port at the bottom right. Any frame containing text with an empty in and/or out port indicates the text is at the beginning or end of the story, respectively.

A port that contains a triangle indicates that the story is linked to another text frame. An out port containing a plus sign (+) indicates existing "overset" text, meaning that there is more copy to flow. To display the rest of the story, you can either make the current text frame larger, or thread the overset text into another frame.

To thread overset text, click the in or out port of a selected text frame with either selection tool and the cursor changes into a loaded text place icon. Click the loaded cursor and a frame is drawn for you automatically using default text frame options, or click and draw a frame (also using default text frame options). In either instance the overset text flows into the new frame. You can also click the loaded text place icon in an existing frame to flow overset text.

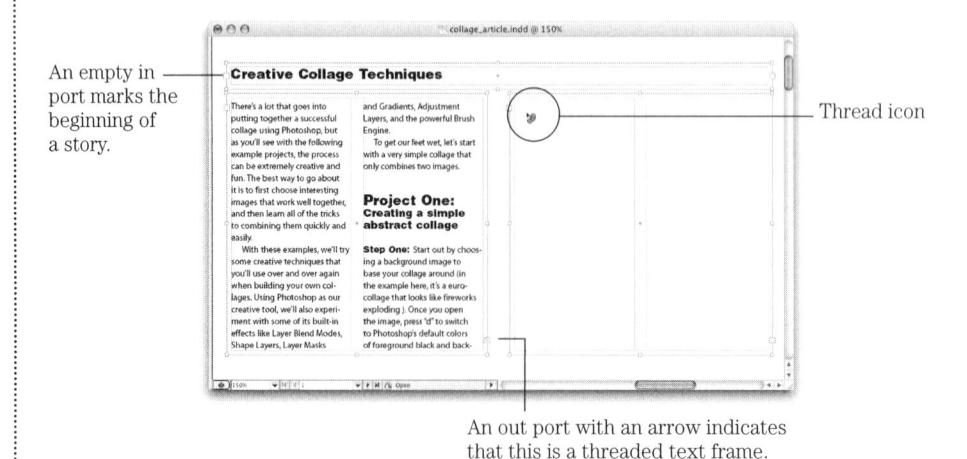

An empty in port marks the beginning of a story.

Thread icon

An out port with an arrow indicates that this is a threaded text frame.

If you have a preexisting text frame that you'd like to thread into, hover the mouse over it until the cursor changes once more—this time into a chain link icon (known as the text *thread* icon).

212

9.2 Threading and Unthreading Text Frames *(continued)*

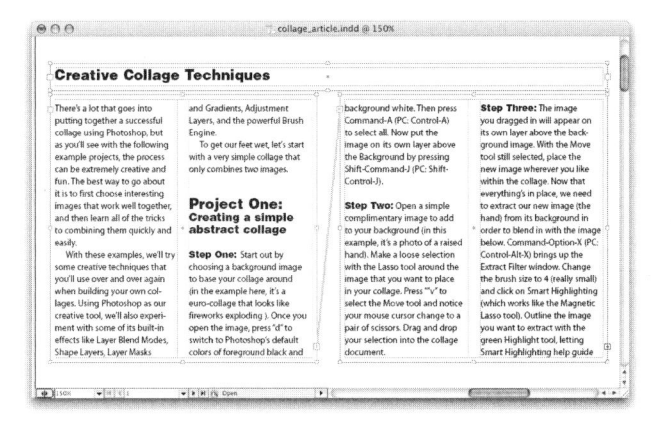

Click the frame and the overset text from the first frame flows into the second. Note: Two text frames containing separate stories can also be threaded this way, merging both stories into one.

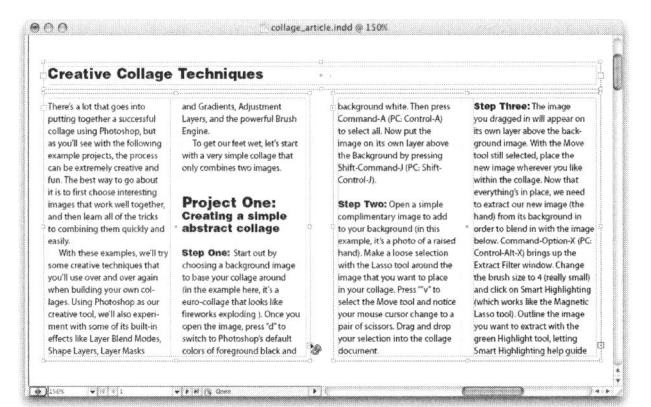

To unthread, click the in or out port of a selected text frame and the cursor again changes into a loaded text place icon. Hover the mouse over either text frame until the cursor changes yet again—this time into a *broken chain link icon* (known as the text *unthread* icon).

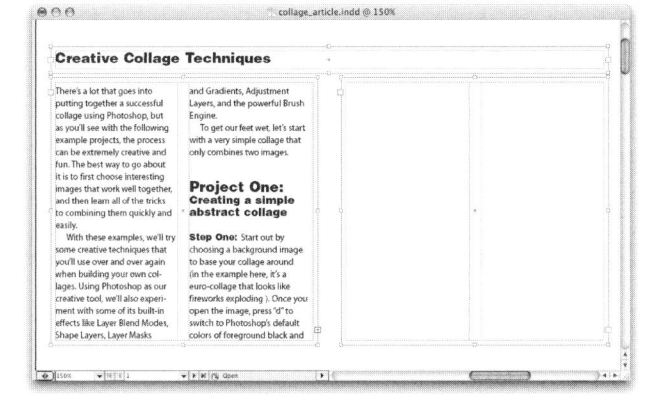

Click either frame and the story unthreads, returning the overset set text to the original frame.

Related Tasks

4.21	Type and Tables Palettes
6.11	Creating Master Pages
7.1	Frame/Shape Overview
9.1	Text Frame Options
9.3	Importing Text
11.5	Creating and Applying Object Styles

Shortcuts

Rectangle tool
Mac and Win: M

Show/hide text threads
Mac: Opt+Cmd+Y
Win: Alt+Ctrl+Y

Show/hide frame edges
Mac: Cmd+H
Win: Ctrl+H

Tip

All text frames can be threaded, even when they are empty, placed on different layers, or locked in position.

9.3 Importing Text

Related Tasks

2.3	File Menu
2.4	Edit Menu
3.6	Type Tools
4.10	Links Palette
4.18	Tags Palette
4.21	Type and Tables Palettes
5.1	General Preferences

Shortcuts

Place
Mac: Cmd+D
Win: Ctrl+D

General Preferences
Mac: Cmd+K
Win: Ctrl+K

Type tool
Mac and Win: T

Copy
Mac: Cmd+C
Win: Ctrl+C

Tip

When importing a text document, hold down the Shift key and click the Open button in the Place dialog to access the import options dialog.

Text can be typed directly into an InDesign document; however, you'll most likely find yourself adding text to your layouts by importing it from outside sources. This is standard fare, as most of us InDesign users are strictly designers and not editors as well. Therefore, it is not uncommon for an editor or a client to send you a text document that has been created in an outside application such as Microsoft Word or BBedit.

You can import text into an InDesign document from an outside source in one of two ways: by copying/pasting, and by using the Place command just as you would with a graphic link.

Copy/Paste

You can copy/paste text from just about any outside source, including other applications, emails, and Web browsers. By default, InDesign ignores any text formatting when copy/pasting. However, if you'd like to preserve formatting when copy/pasting text from an outside source, choose All Information in the When Pasting section of Type Preferences.

Importing Microsoft Word and RTF Text

To import text from a Word or RTF (Rich Text Format) document, choose File > Place and browse to the file's location on your system. Then, check Show Import Options and click Open.

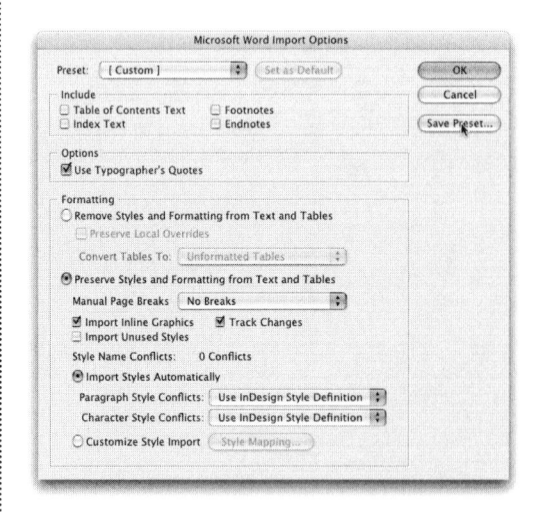

Text imported from a Word doc using the Import Options settings shown above

214

9.3 Importing Text *(continued)*

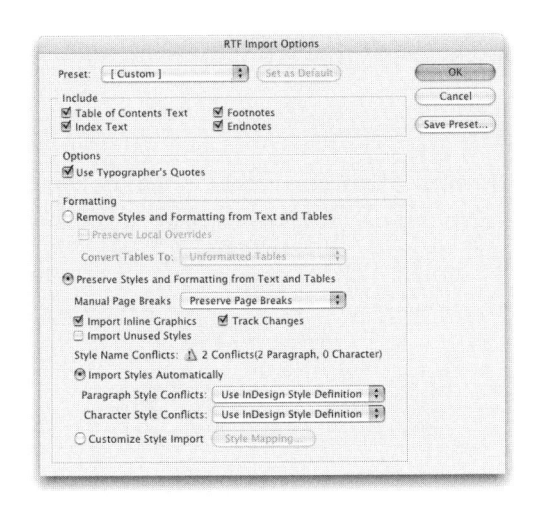

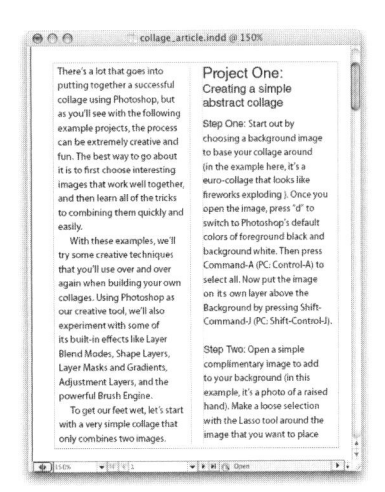

Text imported from an RTF doc using the Import Options settings shown above

The Microsoft Word Import Options and RTF Import Options dialogs are divided into three sections: Include, Options, and Formatting.

Under Include, check the items you'd like to import: Table of Contents Text, Index Text, Footnotes, and Endnotes. It is also recommended that you check Use Typographer's Quotes under Options, as this is standard for most InDesign layouts.

Under Formatting you can choose to either remove or preserve text formatting on import. There are several additional options for preserving formatting, including Manual Page Breaks, Import Inline Graphics, Import Unused Styles, and Track Changes.

You can also choose to import styles automatically or by using a customized style import. When selecting automatic import, InDesign displays style conflicts according to the paragraph and character definitions chosen in the dialog menus. Options include Use InDesign Style Definition, Redefine InDesign Style, and Auto Rename.

Use InDesign Style Definition prefers the InDesign style when a style name conflict occurs. Redefine InDesign Style prefers the imported Word or RTF style and actually changes it without changing its name. Auto Rename changes the InDesign style to match the imported Word or RTF style and also assumes its name.

Customized Style Import allows you to map InDesign styles to imported Word/RTF styles and vice versa.

Related Tasks

5.2 Type Preferences

5.3 Advanced Type Preferences

5.4 Composition Preferences

7.4 Selecting Type

17.6 Exporting as XML

Shortcuts

Paste
Mac: Cmd+V
Win: Ctrl+V

Links palette
Mac: Shift+Cmd+D
Win: Shift+Ctrl+D

Show Structure
Mac: Opt+Cmd+1
Win: Alt+Ctrl+1

Tips

You can choose to either merge or append an existing structure when importing XML into a document.

Unfortunately, you cannot import QuarkXPress tagged text into InDesign.

215

9.4 Importing Tagged and ASCII Text

Related Tasks

2.3	File Menu
2.4	Edit Menu
3.6	Type Tools
4.10	Links Palette
4.18	Tags Palette
4.21	Type and Tables Palettes
5.1	General Preferences

Shortcuts

Place
Mac: Cmd+D
Win: Ctrl+D

General Preferences
Mac: Cmd+K
Win: Ctrl+K

Type tool
Mac and Win: T

Copy
Mac: Cmd+C
Win: Ctrl+C

To import InDesign tagged text, choose File > Place and browse to the file's location on your system. Once selected, check Show Import Options and click Open.

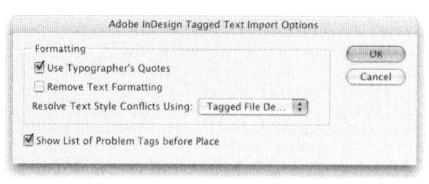

The Adobe InDesign Tagged Text Import Options dialog is much simpler to use and contains fewer options than the import dialogs for Word and RTF documents.

Text imported from an InDesign tagged text file using the Import Options settings shown right.

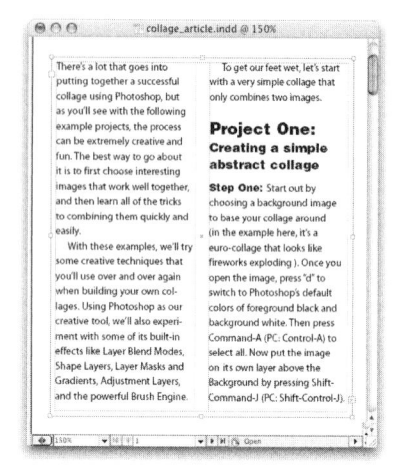

Under Formatting, you can choose to convert straight quotes to typographer's quotes (recommended) and also remove text formatting. To import tagged text formatting, leave the Remove Text Formatting option unchecked and choose a style conflict resolve option from the menu. When a style conflict occurs, you can choose to apply Publication Definition, which applies the InDesign document style, or Tagged File Definition, which applies the Tagged Text style.

To view a list of problem tags before placing imported tagged text, check the Show List option located at the bottom of the dialog.

Importing ASCII and Other Text-Only Formats

To import text-only formats such as ASCII text, choose File > Place and browse to the file's location on your system. Then, check Show Import Options and click Open.

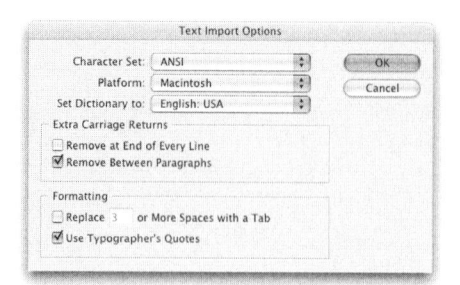

At the top of the Text Import Options dialog, choose a character set from the menu that matches the text-only file you are importing. Macintosh and PC platforms use different character sets. Therefore, to avoid importing strange characters, be sure and choose the platform that the file was originally created on from the menu. You can also choose a dictionary to apply to the imported text from the pop-up menu.

9.4 Importing Tagged and ASCII Text *(continued)*

Text imported from an ASCII file using the Import Option settings shown above

In the center of the dialog, you have the option to remove any extra carriage returns placed at the ends of lines and between paragraphs. Having this option to remove unnecessary forced breaks upon text import can be extremely helpful—it can save you from having to spend an awful lot of time reformatting later.

At the bottom of the dialog are some basic import formatting options. You can choose to replace a specific number of spaces with a tab and also convert straight quotes into typographer's quotes.

ADOBE INCOPY

The Story Editor is also an integral part of the Adobe InDesign/InCopy production workflow. InDesign/InCopy Notes can be added and displayed in the Story Editor as well as in the document window.

The InCopy application is actually nothing more than a glorified Story Editor. Once it's installed, stories can be exported from InDesign using the Edit > InCopy submenu, and then assigned to specific InCopy users through the Assignments palette. Other members of your production team can then open assigned stories in InCopy for editing.

InCopy users can work in any one of three display modes: Story, Galley, or Layout. Story mode works very much like the Story Editor in InDesign. Galley mode is exactly like Story mode except that it also displays line breaks used in the layout. Layout mode allows users to edit copy and also perform a limited amount of graphic editing tasks in the InDesign layout.

Related Tasks

5.2 Type Preferences

5.3 Advanced Type Preferences

5.4 Composition Preferences

7.4 Selecting Type

17.6 Exporting as XML

Shortcuts

Paste
Mac: Cmd+V
Win: Ctrl+V

Links palette
Mac: Shift+Cmd+D
Win: Shift+Ctrl+D

Show structure
Mac: Opt+Cmd+1
Win: Alt+Ctrl+1

Tips

When importing a text document, hold down the Shift key and click the Open button in the Place dialog to access the import options dialog.

You can choose to either merge or append an existing structure when importing XML into a document.

Unfortunately, you cannot import QuarkXPress tagged text into InDesign.

217

9.5 Importing XML

It is also possible to import XML text elements into a document. Choose File > Import XML and browse to the file's location on your system. Once you select the file, check Show XML Import Options and click Open.

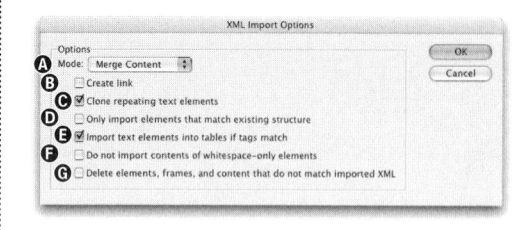

- **A Mode** Choose to merge or append imported XML content into the document's structure.
- **B Create Link** Creates a link for imported XML. The link appears in the Links palette upon import.
- **C Clone Repeating Text Elements** Allows InDesign to automatically clone matched elements in the document to preserve styling.
- **D Only Import Elements That Match Existing Structure** Deletes any existing document elements that do not match the incoming XML.
- **E Import Text Elements Into Tables If Tags Match** Allows InDesign to import XML elements tagged as tables.
- **F Do Not Import Contents Of Whitespace-Only Elements** Prevents the import of XML elements containing nothing but whitespace.
- **G Delete Elements, Frames, And Content That Do Not Match Imported XML** Prevents the import of elements not matching any elements already existing in the document.

Click OK to import. Choose View > Structure > Show Structure to view the imported XML. Upon import, the contents of all imported XML elements are applied to corresponding tagged frames and text objects.

To apply an XML element's contents to an existing untagged frame, click and drag it from the Structure window over the frame in the document layout. Release the mouse button to add the contents of the XML element to the frame.

To apply existing document Paragraph and Character Styles to imported XML tags, choose Map Tags To Styles from the Structure fly-out menu. Select the styles you'd like to map to each tag by clicking its name in the Style menu and choosing from the pop-up menu. If the tags and styles you'd like to map share the same name, click the Map By Name button and InDesign assigns them for you.

Related Tasks

- 4.10 Links Palette
- 4.18 Tags Palette
- 4.21 Type and Tables Palettes
- 5.2 Type Preferences
- 17.6 Exporting as XML

Shortcuts

Place
Mac: Cmd+D
Win: Ctrl+D

General Preferences
Mac: Cmd+K
Win: Ctrl+K

Type tool
Mac and Win: T

Links palette
Mac: Shift+Cmd+D
Win: Shift+Ctrl+D

Show Structure
Mac: Opt+Cmd+1
Win: Alt+Ctrl+1

Tips

When importing a text document, hold down the Shift key and click the Open button in the Place dialog to access the import options dialog.

You can choose to either merge or append an existing structure when importing XML into a document.

Unfortunately, you cannot import QuarkXPress tagged text into InDesign.

9.6 Flowing Text

You can flow text into a document in several ways using the Place command: Manual Text Flow, Semi-Automatic Text Flow, Automatic Text Flow, or Super Autoflow.

Manual Text Flow

Choose File > Place and open the text document you'd like to import. With a loaded text place cursor, click anywhere in the document or draw a frame. InDesign creates a new frame using default text frame options and places the text into it. You can also place text by clicking an existing frame or a series of threaded frames.

The Manual Text Flow icon changes its appearance when you hover the cursor over a frame or guide/grid snap point.

| | The Manual Text Flow icon | | The Manual Text Flow icon when placed over a frame | | The Manual Text Flow icon when placed over a guide/grid snap point |

Semi-Automatic Text Flow

Semi-Automatic Text Flow reloads the text place cursor when a placed story does not end in a drawn or clicked frame (or series of frames). To flow placed text semi-automatically, hold down the Option (Mac) or Alt key (Windows) as you click or draw with the loaded text place cursor.

The Semi-Automatic Text Flow icon changes its appearance when you hover the cursor over a frame.

| | The Semi-Automatic Text Flow icon | | The Semi-Automatic Text Flow icon when placed over a frame |

Automatic Text Flow

Automatic Text Flow adds as many threaded text frames as necessary to fit a story in the existing pages of a document. To flow placed text automatically, hold down Option+Shift (Mac) or Alt+Shift (Windows) as you click or draw with the loaded text place cursor.

| | The Automatic Text Flow icon |

Super Autoflow

SuperAutoflow adds as many threaded text frames *and pages* as necessary to fit an entire story in a document. To Super Autoflow placed text, hold down Shift as you click or draw with the loaded text place cursor.

| | The Super Autoflow icon |

Related Tasks

2.3	File Menu
3.9	Frame Tools
3.10	Shape Tools
4.21	Type and Tables Palettes
5.2	Type Preferences
5.3	Advanced Type Preferences
5.4	Composition Preferences
7.1	Frame/Shape Overview
9.1	Text Frame Options
9.2	Threading and Unthreading Text Frames
9.3	Importing Text
9.7	Filling with Placeholder Text

Shortcuts

Place
Mac: Cmd+D
Win: Ctrl+D

Text frame options
Mac: Cmd+B
Win: Ctrl+B

Rectangle Frame tool
Mac and Win: F

Rectangle tool
Mac and Win: M

Tip

Clicking a loaded text place cursor between column guides creates a text frame that fills the entire column.

9.7 Filling with Placeholder Text

Related Tasks

2.6	Type Menu
3.2	Control Bar
3.3	Selection Tool
3.4	Direct Selection and Position Tools
3.6	Type Tools
3.9	Frame Tools
3.10	Shape Tools
4.21	Type and Tables Palettes
5.19	Keyboard Shortcuts
6.11	Creating Master Pages
7.4	Selecting Type
9.2	Threading and Unthreading Text Frames

Shortcuts

Type tool
Mac and Win: T

Selection tool
Mac and Win: V

Direct Selection tool
Mac and Win: A

Rectangle Frame tool
Mac and Win: F

Rectangle tool
Mac and Win: M

Tip

To Fill with Placeholder Text using the contextual menu, click a frame with either selection tool or the Type tool and Control-click (Mac) or right-click (Windows). Choose Fill With Placeholder Text from the menu.

If you ever have to wait until the last minute for an editor or client to submit text for a layout, you're not alone. This happens all the time. What most people don't realize is that text plays an important role in the *look* of your layout—and trying to design without it is like stumbling through the dark!

Thankfully with InDesign, you don't have to let late text submissions hold up your design work. While you're waiting for the *real text* to arrive in your inbox, go ahead and create a layout using text frames that are filled with placeholder text.

Click a frame with either selection tool or the Type tool, and choose Type > Fill With Placeholder Text. InDesign immediately fills the entire text frame or series of threaded frames with fake-Latin gibberish.

The paragraphs are set up just like real text—perfect for use as placeholders in your layout.

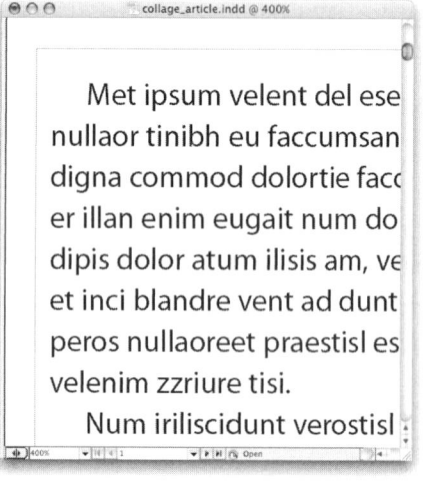

When zoomed out, the placeholder text appears normal—but a closer look reveals the fake-Latin gibberish.

You can also apply character and paragraph styles to placeholder text, if needed to complete a preliminary design. When the real text arrives, copy/paste it into the preexisting frames and it assumes the formatting already applied.

9.8 Editing Using the Story Editor

Warning! Editing large amounts of tiny text on screen has been proven to make you cross-eyed. To save yourself from this miserable fate, try using the Story Editor.

The Story Editor displays all the text for a selected story in a separate, easy-to-read, single-column window (called a "story window"). Unlike the layout window (a.k.a. the document window), the story window does not display any applied line breaks or text formatting (other than bold or italic fonts). To open the Story Editor, choose Edit > Edit in Story Editor, or press Cmd+Y (Mac) or Ctrl+Y (Windows).

The only tool available when using the Story Editor is the Type tool—all other tools appear grayed out in the Toolbox. With the Type tool, you can select and edit text in the story window just as you would in layout view, only without the eyestrain. As you edit or add text in the story window, InDesign updates the story in the layout.

Like with a document window, you can expand, minimize, and close a story window—the controls work exactly the same. Under the Story Editor Preferences, you can change story window display options, such as font, text size, line spacing, and background color.

You can also choose to hide or show the Style Name column and Depth ruler under View > Story Editor. The Style Name column displays all applied paragraph style names to the left of the story. When visible, the Depth ruler also appears in this column, and is used to measure the vertical depth of text in the layout. Adjust the amount of horizontal space the Style Name column uses in the story window by dragging the vertical divider left or right.

One of the best features of the Story Editor is the ability to view and edit any overset text without having to refer back to the layout window. The story window displays a horizontal divider line with the word "Overset" placed before it to indicate where the overset text begins. It also places a colored line along the left side of the ensuing paragraphs to indicate how much text is overset.

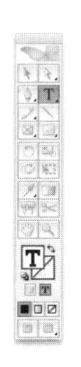

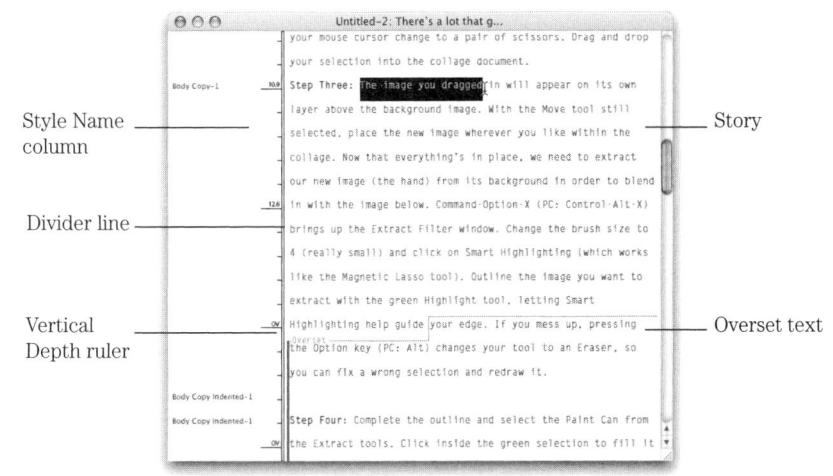

Related Tasks

5.8 Dictionary Preferences
5.9 Spelling Preferences
5.10 Autocorrect Preferences
5.11 Story Editor Display Preferences
6.7 Saving Files for use with InCopy
7.4 Selecting Type
9.2 Threading and Unthreading Text Frames
9.10 Check Spelling
9.11 Editing the Dictionary
9.15 Applying Find/Change

Shortcuts

Edit in Story Editor
Mac: Cmd+Y
Win: Ctrl+Y

Type tool
Mac and Win: T

Check Spelling palette
Mac: Cmd+I
Win: Ctrl+I

Find/Change
Mac: Cmd+F
Win: Ctrl+F

Show/hide hidden characters
Mac: Opt+Cmd+I
Win: Alt+Ctrl+I

Tip

It is possible to have multiple story windows open at the same time in order to edit different sections of the same story or to edit multiple stories at once.

9.9 Changing Case

Related Tasks

2.6	Type Menu
3.2	Control Bar
3.6	Type Tools
4.21	Type and Tables Palettes
7.4	Selecting Type
9.8	Editing Using the Story Editor
11.1	Creating and Applying Character Styles
11.2	Creating and Applying Paragraph Styles
11.6	Editing and Deleting Styles

Shortcuts

Type tool
Mac and Win: T

Paragraph Styles palette
Mac and Win: F11

Character Styles palette
Mac and Win: Shift+F11

Toggle all caps
Mac: Shift+Cmd+K
Win: Shift+Ctrl+K

Toggle small caps
Mac: Shift+Cmd+H
Win: Shift+Ctrl+H

Select all
Mac: Cmd+A
Win: Ctrl+A

Tip

You can assign keyboard shortcuts to the Change Case commands. Choose Edit > Keyboard Shortcuts and select Type Menu from the dialog's Product Area list.

To change case in InDesign, highlight some text with the Type tool and choose Type > Change Case or Control/right-click and select the command from the context menu. Select Uppercase, Lowercase, Title Case, or Sentence Case from the submenu. Title Case capitalizes the first letter of every word, and Sentence Case capitalizes the first letter of every sentence.

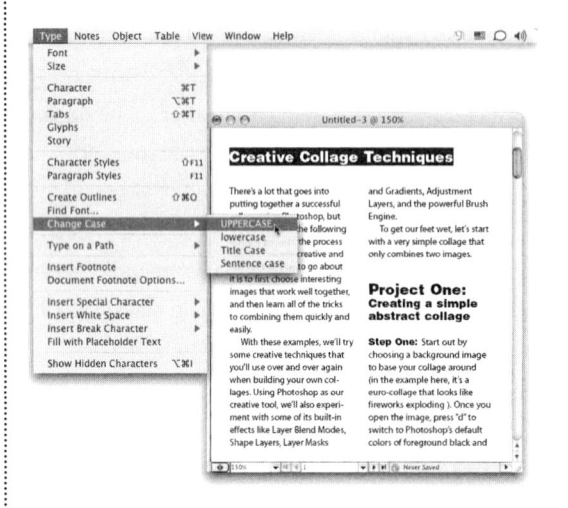

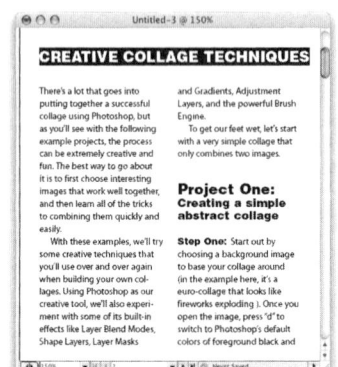

Select some text with the Type tool and apply the Change Case command. The change is applied immediately.

To change case of all text in a story (including overset text), select the frame with either selection tool and apply the Change Case command. Note: If the selected frame is part of a threaded series, you cannot change case for an entire story using this method. To change case for an entire story that is contained in a series of threaded frames, place the Type tool cursor in any one of the threaded frames and choose Edit > Select All, and then apply the command.

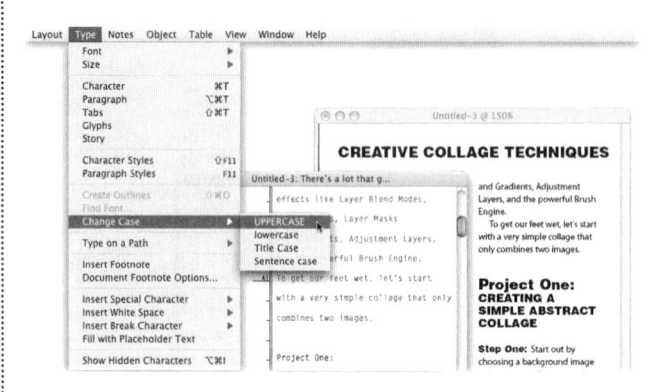

You can also apply Change Case commands to selected text when editing with the Story Editor.

9.10 Check Spelling

To check spelling with the Check Spelling palette, choose Edit > Spelling > Check Spelling or press Command+I (Mac) or Ctrl+I (Windows). You can also access this command under the contextual menu by Control/right-clicking anywhere on the page while working with the Type tool.

Once a search option is selected from the Search menu, click Start. Any words that are misspelled, uncapitalized, unknown, or not in the dictionary appear at the top of the palette. The palette also checks the spelling of any overset text when searching a story or document.

In the Change To data field, enter the correct spelling or choose from the list of suggested corrections (if available). Click the Change button to correct the word in the document and continue the spell-check. To correct every occurrence of the word within the search parameters, click Change All.

If the Check Spelling palette finds a word that is spelled correctly but that is not recognized by the dictionary (such as a proper name or abbreviation), click Skip. To ignore every other occurrence of this word within the search parameters, click Ignore All. You can also add the word to a chosen user dictionary so that it does not come up in future spell-checks. To do so, click Add.

At the bottom of the palette, you can choose to search for misspelled words in a selected story, document, word selection, to the end of a selected story, or in all open documents (if you have more than one open). You can also select from a list of user dictionaries to add words using the Add To menu.

It is also possible to enable the Dynamic Spelling feature, which underlines any found spell-check errors in assigned colors as you type or upon text import. You can turn this option on or off under Edit > Spelling > Dynamic Spelling or in Spelling Preferences.

Related Tasks

2.4	Edit Menu
3.3	Selection Tool
3.4	Direct Selection and Position Tools
3.6	Type Tools
4.14	PageMaker Toolbar
5.8	Dictionary Preferences

Shortcuts

Check Spelling palette
Mac: Cmd+I
Win: Ctrl+I

Type tool
Mac and Win: T

9.10 Check Spelling *(continued)*

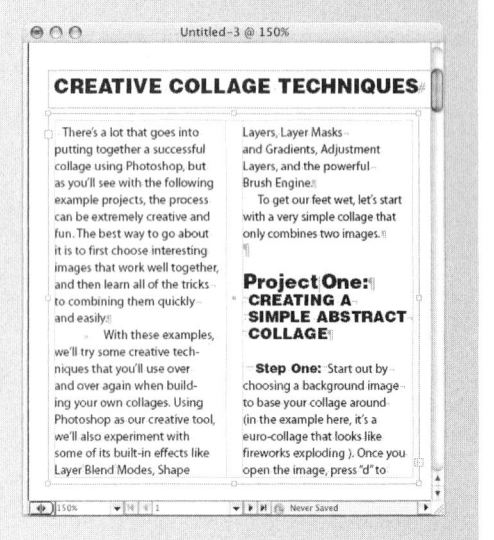

Related Tasks

5.9 Spelling Preferences

5.10 Autocorrect Preferences

7.4 Selecting Type

9.11 Editing the Dictionary

9.12 Using the Dictionary with Foreign Languages

Shortcuts

Find/Change
Mac: Cmd+F
Win: Ctrl+F

General Preferences
Mac: Cmd+K
Win: Ctrl+K

Tips

Although not listed under the Window menu, the Check Spelling, Dictionary, and Find/Change palettes truly are palettes rather than dialogs. The fact that you can switch tools and selections as you're using them gives them away.

You can also open the Check Spelling palette by clicking the Check Spelling button in the PageMaker toolbar.

To automatically correct misspelled words as you type, enable the Autocorrect feature under Edit > Spelling > Autocorrect or in Autocorrect Preferences. Autocorrect only fixes misspelled words that are added to the list in Autocorrect Preferences. Note: Unlike the Dynamic Spelling feature, Autocorrect only works as you type and not upon text import.

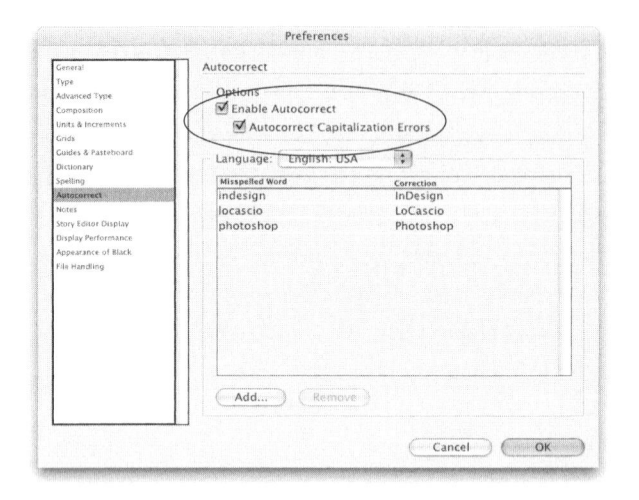

When enabled, Autocorrect fixes capitalization errors for all words located in the default and user dictionaries, not just for words that are added to the Autocorrect Preferences list.

REVEALING HIDDEN CHARACTERS

When editing text in a document, it can help to view any "invisible" characters that have been added. Hidden characters, such as forced line breaks, tabs, or extra spaces, can often create an awkward text flow. By activating the Show Hidden Characters command, you can see where they have been placed in the layout and delete them. Choose Type > Show/Hide Hidden Characters, or press Opt+Cmd+I (Mac) or Alt+Ctrl+I (Windows). You can also access this command from the context menu by Control/right-clicking anywhere on the page while working with the Type tool.

224

9.11 Editing the Dictionary

Proper names, technical terms, abbreviations, and various other slang words are not included in InDesign's default dictionary. To avoid having these words show up repeatedly when running a spell-check, try adding them to a saved user dictionary.

You can add words to user dictionaries as you're running a spell-check. To add words as they are located by the Check Spelling palette, select a user dictionary from the Add To menu and click the Add button. To access and edit user dictionaries with the Dictionary palette while spell-checking, click the Dictionary button.

You can also open the Dictionary palette by choosing Spelling > Dictionary from the Edit menu or the contextual menu. Note: Spelling commands can only be accessed through the contextual menu when the Type tool cursor is placed inside a text frame.

Choose a dictionary to edit from the Target menu located at the top of the Dictionary palette. You must also choose a language to edit with from the Language menu (English: USA is chosen in the example shown below). From the Dictionary List menu, choose to display Added Words, Removed Words, or Ignored Words.

Dynamic Spelling and the Check Spelling palette cannot locate Added Words unless they are spelled incorrectly. Removed Words are erased from the dictionary but can always be added back. Ignored Words are still in the dictionary but go unnoticed by the Check Spelling palette or Dynamic Spelling.

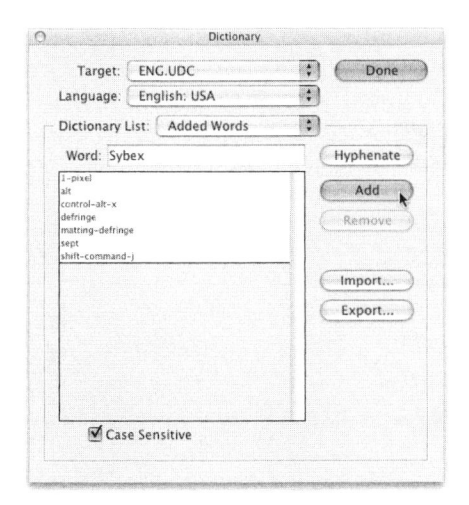

To add a word to any one of the dictionary lists, enter it in the Word field and click the Add button. To remove a word from a dictionary list, select it from the display window and click Remove.

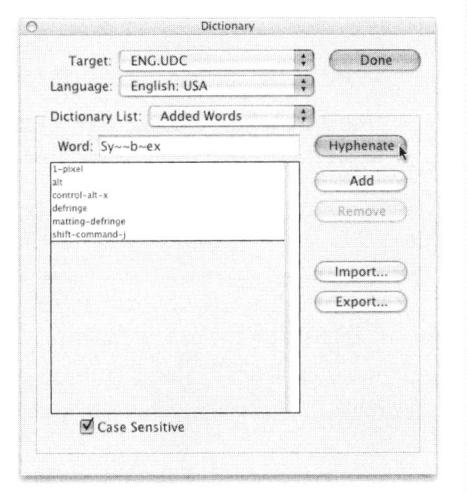

Click the Hyphenate button to view hyphenation points for a word (indicated by a tilde, ~). A single tilde ~ indicates the best hyphenation point, whereas a double tilde ~~ indicates second best and a triple tilde ~~~ third best. You can edit hyphenation points by adding tildes to or deleting them from the word displayed in the Word field.

Related Tasks

2.3	File Menu
4.14	PageMaker Toolbar
5.8	Dictionary Preferences
5.9	Spelling Preferences
5.10	Autocorrect Preferences
9.10	Check Spelling
9.12	Using the Dictionary with Foreign Languages
9.15	Applying Find/Change

Shortcuts

Check Spelling palette
Mac: Cmd+I
Win: Ctrl+I

Find/Change
Mac: Cmd+F
Win: Ctrl+F

General Preferences
Mac: Cmd+K
Win: Ctrl+K

Tip

You can create and add user dictionaries in Dictionary Preferences.

9.12 Using the Dictionary with Foreign Languages

Related Tasks

2.3	File Menu
5.8	Dictionary Preferences
5.9	Spelling Preferences
5.10	Autocorrect Preferences
9.10	Check Spelling
9.11	Editing the Dictionary
9.15	Applying Find/Change

Shortcuts

Check Spelling palette
Mac: Cmd+I
Win: Ctrl+I

Find/Change
Mac: Cmd+F
Win: Ctrl+F

General Preferences
Mac: Cmd+K
Win: Ctrl+K

Tip

You can add foreign language words to any user dictionary.

With InDesign, it is not only possible to use more than one language in a document, you can even mix languages in the same paragraph! There are 28 languages to choose from in the built-in user dictionary. To apply any other languages you must purchase a special language edition of InDesign CS2.

InDesign sees applied languages as a character attribute, unlike QuarkXPress Passport, which considers language a paragraph attribute. You can choose a language to apply to selected text from the Character palette (you must show all options in the palette to access the Language menu), or from the Control bar when working with the Type tool.

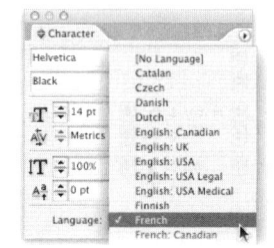

Applying the French language to the top line of the paragraph

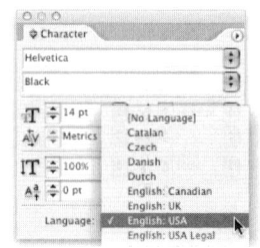

Applying the English language to the bottom line of the paragraph

You can then check spelling for multiple languages in the same paragraph. The Check Spelling palette refers to all available dictionaries when different languages have been applied.

You can select a default language for the document under Dictionary Preferences. It is also possible to edit foreign dictionaries using the Dictionary palette.

Running a French language spell-check

9.13 Font Overview

You can apply any font loaded on your system to selected text through the Type > Font submenu or the Character palette/Control bar Font menus. Note: To access the Font menu in the Control bar, you must first access the Type tool from the Toolbox.

Select a font family and accompanying type style (if available) from the respective menus. Unlike in QuarkXPress no bold or italic type style controls are available in the Character palette or Control bar. You can only apply a bold or italic type style if it is part of a chosen font family.

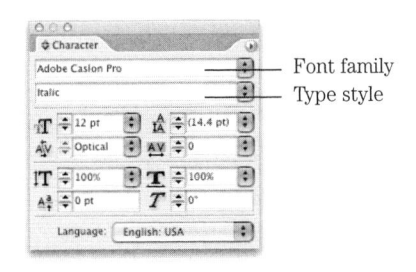

— Font family
— Type style

The Font menu list also displays a PostScript, TrueType, or Open Type icon before each font name as well as a sample preview. You can choose to display sample previews at small, medium, or large sizes under Type Preferences.

Open Type font — Caflisch Script Pro
PostScript font — Cairo
TrueType font — Capitals

A Fonts folder is also located in the InDesign application folder. Any fonts placed in this folder are managed from within InDesign rather than from an outside application or through the operating system. Fonts that do not load properly through the operating system (such as multiple master fonts in OS X) may work in InDesign by placing them in the application Fonts folder.

Like the other applications in the Adobe Creative Suite, InDesign also features full Open Type font support. Open Type fonts are cross platform (usable on a Mac and a PC), and offer many additional characters (called glyphs) and typographical features, such as ligatures and contextual alternates (combined characters), swashes (fancy versions of a letter), ordinal numbers (e.g., 1st, 2nd, 3rd, etc.), tilting characters, and fractions. Some of the Open Type fonts that come with InDesign CS2 include Adobe Caslon Pro, Adobe Garamond Pro, and Caflisch Pro.

Related Tasks

2.6	Type Menu
3.2	Control Bar
3.3	Selection Tool
3.4	Direct Selection and Position Tools
3.6	Type Tools
3.15	Eyedropper Tool
4.21	Type and Tables Palettes
5.2	Type Preferences
9.14	Find/Replace Missing Fonts
11.1	Creating and Applying Character Styles
15.1	Preflighting Fonts

Shortcuts

Type tool
Mac and Win: T

Paragraph Styles palette
Mac and Win: F11

Character Styles palette
Mac and Win: Shift+F11

General Preferences
Mac: Cmd+K
Win: Ctrl+K

Tip

Not sure which font you'd like to use? Select some text with the Type tool and click inside the font data field located in either the Control bar or the Character palette. To preview available fonts as they are applied to the selection, scroll through the list by pressing the up/down arrow keys.

9.14 Find/Replace Missing Fonts

Related Tasks

2.6	Type Menu
3.2	Control Bar
3.3	Selection Tool
3.4	Direct Selection and Position Tools
3.6	Type Tools
3.15	Eyedropper Tool
4.21	Type and Tables Palettes
5.2	Type Preferences
9.13	Font Overview
11.1	Creating and Applying Character Styles
15.1	Preflighting Fonts

Shortcuts

Type tool
Mac and Win: T

Paragraph Styles palette
Mac and Win: F11

Character Styles palette
Mac and Win: Shift+F11

General Preferences
Mac: Cmd+K
Win: Ctrl+K

Tip

You can find and replace fonts using the Find Font dialog even if they are not missing.

Any time you try opening an InDesign document that uses fonts not currently loaded on your system, a warning dialog appears letting you know which fonts are unavailable.

When this happens you can do one of three things:

- Load the fonts on your system.
- Click OK and deal with this later.
- Click the Find Font button and replace missing fonts with something else that you currently have loaded on your system.

If you have the missing font, the smart choice would be to stop what you're doing and load it on your system.

If you don't have the font, you can always choose the second option and click OK to deal with this inconvenience later. All text containing missing fonts appear highlighted in the document, but only if your Composition Preferences are set to highlight substituted fonts (the default setting).

If you don't have the font, or if the font provided is not compatible with your system, you can always replace it with something else. Click the Find Font button in the warning dialog, or if you've already clicked OK, choose Type > Find Font.

Click the Find First button to view the first occurrence of the missing font in the document. Click the Change button to replace it with the selected font. Click the Change All button to replace every occurrence of the missing font in the document. Click Change/Find to locate and replace every occurrence of the missing font with each click of the mouse.

The bottom of the Find Font dialog displays information about the font currently selected from the Fonts In Document list. Click the Less Info button to hide this portion of the dialog. Click the Reveal In Finder button (Mac) or the Reveal In Explorer button (Windows) to browse to the font's location on your system.

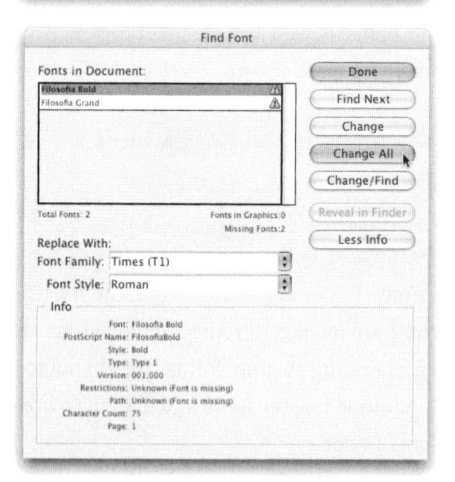

The Find Font dialog displays a list of all fonts being used in the document. Missing fonts appear alphabetically at the top of the list with a warning icon displayed to the right of the window. Click the name of the missing font and choose a replacement font and style from the Font Family and Font Style menus.

9.15 Applying Find/Change

The client loves your layout, but have changed their minds about the custom bullet points. They now would like to use stars rather than bullet points on all 300 pages—and can you provide another proof by tomorrow?

When a situation like this occurs, don't panic! Instead, just remember these two friendly little words: Find/Change.

Before you start to manually change each and every one of those bullet points into a star, choose Edit > Find/Change or press Command+F (Mac) or Ctrl+F (Windows). When the Find/Change palette appears, enter the character(s) you'd like to change into the Find What field. Then proceed to enter the character(s) you'd like to replace with in the Change To field.

From the palette menu, choose to search by document or all open documents (if you have more than one open). To find/change whole words or characters that are case sensitive, check either option in the palette.

Click the Find Next button to locate the first occurrence of the Find character in the document. Click the Change button to replace the Find character with the Change character. Click the Change All button to replace every occurrence of the Find character in the document(s). Click Change/Find to locate and replace every occurrence of the character with each click of the mouse.

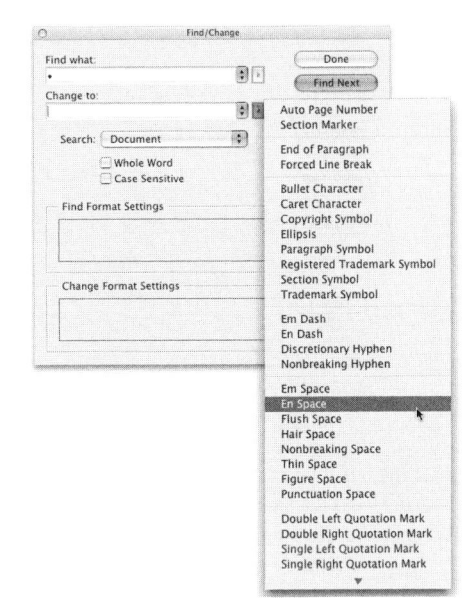

If either of these characters is invisible (or hidden), you can select it from the fly-out menu associated with each field. Metacharacter codes for hidden characters are automatically entered into the Find/Change fields when selected.

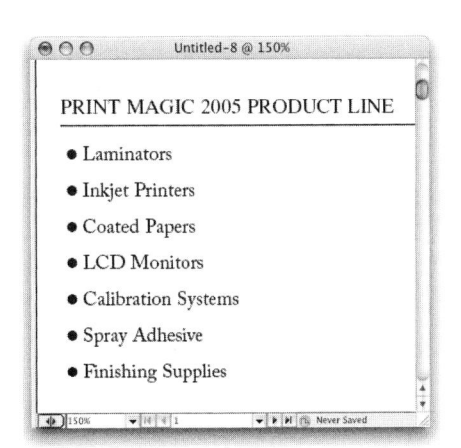

The original product list using bullet points rather than stars

Related Tasks

2.4 Edit Menu
3.3 Selection Tool
3.4 Direct Selection and Position Tools
3.6 Type Tools
7.4 Selecting Type

Shortcuts

Find/Change
Mac: Cmd+F
Win: Ctrl+F

Insert selected text into Find What field
Mac: Cmd+F1
Win: Ctrl+F1

Insert selected text into Find What field and apply Find Next command
Mac and Win: Shift+F1

Find Next
Mac: Shift+F2 or Opt+Cmd+F
Win: Shift+F2 or Alt+Ctrl+F

Insert selected text into Change To field
Mac: Cmd+F2
Win: Ctrl+F2

9.15 Applying Find/Change *(continued)*

Related Tasks

9.10 Check Spelling

9.11 Editing the Dictionary

10.14 Inserting Special Characters

Shortcuts

Replace selection with Change To text
Mac: Cmd+F3
Win: Ctrl+F3

Type tool
Mac and Win: T

Edit in Story Editor
Mac: Cmd+Y
Win: Ctrl+Y

Selection tool
Mac and Win: V

Direct Selection tool
Mac and Win: A

Tip

Using Find/Change, you can convert any unnecessary double spaces into single spaces.

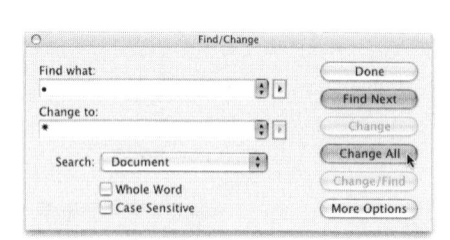

Enter the bullet point character in the Find What field and the star glyph in the Change To field; then click the Change All button.

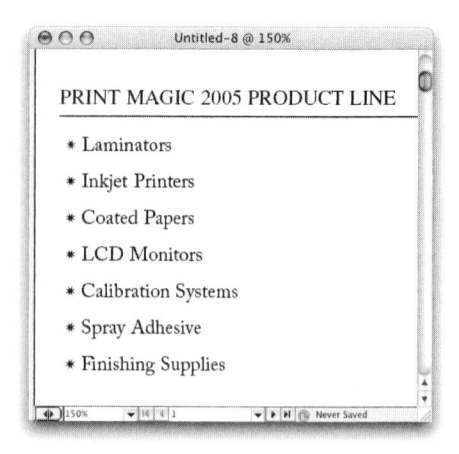

All of the bullet points are instantly replaced with stars!

You can also use Find/Change to locate and replace applied character and paragraph styles. Click the More Options button located in the Find/Change palette to display the Find/Change Format Settings options. For both sections, click the Format button and enter the character and/or paragraph style settings to locate and replace in the document(s). Click the Change, Change All, or Change/Find buttons to replace.

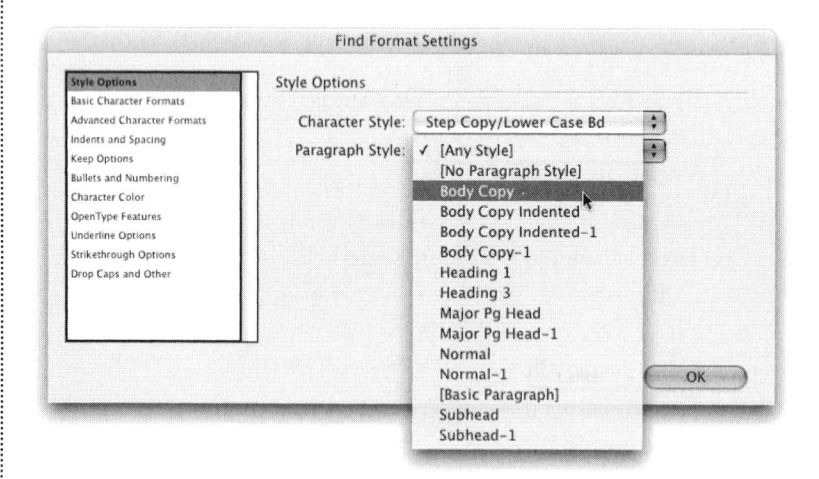

230

CHAPTER **10**

Formatting

AS SOON AS YOU begin formatting text characters in a document, "text" magically becomes "type." So what exactly is "formatting"? Is it the same as applying character and paragraph "styles"?

The answer is yes *and* no. "Formatting" is the process used to alter the look of printed type on the page—something that in the old days before desktop publishing we used to call "typesetting." Styles, although related, are something very different.

Character and paragraph styles are used to save and apply different kinds of formatting. Therefore, to fully understand the power of styles and how best to use them (see Chapter 11, "Styles"), it is important to first learn all of the ins and outs of formatting.

In this chapter we will explore all aspects of character and paragraph formatting, including how to copy and apply format attributes quickly using the Eyedropper tool. In addition, we'll explain how to insert footnotes, drop caps, tab stops, and special characters.

- 10.1 **Kerning and Tracking**
- 10.2 **Scaling and Skewing Type**
- 10.3 **Adjusting Leading and Baseline Shift**
- 10.4 **Underline and Strikethrough**
- 10.5 **Copy/Paste Text Formatting**
- 10.6 **Formatting Paragraphs**
- 10.7 **Creating Drop Caps**
- 10.8 **Applying Keep Options**
- 10.9 **Creating Hanging Indents and Punctuation**
- 10.10 **Change/Apply Hyphenation**
- 10.11 **Change/Apply Justification**
- 10.12 **Bullets and Numbering**
- 10.13 **Setting Tabs**
- 10.14 **Inserting Special Characters**
- 10.15 **Inserting Footnotes**

10.1 Kerning and Tracking

Related Tasks

3.3	Selection Tool
3.4	Direct Selection and Position Tools
3.6	Type Tools
3.15	Eyedropper Tool
4.12	Object Styles Palette
4.21	Type and Tables Palettes
5.2	Type Preferences
5.4	Composition Preferences
7.4	Selecting Type

Shortcuts

Type tool
Mac and Win: T

Increase/decrease kerning and tracking (horizontal type)
Mac: Opt+Left/Right arrow keys
Win: Alt+Left/Right arrow keys

Increase/decrease leading (vertical type)
Mac: Opt+Left/Right arrow keys
Win: Alt+Left/Right arrow keys

Increase spacing between words
Mac: Opt+Cmd+\ (backslash)
Win: Alt+Ctrl+\ (backslash)

Decrease spacing between words
Mac: Opt+Cmd+ Delete
Win: Alt+Ctrl+ Backspace

Change kerning between words by five times
Mac: Shift+Opt+Cmd+ \ (backslash) or Delete
Win: Shift+Alt+Ctrl+ \ (backslash) or Backspace

To maintain the "clean look" of the page and improve legibility, it helps to adjust the amount of space placed between type characters. You can control character spacing in your layouts by adjusting applied kerning and tracking values. The kerning value reflects the amount of space placed between neighboring characters; tracking value reflects the additional amount of intercharacter spacing applied over a range of characters in a series.

Kerning

InDesign offers two different types of auto-kerning: Metrics and Optical. You can choose either method from the fly-out menu located in the Character palette or the Control bar. (Character and Paragraph attributes can only be accessed in the Control bar when working with the Type tool.)

Metrics kerning relies on paired values built into the font by the font's designer. Depending on how well the font's designer prepared the built-in paired kerning values, Metrics may or may not be the most effective method of auto kerning. More often than not, you'll find that the font's designer could have done a much better job.

Optical kerning applies spacing amounts based on character outlines. In general, this results in much more even character spacing than Metrics kerning.

To apply either auto-kerning method, select all of the text in the story with the Type tool and choose Metrics or Optical from the Kerning menu in the Character palette or Control bar. You can also apply auto-kerning to all of the text in a single, unthreaded text frame by selecting the frame with either selection tool and choosing Metrics or Optical.

Once you've applied an auto-kerning method that works best with your font, you can manually adjust any character spaces that appear spaced incorrectly. To increase/decrease kerning values, place the Type cursor between characters and enter a positive or negative value in the Character palette or Control bar kerning field. You can also use the keyboard shortcuts (see the margin).

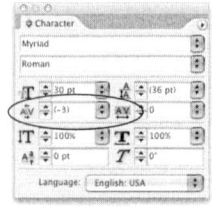

Metrics kerning as applied to all of the type in a selected frame. The Character palette displays the auto-kern amount for the Type tool cursor's current position, between the "C" and "h."

232

10.1 Kerning and Tracking (continued)

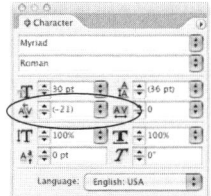

An example of Optical kerning as applied to all of the type in a selected frame. Note that the Character palette now displays a different auto-kern amount between the "C" and "h."

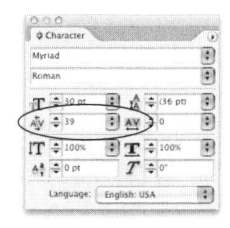

Manually adjusting the kerning between the "C" and "h" characters

Tracking

Tracking applies intercharacter spacing over a range of selected characters, *in addition to* any kerning values applied. To adjust tracking, select two or more characters with the Type tool and enter a positive or negative value in the Tracking field located in the Character palette or Control bar, or select a default tracking value from the fly-out menu. You can also adjust tracking using the same keyboard shortcuts as with kerning.

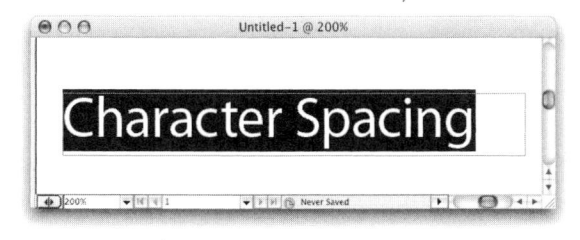

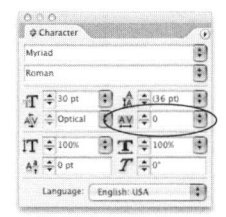

No tracking applied

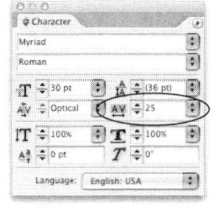

A tracking amount of 25 applied to a selected range of type

Related Tasks

10.5 Copy/Paste Text Formatting

11.1 Creating and Applying Character Styles

11.2 Creating and Applying Paragraph Styles

11.4 Creating and Applying Nested Styles

11.5 Creating and Applying Object Styles

11.6 Editing and Deleting Styles

11.7 Importing Styles

Shortcuts

Reset tracking to zero/clear manual kerning
Mac: Opt+Cmd+Q
Win: Alt+Ctrl+Q

Character palette
Mac: Cmd+T
Win: Ctrl+T

Toggle Control bar character/paragraph attributes
Mac: Cmd+Opt+7
Win: Ctrl+Alt+7

Tip

InDesign displays a kerning value in parentheses when the Auto Kerning feature has been applied. The parentheses indicate that the space between letters has been automatically adjusted using Optical or Metrics kerning.

You can set the default keyboard increment amount for manual kerning in Units & Increments Preferences.

233

10.2 Scaling and Skewing Type

Related Tasks

3.2	Control Bar
3.3	Selection Tool
3.4	Direct Selection and Position Tools
3.6	Type Tools
3.12	Scale Tool
3.13	Shear Tool
3.14	Free Transform Tool
3.15	Eyedropper Tool
4.12	Object Styles Palette
4.21	Type and Tables Palettes

Shortcuts

Type tool
Mac and Win: T

Reset horizontal scale to 100%
Mac: Shift+Cmd+X
Win: Shift+Ctrl+X

Reset vertical scale to 100%
Mac: Shift+Opt+Cmd+X
Win: Shift+Alt+Ctrl+X

Although it is possible to scale or skew type as contents when resizing or shearing a frame container (see Chapter 8), it is also possible to scale and skew type selected within a frame using character formatting. Scaling and skewing type in this fashion allows you to apply various scaling percentages and skewing angles to different characters within the same frame, the same paragraph, and even the same line.

Scaling

Select an area of text with the Type tool and change the Vertical or Horizontal Scale values in the Character palette or Control bar. Note: Scaling selected type with applied character formatting does not affect its point size.

No scaling applied

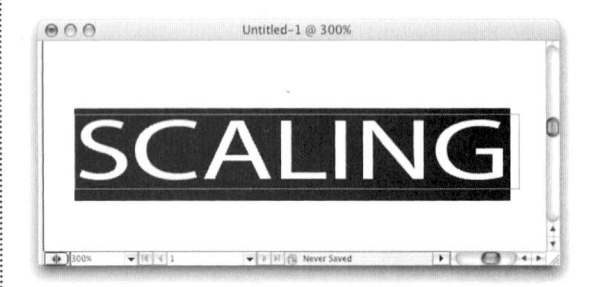

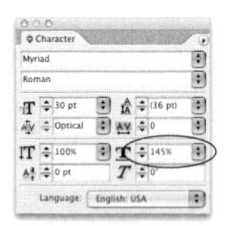

145% horizontal scaling applied

145% vertical scaling applied

10.2 Scaling and Skewing Type (continued)

Skewing

Select an area of text with the Type tool and change the Skew value in the Character palette or Control bar. Positive values skew the selected character(s) to the right and negative values to the left.

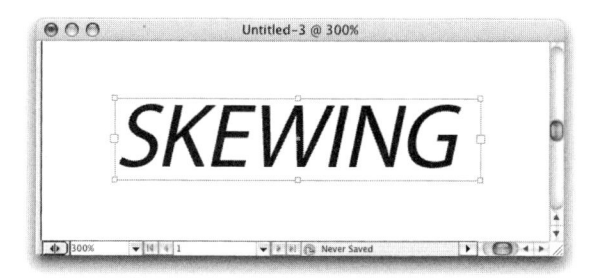

A "fake italic" version of Myriad Roman with a 12° skew applied

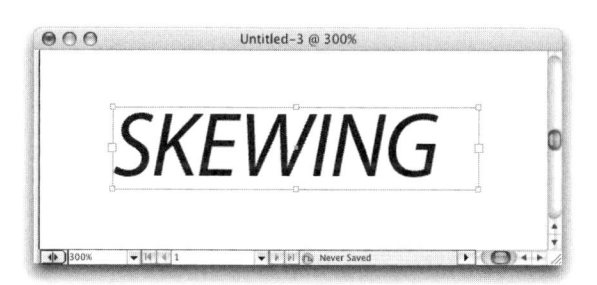

The "real" Myriad Italic; note the much smoother curves in the "S," "C," and "G" characters.

Related Tasks

7.4 Selecting Type
8.2 Resizing Objects
8.5 Shearing Objects
10.5 Copy/Paste Type Formatting
11.1 Creating and Applying Character Styles
11.2 Creating and Applying Paragraph Styles
11.4 Creating and Applying Nested Styles
11.5 Creating and Applying Object Styles
11.6 Editing and Deleting Styles
11.7 Importing Styles

Shortcuts

Character palette
Mac: Cmd+T
Win: Ctrl+T

Toggle Control bar character/paragraph attributes
Mac: Cmd+Opt+7
Win: Ctrl+Alt+7

Tip

Scaling or skewing is considered creating "fake italics" or "fake condensed/expanded type." It is considered "fake" because it distorts the characters from their original font design.

10.3 Adjusting Leading and Baseline Shift

Related Tasks

3.2 Control Bar
3.3 Selection Tool
3.4 Direct Selection and Position Tools
3.6 Type Tools
3.15 Eyedropper Tool
4.12 Object Styles Palette
4.21 Type & Tables Palettes
5.3 Advanced Type Preferences
5.5 Units & Increments Preferences

Shortcuts

Type tool
Mac and Win: T

Character palette
Mac: Cmd+T
Win: Ctrl+T

Increase/decrease leading (horizontal type)
Mac: Opt+Up/Down arrow keys
Win: Alt+Up/Down arrow keys

Increase/decrease leading (vertical type)
Mac: Opt+Left/Right arrow keys
Win: Alt+Left/Right arrow keys

Increase/decrease leading by five times (horizontal type)
Mac: Opt+Cmd+Up/Down arrow keys
Win: Alt+Ctrl+Up/Down arrow keys

Increase/decrease leading by five times (vertical type)
Mac: Opt+Cmd+Left/Right arrow keys
Win: Alt+Ctrl+Left/Right arrow keys

Just as kerning and tracking values control the horizontal space between characters, leading and baseline shift values control the vertical space between baselines.

Leading

Leading reflects the vertical space between baselines of a paragraph (the imaginary lines that each row of characters sits on top of). Increasing the leading pushes baselines further away from each other and decreasing it brings them closer together.

Unlike QuarkXPress, InDesign treats leading as a character attribute rather than a paragraph attribute. However, you can tell InDesign to treat leading as a paragraph attribute (as it would in Quark) by enabling the Apply Leading To Entire Paragraphs option from the Type Preferences dialog. Enabling this option applies the same leading value to all characters in a paragraph. (To get the best of both worlds with this option, keep it enabled and only turn it off to make leading adjustments to individual lines. When you turn the option back on in Type Preferences, the newly applied leading values do not reset.)

To set the leading for a story, select all the text with the Type tool and enter a value in the Leading field of the Character palette or Control bar. You can also apply a leading value to all the text in a single, unthreaded text frame by selecting the frame with either selection tool and entering a value in the Leading field.

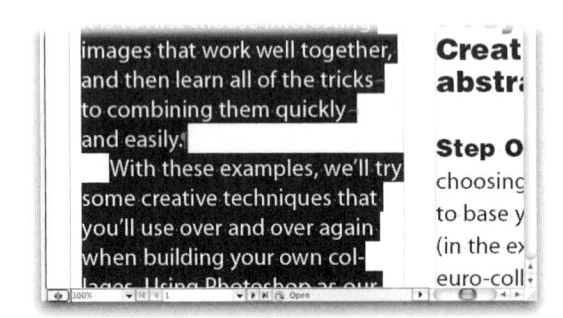

11-point leading applied to selected paragraphs

When you choose Auto from the Leading fly-out menu, InDesign applies a leading value based on a percentage of the largest character on a line. This can often result in uneven leading amounts that appear awkward in your layout. Therefore, it is best to avoid using the Auto Leading feature. (When Auto Leading is used, the leading value appears in parentheses in the Character palette and Control bar.)

10.3 Adjusting Leading and Baseline Shift *(continued)*

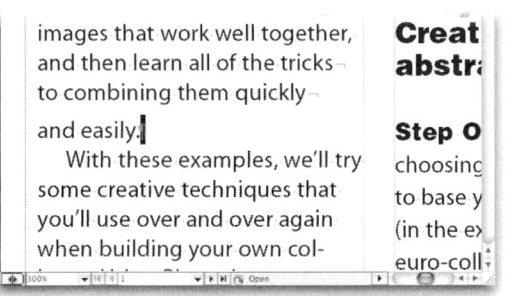

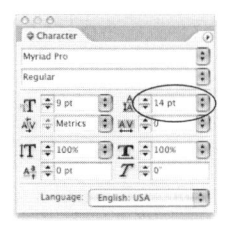

It is also important to select all the characters in a paragraph when setting the leading—including invisible carriage returns. A carriage return hanging at the end of a paragraph can have a different leading value applied to it. This can result in the last line of the paragraph appearing offset from the lines above, like the one shown here.

Baseline Shift

There may be times when you need to move individual characters above or below the baseline. Examples include centering a large lead-in character, such as a bullet point, or repositioning a drop cap that uses an ornate script font.

To shift the baseline of an individual character, select it with the Type tool and enter a value in the Baseline Shift field in the Character palette or Control bar. Entering a positive value positions the selected character farther above the baseline and entering a negative value positions it farther below.

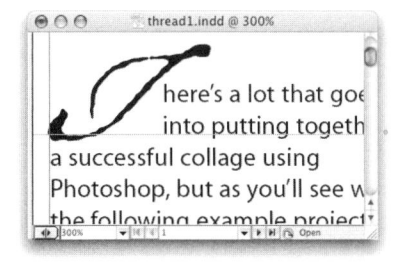

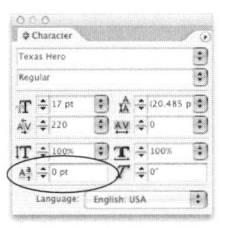

A script drop cap that extends below the baseline

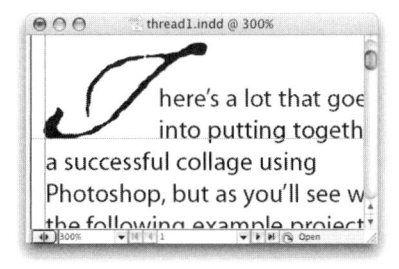

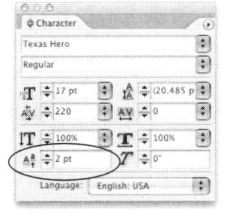

The same script drop cap with a 2-point baseline shift applied

---

Related Tasks

7.4 Selecting Type

10.5 Copy/Paste Type Formatting

11.1 Creating and Applying Character Styles

11.2 Creating and Applying Paragraph Styles

11.5 Creating and Applying Object Styles

11.6 Editing and Deleting Styles

11.7 Importing Styles

Shortcuts

Auto-leading
Mac: Shift+Opt+Cmd+A
Win: Shift+Alt+Ctrl+A

Increase/decrease baseline shift (horizontal type)
Mac: Shift+Opt+Up/Down arrow keys
Win: Shift+Alt+Up/Down arrow keys

Increase/decrease baseline shift by five times (horizontal type)
Mac: Shift+Opt+Cmd+Up/Down arrow keys
Win: Shift+Alt+Ctrl+Up/Down arrow keys

Increase/decrease baseline shift (vertical type)
Mac: Shift+Opt+Left/Right arrow keys
Win: Shift+Alt+Left/Right arrow keys

Toggle Control bar character/paragraph attributes
Mac: Cmd+Opt+7
Win: Ctrl+Alt+7

Tip

You can set the default keyboard increment amount for baseline shift in the Units & Increments Preferences dialog.

237

10.4 Underline and Strikethrough

Related Tasks

3.2	Control Bar
3.6	Type Tools
3.15	Eyedropper Tool
4.12	Object Styles Palette
4.16	Stroke Palette
4.21	Type and Tables Palettes
5.5	Units & Increments Preferences
7.4	Selecting Type
9.15	Applying Find/Change

Shortcuts

Underline
Mac: Shift+Cmd+U
Win: Shift+Ctrl+U

Strikethrough
Mac: Shift+Cmd+/ (forward slash)
Win: Shift+Ctrl+/ (forward slash)

Rather than drawing an underline or strikethrough with the Line or Pen tools, you can apply them using text effects.

Underline

To apply an underline, select an area of text with the Type tool and choose Underline from the Character palette fly-out menu, or click the Underline toggle button in the Control bar. To add an underline to all the text in a single, unthreaded frame, select the frame with either selection tool and apply the Underline command.

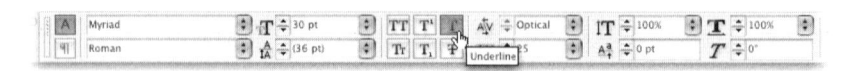

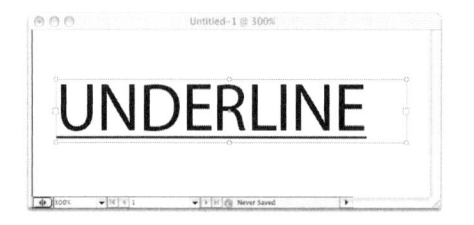

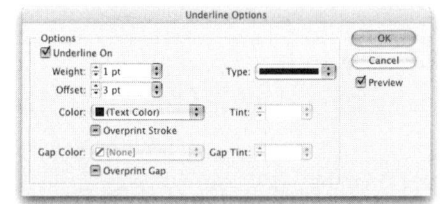

To customize an underline's appearance, access the Underline Options dialog by choosing Underline Options from the Character palette menu. When the dialog opens, click the Underline On option to access the settings. The rest of the dialog is set up like the Stroke palette, allowing you to choose an underline weight, offset, type, color, tint, and—when applying an open stroke type—gap color, and gap tint. You can also choose to overprint any applied underline or gap olors.

Although you cannot save these settings as an underline style, you can save them as part of a character style.

The underline effect automatically applies itself to any selected spaces. If your design requires that word spaces not have underlines, you can always replace them using Find/Change.

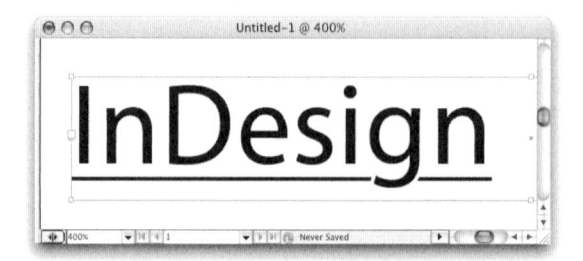

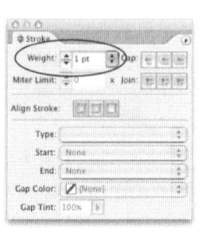

Formatted underlines also overlap any descending characters (such as lowercase "g" or "y"). It is possible to create a simulated break in the underline for these characters by applying a thin white stroke to the outside of the type.

10.4 Underline and Strikethrough *(continued)*

Strikethrough

To apply the strikethrough effect, select an area of text with the Type tool and choose Strikethrough from the Character palette fly-out menu, or click the Strikethrough toggle button in the Control bar. To add a strikethrough to all of the text in a single, unthreaded frame, select the frame with either selection tool and apply the Strikethrough command.

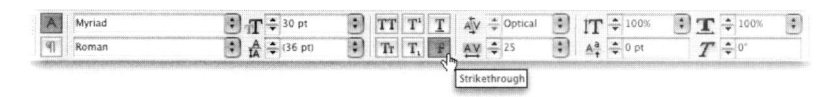

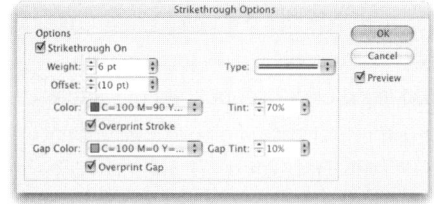

To customize a strikethrough's appearance, access the Strikethrough Options dialog by choosing Strikethrough Options from the Character palette menu. When the dialog opens, click the Strikethrough On option to access the settings. The rest of the dialog is set up exactly like the Underline Options dialog.

To avoid difficult registration on press, it is recommended that you enable the overprint option in this dialog when applying strikethrough or gap colors.

Unfortunately, just as with underlines, you cannot create and save a strikethrough style—but you can save these settings as part of a character style.

DRAG-AND-DROP TEXT EDITING

In the Type Preferences dialog, you can enable drag-and-drop text editing for use in both Layout View and the Story Editor. With these options enabled, you can move text by highlighting it with the Type tool and dragging it to another place in the story. This is a quick way to edit paragraphs without having to use copy/paste commands. You can also duplicate a type selection by holding down the Option/Alt key as you click and drag.

Related Tasks

10.5 Copy/Paste Type Formatting

11.1 Creating and Applying Character Styles

11.2 Creating and Applying Paragraph Styles

11.4 Creating and Applying Nested Styles

11.5 Creating and Applying Object Styles

11.6 Editing and Deleting Styles

11.7 Importing Styles

16.3 Creating and Assigning Trap Presets

Shortcuts

Type tool
Mac and Win: T

Character palette
Mac: Cmd+T
Win: Ctrl+T

Tip

You can access the Underline and Strikethrough dialogs by Option/Alt-clicking their respective buttons in the Control bar.

10.5 Copy/Paste Text Formatting

Related Tasks

3.2	Control Bar
3.6	Type Tools
3.15	Eyedropper Tool
4.21	Type and Tables Palettes
7.4	Selecting Type
11.1	Creating and Applying Character Styles
11.2	Creating and Applying Paragraph Styles
11.4	Creating and Applying Nested Styles
11.5	Creating and Applying Object Styles

Shortcuts

Eyedropper tool
Mac and Win: I

Character palette
Mac: Cmd+T
Win: Ctrl+T

Drop Shadow dialog
Mac: Opt+Cmd+M
Win: Alt+Ctrl+M

Tip

You can also use the Eyedropper tool to sample and apply drop shadow settings to editable type.

The Eyedropper tool allows you to sample and apply text formatting quickly and easily throughout your documents. Although it is a good idea to save formatting as part of a style, you might want to preview it being used in several places in your layout first. You might also be on such a tight deadline that you simply *don't have time* to stop and create a style!

If you like what you see, you can always create a style based on this formatting later and reapply as needed. You can also use the Eyedropper tool to sample and apply styles and object-level formatting, such as stroke styles and fill colors/gradients.

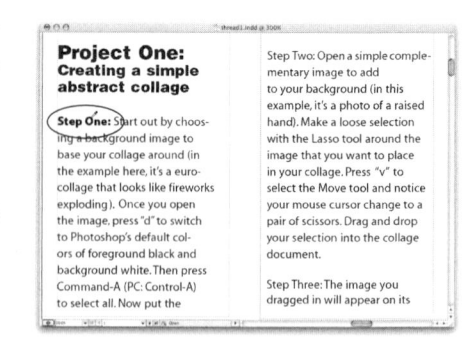

You can sample formatted text by hovering over it with the Eyedropper tool and clicking. You'll know it has been sampled when the Eyedropper icon appears full.

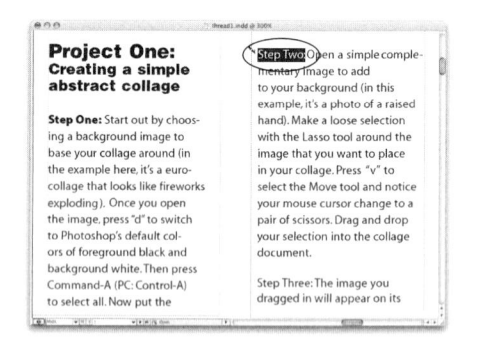

You can then proceed to highlight any text you'd like to apply the sampled formatting to.

Continue applying without having to resample all over again.

10.6 Formatting Paragraphs

InDesign considers a "paragraph" any sequence of characters that ends in a carriage return (also referred to as a paragraph return). Many other attributes make up paragraph formatting in InDesign, but the basics include horizontal alignment, left/right indents, first/last-line indents, and space before/space after. These attributes determine the "shape" of a paragraph.

To apply these characteristics, insert the Type tool cursor in a paragraph or highlight one or more paragraphs. Then click the appropriate button (for alignment) or set the desired value (for indents and space before/after) in the Control bar or Paragraph palette.

You can also apply these characteristics to *all* of the paragraphs in a single, unthreaded text frame by selecting the frame with either selection tool and clicking the appropriate button or setting the value in the Control bar or Paragraph palette.

Setting Paragraph Horizontal Alignment

You can choose to align selected paragraphs to the left, center, right, or justified. Justified options also include the ability to align the last line of the paragraph left, center, right, or justified. You can also align the paragraph toward or away from the spine.

Align Left

Align Center

Align Right

Justify With Last Line Aligned Left

Justify With Last Line Aligned Center

Justify With Last Line Aligned Right

Justify All Lines

Related Tasks

2.6 Type Menu
3.2 Control Bar
3.3 Selection Tool
3.4 Direct Selection and Position Tools

Shortcuts

Align left
Mac: Shift+Cmd+L
Win: Shift+Ctrl+L

Align right
Mac: Shift+Cmd+R
Win: Shift+Ctrl+R

Align center
Mac: Shift+Cmd+C
Win: Shift+Ctrl+C

10.6 Formatting Paragraphs *(continued)*

Related Tasks

3.6	Type Tools
3.15	Eyedropper Tool
4.21	Type and Tables Palettes
5.2	Type Preferences

Shortcuts

Justify all lines
Mac: Shift+Cmd+F
Win: Shift+Ctrl+F

Justify all lines (but last line)
Mac: Opt+Shift+Cmd+J
Win: Alt+Shift+Ctrl+J

Justification dialog
Mac: Opt+Cmd+J
Win: Alt+Ctrl+J

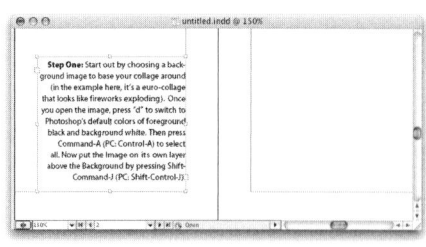

Align Towards Spine works just like Align Right when applied to a paragraph on a left page.

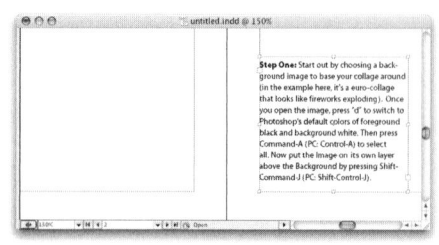

When you move the frame to a right page, the text automatically aligns toward the spine.

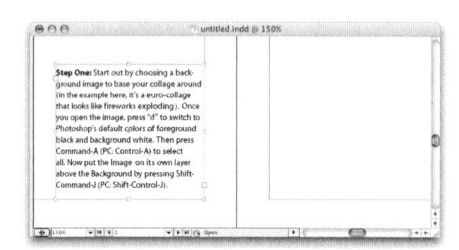

Align Away From Spine works just like Align Left when applied to a paragraph on a left page.

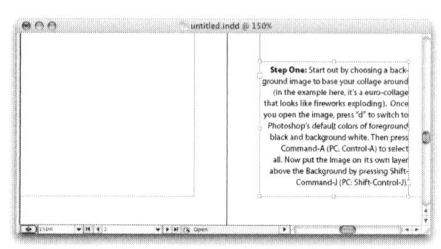

When you move the frame to a right page, the text automatically aligns away from the spine.

Setting Left and Right Paragraph Indents

You can set left and right paragraph indents using the controls located in the Paragraph palette, Control bar, or the Tabs palette.

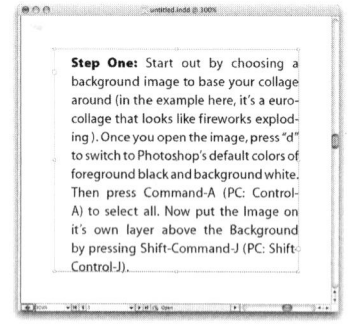

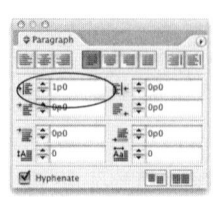

Setting a left indent with the Paragraph palette

242

10.6 Formatting Paragraphs *(continued)*

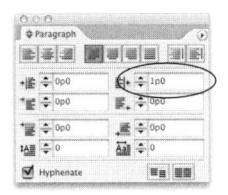

Setting a right indent with the Paragraph palette

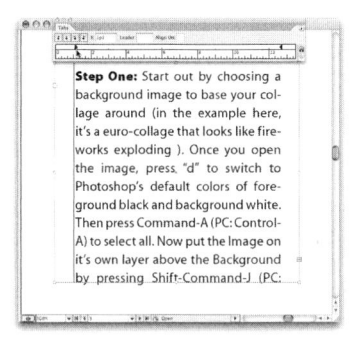

To set left/right indents using the Tabs palette, select a paragraph with the Type tool and choose Window > Type and Tables > Tabs, or press Shift+Command+T (Mac) or Shift+Ctrl+T (Windows). When the Tabs palette appears, you can set a left indent by clicking the bottom-left arrow (the Left Indent icon) and dragging it to the right, or entering a value in the X field; to set a right indent, click and drag the right arrow (the Right Indent icon) to the left, or enter a value in the X field. A vertical guide appears in the text frame as you drag the left/right indent icons.

Setting First and Last Line Indents

InDesign also allows you to set first and last line indents using the controls located in the Paragraph palette and Control bar. In addition, you can also set first line (but not last line) indents using the Tabs palette.

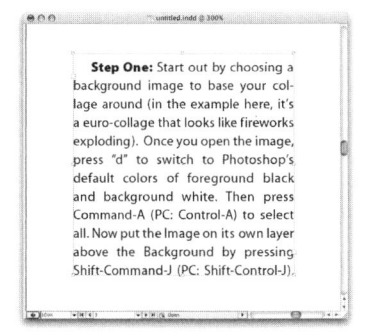

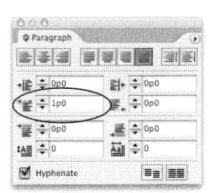

Setting a first line indent

Related Tasks

7.4 Selecting Type

10.9 Creating Hanging Indents and Punctuation

11.1 Creating and Applying Character Styles

Shortcuts

Paragraph palette
Mac: Opt+Cmd+T
Win: Alt+Ctrl+T

Tabs palette
Mac: Shift+Cmd+T
Win: Shift+Ctrl+T

10.6 Formatting Paragraphs (continued)

Related Tasks

11.2 Creating and Applying Paragraph Styles

11.4 Creating and Applying Nested Styles

11.5 Creating and Applying Object Styles

Shortcuts

Switch between Tabs palette alignment options
Mac: Opt+click tab marker in palette
Win: Alt+click tab marker in palette

Toggle Control bar character/paragraph attributes
Mac: Cmd+Opt+7
Win: Ctrl+Alt+7

Tips

For more precise paragraph spacing, try using Snap To Baseline Grid along with Space Before/Space After.

It is possible to apply different left/right and first/last line indents to separate paragraphs within the same text frame and story.

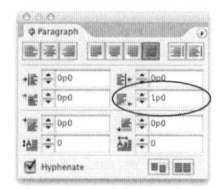

Setting a last-line indent

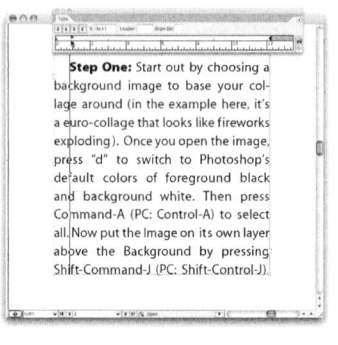

To set a first line indent using the Tabs palette, select a paragraph and choose Window > Type and Tables > Tabs. When the Tabs palette appears above the paragraph, drag the top-left arrow (the First Line Indent icon) to the right or enter an indent value in the X field.

Putting Space Before and After Paragraphs

You can avoid adding unnecessary paragraph returns to the text in your layouts by applying Space Before and Space After instead.

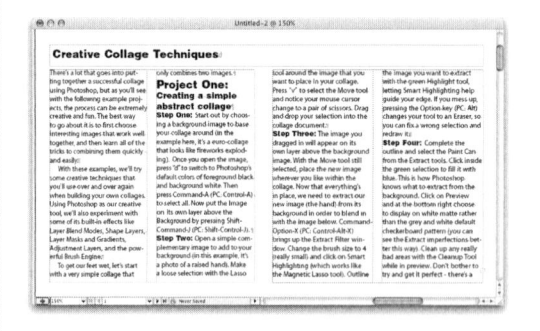

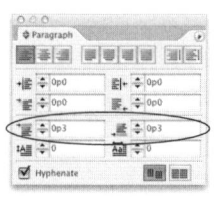

Left: No spacing applied. Right: With 0p3 Space Before/Space After applied.

Space Before values have no effect on paragraphs positioned at the top of a text frame column, and Space After values have no effect on paragraphs positioned at the bottom.

244

10.7 Creating Drop Caps

To apply a drop cap, insert the Type tool cursor anywhere in the paragraph, and enter a value in the Drop Cap Number Of Lines field located in the Paragraph palette or Control bar. This number determines the size and baseline shift for the drop cap character. You can apply this effect to additional characters by entering a larger value in the Drop Cap One Or More Characters field.

Drop cap characters can be selected and formatted just like any other character. To enhance a drop cap's appearance, select it with the Type tool and change the applied font, type size, kerning, and baseline shift.

Drop caps can also be applied as part of a nested style.

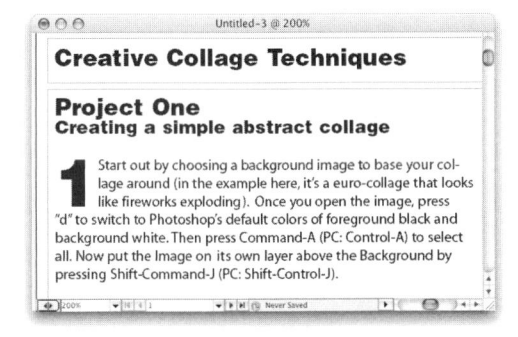

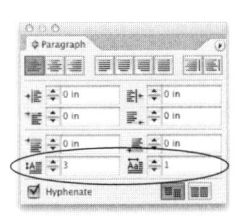

Applying a single-character drop cap

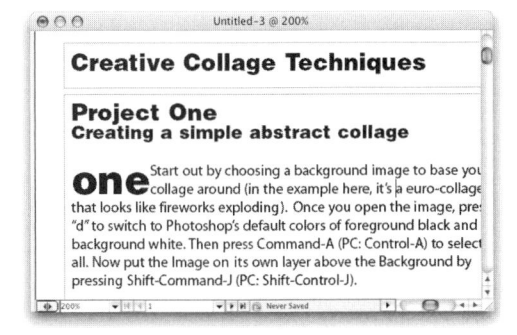

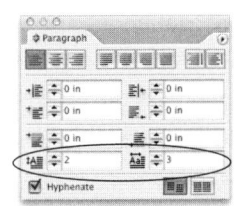

Applying a multicharacter drop cap

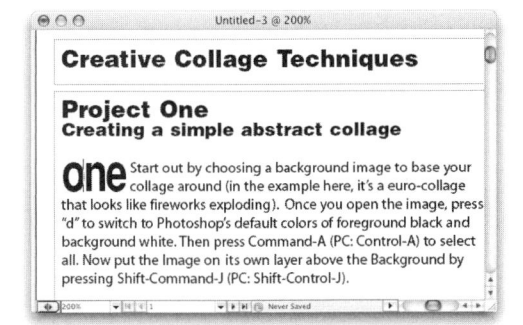

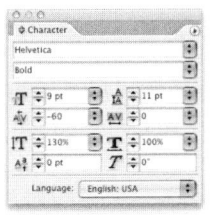

Formatting a multi-character drop cap

Related Tasks

3.2	Control Bar
3.3	Selection Tool
3.4	Direct Selection and Position Tools
3.6	Type Tools
3.15	Eyedropper Tool
4.21	Type and Tables Palettes
7.4	Selecting Type
10.5	Copy/Paste Type Formatting
10.9	Creating Hanging Indents and Punctuation
11.2	Creating and Applying Paragraph Styles
11.4	Creating and Applying Nested Styles
11.5	Creating and Applying Object Styles

Shortcuts

Paragraph palette
Mac: Opt+Cmd+T
Win: Alt+Ctrl+T

Type tool
Mac and Win: T

Toggle Control bar character/paragraph attributes
Mac: Cmd+Opt+7
Win: Ctrl+Alt+7

Tip

To place a drop cap outside a column, insert a hanging indent after it by pressing Command+\ (Mac) or Ctrl+\ (Windows). You can also insert a hanging indent by choosing Type > Insert Special Character > Indent To Here.

245

10.8 Applying Keep Options

Related Tasks

2.6	Type Menu
3.6	Type Tools
4.21	Type and Tables Palettes
5.4	Composition Preferences
7.4	Selecting Type
9.6	Flowing Text
10.6	Formatting Paragraphs

Shortcuts

Keep Options dialog
Mac: Opt+Cmd+K
Win: Alt+Ctrl+K

Paragraph palette
Mac: Opt+Cmd+T
Win: Alt+Ctrl+T

By applying InDesign's Keep Options feature, you can prevent widows and orphans from appearing throughout the text of your layout. A *widow* is the last line of a paragraph that ends up by itself at the top of a column, separated from the rest of the paragraph. An *orphan* is the first line of a paragraph that ends up on its own line at the end of a column. Additionally, a word that gets separated from the rest of a paragraph and ends up on its own line is also considered a widow.

Not only do these little annoyances affect readability, but they are also a terrible eyesore! To ward off these typographical gremlins, select a paragraph (or multiple paragraphs) with the Type tool and choose Keep Options from the Paragraph palette menu, or press Option+Command+K (Mac) or Alt+Ctrl+K (Windows).

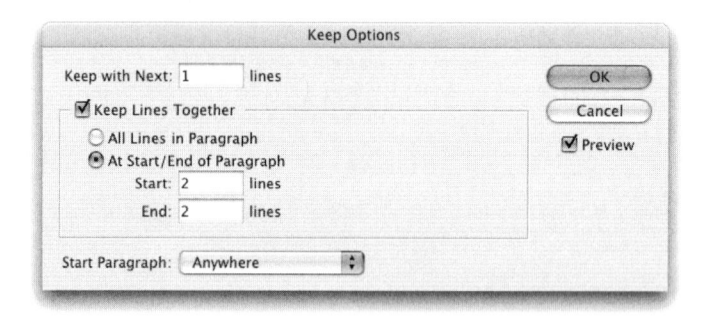

The Keep Options dialog is divided into three sections: Keep With Next, Keep Lines Together, and Start Paragraph.

Keep With Next: By entering a value of one in the Keep with Next field, you can ensure that headers always remain positioned above the paragraph that follows. Should any text or frame edits push the paragraph into a new column, new page, or a text wrap, the header will follow.

Keep Lines Together: You can safeguard your text from any sneaky widows and orphans appearing by enabling the Keep Lines Together option and choosing At Start/End Of Paragraph. To keep paragraphs together during editing, enter a value in the Start and End fields. These values tell InDesign the minimum number of lines allowed to separate at the start or end of a paragraph should it be pushed into a new column or page; therefore, entering a value of 2 ensures that a widow or orphan never appears.

Choosing All Lines In Paragraph from the Keep Lines Together option does not allow for any lines to be separated from a paragraph should editing push it into a new column or page. Instead, the whole paragraph is moved.

10.8 Applying Keep Options (continued)

Start Paragraph: The Start Paragraph menu contains options for forcing a column or page break before the selected paragraph. Choose one of these options to ensure the paragraph's position in the layout. Options include: Anywhere (the default), In Next Column, In Next Frame, On Next Page, On Next Odd Page, and On Next Even Page.

An orphaned paragraph

The same paragraph with Keep Options applied

SUPERSCRIPT AND SUBSCRIPT

Although it is possible to position characters such as copyright and registered trademark symbols by lowering their point size and shifting their baselines, it is quicker to apply InDesign's built-in effects. Select the character(s) with the Type tool and choose Superscript or Subscript from the Character palette menu or click the appropriate button in the Control bar. InDesign scales and shifts the baseline of the character(s) using the percentages entered in the Advanced Type Preferences dialog.

Related Tasks

10.9 Creating Hanging Indents and Punctuation

10.10 Change/Apply Hyphenation

10.11 Change/Apply Justification

11.2 Creating and Applying Paragraph Styles

11.4 Creating and Applying Nested Styles

11.5 Creating and Applying Object Styles

Shortcuts

Type tool
Mac and Win: T

Toggle Control bar character/paragraph attributes
Mac: Cmd+Opt+7
Win: Ctrl+Alt+7

Tip

You can choose to highlight Keep Violations in Composition Preferences.

10.9 Creating Hanging Indents and Punctuation

Related Tasks

2.6	Type Menu
3.2	Control Bar
3.6	Type Tools
4.21	Type and Tables Palettes
7.4	Selecting Type
9.6	Flowing Text

Shortcuts

Paragraph palette
Mac: Opt+Cmd+T
Win: Alt+Ctrl+T

Insert Indent To Here character
Mac: Cmd+\ (backslash)
Win: Ctrl+\ (backslash)

Hanging indents are great for creating custom bulleted or number lists. By placing a hanging indent after a lead-in character (a bullet point, a number, etc.), you can force the subsequent lines of the paragraph to line up evenly with the indent.

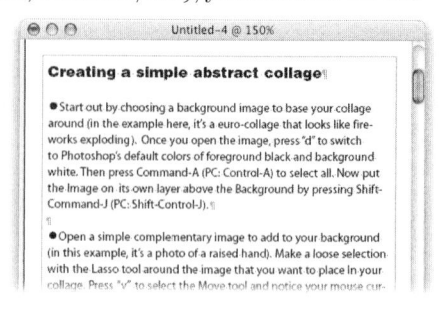

You can also clean up the overall look of your text by allowing punctuation marks—such as periods, commas, and quotation marks—to hang outside the column.

InDesign provides three ways to create hanging indents:

- By entering a positive value in the Left Indent field and a negative value in First Line indent field of the Paragraph palette or Control bar
- By inserting a tab and the special Indent To Here character
- By applying a tab stop and a first line indent with the Tabs palette

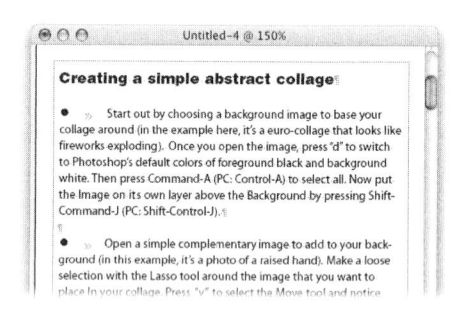

Paragraphs in need of some hanging indents

Paragraph Palette/Control Bar Indent Fields

To create a hanging indent using the Paragraph palette/Control bar indent fields, perform the following steps:

1. In the first line of each paragraph, insert a tab after the lead-in character.
2. Enter a positive value in the Left Indent field of the Paragraph palette or Control bar.
3. Enter the negative of the value in the First Line Indent field of the Paragraph palette or Control bar.

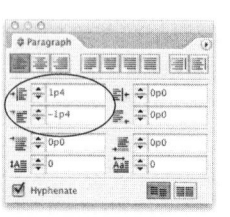

10.9 Creating Hanging Indents and Punctuation *(continued)*

Indent To Here Character

1. In the first line of each paragraph, insert a tab after the lead-in character.
2. Place the Type tool cursor just after the tab in each paragraph and choose Type > Insert Special Character > Indent To Here.
3. If necessary, select the paragraphs with the Type tool and adjust the tab indents using the Tabs palette.

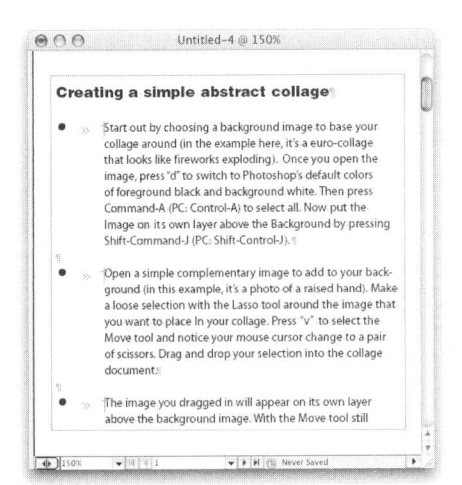

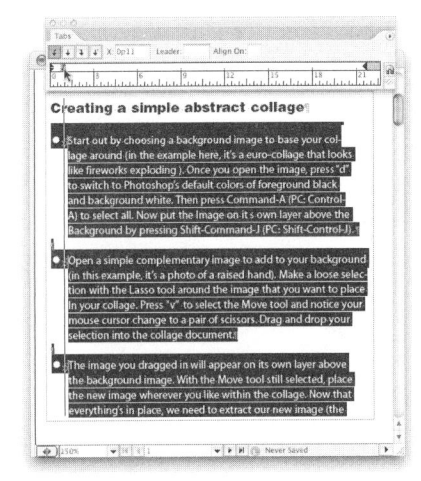

Tabs Palette

You can also create a hanging indent using the Tabs palette.

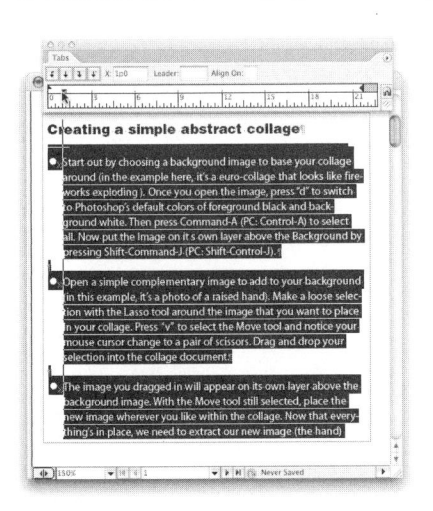

In the first line of each paragraph, insert a tab after the lead-in character. Select the paragraphs with the Type tool and press Command+Shift+T/Ctrl+Shift+T to open the Tabs palette. Hold down the Shift key and drag the bottom-left arrow (the Left Indent icon) to the right.

Related Tasks

10.6 Formatting Paragraphs

10.7 Creating Drop Caps

10.10 Change/Apply Hyphenation

10.11 Change/Apply Justification

10.13 Setting Tabs

Shortcuts

Type tool
Mac and Win: T

Tabs palette
Mac: Shift+Cmd+T
Win: Shift+Ctrl+T

249

10.9 Creating Hanging Indents and Punctuation *(continued)*

Related Tasks

10.14 Inserting Special Characters

11.2 Creating and Applying Paragraph Styles

11.4 Creating and Applying Nested Styles

11.5 Creating and Applying Object Styles

Shortcut

Toggle Control bar character/paragraph attributes
Mac: Cmd+Opt+7
Win: Ctrl+Alt+7

Tip

One benefit to creating hanging indents with the Paragraph or Tabs palette is the ability to save them as part of a paragraph style—an option you do not have when inserting the Indent To Here character.

Hanging Punctuation

You can greatly improve the "look" of your text by hanging punctuation marks outside the column edge. You can do this by applying the Optical Margin Alignment option located in the Story palette. When you enable this feature, InDesign not only adjusts the punctuation, but also makes a slight adjustment to the edges of any characters extending outside the column edge (a common occurrence with capital serifs).

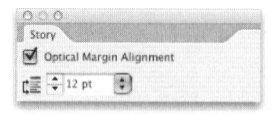

Select a text frame with either selection tool and then open the Story palette by choosing Window > Type & Tables > Story. Click the Optical Margin Alignment check box to allow InDesign to instantly adjust the punctuation and extended character alignment. Optical Margin Alignment carries through to all linked frames in a story.

To adjust the applied "hang" amount, increase or decrease the value entered in the Align Based On Size field.

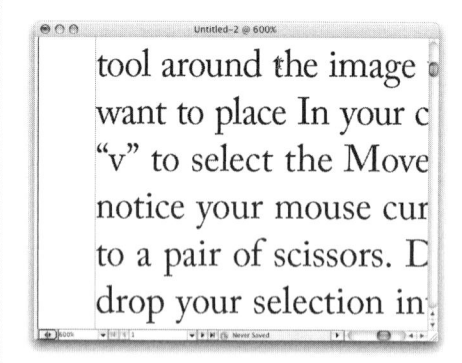

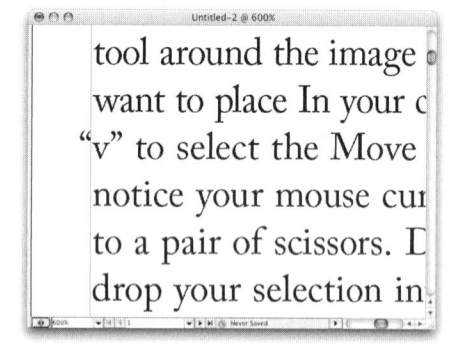

Before (left) and after (right) applying Optical Margin Alignment

10.10 Change/Apply Hyphenation

InDesign allows you to apply specific hyphenation settings to a document or selected paragraph. You can do this using the Hyphenation Settings dialog, which you can access by choosing Hyphenation from the Paragraph palette menu.

To set document-wide hyphenation settings, choose Edit > Deselect All. In the resulting dialog, the settings you specify are applied to all added and imported text (untagged and unformatted), while preexisting paragraphs retain their applied hyphenation settings.

To adjust hyphenation settings for a specific paragraph (or paragraphs), insert the Type tool cursor anywhere in the paragraph (or highlight multiple paragraphs) and access the Hyphenation Settings dialog.

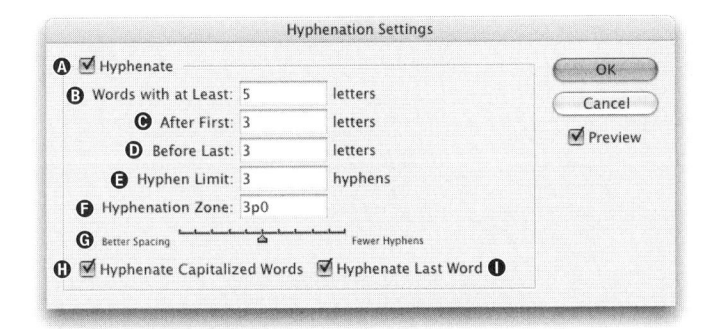

Related Tasks

2.6 Type Menu
3.6 Type Tools
4.21 Type and Tables Palettes
5.4 Composition Preferences
7.4 Selecting Type
9.3 Importing Text

Shortcuts

Paragraph palette
Mac: Opt+Cmd+T
Win: Alt+Ctrl+T

Type tool
Mac and Win: T

A Hyphenate Click to access and apply hyphenation settings.

B Words With At Least Enter a value indicating how many letters a word must contain before hyphenation can occur. Higher values result in fewer hyphenations.

C After First Enter a value indicating how many letters a word fragment must contain preceding a hyphen. To avoid two-letter fragments, enter a value of 3 or higher.

D Before Last Enter a value indicating how many letters a word fragment must contain following a hyphen. To avoid two-letter fragments, enter a value of 3 or higher.

E Hyphen Limit Enter a value to limit the number of consecutive hyphens allowed at the left edge of the column.

F Hyphenation Zone Enter a value indicating the inset of the imaginary "hyphenation zone" along the right column edge. Higher values result in fewer hyphenations but more ragged lines. Note: Hyphenation Zone does not apply to justified text.

G Hyphenation Slider Drag the slider to the left for Better Spacing; drag to the right for Fewer Hyphens. Click the Preview button to see the effect as it is applied.

H Hyphenate Capitalized Words Uncheck this option to prevent hyphenation of proper names and other capitalized words.

I Hyphenate Last Word Check this option to allow hyphenation of the last word of a paragraph.

10.10 Change/Apply Hyphenation *(continued)*

Related Tasks

9.11 Editing the Dictionary

10.6 Formatting Paragraphs

10.11 Change/Apply Justification

11.2 Creating and Applying Paragraph Styles

11.4 Creating and Applying Nested Styles

11.5 Creating and Applying Object Styles

Shortcuts

Toggle Control bar character/paragraph attributes
Mac: Cmd+Opt+7
Win: Ctrl+Alt+7

Insert discretionary hyphen
Mac: Shift+Cmd+Hyphen
Win: Shift+Ctrl+Hyphen

Tip

You can tell InDesign how you'd like to hyphenate certain words by editing their hyphenation points in the Dictionary palette.

Using InDesign's default hyphenation settings: more hyphens—fewer ragged lines.

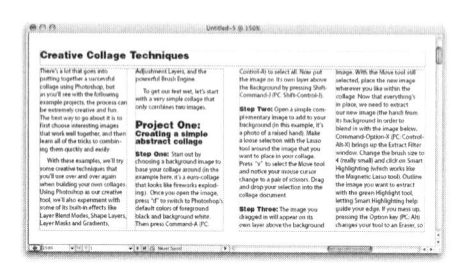

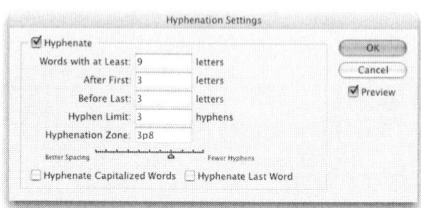

Using custom hyphenation settings: fewer hyphens—more ragged lines.

To set customized application-wide default hyphenation settings, make your adjustments in the dialog without any documents open. These settings are then applied to all added and imported text (untagged and unformatted, of course) in all your documents. Preexisting paragraphs will retain their applied hyphenation settings.

DISCRETIONARY HYPHENS

Another way to control hyphenation in InDesign is to insert Discretionary Hyphen characters. Place the Type tool cursor at a preferred hyphenation point in a word, and choose Type > Insert Special Character > Discretionary Hyphen. By doing so, you're not forcing a word to hyphenate; instead, you're telling InDesign "it's okay to hyphenate this word here, but only if you really need to."

10.11 Change/Apply Justification

The Justification dialog, which you can access by choosing Justification from the Paragraph palette menu, allows you to control how InDesign handles word and letter spacing. The values entered in the Minimum, Desired, and Maximum fields of this dialog are percentages of the standard word and letter spaces embedded in the font by its designer.

The Justification dialog also lets you adjust the default Auto Leading percentage, specify a Single-Line or Paragraph Composer, and choose from available Single Word Justification options.

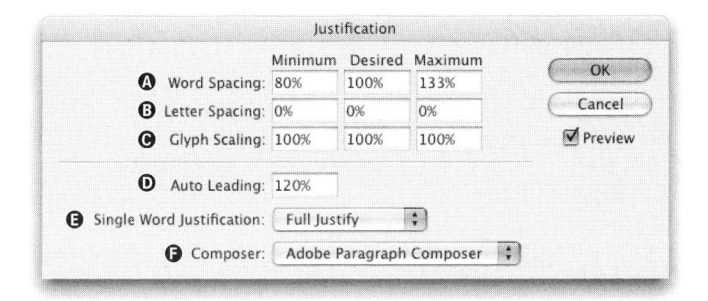

Related Tasks

2.6	Type Menu
3.6	Type Tools
4.21	Type and Tables Palettes
5.4	Composition Preferences
7.4	Selecting Type
9.3	Importing Text

Shortcuts

Justification dialog
Mac: Opt+Shift+Cmd+J
Win: Alt+Shift+Ctrl+J

Paragraph palette
Mac: Opt+Cmd+T
Win: Alt+Ctrl+T

- **Ⓐ Word Spacing** Enter a value to apply Minimum, Desired, and Maximum percentages of word spacing. Nonjustified text only responds to the Desired value.
- **Ⓑ Letter Spacing** Enter a value to apply the Minimum, Desired, and Maximum amount of character spacing. As with Word Spacing, nonjustified text only responds to the Desired value.
- **Ⓒ Glyph Scaling** Enter a value to apply the Minimum, Desired, and Maximum amount of horizontal glyph scaling allowed. This option is genuinely weird. Glyph scaling fits characters into a line by stretching them, except it uses different scaling percentages, resulting in all different character shapes from line to line. Unless you're purposely trying to make your type look bad, it is recommended that you keep these values set at 100%.
- **Ⓓ Auto Leading** Enter a value for InDesign to apply to paragraphs set to Auto Leading. Auto Leading is calculated using a percentage (entered here) of the largest character on a line.
- **Ⓔ Single Word Justification** Choose a justification method for InDesign to use when faced with a single-word line in a paragraph (usually the result of a really long word or a really narrow column). Options include: Full Justify, Align Left, Align Center, and Align Right.
- **Ⓕ Composer** Choose a paragraph composition method. Options include Adobe Single-Line Composer or Adobe Paragraph Composer. Single-line composition calculates word and letter spacing on a per-line basis. This adds greater space variation to the text and can make it harder to read. Paragraph composition considers all lines in a paragraph when calculating word and letter spacing. Paragraph (or multiline) composition generally results in better-looking text that is much easier to read.

10.11 Change/Apply Justification (continued)

Related Tasks

9.11 Editing the Dictionary

10.6 Formatting Paragraphs

10.14 Inserting Special Characters

11.2 Creating and Applying Paragraph Styles

11.4 Creating and Applying Nested Styles

11.5 Creating and Applying Object Styles

Shortcuts

Type tool
Mac and Win: T

Toggle Control bar character/paragraph attributes
Mac: Cmd+Opt+7
Win: Ctrl+Alt+7

Tips

Inserting a Flush Space character at the end of a paragraph that is set to Justify All Lines allows you to flush the last line to the left. Choose Type > Insert White Space > Flush Space.

To help balance out uneven line widths, insert the Type tool cursor anywhere in a ragged paragraph and choose Balance Ragged Lines from the Paragraph palette menu.

Using InDesign's default justification settings (shown above): fairly wide word spacing, no extra letter spacing.

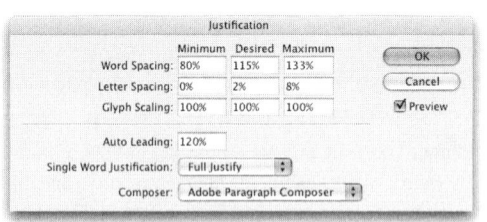

Using custom justification settings: extra-wide word spacing, slightly extra letter spacing. As a result, paragraphs are a little less ragged.

To set application-wide default justification settings, make your adjustments in the dialog without any documents open. These settings are then applied to all added and imported text (untagged and unformatted, of course) in all your documents. Preexisting paragraphs retain their applied justification settings.

10.12 Bullets and Numbering

InDesign CS2 allows you to place a bullet or number before each paragraph in a list using paragraph formatting. You can also save bulleted and numbered list attributes as part of a paragraph style.

To set and apply bullet and numbering attributes, select the list with the Type tool and choose Bullets and Numbering from the Paragraph palette menu. InDesign launches the Bullets and Numbering dialog. In the dialog, choose Bullets or Numbers from the List Type menu.

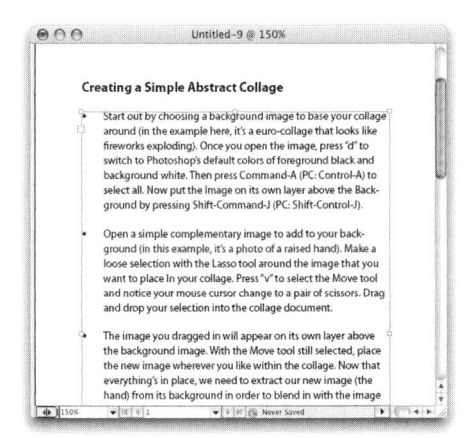

Related Tasks

2.6 Type Menu
3.6 Type Tools
4.21 Type and Tables Palettes
7.4 Selecting Type

Shortcuts

Paragraph palette
Mac: Opt+Cmd+T
Win: Alt+Ctrl+T

Type tool
Mac and Win: T

Toggle Control bar character/paragraph attributes
Mac: Cmd+Opt+7
Win: Ctrl+Alt+7

When you select the Bullets option, the dialog displays a glyphs icon grid that allows you to select a character to place before each paragraph in the selected list. You can also choose a font family and style, point size, and color to apply to the selected bullet character. At the bottom of the dialog, define the bullet position by choosing Hanging or Flush Left from the Position menu, or by entering values in the Left Indent, First Line Indent, and Tab Position fields. Check the Preview option to see the settings applied as you enter them.

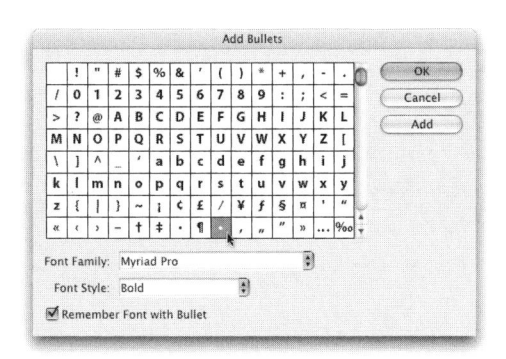

You can add characters to the bullet glyph set by clicking the Add button. InDesign launches the Add Bullets dialog, which allows you to select characters from a chosen font and add them to the bullet glyph set. To insure that an added bullet character is applied using the selected font, check the Remember Font with Bullet option. Click OK to add the selected character to the bullet glyph set and close the dialog. Click the Add button to add the selected character and keep the dialog open.

255

10.12 Bullets and Numbering (continued)

Related Tasks

10.6 Formatting Paragraphs

10.14 Inserting Special Characters

11.2 Creating and Applying Paragraph Styles

11.4 Creating and Applying Nested Styles

Tips

Bullet glyph characters without a remembered font appear in the Bullets and Numbering dialog grid with a "u" (for Unicode) next to it.

Formatted numbers are updated automatically when editing a paragraph list.

Formatted bullets and numbers cannot be selected with the Type tool. To convert formatted bullets or numbering to selectable text, choose Convert Numbering to Text or Convert Bullets to Text from the Paragraph palette menu.

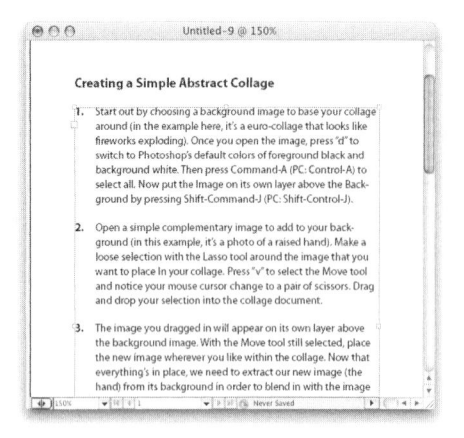

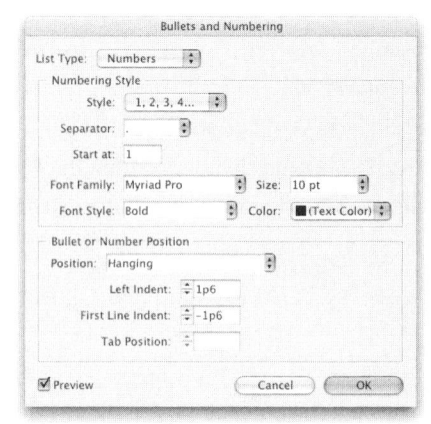

When you select the Numbers option, choose a style and separator character from the menus. You can also enter a separator character in the field. Enter a number to start the list with in the Start At field, then choose a font family and style, point size, and color to apply. At the bottom of the dialog, define the bullet position using the Position menu or by entering values in the Indent/Position fields. Check the Preview option to see the settings applied as you enter them.

To apply the document default list attributes to a selected list, click the Bulleted or Numbered List buttons in the Control bar or PageMaker Toolbar.

CREATING JUMP LINES

You may run into an instance, especially in book or magazine publishing, where you need to indicate what page a story continues on. Thankfully, InDesign has special characters devoted to creating auto jump lines. Using these characters, InDesign automatically identifies the page you are jumping to or from.

In a separate text frame that overlaps the main story, type a jump line followed by the Next Page Number or Previous Page Number character. To insert either character, choose Type > Insert Special Character > Next/Previous Page Number. You can also insert these characters using the contextual menu by Control/right-clicking.

10.13 Setting Tabs

You can adjust tab stops for selected tab characters using the Tabs palette. Insert the Type tool cursor on a line of a paragraph containing a tab character (or multiple tab characters), and open the Tabs palette by choosing Window > Type & Tables > Tabs.

To position the stops for all tab characters placed in the paragraphs of a single, unthreaded text frame, select the frame with either selection tool and open the Tabs palette.

Click the Magnet button located in the bottom right of the Tabs palette to position it (when possible) directly above the selected text frame. Click above the tab ruler to position a tab stop, or enter a specific measurement value in the X field. With the tab stop icon selected, click one of five alignment option buttons.

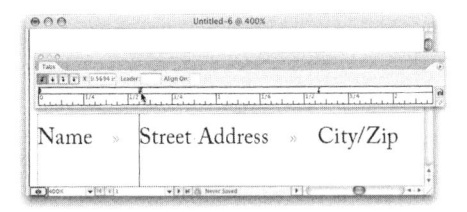

Left Tab Stop: Aligns text to the left of the tab stop position

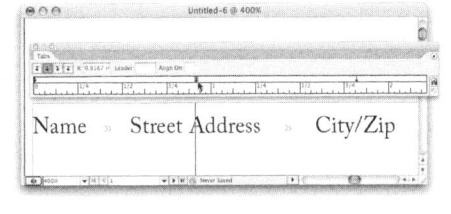

Centered Tab Stop: Aligns text to the center of the tab stop position

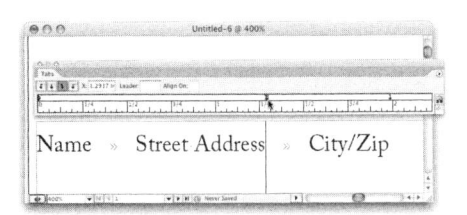

Right Tab Stop: Aligns text to the right of the tab stop position

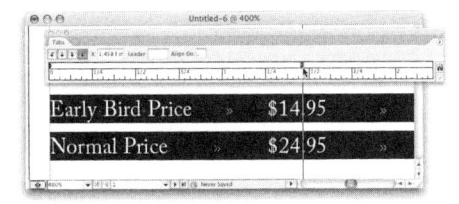

Decimal Tab Stop: Aligns decimal points and other nonnumeric characters to the tab stop position

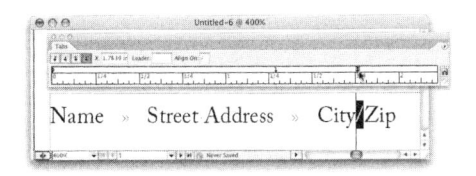

Align to Character Tab Stop: Aligns the character specified in the Align On field to the tab stop position. If InDesign cannot locate the specified character in the text, it treats the tab as a Right Tab Stop.

To remove a tab stop, simply drag it off the palette. To remove all tab stops from a selected area of text, choose Clear All from the palette menu.

Related Tasks

2.6 Type Menu
3.6 Type Tools
4.21 Type and Tables Palettes
7.4 Selecting Type
9.3 Importing Text
10.6 Formatting Paragraphs

Shortcuts

Tabs palette
Mac: Shift+Cmd+T
Win: Shift+Ctrl+T

Switch between Tabs palette alignment options
Mac: Opt-click tab marker in palette
Win: Alt-click tab marker in palette

10.13 Setting Tabs *(continued)*

Related Tasks

10.9 Creating Hanging Indents and Punctuation

10.14 Inserting Special Characters

11.2 Creating and Applying Paragraph Styles

11.4 Creating and Applying Nested Styles

11.5 Creating and Applying Object Styles

Shortcuts

Type tool
Mac and Win: T

Toggle Control bar character/paragraph attributes
Mac: Cmd+Opt+7
Win: Ctrl+Alt+7

Tips

When setting tab stops with the Tabs palette, you cannot select and move more than one tab stop icon at a time.

Tab stops can also be saved as part of a paragraph style.

Changing Tab Stop Alignment and Position

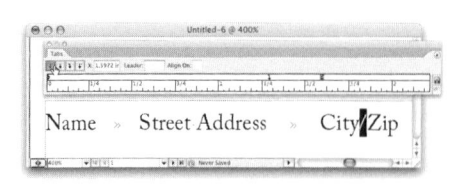

Tab stop alignment can be changed at any time by selecting the tab stop icon and clicking a different alignment button.

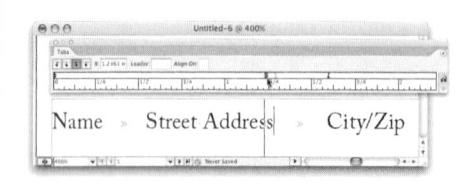

You can reposition a tab stop by dragging it to the left or right above the tab ruler. As you do, a vertical guide follows your movements in the text frame and a grayed-out tab stop icon appears in its previous position. You can also reposition a tab stop by selecting it and entering a new measurement value in the X field.

Repeating Tab Stops

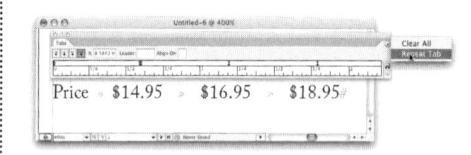

To position a series of tab stops spaced an equal distance apart from each other, select a tab stop icon and choose Repeat Tab from the palette menu. The tab stop is repeated and applied to all tab characters across the length of the column, replacing any preexisting tab stops.

Tab Leaders

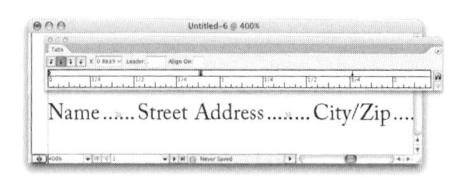

To fill a tab space with series of characters (called leaders), select the tab stop icon and enter a leader character (period, dash, bullet point, etc.) into the Leader field of the Tabs palette. Leader characters can be selected and formatted just like any other type character.

10.14 Inserting Special Characters

Unlike QuarkXPress, InDesign does not expect you to memorize a lot of keyboard shortcuts in order to insert special characters (such as an em dash, hair space, copyright symbol, or forced line break). Instead it allows you to access them under the Type menu. Of course, if you're really into keyboard shortcuts, you can still use them—you just don't have to memorize them!

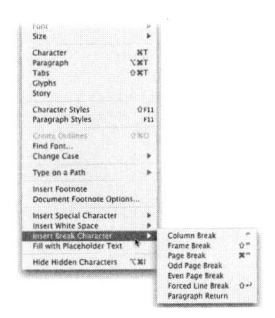

The Type menu includes submenus for inserting special characters, white space characters, and break characters. Position the Type tool cursor anywhere you'd like to insert a special character and select it from any one of these submenus.

Glyphs Palette

Another way to access and insert special characters is through the Glyphs palette. These characters (called glyphs) are actually built into the selected font and can be previewed and applied using the palette. You can open it by choosing Type > Glyphs or Window > Type & Tables > Glyphs.

The palette Show menu allows you to display available glyph characters for an entire font or alternates for a type selection. You can also choose to display additional glyph subsets such as Small Capitals, Discretionary Ligatures, or Slashed Zeros, for OpenType fonts that contain them.

Related Tasks

4.21 Type and Tables Palettes

9.15 Applying Find/Change

Shortcuts

Type tool
Mac and Win: T

Show/hide hidden characters
Mac: Opt+Cmd+I
Win: Alt+Ctrl+I

Auto Page Number
Mac: Opt+Shift+Cmd+N
Win: Alt+Shift+Ctrl+N

Bullet character
Mac: Opt+8
Win: Alt+8

Copyright symbol
Mac: Opt+G
Win: Alt+G

Ellipsis
Mac: Opt+; (semicolon)
Win: Alt+; (semicolon)

Paragraph symbol
Mac: Opt+7
Win: Alt+7

Registered trademark symbol
Mac: Opt+R
Win: Alt+R

Section symbol
Mac: Opt+6
Win: Alt+6

Em dash
Mac: Opt+Shift+- (dash)
Win: Alt+Shift+- (dash)

Tip

When working with the Type tool, you can insert special characters through the contextual menu by Control/right-clicking.

10.14 Inserting Special Characters *(continued)*

Related Tasks

10.6 Formatting Paragraphs

10.9 Creating Hanging Indents and Punctuation

10.13 Setting Tabs

11.2 Creating and Applying Paragraph Styles

11.4 Creating and Applying Nested Styles

11.5 Creating and Applying Object Styles

Shortcuts

En dash
Mac: Opt+- (dash)
Win: Alt+- (dash)

Discretionary hyphen
Mac: Opt+Cmd+- (dash)
Win: Alt+Ctrl+- (dash)

Nonbreaking hyphen
Mac: Opt+Cmd+- (dash)
Win: Alt+Ctrl+- (dash)

Right indent tab
Mac and Win:
Shift+Tab

Indent To Here
Mac: Cmd+\ (backslash)
Win: Ctrl+\ (backslash)

Em space
Mac: Shift+Cmd+M
Win: Shift+Ctrl+M

En space
Mac: Shift+Cmd+N
Win: Shift+Ctrl+N

Nonbreaking space
Mac: Opt+Cmd+X
Win: Alt+Ctrl+X

Thin space
Mac: Opt+Shift+Cmd+M
Win: Alt+Shift+Ctrl+M

To insert a glyph, position the Type tool cursor anywhere you'd like the glyph to appear and double-click the character in the palette.

The Glyphs palette also allows you to create and save all your favorite glyph characters in a custom glyph set. To create a set, choose New Glyph Set from the palette menu, enter a name for it, and click OK. Choose a font from the menu at the bottom of the palette and then select a glyph to add to the set. Choose Add To Glyph Set from the palette menu and select your set's name from the submenu list. You can continue to select and add as many glyphs as you like.

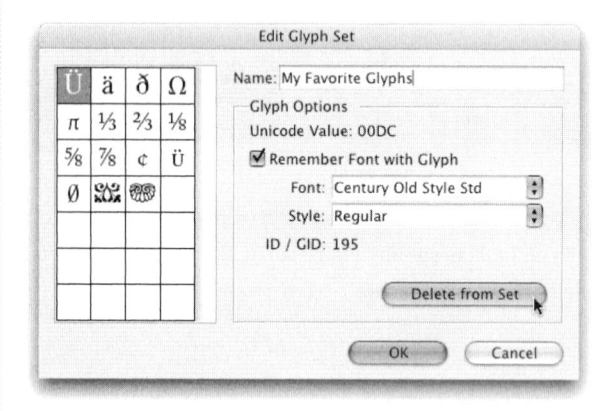

To edit a set, choose Edit Glyph Set from the palette menu and select a set from the submenu. To remove a glyph from the set, select it from the Edit Glyph Set dialog display and click the Delete From Set button. You can also apply a different font and style to a selected glyph character in this dialog.

OpenType Fonts

Certain OpenType fonts also contain special characters (such as fractions and discretionary ligatures) that can be applied automatically through the Character palette menu. You can turn these automatic special character options on and off by selecting them from the OpenType submenu.

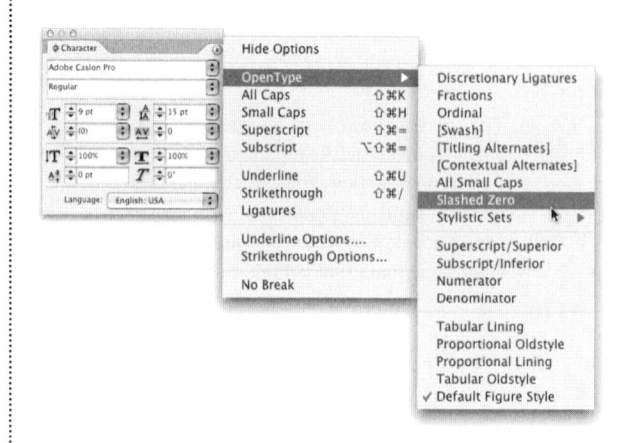

An option that appears in brackets, such as [Contextual Alternates], indicates that it is not available for the currently selected font. When available, you can also apply a Stylistic Set from the OpenType submenu. When chosen, set glyphs are applied over the font's default glyphs.

10.15 Inserting Footnotes

InDesign allows you to create footnote references that automatically number themselves. To insert a footnote, position the Type tool cursor at the end of a word and choose Type > Insert Footnote. InDesign creates a superscript number and places the corresponding reference at the bottom of the column for you to enter footnote text.

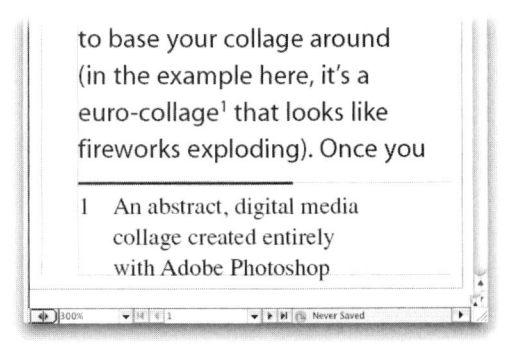

As you type, the footnote text area automatically expands up the column as needed, but not past the footnote reference number. If you allow it to split, overset footnote text carries over to the next text frame column or threaded frame. If not, the footnote reference is either moved to the next column or an overset icon appears. When this happens you can either resize the frame or change the text formatting.

Footnote numbering restarts with each story. You can change footnote numbering, formatting, and layout in the Footnote Options dialog (Type > Document Footnote Options).

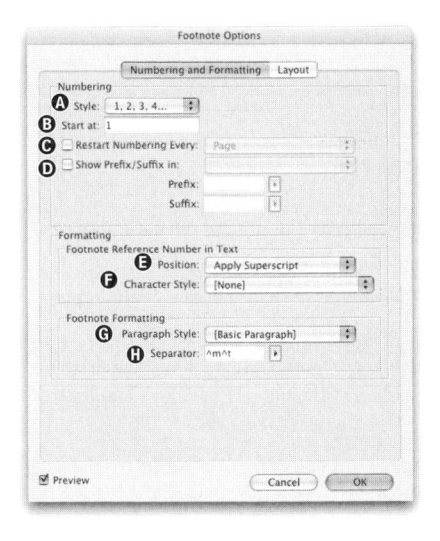

Ⓐ Style Choose a footnote numbering style from the menu.

Ⓑ Start At Specify the start number for the first footnote of the story.

Ⓒ Restart Numbering Every Enable to allow renumbering to start within the document. Choose Page, Spread, or Section from the menu to indicate when renumbering should begin.

Ⓓ Show Prefix/Suffix In Enable to display prefixes or suffixes in the footnote reference. This option is useful for displaying footnote text or references in parentheses or brackets, such as (1) or [1].

Ⓔ Position Reference number display method. Options include Apply Superscript, Apply Subscript, and Apply Normal.

Ⓕ Character Style Style for the footnote reference number. To apply no style, choose None from the menu.

Ⓖ Paragraph Style Style for the footnote reference text. To apply no style, choose None from the menu.

Ⓗ Separator White space characters to place between the footnote number and the start of the footnote text. To change the existing separator, delete it first, and then select a new one from the menu.

Related Tasks

2.6 Type Menu
3.6 Type Tools
4.21 Type and Tables Palettes
7.4 Selecting Type
9.1 Text Frame Options
10.14 Inserting Special Characters

Shortcuts

Type tool
Mac and Win: T

Show/hide character styles
Mac and Win: Shift+F11

Show/hide Paragraph Styles palette
Mac and Win: F11

10.15 Inserting Footnotes *(continued)*

Related Tasks

11.1 Creating and Applying Character Styles

11.2 Creating and Applying Paragraph Styles

13.4 Creating Paragraph Rules

Shortcuts

Em space
Mac: Shift+Cmd+M
Win: Shift+Ctrl+M

En space
Mac: Shift+Cmd+N
Win: Shift+Ctrl+N

Tips

To set default footnote options, enter preferred settings in the dialog without any documents open.

You can import footnotes from Microsoft Word and RTF documents.

Layout Options

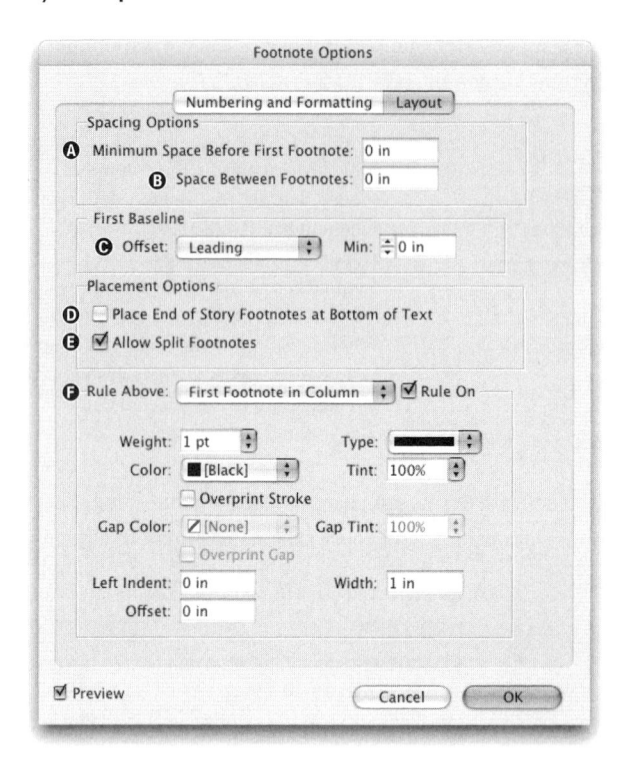

- **A** **Minimum Space Before First Footnote** Enter a value to specify the amount of space between the bottom of the column and the first line of the footnote.

- **B** **Space Between Footnotes** Enter a value to specify the amount of space between paragraphs of footnote text.

- **C** **Offset** This option specifies the amount of space between the footnote divider and the first line of footnote text. Choose to apply Ascent, Cap Height, Leading, X Height, or Fixed first baseline offset to the footnote.

- **D** **Place End Of Story Footnotes At Bottom Of Text** Enable this option to allow footnotes placed in the last column to appear directly below the last frame of the story rather than at the bottom of the column.

- **E** **Allow Split Footnotes** Enable this option to allow overset footnotes to carry over to the next text frame column or threaded frame.

- **F** **Ruler Above** Specify appearance and location options for the footnote divider line. These options are similar to those available for creating paragraph rules. For no rule to appear, uncheck the Rule On option.

262

CHAPTER 11

Styles

STYLES ALLOW YOU TO save and apply various character, paragraph, and object formatting attributes. Once you create a winning combination of attributes, you can save it as a style and apply it to other text or object selections with one simple click. Also, applying styles identifies what role each item plays in a document—an important function when working with XML.

To make good use of this chapter, you might want to familiarize yourself with some "style language" and the following terms:

Global formatting: Applying attributes with styles; so called because all text items or objects formatted this way throughout the document are affected by any changes made to the style.

Local formatting: Applying attributes directly (without styles). Any changes made affect the selected text only.

Overriding: Adding local formatting to stylized text. It is possible to add overridden attributes to a style, and also remove them from stylized text.

Default character/paragraph formatting: The attribute settings entered in the Character and Paragraph palettes and Control bar at application launch.

Undefined attributes: Attributes left unchanged by an applied style.

A magazine page created in InDesign using styles

OK, now that we're well versed in style terminology, let's get started!

- 11.1 **Creating and Applying Character Styles**
- 11.2 **Creating and Applying Paragraph Styles**
- 11.3 **Creating and Applying Parent/Child Styles**
- 11.4 **Creating and Applying Nested Styles**
- 11.5 **Creating and Applying Object Styles**
- 11.6 **Editing and Deleting Styles**
- 11.7 **Importing Styles**

11.1 Creating and Applying Character Styles

Related Tasks

2.6	Type Menu
3.2	Control Bar
3.6	Type Tools
4.4	Automation Palettes
4.21	Type and Tables Palettes
5.2	Type Preferences
7.4	Selecting Type
7.12	Filling Text

Shortcuts

Character Styles palette
Mac and Win: Shift+F11

Paste without formatting
Mac: Shift+Cmd+V
Win: Shift+Ctrl+V

Redefine character style (match selected text)
Mac: Opt+Shift+Cmd+C
Win: Alt+Shift+Ctrl+C

Character styles only allow you to save and apply *character* attributes, such as kerning and tracking, not paragraph attributes such as justification and alignment. Items that repeat in a publication—headings, subheads, or custom drop caps, for example—are all prime candidates for character styles.

Creating Character Styles

There are three ways to set up a character style: from scratch, by basing the new style on preformatted text you've selected, or by basing it on an existing style:

- To create a character style from scratch—with no attributes already set, make sure that no text is selected and no style is highlighted in the palette, then Option/Alt-click the Create New Style button at the bottom of the Character Styles palette or choose New Character Style from the palette menu.

- To create a character style and have it start out inheriting all the attributes of another style, highlight the existing style in the Character Styles palette, make sure no text is selected, then click the Create New Style button or choose New Character Style from the palette menu.

- To create a character style and have it start out using all the attributes of some text that has already been formatted locally, select the formatted text with the Type tool, then Option/Alt-click the Create New Style button. This is probably the easiest way to create a new style.

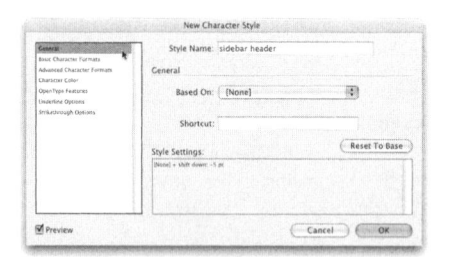

In all three cases, you'll be presented with the New Character Style dialog, where you can enter your preferred values for the style. Each of this dialog's panels mirrors the formatting controls located in the corresponding palette or dialog. You can access a panel by clicking its name in the menu to the left.

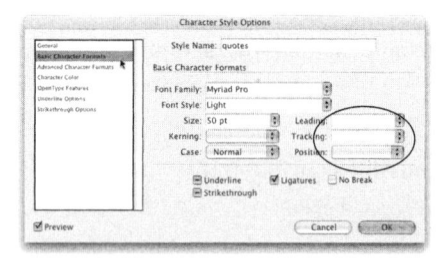

To edit an existing style's definition, double-click the style name in the palette or choose Style Options from the palette menu; the Character Style Options dialog includes the same set of category panels. You'll notice that some of the fields in the dialog appear blank. This is because InDesign only adds those attributes to the style that have been changed from the defaults. Therefore, when you apply a character style to selected text in InDesign, only the attributes defined by the style are changed—all other local formatting remains unchanged.

11.1 Creating and Applying Character Styles (continued)

Click OK when you've finished defining or editing the style. Once you've created a new style, InDesign does not automatically apply it to a text selection. After all, you can't expect InDesign to do *everything* for you!

To save *all* of the character attributes applied to the selected text as a style, you can either enter all of the missing values manually in the Character Style Options dialog, or run the CreateCharacterStyle script available on the InDesign CS2 installation CD.

Applying Character Styles

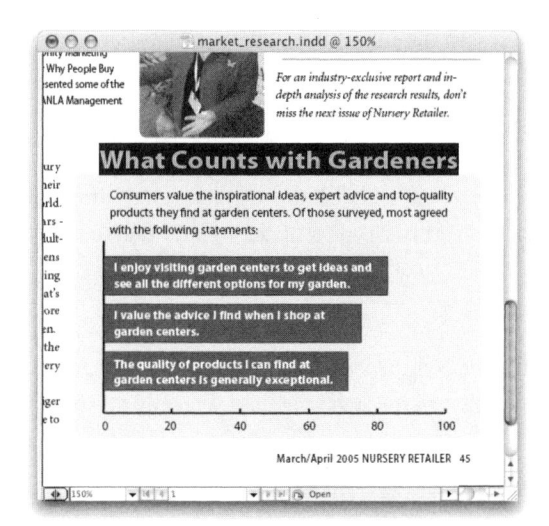

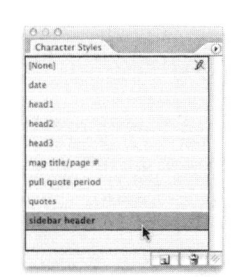

To apply a character style, make a text selection with the Type tool and click the style name in the Character Styles palette. Once again, only the attributes *defined by the style* are applied—all other attributes remain local.

Once applied, the style is linked to the text and can only be removed by selecting the text and clicking None in the Character Styles palette or choosing Break Link To Style from the palette menu. You can also choose None from the Character Style menu located in the Control bar.

When breaking a style link, stylized attributes become local and are not removed from the text. To break the link and reformat using default attributes, hold down Option/Alt as you select the command from the palette menu, or apply the None style.

Related Tasks

7.14 Stroking Text
10.1 Kerning and Tracking
10.2 Scaling and Skewing Type
10.3 Adjusting Leading and Baseline Shift
10.4 Underline and Strikethrough
11.6 Editing and Deleting Styles
11.7 Importing Styles

Shortcuts

Edit style options without applying style
Mac: Opt+Shift+Cmd-double-click style
Win: Alt+Shift+Ctrl-double-click style

Remove local formatting
Mac: Opt-click style name in palette
Win: Alt-click style name in palette

Quick Apply
Mac: Cmd+Return
Win: Ctrl+Enter

Tip

To open the New Character Style dialog, double-click the character style icon in the Control bar.

11.2 Creating and Applying Paragraph Styles

Related Tasks

6.20	Aligning to Baseline Grid
7.4	Selecting Type
7.12	Filling Text
7.14	Stroking Text
9.15	Applying Find/Change
10.1	Kerning and Tracking
10.2	Scaling and Skewing Type
10.3	Adjusting Leading and Baseline Shift
10.4	Underline and Strikethrough
10.6	Formatting Paragraphs
10.7	Creating Drop Caps
10.8	Applying Keep Options

Shortcuts

Paragraph Styles palette
Mac and Win: F11

Paste without formatting
Mac: Shift+Cmd+V
Win: Shift+Ctrl+V

Redefine character style (match selected text)
Mac: Opt+Shift+Cmd+C
Win: Alt+Shift+Ctrl+C

Redefine paragraph style (match selected text)
Mac: Opt+Shift+Cmd+R
Win: Alt+Shift+Ctrl+R

Edit style options without applying style
Mac: Opt+Shift+Cmd-double-click style in palette
Win: Alt+Shift+Ctrl-double-click style in palette

Paragraph styles include both paragraph *and* character formatting, and are ideal for applying to items such as body text or captions.

Creating Paragraph Styles

There are three ways to set up a paragraph style: from scratch, by basing the new style on preformatted text you've selected, or by basing it on an existing style:

- To create a paragraph style from scratch, with no attributes already set, make sure that no text is selected and no style is highlighted in the palette, then Option/Alt-click the Create New Style button at the bottom of the Paragraph Styles palette or choose New Paragraph Style from the palette menu.

- To create a paragraph style and have it start out inheriting all the attributes of another style, highlight the existing style in the Character Styles palette, make sure no text is selected, then click the Create New Style button or choose New Paragraph Style from the palette menu.

- To create a paragraph style and have it start out using all the attributes of a paragraph that has already been formatted locally, insert the Type tool cursor anywhere in the paragraph, then Option/Alt-click the Create New Style button. This is probably the easiest way to create a new style.

Click OK when you have finished defining the style. Once you create the new paragraph style, InDesign does not automatically apply it to the text selection. You must do so manually.

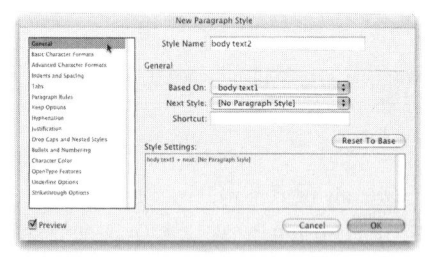

In all three cases, you'll be presented with the New Paragraph Style dialog, which includes 15 different panels. Each panel mirrors the formatting controls located in the corresponding palette or dialog. You can access each one by clicking its name in the menu located on the left.

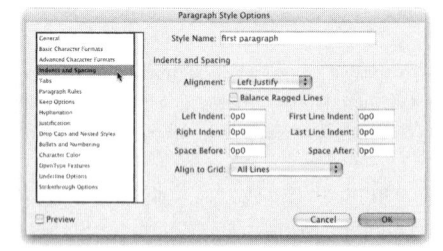

To edit an existing style's definition, double-click the style name in the palette or choose Style Options from the palette menu; the Paragraph Style Options dialog includes the same set of category panels. Unlike with character styles, InDesign adds all of the applied character and paragraph formatting from the selected text to the new paragraph style.

11.2 Creating and Applying Paragraph Styles *(continued)*

Applying Paragraph Styles

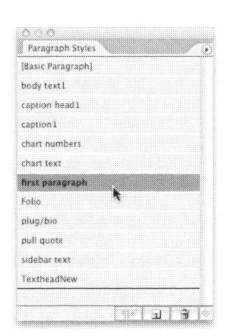

To apply a paragraph style, make a text selection with the Type tool and click the style name in the Paragraph Styles palette. When applying a paragraph style this way, InDesign retains local formatting undefined by the style, except when it applies to *all* of the characters in the paragraph, in which case local formatting is removed.

Once applied, the style is linked to the text and can only be removed by choosing Break Link To Style from the palette menu, or by choosing No Paragraph Style from the menu in the Control bar.

When you break a style link, stylized attributes become local and are not removed from the text. To reformat using default attributes, apply the Basic Paragraph style.

Applying Next Style

When you create a paragraph style, InDesign allows you to automatically assign a different, preexisting style to the next paragraph following a carriage return. For example, if you create and apply a style for an item such as a pull quote (a short excerpt or quoted paragraph, inserted between or to one side of paragraphs of body text), you can set up your styles so that the paragraph immediately following automatically has the body text style.

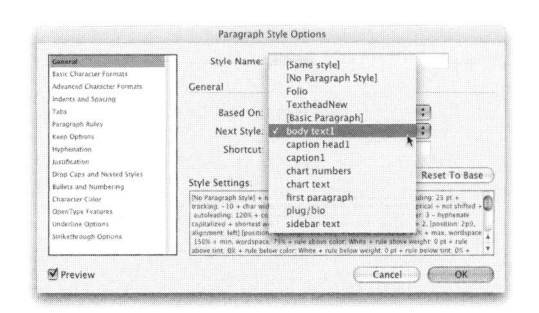

Select the pull quote style in the Paragraph Styles palette and choose Style Options from the palette menu. In the General panel of the options dialog, select the body text style from the Next Style menu. Click OK and type the pull quote. When you press Return/Enter, the chosen style is automatically applied.

Related Tasks

10.13 Setting Tabs

10.14 Inserting Special Characters

10.15 Inserting Footnotes

11.6 Editing and Deleting Styles

11.7 Importing Styles

Shortcuts

Remove local formatting and apply style
Mac: Opt-click style name in palette
Win: Alt-click style name in palette

Clear character overrides only
Mac: Cmd-click Clear Overrides button
Win: Ctrl-click Clear Overrides button

Clear paragraph-level overrides only
Mac: Cmd+Shift-click Clear Overrides button
Win: Ctrl+Shift-click Clear Overrides button

Remove local formatting including character styles and apply paragraph styles
Mac: Opt+Shift-click style name in palette
Win: Alt+Shift-click style name in palette

Quick Apply
Mac: Cmd+Return
Win: Ctrl+Enter

Tip

The whole idea behind using styles is to save time, not waste it. That's why it is *always* a good idea to name your styles. You won't waste time trying to find the one you need.

267

11.3 Creating and Applying Parent/Child Styles

Related Tasks

7.4 Selecting Type
11.6 Editing and Deleting Styles
11.7 Importing Styles

Shortcuts

Character Styles palette
Mac and Win: Shift+F11

Paragraph Styles palette
Mac and Win: F11

Paste without formatting
Mac: Shift+Cmd+V
Win: Shift+Ctrl+V

Redefine paragraph style (match selected text)
Mac: Opt+Shift+Cmd+R
Win: Alt+Shift+Ctrl+R

Edit style options without applying style
Mac: Opt+Shift+Cmd-double-click style
Win: Alt+Shift+Ctrl-double-click style

Quick Apply
Mac: Cmd+Return
Win: Ctrl+Enter

Tip

When you're creating a new style, InDesign automatically bases it on the style that is applied wherever the Type tool cursor is placed. If you do not want to base the new style on another, be sure to choose No Paragraph Style from the Based On menu.

InDesign allows you to create a style that is based on another style. When you do this, shared attributes change dynamically throughout all of the "children" when the "parent" style is edited.

All styles in InDesign can be based on another style of the same type. For example, a character style can be based on another character style but not on a paragraph or object style. Paragraph styles can be based on other paragraph styles, and object styles can be based on other object styles.

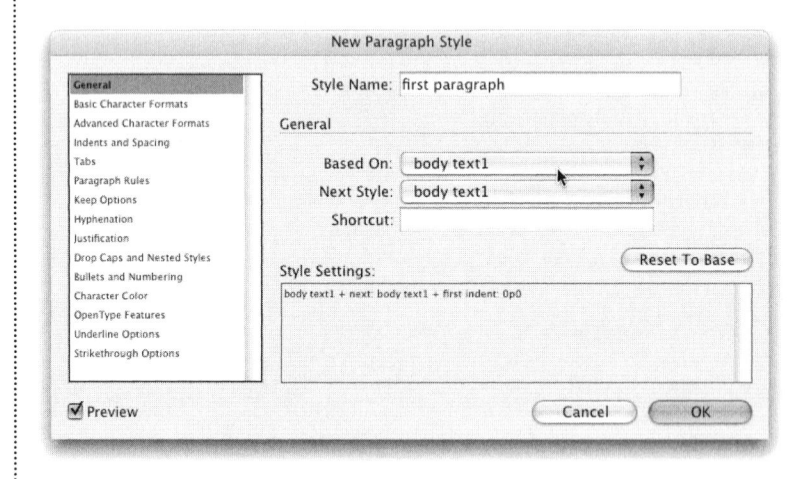

To create a new style that is based on an existing "parent" style, access the New Style dialog from the Styles palette menu. Choose a parent style from the Based On pop-up menu.

Be sure and change any attributes you do not want affected by edits made to the parent style. InDesign keeps track of which attributes are shared and which are not. When you've finished, click OK to add the new style to the Styles palette list.

11.4 Creating and Applying Nested Styles

With nested styles, you can automatically format a paragraph using several character styles. Rather than apply multiple character styles one at a time, you can select multiple lines and/or paragraphs of text and apply the styles all at once.

1. Select some text and choose Drop Caps And Nested Styles from the Paragraph palette menu or Control bar menu. At the bottom of the dialog, click the New Nested Style button.

2. From the menu that appears, choose a character style to apply to the initial characters.

3. Click the word to the right of the character style menu to activate a second menu: Choose "through" to apply the selected character style up to *and including* the specified characters. Choose "up to" to apply the style up to *but not including* the specified characters.

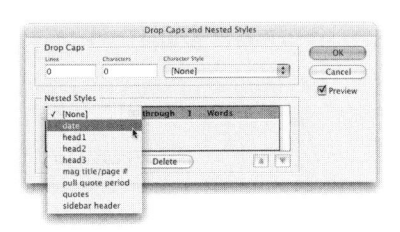

4. Click the number to the right of the through/up to menu to activate the data field. Enter the number of characters you'd like to apply the character style to.

5. Click the field at the far right to activate the character menu/data field. Choose a delimiting character from the list or enter one in the data field. You can also enter metacharacters like the one shown here for an en space.

6. To continue adding nested styles, click the New Nested Style button again and repeat steps 2–5. When you've finished, click OK to apply the nested style to the selection. Check the Preview option in the dialog to see the nested styles applied as you create them.

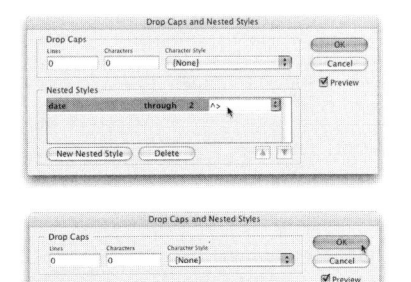

Nested Style 1   Nested Style 2

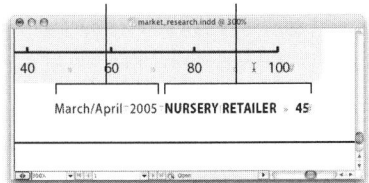

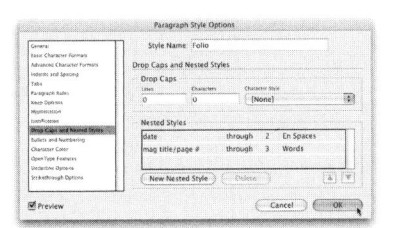

Nested styles become even more powerful when you save them as part of a paragraph style. To do this, open the New Paragraph Style or Paragraph Style Options dialog and click the Drop Caps And Nested Styles panel. Follow the steps above to add more formatting to a paragraph style than you ever realized you could.

Related Tasks

7.4 Selecting Type
7.12 Filling Text
10.7 Creating Drop Caps
10.13 Setting Tabs
11.6 Editing and Deleting Styles
11.7 Importing Styles

Shortcuts

Drop caps and nested styles
Mac: Opt+Cmd+R
Win: Alt+Ctrl+R

Character Styles palette
Mac and Win: Shift+F11

Paste without formatting
Mac: Shift+Cmd+V
Win: Shift+Ctrl+V

Edit style options without applying style
Mac: Opt+Shift+Cmd-double-click style
Win: Alt+Shift+Ctrl-double-click style

Quick Apply
Mac: Cmd+Return
Win: Ctrl+Enter

Tip

You can insert the special End Nested Style Here character at a point in the paragraph where you'd like to stop applying the style. Place the Type tool cursor at the preferred stopping point and choose Type > Insert Special Character > End Nested Style Here.

11.5 Creating and Applying Object Styles

Related Tasks

4.12 Object Styles Palette

7.5 Drawing Rectangles, Ellipses, and Polygons

7.6 Drawing Custom Shapes

7.7 Drawing Freeform Shapes

7.10 Filling with Solid and Transparent Colors

7.11 Filling with Gradients

7.13 Stroking Frames, Shapes, and Paths

Shortcuts

Object Styles palette
Mac: Cmd+F7
Win: Ctrl+F7

Edit style options without applying style
Mac: Opt+Shift+Cmd-double-click style
Win: Alt+Shift+Ctrl-double-click style

Object styles are used to format shapes and frames rather than text. They are structured the same way as character and paragraph styles, allowing you to create, apply, edit, and override styles, as well as create parent/child relationships. You can apply them to objects, groups, graphic frames, and text frames. You can stylize fill color, stroke, text wrap, drop shadow settings, and transparency, and even include paragraph styles!

Creating Object Styles

There are three ways to set up an object style: from scratch, by basing the new style on an object you've selected, or by basing it on an existing style:

- To create an object style from scratch, with no attributes already set, make sure that no object is selected and no style is highlighted in the palette, then Option/Alt-click the Create New Style button at the bottom of the Object Styles palette or choose New Object Style from the palette menu.

- To create an object style and have it start out inheriting all the attributes of another style, make sure that no object is selected, highlight the existing style in the Object Styles palette, then click the Create New Style button or choose New Object Style from the palette menu.

- To create an object style and have it start out using all the attributes of an object that has already been formatted locally, select the object or text frame with either selection tool, then Option/Alt-click the Create New Style button. This is probably the easiest way to create a new style.

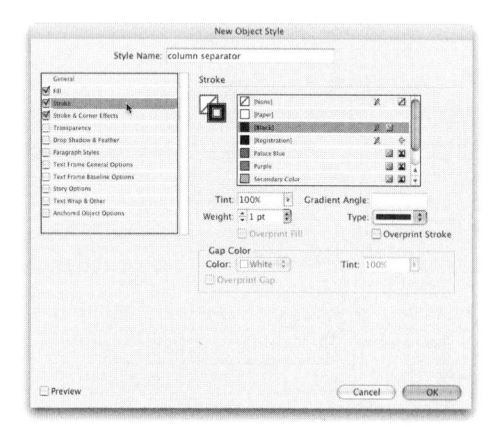

In all three cases, you're presented with the New Object Style dialog, where you can enter your preferred values for the style. Each of this dialog's panels mirrors the formatting controls located in the corresponding palette or dialog. You can access a panel by clicking its name in the menu to the left.

11.5 Creating and Applying Object Styles (continued)

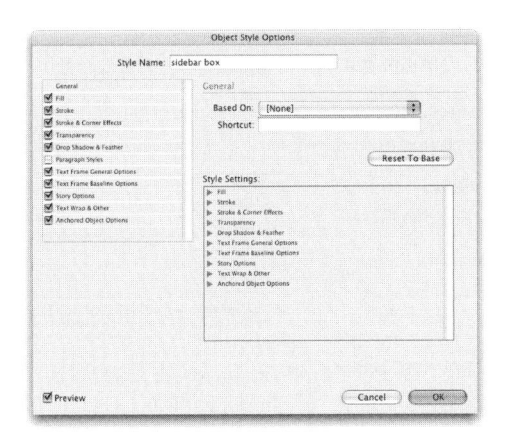

To edit an existing style's definition, double-click the style name in the palette or choose Style Options from the palette menu; the Object Style Options dialog includes the same set of category panels.

InDesign adds all of the formatting applied to the selected object to the new style (except paragraph styles, which stays turned off by default). Type a name for the style and add or remove any formatting using the different panels of the options dialog or by checking/unchecking any of the attribute options listed in the menu. Click the category arrows in the Style Settings portion of the General panel to display a summary of applied attributes.

Click OK when you've finished defining the style. Once you create a new object style, InDesign does not automatically apply it to the selected object. You must do so manually.

Applying Object Styles

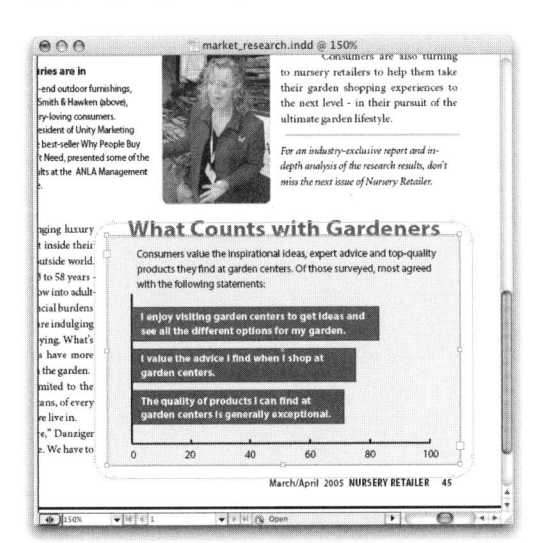

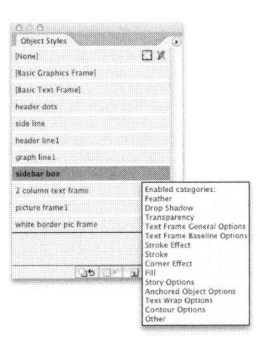

To apply an object style, select an object (frame or group) with either selection tool and click the style name in the Object Styles palette or choose one from the Control bar menu. Hovering over the style name in the palette displays a tooltip containing a list of applied attributes.

Related Tasks

7.15 Aligning Strokes

7.16 Applying Stroked Path Start and End Styles

7.17 Saving and Applying Custom Strokes

7.18 Applying Gap Color to Open Stroke Styles

7.19 Applying Corner Effects

7.20 Applying and Editing Compound Paths

Shortcuts

Remove local formatting
Mac: Opt-click style name in palette
Win: Alt-click style name in palette

Quick Apply
Mac: Cmd+Return
Win: Ctrl+Enter

271

11.5 Creating and Applying Object Styles *(continued)*

Related Tasks

- 7.21 Creating Custom Shapes with Pathfinder
- 11.6 Editing and Deleting Styles
- 11.7 Importing Styles
- 14.8 Changing an Object's Opacity Level
- 14.9 Applying Blend Modes
- 14.10 Adding Drop Shadows
- 14.11 Feathering

Tip

To create a shortcut for applying styles, turn Num Lock on and enter any combination of Shift, Option, Command (Mac) or Shift, Alt, Ctrl (Windows) plus a number from the numeric keypad into the Shortcut field of the New Style or Style Options dialog. Letters and non-keypad numbers cannot be used with style shortcuts.

You can also drag and drop the style from the palette onto the selection. When you apply an object style to a group, the style is applied to *every* object in the group.

When you break an object style link, stylized attributes become local and are not removed from the object. To remove the style *and* its applied attributes, change the Object Style to None rather than breaking the link.

Using Default Object Styles

Every document contains three default object styles: Basic Graphics Frame, Basic Text Frame, and None. By default, the Basic Text Frame style is applied to any new text frame created with the Type tool; the Basic Graphics Frame style is applied to any new shapes drawn with Shape, Pen, and Pencil tools; and the None style is applied to any new frame drawn with the Frame tools.

To set the default object style for text or graphic frames, select an object style from the palette with nothing selected in the document.

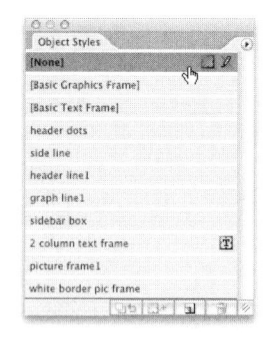

Once applied, the style is linked to the object and can only be removed by clicking None in the Object Styles palette or choosing Break Link To Style from the palette menu. You can also choose None from the Object Style menu located in the Control bar.

The Basic Graphics Frame and Basic Text Frame object styles can be edited but not deleted. The None style cannot be edited or deleted.

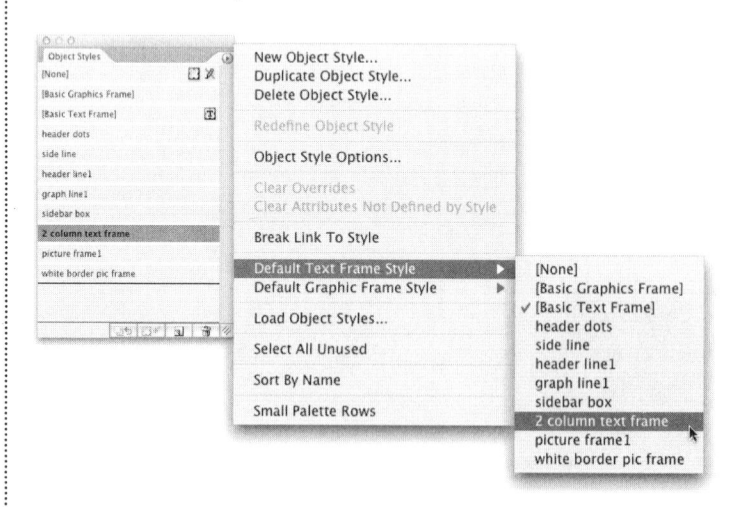

To change the object style defaults, choose Default Text/Graphic Frame Style from the Object Styles palette menu and select a different style from the list. You can also change defaults by dragging the object type icon (text or graphics) from the current default style in the palette to another.

11.6 Editing and Deleting Styles

Character, paragraph, and object styles can all be edited, overridden, and redefined. Note that simply double-clicking a style name in the palette not only opens its options dialog, but also applies the style to your current selection.

Editing Styles

To edit a style with the Style Options dialog, do *one* of the following:

- Press Shift+Opt+Cmd (Mac) or Shift+Alt+Ctrl (Windows) and double-click the style name in the palette.

- Make sure nothing is selected in the document, then click the style name in the palette and choose Style Options from the palette menu.

Proceed to adjust the settings located in the different panels of the dialog. Once you click OK, the changes affect all of the text items or objects where the style is applied in the document.

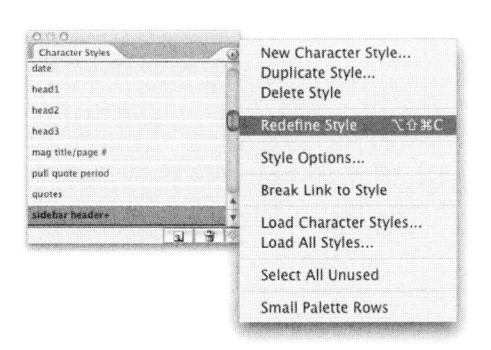

You can also edit styles using local formatting rather than with style options dialogs. Select the text or object that is tagged with the style you'd like to edit and apply some local formatting. Before you deselect, choose Redefine Style from the palette menu. InDesign adjusts the style to match. Note: The Redefine Object Styles command only redefines attributes for categories that are checked in the options dialog. If the attribute's category is not checked, you must add it to the style separately.

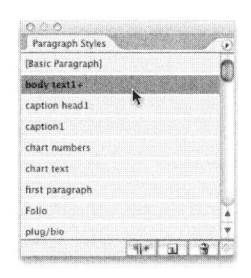

You may be wondering why a plus sign occasionally appears next to the selected style name in the palette. When the plus icon appears, it means that the applied style has been *overridden*. A style appears overridden in the palette when you apply local formatting to a selection *in addition* to the style.

Related Tasks

6.20 Aligning to Baseline Grid
7.4 Selecting Type
7.12 Filling Text
7.14 Stroking Text
9.15 Applying Find/Change
10.1 Kerning and Tracking

Shortcuts

Character Styles palette
Mac and Win: Shift+F11

Paragraph Styles palette
Mac and Win: F11

Paste without formatting
Mac: Shift+Cmd+V
Win: Shift+Ctrl+V

11.6 Editing and Deleting Styles *(continued)*

Related Tasks

10.2 Scaling and Skewing Type

10.3 Adjusting Leading and Baseline Shift

10.4 Underline and Strikethrough

10.6 Formatting Paragraphs

10.7 Creating Drop Caps

10.8 Applying Keep Options

Shortcuts

Redefine paragraph style (match selected text)
Mac: Opt+Shift+Cmd+R
Win: Alt+Shift+Ctrl+R

Edit style options without applying style
Mac: Opt+Shift+Cmd-double-click style
Win: Alt+Shift+Ctrl-double-click style

Remove local formatting
Mac: Opt-click style name in palette
Win: Alt-click style name in palette

To remove all character, paragraph, or object style overrides in a selection, Option/Alt-click the style name in the respective styles palettes. You can also remove paragraph and object style overrides by clicking the Clear Overrides button in the Paragraph Styles palette or Object Styles palette or its equivalent in the Control bar. The Character Styles palette does not have a clear overrides button.

Overrides are handled a little differently with object styles than with character and paragraph styles. With object styles, overrides are not displayed unless they are part of the style. Therefore, any formatting added outside of the style is not considered an override, and is not removed by clicking the Clear Overrides button. To remove all added formatting, you must click the Clear Attributes Not Defined By Style button located in the Control bar or at the bottom of the Object Styles palette. Clicking this button also resets any disabled categories in the style to None.

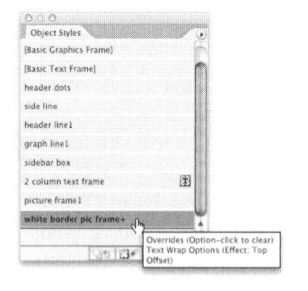

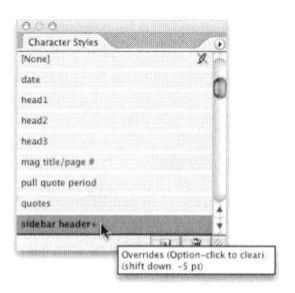

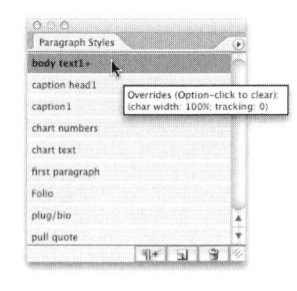

For all three style types (character, paragraph, and object), you can identify what attributes have been overridden by hovering your mouse over the style name in the palette; the tooltip lists them for you.

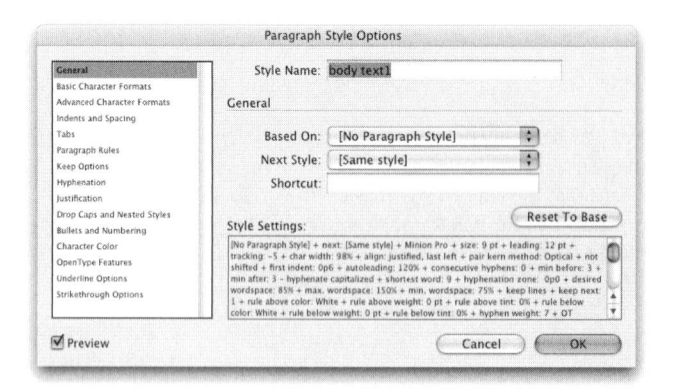

The Style Settings window in the General panel of the Style Options dialog also contains a list of attributes that differ from the style.

11.6 Editing and Deleting Styles *(continued)*

Deleting Styles

To delete a style, first Deselect All (Mac: Shift+Cmd+A; Windows: Shift+Ctrl+A) to avoid applying the style to a selection; then select the style from the palette and click the Delete Selected Styles button. You can also choose the Delete Style command from the palette menu or drag the style to the Delete button trash icon.

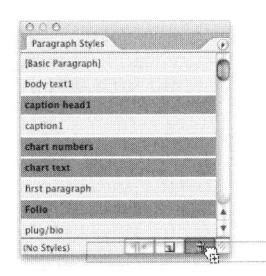

To delete multiple styles at a time, Command/Ctrl-click the styles in the palette and click the Delete Selected Styles button or choose Delete Style from the palette menu. Shift-click to select and delete consecutive styles. You can also choose Select All Unused from the palette menu and delete.

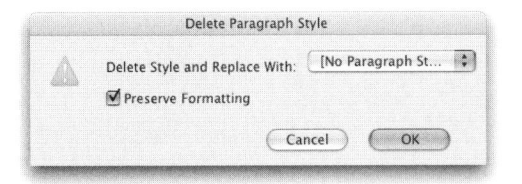

Before deleting a style that is in use InDesign displays a dialog, asking you what you would like to replace the style with. Choose a replacement style from the menu and click OK.

When replacing a deleted style with No Paragraph Style or None (character or object styles), you can keep the formatting applied by checking the Preserve Formatting option in the Delete Style dialog before clicking OK. InDesign applies the deleted style's formatting as local formatting.

QUICK APPLY

If you have so many styles saved in your document that it takes a long time to scroll through the styles palette to find the one you need, try using Quick Apply. Click the Quick Apply button in the Control bar, or choose Edit > Quick Apply to open the Quick Edit list. Type the name (or even just the first two letters) of the style you're trying to locate in the search field. Quick Apply then displays any characters that match your search in the Quick Edit list below. Once you locate the style, press Return (Mac) or Enter (Windows) to apply it to your selection. The Quick Edit list automatically closes once a style is applied. If you can't find the style you're looking for, press Esc, or click the Quick Apply button to close the Quick Edit list.

Related Tasks

10.9 Creating Hanging Indents and Punctuation

10.10 Change/Apply Hyphenation

10.11 Change/Apply Justification

10.13 Setting Tabs

10.14 Inserting Special Characters

10.15 Inserting Footnotes

Shortcuts

Remove local formatting including character styles
Mac: Opt+Shift-click style name in palette
Win: Alt+Shift-click style name in palette

Quick Apply
Mac: Cmd+Return
Win: Ctrl+Enter

Tip

You can also edit or delete a style through the contextual menu by Control-clicking (Mac) or right-clicking (Windows) its name in the palette. This is another quick and easy way to delete or edit a style without accidentally applying it to a selection in the document.

11.7 Importing Styles

Once you create a set of styles that you like, you can apply them to other InDesign documents using the Load feature.

1. To import character, paragraph, or object styles, choose Load Styles from the respective palette's menu.

2. When the Open A File dialog appears, locate and select the document containing the styles you'd like to import. Click the Open button to access the Load Styles dialog.

3. The Load Styles dialog displays a list of available styles. Check the boxes next to the styles that you'd like to import. You can also use the Check All or Uncheck All button.

4. You can tell InDesign how you'd like to handle conflicting style names in the Conflict With Existing Style column of the dialog. If a style conflict exists, that column displays an option. To change the option, select the style and choose Auto-Rename or Use Incoming Style Definition from the menu that appears in the column. Style differences are listed below in the Incoming Style Definition and Existing Style Definition sections of the dialog.

5. Click OK. That's all there is to it! InDesign displays the imported styles in the palette.

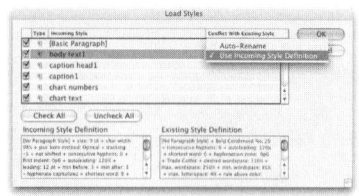

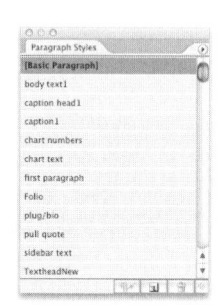

To import *all* of the character and paragraph styles from a specific document, choose Load All Styles from the Character Styles or Paragraph Styles palette menus.

InDesign also adds styles to a document when you copy/paste or drag and drop stylized text or objects from one InDesign document to another. If a style of the same name already exists, the added style is overridden by the existing style.

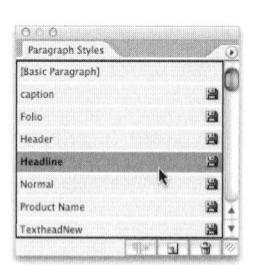

Styles contained in converted QuarkXPress documents, PageMaker documents, and imported Microsoft Word and RTF files are also added. You can identify them by the floppy disk icon that appears next to the style's name in the palette.

Related Tasks

9.4 Importing Tagged and ASCII Text
9.5 Importing XML
17.6 Exporting as XML

Shortcuts

Character Styles palette
Mac and Win: Shift+F11

Paragraph Styles palette
Mac and Win: F11

Paste without formatting
Mac: Shift+Cmd+V
Win: Shift+Ctrl+V

Redefine paragraph style (match selected text)
Mac: Opt+Shift+Cmd+R
Win: Alt+Shift+Ctrl+R

Edit style options without applying style
Mac: Opt+Shift+Cmd-double-click style
Win: Alt+Shift+Ctrl-double-click style

Remove local formatting
Mac: Opt-click style name in palette
Win: Alt-click style name in palette

Quick Apply
Mac: Cmd+Return
Win: Ctrl+Enter

Place
Mac: Cmd+D
Win: Ctrl+D

Tip

InDesign's Book palette allows you to synchronize styles among multiple documents.

CHAPTER **12**

Placed Images

A PAGE LAYOUT JUST wouldn't be a page layout without including some placed images. To add visual interest to a design, you'll probably want to include a few photographs. And even though you can create custom-drawn logos and shapes in InDesign, you may also want to add images created in other vector-based drawing programs, such as Adobe Illustrator.

In this chapter we'll explain how to import images of all types into your InDesign documents, including TIFFs, EPS files, layered and multipage PDFs, and native file formats such as AI (Adobe Illustrator format) and layered PSDs (Photoshop Documents). We'll also explain how to manage links and embed images using the Links palette, and how to apply, create, and edit clipping paths.

- 12.1 **Importing a Graphic Image**
- 12.2 **Setting Import Options**
- 12.3 **Object Layer Options and Placed PSDs**
- 12.4 **Copying to and from Adobe Illustrator**
- 12.5 **Resizing Placed Images**
- 12.6 **Updating Missing and Modified Links**
- 12.7 **Embedding Images**
- 12.8 **Object-Level Display Settings**
- 12.9 **Applying and Editing a Photoshop Clipping Path**
- 12.10 **Creating and Editing an InDesign Clipping Path**

12.1 Importing a Graphic Image

Related Tasks

2.3	File Menu
3.3	Selection Tool
3.4	Direct Selection and Position Tools
4.10	Links Palette
4.14	PageMaker Toolbar
5.12	Display Performance Preferences
5.14	File Handling Preferences

Shortcuts

Place
Mac: Cmd+D
Win: Ctrl+D

Copy to Clipboard
Mac: Cmd+C
Win: Ctrl+C

Paste from Clipboard
Mac: Cmd+V
Win: Ctrl+V

Links palette
Mac: Shift+Cmd+D
Win: Shift+Ctrl+D

Selection tool
Mac and Win: V

Tip

You can drag and drop multiple images at once from a folder on your system into an InDesign document.

You can import graphics using the File > Place command (Mac: Cmd+D, Windows: Ctrl+D). When the Place dialog opens, browse to a graphic image on your system and click the Open button. With the loaded Place cursor, you can then click on an existing frame, draw a frame, or click once anywhere on the page for InDesign to draw a frame for you. In all three scenarios, the image is automatically placed in the frame.

The loaded Place cursor

The loaded Place cursor positioned over a frame

The loaded Place PDF cursor

The loaded Place PDF cursor positioned over a frame

To import a graphic image as you would in QuarkXPress, select an existing frame and choose the Place command. In the resulting dialog, browse to the image and click the Open button. The image appears at 100% of its size in the graphic frame. You can then resize the image or apply one of the fitting commands, from the Object > Fitting submenu.

1. Select a frame.

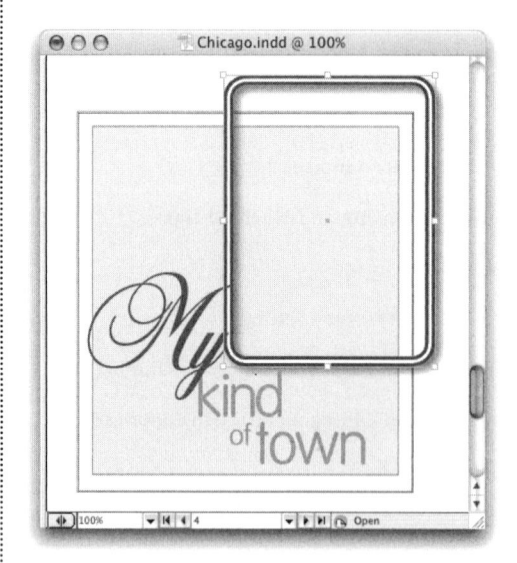

12.1 Importing a Graphic Image (continued)

2. Choose File > Place to access the Place dialog and browse to the image.

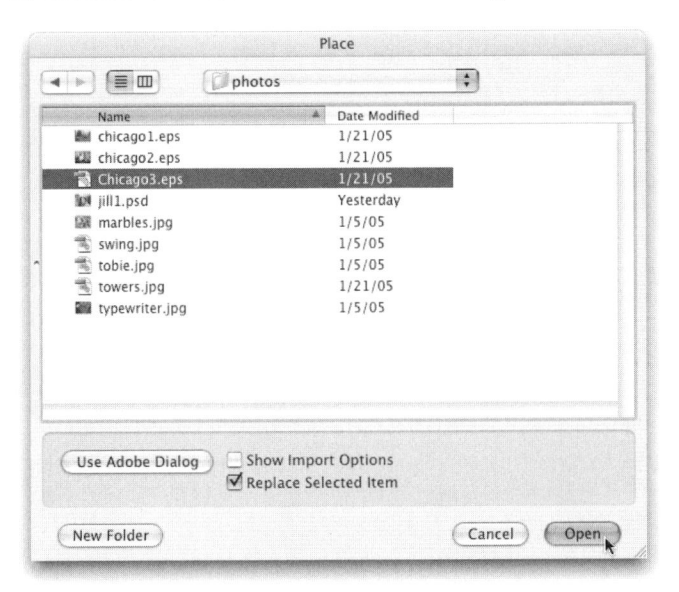

3. Click Open to Place the image at 100% of its size (below left).

4. Apply the Fill Frame Proportionally command (Object > Fitting > Fill Frame Proportionally) (below right).

For additional options, click Show Import Options in the Place dialog, or press the Shift key as you click Open. It is also possible to import graphic images by dragging and dropping them from a folder on your system into a document window. You can even drag an image onto an existing frame to place it inside the frame.

Related Tasks

7.1 Frame/Shape Overview

7.2 Selection Tool vs. Direct Selection Tool

11.5 Creating and Applying Object Styles

12.4 Object Layer Options and Placed PSDs

12.5 Copying to and from Adobe Illustrator

12.6 Resizing Placed Images

14.2 Color-Managing Imported Graphics

Shortcuts

Direct Selection tool
Mac and Win: A

Fit content proportionally
Mac: Opt+Shift+Cmd+E
Win: Alt+Shift+Ctrl+E

Fill frame proportionally
Mac: Opt+Shift+Cmd+C
Win: Alt+Shift+Ctrl+C

Fit content to frame
Mac: Opt+Cmd+E
Win: Alt+Ctrl+E

Fit frame to content
Mac: Opt+Cmd+C
Win: Alt+Ctrl+C

Tip

Dragging a graphic over a palette or document title bar cancels the import.

279

12.2 Setting Import Options

Related Tasks

2.3	File Menu
3.3	Selection Tool
3.4	Direct Selection and Position Tools
4.10	Links Palette
4.14	PageMaker Toolbar

Shortcuts

Place
Mac: Cmd+D
Win: Ctrl+D

Links palette
Mac: Shift+Cmd+D
Win: Shift+Ctrl+D

Selection tool
Mac and Win: V

Tip

You can access import options by holding down Shift as you click Open in the Place dialog.

InDesign accepts all graphic file formats used for prepress including TIFF, EPS, PDF, DCS, as well as native file formats such as AI (Adobe Illustrator format), and PSD (Photoshop document).

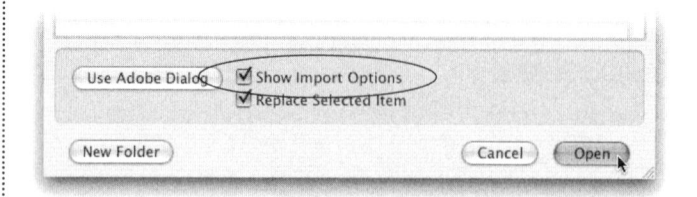

To access additional import options, click Show Import Options in the Place dialog, or press Shift as you click Open.

Import options vary depending on selected file type. PDFs and EPS files have their own options dialogs, while all other file types are handled with the Image Import Options dialog.

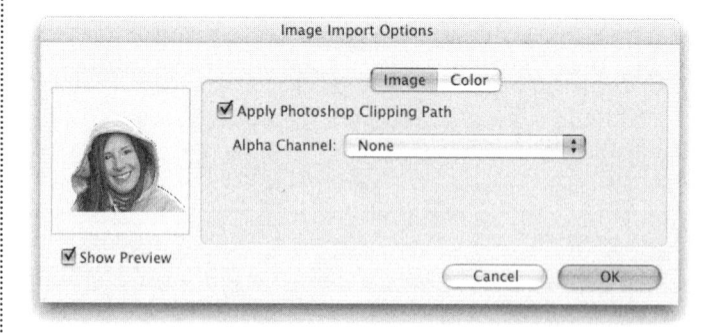

Clipping paths and alpha channels allow you to extract an image from a photograph. If the image you are importing contains a Photoshop clipping path or alpha channel, the Image panel of the Image Import Options dialog allows you to apply and edit the path in InDesign. To do so, check the Apply Photoshop Clipping Path box or choose an alpha channel from the menu. You can apply this option later if you decide to leave it off during import.

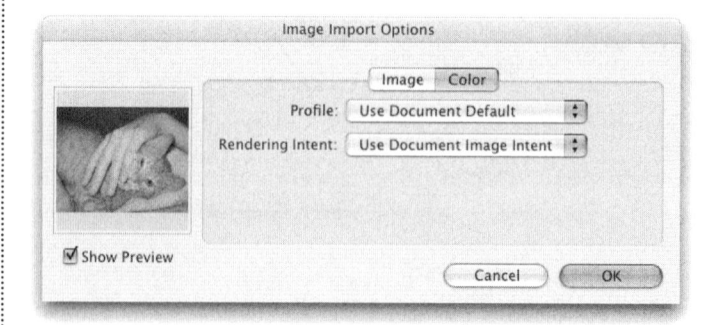

In the Color panel, you can tell InDesign how you would like to color-manage the image you are importing. Select and apply a color profile and rendering intent.

12.2 Setting Import Options (continued)

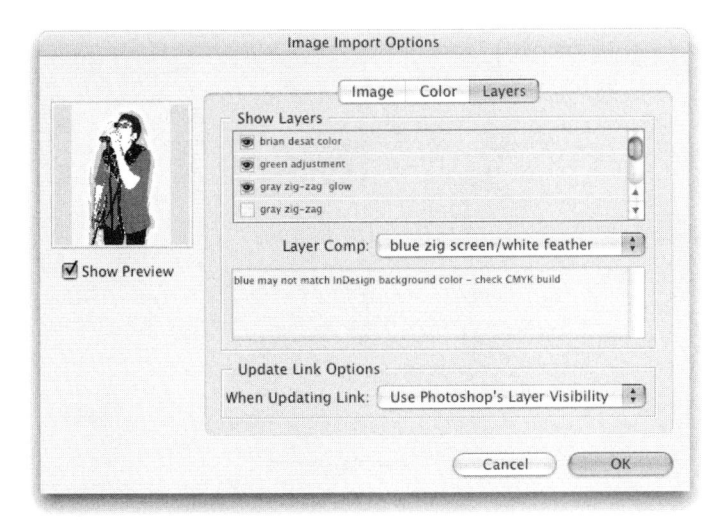

The Layers panel only appears when importing a native Photoshop PSD. In the Show Layers section of the dialog, an eye icon appears next to each layer's name; click the icon to turn a layer's visibility on or off. If the image contains Photoshop layer comps, you can choose to display one in InDesign by selecting it from the Layer Comp drop-down menu. When editing a placed PSD in Photoshop and then updating in InDesign, you have the option to keep the layer visibility overrides chosen upon import, or to view layers as they are saved in the PSD; select either option from the When Updating Link drop-down menu.

EPS Import Options Dialog

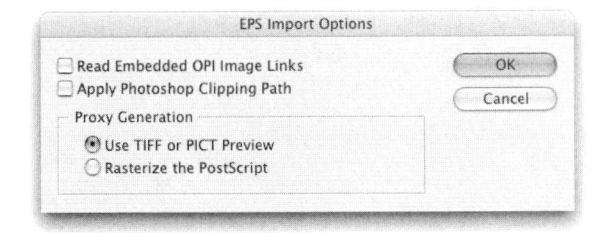

Read Embedded OPI Image Links: An Open Prepress Interface (OPI) workflow allows you to place low-res EPS images that are used to reference high-res versions from an OPI server during output. Enable this option to allow InDesign to act as an OPI server.

Apply Photoshop Clipping Path: If the EPS image you are importing contains a Photoshop clipping path, the EPS Import Options dialog allows you to apply it in InDesign. Unlike with a clipping path applied to a TIFF or PSD, you cannot edit a Photoshop path applied to an EPS file in InDesign.

Proxy Generation: To use the preview embedded in the EPS image, select Use TIFF Or PICT Preview. To create a preview in InDesign, select Rasterize The PostScript.

Related Tasks

5.12 Display Performance Preferences

5.14 File Handling Preferences

7.1 Frame/Shape Overview

7.2 Selection Tool vs. Direct Selection Tool

Shortcuts

Direct Selection tool
Mac and Win: A

Fit content proportionally
Mac: Opt+Shift+Cmd+E
Win: Alt+Shift+Ctrl+E

Fill frame proportionally
Mac: Opt+Shift+Cmd+C
Win: Alt+Shift+Ctrl+C

Tip

The following graphic file formats are not recommended for prepress work: BMP, GIF, PCX, PNG, PICT, WMF, and low-res JPEG.

12.2 Setting Import Options *(continued)*

Related Tasks

11.5 Creating and Applying Object Styles

12.4 Object Layer Options and Placed PSDs

12.5 Copying to and from Adobe Illustrator

14.2 Color-Managing Imported Graphics

Shortcuts

Fit content to frame
Mac: Opt+Cmd+E
Win: Alt+Ctrl+E

Fit frame to content
Mac: Opt+Cmd+C
Win: Alt+Ctrl+C

Place PDF Dialog

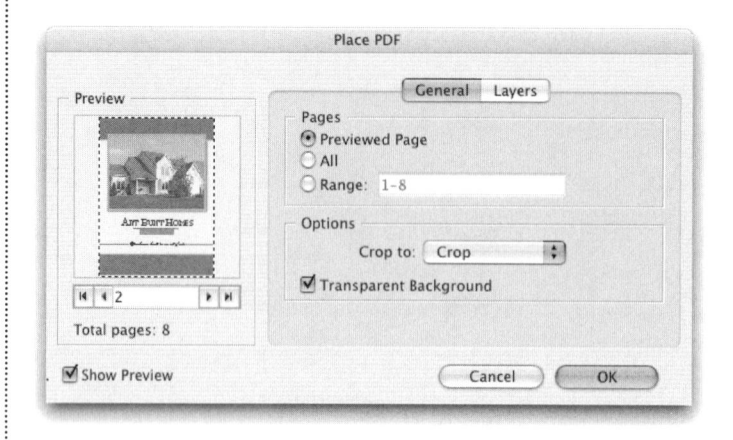

Pages: You can choose to import a specific page, all pages, or a range of pages from a PDF document into InDesign. It is also possible to select which page you would like to import by entering a page number or clicking the left/right arrows under the preview window and selecting the Previewed Page option.

Crop To: Choose how much of the page you would like to import. From the Crop To drop-down menu, select Bounding Box, Art, Crop, Trim, Bleed, or Media.

Transparent Background: Enable this option to allow imported PDFs containing transparent backgrounds to remain transparent in InDesign.

With the exception of layer comps, the Layers panel of the Place PDF dialog has the same functionality as the Layers panel of the Image Import Options dialog.

12.3 Object Layer Options and Placed PSDs

Clipping paths are great for extracting images from placed photographs. The downside is that they can take a long time to draw, and their edges often appear too sharp. To get around this, try extracting your images in Adobe Photoshop and then placing transparent PSDs in InDesign CS2. It's quicker and easier, and produces better-looking images overall. Plus, you can take advantage of InDesign's new Object Layer Options dialog, which allows you to control layer visibility in placed PSDs—including layer comps.

1. Open the photograph in Photoshop CS2.
2. Extract the image using the Extract filter.
3. Create some effects using layers. You can also save your favorite layer effect combinations as layer comps. When you've finished, save the file as a PSD and close it.

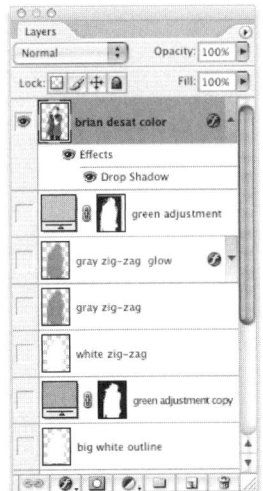

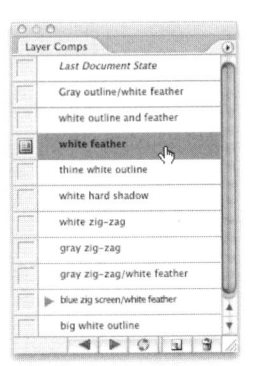

4. Import the PSD into your InDesign document using the File > Place command (Mac: Cmd+D, Windows: Ctrl+D). To access the Image Import Options dialog, enable Show Import Options before clicking Open.

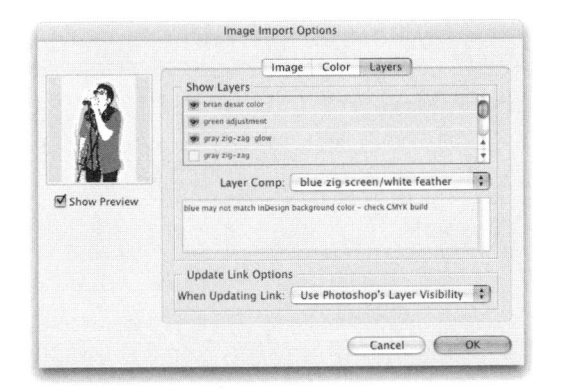

Related Tasks

2.3 File Menu
3.3 Selection Tool
3.4 Direct Selection and Position Tools
4.10 Links Palette
4.14 PageMaker Toolbar

Shortcuts

Place
Mac: Cmd+D
Win: Ctrl+D

Links palette
Mac: Shift+Cmd+D
Win: Shift+Ctrl+D

Tip

The Object Layer Options dialog also allows you to control layer visibility for placed PDFs.

12.3 Object Layer Options and Placed PSDs *(continued)*

Related Tasks

5.12 Display Performance Preferences

5.14 File Handling Preferences

7.1 Frame/Shape Overview

7.2 Selection Tool vs. Direct Selection Tool

11.5 Creating and Applying Object Styles

Shortcuts

Selection tool
Mac and Win: V

Tip

Changing PSD layer visibility or layer comps in InDesign does not alter the original Photoshop file.

5. Click the Layers tab at the top of the dialog to access the Layers panel. In the Show Layers section, choose which layers to display by clicking the eye icons that appear next to each layer's name, or choose a layer comp from the menu. Any layer comp comments saved in the PSD are displayed in the window beneath the Layer Comp drop-down menu.

6. Click OK to place the PSD.

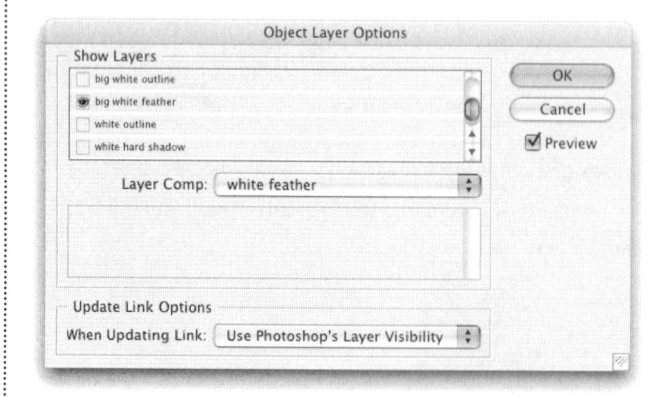

284

12.3 Object Layer Options and Placed PSDs *(continued)*

7. To adjust layer visibility after the PSD is placed, choose Object **>** Object Layer Options. In the resulting dialog, choose to show or hide different layers or select a different layer comp from the menu. Check the Preview option to view your changes in the document as you make them. When you've finished, click OK to close the dialog and apply your changes.

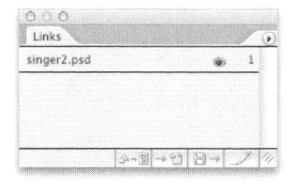

InDesign places an eye icon next to the link's name in the Links palette, indicating that the image now contains layer visibility overrides.

Related Tasks

12.1 Importing a Graphic Image

12.2 Setting Import Options

12.5 Copying to and from Adobe Illustrator

14.2 Color-Managing Imported Graphics

Shortcuts

Direct Selection tool
Mac and Win: A

12.4 Copying to and from Adobe Illustrator

Related Tasks

2.3 File Menu
3.3 Selection Tool
3.4 Direct Selection and Position Tools
4.10 Links Palette
4.14 PageMaker Toolbar
5.12 Display Performance Preferences
5.14 File Handling Preferences

Shortcuts

Place
Mac: Cmd+D
Win: Ctrl+D

Copy to Clipboard
Mac: Cmd+C
Win: Ctrl+C

Paste from Clipboard
Mac: Cmd+V
Win: Ctrl+V

Tip

An Illustrator graphic must be saved in layered PDF format in order to adjust its layer visibility in InDesign using the Object Layer Options dialog.

In addition to placing native .AI (Adobe Illustrator format) files, you can copy/paste or drag and drop Illustrator objects into an InDesign document. With the proper settings enabled, it is possible to edit simple objects in InDesign that have been copied from Illustrator, and vice versa.

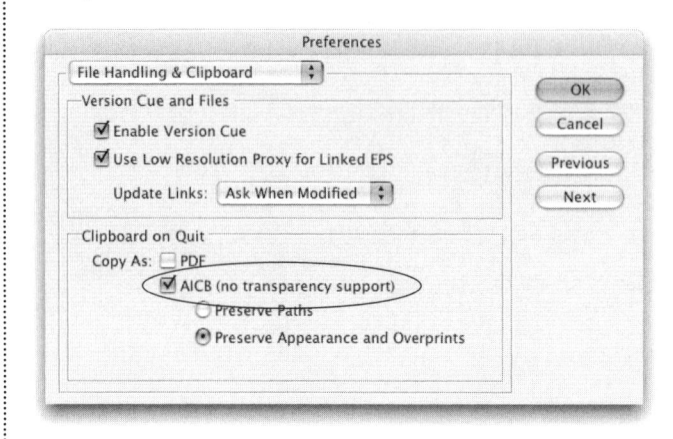

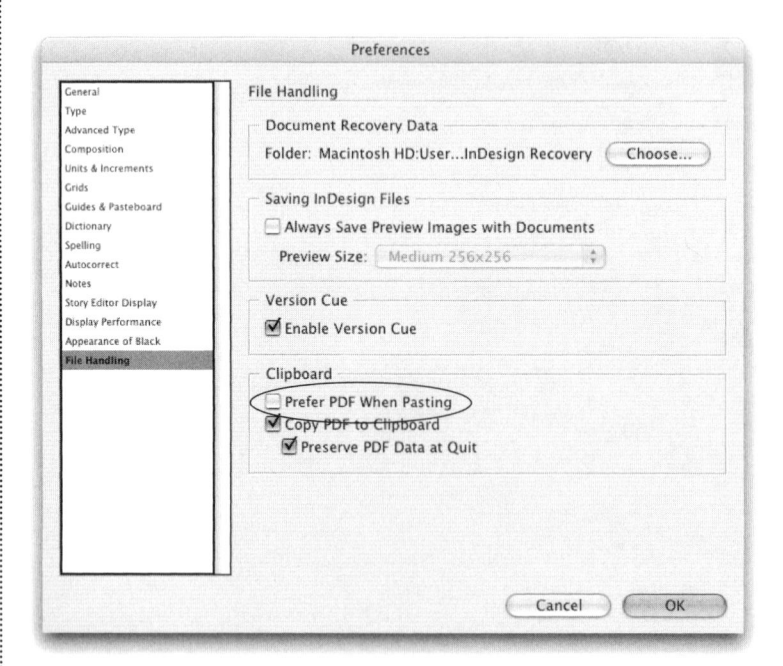

To edit Illustrator objects in InDesign, you must enable the AICB option—Adobe Illustrator Clipboard—in Illustrator's File Handling & Clipboard preferences (top), and disable the Prefer PDF When Pasting option in InDesign's File Handling preferences (right). Once these preferences are set, you can edit Illustrator paths using InDesign's drawing tools.

12.4 Copying to and from Adobe Illustrator *(continued)*

When you're copy/pasting or dragging and dropping an Illustrator graphic into InDesign, paths are automatically grouped. Ungroup to edit them with InDesign's drawing tools.

Of course, there are some limitations to the kinds of objects you can copy/paste and the kinds of edits you can make. For example, InDesign converts any editable text copied from Illustrator into objects that can be transformed but not edited with the Type tool. InDesign also does not accept compound shapes or applied transparency (such as blend modes and drop shadows).

However, colors and simple gradients copied from Illustrator *can* be edited in InDesign using the Color and Gradient palettes.

To copy/paste or drag and drop editable paths from InDesign into Illustrator, enable the Copy PDF To Clipboard option in InDesign's preferences.

Related Tasks

7.1	Frame/Shape Overview
7.2	Selection Tool vs. Direct Selection Tool
11.5	Creating and Applying Object Styles
12.1	Importing a Graphic Image
12.2	Setting Import Options
12.4	Object Layer Options and Placed PSDs
14.2	Color-Managing Imported Graphics

Shortcuts

Ungroup
Mac: Shift+Cmd+G
Win: Shift+Ctrl+G

Links palette
Mac: Shift+Cmd+D
Win: Shift+Ctrl+D

Selection tool
Mac and Win: V

Direct Selection tool
Mac and Win: A

Tip

Objects copy/pasted from Illustrator into InDesign are not treated as links, and therefore do not appear in the Links palette.

12.5 Resizing Placed Images

Related Tasks

2.7 Object Menu
3.2 Control Bar
3.3 Selection Tool
3.4 Direct Selection and Position Tools
3.12 Scale Tool
3.14 Free Transform Tool

Shortcuts

Links palette
Mac: Shift+Cmd+D
Win: Shift+Ctrl+D

Selection tool
Mac and Win: V

Direct Selection tool
Mac and Win: A

Scale tool
Mac and Win: S

Free Transform tool
Mac and Win: E

Transform palette
Mac and Win: F9

To resize a placed image within a frame, you must select it with the Direct Selection tool, and then perform any one of the following actions:

- Drag any one of the image bounding box nodes. Press the Shift key to constrain your image to its original proportions as you drag.

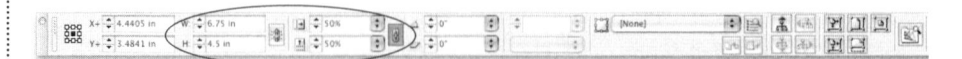

- Enter new Scale X and Y Percentages or new Width and Height values in either the Transform palette or Control bar.

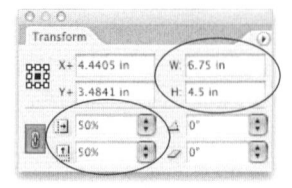

288

12.5 Resizing Placed Images *(continued)*

- Press S to access the Scale tool, then click and drag. Press the Shift key to constrain your image to its original proportions or to limit the scale to one axis.

- Access the Scale dialog by choosing Object > Transform > Scale. Enter values for Uniform or Non-Uniform scaling and click OK.

- Press E to access the Free Transform tool and click and drag one of the image bounding box nodes. Press the Shift key to constrain your image to its original proportions.

- Use either of the keyboard shortcuts for incremental resizing (1% or 5%).

To resize a placed image and its frame container at the same time, select the frame with the Selection tool and use any of the resizing methods described above while holding the Command key (Mac) or the Ctrl key (Windows).

You can also resize an image within a frame by selecting it with the Direct Selection tool and applying one of the commands from the Object > Fitting submenu: Fit Content To Frame, Fit Content Proportionally, Fill Frame Proportionally.

Related Tasks

4.10 Links Palette

4.11 Object and Layout Palettes

7.1 Frame/Shape Overview

7.2 Selection Tool vs. Direct Selection Tool

8.2 Resizing Objects

Shortcuts

Increase/decrease size of selected object by 1%
Mac: Cmd+> (increase)/ Cmd+< (decrease)
Win: Ctrl+> (increase)/ Ctrl+< (decrease)

Increase/decrease size of selected object by 5%
Mac: Opt+Cmd+> (increase)/Opt+Cmd+< (decrease)
Win: Alt+Ctrl+> (increase)/Alt+Ctrl+< (decrease)

Fit content to frame
Mac: Opt+Cmd+E
Win: Alt+Ctrl+E

Fit frame to content
Mac: Opt+Cmd+C
Win: Alt+Ctrl+C

Tip

You can apply Fitting, commands to a graphic selection by using the buttons located on the far right of the Control bar.

12.6 Updating Missing and Modified Links

Related Tasks

3.3 Selection Tool
3.4 Direct Selection and Position Tools
4.10 Links Palette
4.14 PageMaker Toolbar
7.2 Selection Tool vs. Direct Selection Tool
12.8 Embedding and Unembedding Images

Shortcuts

Links palette
Mac: Shift+Cmd+D
Win: Shift+Ctrl+D

Selection tool
Mac and Win: V

Direct Selection tool
Mac and Win: A

Go To Link
Mac: Opt-double-click filename in Links palette
Win: Alt-double-click filename in Links palette

Tips

You can select all of the filenames in the Links palette at once by Command/Ctrl-double-clicking any one of them.

To locate where a link is placed in a document, select it in the Links palette and click the Go To Link button.

To locate a link on your system, select it in the palette and choose Reveal In Finder (Mac), Reveal In Explorer (Windows), or Reveal In Bridge from the palette menu.

The Links palette is similar to the Picture Usage feature in QuarkXPress in that it allows you to update and relink modified and missing links. When a link is edited outside InDesign, it is considered "modified." When a link is moved from its previous location on your system, it is considered "missing." In either scenario, InDesign displays a missing or modified icon next to the link name in the palette.

When the Sort By Status option is enabled in the Links palette menu, missing and modified links always appear at the top of the palette list. You can also choose to sort by name or by page.

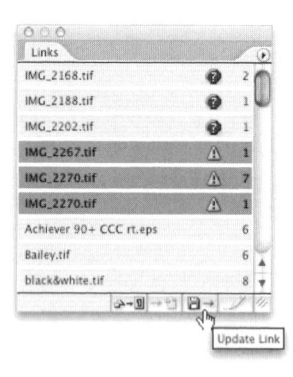

To update a modified link, select it in the Links palette and click the Update Link button located in the palette footer controls, or choose Update Link from the palette menu. You can also select and update several modified links at once.

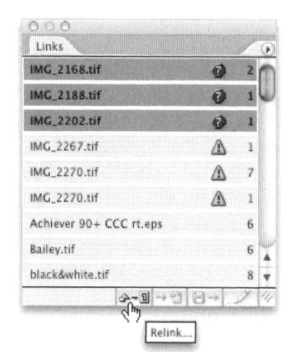

To relink a missing item, select it in the palette and click the Relink button, or choose Relink from the palette menu. When the Locate File dialog opens, browse to the link on your system and then click Open. It is also possible to select and relink several missing items at once.

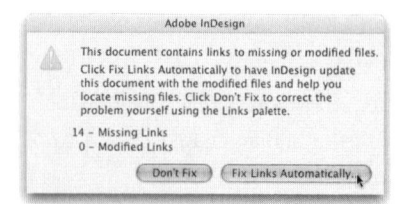

When opening a document containing missing or modified links, InDesign gives you the option to update and/or relink immediately. To do so, click the Fix Links Automatically button or click Don't Fix to update later.

12.7 Emdedding Images

The more pages you add to a document, the more images you are going to place. As the links add up, keeping track of all of them on your system grows increasingly harder. It's the nature of the beast, unfortunately. However, there is something you can do to make it a little easier: *embed* the smaller links in the document.

When you embed an image it becomes part of the document, thereby eliminating the need to refer to a separate file on your system. However, embedding images adds to a document's file size, which is why it is best to only embed smaller graphics such as end mark icons and small vector graphics.

To embed an image, select it in the document or click the link name in the Links palette and choose Embed File from the palette menu. You can also select and embed several links at once.

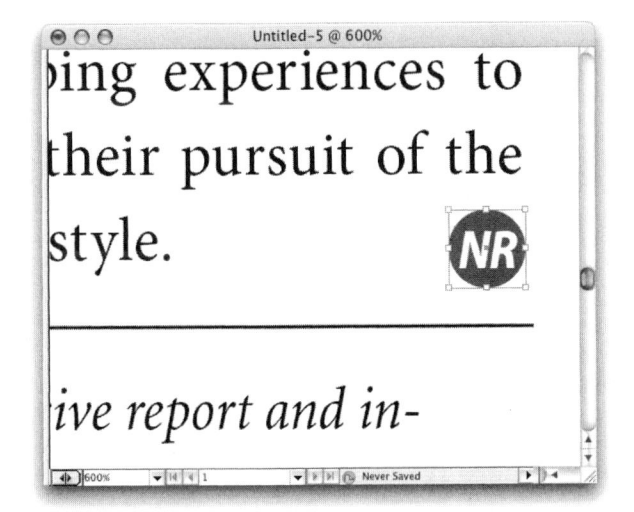

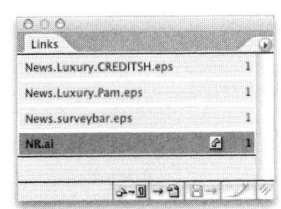

Once you embed a file, an Embedded icon appears in the palette next to the link name.

To relink an embedded file, select it and choose Unembed File from the palette menu. As with embedding, you can also select and unembed several links at once.

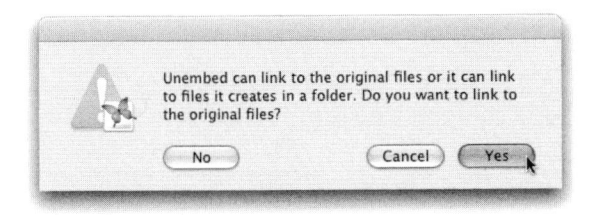

After choosing the Unembed File command, InDesign displays a dialog asking if you'd like to relink to the original file or create a new file. Click Yes to relink to the original and No if you'd like InDesign to create a new file.

Unless it has been moved to a new location on your system, InDesign remembers the original file location when relinking. When creating a new file, you must select a file location from the Choose A Folder (Mac) or Browse For Folder (Windows) dialog and click the Choose button.

Related Tasks

3.3 Selection Tool
3.4 Direct Selection and Position Tools
4.10 Links Palette
7.2 Selection Tool vs. Direct Selection Tool
12.1 Importing a Graphic Image

Shortcuts

Links palette
Mac: Shift+Cmd+D
Win: Shift+Ctrl+D

Selection tool
Mac and Win: V

Direct Selection tool
Mac and Win: A

Go To Link
Mac: Opt-double-click filename in Links palette
Win: Alt-double-click filename in Links palette

Tip

To embed a text link, select the filename in the Links palette and choose Unlink from the palette menu. The filename is removed from the Links palette.

12.8 Object-Level Display Settings

Related Tasks

1.4	Interface Objects
2.7	Object Menu
2.9	View Menu
3.3	Selection Tool
3.4	Direct Selection and Position Tools
4.10	Links Palette
5.12	Display Performance Preferences

Shortcuts

Links palette
Mac: Shift+Cmd+D
Win: Shift+Ctrl+D

Selection tool
Mac and Win: V

Direct Selection tool
Mac and Win: A

Go to link
Mac: Opt-double-click filename in Links palette
Win: Alt-double-click filename in Links palette

Tip

Vector EPS images never preview well on screen. Thankfully in InDesign, you can change the display setting by selecting the image and choosing Object > Display Performance > High Quality Display.

InDesign allows you to apply settings from the Display Performance submenu not only to an entire document, but to individual objects as well. This means that you can override document-level display settings by applying the Fast Display, Typical Display, or High Quality Display setting to selected objects.

For example, if working with High Quality Display enabled slows down your computer, you may want to consider switching to Typical Display and then applying High Quality Display overrides to specific objects as needed.

To do this, you must enable the Allow Object-Level Display Settings option in the View > Display Performance submenu. With the document display set to Typical Display, select an object (or objects) with either selection tool and choose Object > Display Performance > High Quality Display.

You can also set object-level display settings through the contextual menu. Select an object (or objects) with either selection tool and Control-click (Mac) or right-click (Windows) to access the Display Performance commands.

You can change object-level display at any time by selecting the object(s) and choosing a different setting under the Object > Display Performance submenu. To clear local display settings for a selected object (or objects), choose Use View Setting.

To clear all object-level display overrides and display all images in the document with the chosen View setting, select View > Display Performance > Clear Object-Level Display Settings.

Fast Display setting    Typical Display setting    High Quality Display setting

12.9 Applying and Editing a Photoshop Clipping Path

If the TIFF, JPEG, or PSD you are importing contains a Photoshop clipping path, you can apply it via the Image panel of the Image Import Options dialog or the Clipping Path dialog. You can then edit the Photoshop path using InDesign's path editing tools. Any edits made to a Photoshop clipping path in InDesign are not applied to the original file—they only affect the image as it appears in InDesign. (InDesign does not allow you to edit Photoshop clipping paths applied to EPS files).

To apply a Photoshop path when placing an image, check the Apply Photoshop Clipping Path box in the Image Import Options dialog.

To apply a Photoshop path after the image has been placed, select it with either selection tool and choose Object > Clipping Path. At the top of the Clipping Path dialog, choose Photoshop Path from the Type menu. If the image contains more than one Photoshop path, you can select which one to apply in the Path menu below. To see the path as you are applying it, click the Preview check box.

To remove any extraneous black or white edges from the path, contract it by entering a value in the Inset Frame field. You can also invert a Photoshop path by clicking the Invert check box.

Related Tasks

2.3	File Menu
3.3	Selection Tool
3.4	Direct Selection and Position Tools
3.5	Pen Tools
3.7	Pencil Tools
3.19	Scissors Tool
4.10	Links Palette
4.19	Text Wrap Palette

Shortcuts

Clipping path
Mac: Opt+Shift+Cmd+K
Win: Alt+Shift+Ctrl+K

Place
Mac: Cmd+D
Win: Ctrl+D

Links palette
Mac: Shift+Cmd+D
Win: Shift+Ctrl+D

Selection tool
Mac and Win: V

Direct Selection tool
Mac and Win: A

Pen tool
Mac and Win: P

Add Anchor Point tool
Mac and Win: =

Tip

To open and edit an image in Photoshop, select it and click the Edit Original button located at the bottom of the Links palette. Once you save and close the image in Photoshop, InDesign automatically updates it in the InDesign document.

12.9 Applying and Editing a Photoshop Clipping Path *(continued)*

Related Tasks

7.2 Selection Tool vs. Direct Selection Tool

12.1 Importing a Graphic Image

12.2 Setting Import Options

12.12 Creating a Clipping Path in InDesign

13.1 Placing and Editing Text Wraps

Shortcuts

Delete Anchor Point tool
Mac and Win: -

Convert Direction Point tool
Mac and Win: Shift+C

Pencil tool
Mac and Win: N

Scissors tool
Mac and Win: C

Temporarily select Convert Direction Point tool
Mac: Pen tool+Opt, or Direct Selection tool+Opt+Cmd
Win: Pen tool+Alt, or Direct Selection tool+Alt+Ctrl

Temporarily switch between Add/Delete Anchor Point tools
Mac: Opt
Win: Alt

Text Wrap palette
Mac: Opt+Cmd+W
Win: Alt+Ctrl+W

The original image

Applying a Photoshop clipping path

Once you've applied points, you can move them on the Photoshop path using the Direct Selection tool. You can also use the path editing tools included in the Pen and Pencil toolsets to add or delete points, or convert their direction, or you can cut the path using the Scissors tool.

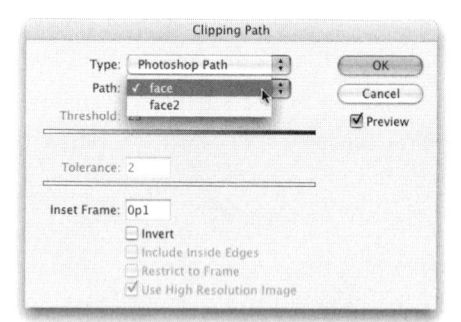

CONVERTING CLIPPING PATHS TO FRAMES

You can convert a clipping path (applied from Photoshop or created in InDesign) into a graphic frame. To do this, select the image with the Direct Selection tool, Control-click (Mac) or right-click (Windows) to access the contextual menu, and choose Convert Clipping Path To Frame. Once the command is applied, InDesign removes the clipping path and replaces it with a graphic frame of the same shape.

12.10 Creating and Editing an InDesign Clipping Path

One way to extract an image from a photograph is to create a clipping path—but be wary of the InDesign clipping path controls. They are clumsy and not very precise. It makes more sense to create a clipping path in Photoshop and apply it to the image in InDesign. However, if all you need to do is remove a simple solid-color background, an InDesign path will suffice.

To create an InDesign clipping path, select a placed image with either selection tool and choose Object **>** Clipping Path. At the top of the Clipping Path dialog, choose Detect Edges from the Type menu. You can then adjust the Threshold and Tolerance settings by entering values in the respective fields or dragging the sliders. To see the path as you are applying it, click the Preview check box.

The Threshold slider determines how close a color must be to white before it is removed. Apply lower values to drop a light color background and higher values to drop a dark one. The Tolerance slider determines how close a pixel must be to the Threshold value in order to be removed by the clipping path. Once the Threshold and Tolerance values are set, you can contract the resulting path and remove any black or white edges by entering a value in the Inset Frame field.

The original image

Related Tasks:

2.3	File Menu
3.3	Selection Tool
3.4	Direct Selection and Position Tools
4.10	Links Palette
4.19	Text Wrap Palette

Shortcuts

Clipping path
Mac: Opt+Shift+Cmd+K
Win: Alt+Shift+Ctrl+K

Place
Mac: Cmd+D
Win: Ctrl+D

Links palette
Mac: Shift+Cmd+D
Win: Shift+Ctrl+D

Tip

To eliminate the need to create a clipping path, try placing a transparent Photoshop file (.PSD) instead.

12.10 Creating and Editing an InDesign Clipping Path *(continued)*

Related Tasks:

7.2 Selection Tool vs. Direct Selection Tool

12.1 Importing a Graphic Image

12.11 Altering an Embedded Photoshop Path

13.1 Placing and Editing Text Wraps

Shortcuts

Selection tool
Mac and Win: V

Direct Selection tool
Mac and Win: A

Text Wrap palette
Mac: Opt+Cmd+W
Win: Alt+Ctrl+W

Tip

InDesign also allows you to apply alpha channels embedded in a placed Photoshop image (.PSD). You can select and apply an alpha channel in the Import Options or Clipping Path dialog.

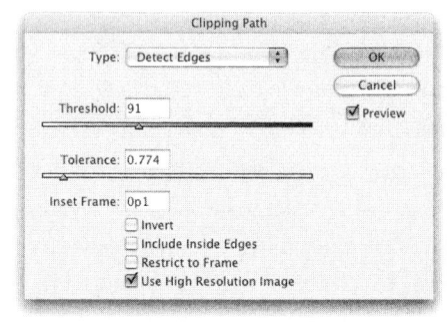

Dropping the sky area of the image by applying an InDesign clipping path

To allow the clipping path to recognize any areas inside of an image as defined by the Threshold and Tolerance settings, enable the Include Inside Edges feature. You can also invert an InDesign path by clicking the Invert check box.

Enabling the Restrict To Frame option limits the clipping path to include only the image areas within the graphic frame and not the areas cropped outside. With this option on, adjusting the crop means re-creating the path. Therefore, in most cases it is best to leave this option off.

You can edit the path later using the same dialog. To do so, select the image and choose Object > Clipping Path. Using the dialog, you can adjust the settings or turn off the path by choosing None from the Type menu.

You can also adjust an InDesign clipping path by selecting the image with the Direct Selection tool and editing the points using the various drawing tools, including the Pen toolset, the Pencil toolset, the Scissors tool, and the Direct Selection tool.

Combining Graphics with Text

GRAPHIC IMAGES AND TEXT are two very different page elements that complement each other well in a layout, but in some instances the two merge to become one.

In this chapter we show you the various ways of combining graphics with text in InDesign CS2, including wrapping text, creating type on a path, inserting paragraph rules, and building tables.

- 13.1 Placing and Editing Text Wraps
- 13.2 Converting Text to Outlines
- 13.3 Creating and Editing Type on a Path
- 13.4 Creating Paragraph Rules
- 13.5 Creating a New Table
- 13.6 Making Table Selections
- 13.7 Adding and Deleting Rows and Columns
- 13.8 Merging and Splitting Cells
- 13.9 Adjusting Cell Spacing and Alignment
- 13.10 Resizing Tables
- 13.11 Setting Table Borders, Strokes, and Fills
- 13.12 Creating and Editing Table Headers and Footers
- 13.13 Importing Tables from Microsoft Word or Excel

13.1 Placing and Editing Text Wraps

Related Tasks

3.4 Direct Selection and Position Tools
3.9 Frame Tools
3.10 Shape Tools

Shortcuts

Text Wrap palette
Mac: Opt+Cmd+W
Win: Alt+Ctrl+W

Text frame options
Mac: Cmd+B
Win: Ctrl+B

Tip

As you move a text wrap object, you can watch the surrounding text shift. To do this, select the object and hold for a second, then drag it to a new location on the page. As you drag, the surrounding text rewraps in real time.

You can insert an image into a body of text by applying a text wrap to any custom shape or graphic frame. To place a text wrap, select an object and click one of the buttons located at the top of the Text Wrap palette. Options include: No Text Wrap, Wrap Around Bounding Box, Wrap Around Object Shape, Jump Object, and Jump To Next Column.

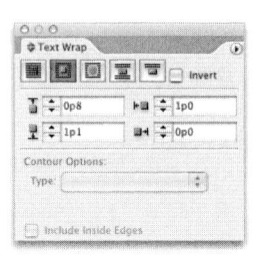

The Wrap Around Bounding Box option allows you to apply a text wrap to the top, bottom, left, and right sides of a frame.

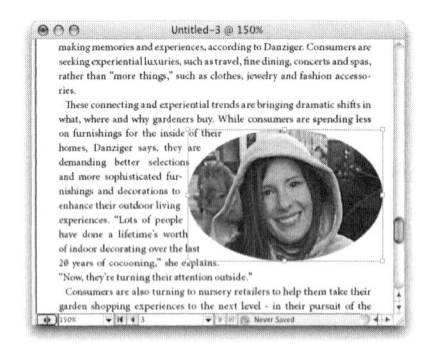

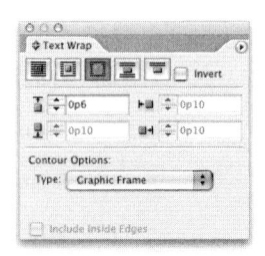

The Wrap Around Object Shape option applies one offset value around an entire object.

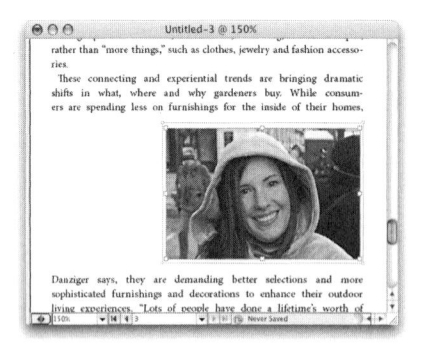

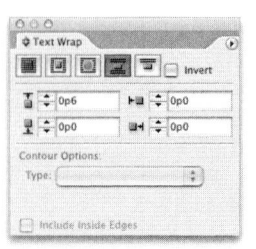

The Jump Object option applies a wrap that "jumps" text over an object, resulting in text above and below the offset, but not to the left or right.

13.1 Placing and Editing Text Wraps *(continued)*

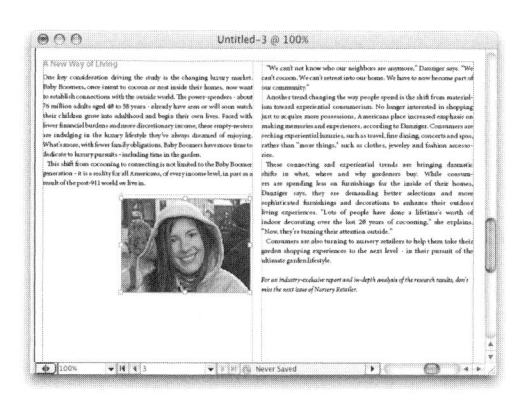

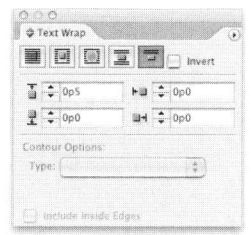

Related Tasks

4.12 Object Styles Palette

4.19 Text Wrap Palette

5.4 Composition Preferences

Shortcuts

Direct Selection tool
Mac and Win: A

Rectangle Frame tool
Mac and Win: F

Rectangle tool
Mac and Win: M

Tip

To permit a selected text frame not to be affected by surrounding text wraps, access the Text Frame Options dialog and enable the Ignore Text Wrap option.

Jump To Next Column applies a wrap that "jumps" text to the next column, stopping the text at the top of the offset.

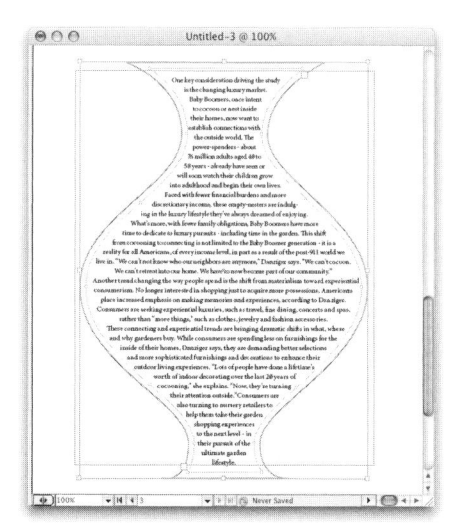

To create an "inside-out" wrap, place a check in the Invert check box. This feature works well with the Wrap Around Object Shape option.

For objects set to Wrap Around Bounding Box, Jump Object, or Jump To Next Column, you can enter an offset distance amount in any of the top, bottom, left, and right offset fields of the palette. For objects set to Wrap Around Object Shape, you must enter a single offset distance amount in the Top Offset field.

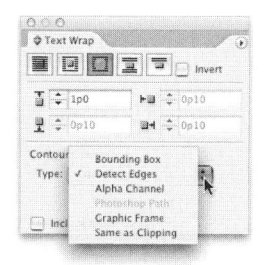

When applying the Wrap Around Object Shape option to a frame containing a placed image, InDesign activates the Contour Options portion of the palette. To access these options, choose Show Options from the palette menu.

13.1 Placing and Editing Text Wraps *(continued)*

Related Tasks

7.5 Drawing Rectangles, Ellipses, and Polygons

7.6 Drawing Custom Shapes

7.7 Drawing Freeform Shapes

Shortcuts

Direct Selection tool
Mac and Win: A

Rectangle Frame tool
Mac and Win: F

Rectangle tool
Mac and Win: M

Tip

As you move a text wrap object, you can watch the surrounding text shift. To do this, select the object and hold for a second, then drag it to a new location on the page. As you drag, the surrounding text rewraps in real time.

The Type menu lets you choose a contour type (such as a clipping path) to base the text wrap on. Options include Bounding Box, Detect Edges, Alpha Channel, Photoshop Path, Graphic Frame, and Same As Clipping.

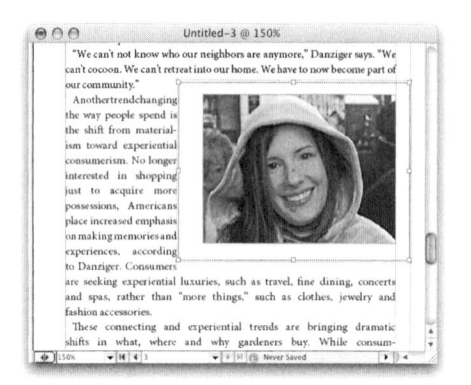

The Bounding Box option applies a text wrap to the outer edge of the placed graphic (this includes all areas cropped by a graphic frame).

The Detect Edges option applies a text wrap based on edges calculated by existing white areas in a placed graphic. Check the Include Inside Edges box to allow areas inside the clipping path to appear transparent.

The Alpha Channel or Photoshop Path option applies a text wrap to the contour of an embedded Photoshop path or alpha channel. If the placed image contains more than one Photoshop path or alpha channel, select which one you'd like to apply the clipping path to from the Path menu.

The Graphic Frame option applies one offset value to all sides of the frame container.

13.1 Placing and Editing Text Wraps *(continued)*

The Same As Clipping option allows you to apply a text wrap based on a clipping path that is created in InDesign.

You can edit a text wrap by selecting and repositioning points on the boundary path with the Direct Selection tool. You can also add, delete, or convert points using the various Pen tools. You *cannot* add points using the Pencil tool, erase points using the Erase tool, smooth points using the Smooth tool, or cut points and line segments using the Scissors tool.

Related Tasks

10.8 Applying Keep Options

11.5 Creating and Applying Object Styles

12.11 Altering an Embedded Photoshop Path

12.12 Creating a Clipping Path in InDesign

Shortcuts

Text Wrap palette
Mac: Opt+Cmd+W
Win: Alt+Ctrl+W

Text frame options
Mac: Cmd+B
Win: Ctrl+B

Tips

As you move a text wrap object, you can watch the surrounding text shift. To do this, select the object and hold for a second, then drag it to a new location on the page. As you drag, the surrounding text rewraps in real time.

To permit a selected text frame not to be affected by surrounding text wraps, access the Text Frame Options dialog and enable the Ignore Text Wrap option.

301

13.2 Converting Text to Outlines

Related Tasks

2.6	Type Menu
3.3	Selection Tool
3.4	Direct Selection and Position Tools
3.6	Type Tools
7.2	Selection Tool vs. Direct Selection Tool
7.4	Selecting Type
7.8	Modifying Paths and Frames
8.6	Grouping and Ungrouping Objects
8.7	Selecting Objects within a Group

Shortcuts

Create outlines
Mac: Shift+Cmd+O
Win: Shift+Ctrl+O

Selection tool
Mac and Win: V

Direct Selection tool
Mac and Win: A

Type tool
Mac and Win: T

Group
Mac: Cmd+G
Win: Ctrl+G

Ungroup
Mac: Shift+Cmd+G
Win: Shift+Ctrl+G

Tip

You can nest text and graphic frames into a character outline frame.

InDesign allows you to convert text characters into editable paths. Once the text is converted, you can't edit it with the Type tool, but you can with the drawing tools.

To convert all of the text characters in a selected frame into editable paths, select the text frame with either selection tool and choose Type > Create Outlines. InDesign instantly converts all of the characters in the frame and groups them. Characters such as "P" and "A" are automatically converted into compound paths.

To convert individual selected characters in a text frame into editable paths, highlight them with the Type tool and choose Type > Create Outlines.

InDesign converts the selected characters into outlines and treats them as nested inline objects.

Just like with any other custom shape, you can edit a character outline by selecting and repositioning points on the path with the Direct Selection tool. You can also add, delete, or convert points using the various Pen tools; add points using the Pencil tool; erase points using the Erase tool; cut points and line segments using the Scissors tool; and smooth points using the Smooth tool. Outline characters can also be transformed using the Scale, Shear, Rotate, Free Transform, and selection tools.

13.3 Creating and Editing Type on a Path

InDesign's Type On A Path tool allows you to place editable type along the contour of any open or closed path. Like all other editable text, you can select type on a path with the Type tool, format it, apply styles to it, and even edit it with the Story Editor.

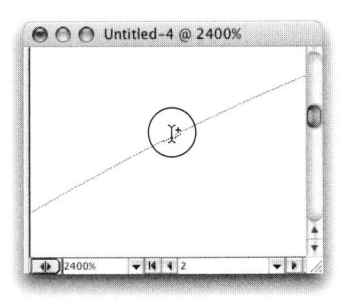

To create type on a path, press Shift+T to access the Type On A Path tool, and position the cursor over any open or closed path. When the cursor changes to display a plus sign, you can place it by clicking the path.

Clicking once positions the cursor using the default document paragraph alignment. To define the area of the path you'd like to add text to, click and drag with the tool.

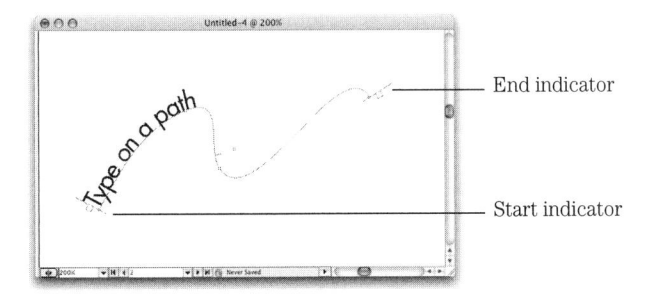

End indicator

Start indicator

As you type, the added text follows the contour of the path.

You can also add text to the path by pasting from the Clipboard, or importing with the Place command. InDesign also lets you thread type on a path object using the available in and out ports. Any text that does not fit is stored as overset text.

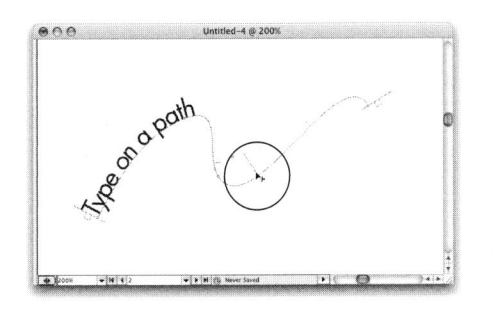

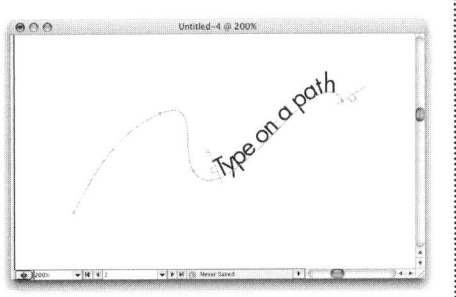

To change the position of type on a path, select the Start indicator or End indicator with the Selection tool, hold the mouse button down and drag it along the path. Release the mouse button to reposition the text.

Related Tasks

2.6	Type Menu
3.2	Control Bar
3.4	Direct Selection and Position Tools
3.5	Pen Tools
3.6	Type Tools
3.7	Pencil Tools
3.8	Line Tool

Shortcuts

Type On A Path tool
Mac and Win: Shift+T

Character palette
Mac: Cmd+T
Win: Ctrl+T

Character Styles palette
Mac and Win: Shift+F11

Tip

With the cursor inserted, you can access the Type On A Path Options dialog by double-clicking the tool's icon in the Toolbox.

13.3 Creating and Editing Type on a Path *(continued)*

Related Tasks

3.19 Scissors Tool

4.21 Type and Tables Palettes

7.6   Drawing Custom Shapes

7.7   Drawing Freeform Shapes

7.8   Modifying Paths and Frames

9.2   Threading and Unthreading Text Frames

9.6   Flowing Text

Shortcuts

Copy to Clipboard
Mac: Cmd+C
Win: Ctrl+C

Paste from Clipboard
Mac: Cmd+V
Win: Ctrl+V

Place
Mac: Cmd+D
Win: Ctrl+D

Direct Selection tool
Mac and Win: A

Pen tool
Mac and Win: P

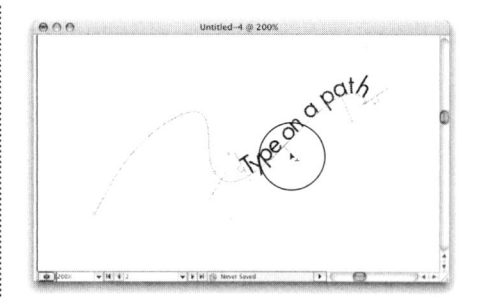

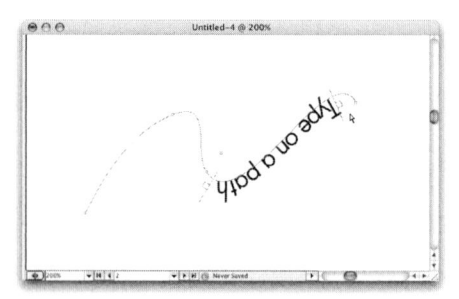

To flip the type, select the Flip indicator located in the center of the text, hold the mouse button down, and drag it to the other side of the path. Release the mouse button to flip the text.

Type On A Path Options

Access the Type On A Path Options dialog by selecting any path text object and choosing Type > Type On A Path > Options. The dialog allows you to apply specific type effects to selected type on a path. It also lets you change character alignment and spacing, flip the type, or delete it.

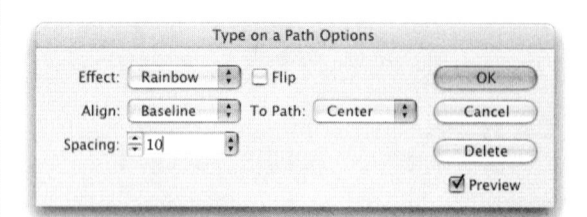

To apply a type effect to a selected path text object, simply choose one from the dialog's Effect menu. Options include Rainbow, Skew, 3D Ribbon, Stair Step, and Gravity. Check the Preview option to see the effect as it is applied.

Rainbow

Skew

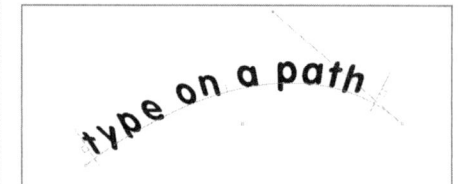

3D Ribbon

Stair Step

304

13.3 Creating and Editing Type on a Path *(continued)*

Gravity

The Align menu lets you choose a method for aligning the type to the path.

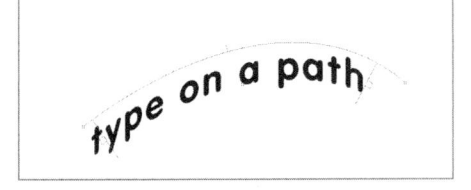

Ascender aligns the top of the capital letters to the path.

Descender aligns the bottoms of the characters to the path.

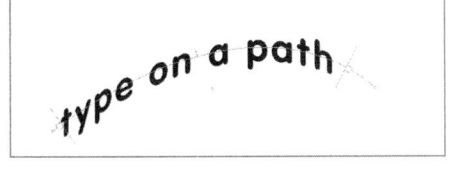

Center aligns the text to the path at the vertical center point of the capital letters.

Baseline aligns the baseline of the characters to the path.

Use the To Path menu to choose a method for aligning the type to the stroke of the path. Options include Top, Bottom, and Center.

Enter a point value in the Spacing field to control the amount of character spacing applied to the type around the curves of the path. You can also choose a value by clicking the up/down arrows to the left of the field, or by selecting a preset value from the menu. Note that the spacing value does not affect the character spacing of type placed on straight-line segments.

To flip the type, check the Flip option located in the center of the dialog.

Delete type on a path by clicking the Delete button in the dialog or by choosing Type > Type On A Path > Delete Type From Path. The delete option is only available in the dialog or from the menu when a path text object is selected with one of the selection tools (not one of the Type tools).

Related Tasks

9.8 Editing Using the Story Editor
9.9 Changing Case
10.1 Kerning and Tracking
10.2 Scaling and Skewing Type
10.3 Adjusting Leading and Baseline Shift
11.1 Creating and Applying Character Styles

Shortcuts

Add Anchor Point tool
Mac and Win: =

Delete Anchor Point tool
Mac and Win: -

Convert Direction Point tool
Mac and Win: Shift+C

Pencil tool
Mac and Win: N

Scissors tool
Mac and Win: C

Tip

With the cursor inserted, you can access the Type On A Path Options dialog by double-clicking the tool's icon in the Toolbox.

305

13.4 Creating Paragraph Rules

Related Tasks

3.2	Control Bar
3.6	Type Tools
4.21	Type and Tables Palettes
10.5	Copy/Paste Type Formatting
10.6	Formatting Paragraphs
11.2	Creating and Applying Paragraph Styles
11.6	Editing and Deleting Styles

Shortcuts

Paragraph Rules dialog
Mac: Opt+Cmd+J
Win: Alt+Ctrl+J

Type tool
Mac and Win: T

Eyedropper tool
Mac and Win: I

Paragraph palette
Mac: Opt+Cmd+T
Win: Alt+Ctrl+T

Paragraph Styles palette
Mac and Win: F11

Tips

You cannot apply paragraph rules to type on a path.

By experimenting with the Weight, Color, Offset, and Indent settings in the Paragraph Rules dialog, you can place a tinted box behind a paragraph. You can also create vertical paragraph rules or a paragraph-bounding box.

You can create and apply evenly spaced rules above and/or below selected paragraphs as part of their formatting, or as part of a paragraph style. To create a formatted paragraph rule, insert the Type tool cursor in a paragraph and choose Paragraph Rules from the Paragraph palette menu.

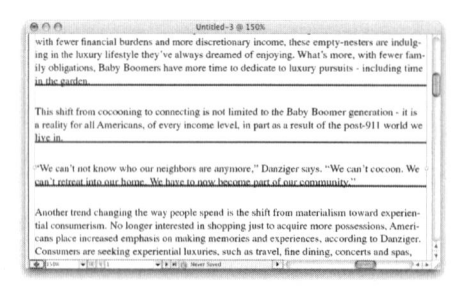

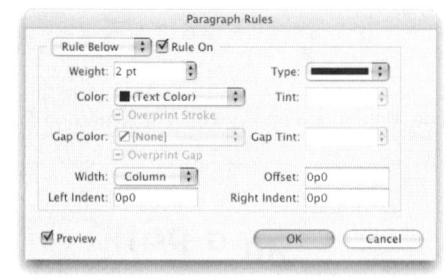

At the top of the Paragraph Rules dialog, select Rule Above or Rule Below from the menu and check the Rule On option. By default, InDesign places formatted rules behind the paragraph text.

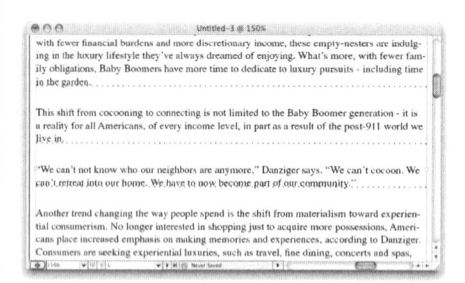

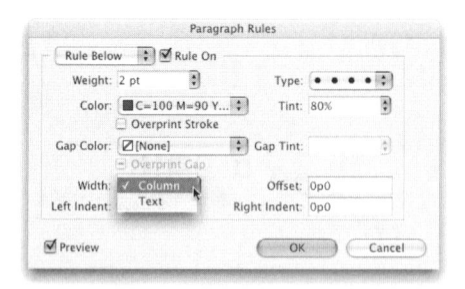

Proceed to choose Weight, Type, Color, Tint, Gap Color, and Gap Tint settings for the rule stroke. You can also choose to overprint any applied stroke colors or gap colors. Check the Preview option at the bottom left of the dialog to see the settings applied as you adjust them. Use the Width menu to apply the rule across the width of the column or across the first line of text in the paragraph.

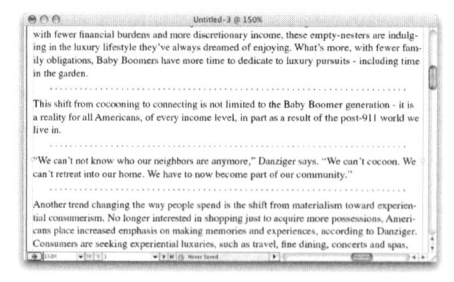

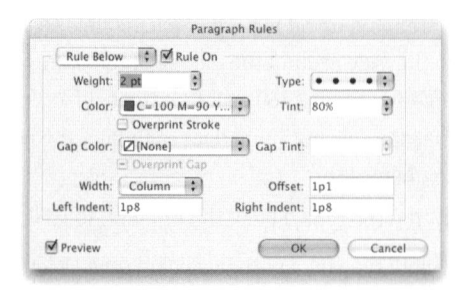

Enter a value in the Offset field to move the rule above or below the baseline. Enter higher values to move a Rule Above up or a Rule Below down. To apply a left/right indent to the rule, enter a value in the Left Indent and Right Indent fields.

306

13.5 Creating a New Table

In the past, building complicated tables has been an arduous task in any page layout program. Thankfully, InDesign CS2 now makes building tables easier than ever.

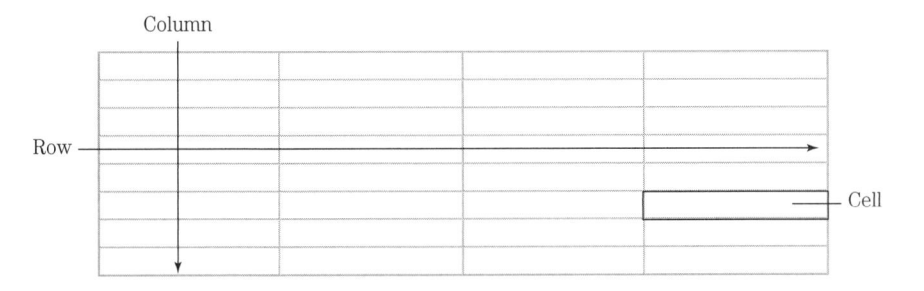

[Diagram showing a table grid with labels: Column, Row, Cell]

A table is nothing more than a grid made up of horizontal *rows* and vertical *columns*. Each area of grid intersection is called a *cell*. You can insert text or an inline graphic into a table cell.

Creating a Table "from Scratch"

A table in InDesign is treated like a very large inline character placed inside a text frame (not a graphic frame). This means that you must use the Type tool (not the Selection tools) to create a new table. Start out by inserting the Type tool into a text frame and choosing Table > Insert Table.

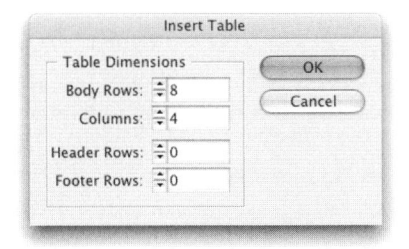

[Insert Table dialog box image]

When the Insert Table dialog appears, define the number of body rows, columns, header rows, and footer rows by entering values in the respective fields. You can also choose values by clicking the up/down arrows located next to each field.

Click OK for InDesign to insert the table into the frame. You can then place the Type tool cursor inside any cell and add text by typing. As you type, the table column expands vertically to fit the added text. Add text or inline graphics to a table cell by pasting from the Clipboard or importing with the Place command.

Any added text or inline graphics that do not fit into a table cell are stored as overset items. InDesign indicates overset text or graphics by displaying a red dot in the bottom-right corner of the cell.

Converting Text into Tables

You can convert text into tables by highlighting a range of text with the Type tool and choosing Table > Convert Text To Table.

Related Tasks

2.8	Table Menu
3.6	Type Tools
4.21	Type and Tables Palettes
7.19	Applying Corner Effects
7.21	Creating Custom Shapes with Pathfinder
8.13	Saving Objects to a Library

Shortcuts

Insert table
Mac: Opt+Shift+Cmd+T
Win: Alt+Shift+Ctrl+T

Table Options dialog
Mac: Opt+Shift+Cmd+B
Win: Alt+Shift+Ctrl+B

Table palette
Mac and Win: Shift+F9

13.5 Creating a New Table *(continued)*

Related Tasks

13.6 Making Table Selections

13.7 Adding and Deleting Rows and Columns

13.8 Merging and Splitting Cells

13.9 Adjusting Cell Spacing and Alignment

13.10 Resizing Tables

13.11 Setting Table Borders, Strokes, and Fills

13.12 Creating and Editing Table Headers and Footers

Shortcuts

Toggle between text selection and cell selection
Mac and Win: Esc

Type tool
Mac and Win: T

Tip

You can add text before and after a table in a story (a.k.a. a text frame).

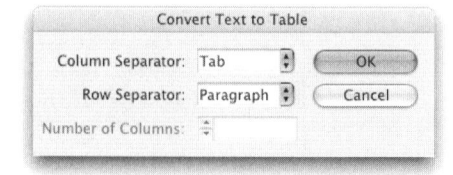

When the Convert Text To Table dialog appears, choose delimiter characters for table column and row separators from the respective menus. The Number Of Columns field only becomes active when the Paragraph option is chosen as the delimiter character for both column and row separators.

Click OK to convert the text into a table.

FIXING OVERSET TEXT AND GRAPHICS IN A TABLE CELL

Table cells automatically expand when adding text or graphics. However, when adding text or graphics to a cell containing a set fixed height amount, any items that exceed that height are automatically stored as overset. InDesign indicates when a cell contains overset items by displaying a red dot in the bottom right corner of the cell.

To display overset text and graphics in an overset cell, expand the cell or reduce the size of the text or graphics. You can also select the cell and adjust the fixed height amount, the inset spacing, or the first baseline offset.

It is also possible to thread text frames containing overset tables and repeat any existing header and footer rows.

13.6 Making Table Selections

InDesign allows you to select table rows, columns, cells, cell contents, or all of the above. To make a table selection, press T to access the Type tool and hover the cursor over the edge of any row, column, or cell. Notice the cursor icon change as you reposition it over different areas of the table. The different cursor icons indicate the type of selection you can make by clicking that area of the table.

ICON	APPEARS	ACTION
↘	When hovering over the top-left corner of the table	Click to select the entire table.
→	When hovering over the left edge of a row	Click to select the row.
↓	When hovering over the top of a column	Click to select the column.
↔	When hovering over the right or left edge of a cell	Drag to resize the column.
↕	When hovering over the top or bottom of a cell	Drag to resize the row.
↘	When hovering over the bottom-right corner of the table	Drag to resize the table.

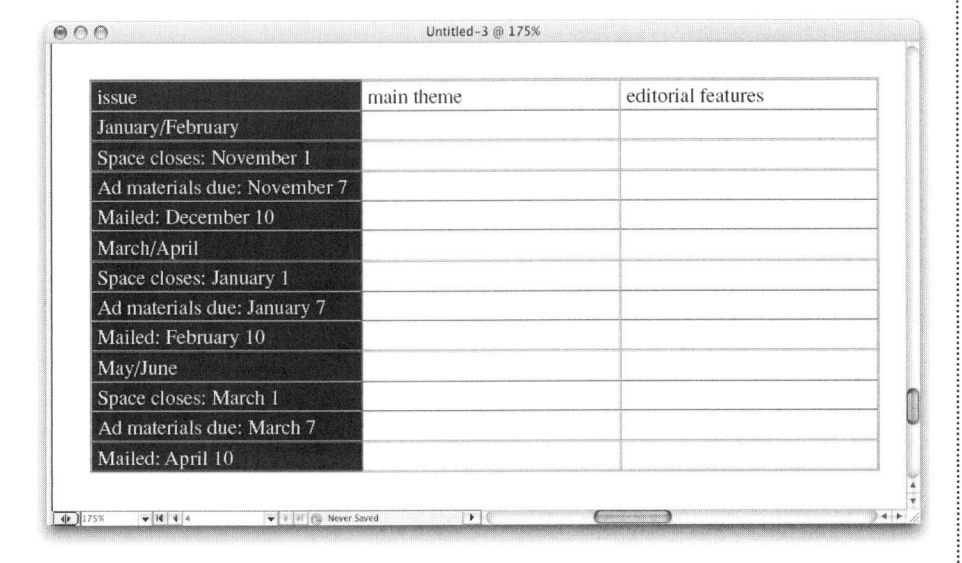

Select a cell and its contents (or a range of adjacent cells and their contents) by clicking and dragging with the Type tool.

You can also select any text or inline graphics placed in a table cell without selecting the cell itself. To select cell contents, use the same methods you would use to select text or inline graphics in a text frame.

Related Tasks

2.8 Table Menu
3.6 Type Tools
7.4 Selecting Type
13.7 Adding and Deleting Rows and Columns
13.8 Merging and Splitting Cells

Shortcuts

Select cell
Mac: Cmd+/
Win: Ctrl+/

Select row
Mac: Cmd+3
Win: Ctrl+3

Select column
Mac: Opt+Cmd+3
Win: Alt+Ctrl+3

Select table
Mac: Opt+Cmd+A
Win: Alt+Ctrl+A

Select cell above/below current cell
Mac and Win: Shift+Up/Down arrow

Select cell to the right or left of current cell
Mac and Win: Shift+Right/Left arrow

Toggle between text selection and cell selection
Mac and Win: Esc

Tip

To select a series of table rows or columns, hold down the Shift key and click the left edge of each row or the top of each column.

13.7 Adding and Deleting Rows and Columns

Related Tasks

2.8 Table Menu
3.6 Type Tools
4.21 Type and Tables Palettes
7.4 Selecting Type

Shortcuts

Insert table
Mac: Opt+Shift+Cmd+T
Win: Alt+Shift+Ctrl+T

Insert row
Mac: Cmd+9
Win: Ctrl+9

Insert column
Mac: Opt+Cmd+9
Win: Alt+Ctrl+9

Delete row
Mac: Cmd+Delete
Win: Ctrl+Backspace

Delete column
Mac: Shift+Delete
Win: Shift+Backspace

Table Options dialog
Mac: Opt+Shift+Cmd+B
Win: Alt+Shift+Ctrl+B

Once you create or import a table, you can edit it by adding and deleting rows and columns. InDesign offers several ways to do this.

Adding Rows and Columns

The four ways to add rows and columns to a table are as follows:

Insert commands: Select a cell with the Type tool and choose Insert > Row/Column from the context menu, the Table menu, or the Table palette menu.

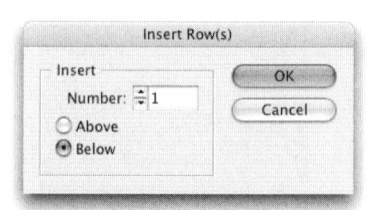

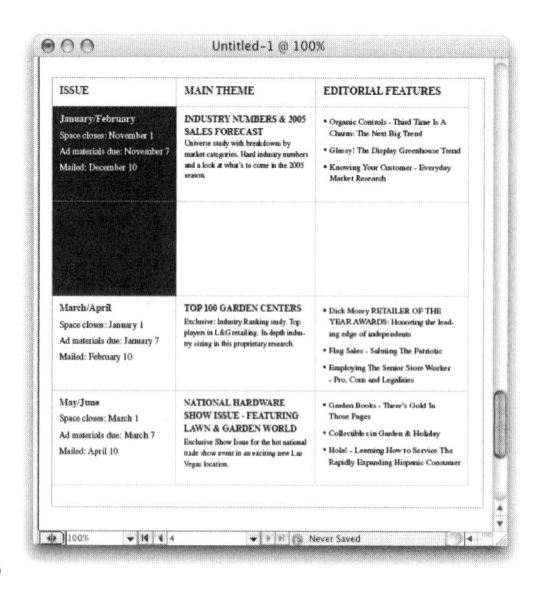

When the Insert Row/Column dialog appears, enter the number of rows or columns you would like to add in the Number field. At the bottom of the dialog, choose whether to place the new rows above or below (or the new columns to the left or right) of the selected cell. Click OK to add the rows or columns.

310

13.7 Adding and Deleting Rows and Columns *(continued)*

Table palette and Control bar: You can also add rows and columns using the controls located in the Table palette and Control bar. The Number Of Rows and Number Of Columns fields each displays the current number of rows and columns in the table. New rows are added at the bottom of the table, and new columns to the right.

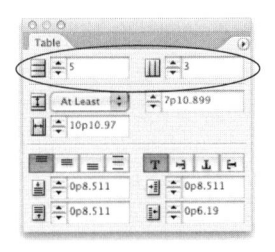

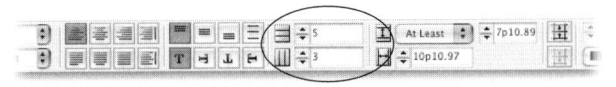

To add rows or columns, place the Type tool cursor in a cell and enter the total number of rows or columns you would like the table to contain in the Number field. You can also add rows and columns by clicking the up/down arrows next to the Number.

Option/Alt-dragging: Position the Type tool cursor over the top or bottom of a cell, click and hold the mouse button down, then Option/Alt-drag to create a new row or column.

Table Options dialog: Place the Type tool cursor in a cell and choose Table > Table Options > Table Setup. In the Table Setup panel of the dialog, enter the total number of rows and columns you would like the table to contain in the Body Rows and Columns fields. You can also add rows or columns by clicking the up/down arrows next to the number fields. Rows are added at the bottom of the table and columns to the right.

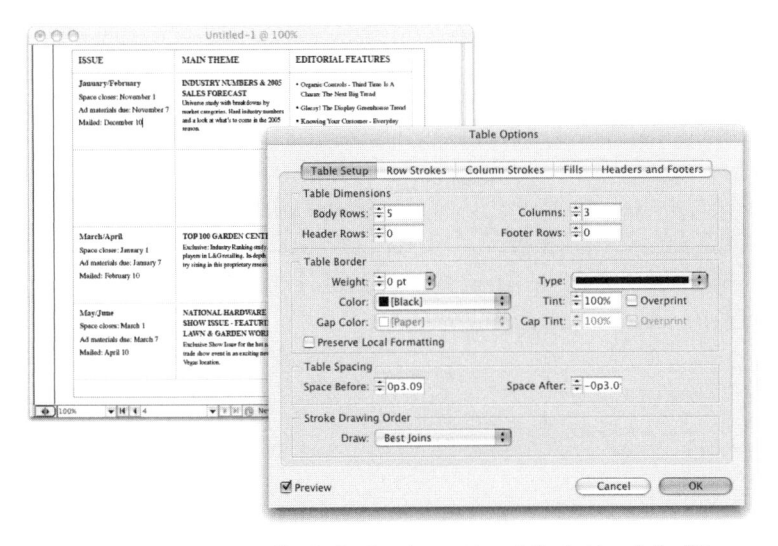

Check the Preview option at the bottom left of the dialog to see the settings applied as you adjust them. When you're ready, click OK to apply.

Related Tasks

13.6 Making Table Selections

13.8 Merging and Splitting Cells

13.9 Adjusting Cell Spacing and Alignment

13.10 Resizing Tables

Shortcuts

Table palette
Mac and Win: Shift+F9

Select cell
Mac: Cmd+/
Win: Ctrl+/

Select row
Mac: Cmd+3
Win: Ctrl+3

Select column
Mac: Opt+Cmd+3
Win: Alt+Ctrl+3

Select table
Mac: Opt+Cmd+A
Win: Alt+Ctrl+A

Move to next/previous cell
Mac and Win: Tab/Shift+Tab

311

Related Tasks

13.11 Setting Table Borders, Strokes, and Fills

13.12 Creating and Editing Table Headers and Footers

13.13 Importing Tables from Microsoft Word or Excel

Shortcuts

Move to first/last cell in column
Mac: Opt+Page Up/Page Down
Win: Alt+Page Up/Page Down

Move to first/last cell in row
Mac: Opt+Home/End
Win: Alt+Home/End

Move to first/last row in frame
Mac and Win: Page Up/Page Down

Select cell above/below current cell
Mac and Win: Shift+Up/Down arrow

Select cell to the right or left of current cell
Mac and Win: Shift+Right/Left arrow

Toggle between text selection and cell selection
Mac and Win: Esc

Tip

You can add a single row to the bottom of a table by placing the Type tool cursor in the last cell of the existing bottom row and pressing the Tab key.

13.7 Adding and Deleting Rows and Columns *(continued)*

Deleting Rows and Columns

The three ways to delete rows and columns from a table are as follows:

Delete commands: Place the Type tool cursor in a cell and choose Delete > Row/Column from the context menu, the Table menu, or the Table palette menu. InDesign immediately deletes the row or column that the cursor is positioned in. You can also select multiple rows or columns and delete them using the Delete command.

Table palette and Control bar: You can also delete rows and columns using the controls located in the Table palette and Control bar. The Number Of Rows and Number Of Columns fields each displays the current number of rows and columns in the table. To delete rows or columns, place the Type tool cursor in a cell and enter the total number of rows or columns you would like the table to contain in the Number field. You can also delete rows and columns by clicking the up/down arrows next to the Number.

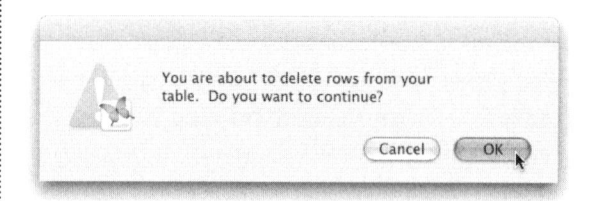

InDesign displays a warning dialog whenever new values are entered into the Number Of Rows and Number Of Columns fields. If you are sure you want to delete, click OK. Rows are deleted from the bottom of the table, and columns from the right, regardless of what you may have selected in the table.

Table Options dialog: Place the Type tool cursor in a cell and choose Table > Table Options > Table Setup. In the Table Setup panel of the dialog, enter the total number of rows and columns you would like the table to contain in the Body Rows and Columns fields. You can also delete rows or columns by clicking the up/down arrows next to the number field. Rows are deleted from the bottom of the table and columns from the right. Check the Preview option at the bottom left of the dialog to see the settings applied as you adjust them. When you're ready, click OK to apply.

13.8 Merging and Splitting Cells

When working with InDesign tables, adjusting the height of a cell also adjusts the height of a row. Likewise, adjusting the width of a cell also adjusts the width of a column. Despite this, it is possible to create cells that are wider or taller than the rows or columns they are positioned in by merging and splitting.

Merging and Unmerging Cells

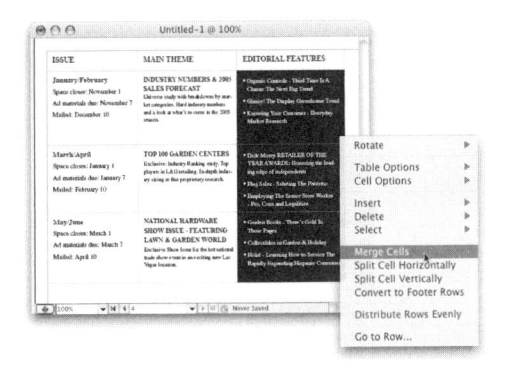

To merge two or more cells in a table, select the cells with the Type tool and choose Merge Cells from the Table menu, the Table palette menu, or the context menu.

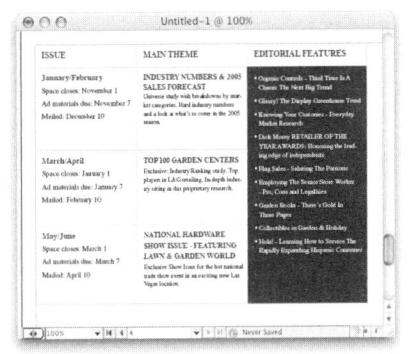

InDesign places any text or graphics contained in the selected cells into one merged cell.

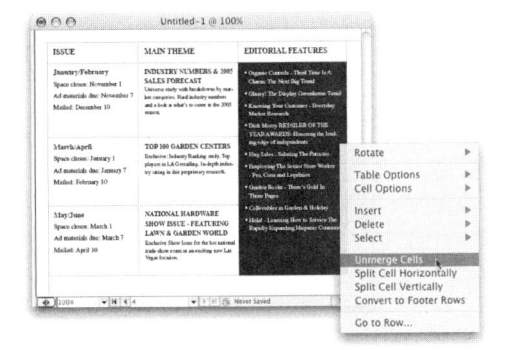

To restore a merged cell back to its original state, select the cell and choose Unmerge Cells from the Table menu, the Table palette menu, or the context menu.

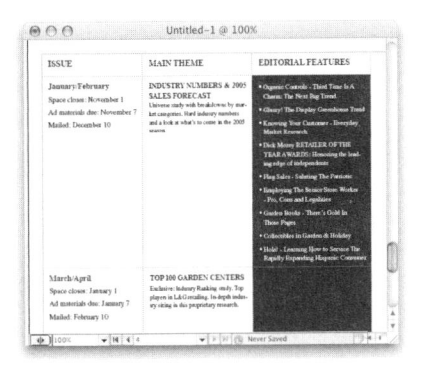

Note that unmerging places all merged cell contents into a single cell and does not restore contents to their original cells.

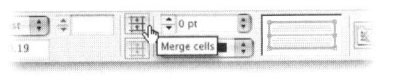

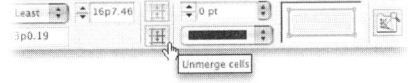

You can also merge and unmerge selected cells by clicking either the Merge Cells or Unmerge Cells button located in the Control bar.

Related Tasks

2.8 Table Menu
3.6 Type Tools
4.21 Type and Tables Palettes
7.4 Selecting Type
13.6 Making Table Selections
13.7 Adding and Deleting Rows and Columns

Shortcuts

Insert table
Mac: Opt+Shift+Cmd+T
Win: Alt+Shift+Ctrl+T

Table palette
Mac and Win: Shift+F9

Move to next/previous cell
Mac and Win: Tab/Shift+Tab

Move to first/last cell in column
Mac: Opt+Page Up/Page Down
Win: Alt+Page Up/Page Down

Move to first/last cell in row
Mac: Opt+Home/End
Win: Alt+Home/End

Move to first/last row in frame
Mac and Win: Page Up/Page Down

Select cell
Mac: Cmd+/
Win: Ctrl+/

Select row
Mac: Cmd+3
Win: Ctrl+3

313

13.8 Merging and Splitting Cells *(continued)*

Related Tasks

13.9 Adjusting Cell Spacing and Alignment

13.10 Resizing Tables

13.11 Setting Table Borders, Strokes, and Fills

13.12 Creating and Editing Table Headers and Footers

13.13 Importing Tables from Microsoft Word or Excel

Shortcuts

Select column
Mac: Opt+Cmd+3
Win: Alt+Ctrl+3

Select table
Mac: Opt+Cmd+A
Win: Alt+Ctrl+A

Select cell above/ below current cell
Mac and Win:
Shift+Up/Down arrow

Select cell to the right or left of current cell
Mac and Win:
Shift+Right/Left arrow

Toggle between text selection and cell selection
Mac and Win: Esc

Tip

The text rotation buttons in the Table palette and Control bar only allow you to rotate text in 90° increments. However, you can place text rotated at another angle by creating it outside of the table and nesting it into a table cell.

Splitting Cells

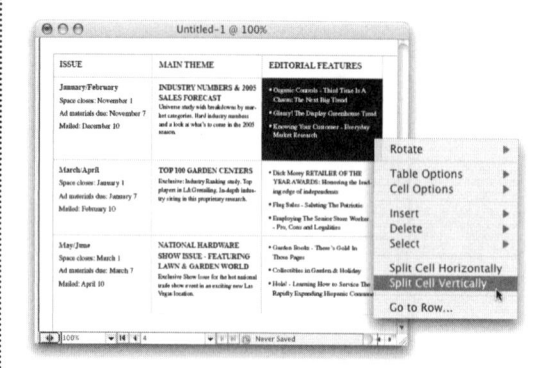

To divide a cell, select it with the Type tool and choose Split Cell Horizontally or Split Cell Vertically from the Table menu, the Table palette menu, or the context menu.

InDesign places any text or graphics contained in the cell into the left or top half.

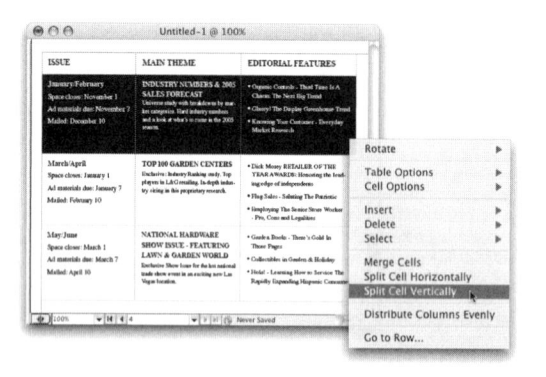

You can also select an entire row or column (or multiple rows/columns) and apply the Split Cell Horizontally or Split Cell Vertically command to all the cells in the selection.

InDesign places any text or graphics contained in the cell into the left or top half.

PLACING A GRAPHIC IN A TABLE CELL

InDesign allows you to place a graphic in a table cell using exactly the same method that you would to insert a graphic into a line of text. Because table cells behave like miniature text frames, placed graphics are treated as nested inline objects.

To place a graphic in a table cell, click an insertion point with the Type tool and import using the Place command or by copying and pasting.

13.9 Adjusting Cell Spacing and Alignment

Table cells behave like little text frames in that they allow you to insert text and inline graphics. Because of this, you can also apply some of the same text frame settings, including inset spacing amounts, vertical justification, and horizontal text alignment.

You can apply table cell settings using the Cell Options dialog in the same way you would apply text frame settings using the Text Frame Options dialog.

To access the dialog, insert the Type tool cursor in a table cell and choose Cell Options > Text from the Table Menu or the Table palette menu. The Cell Options dialog is only accessible through the context menu when a cell (or series of cells) is selected.

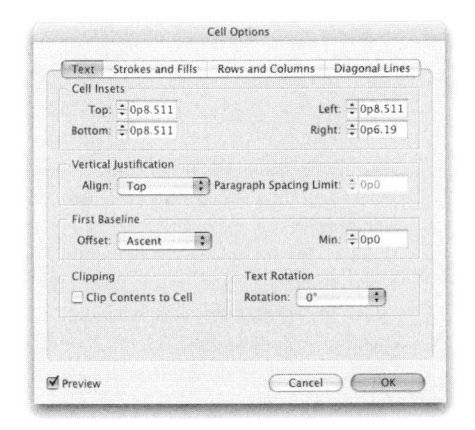

In the Text panel of the Cell Options dialog, enter top, bottom, left, and right cell inset spacing amounts in the respective fields. You can also enter inset spacing amounts by clicking the up/down arrows located next to each field.

To apply vertical justification to the selected cell(s), choose Top, Center, Bottom, or Justify from the Align menu. To apply a limit for paragraph spacing when applying justified vertical alignment, enter a value or click the up/down arrows in the Paragraph Spacing Limit field. This value sets the maximum amount of space allowed between paragraphs in the cell when justified. InDesign adjusts the leading of each line up to the amount entered. Enter higher values to prevent a change in leading.

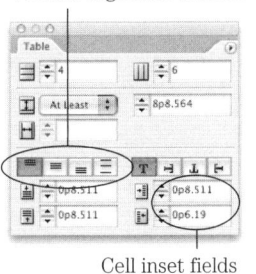

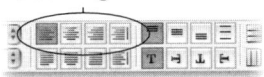

Vertical alignment buttons

Vertical alignment buttons

Cell inset fields

If you prefer palettes to dialogs, you can also enter inset spacing amounts for a selected cell (or series of cells) in the top, bottom, left, and right cell inset fields of the Table palette. You can also apply vertical justification settings by clicking one of the vertical alignment buttons located in the Table palette or Control bar. Options include Align Top, Align Bottom, Align Center, or Justify Vertically.

To adjust the horizontal alignment of text placed in a table cell, insert the Type tool cursor into a paragraph contained in a cell (or highlight multiple paragraphs) and click one of the alignment buttons located in the Paragraph palette or Control bar.

Related Tasks

2.8 Table Menu
4.21 Type and Tables Palettes
13.6 Making Table Selections

Shortcuts

Insert table
Mac: Opt+Shift+Cmd+T
Win: Alt+Shift+Ctrl+T

Cell Options dialog
Mac: Opt+Cmd+B
Win: Alt+Ctrl+B

Table palette
Mac and Win: Shift+F9

Select cell
Mac: Cmd+/
Win: Ctrl+/

Select row
Mac: Cmd+3
Win: Ctrl+3

Select column
Mac: Opt+Cmd+3
Win: Alt+Ctrl+3

Tip

To adjust a table's horizontal alignment in relation to its text frame container, insert the Type tool cursor before or after the table in the frame, and click one of the horizontal alignment buttons located in the Paragraph palette or Control bar.

Unfortunately, you cannot save any table formatting as part of a character, paragraph, or object style. Hopefully table styles will one day find their way into InDesign, but until then, try saving your tables into a library.

13.10 Resizing Tables

Related Tasks

2.8 Table Menu
3.3 Selection Tool
3.4 Direct Selection and Position Tools
3.6 Type Tools
3.12 Scale Tool
3.14 Free Transform Tool

Shortcuts

Insert table
Mac: Opt+Shift+Cmd+T
Win: Alt+Shift+Ctrl+T

Table Options dialog
Mac: Opt+Shift+Cmd+B
Win: Alt+Shift+Ctrl+B

Table palette
Mac and Win: Shift+F9

Select table
Mac: Opt+Cmd+A
Win: Alt+Ctrl+A

You can resize an entire table, or adjust column width and row height, interactively by clicking and dragging with the Type tool. You can also resize numerically by entering measurements in the Row Height and Column Width fields of the Rows and Columns panel of the Cell Options dialog, or in the Table palette/Control bar.

Resizing an Entire Table Interactively

To resize a table interactively, click the Type tool in any cell and then position the cursor over the bottom-right corner of the table.

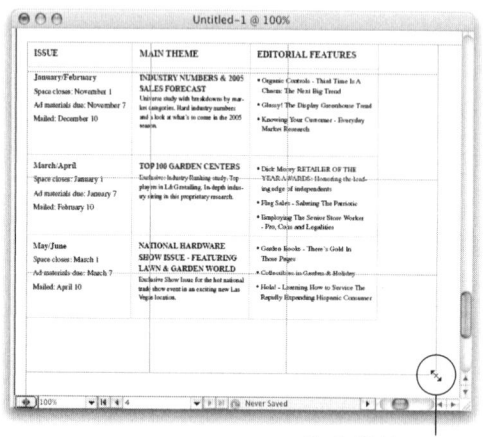

Scale Table cursor

When the cursor icon changes to display a diagonal, double-headed arrow, click and drag to scale. Hold down the Shift key as you drag to scale the table proportionately. When resizing a table using this method, InDesign does not scale any existing cell contents along with the table. To resize a table and its contents together, you must scale the text frame using one of the methods described in Section 8.2, "Resizing Objects."

Resizing Columns and Rows Interactively

To resize a column interactively, insert the Type tool anywhere in the table and then position the cursor over the right or left edge of a cell.

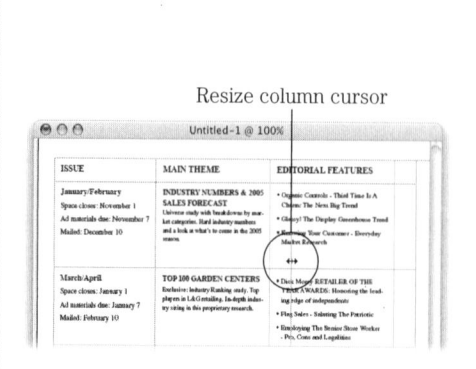

Resize column cursor

Resize Column cursor

Table edge

Text frame edge

When the cursor icon changes to display a horizontal, double-headed arrow, click and drag to change the column width.

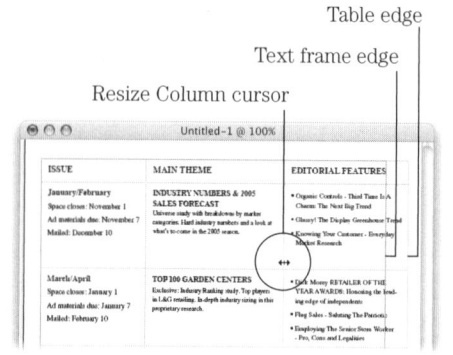

Note that columns can be expanded beyond the right edge of a text frame (except when the table is right justified within the text frame).

13.10 Resizing Tables *(continued)*

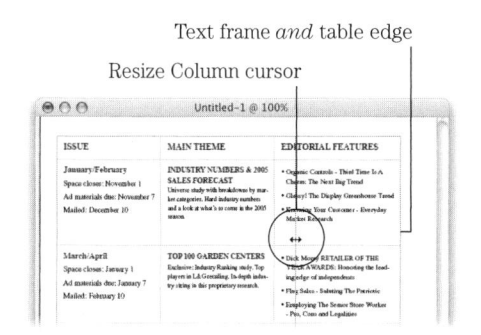

Resize Column cursor — Text frame *and* table edge

Resize Column cursor

To resize a column without expanding the table beyond the boundaries of the text frame, hold down the Shift key as you drag.

To change the width of all columns proportionately, hold down the Shift key as you drag the right edge of the table.

To resize a row interactively, insert the Type tool anywhere in the table and then position the cursor over the top or bottom of a cell.

Resize Row cursor

Resize Row cursor — Table edge / Text frame edge

When the cursor icon changes to display a vertical, double-headed arrow, click and drag to change the row height.

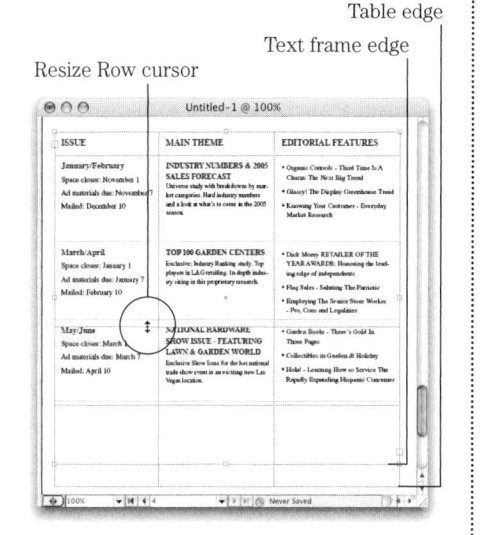

Note that rows can be expanded beyond the bottom edge of a text frame.

Related Tasks

- 7.4 Selecting Type
- 8.2 Resizing Objects
- 9.2 Threading and Unthreading Text Frames
- 9.6 Flowing Text
- 13.6 Making Table Selections

Shortcuts

Move to next/previous cell

Mac and Win: Tab/Shift+Tab

Move to first/last cell in column
Mac: Opt+Page Up/Page Down
Win: Alt+Page Up/Page Down

Move to first/last cell in row
Mac: Opt+Home/End
Win: Alt+Home/End

317

13.10 Resizing Tables (continued)

Related Tasks

13.7 Adding and Deleting Rows and Columns

13.8 Merging and Splitting Cells

13.9 Adjusting Cell Spacing and Alignment

13.12 Creating and Editing Table Headers and Footers

13.13 Importing Tables from Microsoft Word or Excel

Shortcuts

Move to first/last row in frame
Mac and Win: Page Up/Page Down

Select cell above/below current cell
Mac and Win: Shift+Up/Down arrow

Select cell to the right or left of current cell
Mac and Win: Shift+Right/Left arrow

Toggle between text selection and cell selection
Mac and Win: Esc

Tip:

You can evenly distribute the cell spacing of an entire table. With the type tool cursor inserted, press Opt+Cmd+A (Mac) or Alt+Ctrl+A (Windows) to select the table, then choose Distribute Rows/Columns Evenly from the Table menu, context menu, or Table palette menu.

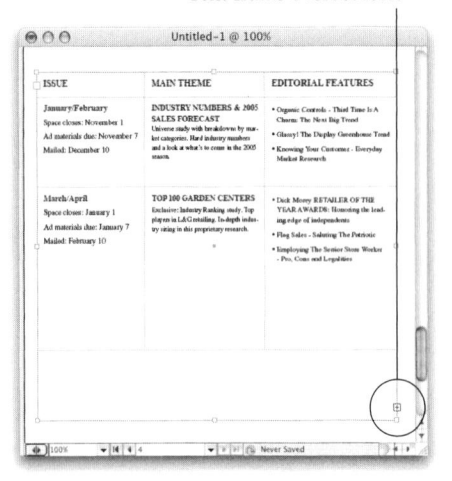

Any rows that are resized beyond the boundaries of the text frame are stored as overset items.

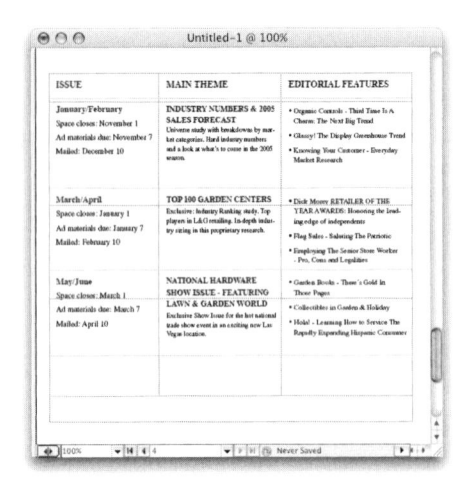

To change the height of all rows proportionately, hold down the Shift key as you drag the bottom edge of the table.

Resizing Columns and Rows Numerically

You can resize selected rows and columns numerically using the Cell Options dialog. To do so, choose Cell Options > Rows And Columns from the Table menu, the context menu, or the Table palette/Control bar menus.

Choose At Least or Exactly from the Row Height menu and enter a measurement value in the field. To apply a maximum row height, enter a value in the Maximum field. To resize selected column widths numerically, enter a measurement value in the Column Width field. You can also apply measurement values by clicking the up/down arrows located next to the Row Height and Column Width fields.

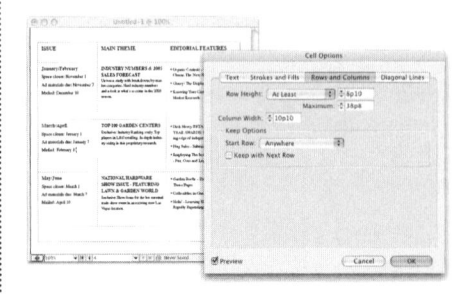

Check the Preview option at the bottom left of the dialog to see the settings applied as you adjust them. When you're ready, click OK to apply.

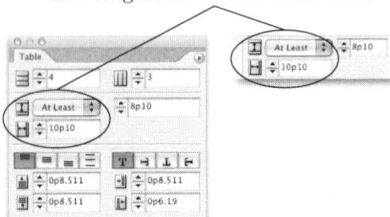

These settings can also be applied by entering measurement values in the Row Height and Column Width fields located in the Table palette and Control bar.

318

13.11 Setting Table Borders, Strokes, and Fills

InDesign allows you to apply stroke and fill attributes to an entire table *and* to its individual cells. Table cell strokes and fills are applied globally using the Table Options dialog and locally using the Cell Options dialog. The table border (i.e., the stroke that surrounds the *entire* table) can be set using the controls in the Table Options dialog or in the Control bar.

Setting the Table Border

To set the table border, choose Table Options > Table Setup from the Table menu, the Table palette menu, or the context menu.

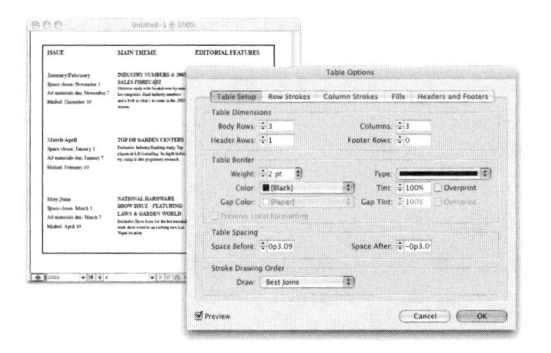

Choose a stroke Weight, Type, Color, and Tint. You can also choose a Gap Color and Tint value when applying an open stroke style. To overprint, enable the Overprint option.

If you have already applied a cell border locally to one or more cells positioned at the top, bottom, right, or left edges of the table using the Cell Options dialog or Control bar, applying a table border using the Table Options dialog overrides it. To maintain local cell formatting, enable the Preserve Local Formatting option.

To apply a table border locally using the Cell Options dialog, select the entire table with the Type tool and choose Cell Options > Strokes And Fills from the Table menu, the Table palette menu, or the context menu. In the center of the cell diagram at the top of the dialog, click the intersecting horizontal and vertical lines. By clicking these lines, you are telling InDesign to apply a stroke to the *surrounding edges* of the table, and *not* to the interior cell edges.

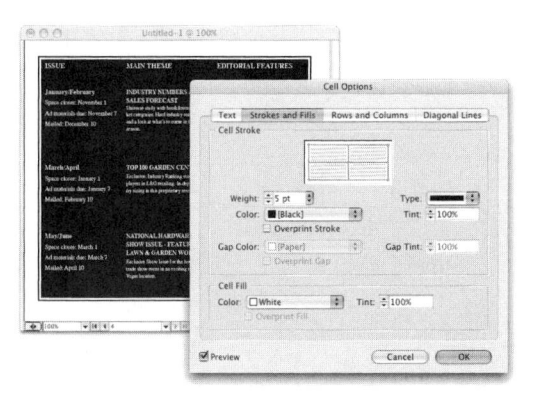

Choose a stroke Weight, Type, Color, and Tint setting. You can also choose a Gap Color and Tint value when applying an open stroke style. To overprint, enable the Overprint options.

Related Tasks

2.8 Table Menu
3.6 Type Tools
3.15 Eyedropper Tool
3.17 Gradient Tool

Shortcuts

Insert table
Mac: Opt+Shift+Cmd+T
Win: Alt+Shift+Ctrl+T

Table Options dialog
Mac: Opt+Shift+Cmd+B
Win: Alt+Shift+Ctrl+B

Cell Options dialog
Mac: Opt+Cmd+B
Win: Alt+Ctrl+B

Table palette
Mac and Win: Shift+F9

Select cell
Mac: Cmd+/
Win: Ctrl+/

Select row
Mac: Cmd+3
Win: Ctrl+3

13.11 Setting Table Borders, Strokes, and Fills *(continued)*

Related Tasks

4.5	Color Palette
4.6	Gradient Palette
4.17	Swatches Palette
4.21	Type and Tables Palettes
7.4	Selecting Type

Shortcuts

Select column
Mac: Opt+Cmd+3
Win: Alt+Ctrl+3

Select table
Mac: Opt+Cmd+A
Win: Alt+Ctrl+A

Move to next/previous cell

Mac and Win:
Tab/Shift+Tab

Move to first/last cell in column

Mac: Opt+Page Up/Page Down
Win: Alt+Page Up/Page Down

Move to first/last cell in row
Mac: Opt+Home/End
Win: Alt+Home/End

You can also apply a table border locally using the cell diagram and stroke type and weight controls located in the Control bar.

Setting Strokes and Fills with the Table Options Dialog

To set cell strokes and fills globally using the Table Options dialog, insert the Type tool cursor anywhere in the table and choose Table Options > Alternating Row Strokes, Alternating Column Strokes, or Alternating Fills from the Table menu, the Table palette menu, or the context menu. From the Alternating Pattern menu at the top of the dialog, choose to apply a stroke or fill to Every Other, Every Second, Every Third, or Custom Row/Column.

Proceed to choose a fill color and tint or a stroke weight, type, color, and tint for the first and next rows or columns. You can also choose a Gap Color and Tint value when applying an open stroke style. To overprint, enable the Overprint options.

You can also choose to skip rows or columns in the alternating stroke or fill pattern by entering a value in the Skip First or Skip Last field.

To maintain local cell formatting already applied using the Cell Options dialog or Control bar, enable the Preserve Local Formatting option.

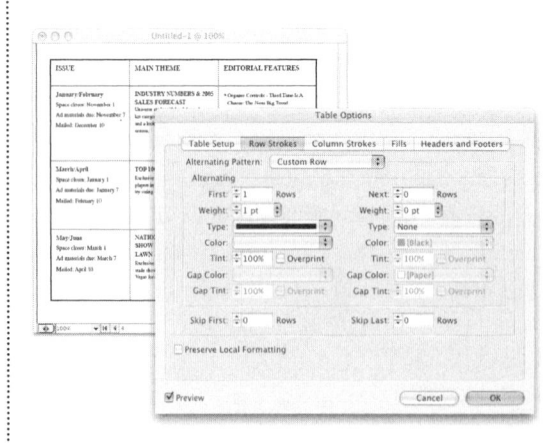

To apply a stroke or fill to *every* row or column in a table, choose Custom Row /Column from the Alternating Pattern menu and enter a value of one in the First field, and a value of 0 in the Next field.

13.11 Setting Table Borders, Strokes, and Fills *(continued)*

Setting Strokes and Fills with the Cell Options Dialog

To set cell strokes and fills locally using the Cell Options dialog, select the cells you would like to format and choose Cell Options > Strokes And Fills from the Table menu, the Table palette menu, or the context menu.

From the cell diagram at the top of the dialog, click to highlight the edges you would like to apply a stroke to. Proceed to choose a stroke weight, type, color, and tint. You can also choose a Gap Color and Tint value when applying an open stroke style. At the bottom of the dialog, choose a fill color and tint to apply to the selected cells. To overprint cell strokes and fills, enable the Overprint options.

Check the Preview option at the bottom left of the dialog to see the settings applied as you adjust them. When you're ready, click OK to apply.

To apply a stroke or fill to *every* row or column in a table, select the entire table and apply settings using the controls in the Strokes And Fills panel of the Cell Options dialog.

You can also apply strokes locally to selected cells using the cell diagram and stroke type and weight controls located in the Control bar.

PLACING DIAGONAL LINES IN TABLE CELLS

You can apply diagonal lines to a selected table cell (or series of cells) using the Diagonal Lines panel of the Cell Options dialog. Choose Cell Options > Diagonal Lines from the Table menu, the Table palette menu, or the context menu. Click one of the option buttons located at the top of the dialog and then choose stroke weight, type, color, and tint. To overprint, enable the Overprint options. From the Draw menu, choose Content In Front or Diagonal In Front.

Related Tasks

7.17 Saving and Applying Custom Strokes

7.18 Applying Gap Color to Open Stroke Styles

13.6 Making Table Selections

13.11 Setting Table Borders, Strokes, and Fills

Shortcuts

Move to first/last row in frame
Mac and Win: Page Up/Page Down

Select cell above/below current cell
Mac and Win: Shift+Up/Down arrow

Select cell to the right or left of current cell
Mac and Win: Shift+Right/Left arrow

Toggle between text selection and cell selection
Mac and Win: Esc

Tips

You can apply a sampled color to a selected table cell using the Eyedropper tool.

You can also set cell strokes and fills locally using the Stroke palette and Swatches palette—just as you would with any text frame.

You can apply a gradient fill to a selected table cell (or series of cells) using the Gradient tool.

13.12 Creating and Editing Table Headers and Footers

Related Tasks

2.8 Table Menu
3.6 Type Tools
4.21 Type and Tables Palettes
7.4 Selecting Type

Shortcuts

Insert table
Mac: Opt+Shift+Cmd+T
Win: Alt+Shift+Ctrl+T

Table Options dialog
Mac: Opt+Shift+Cmd+B
Win: Alt+Shift+Ctrl+B

Table palette
Mac and Win: Shift+F9

Move to next/previous cell

Mac and Win: Tab/Shift+Tab

Move to first/last cell in column
Mac: Opt+Page Up/Page Down
Win: Alt+Page Up/Page Down

InDesign gives you the option to create header and footer rows that repeat as a table flows across multiple text frames, text columns, or pages.

Adding Table Headers and Footers

You can include header and footer rows when creating a new table, or add them to an existing one. You can also convert selected table rows into repeating headers or footers.

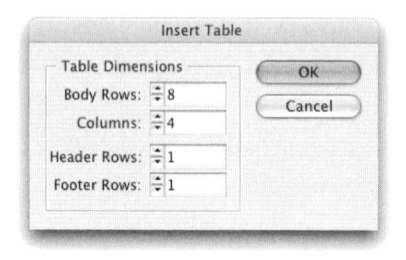

To include header or footer rows upon insert of a new table, define the number of rows you'd like to include by entering values in the respective fields of the Insert Table dialog.

You can add header or footer rows to an existing table using the Table Options dialog. To access the dialog, select a cell, row, column, or table with the Type tool and choose Table Options > Headers And Footers from the Table menu, the Table palette menu, or the context menu. In the Headers And Footers panel of the dialog, define the number of rows you'd like to include by entering values in the respective fields. You can also apply row numbers by clicking the up/down arrows located next to the Header Rows and Footer Rows fields.

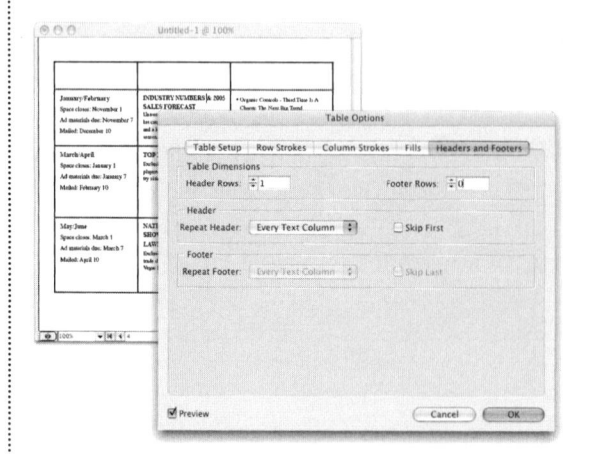

From the Repeat Header/Footer menus, choose to repeat the row on every text column, once per frame, or once per page. Enable the Skip First option to prevent the header from appearing in the first row of the table. Enable the Skip Last option to prevent the footer from appearing in the last row of the table. Check the Preview option at the bottom left of the dialog to see the settings applied as you adjust them. When you're ready, click OK to apply.

13.12 Creating and Editing Table Headers and Footers *(continued)*

Converting Existing Rows into Headers and Footers

To convert an existing row into a header, select the first row of the table with the Type tool and choose Convert Rows > To Header from the Table menu or the Table palette menu, or choose Convert To Header Rows from the context menu.

To convert an existing row into a footer, select the last row of the table with the Type tool and choose Convert Rows > To Footer from the Table menu or the Table palette menu. You can also choose Convert To Footer Rows from the context menu.

It is also possible to convert multiple rows into headers or footers. Select the first or last row, Shift+click to select additional rows, then choose the appropriate command.

Editing Table Headers and Footers

The first instance of a header or footer can be edited just like any other row, but it is important to note that any edits made affect all repeated instances of the header or footer throughout the table.

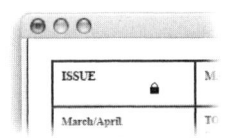

InDesign displays a lock icon when hovering the cursor over subsequent headers and footers.

Header and Footer options can be edited using the controls located in the Headers And Footers panel of the Table Options dialog.

To convert an existing header or footer into a body row, select the first instance of the header or footer with the Type tool (or choose Edit Header/Footer from the context menu) and choose Convert Rows > To Body from the Table menu or the Table palette menu.

SETTING TABS IN TABLE CELLS

When you press the Tab key with the Type tool cursor inserted in a table cell, it moves the cursor to the next cell. So does this mean that you can't enter a Tab character into a cell? Thankfully, no—you can enter a tab character by inserting the Type tool cursor and choosing Insert Special Character > Tab from the Type menu or the context menu, or if you're on the Mac platform, press Opt+Tab.

Related Tasks

13.6 Making Table Selections

13.9 Adjusting Cell Spacing and Alignment

13.10 Resizing Tables

13.13 Importing Tables from Microsoft Word or Excel

Shortcuts

Move to first/last cell in row
Mac: Opt+Home/End
Win: Alt+Home/End

Move to first/last row in frame
Mac and Win: Page Up/Page Down

Select cell above/below current cell
Mac and Win: Shift+Up/Down arrow

Select cell to the right or left of current cell
Mac and Win: Shift+Right/Left arrow

Toggle between text selection and cell selection
Mac and Win: Esc

Tip

Tables have their own Keep Option settings that allow you to control where a row breaks when threading tables across multiple text frames. You can apply these settings to a selected row in the Rows And Columns panel of the Cell Options dialog.

323

13.13 Importing Tables from Microsoft Word or Excel

Related Tasks

2.8   Table Menu
4.21 Type and Tables Palettes
9.3   Importing Text

Shortcuts

Table Options Dialog
Mac: Opt+Shift+Cmd+B
Win: Alt+Shift+Ctrl+B

Table palette
Mac and Win: Shift+F9

Move to next/previous cell
Mac and Win: Tab/Shift+Tab

Move to first/last cell in column
Mac: Opt+Page Up/Page Down
Win: Alt+Page Up/Page Down

Move to first/last cell in row
Mac: Opt+Home/End
Win: Alt+Home/End

Move to first/last row in frame
Mac and Win: Page Up/Page Down

Select cell above/below current cell
Mac and Win: Shift+Up/Down arrow

Select cell to the right or left of current cell
Mac and Win: Shift+Right/Left arrow

Toggle between text selection and cell selection
Mac and Win: Esc

When importing Microsoft Word or Excel documents containing tables, you have the option to convert them into unformatted InDesign tables, or into InDesign tables tagged with preserved Word or Excel styles and formatting.

Choose File > Place and browse to the Word or Excel document on your system. To access the Import Options dialog, check Show More Options or hold down the Shift key and click the Open button.

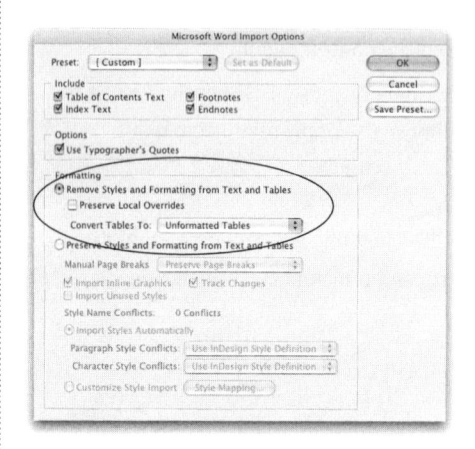

In the Formatting section of the Microsoft Word Import Options dialog, choose to either remove or preserve styles and formatting. When choosing to remove styles and formatting, select Unformatted Tables from the Convert Tables To menu.

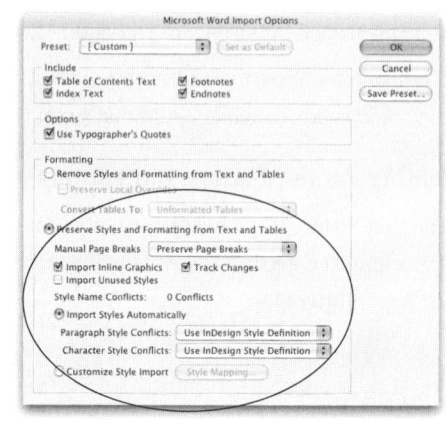

When choosing to preserve styles and formatting, there are several additional options for preserving formatting, including Manual Page Breaks, Inline Graphics, Unused Styles, and Track Changes. You can also choose to import styles automatically or by using a customized style import. The Customized Style Import option allows you to map InDesign styles to imported Word/RTF styles and vice versa.

You can also copy/paste tables from Word or Excel documents. By default, InDesign removes any styles and formatting when copying/pasting. However, if you'd like to preserve styles and formatting when copying/pasting, choose All Information under the When Pasting section of InDesign's Type Preferences.

CONVERTING TABLES TO TEXT

You can convert tables into text by inserting the Type tool cursor anywhere inside the table and choosing Table > Convert Table To Text. When the Convert Table To Text dialog appears, choose the delimiter characters you'd like to use and click OK.

CHAPTER **14**

Color and Transparency

WHEN IT COMES TO design, color truly is the great communicator. There is no better way to incite a reaction from an audience than through good use of color. Colors can inspire, stimulate, and influence all of us, which is why we rely on its effectiveness.

Not only does InDesign CS2 make working with color incredibly easy, but you can also add transparency effects. This chapter shows you how to use InDesign's enhanced color management features, as well as how to use the Ink Manager and other Swatches palette options. In addition, I explain how the different blend modes can help when you're working with transparent objects, and show you how to create cool drop shadows and feathered edges.

- 14.1 **Using Color Settings**
- 14.2 **Color-Managing Imported Graphics**
- 14.3 **Using Proof Setup for Soft Proofing**
- 14.4 **Creating and Saving Mixed-Ink Swatches and Groups**
- 14.5 **Accessing Colors Stored in Libraries**
- 14.6 **Converting Spot Colors to Process**
- 14.7 **Importing Colors from Other Documents**
- 14.8 **Changing an Object's Opacity Level**
- 14.9 **Applying Blend Modes**
- 14.10 **Adding Drop Shadows**
- 14.11 **Feathering**
- 14.12 **Importing Transparent TIFFs**

14.1 Using Color Settings

Related Tasks

- 5.13 Appearance of Black Preferences
- 12.1 Importing a Graphic Image
- 12.2 Setting Import Options
- 14.2 Color-Managing Imported Graphics
- 14.3 Using Proof Setup for Soft Proofing
- 15.4 Preflighting Colors and Inks
- 16.1 Printing a Document
- 16.2 Creating Transparency Flattener Presets
- 17.1 Exporting as Adobe PDF

Shortcuts

Launch Adobe Bridge (Browse)
Mac: Opt+Cmd+O
Win: Alt+Ctrl+O

Separations Preview
Mac and Win: Shift+F6

Overprint Preview
Mac: Opt+Shift+Cmd+Y
Win: Alt+Shift+Ctrl+Y

Tip

You can load and apply color settings created in Photoshop and Illustrator into InDesign.

Often when designing, colors can appear one way on your monitor but appear drastically different when printed. Thankfully, InDesign CS2 contains enhanced color management features that can make screen colors come as close as possible to what you'll see in the final printed piece. These color settings can also be synchronized with the other applications in the Creative Suite 2 (such as Photoshop and Illustrator) through the Adobe Bridge application when Version Cue is installed.

The InDesign and CS2 color settings are enabled by default. You can enable or disable color management from the Color Settings dialog (Edit > Color Settings).

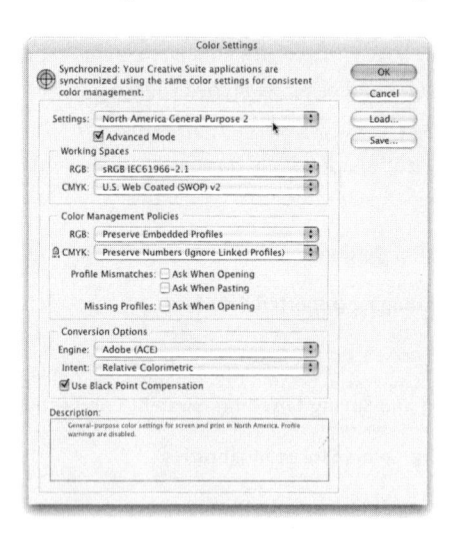

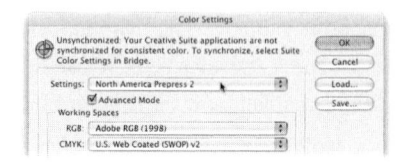

To unsynchronize, choose a different setting from the Settings menu. For more information on a chosen color setting, hover the cursor over the Settings menu and refer to the bottom of the dialog for a brief description. To resynchronize, choose the same setting applied in the Adobe Bridge application Suite Color Settings dialog. A brief description is listed under each setting name.

At the top of the dialog, InDesign displays whether the current color settings are synchronized with the other applications in CS2.

The setting you choose applies specific working space profiles and color management policies for both RGB and CMYK color spaces. It also applies specific conversion options, which you can view in the dialog by clicking the Advanced Mode checkbox. For more on a working space profile, color management policy, or conversion option (color engine and rendering intent), hover the cursor over the respective menu and see the bottom of the dialog for a brief description.

If you prefer, choose your own custom working space profiles, color management policies, and conversion options and save them as a custom setting. Click Save and enter a name for the setting in the Save Color Settings dialog. Click Save again to add the custom setting to the menu.

To profile mismatch or missing profile warning dialogs when opening documents, disable both Ask When Opening options. To disable color management policies, choose Off from the RGB and CMYK menus.

14.2 Color-Managing Imported Graphics

InDesign allows you to color-manage individual graphics at the time of import or after they've already been placed.

To color-manage a graphic upon import, choose File > Place and browse to the file's location on your system using the Place dialog. Before you click the Open button, turn on Show Import Options.

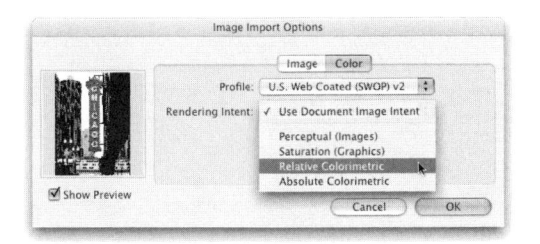

In the Color panel of the Image Import Options dialog you can tell InDesign how you would like to color-manage the image. Select and apply a color profile and rendering intent from the respective menus. To apply document color settings to the image, choose Use Document Default and Use Document Image Intent from the menus.

To color-manage a graphic that has already been placed in a layout, select it with either selection tool and choose Object > Image Color Settings. You can't apply Image Color Settings to placed EPS and PDF files, but you can with placed TIFFs and PSDs.

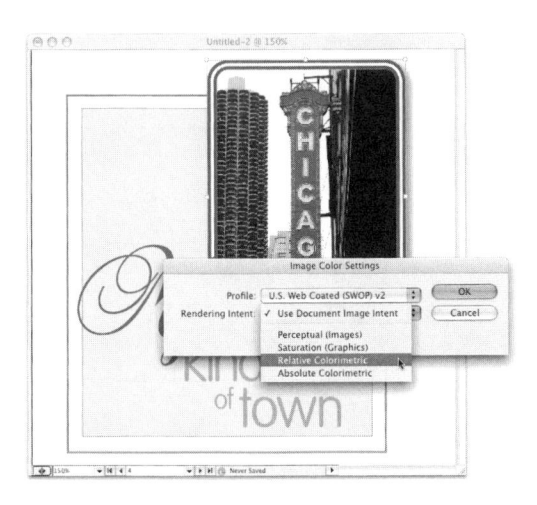

Select and apply a color profile and rendering intent from the respective menus. To apply document color settings to the image, choose Use Document Default and Use Document Image Intent from the menus.

Related Tasks

2.3	File Menu
2.7	Object Menu
3.3	Selection Tool
3.4	Direct Selection and Position Tools
4.13	Output Palettes
12.1	Importing a Graphic Image
12.2	Setting Import Options
14.1	Using Color Settings
14.3	Using Proof Setup for Soft Proofing
15.3	Preflighting Colors and Inks
16.1	Printing a Document

Shortcuts

Place
Mac: Cmd+D
Win: Ctrl+D

Links palette
Mac: Shift+Cmd+D
Win: Shift+Ctrl+D

Separations Preview
Mac and Win: Shift+F6

Overprint Preview
Mac: Opt+Shift+Cmd+Y
Win: Alt+Shift+Ctrl+Y

Tip

You can also access object-level color management options by selecting a placed image and choosing Graphics > Image Color Settings from the context menu (Mac: Control-click; Windows: right-click).

14.3 Using Proof Setup for Soft Proofing

Related Tasks

2.9	View Menu
4.13	Output Palettes
5.13	Appearance of Black Preferences
12.1	Importing a Graphic Image
12.2	Setting Import Options
14.1	Using Color Settings
14.2	Color-Managing Imported Graphics
15.3	Preflighting Colors and Inks
16.1	Printing a Document

Shortcuts

Launch Adobe Bridge (Browse)
Mac: Opt+Cmd+O
Win: Alt+Ctrl+O

Place
Mac: Cmd+D
Win: Ctrl+D

Links palette
Mac: Shift+Cmd+D
Win: Shift+Ctrl+D

Separations Preview
Mac and Win: Shift+F6

Overprint Preview
Mac: Opt+Shift+Cmd+Y
Win: Alt+Shift+Ctrl+Y

Tip

To achieve the best possible results when soft-proofing, choose Display Performance > High Quality Display from the View menu.

InDesign's proof setup feature lets you preview how a document is going to print as you design on screen (a process called *soft proofing*). Under the View **>** Proof Setup submenu, choose one of three options:

Custom Choosing this option opens the Customize Proof Condition dialog. Select a device profile to proof with from the Device To Simulate menu. InDesign simulates on screen how the document's color settings should appear based on the profile of the medium selected. Under Display Options (On-Screen), enable the Simulate Paper Color and Simulate Black Ink options to preview a selected profile's dynamic range. If Simulate Paper Color is selected, Simulate Black Ink is automatically selected then grayed out. For more information on the Display Options or a chosen device profile, hover the cursor over a heading and refer to the bottom of the dialog for a brief description.

Document CMYK Choosing this option tells InDesign to use the *document* CMYK profile to soft-proof with. By default InDesign uses the assigned Working Space profile set in Color Settings as the document CMYK profile. However, you can assign a different document CMYK profile using the Assign Profiles dialog, accessible under the Edit menu.

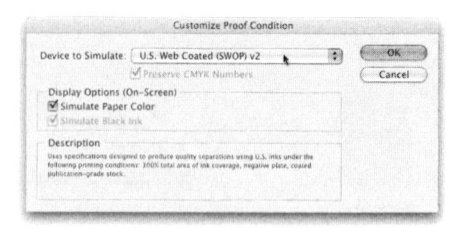

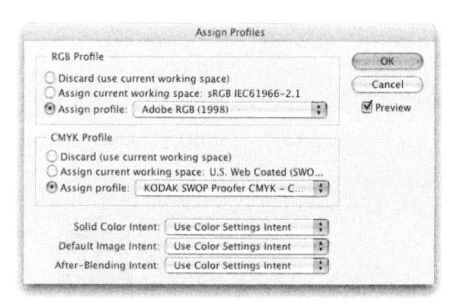

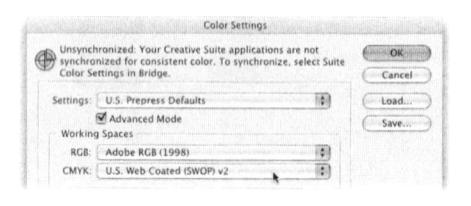

Working CMYK Choosing this option tells InDesign to use the Working Space profile set in the Color Settings dialog to soft-proof with.

Once you've picked a proof setup, you can toggle a soft proof of the document on or off by choosing View **>** Proof Colors.

You can change a document's color definitions permanently using the Convert To Profile dialog, accessible under the Edit menu. The current document space is always listed at the top of the dialog. Choose the RGB and CMYK profiles you'd like to convert to from the menus in the Destination Space portion below. Note that converting to the wrong profile can mess up the colors in your document, so be careful!

14.4 Creating and Saving Mixed-Ink Swatches and Groups

InDesign allows you to create a single "mixed-ink" swatch by combining varying percentages of two different spot colors. You can use these colors to jazz up those boring old two- and three-color designs.

Creating a Mixed-Ink Swatch

To create a mixed-ink swatch, choose New Mixed Ink Swatch from the Swatches palette menu. You must have at least one spot color saved in the Swatches palette to access the New Mixed Ink Swatch dialog.

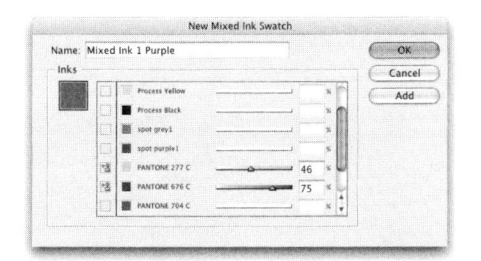

In the dialog, choose a color to add to the mixed-ink swatch by clicking the box to the left of its name. You can then indicate what ink percentage to use by dragging the slider left or right or entering a value in the percentage field. As you add colors, refer to the preview swatch in the upper left of the dialog.

When you create a mixed-ink swatch that you like, enter a name for it and click OK to save it in the Swatches palette and close the dialog. To save it in the Swatches palette without closing the dialog, click the Add button. You can then continue creating mixed-ink swatches and adding them to the palette.

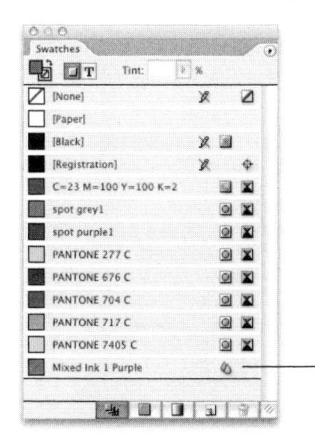

InDesign places a special mixed-ink icon next to the swatch name in the palette.

When printing, InDesign places each color in the mixed-ink swatch on its own separate plate. However, to prevent moiré patterns or dot-doubling from occurring, print each color at the correct halftone angle.

Related Tasks

3.1 Toolbox
3.22 Other Toolbox Functions
4.5 Color Palette
4.13 Output Palettes
4.17 Swatches Palette
7.10 Filling with Solid and Transparent Colors

Shortcuts

Swatches palette
Mac and Win: F5

Color palette
Mac and Win: F6

Create new swatch based on selected swatch in palette
Mac: Opt-click New Swatch button
Win: Alt-click New Swatch button

Tip

To get an idea of how well colors will mix on press, always consult your printer first before using mixed-ink colors.

14.4 Creating and Saving Mixed-Ink Swatches and Groups (continued)

Related Tasks

7.13 Stroking Frames, Shapes, and Paths

14.5 Accessing Colors Stored in Libraries

14.7 Importing Colors from Other Documents

15.3 Preflighting Colors and Inks

16.1 Printing a Document

Shortcuts

Create spot color swatch based on selected swatch in palette
Mac: Opt+Cmd-click New Swatch button
Win: Alt+Ctrl-click New Swatch button

Change swatch options without applying swatch
Mac: Shift+Opt+Cmd-double-click swatch
Win: Shift+Alt+Ctrl-double-click swatch

Tip

You can delete all the swatches in a mixed-ink group from the Swatches palette at once by deleting the mixed-ink group swatch.

Creating a Mixed-Ink Group

To create a mixed-ink group, choose New Mixed Ink Group from the Swatches palette menu. You must have at least one spot color saved in the Swatches palette to access the New Mixed Ink Group dialog.

For each color in the group, enter an Initial tint percentage, Repeat amount, and Increment percentage in the respective fields. You can also use the drop-down sliders to apply percentage amounts.

The Initial tint value tells InDesign what percentage of ink you'd like to start out with for each color in the group. The Repeat value indicates how many swatches InDesign should create. The Increment value tells InDesign how much ink to add with each repeat.

When you're ready, click the Preview Swatches button to display a list of mixed-ink swatches that InDesign can generate using these settings. To save the mixed-ink group, enter a name for it and click OK to add all the swatches in the group to the Swatches palette.

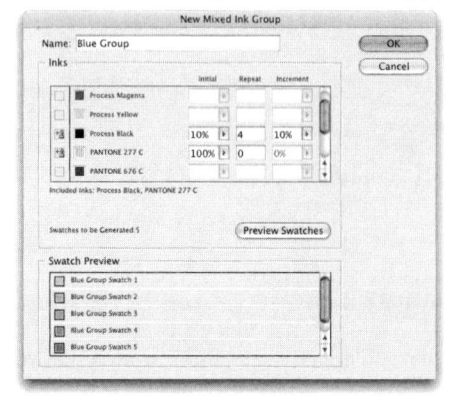

In the dialog, choose which colors to add to the mixed-ink group by clicking the boxes to the left. You must include at least two colors in a mixed-ink group and at least one spot color. It's also possible to include process colors in a mixed-ink group (Cyan, Magenta, Yellow, and Black).

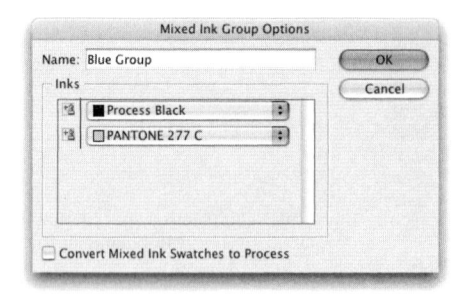

InDesign also adds a group swatch to the Swatches palette. Double-click the group swatch to access the options dialog and rename the group, delete or apply different colors to the mixed-ink group, or convert all the mixed-ink swatches to process.

330

14.5 Accessing Colors Stored in Libraries

You can access colors stored in swatch libraries (such as Pantone colors) through the Color Mode menu of the New Color Swatch dialog. To access the dialog, choose New Color Swatch from the palette menu.

To save a library color in the Swatches palette and close the dialog, select it from the list and click OK. To save the color in the Swatches palette without closing the dialog, click the Add button. You can then continue selecting library swatches and adding them to the palette.

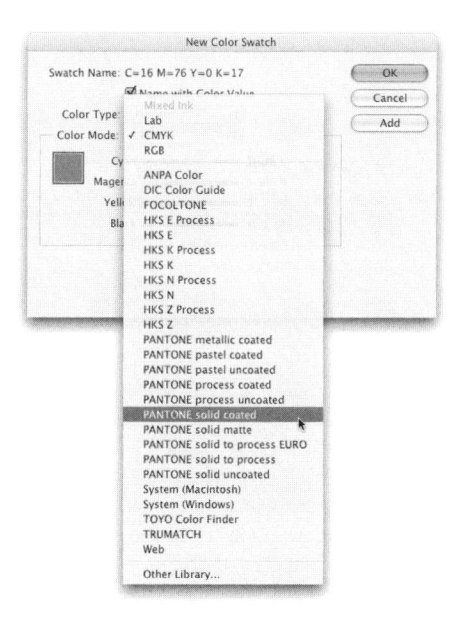

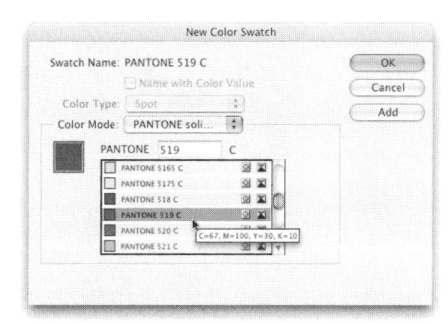

If you know the number of a specific library swatch that you'd like to locate and use, enter it in the search field and let InDesign select it for you. Hover the cursor over any swatch name in the library list and a tooltip displays its color build.

From the Color Mode menu, choose a swatch library to display.

ADDING SWATCHES FROM ADOBE ILLUSTRATOR FILES

InDesign lets you access color swatches stored in Adobe Illustrator 8.x files. To do so, choose Other Library from the Color Mode menu in the New Color Swatch dialog. InDesign launches the Open A File dialog, where you can browse to an Illustrator 8.x file on your system. Click the Open button to add all the stored swatches to the New Color Swatch dialog. You can then select the swatches you'd like to use and add them to the Swatches palette by clicking the Add button.

Related Tasks

4.17 Swatches Palette

7.10 Filling with Solid and Transparent Colors

7.13 Stroking Frames, Shapes, and Paths

14.4 Creating and Saving Mixed-Ink Swatches and Groups

14.7 Importing Colors from Other Documents

Shortcuts

Swatches palette
Mac and Win: F5

Create new swatch based on selected swatch in palette
Mac: Opt-click New Swatch button
Win: Alt-click New Swatch button

Create spot color swatch based on selected swatch in palette
Mac: Opt+Cmd-click New Swatch button
Win: Alt+Ctrl-click New Swatch button

Change swatch options without applying swatch
Mac: Shift+Opt+Cmd-double-click swatch
Win: Shift+Alt+Ctrl-double-click swatch

Tip

Colors applied to objects but not added to the Swatches palette are considered "unnamed." You can add all of them to the palette at once by choosing Add Unnamed Colors from the Swatches palette menu.

14.6 Converting Spot Colors to Process

Related Tasks

4.17 Swatches Palette
7.10 Filling with Solid and Transparent Colors
7.12 Filling Text
7.13 Stroking Frames, Shapes, and Paths
7.14 Stroking Text
14.7 Importing Colors from Other Documents
15.3 Preflighting Colors and Inks
16.1 Printing a Document

Shortcuts

Swatches palette
Mac and Win: F5

Create new swatch based on selected swatch in palette
Mac: Opt-click New Swatch button
Win: Alt-click New Swatch button

Create spot color swatch based on selected swatch in palette
Mac: Opt+Cmd-click New Swatch button
Win: Alt+Ctrl-click New Swatch button

Change swatch options without applying swatch
Mac: Shift+Opt+Cmd-double-click swatch
Win: Shift+Alt+Ctrl-double-click swatch

Tip

Access the Swatch Options dialog by double-clicking a swatch name in the Swatches palette.

You can convert spot colors to process using the Ink Manager, or by changing a selected color's mode and type settings in the Swatch Options dialog.

The Ink Manager converts spot colors to process during output without changing the color swatch definitions in the document. To convert spot colors to process using the Ink Manager, choose Ink Manager from the Swatches palette menu.

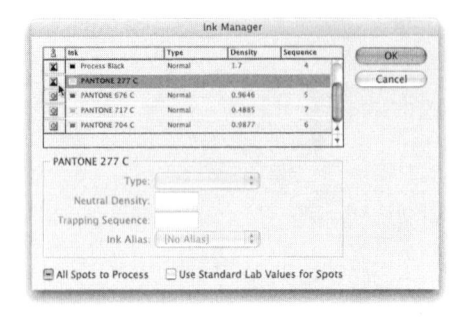

Locate a spot color from the list and click its color mode icon in the far-left column to toggle from spot to process.

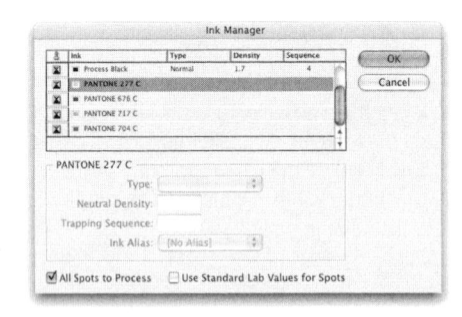

To convert *all* spot colors in the document to process, check the All Spots To Process option in the bottom left of the dialog.

Unlike with the Ink Manager, converting a spot color to process using the Swatch Options dialog actually alters the swatch definition in the document. To convert a spot color to process using the Swatch Options dialog, select a spot color from the Swatches palette and choose Swatch Options from the palette menu.

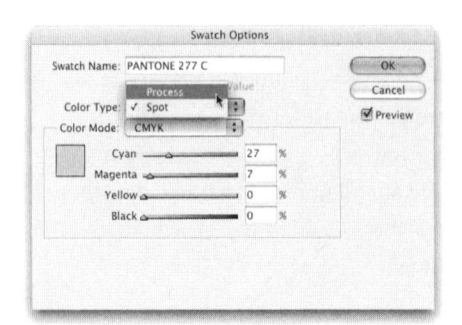

Choose CMYK from the Color Mode menu and Process from the Color Type menu. Click OK to convert the color and close the dialog.

14.7 Importing Colors from Other Documents

You can import colors from other InDesign documents in three ways:

Choose Load Swatches from the Swatches palette menu. Use the Open A File dialog to browse to an InDesign file on your system and click the Open button. All of the stored swatches are added to the Swatches palette.

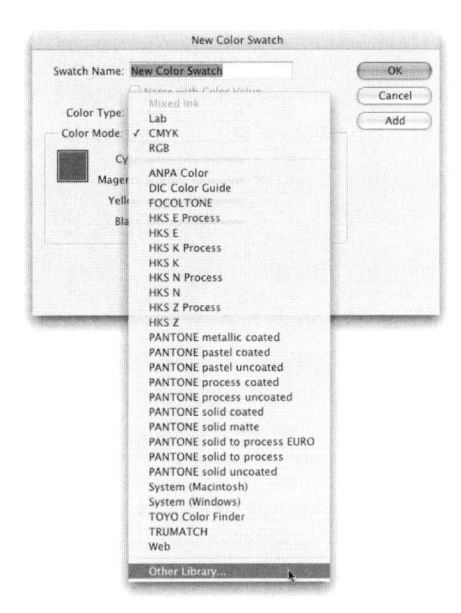

Choose New Color Swatch from the Swatches palette menu and select Other Library from the Color Mode menu. InDesign launches the Open A File dialog, where you can browse to an InDesign file on your system. Click the Open button to add all of the stored swatches to the New Color Swatch dialog. You can then select the swatches you'd like to use and add them to the Swatches palette by clicking the Add button.

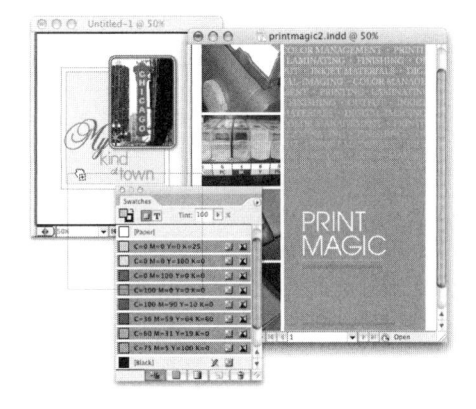

Select colors from the Swatches palette and drag them from one InDesign document to another.

Related Tasks

4.17 Swatches Palette
7.10 Filling with Solid and Transparent Colors
7.12 Filling Text
7.13 Stroking Frames, Shapes, and Paths
7.14 Stroking Text
14.4 Creating and Saving Mixed-Ink Swatches and Groups
14.6 Converting Spot Colors to Process

Shortcuts

Swatches palette
Mac and Win: F5

Create new swatch based on selected swatch in palette
Mac: Opt-click New Swatch button
Win: Alt-click New Swatch button

Create spot color swatch based on selected swatch in palette
Mac: Opt+Cmd-click New Swatch button
Win: Alt+Ctrl-click New Swatch button

Change swatch options without applying swatch
Mac: Shift+Opt+Cmd-double-click swatch
Win: Shift+Alt+Ctrl-double-click swatch

Tip

When converting QuarkXPress or PageMaker documents, or placing Illustrator files, InDesign automatically adds all document swatches to the Swatches palette.

14.8 Changing an Object's Opacity Level

Related Tasks

3.3	Selection Tool
3.4	Direct Selection and Position Tools
4.10	Links Palette
4.12	Object Styles Palette
4.13	Output Palettes
4.20	Transparency Palette
7.10	Filling with Solid and Transparent Colors
11.5	Creating and Applying Object Styles
14.9	Applying Blend Modes
16.1	Printing a Document
16.2	Creating Transparency Flattener Presets
17.1	Exporting as Adobe PDF

Shortcuts

Transparency palette
Mac and Win:
Shift+F10

Links palette
Mac: Shift+Cmd+D
Win: Shift+Ctrl+D

Object Styles palette
Mac: Cmd+F7
Win: Ctrl+F7

Tip

You can adjust the opacity level of a selected group. Ungrouping sets the opacity level of all objects back to 100%.

Lowering a selected object's opacity level allows you to see through it. You can do this in InDesign using the controls located in the Transparency palette. Any adjustments made to a selected object's opacity level affects the entire object (fill and stroke), as well as any frame contents (placed graphic or text). It is not possible to apply different transparency effects or values to the fill and stroke of an object or to individual text characters or layers.

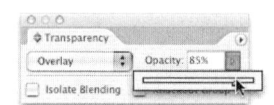

To change an object's opacity level, select it with either selection tool and enter a value in the Opacity field of the Transparency palette. You can also enter an opacity value using the drop-down slider.

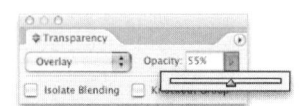

The lower the opacity level, the more transparent the selected object becomes.

The Opacity control in the Transparency palette should not to be confused with the Tint control in the Swatches palette. Although both controls can appear to lighten a selected fill color, lowering the Opacity value also allows you to see through the object—something the Tint control does not do. For visual examples of these differences, refer to the color section.

14.9 Applying Blend Modes

InDesign allows you to apply transparent blend modes to selected objects. Similar to the transparency effects found in Photoshop and Illustrator, applying blend modes lets you control how transparent objects blend with the colors underneath. Here's what each of them does:

Normal At 100% opacity, a selected object's color does not blend with the colors of the objects underneath.

Multiply Darkens a selected object's color by multiplying its values with the values of the colors underneath. White colors are not affected. This is the default blend mode for drop shadows.

Screen Lightens a selected object's color by multiplying the inverse of the base and blend colors. Screening lighter colors produces greater changes; black is not affected.

Overlay Darkens (multiplies) or lightens (screens) a selected object's color while preserving luminosity. Contrasting colors produce greater changes; black, white, and 50% gray are not affected.

Soft Light Darkens (multiplies) or lightens (screens) a selected object's color without preserving highlight and shadow values. Blend colors above 50% darken the base color; blend colors below 50% lighten the base color. Black, white, and 50% gray are not affected.

Hard Light Produces the same effect as Soft Light but with more contrast.

Color Dodge A selected object's pixels are colorized using the hue of the pixels underneath. Color Dodge has a greater effect on lighter colors.

Color Burn A selected object's pixels are colorized using the hue of the pixels underneath. Color Burn has a greater effect on darker colors.

Darken When selected object's color is lighter than those beneath, darker color is used.

Lighten When selected object's color is darker than those beneath, lighter color is used.

Difference Applies the color that results when blend and base colors are subtracted from each other. White inverts the base color; black has no effect.

Exclusion Produces the same effect as Difference but with less contrast.

Hue Applies the hue of the blend color to the luminance and saturation of the base color.

Saturation Applies saturation of the blend color to luminance and hue of the base color.

Color Applies the hue and saturation of the blend color to the luminance of the base color.

Luminosity Applies luminance of the blend color to hue and saturation of the base.

For visual examples of the different blend modes, refer to the color section.

Related Tasks

3.3 Selection Tool
3.4 Direct Selection and Position Tools
4.10 Links Palette
4.13 Output Palettes
4.17 Swatches Palette
4.20 Transparency Palette
7.10 Filling with Solid and Transparent Colors
16.1 Printing a Document
16.2 Creating Transparency Flattener Presets
17.1 Exporting as Adobe PDF

Shortcuts

Transparency palette
Mac and Win: Shift+F10

Links palette
Mac: Shift+Cmd+D
Win: Shift+Ctrl+D

Object Styles palette
Mac: Cmd+F7
Win: Ctrl+F7

Selection tool
Mac and Win: V

Direct Selection tool
Mac and Win: A

Tip

For a more accurate display, select the Document CMYK Transparency Blend Space option under the Edit menu when applying transparency to layouts intended for print.

14.10 Adding Drop Shadows

Related Tasks

2.7	Object Menu
3.3	Selection Tool
3.4	Direct Selection and Position Tools
3.15	Eyedropper Tool
4.10	Links Palette
4.12	Object Styles Palette
4.13	Output Palettes

Shortcuts

Drop shadow
Mac: Opt+Cmd+M
Win: Alt+Ctrl+M

Selection tool
Mac and Win: V

Direct Selection tool
Mac and Win: A

Let's face it—drop shadows are cool. What's *not* cool is interrupting your design process to create them in other applications such as Adobe Photoshop. Adobe understands this, and that's why they've made it possible to create transparent drop shadows right in InDesign.

You can apply drop shadows to imported graphics, shapes, lines, tables, text frames, and editable text characters. One of the great things about InDesign drop shadows is that they are not permanent effects. You can turn them on or off at any time.

To apply a drop shadow in InDesign, select an object with either selection tool and choose Object > Drop Shadow. InDesign launches the Drop Shadow dialog.

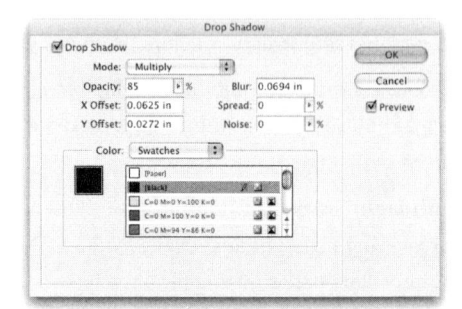

Check the Drop Shadow option in the upper left of the dialog. Enter an Opacity value, Blur amount, and X and Y Offset amount. You can also apply Spread and Noise percentages. To see the settings applied as you enter them, check the Preview option. Select a color to apply to the drop shadow from the Swatches list (the default is Black). To view and edit the color build of a chosen swatch, choose RGB, CMYK, or Lab from the Color menu. Note that adjusting the color build of a chosen swatch does not change its color build in the Swatches palette.

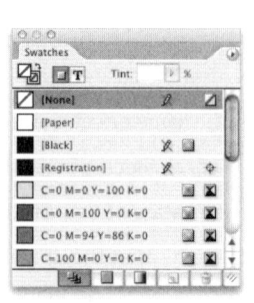

If you want to apply a drop shadow to editable text characters, the text frame must have a fill of None applied.

14.10 Adding Drop Shadows (continued)

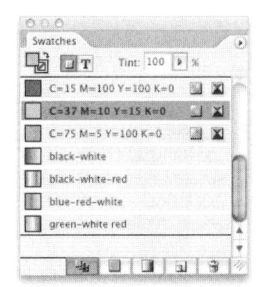

A drop shadow is added to the *text frame* rather than the text when a fill color (other than None) is applied.

Copy/Pasting Drop Shadows

You can sample and apply your favorite drop shadow settings to multiple objects in a document using the Eyedropper tool. To do this, it helps if you show frame edges in the document by pressing Cmd+H (Mac) or Ctrl+H (Windows). Then select the objects you would like to apply the drop shadow to with the Selection tool. Press I to switch to the Eyedropper and click directly on the frame edge of the object containing the drop shadow you'd like to sample. InDesign places the sampled drop shadow on all of the selected objects at once—and you don't have to reenter any dialog settings!

TINT SWATCHES

InDesign allows you to create a new swatch based on a tint of a selected color. To create a tint swatch, select a color from the Swatches palette and choose New Tint Swatch from the palette menu. When the New Tint Swatch dialog appears, enter a value in the Tint field or drag the slider. Click OK to add the tint swatch to the Swatches palette and close the dialog.

Related Tasks

4.17 Swatches Palette

4.20 Transparency Palette

11.5 Creating and Applying Object Styles

14.9 Applying Blend Modes

16.1 Printing a Document

16.2 Creating Transparency Flattener Styles

17.1 Exporting as Adobe PDF

Shortcuts

Links palette
Mac: Shift+Cmd+D
Win: Shift+Ctrl+D

Object Styles palette
Mac: Cmd+F7
Win: Ctrl+F7

Tips

Adjusting the opacity level of a selected object also adjusts the opacity level of its drop shadow.

You can save drop shadow settings as part of an object style.

337

14.11 Feathering

InDesign allows you to apply a soft edge (referred to as a *feather*) to any selected object, including imported graphics, shapes, and editable text. To create a feathered edge using the Feather dialog, select an object and choose Object > Feather.

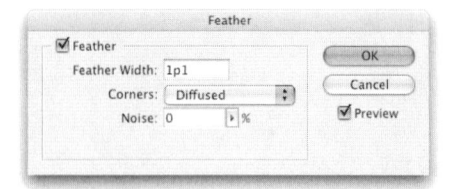

Check the Feather option in the upper left of the dialog, then enter a value in the Feather Width field. Larger values produce softer edges. To see the settings applied as you enter them, check the Preview option on the right.

Choose a corner option from the pop-up menu. Options include Sharp, Rounded, and Diffused (the default).

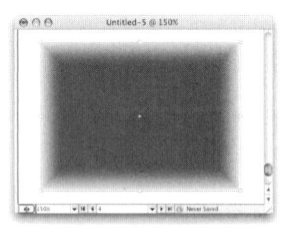

The Sharp option applies the feather along the outline of the path.

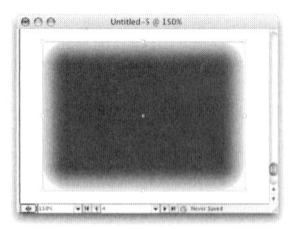

The Rounded option also applies the feather along the outline of the path, but "rounds" the edges of the feather around sharp corners.

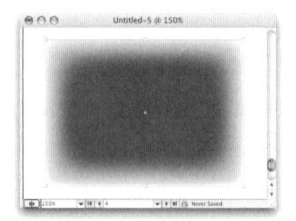

The Diffused option applies a transparent fade from the center of the object rather than along the outline of the path.

If you want to apply a feather to editable text characters, the text frame must have a fill of None applied.

A feather is added to the *text frame* rather than the text when a fill color (here, Paper) is applied.

Related Tasks

- 2.7 Object Menu
- 3.3 Selection Tool
- 3.4 Direct Selection and Position Tools
- 3.15 Eyedropper Tool
- 4.10 Links Palette
- 4.12 Object Styles Palette
- 4.13 Output Palettes
- 4.20 Transparency Palette
- 11.5 Creating and Applying Object Styles
- 16.1 Printing a Document
- 16.2 Creating Transparency Flattener Presets
- 17.1 Exporting as Adobe PDF

Shortcuts

Links palette
Mac: Shift+Cmd+D
Win: Shift+Ctrl+D

Selection tool
Mac and Win: V

Direct Selection tool
Mac and Win: A

Transparency palette
Mac and Win: Shift+F10

Tip

You can also apply feathering to selected lines and tables.

14.12 Importing Transparent TIFFs

Not only does InDesign allow you to import layered PSDs and PDFs, but you can also import transparent TIFFs.

Open a layered PSD or TIFF file in Adobe Photoshop. In the Layers palette, delete the Background and any other unnecessary layers until only one transparent image layer is left in the document. Then Choose File > Save As.

Now open a document in InDesign and choose File > Place. In the Place dialog, browse to the file location on your system and click Open.

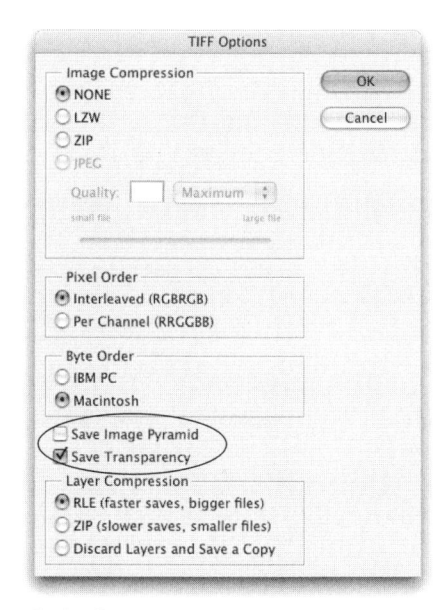

Click the loaded Place cursor anywhere on the page to import the graphic. You can then position and resize the transparent graphic however you like.

In the Save As dialog, choose TIFF from the Format menu. Enter a name for the TIFF and click the Save button. In the TIFF Options dialog, check the Save Transparency option and click OK.

Related Tasks

2.3	File Menu
3.9	Frame Tools
3.10	Shape Tools
4.10	Links Palette
4.13	Output Palettes
12.1	Importing a Graphic Image
12.2	Setting Import Options
12.4	Object Layer Options and Placed PSDs
16.1	Printing a Document
16.2	Creating Transparency Flattener Presets
17.1	Exporting as Adobe PDF

Shortcuts

Place
Mac: Cmd+D
Win: Ctrl+D

Links palette
Mac: Shift+Cmd+D
Win: Shift+Ctrl+D

Selection tool
Mac and Win: V

Direct Selection tool
Mac and Win: A

Tip

You can save and import transparent TIFFs using Grayscale, RGB, CMYK, or Lab color space.

InDesign in Color

The Color Picker

InDesign CS2 features a Color Picker, similar to the one found in Photoshop or Illustrator. To open the Color Picker, double-click the Stroke or Fill swatches located at the bottom of the Toolbox or in the Color palette. When the dialog opens, you can click anywhere in the color field to locate a specific RGB, CMYK, or Lab build.

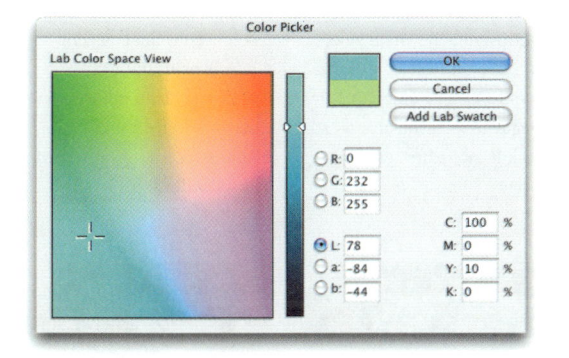

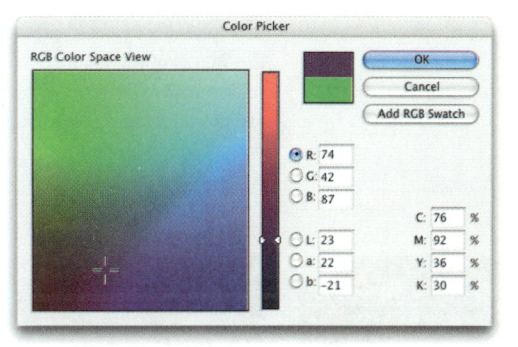

To change the color spectrum displayed in the Color Picker, click a letter: R (red), G (green), or B (blue); or L (luminance), a (green-red axis), or b (blue-yellow axis).

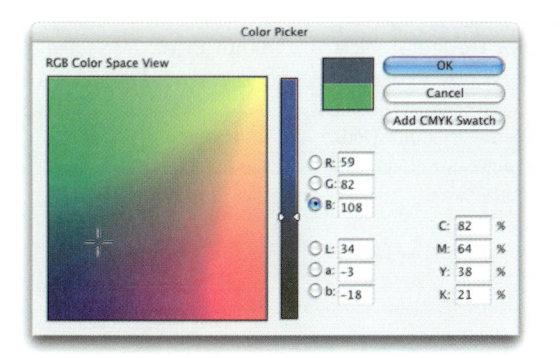

To add the chosen color to the Swatches palette, click the Add Swatch button. Click inside any of the RGB, Lab, or CMYK percentage fields to display the Add RGB, Lab, or CMYK Swatch button. Click OK to display the chosen color in the Fill or Stroke swatch (whichever is placed in front) and apply it to any selected objects.

Blend Modes

InDesign allows you to apply blend modes to selected objects, similar to the blend modes found in Photoshop and Illustrator. Applying blend modes allows you to control how transparent objects blend with the colors underneath.

Normal: At 100% opacity, a selected object's color does not blend with the colors of the objects underneath.

Multiply: Darkens a selected object's color by multiplying its values with the values of the colors underneath. White colors are not affected. This is the default blend mode for drop shadows.

Screen: Lightens a selected object's color by multiplying the inverse of the base and blend colors. Screening lighter colors produces greater changes; black is not affected.

Overlay: Darkens (multiplies) or lightens (screens) a selected object's color while preserving luminosity. Contrasting colors produce greater changes; black, white, and 50% gray are not affected.

Soft Light: Darkens (multiplies) or lightens (screens) a selected object's color without preserving highlight and shadow values. Blend colors above 50% darken the base color; blend colors below 50% lighten the base color. Black, white, and 50% gray are not affected.

Hard Light: Produces the same effect as Soft Light but with more contrast.

Color Dodge: A selected object's pixels are colorized using the hue of the pixels underneath. Color Dodge has a greater effect on lighter colors.

Color Burn: A selected object's pixels are colorized using the hue of the pixels underneath. Color Burn has a greater effect on darker colors.

Darken: When a selected object's color is lighter than the colors underneath, the darker color is applied.

Lighten: When a selected object's color is darker than the colors underneath, the lighter color is applied.

Difference: Applies the color that results when blend and base colors are subtracted from each other. White inverts the base color; black has no effect.

Exclusion: Produces the same effect as Difference but with less contrast.

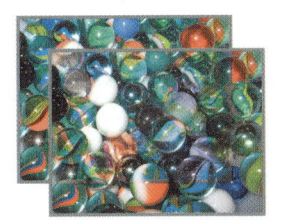

Hue: Applies the hue of the blend color to the luminance and saturation of the base color.

Saturation: Applies the saturation of the blend color to the luminance and hue of the base color.

Color: Applies the hue and saturation of the blend color to the luminance of the base color.

Luminosity: Applies the luminance of the blend color to the hue and saturation of the base color.

THE COLOR PICKER

BLEND MODES

COLORIZING GRAPHICS

PREVIEWS

Tint vs. Transparency

The Fill color of a selected object (or objects) can be made transparent by adjusting the Opacity control located in the Transparency palette. Don't confuse this with the Tint control located in the Swatches palette. Although both controls appear to lighten a selected fill color, lowering the Opacity value also lets you see through the object—something the Tint control does not do.

Two overlapping frames, one with a fill color of green and one with a fill color of yellow. In this figure, the green frame has a 60% tint applied and is placed in front of the yellow frame.

The same two frames, but this time with 60% transparency applied to the forefront green frame. Notice that you can see through the transparent green frame to the yellow frame underneath. The overlapping area creates a whole new color.

Colorizing Graphics

You can colorize a placed grayscale TIFF or PSD by selecting it with the Direct Selection tool and applying a color with the Swatches or Color palette, Color Picker, or Eyedropper tool.

To create a duotone effect in InDesign, select a placed grayscale TIFF or PSD with the Selection tool (not the Direct Selection tool) and drag in a color from the Swatches palette. This colorizes the shadow areas of the image. To colorize the highlight areas, click a second swatch in the palette (but don't drag it onto the image).

Soft Proofing

You can use InDesign's proof setup feature to preview how a document is going to print as you design on screen (a process called *soft proofing*). Under the View > Proof Setup submenu, choose one of three options: Working CMYK, Document CMYK, or Custom. To soft-proof the document, choose Proof Colors from the View menu.

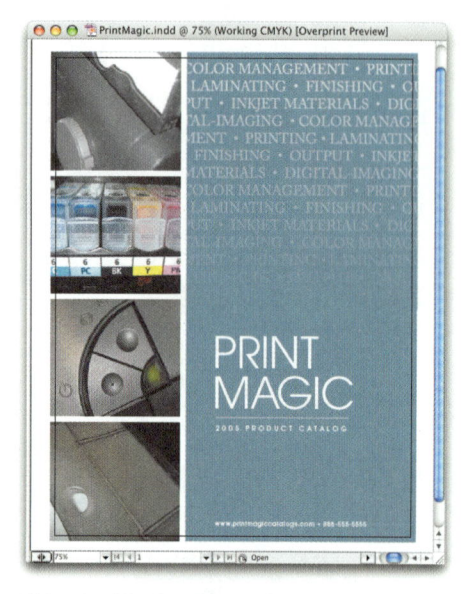

Using the Working Space profile set in Color Settings to soft-proof with (North American Prepress 2)

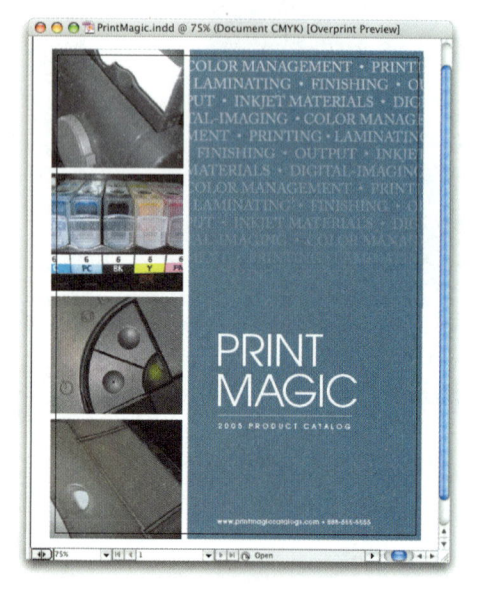

Using the assigned document CMYK profile to soft-proof with (KODAK SWOP Proofer CMYK—Coated Stock)

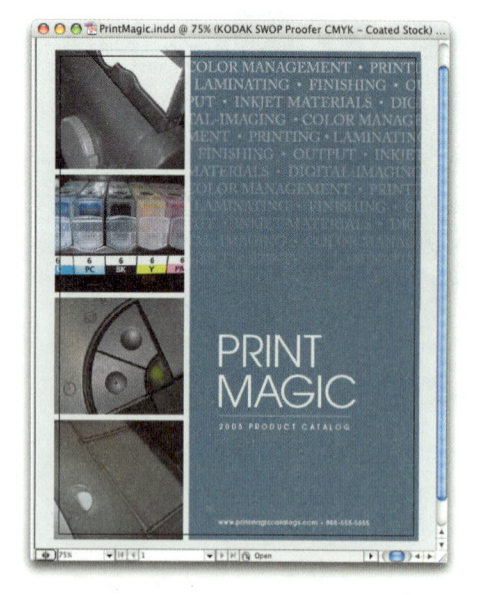

Using the assigned document CMYK profile (KODAK SWOP Proofer CMYK–Coated Stock) and enabling the Simulate Paper Color option in the Custom Proof Setup dialog

Flattener and Separations Previews

The Window > Output palettes can assist you in troubleshooting any potential printing and exporting problems you might encounter with your InDesign documents.

The Flattener Preview palette allows you to highlight areas in a document that are affected by transparency flattening during output. You can create, save, and apply your own custom presets in the Transparency Flattener Presets dialog accessible through the Flattener Preview palette menu.

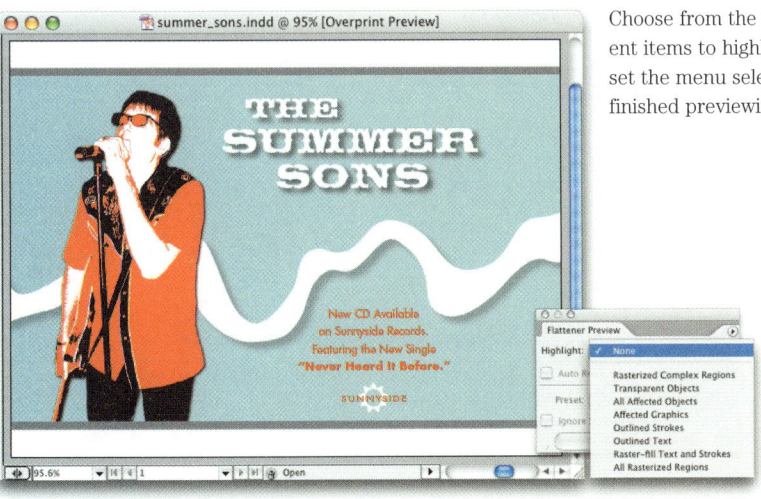

Choose from the default list of potential transparent items to highlight in the document. Be sure to set the menu selection back to None when you've finished previewing.

Continues

Flattener and Separations Previews *(Continued)*

The Separations Preview palette allows you to preview CMYK process plates individually on screen, before outputting. You can use the separations preview to check rich black builds, total ink coverage (to make sure it does not exceed press limitations), and overprinting (including transparency and blends).

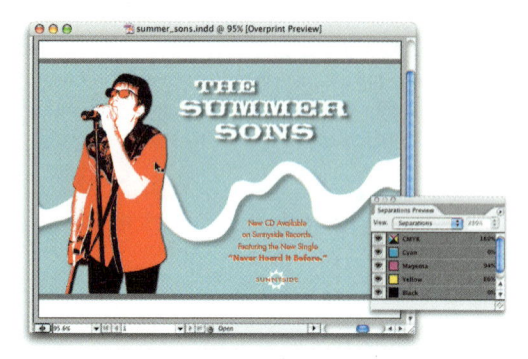

Hover your mouse over any area in the document to view the CMYK numerical build for a specific color. The percentage numbers appear next to each plate color, and change as you move your mouse around the document.

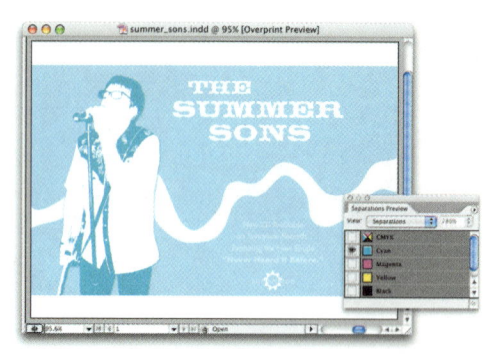

You can choose to view each plate in its actual color (Cyan, Magenta, Yellow, or Black).

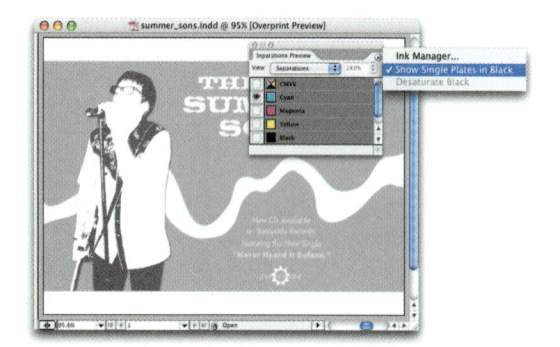

Or you can choose to view each plate in black.

The Ink Limit preview displays any exceeding ink coverage in red.

CHAPTER **15**

Preflighting and Packaging

BEFORE YOU SEND YOUR publication off to the printer, it's *always* a good idea to use InDesign's built-in Preflight plug-in to check for any potential output problems. When you run a preflight check, InDesign inspects the document for missing fonts and links, and searches for placed RGB images that should be converted to CMYK.

Once you know that your document is trouble-free, you can use InDesign's Package feature to collect all the fonts and links needed for printing. You can also package all of the document's stories and graphics in a web-ready format and create a web version of your layout in Adobe GoLive CS2.

- 15.1 **Preflighting Fonts**
- 15.2 **Preflighting Links and Images**
- 15.3 **Preflighting Colors and Inks**
- 15.4 **Preflighting Print Settings**
- 15.5 **Packaging**
- 15.6 **Packaging for GoLive**

15.1 Preflighting Fonts

Related Tasks

2.3	File Menu
3.2	Control Bar
3.6	Type Tools
4.21	Type and Tables Palettes
9.13	Font Overview
9.14	Find/Replace Missing Fonts
15.5	Packaging
18.7	Preflighting, Printing, and Exporting Books

Shortcuts

Preflight
Mac: Opt+Shift+Cmd+F
Win: Alt+Shift+Ctrl+F

Package
Mac: Opt+Shift+Cmd+P
Win: Alt+Shift+Ctrl+P

Tip

Click the Report button to generate a text file of the preflight information.

Any time you run an InDesign preflight check on a document (choose File > Preflight), a dialog appears displaying a summary of what it found.

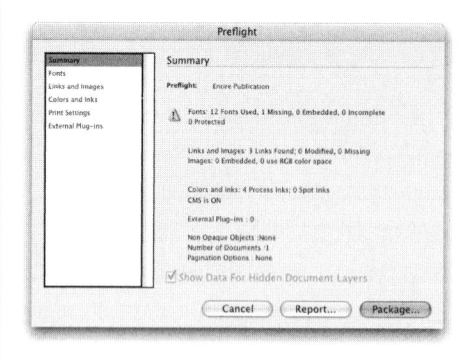

The Preflight dialog contains six panels: Summary, Fonts, Links And Images, Colors And Inks, Print Settings, and External Plug-ins. The Summary panel displays a brief description of what is found for each category. When a potential output problem exists, InDesign places a warning icon next to the category in the summary.

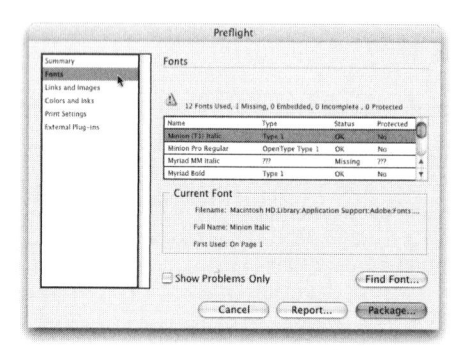

Click the Fonts category on the left to display the panel in the Preflight dialog. Click to select from the list of fonts used in the document. InDesign displays more information about the font in the Current Font section of the panel, including where the font is located on your system, the full font name, and where it is first used in the document.

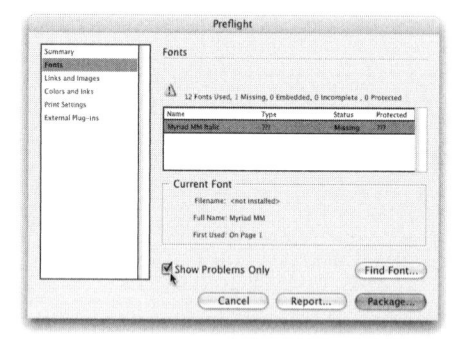

Check the Show Problems Only option to display missing fonts exclusively. Click the Find Font button to relink or replace any missing fonts using the Find Font dialog.

342

15.2 Preflighting Links and Images

The Preflight dialog Summary panel displays a brief description of what is found for each preflight category, including fonts, links and images, colors and inks, print settings, and external plug-ins.

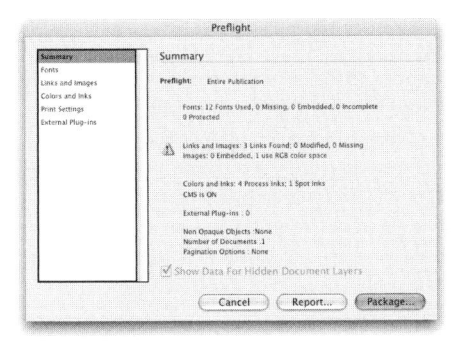

When a potential output problem exists regarding links and images, InDesign places a warning icon next to that category in the summary.

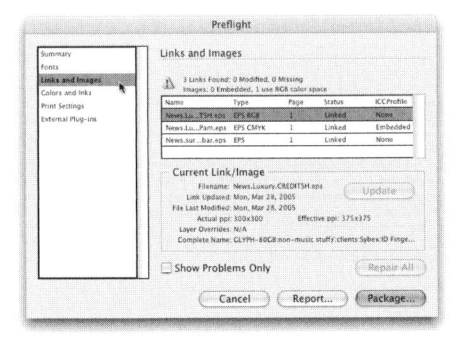

Click the Links And Images category on the left to display the panel in the Preflight dialog. In the center of the panel, click to select from the list of links placed in the document. InDesign displays more information about the link/image in the Current Link/Image section of the panel, including where it is located on your system, its full name and Actual ppi, and when it was last updated or modified.

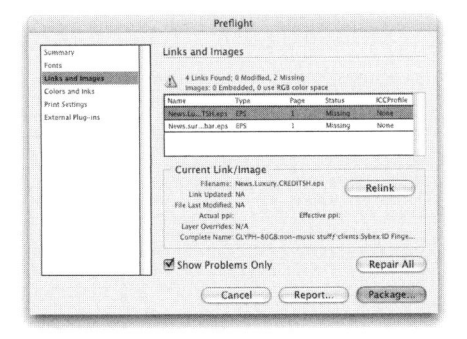

Check the Show Problems Only option to display missing and modified links exclusively. To relink or update a link, select it from the list and click the Relink or Update button. Click the Repair All button to update and/or relink all missing and modified links at once.

Related Tasks

2.3	File Menu
4.10	Links Palette
12.1	Importing a Graphic Image
12.2	Setting Import Options
12.4	Object Layer Options and Placed PSDs
12.7	Updating Missing and Modified Links
14.12	Importing Transparent TIFFs
15.5	Packaging
18.7	Preflighting, Printing, and Exporting Books

Shortcuts

Preflight
Mac: Opt+Shift+Cmd+F
Win: Alt+Shift+Ctrl+F

Package
Mac: Opt+Shift+Cmd+P
Win: Alt+Shift+Ctrl+P

Links palette
Mac: Shift+Cmd+D
Win: Shift+Ctrl+D

Tip

In addition to filename and status, the Links And Images panel lists the page number each link is placed on in the document and whether it has an ICC profile embedded.

15.3 Preflighting Colors and Inks

Related Tasks

- 4.5 Color Palette
- 4.17 Swatches Palette
- 7.10 Filling with Solid and Transparent Colors
- 7.12 Filling Text
- 14.4 Creating and Saving Mixed-Ink Swatches and Groups
- 14.5 Accessing Colors Stored in Libraries
- 14.6 Converting Spot Colors to Process
- 14.7 Importing Colors from Other Documents

Shortcuts

Preflight
Mac: Opt+Shift+Cmd+F
Win: Alt+Shift+Ctrl+F

Package
Mac: Opt+Shift+Cmd+P
Win: Alt+Shift+Ctrl+P

Swatches palette
Mac and Win: F5

Separations Preview palette
Mac and Win: Shift+F6

Overprint preview
Mac: Opt+Shift+Cmd+Y
Win: Alt+Shift+Ctrl+Y

Tip

The Ink Manager converts spot colors to process during output without changing the color swatch definitions in the document.

The Preflight dialog Summary panel displays a brief description of what is found for each preflight category, including fonts, links and images, colors and inks, print settings, and external plug-ins.

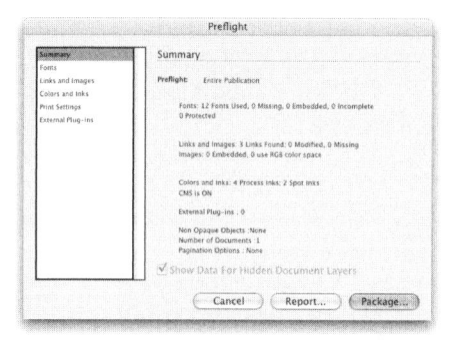

The Summary panel lists the number of process and spot inks used in the document and whether a color management system (CMS) is being used. Because some print jobs require them, spot inks do not trigger a warning icon. If a preflight check reveals spot colors that should be process, click the Cancel button and convert them using the Ink Manager or Swatch Options dialog (both accessible through the Swatches palette).

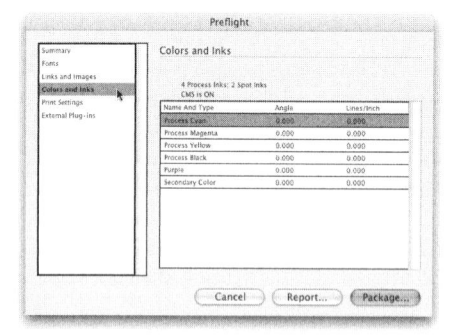

Click the Colors And Inks category on the left to display the panel in the Preflight dialog. In the center of the panel, InDesign displays a list of all colors and inks used in the document as well as their halftone screen angles and lines per inch (if applicable).

15.4 Preflighting Print Settings

The Preflight dialog Summary panel displays a brief description of what is found for each preflight category, including fonts, links and images, colors and inks, print settings, and external plug-ins. Clicking the Print Settings category displays a list of document information relevant to output.

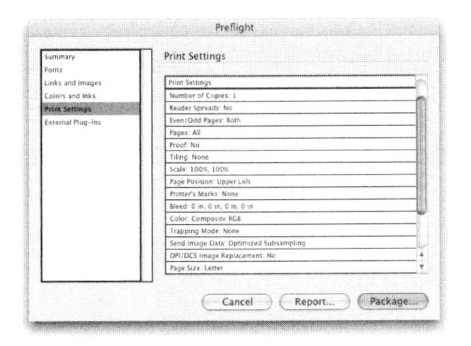

In the center of the panel is a list of document information relevant to output, including bleed amounts, page size and position, and whether the document is set up in reader or printer spreads.

PREFLIGHTING EXTERNAL PLUG-INS

The last panel of the Preflight dialog displays a list of external plug-ins used in the document. Your printer or service provider must have these plug-ins installed in order to output your document properly. To display the list, click the External Plug-ins category on the left of the Preflight dialog.

Related Tasks

2.3	File Menu
5.16	Print Presets
15.5	Packaging
16.1	Printing a Document
16.2	Creating Transparency Flattener Presets
16.3	Creating and Assigning Trap Presets
18.7	Preflighting, Printing, and Exporting Books

Shortcuts

Preflight
Mac: Opt+Shift+Cmd+F
Win: Alt+Shift+Ctrl+F

Package
Mac: Opt+Shift+Cmd+P
Win: Alt+Shift+Ctrl+P

Print
Mac: Cmd+P
Win: Ctrl+P

Separations Preview palette
Mac and Win: Shift+F6

Overprint preview
Mac: Opt+Shift+Cmd+Y
Win: Alt+Shift+Ctrl+Y

Tip

InDesign allows you to save custom print presets.

345

15.5 Packaging

Related Tasks

2.3	File Menu
4.10	Links Palette
9.13	Font Overview
9.14	Find/Replace Missing Fonts
15.1	Preflighting Fonts
15.2	Preflighting Links and Images
15.3	Preflighting Colors and Inks
15.4	Preflighting Print Settings
15.6	Packaging for GoLive
18.7	Preflighting, Printing, and Exporting Books

Shortcuts

Preflight
Mac: Opt+Shift+Cmd+F
Win: Alt+Shift+Ctrl+F

Package
Mac: Opt+Shift+Cmd+P
Win: Alt+Shift+Ctrl+P

Tip

Packaging places a copy of the document as well as copies of all fonts and links into the package folder. It does not move the original files from their location on your system.

InDesign's Package feature allows you to collect all the fonts and links needed for printing. In QuarkXPress this task is called "Collect For Output"; in Adobe PageMaker it's called "Save For Service Provider."

To package a document, choose File > Package. Note that any time you choose this command, InDesign runs a preflight check first. If problems are detected, you can choose to either view the preflight info or continue on with packaging. If everything checks out, InDesign displays the Printing Instructions dialog. When the document contains unsaved changes, InDesign always prompts you to save before packaging.

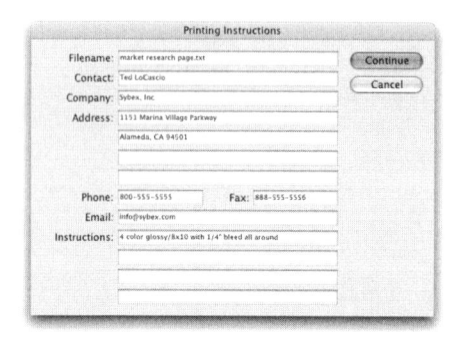

Enter your contact information and any necessary printing instructions in the dialog. This information is added to the text report included in the final package. When you've finished entering the information, click Continue.

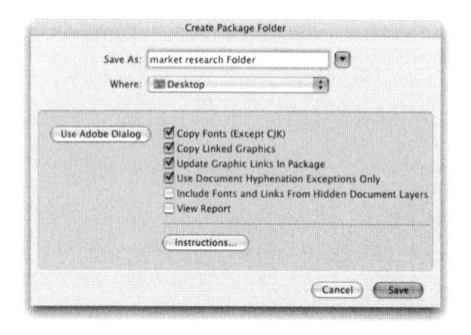

In the Create Package Folder dialog (Mac) or the Package Publication dialog (Windows), enter a folder name (InDesign adds the word "Folder" to the existing filename by default), and choose a folder location on your system.

Check the Copy Fonts (Except CJK) and Copy Linked Graphics options to collect all fonts and links into the folder. Check the Update Graphic Links In Package option to tell InDesign to link to the copied images in the package folder and not to the original files.

Check the Use Document Hyphenation Exceptions Only option to prevent the reflow of text when opening the document on another system containing different dictionaries and hyphenation settings.

To include fonts and links from hidden document layers and to view the package report, check the options of the same name. If necessary, click the Instructions button to relaunch the Printing Instructions dialog and edit the information.

Click Save (Mac) or Package (Windows) to package the document.

15.6 Packaging for GoLive

The Package For GoLive feature allows you to create web versions of InDesign print or PDF documents. A GoLive package includes a document preview as well as all of the text and graphic files needed to create a web version of the document in GoLive. You can open the package in GoLive CS2 and drag objects from the preview into a GoLive web page. Note that the InDesign CS2 Package for GoLive feature is only compatible with Adobe GoLive CS2 and not CS.

When packaging for GoLive, all InDesign stories are converted to XML files with the .incd filename extension (threaded text frames are converted into a single XML file). All applied paragraph and character styles are converted to Cascading Style Sheets (CSS) in GoLive.

All placed images and graphics are converted to TIFF for faster web display. You can also save applied graphic transformations such as scaling, shearing, and rotating. Native and custom drawn InDesign shapes can be dragged into a GoLive webpage from the InDesign Layout tab in GoLive. InDesign shapes are converted to GIF but are not added to the Assets folder.

To create a GoLive package of an InDesign document, choose File > Package For GoLive. In the first dialog (Package Publication For GoLive), choose a name and system location and click Package; then InDesign launches the Package For GoLive dialog.

In the Pages section of the Package For GoLive dialog, choose All, Range, or Selection: The All option packages all pages in the document; the Range option allows you to specify which pages to package by entering a range in the field provided; the Selection option packages only selected objects. Note that nonselected objects also appear on the preview page but cannot be dragged into a GoLive webpage. Check the Include Hidden Layers option to package linked objects on hidden layers.

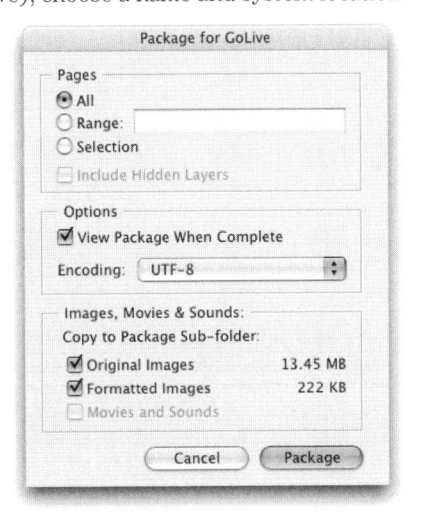

Related Tasks

2.3	File Menu
4.10	Links Palette
9.13	Font Overview
11.1	Creating and Applying Character Styles

Shortcut

Show Structure
Mac: Opt+Cmd+1
Win: Alt+Ctrl+1

15.6 Packaging for GoLive *(continued)*

Related Tasks

11.2 Creating and Applying Paragraph Styles

11.3 Creating and Applying Parent/Child Styles

15.5 Packaging

Tip

You can also package for GoLive by clicking the Package For GoLive button located in the PageMaker toolbar.

In the Options portion of the dialog, check the View Package When Complete option to open the package in GoLive CS2 immediately after. You can also select an encoding format from the menu. Options include UTF-8 (8-bit), UTF-16 (16-bit), and Shift-JIS (for Japanese characters).

In the Images, Movies & Sounds portion of the dialog, choose how you would like to package these file types. Check the Original Images option to copy the original graphics files and format the images later in GoLive. Check the Formatted Images option to copy the images as they appear in InDesign (such as cropped images). Check the Movies And Sounds option to copy the original movie and sound files.

When you're ready, click Package. You can then open the .idpk file in GoLive and re-create the layout for web display.

CHAPTER **16**

Printing

UNLESS YOU'RE USING INDESIGN CS2 exclusively for PDF output, your layouts and designs are created especially for *printing*. The InDesign Print dialog makes it easy to set up your preferred printing options and save them as print presets. InDesign also lets you save and apply transparency flattening and trapping presets. Using presets, you can print your documents quickly and successfully without having to stop and reenter any settings in a dialog.

- 16.1 **Printing a Document**

    The General Panel

    The Setup Panel

    The Marks and Bleed Panel

    The Output Panel

    The Graphics Panel

    The Color Management Panel

    The Advanced Panel

    The Summary Panel

- 16.2 **Creating Transparency Flattener Presets**
- 16.3 **Creating and Assigning Trap Presets**

16.1 Printing a Document

Related Tasks

2.3	File Menu
4.3	Attributes Palette
4.13	Output Palettes
4.14	PageMaker Toolbar

Shortcuts

Print
Mac: Cmd+P
Win: Ctrl+P

Scroll through Print dialog panels
Mac: Cmd+Up/Down arrow
Win: Ctrl+Up/Down arrow

Preflight
Mac: Opt+Shift+Cmd+F
Win: Alt+Shift+Ctrl+F

Separations Preview
Mac and Win: Shift+F6

Overprint Preview
Mac: Opt+Shift+Cmd+Y
Win: Alt+Shift+Ctrl+Y

Tip

Access the Print dialog by clicking the Print button in the PageMaker toolbar.

To access the Print dialog, choose File > Print. The dialog contains eight panels: General, Setup, Marks And Bleed, Output, Graphics, Color Management, Advanced, and Summary. Display any of these panels in the dialog by clicking its name in the category list on the left.

Whenever you print a document for the first time, inspect each panel of the dialog to make sure the proper settings are applied. Once the Print dialog setup is complete, you can save it as a Print Preset to use again and again, without having to reenter any settings. Click the Save Preset button, enter a name for the setup in the Save Preset dialog, and click OK to add the preset to the Print Preset menu.

Beneath the category list is a visual preview of the print settings entered in each panel. Click once to display more information about the print job. Click twice to reveal the print job's color space and to display the page versus paper path. Click a third time to return to the original preview.

If you created a Print Preset that you'd like to use, choose it from the Print Preset menu at the top of the dialog. From the Printer menu, choose any of the printers installed on your system. InDesign automatically displays the PostScript Printer Driver associated with the chosen printer as grayed out in the PPD menu. If there is no PPD for the chosen printer, the menu remains grayed out and blank.

When you're ready to print the document using the applied settings, click Print.

16.1 Printing a Document (continued)

The General Panel

The General panel is the first to appear when you open the Print dialog. With the dialog box open, you can access it by clicking General in the category list or by pressing Command+1 (Mac) or Ctrl+1 (Windows).

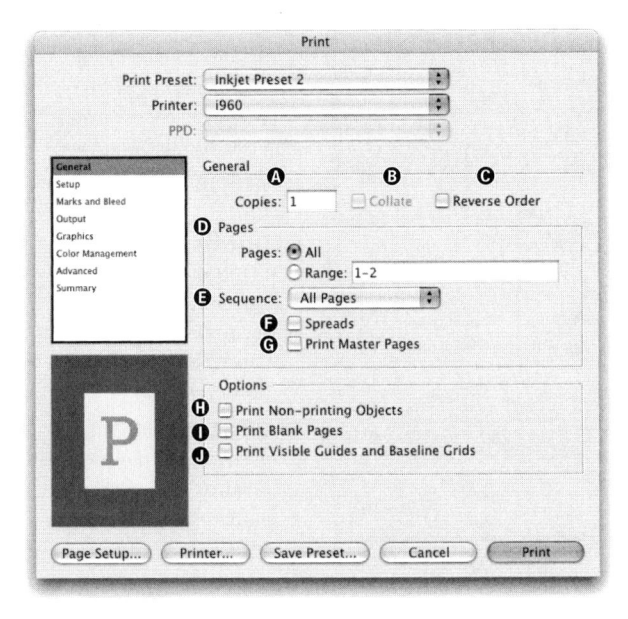

A **Copies** Enter the number of copies to print (up to 999).

B **Collate** Collates the print job (this slows printing).

C **Reverse Order** Prints the last page first.

D **Pages** Choose to print all the pages or a range of specific pages. In the Range field, enter the page numbers in numerical order separated by either commas (to indicate individual pages) or dashes (to indicate a series of pages).

E **Sequence** Choose to print All Pages (even and odd), Even Pages Only, or Odd Pages Only. Each option prints the chosen sequence within the specified range. These options are not available when printing spreads or master pages.

F **Spreads** Prints each spread on a single sheet of paper (or other output media).

G **Print Master Pages** Prints all the master pages (rather than document pages) and does not allow you to specify a page range.

H **Print Non-printing Objects** Overrides the Attributes palette's Nonprinting checkbox and prints every object placed on the specified pages.

I **Print Blank Pages** Prints any blank pages positioned within the specified page range.

J **Print Visible Guides and Baseline Grids** Allows any visible margin guides, page guides, and baseline grids to print. Enabling this option does not print the document grid.

Related Tasks

5.16 Print Presets
6.11 Creating Master Pages
6.18 Adjusting Ruler Guides
6.19 Adjusting Margin and Column Guides
6.20 Aligning to Baseline Grid

Shortcuts

Print
Mac: Cmd+P
Win: Ctrl+P

Scroll through Print dialog panels
Mac: Cmd+Up/Down arrow
Win: Ctrl+Up/Down arrow

Preflight
Mac: Opt+Shift+Cmd+F
Win: Alt+Shift+Ctrl+F

Separations Preview
Mac and Win: Shift+F6

Overprint Preview
Mac: Opt+Shift+Cmd+Y
Win: Alt+Shift+Ctrl+Y

Tips

To print from a specific page to the end of the document, enter the page number followed by a dash (e.g., 5 –) in the Range field of the General panel.

To print from the beginning of a document to a specific page, enter the page number preceded by a dash (e.g., – 5) in the Range field of the General panel.

16.1 Printing a Document (continued)

Related Tasks

6.19 Adjusting Margin and Column Guides

6.20 Aligning to Baseline Grid

7.12 Filling Text

Shortcuts

Print
Mac: Cmd+P
Win: Ctrl+P

Scroll through Print dialog panels
Mac: Cmd+Up/Down arrow
Win: Ctrl+Up/Down arrow

Preflight
Mac: Opt+Shift+Cmd+F
Win: Alt+Shift+Ctrl+F

Separations Preview
Mac and Win: Shift+F6

Overprint Preview
Mac: Opt+Shift+Cmd+Y
Win: Alt+Shift+Ctrl+Y

The Setup Panel

Click Setup in the category list to display the Setup panel of the Print dialog, or press Command+2 (Mac) or Ctrl+2 (Windows).

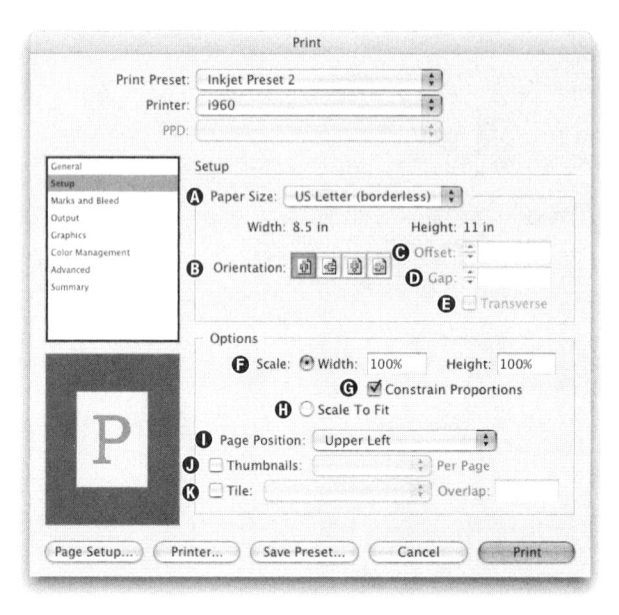

A **Paper Size** Choose a paper size (available options defined by the chosen printer's PPD). When you choose a non-PostScript printer, the menu displays Defined By Driver.

B **Orientation** Click one of the four 90° rotation buttons to control how the page is rotated on the paper. Refer to the page preview at the bottom left.

C **Offset** Controls the placement of the document relative to the edge of the output media (e.g., paper or film).

D **Gap** When printing to a roll-fed printer, defines the amount of blank space placed between each document page.

E **Transverse** When printing to a roll-fed printer and Paper Size is set to Custom, places the width of the paper along the length of the roll.

F **Scale** Enter a scale percentage (from 1 to 1000) in the Width and Height fields. See the page preview at the bottom left.

G **Constrain Proportions** Forces both the scale width and scale height settings to reflect the same percentage.

H **Scale To Fit** Allows InDesign to scale the page to fit the chosen paper size, including any printer's marks selected in the Marks And Bleed panel.

I **Page Position** When selecting a paper size larger than the document, specifies where to position the page: Upper Left, Center Horizontally, Center Vertically, or Centered.

J **Thumbnails** Prints an overview of a document. Specify a number of thumbnails to place per page (e.g., 1×2, 2×2, 3×3). See the page preview in the bottom left.

K **Tile** Prints a document that is larger than the selected paper size using tiling. Auto tiling fits as much of the document as possible on the selected paper size, starting from the upper-left corner. Specify an overlap amount for printing successive tiles in the Overlap field. Auto Justified tiling does the same without having to enter an overlap amount and without leaving any extra white space to the right or under the image. Manual tiling only prints one tile per document page and uses the ruler zero point as the origin for printing. You must manually move the zero point to print successive tiles.

16.1 Printing a Document *(continued)*

The Marks And Bleed Panel

Click Marks and Bleed in the category list to display the Marks and Bleed panel of the Print dialog, or press Command+3 (Mac) or Ctrl+3 (Windows).

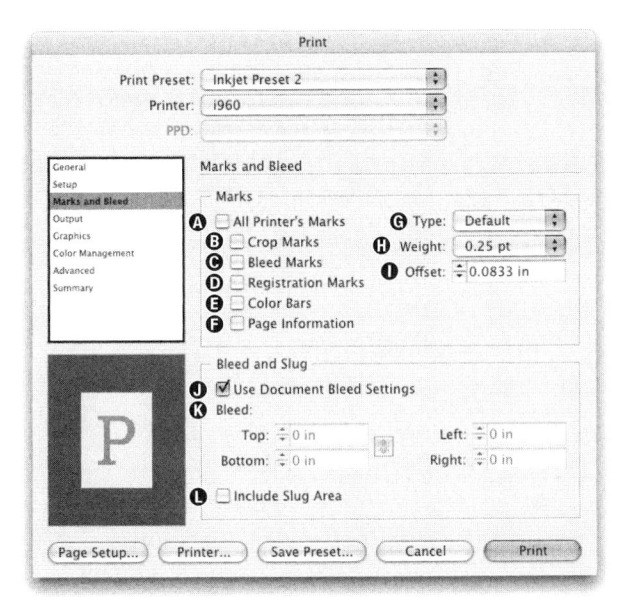

Ⓐ All Printer's Marks Prints all printer's marks.

Ⓑ Crop Marks Prints lines that define the page area (also referred to as "trim marks").

Ⓒ Bleed Marks Prints lines that define the bleed area.

Ⓓ Registration Marks Prints small targets around the edge of each page; used for lining up color separations.

Ⓔ Color Bars Prints small square color samples outside the bleed area; used for matching colors on press.

Ⓕ Page Information Prints the filename and publication date on every page of the document. When printing separations, also prints the name of the color plate.

Ⓖ Type Lets you select additional sets of printer's marks created by other developers. InDesign CS2 only ships with one default set.

Ⓗ Weight Change the stroke weight of the printer's marks by choosing 0.125 pt, 0.25 pt., or 0.50 pt.

Ⓘ Offset Defines how far from the page edge the printer's marks should print.

Ⓙ Use Document Bleed Settings Applies the Bleed settings entered in the Document Setup dialog.

Ⓚ Bleed Defines the amount of bleed area off the top, bottom, inside, and outside edges of the page. Click the chain link icon to make all the settings the same.

Ⓛ Include Slug Area Prints the slug area defined in the Document Setup dialog.

Related Tasks

6.18 Adjusting Ruler Guides
8.16 Placing Objects on Layers
9.13 Font Overview
9.14 Find/Replace Missing Fonts

Shortcuts

Print
Mac: Cmd+P
Win: Ctrl+P

Scroll through Print dialog panels
Mac: Cmd+Up/Down arrow
Win: Ctrl+Up/Down arrow

Preflight
Mac: Opt+Shift+Cmd+F
Win: Alt+Shift+Ctrl+F

Separations Preview
Mac and Win: Shift+F6

Overprint Preview
Mac: Opt+Shift+Cmd+Y
Win: Alt+Shift+Ctrl+Y

16.1 Printing a Document *(continued)*

Related Tasks

12.2 Setting Import Options

16.3 Creating and Assigning Trap Presets

Shortcuts

Print
Mac: Cmd+P
Win: Ctrl+P

Scroll through Print dialog panels
Mac: Cmd+Up/ Down arrow
Win: Ctrl+Up/ Down arrow

Preflight
Mac: Opt+Shift+Cmd+F
Win: Alt+Shift+Ctrl+F

Separations Preview
Mac and Win: Shift+F6

Overprint Preview
Mac: Opt+Shift+Cmd+Y
Win: Alt+Shift+Ctrl+Y

The Output Panel

Click Output in the category list to display the Output panel of the Print dialog, or press Command+4 (Mac) or Ctrl+4 (Windows).

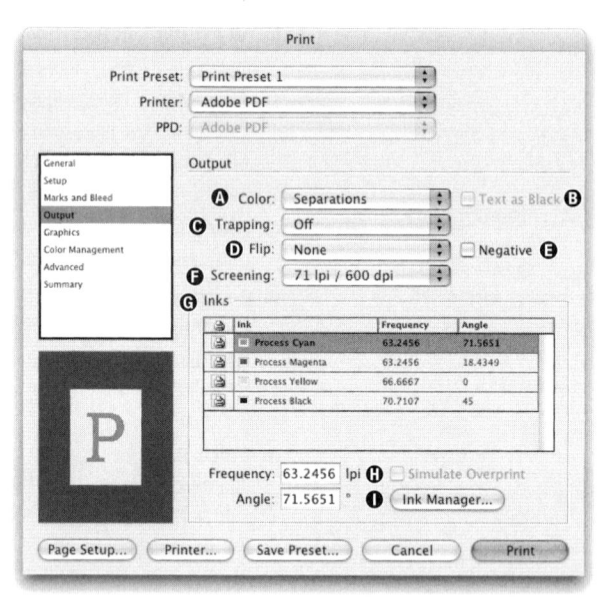

Ⓐ Color Prints a color composite or color separations. Most inkjet printers require Composite RGB data. PostScript printers prefer Composite CMYK data. Choosing Separations activates the Inks list.

Ⓑ Text As Black Prints all colored text as black, except text filled with white, Paper color, or None.

Ⓒ Trapping Choose Off if you've set trapping manually using fills and strokes. Choose Application Built-In to allow InDesign to handle trapping as you send the document to the printer. Choose Adobe In-RIP to let the RIP in your printer handle trapping.

Ⓓ Flip Choose Horizontal, Vertical, or Horizontal and Vertical to mirror the image. Choose None to leave the Flip option off.

Ⓔ Negative Inverts the page.

Ⓕ Screening When printing separations, defines the halftone frequency and screen angle for the inks shown in the Inks list. These numbers are defined by the chosen printer's PPD.

Ⓖ Inks Displays the four process inks and any defined spot inks as well as their halftone frequency and screen angle. Override the optimized screen settings for any ink by selecting it and entering a new value in the Frequency and Angle fields. Click the printer icon to the left of an ink name to tell InDesign not to print that separation.

Ⓗ Simulate Overprint Enable this option when printing to a composite output device that does not support overprinting (such as laser printers or inkjets). The Simulate Overprint feature is helpful when proofing your documents.

Ⓘ Ink Manager Opens the Ink Manager dialog.

16.1 Printing a Document *(continued)*

The Graphics Panel

Click Graphics in the category list to display the Graphics panel of the Print dialog, or press Command+5 (Mac) or Ctrl+5 (Windows).

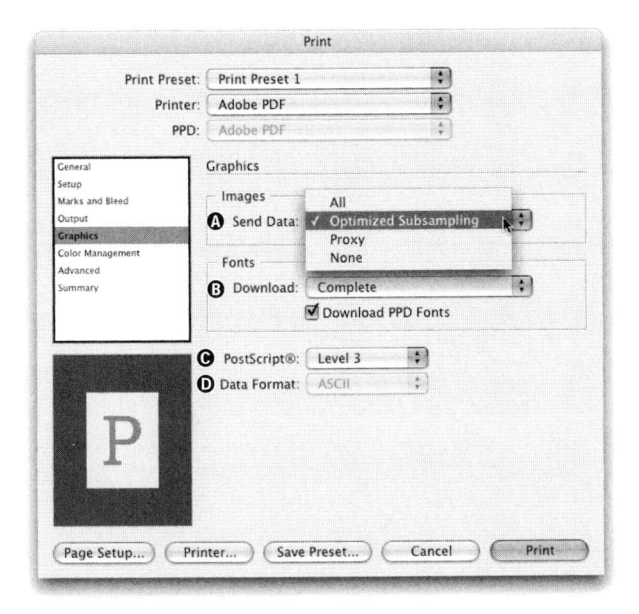

Ⓐ Send Data Choose how you want to send the image data included in your document to the printer. Choosing All sends all of the image data to the printer and can slow down the printing process. Choosing Optimized Subsampling sends only as much information as is necessary to produce a quality print, and can speed up the printing process. Choosing Proxy sends only the low-resolution preview images displayed on screen using Typical Display Performance. Choosing None sends no image data.

Ⓑ Download Choose how you want to send the font data included in your document (that is not available in the printer PPD) to the printer. Choosing None sends no data and replaces the font with the printer's default font (e.g., Courier). Choosing Subset sends only the characters required to print the document, which can accelerate printing. Choosing Complete automatically enables the Download PPD Fonts option and sends all fonts used in the document to the printer's memory. Disabling the Download PPD Fonts option sends all fonts used in the document that are not listed in the PPD. Fonts are downloaded once for each page, which adds to the time it takes to print.

Ⓒ PostScript InDesign generally reads the printer's PostScript Level from the PPD, so you do not have to choose one. Select Level 2 or Level 3 when creating a device-independent PostScript file.

Ⓓ Data Format Choose a format for sending bitmap image data. Options include Binary or ASCII.

Related Tasks

12.7 Updating Missing and Modified Links

12.8 Embedding and Unembedding Images

14.1 Using Color Settings

14.3 Using Proof Setup for Soft Proofing

Shortcuts

Print
Mac: Cmd+P
Win: Ctrl+P

Scroll through Print dialog panels
Mac: Cmd+Up/Down arrow
Win: Ctrl+Up/Down arrow

Preflight
Mac: Opt+Shift+Cmd+F
Win: Alt+Shift+Ctrl+F

Separations Preview
Mac and Win: Shift+F6

Overprint Preview
Mac: Opt+Shift+Cmd+Y
Win: Alt+Shift+Ctrl+Y

16.1 Printing a Document *(continued)*

Related Tasks

14.2 Color Managing Imported Graphics

14.4 Creating and Saving Mixed-Ink Swatches and Groups

14.6 Converting Spot Colors to Process

14.9 Applying Blend Modes

Shortcuts

Print
Mac: Cmd+P
Win: Ctrl+P

Scroll through Print dialog panels
Mac: Cmd+Up/Down arrow
Win: Ctrl+Up/Down arrow

Preflight
Mac: Opt+Shift+Cmd+F
Win: Alt+Shift+Ctrl+F

Separations Preview
Mac and Win: Shift+F6

Overprint Preview
Mac: Opt+Shift+Cmd+Y
Win: Alt+Shift+Ctrl+Y

The Color Management Panel

Click Color Management in the category list to display the Color Management panel of the Print dialog, or press Command+6 (Mac) or Ctrl+6 (Windows).

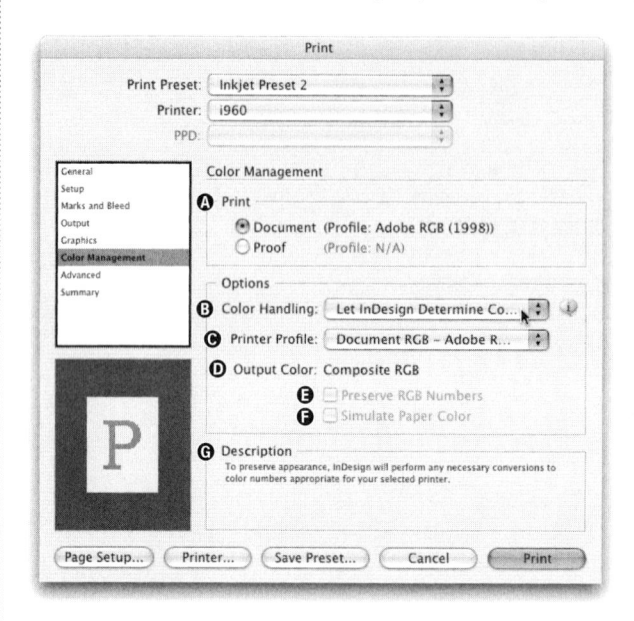

- **A Print** Prints a color-managed document or a color-managed proof.
- **B Color Handling** Choose whether to handle color management in the application or in the output device. Options include Let InDesign Determine Colors or PostScript Printer Determines Colors.
- **C Printer Profile** Choose a valid profile for your printer and output media.
- **D Output Color** Displays the name of the option selected in the Output panel of the Print dialog.
- **E Preserve RGB/CMYK Numbers** Sends color numbers for objects (such as placed graphics) directly to the printer. Deselect to allow InDesign to convert the color numbers to the color space of the printer. Preserving numbers is recommended for proofing CMYK documents; do not preserve numbers when printing RGB documents.
- **F Simulate Paper Color** Simulates how colors will print on the output media of a selected device.
- **G Description** Displays a description for each available option in the Color Management panel. Position the pointer over a heading to view the description.

356

16.1 Printing a Document *(continued)*

The Advanced Panel

Click Advanced in the category list to display the Advanced panel of the Print dialog, or press Command+7 (Mac) or Ctrl+7 (Windows).

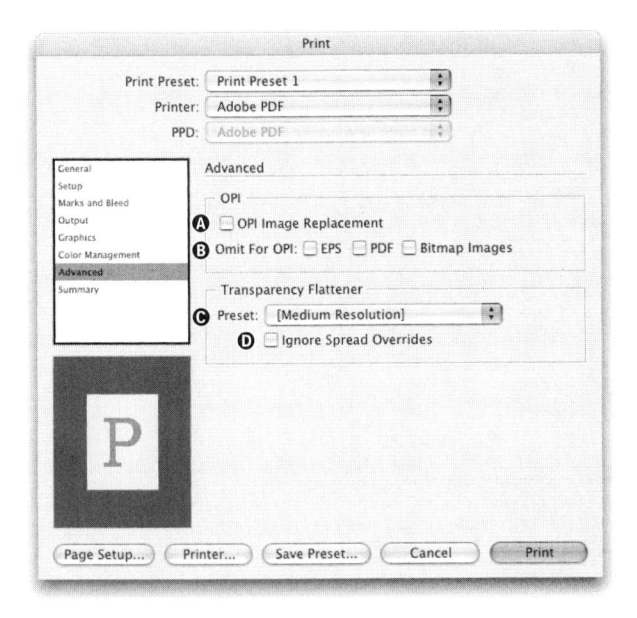

Ⓐ OPI Image Replacement Allows InDesign to act as an OPI server when printing.

Ⓑ Omit for OPI Choose which images to replace with low-res proxy OPI links by checking EPS, PDF, and/or Bitmap Images. InDesign must have access to the drive containing high-res versions of the images in order to link to them.

Ⓒ Preset Choose a default Flattener setting for the print job.

Ⓓ Ignore Spread Overrides Tells InDesign to disregard any Transparency Flattener settings applied using the Pages palette override option.

Related Tasks

15.1 Preflighting Fonts

15.2 Preflighting Links and Images

15.3 Preflighting Colors and Inks

16.2 Creating Transparency Flattener Presets

Shortcuts

Print
Mac: Cmd+P
Win: Ctrl+P

Scroll through Print dialog panels
Mac: Cmd+Up/Down arrow
Win: Ctrl+Up/Down arrow

Preflight
Mac: Opt+Shift+Cmd+F
Win: Alt+Shift+Ctrl+F

Separations Preview
Mac and Win: Shift+F6

Overprint Preview
Mac: Opt+Shift+Cmd+Y
Win: Alt+Shift+Ctrl+Y

Tips

The Transparency Flattener does not work with transparent DCS files and OPI workflows.

16.1 Printing a Document *(continued)*

Related Tasks

15.4 Preflighting Print Settings

18.7 Preflighting, Printing, and Exporting Books

Shortcuts

Print
Mac: Cmd+P
Win: Ctrl+P

Scroll through Print dialog panels
Mac: Cmd+Up/Down arrow
Win: Ctrl+Up/Down arrow

Preflight
Mac: Opt+Shift+Cmd+F
Win: Alt+Shift+Ctrl+F

Separations Preview
Mac and Win: Shift+F6

Overprint Preview
Mac: Opt+Shift+Cmd+Y
Win: Alt+Shift+Ctrl+Y

Tips

To print from the beginning of a document to a specific page, enter the page number preceded by a dash (e.g., –5) in the Range field of the General panel.

The Transparency Flattener does not work with transparent DCS files and OPI workflows.

The Summary Panel

Click Summary in the category list to display the Summary panel of the Print dialog, or press Command+8 (Mac) or Ctrl+8 (Windows).

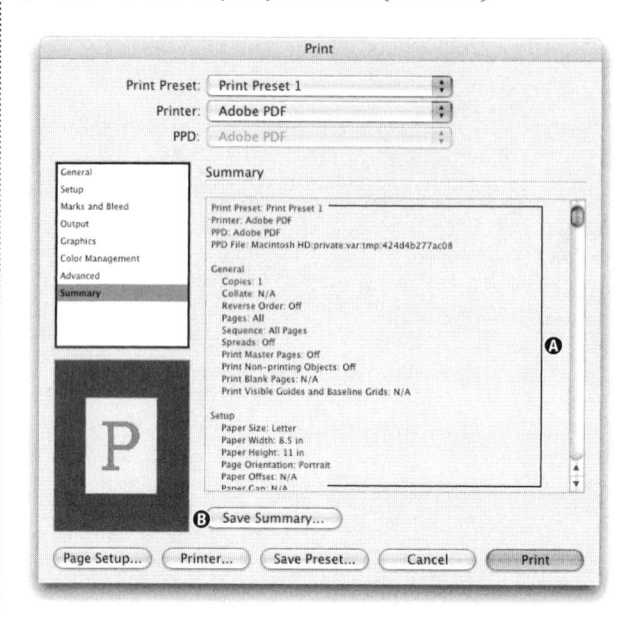

Ⓐ Summary Displays a summary of every setting applied in all panels of the Print dialog.

Ⓑ Save Summary Saves the Summary list as a text file.

CREATING A POSTSCRIPT FILE

You can save a PostScript file to disk using the Print dialog. To do so, choose PostScript File from the Printer pop-up menu. You must also choose a printer description, or Device Independent from the PPD menu. You can then enter preferred output settings in the various panels of the Print dialog and click Save.

16.2 Creating Transparency Flattener Presets

Any time you adjust an object's opacity level, apply a blend mode, import a transparent graphic, or apply a drop shadow or feather effect, you are applying transparency. InDesign lets you know which pages in the document contain transparency by displaying a checkerboard pattern in each page's icon in the Pages palette.

To print transparent objects, they must be flattened so that PostScript language can understand them. At output time, InDesign applies the transparency flattener presets that you choose. You can print using one of the noneditable default settings (Low, Medium, or High Resolution), or create and apply a custom preset.

To create a custom Flattener preset, choose Edit > Transparency Flattener Presets from the main menu. Then click New in the Transparency Flattener Presets dialog. InDesign opens the Transparency Flattener Preset Options dialog.

Ⓐ Name Enter a name for the flattener preset.

Ⓑ Raster/Vector Balance Push the slider all the way to the left to rasterize all images and print faster. Push the slider to the right to maintain vectors but print slower.

Ⓒ Line Art And Text Resolution Enter a ppi value for rasterizing vector objects. The value you enter should be applicable to the chosen output media and device (e.g., 800 ppi for newsprint, 1600 ppi for glossy stock).

Ⓓ Gradient And Mesh Resolution Enter a ppi value for rasterizing transparent objects such as drop shadows, feathers, and gradients. Generally, desktop printers require no more than 100 ppi, and high-res output devices require no more than 200 ppi.

Ⓔ Convert All Text To Outlines For some output devices (but generally not high-res printers) transparent text appears bolder than the rest of the text in the document when printed. When this happens, check this option to make all text items (transparent and opaque) output the same. With this option enabled, the flattener converts all text to outlines at print time.

Ⓕ Convert All Strokes To Outlines Thin lines can also print bolder than the rest of the lines in the document when transparency is applied. Check this option to make all lines (transparent and opaque) output the same. With this option enabled, the flattener converts all strokes to outlines at print time.

Ⓖ Clip Complex Regions Prevents any unwanted lines from printing when rasterizing vectors. Enabling this option produces a higher-quality print, but increases the amount of time it takes to output.

Related Tasks

2.4 Edit Menu
4.13 Output Palettes
5.16 Print Presets
15.2 Preflighting Links and Images
15.3 Preflighting Colors and Inks
15.4 Preflighting Print Settings

Shortcuts

Print
Mac: Cmd+P
Win: Ctrl+P

Scroll through Print dialog panels
Mac: Cmd+Up/Down arrow
Win: Ctrl+Up/Down arrow

Preflight
Mac: Opt+Shift+Cmd+F
Win: Alt+Shift+Ctrl+F

Separations Preview
Mac and Win: Shift+F6

Overprint Preview
Mac: Opt+Shift+Cmd+Y
Win: Alt+Shift+Ctrl+Y

Tip

You can base a custom flattener preset on one of the default presets. Select the default preset from the Transparency Flattener Presets dialog and click the New button. The default settings appear in the Transparency Flattener Preset Options dialog that launches.

16.3 Creating and Assigning Trap Presets

Related Tasks

4.13 Output Palettes
5.16 Print Presets
15.4 Preflighting Print Settings

Shortcuts

Print
Mac: Cmd+P
Win: Ctrl+P

Scroll through Print dialog panels
Mac: Cmd+Up/Down arrow
Win: Ctrl+Up/Down arrow

Preflight
Mac: Opt+Shift+Cmd+F
Win: Alt+Shift+Ctrl+F

Separations Preview
Mac and Win: Shift+F6

Overprint Preview
Mac: Opt+Shift+Cmd+Y
Win: Alt+Shift+Ctrl+Y

Tip

You cannot adjust the trap preset for individual objects on a page.

The default trap settings in InDesign are great for most print jobs; however, certain print jobs may require that you assign a custom trap preset to a specific page range, or to the entire document.

You can create a trapping preset using the Trap Presets palette. To open the palette, choose Window > Output > Trap Presets. To access the New Trap Preset dialog, choose New Preset from the palette menu.

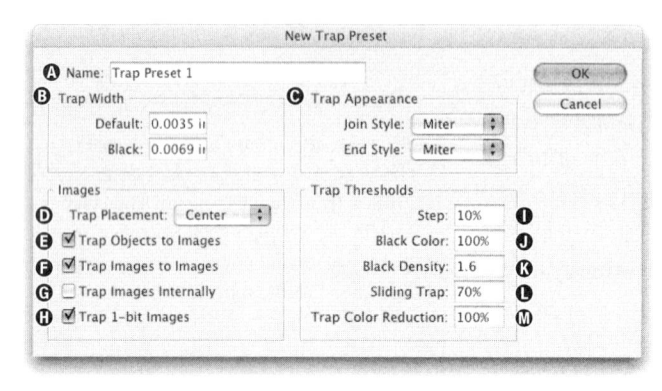

Ⓐ Name Enter a name for the trap preset.

Ⓑ Trap Width Sets the trap width for all inks (except solid black). Enter a value in the Black field to set the trap width for solid black.

Ⓒ Trap Appearance Choose Miter, Round, or Bevel from the Join Style menu to define how corner points in trap segments appear. Choose Miter or Overlap from the End Style menu to define how trap line end points appear.

Ⓓ Trap Placement Center applies a trap that expands uniformly on either side of the image boundary. Choke applies a trap that extends into the image area. Neutral Density applies a trap based on the ink neutral density of the neighboring colors. Spread bleeds the colors from the image into the adjacent InDesign object.

Ⓔ Trap Objects To Images Automatically applies trapping to InDesign objects that are adjacent to imported images. The chosen Trap Placement option is applied.

Ⓕ Trap Images To Images Automatically applies trapping to imported images that are adjacent to each other.

Ⓖ Trap Images Internally Automatically applies in-RIP trapping to color areas inside imported bitmap images (such as screen shots).

Ⓗ Trap 1-bit Images Automatically applies trapping to black-and-white images that are adjacent to InDesign objects.

Ⓘ Step Sets the percentage of difference required between each color element in order to activate automatic trapping.

Ⓙ Black Color Sets the percentage of black that must be present in a color before applying Black Trap Width.

Ⓚ Black Density Sets the level of black ink neutral density required in order to activate automatic trapping.

Ⓛ Sliding Trap Defines at what percentage a trap changes from a spread to a centerline trap, or a centerline trap to a choke.

Ⓜ Trap Color Reduction Defines the colors InDesign creates as it builds traps.

CHAPTER **17**

Exporting

NOWADAYS, CREATING A LAYOUT solely for print isn't enough. As a graphic designer, you're expected to also create a PDF version. Not only do PDFs provide an easy and practical way to send proofs to your clients, but you can also post a PDF of a finalized layout for online download and reach a much larger audience.

InDesign also allows you to create interactive PDFs that include hyperlinks, bookmarks, buttons, and even movie and sound files. In this chapter, we'll show you how to export PDFs of all types, as well as how to export as EPS, JPEG, and XML.

- 17.1 **Exporting as Adobe PDF**

    The Export Adobe PDF General Panel

    The Export Adobe PDF Compression Panel

    The Export Adobe PDF Marks And Bleeds Panel

    The Export Adobe PDF Output Panel

    The Export Adobe PDF Advanced Panel

    The Export Adobe PDF Security Panel

    The Export Adobe PDF Summary Panel

- 17.2 **Embedding PDF Hyperlinks**
- 17.3 **Embedding Movies and Sound in PDFs**
- 17.4 **Exporting as EPS**
- 17.5 **Exporting as JPEG**
- 17.6 **Exporting as XML**

17.1 Exporting as Adobe PDF

Related Tasks

2.3 File Menu
3.18 Button Tool
4.3 Attributes Palette
4.8 Interactive Palettes

Shortcuts

Export
Mac: Cmd+E
Win: Ctrl+E

Show Structure
Mac: Opt+Cmd+1
Win: Alt+Ctrl+1

Tips

You can access the Export dialog by clicking the Export Adobe PDF button in the PageMaker toolbar.

To export from the beginning of a document to a specific page, enter the page number preceded by a dash (e.g., –5) in the Pages Range field of the General panel.

To access the Export dialog, choose File > Export. Enter a name for the PDF and specify where you'd like to save it on your system. At the bottom of the dialog, choose Adobe PDF from the Format menu (Mac) or the Save As Type menu (Windows) and click Save.

InDesign launches the Export Adobe PDF dialog, which contains seven panels: General, Compression, Marks And Bleeds, Output, Advanced, Security, and Summary. You can display any of these panels in the dialog by clicking its name in the category list on the left.

Whenever you export a document as Adobe PDF for the first time, inspect each panel of the dialog to make sure the proper settings are applied. Once the dialog setup is complete, you can save it as an Adobe PDF Preset to use again and again, without having to reenter any settings. Click the Save Preset button, enter a name for the setup in the Save Preset dialog, and click OK to add the preset to the Adobe PDF Preset menu.

If you'd like to use a default or custom Adobe PDF Preset, choose it from the Adobe PDF Preset menu located at the top of the dialog. To export as PDF/X, choose one of the PDF/X presets or select a PDF/X option from the Standard menu. You can also choose to make the PDF compatible with older versions of Acrobat by selecting an option (versions 4 through 7) from the Compatibility menu.

When you're ready to export the document using the applied settings, click Export.

The Export Adobe PDF General Panel

The General panel is the first to appear when the Export Adobe PDF dialog opens. You can access it by clicking General in the category list.

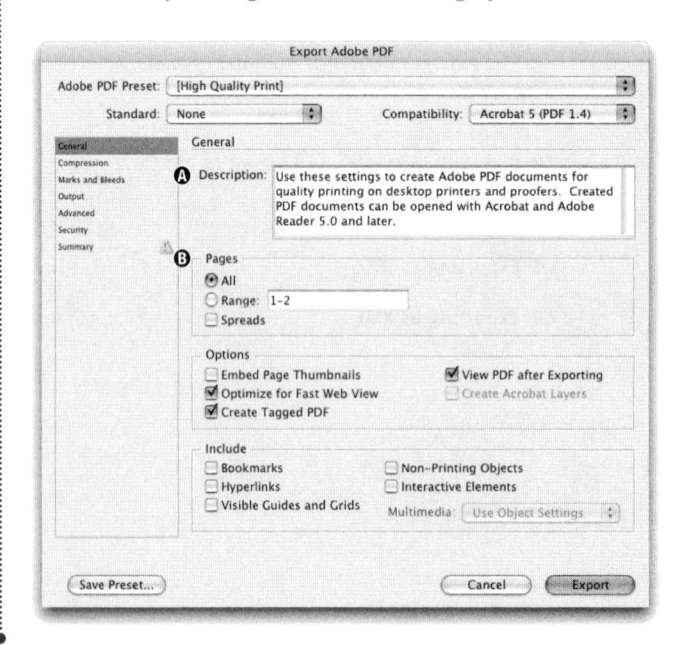

A Description Summary for each preset that is selected from the Adobe PDF Preset menu.

B Pages Export all the pages or a range of specific pages. In the Range field, enter the page numbers in numerical order separated by either commas (to indicate individual pages) or dashes (to indicate a series of pages).

17.1 Exporting as Adobe PDF *(continued)*

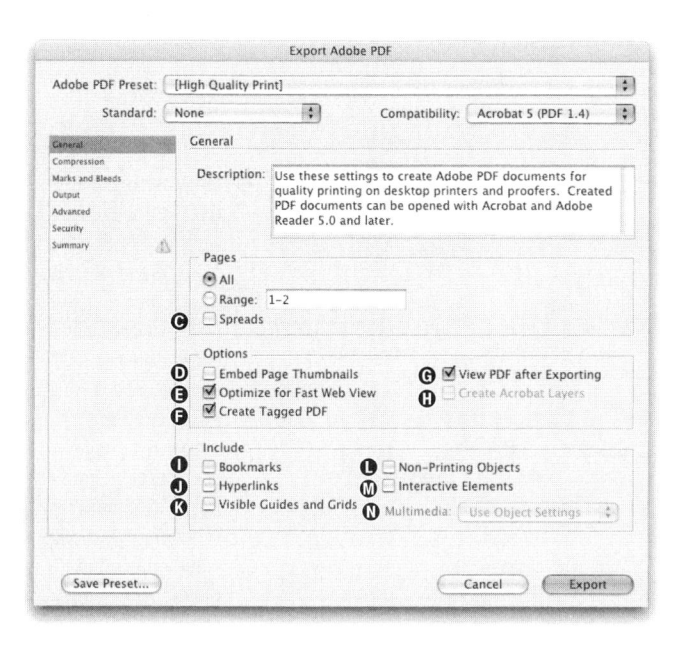

Ⓒ Spreads Exports each spread on a single PDF page.

Ⓓ Embed Page Thumbnails Creates a preview image for each page or spread you export. Embedding thumbnails increases the PDF file size.

Ⓔ Optimize For Fast Web View Check when creating PDFs for online viewing; it reduces the file size of the PDF without changing the appearance of the pages. It also creates PDFs that can be downloaded one page at a time from a web server, rather than all at once.

Ⓕ Create Tagged PDF Automatically adds an XML structure to a generated PDF by tagging elements to each story in the document. To reduce file size, tags can be compressed when exporting PDFs compatible with Acrobat 6 (PDF 1.5) or 7 (PDF 1.6).

Ⓖ View PDF After Exporting Opens the PDF in Acrobat or Reader immediately after exporting.

Ⓗ Create Acrobat Layers Converts all InDesign document layers (including hidden layers) into Acrobat layers. Any added printer's marks are placed on a separate layer as well. Only available when exporting PDFs compatible with Acrobat 6 (PDF 1.5) or 7 (PDF 1.6).

Ⓘ Bookmarks Adds any bookmarks created using the Bookmarks palette or the table of contents feature to the PDF.

Ⓙ Hyperlinks Adds any hyperlinks created using the Hyperlinks palette to the PDF; also adds PDF hyperlinks to any table of contents or index created in InDesign.

Ⓚ Visible Guides And Grids Exports any visible margin guides, page guides, and baseline grids, but does not export the document grid.

Ⓛ Non-Printing Objects Overrides the Attributes palette Nonprinting checkbox and exports every object placed on the specified pages.

Ⓜ Interactive Elements Includes any buttons, movies, or sounds contained in the document in the exported PDF.

Ⓝ Multimedia When including interactive elements, choose to embed them all in the PDF, link them all to disk, or use object-level settings. Link All and Embed All options override existing object-level settings.

Related Tasks

4.9 Layers Palette
4.13 Output Palettes
4.14 PageMaker Toolbar
4.17 Swatches Palette

Shortcuts

Export
Mac: Cmd+E
Win: Ctrl+E

Show Structure
Mac: Opt+Cmd+1
Win: Alt+Ctrl+1

Tip

To export from a specific page to the end of the document, enter the page number followed by a dash (e.g., 5 –) in the Pages Range field of the General panel.

17.1 Exporting as Adobe PDF (continued)

Related Tasks

4.18 Tags Palette
5.17 Adobe PDF Presets

Shortcuts

Export
Mac: Cmd+E
Win: Ctrl+E

Show Structure
Mac: Opt+Cmd+1
Win: Alt+Ctrl+1

The Export Adobe PDF Compression Panel

Click Compression in the category list to display the Compression panel of the Export Adobe PDF dialog.

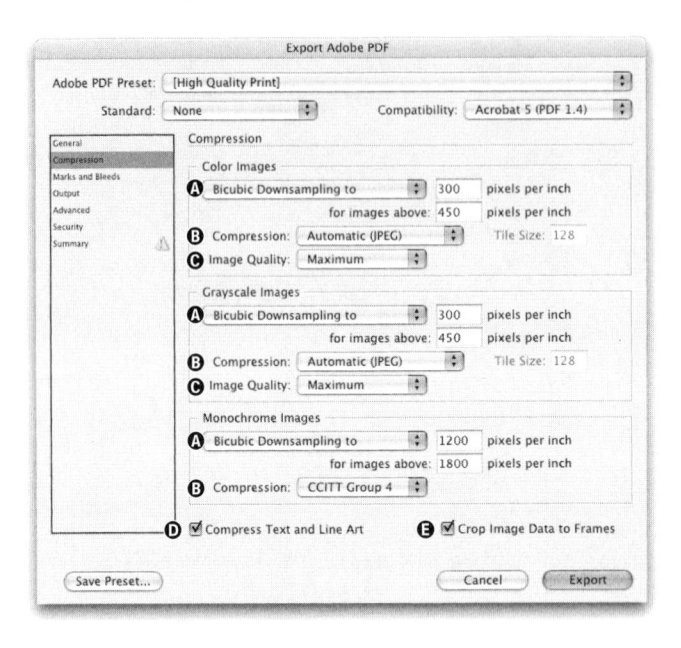

Ⓐ Downsampling lists Choose a downsampling option for color, grayscale, and monochrome images: Do Not Downsample maintains original resolution. Average Downsampling decreases image resolution by converting an area of pixels (specified by the ppi value entered in the neighboring Downsampling To and For Images Above fields) into one large pixel based on the *average value* of all pixels in the area. Subsampling converts the specified pixel area into one large pixel based on a *single pixel* located in the center, resulting in faster conversion times but poorer image results. Bicubic Downsampling uses a more precise *weighted average;* this provides the smoothest tonal gradations but takes longest to convert.

Ⓑ Compression lists Choose a compression option for color, grayscale, and monochrome images: None leaves images uncompressed. The Automatic (JPEG) and Automatic (JPEG 2000) options let InDesign determine the best quality but are only available when exporting PDFs compatible with Acrobat 6 (PDF 1.5) or 7 (PDF 1.6). The JPEG option applies a *lossy* compression (*loss* of image data), which reduces image quality while decreasing file size and conversion time. ZIP compression is lossless and works best with images containing lots of solid color areas and sharp edges (such as screen captures). The JPEG 2000 option compresses images to an even smaller size and produces a higher-quality image, but is only available when exporting PDFs compatible with Acrobat 6 (PDF 1.5) or 7 (PDF 1.6).

CCITT Group 4 compression works best with most monochrome images. CCITT Group 3 applies compression to monochrome images one row at a time. Run Length compression works best with images that contain large areas of solid black or white.

Ⓒ Image Quality lists The amount of JPEG or JPEG 2000 compression that is applied: Minimum, Low, Medium, High, and Maximum.

Ⓓ Compress Text And Line Art Applies compression to all text and paths in the document.

Ⓔ Crop Image Data To Frames Exports only the data for the visible areas of cropped images in the document; can greatly reduce the file size of the exported PDF.

17.1 Exporting as Adobe PDF *(continued)*

The Export Adobe PDF Marks And Bleeds Panel

Click Marks And Bleeds in the category list to display the Marks And Bleeds panel of the Export Adobe PDF dialog.

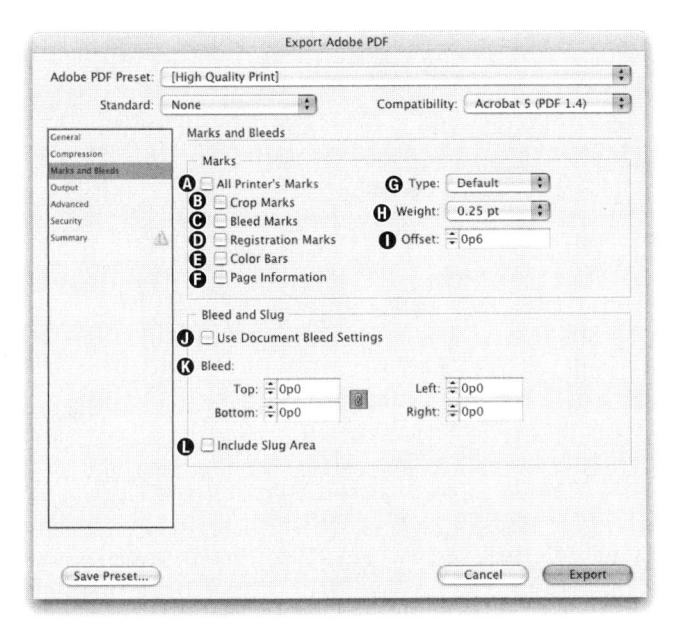

Related Tasks

9.13 Font Overview
9.14 Find/Replace Missing Fonts

Shortcuts

Export
Mac: Cmd+E
Win: Ctrl+E

Show Structure
Mac: Opt+Cmd+1
Win: Alt+Ctrl+1

Ⓐ All Printer's Marks Includes all printer's marks.

Ⓑ Crop Marks Includes lines that define the page area (also referred to as "trim marks").

Ⓒ Bleed Marks Includes lines that define the bleed area.

Ⓓ Registration Marks Includes small targets around the edge of each page; used for lining up color separations.

Ⓔ Color Bars Includes small square color samples outside the bleed area; used for matching colors on press.

Ⓕ Page Information Includes the filename and publication date on every page of the document.

Ⓖ Type Intended for selecting additional sets of printer's marks created by other developers; however, InDesign CS2 only ships with one Default set.

Ⓗ Weight Change the stroke weight of the printer's marks by choosing 0.125 pt, 0.25 pt, or 0.50 pt from the menu.

Ⓘ Offset Defines how far from the page edge the printer's marks should appear.

Ⓙ Use Document Bleed Settings Applies the Bleed settings entered in the Document Setup dialog.

Ⓚ Bleed Defines the amount of bleed area off the top, bottom, left, and right edges of the page. Click the chain link icon to make all the settings the same.

Ⓛ Include Slug Area Includes the slug area defined in the Document Setup dialog.

17.1 Exporting as Adobe PDF *(continued)*

Related Tasks

14.1 Using Color Settings

14.2 Color-Managing Imported Graphics

14.4 Creating and Saving Mixed-Ink Swatches and Groups

14.8 Changing an Object's Opacity Level

Shortcuts

Export
Mac: Cmd+E
Win: Ctrl+E

Show Structure
Mac: Opt+Cmd+1
Win: Alt+Ctrl+1

The Export Adobe PDF Output Panel

Click Output in the category list to display the Output panel of the Export Adobe PDF dialog.

Ⓐ Color Conversion Choose how to convert process colors in the PDF: No Color Conversion leaves the color data as is. Convert To Destination converts the document colors to the profile selected in the Destination menu below. Convert To Destination (Preserve Numbers) only converts document colors with color spaces or embedded profiles that differ from the Destination profile. Colors without embedded profiles and native objects (such as type) are not converted. The Convert To Destination (Preserve Numbers) option is only available when color management is enabled.

Ⓑ Destination Choose a profile for the target output device (such as a monitor or inkjet printer). InDesign converts the document's source profile (defined in the Working Spaces section of the Color Settings dialog) to that profile.

Ⓒ Profile Inclusion Policy Choose whether or not to embed any color profiles in the PDF. Options vary depending on which Color Conversion setting is chosen, whether color management is enabled, and if one of the PDF/X standards is selected.

Ⓓ Simulate Overprint Creates a simulated overprint PDF soft proof of the document, viewable in Acrobat 4. This option is only available when choosing Convert Colors To Destination or Convert Colors To Destination (Preserve Numbers) from the Color Conversion menu, and Acrobat 4 from the Compatibility menu.

Ⓔ Ink Manager Opens the Ink Manager dialog, where you can manage spot color conversion.

Ⓕ Output Intent Profile Name This menu and the field below are only available when exporting a PDF/X file. When color management is disabled, the menu is limited to profiles that match the destination profile's color space. When color management is on, the output intent profile matches the destination profile.

Ⓖ Output Condition Name Enter a description of the output condition. Any text entered is stored in the PDF/X output file.

Ⓗ Description Displays a description for each available option in the Output panel. Position the pointer over a heading to view the description.

17.1 Exporting as Adobe PDF *(continued)*

The Export Adobe PDF Advanced Panel

Click Advanced in the category list to display the Advanced panel of the Export Adobe PDF dialog.

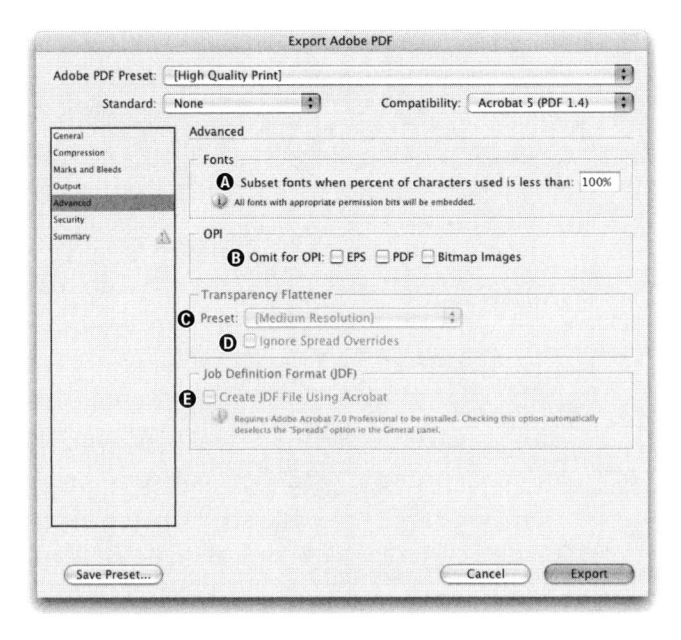

Ⓐ Subset Fonts When Percent Of Characters Used Is Less Than Sets the threshold (in percentage of characters used in the document) for embedding complete fonts in the PDF. When the specified percentage is exceeded, InDesign embeds the complete font, which adds to the file size.

Ⓑ Omit For OPI Choose which types of images, if any, to replace with low-res proxy OPI links by checking EPS, PDF, and/or Bitmap Images. InDesign must have access to the drive containing high-res versions of the images in order to link to them.

Ⓒ Transparency Flattener Preset Choose a Flattener setting for the PDF.

Ⓓ Ignore Spread Overrides Tells InDesign to disregard any Transparency Flattener settings applied using the Pages palette override option.

Ⓔ Create JDF File Using Acrobat Launches Acrobat 7.0 Professional (must be previously installed on your system) and creates a Job Definition Format file.

Related Tasks

14.9 Applying Blend Modes
14.10 Adding Drop Shadows
14.11 Feathering
4.20 Transparency Palette
16.2 Creating Transparency Flattener Presets

Shortcuts

Export
Mac: Cmd+E
Win: Ctrl+E

Show Structure
Mac: Opt+Cmd+1
Win: Alt+Ctrl+1

Drop Shadow
Mac: Opt+Cmd+M
Win: Alt+Ctrl+M

Transparency Palette
Mac and Win: Shift+F10

Tip

The Transparency Flattener does not work with transparent DCS files and OPI workflows.

17.1 Exporting as Adobe PDF *(continued)*

Related Tasks

14.12 Importing Transparent TIFFs

17.2 Embedding PDF Hyperlinks

Shortcuts

Export
Mac: Cmd+E
Win: Ctrl+E

Show Structure
Mac: Opt+Cmd+1
Win: Alt+Ctrl+1

Tips

You can access the Export dialog by clicking the Export Adobe PDF button in the PageMaker toolbar.

To export from a specific page to the end of the document, enter the page number followed by a dash (e.g., 5 –) in the Pages Range field of the General panel.

The Export Adobe PDF Security Panel

Click Security in the category list to display the Security panel of the Export Adobe PDF dialog.

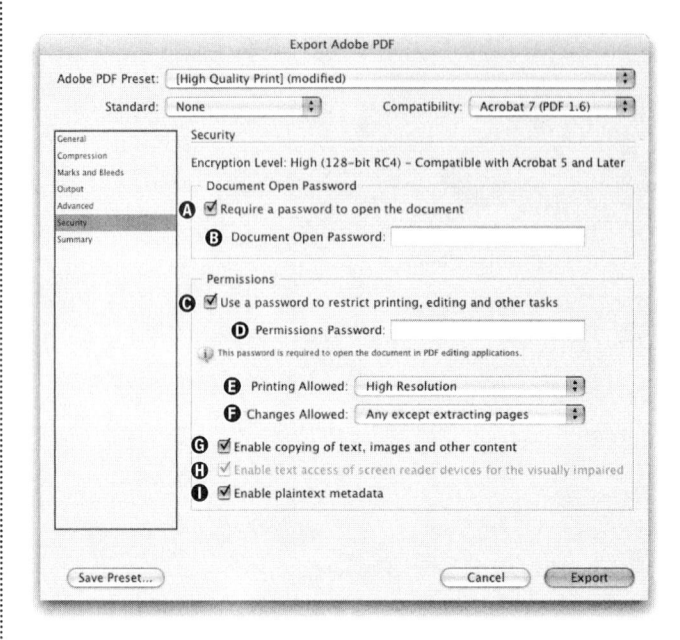

- **Ⓐ Require A Password To Open The Document** Enables document password protection, requiring that users enter a password to open the PDF.
- **Ⓑ Document Open Password** Enter the password required to open the PDF.
- **Ⓒ Use A Password To Restrict Printing, Editing And Other Tasks** Enables permissions password protection, requiring that users enter a password to print, make changes to, or copy content from the PDF (depending on which options you select from the menus below).
- **Ⓓ Permissions Password** Enter the permissions password required to print, make changes to, or copy content from the PDF (depending on which options you select from the menus below).
- **Ⓔ Printing Allowed** Choose the print resolution allowed once the password is entered. Options include None (to prohibit printing), Low Resolution, and High Resolution. If Acrobat 4 is selected in the Compatibility field, Low Resolution is not an option.
- **Ⓕ Changes Allowed** Choose the editing actions allowed once the password is entered: None (to prohibit editing); Inserting, Deleting, And Rotating Pages; Filling In Form Fields And Signing; Commenting, Filling In Form Fields, And Signing; and Any Except Extracting Pages. If Acrobat 4 is selected in the Compatibility field, Low Resolution is not an option.
- **Ⓖ Enable Copying Of Text, Images And Other Content** Allows users to copy and extract PDF content.
- **Ⓗ Enable Text Access Of Screen Reader Devices For The Visually Impaired** Allows users to access PDF content using tools for the visually impaired.
- **Ⓘ Enable Plaintext Metadata** Allows search engines to access metadata stored in the PDF.

17.1 Exporting as Adobe PDF *(continued)*

The Export Adobe PDF Summary Panel

Click Summary in the category list to display the Summary panel of the Export Adobe PDF dialog.

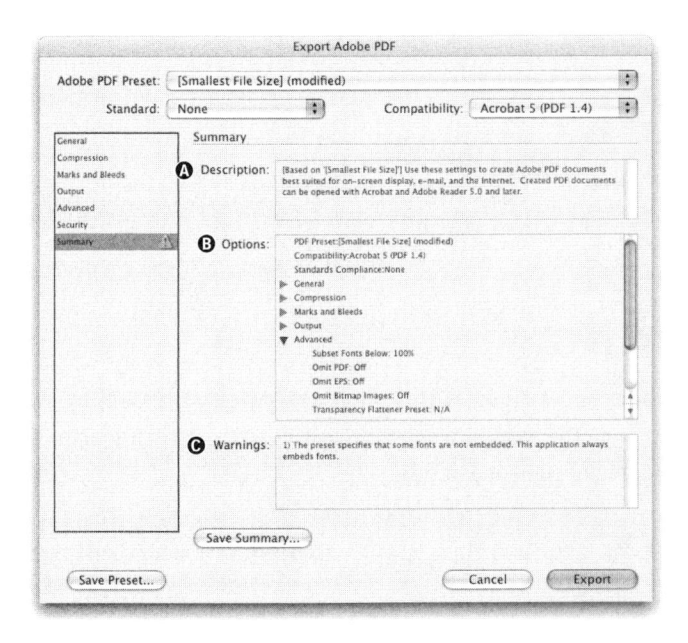

Ⓐ Description Displays a description for each preset selected from the Adobe PDF Preset menu.

Ⓑ Options Displays a summary of settings applied in all panels of the Export Adobe PDF dialog.

Ⓒ Warnings Displays explanatory text when the settings of a PDF preset cannot be honored.

Related Tasks

17.3 Embedding Movies and Sound in PDFs

18.4 Building a Table of Contents

18.7 Preflighting, Printing, and Exporting Books

Shortcuts

Drop Shadow
Mac: Opt+Cmd+M
Win: Alt+Ctrl+M

Transparency Palette
Mac and Win:
Shift+F10

Tips

To export from the beginning of a document to a specific page, enter the page number preceded by a dash (e.g., –5) in the Pages Range field of the General panel.

The Transparency Flattener does not work with transparent DCS files and OPI workflows.

17.2 Embedding PDF Hyperlinks

Related Tasks

2.3	File Menu
3.18	Button Tool
4.8	Interactive Palettes
4.13	Output Palettes

Using the Hyperlinks palette, you can add interactive web, e-mail, page, and text anchor links to your exported PDFs. The palette displays a list of hyperlink sources that you've created (not destinations). When adding hyperlinks to a document, create destinations first, before applying them to a hyperlink source. To do so, choose New Hyperlink Destination from the Hyperlinks palette menu.

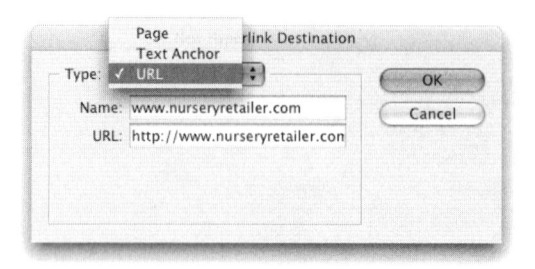

In the New Hyperlink Destination dialog that opens, choose a destination type from the Type menu. Enter a name for it (and URL address if creating a URL hyperlink) and click OK.

In the document, select an object or text item as the source and click the Create New Hyperlink button at the bottom of the palette. When the dialog appears, enter a source name and choose the destination document and type.

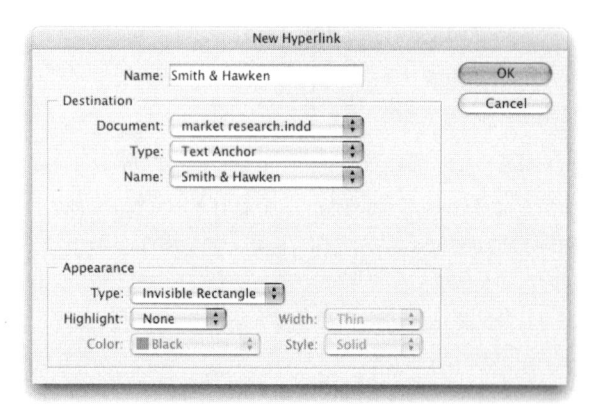

You can choose one of your preset destinations from the Name menu. If you did not save your destination ahead of time when creating a hyperlink to a page or a URL (but not a text anchor), choose Unnamed from the Name menu and enter the page number or URL address in the field. At the bottom of the dialog, enter your preferred appearance settings for the hyperlink.

17.2 Embedding PDF Hyperlinks *(continued)*

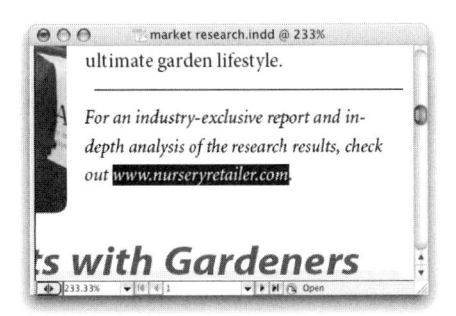

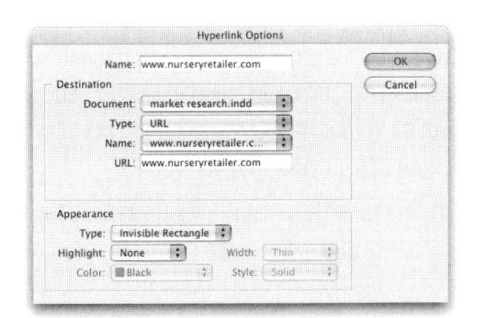

To create a basic URL link, highlight the typed URL in the document with the Type tool and choose New Hyperlink From URL from the Hyperlinks palette menu. InDesign automatically adds the URL destination to the link and uses the URL as the source name that appears in the palette. When exporting the document, be sure and check the Include Hyperlinks option in the Export Adobe PDF dialog.

Related Tasks

5.17 Adobe PDF Presets

17.1 Exporting as Adobe PDF

17.3 Embedding Movies and Sound in PDFs

Shortcut

Export
Mac: Cmd+E
Win: Ctrl+E

Tip

To locate a hyperlink in a document (especially if its appearance is set to Invisible Rectangle), select it from the Hyperlinks palette and click the Go To Hyperlink Source button, or choose Go To Source from the palette menu.

371

17.3 Embedding Movies and Sound in PDFs

Related Tasks

2.3	File Menu
3.18	Button Tool
4.8	Interactive Palettes
4.13	Output Palettes

Shortcuts

Export
Mac: Cmd+E
Win: Ctrl+E

Place
Mac: Cmd+D
Win: Ctrl+D

InDesign CS2 allows you to embed movie and sound clips in exported PDFs. Sounds crazy, but it's true. InDesign supports WAV, AIF, and AU sound files, and QuickTime, AVI, MPEG, and SWF movie files. You must have QuickTime version 6 (or later) to embed movie and sound files in your PDFs.

You can import a movie or sound file using the Place command. When you place a movie file in the document, resize the frame to match the media. To ensure this, select the frame and choose Object > Fitting > Fit Frame To Content or Fit Content Proportionately.

You can also import a movie or sound file through the Movie/Sound Options dialog, accessible through the Object > Interactive submenu. In the Movie Options dialog, click Choose A File and then click Choose (Mac) or Browse (Windows). In the Sound Options dialog, click Choose (Mac) or Browse (Windows). InDesign launches the Choose Sound/Movie dialog, where you can browse to the file on your system. Select the movie or sound file and click Open. Again, when placing a movie file, adjust the frame size to match the imported media.

Double-click the placed movie or sound file with either Selection tool to access the Movie/Sound Options dialog. Enter the preferred settings and click Export.

These options are explained in the list on the following page.

17.3 Embedding Movies and Sound in PDFs *(continued)*

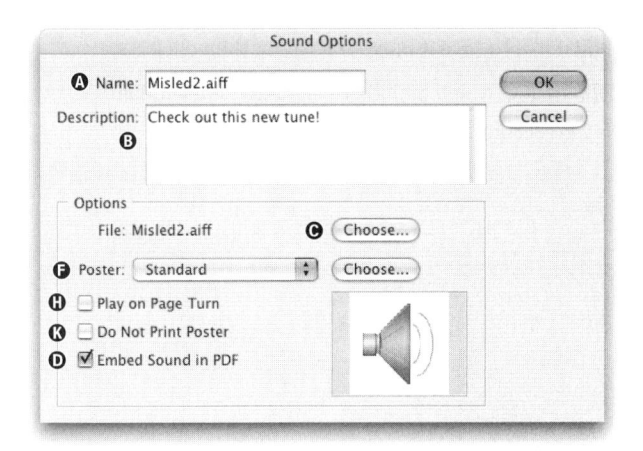

Related Tasks

5.17 Adobe PDF Presets

17.1 Exporting as Adobe PDF

17.2 Embedding PDF Hyperlinks

Shortcuts

Export
Mac: Cmd+E
Win: Ctrl+E

Place
Mac: Cmd+D
Win: Ctrl+D

Tip

InDesign does not allow you to embed MP3 files in an exported PDF.

Ⓐ Name The name of the media file—especially important when creating a button event for controlling sound.

Ⓑ Description A media file description to be displayed as a tooltip when the user hovers the mouse over the object in the PDF. The media must have a poster image displayed in order for the tooltip description to appear.

Ⓒ Choose A File/Choose button (Mac); Browse button (Windows) Browse to a media file on your system.

Ⓓ Embed Movie/Sound In PDF Embeds the media file in an exported PDF of the document. The Interactive Elements Multimedia setting located in the general panel of the Export As Adobe PDF dialog overrides this object-level setting.

Ⓔ Specify A URL Enter a URL where InDesign can stream a movie from. Click the Verify URL And Movie Size button to download the movie dimensions and match the frame to them.

Ⓕ Poster Choose a still image to display before the media file is played. Choosing None displays no image. Standard displays a default filmstrip or speaker image. Default Poster displays the first frame of the movie. Choose Image As Poster allows you to select an image to display. Choose Movie Frame As Poster allows you to select a frame from the movie. Sound Poster options are limited to None, Standard, and Choose Image As Poster.

Ⓖ Mode Controls what happens when the movie stops playing: Play Once Then Stop (the default), Play Once Stay Open (if playing in a free-floating window), or Repeat Play.

Ⓗ Play On Page Turn Plays the media file as soon as the page is displayed.

Ⓘ Show Controller During Play Displays the standard QuickTime movie controller buttons while the movie is playing. Disable this option if you've created your own buttons.

Ⓙ Floating Window Plays the movie in a floating window rather than in the PDF. Specify the size and position of the window from the menus below.

Ⓚ Do Not Print Poster Prohibits printing of the Sound poster image.

17.4 Exporting as EPS

Related Tasks

2.3	File Menu
4.13	Output Palettes
14.4	Creating and Saving Mixed-Ink Swatches and Groups
14.6	Converting Spot Colors to Process
16.1	Printing a Document
16.2	Creating Transparency Flattener Presets

Shortcut

Export
Mac: Cmd+E
Win: Ctrl+E

To access the Export dialog, choose File > Export. At the bottom of the dialog, choose EPS from the Format menu (Mac) or the Save As Type menu (Windows). Enter a name for the EPS and choose where you'd like to save it on your system, then click Save.

InDesign launches the Export EPS dialog, which includes a General panel and an Advanced panel. Enter the preferred settings in each panel and click Export.

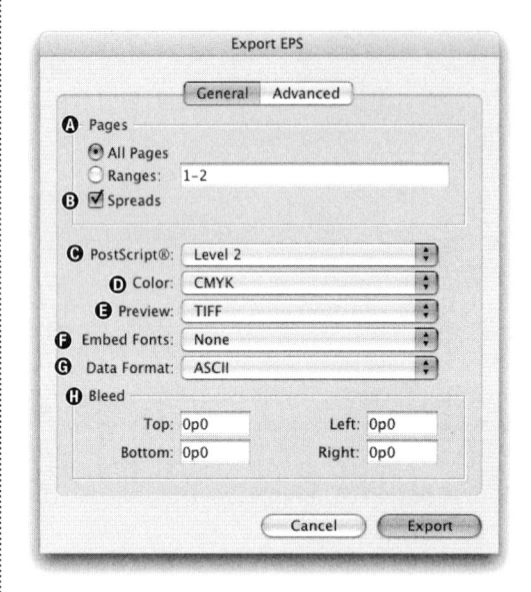

- **Ⓐ Pages** All Pages exports all the pages in the document; Ranges exports specific pages. In the Ranges field, enter the page numbers in numerical order separated by either commas (to indicate individual pages) or dashes (to indicate a series of pages).
- **Ⓑ Spreads** Exports each spread in the document on a single page.
- **Ⓒ PostScript** Choose the PostScript Level of the printer you expect to print the EPS with.
- **Ⓓ Color** Choose a color space for converting images exported to EPS: Leave Unchanged, CMYK, Gray, RGB, or PostScript Color Management.
- **Ⓔ Preview** Choose a file format for creating a low-res preview image of the EPS, to be used for onscreen display. Options: None, TIFF, and PICT (Mac only).
- **Ⓕ Embed Fonts** Choose how you would like to export the font data included in your document. Complete exports all fonts used in the document (larger file size). Subset sends only the characters required to print the document (smaller file size).
- **Ⓖ Data Format** Choose a data format for exporting. Choose ASCII if you plan to edit the EPS using a text editor; choose Binary to create a smaller, compressed file.
- **Ⓗ Bleed** Defines the amount of bleed area to include in the EPS. Enter values for bleed areas off the top, bottom, inside, and outside edges of the page.

17.4 Exporting as EPS *(continued)*

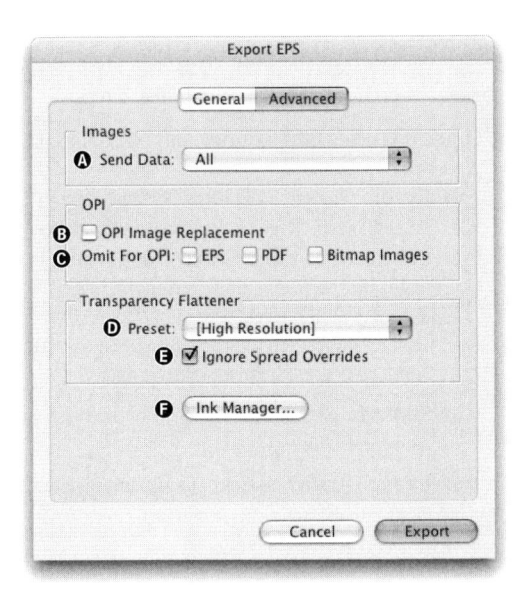

Related Tasks

16.3 Creating and Assigning Trap Presets

17.1 Exporting as Adobe PDF

17.5 Exporting as JPEG

Shortcut

Export
Mac: Cmd+E
Win: Ctrl+E

Tip

InDesign creates multiple EPS files when exporting multiple pages at a time (one for each page).

Ⓐ Send Data Choose whether to export using full resolution (All) or low-resolution (Proxy). Choose All if you intend to print the exported EPS, and Proxy if you intend to use the EPS exclusively for onscreen viewing.

Ⓑ OPI Image Replacement Allows InDesign to act as an OPI server when exporting.

Ⓒ Omit For OPI Choose which images to replace with low-res proxy OPI links by checking EPS, PDF, and/or Bitmap Images. InDesign must have access to the drive containing high-res versions of the images to link to them.

Ⓓ Transparency Flattener Preset Choose a Flattener setting for the EPS.

Ⓔ Ignore Spread Overrides Tells InDesign to disregard any Transparency Flattener settings applied using the Pages palette override option.

Ⓕ Ink Manager Opens the Ink Manager dialog.

17.5 Exporting as JPEG

Related Tasks

2.3 File Menu
17.1 Exporting as Adobe PDF
17.4 Exporting as EPS

Shortcuts

Export
Mac: Cmd+E
Win: Ctrl+E

Tip

InDesign creates multiple JPEG files when exporting multiple pages at a time (one for each page).

To access the Export dialog, choose File > Export. At the bottom of the dialog, choose JPEG from the Format menu (Mac) or the Save As Type menu (Windows). Enter a name for the JPEG and choose where you'd like to save it on your system, then click Save.

InDesign launches the Export JPEG dialog. Enter the preferred settings and click Export.

A **Export** Selection exports only the selected objects on the page. All exports all the pages in the document, and Range exports specific pages. In the Range field, enter the page numbers in numerical order separated by either commas (to indicate individual pages) or dashes (to indicate a series of pages).

B **Spreads** Exports each spread in the document on a single page.

C **Image Quality** Exports in Maximum, High, Medium, or Low image quality.

D **Format Method** Progressive displays the image in stages from low to high resolution; Baseline does not.

EXPORTING AS SVG

You can export InDesign pages or selected objects to SVG format (Scalable Vector Graphics). Choose File > Export, and at the bottom of the dialog, choose SVG or SVG Compressed from the Format menu (Mac) or Save As Type menu (Windows). Enter a name for the SVG file and choose where you'd like to save it on your system, then click Save. InDesign launches the SVG Options dialog. For more information about the different settings in the dialog, hover your mouse over each heading and refer to the description below. Once you've entered your preferred settings, click Export. You can then open the SVG file in a compatible program for editing.

17.6 Exporting as XML

To export a document to XML, you must first create an XML structure by tagging all of the document's page items. Once the XML structure is complete, you can access the Export dialog by choosing File > Export. At the bottom of the dialog, choose XML from the Format menu (Mac) or the Save As Type menu (Windows). Enter a name for the XML file and choose where you'd like to save it on your system, then click Save.

InDesign launches the Export XML dialog, which includes a General panel and an Images panel. Enter the preferred settings in each panel and click Export.

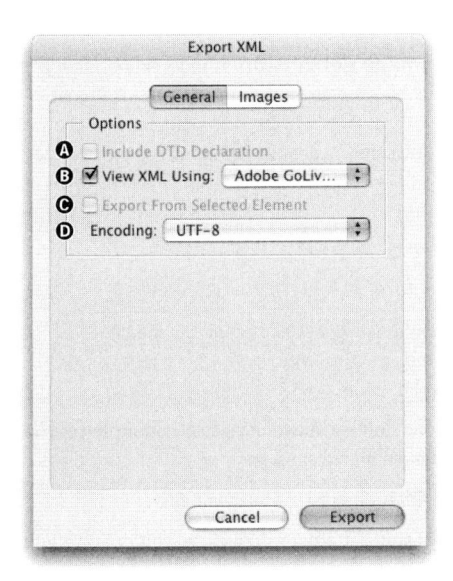

Ⓐ Include DTD Declaration Correlates a loaded DTD file with the exported XML file. You must have a DTD file loaded to enable this option.

Ⓑ View XML Using Lets you view the XML file immediately after exporting. Choose which application to open the XML file in from the menu.

Ⓒ Export From Selected Element Lets you start exporting from a selected XML element in the document. You must have an XML element selected to enable this option.

Ⓓ Encoding Choose an encoding format from the menu: UTF-8 (8-bit), UTF-16 (16-bit), and Shift-JIS (for Japanese characters).

Related Tasks

2.3	File Menu
4.18	Tags Palette
9.5	Importing XML
15.6	Packaging for GoLive
17.1	Exporting as Adobe PDF

Shortcuts

Export
Mac: Cmd+E
Win: Ctrl+E

Show Structure
Mac: Opt+Cmd+1
Win: Alt+Ctrl+1

17.6 Exporting as XML *(continued)*

Related Tasks

2.3	File Menu
4.18	Tags Palette
9.5	Importing XML
15.6	Packaging for GoLive
17.1	Exporting as Adobe PDF

Shortcuts

Export
Mac: Cmd+E
Win: Ctrl+E

Show Structure
Mac: Opt+Cmd+1
Win: Alt+Ctrl+1

Tip

When exporting a document to XML, only the tagged content is exported, not its formatting or layout.

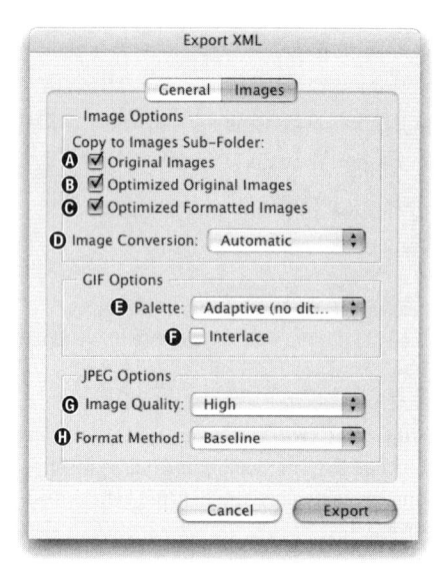

Ⓐ Original Images Places a copy of the original images in an images subfolder.

Ⓑ Optimized Original Images Optimizes the original images and places copies of them in an images subfolder.

Ⓒ Optimized Formatted Images Optimizes and copies only the original images that have applied transformations (such as cropped or rotated images).

Ⓓ Image Conversion Choose an option for converting images during export: Automatic, GIF, and JPEG. The Automatic option allows InDesign to decide which file type to convert to based on the image.

Ⓔ Palette Choose the color palette that InDesign should use when converting the image to GIF format: Adaptive (no dither), Web, System (Mac), and System (Windows). The Adaptive (no dither) option works best for images with primary solid colors.

Ⓕ Interlace Allows a preview of the image to download quickly; downloads every other line of the image with each pass rather than downloading the whole image at once.

Ⓖ Image Quality Export images in Maximum, High, Medium, or Low image quality.

Ⓗ Format Method Progressive displays the image in stages from low to high resolution; Baseline does not.

SNIPPETS

A snippet is a type of XML file used to export and import page content. Snippets are based on the InDesign Interchange format and use the .inds extension. To export snippets, select one or more objects and choose File > Export. At the bottom of the dialog, choose InDesign Snippet from the Format menu (Mac) or the Save As Type menu (Windows). Enter a name for the snippet file and choose where you'd like to save it on your system, then click Save. You can also drag the selected objects (or items selected from the Structure menu) to your desktop. A snippet file is automatically created when dragging from the document. Snippets can also be imported into an InDesign document using the Place command, or by dragging.

CHAPTER **18**

Books and Other Large Documents

INDESIGN CS2 MAKES IT easy to create and manage large documents such as books, magazines, newsletters, and catalogs. Using the Book palette, you can divide your project into small documents and manage them. The palette allows you to control automatic page numbering and applied styles for all the documents in your project. You can also preflight, print, and export one or more documents from the Book palette without even having to open them.

InDesign also contains options for creating a table of contents and an index.

- 18.1 **Creating a New Book File**
- 18.2 **Synchronizing Book Chapters**
- 18.3 **Page Numbering across Book Documents**
- 18.4 **Building a Table of Contents**
- 18.5 **Creating and Saving a TOC Style**
- 18.6 **Building an Index**
- 18.7 **Preflighting, Printing, and Exporting Books**

18.1 Creating a New Book File

Related Tasks

2.3	File Menu
2.5	Layout Menu
4.8	Interactive Palettes
4.21	Type and Tables Palettes
4.22	Book and Library Palettes
18.2	Synchronizing Book Chapters
18.3	Page Numbering across Book Documents
18.4	Building a Table of Contents
18.5	Creating and Saving a TOC Style
18.6	Building an Index

Shortcut

Open
Mac: Cmd+O
Win: Ctrl+O

Tip

You can add documents to a book by dragging them from any folder on your system into the Book palette.

To create a new Book file, choose File > New > Book. When the New Book dialog appears, enter a name for the book and choose where you'd like to save the file on your system. Click Save to display the Book palette.

Each book you create is displayed in its own Book palette. The name of the book appears in the palette tab.

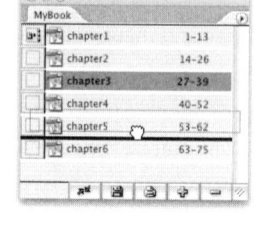

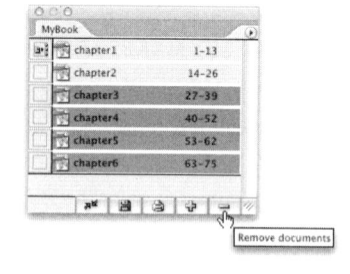

To add a document, click the Add Documents button at the bottom of the palette or choose Add Document from the palette menu. When the Add Documents dialog appears, select a document from your system and click Open. If you select a document from the palette first before clicking the Add Documents button, the added document is placed after the selection; otherwise, it is placed at the bottom of the list.

You can move documents to a new location in the book by clicking and dragging them up or down in the palette list.

To remove a document (or multiple documents), select the document(s) from the palette and click the Remove Documents button or choose Remove Document from the palette menu.

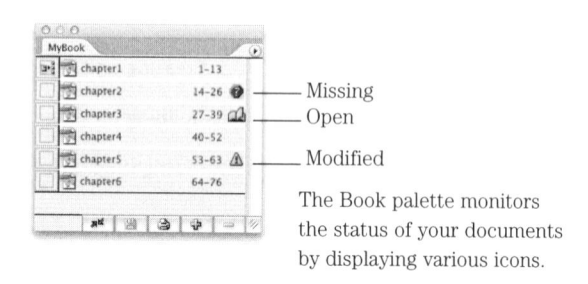

The Book palette monitors the status of your documents by displaying various icons.

The Open icon appears when a book document is open in InDesign.

The Missing icon appears when a document has been moved to a new location. To relink, double-click the document in the list. When the Replace Document dialog appears, browse to the new file location on your system and click Open.

The Modified icon appears when a document has been changed without the Book palette open. To update, select Repaginate from the palette menu.

380

18.2 Synchronizing Book Chapters

The Book palette allows you to choose a master document as the style source. Any styles or color swatches defined in the master document are added to all the other documents in the palette when you click the synchronize button.

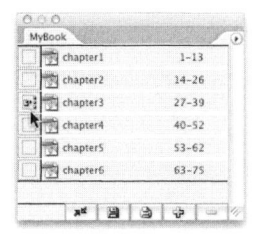

To set which document is to be used as the master style source, click in the left column next to the filename (by default, it's the first document added to the palette).

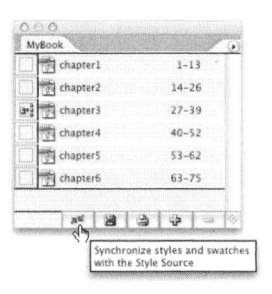

Select the documents you'd like to synchronize in the Book palette and click the Synchronize Styles And Swatches button or choose Synchronize Selected Documents from the Book palette menu. To synchronize all the documents in the palette, either select them all or select no documents and click the synchronize button.

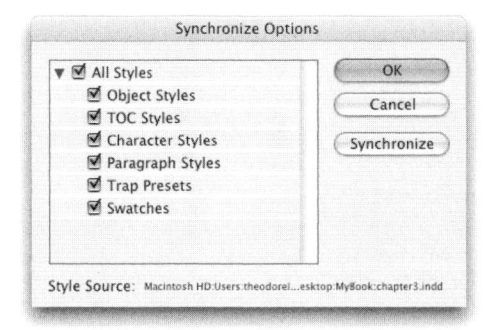

You can choose which settings to synchronize in the Synchronize Options dialog. To access the dialog, choose Synchronize Options from the Book palette menu.

Related Tasks

2.3 File Menu
2.5 Layout Menu
4.8 Interactive Palettes
4.21 Type and Tables Palettes
4.22 Book and Library Palettes
11.1 Creating and Applying Character Styles
11.2 Creating and Applying Paragraph Styles
18.1 Creating a New Book File
18.3 Page Numbering across Book Documents
18.4 Building a Table of Contents
18.5 Creating and Saving a TOC Style
18.6 Building an Index

Shortcuts

Open
Mac: Cmd+O
Win: Ctrl+O

Paragraph Styles palette
Mac and Win: F11

Character Styles palette
Mac and Win: Shift+F11

Quick Apply
Mac: Cmd+Return
Win: Ctrl+Enter

Tip

The quickest way to open a book document is to double-click it in the Book palette.

381

18.3 Page Numbering across Book Documents

Related Tasks

2.3	File Menu
2.5	Layout Menu
4.8	Interactive Palettes
4.21	Type and Tables Palettes
4.22	Book and Library Palettes
6.17	Adding Page Numbers to Sections
18.1	Creating a New Book File
18.2	Synchronizing Book Chapters
18.4	Building a Table of Contents
18.5	Creating and Saving a TOC Style
18.6	Building an Index

Shortcuts

Auto Page Number
Mac: Opt+Shift+Cmd+N
Win: Alt+Shift+Ctrl+N

Type tool
Mac and Win: T

Open
Mac: Cmd+O
Win: Ctrl+O

Tip

You can access the Document Page Numbering Options dialog by double-clicking the page numbers that appear next to the document file name in the Book palette.

Here is one of the best features of InDesign's Book palette—it keeps track of page numbering for you! As long as you apply automatic page numbering to all the documents, InDesign updates the page numbers whenever you add or delete pages.

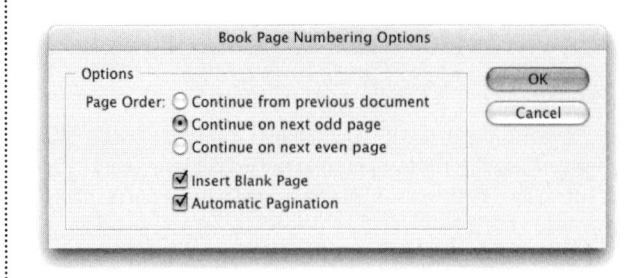

To set options for automatic book page numbering; choose Book Page Numbering Options from the palette menu. In the dialog, you can choose to continue numbering on the next even or odd page, and insert a blank page at the end of a document when necessary to match the numbering scheme.

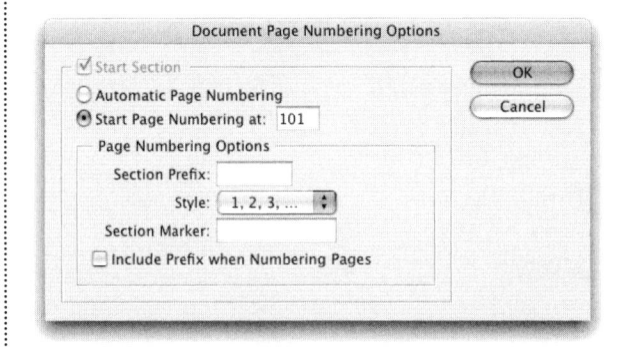

You can also create a section start using the Document Page Numbering Options dialog. To do so, select a document from the palette and choose Document Page Numbering Options from the palette menu. Choose the Start Page Numbering At option and enter a page number in the field. Click OK to apply.

18.4 Building a Table of Contents

To create a table of contents, choose Layout > Table Of Contents to display the Table Of Contents dialog. If you've created a TOC style you'd like to apply, choose it from the TOC Style menu at the top of the dialog; otherwise leave the style setting at [Default]. Enter a name for the TOC in the Title field, and choose a paragraph style to apply to it from the neighboring Style menu. The title that you enter is placed at the beginning of the TOC.

Choose the paragraph styles you'd like to include from the Other Styles list on the right and click Add. You can also add styles by double-clicking them. Styles are added alphabetically to the Include Paragraph Styles list, but can be rearranged by clicking and dragging.

Proceed to select each style name in the Include Paragraph Styles list and choose a paragraph style to apply to it from the Entry Style menu. Note that you can also choose the "TOC body text" paragraph style that InDesign adds to the Entry Style menu.

Click the More Options button to display additional Style options in the dialog. From the Page Number menu, choose how you would like to display page numbers in the TOC: After Entry, Before Entry, or No Page Number. You can choose which characters to place between the entries and page numbers from the Between Entry and Number menu, or by entering a metacharacter in the field (by default it's a tab character). Choose a character style to apply to the page numbers and "between" dot leaders from the neighboring Style menus. You may want to enable the Sort Entries In Alphabetical Order option when creating a list rather than a Book TOC.

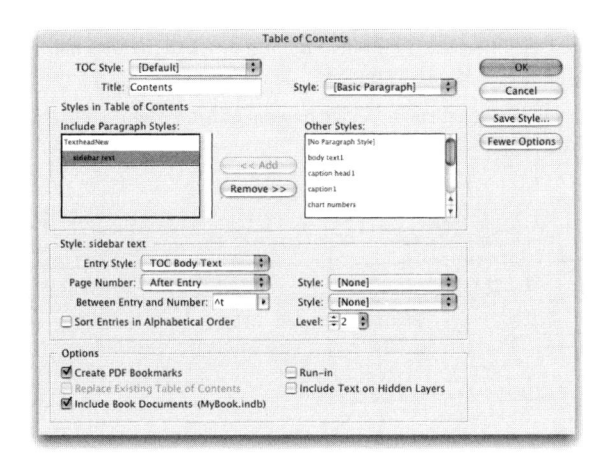

You can choose to include the entire book in the TOC by enabling the Include Book Documents option at the bottom of the dialog. To place all of the headings in a paragraph separated by semicolons, enable the Run-in option. Other options include Create PDF Bookmarks, Replace Existing Table Of Contents, and Include Text On Hidden Layers.

When you click OK, InDesign generates the TOC (this could take a while depending on how many entries there are). When it's finished, a loaded place cursor is displayed. Click to place the new TOC into a text frame.

Related Tasks

2.3	File Menu
2.5	Layout Menu
4.8	Interactive Palettes
4.21	Type and Tables Palettes
4.22	Book and Library Palettes
9.3	Importing Text
18.1	Creating a New Book File
18.2	Synchronizing Book Chapters
18.3	Page Numbering across Book Documents
18.5	Creating and Saving a TOC Style
18.6	Building an Index

Shortcut

Open
Mac: Cmd+O
Win: Ctrl+O

Tips

Any object tagged with a paragraph style can be built into a list using the table of contents feature.

You can define the amount of indent used for each paragraph style in the Include Paragraph Styles list of the TOC dialog by entering a value in the Level field.

383

18.5 Creating and Saving a TOC Style

Related Tasks

2.3	File Menu
2.5	Layout Menu
4.8	Interactive Palettes
4.21	Type and Tables Palettes
4.22	Book and Library Palettes
18.1	Creating a New Book File
18.2	Synchronizing Book Chapters
18.3	Page Numbering across Book Documents
18.4	Building a Table of Contents
18.6	Building an Index

Shortcut

Open
Mac: Cmd+O
Win: Ctrl+O

Tip

To update a TOC, select the text frame containing the list and choose Layout > Update Table Of Contents.

You can define several different TOC styles in one document. To do so, choose Layout > Table Of Contents to access the Table Of Contents dialog. Enter your preferred settings and click Save Style. When the Save Style dialog appears, enter a name for the style and click OK. The new style is added to the TOC Style menu.

You can also create, edit, delete, and load TOC styles by choosing Layout > Table Of Contents Styles. Doing so opens the Table Of Contents Styles dialog.

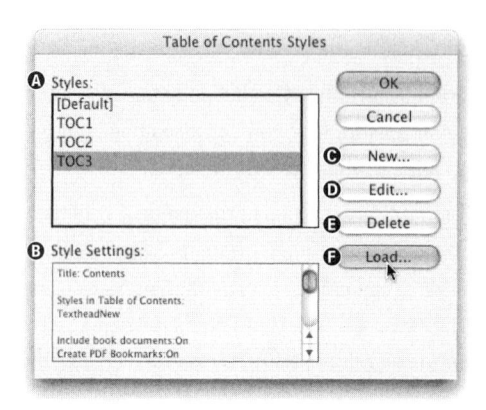

Ⓐ Styles Displays a list of saved TOC Styles. Click a style name to select; double-click to edit.

Ⓑ Style Settings Displays a summary of TOC dialog settings for the selected TOC style.

Ⓒ New Click to access the New Table Of Contents Style dialog and choose your preferred settings. Click OK to save the style and add it to the list.

Ⓓ Edit Select a style from the list and click the Edit button to adjust the settings in the Edit Table Of Contents Style dialog. Click OK to save your changes and return to the Table Of Contents Styles dialog.

Ⓔ Delete Select a style from the list and click the Delete button to remove it. When the warning dialog appears, click OK to commit (this action cannot be undone).

Ⓕ Load Click to access the Open A File dialog. Locate an InDesign document from your system and then click Open to load its TOC styles.

18.6 Building an Index

With InDesign's Index palette, you can create, edit, and preview an index for a large document or book. To create an index in InDesign CS2, you must add topic entries and references to those topics using the Index palette. To add an index entry:

1. If a word that describes the topic appears on the page, select it with the Type tool and click the Create A New Index Entry button at the bottom of the Index palette. If no word on the page describes the topic, place the Type tool cursor anywhere in the related text and click the Create A New Index Entry button. InDesign displays the New Page Reference dialog.

2. If necessary, edit the text in the Topic Levels field. Any text entered is what InDesign displays in the index.

3. Enter a word in the Sort By field to place the index entry in a specific alphabetical position (e.g., to place "16 volt" under "S" rather than before "A").

4. Choose an indexing page range from the Type menu. Options include Current Page, To Next Style Change, To Next Use Of Style, To End Of Story, To End Of Document, To End Of Section, For Next # Of Paragraphs, For Next # Of Pages, and Suppress Page Range. Choose Suppress Page Range when adding second-level entries. At the bottom of the menu are six cross-reference options including: See [also], See, See Also, See Herein, See Also Herein, and [Custom Cross Reference]. Choosing one of the cross-reference options changes the dialog to display a Referenced field. Enter any cross-reference words or phrases in this field.

5. If you prefer, enable the Number Style Override option to apply a specific character style to the page number(s).

6. Click OK to add the index entry to the Index palette. If the indexed text appears on a master page or the Pasteboard, the palette displays the master page label or "PB."

Related Tasks

2.3 File Menu
2.5 Layout Menu
4.8 Interactive Palettes

Shortcuts

Index palette
Mac and Win: Shift+F8

Create index entry without dialog
Mac: Shift+Cmd+Opt+[(left bracket)
Win: Shift+Ctrl+Alt+[(left bracket)

18.6 Building an Index *(continued)*

Related Tasks

4.21 Type and Tables Palettes

4.22 Book and Library Palettes

18.1 Creating a New Book File

Shortcuts

Open New Page Reference dialog
Mac: Cmd+U
Win: Ctrl+U

Create proper name entry (last name first)
Mac: Shift+Cmd+Opt+]
(right bracket)
Win: Shift+Ctrl+Alt+]
(right bracket)

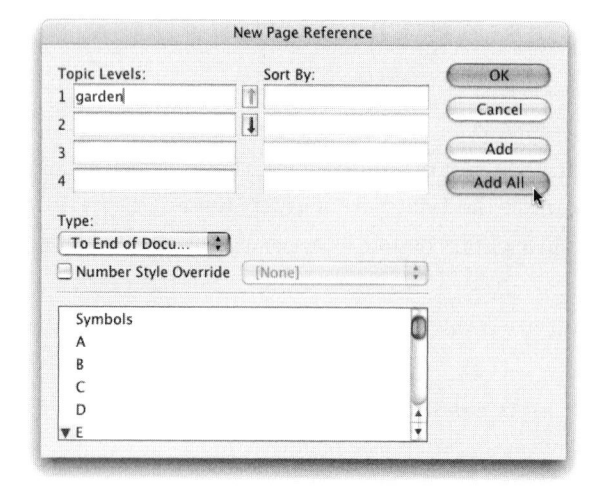

To add an index entry without closing the New Page Reference dialog, click Add. Click Add All to search the document for every instance of the entry text (exact matches only) and add it to the index.

To add a reference to an index entry:

1 Place the Type tool cursor anywhere in the related text.

2 Click the index entry in the Index palette.

3 Option-click (Mac) or Alt-click (Windows) the Create A New Index Entry button. Set up the New Page Reference dialog accordingly and click OK to add the reference.

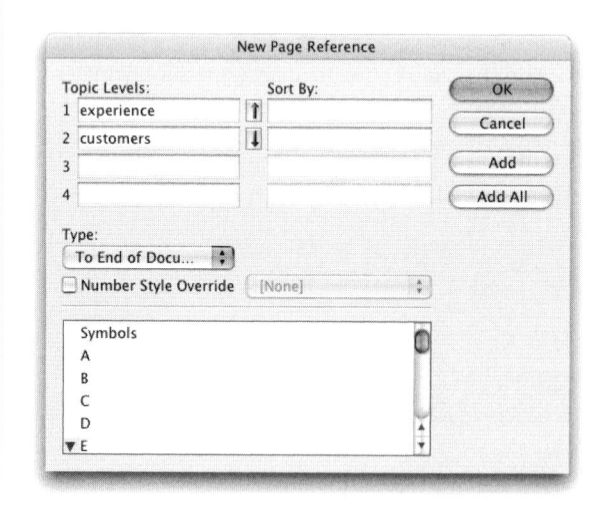

To create a second-level entry, follow the same steps as you would to create a first-level entry, but include two extra steps. When the New Page Reference dialog appears, click the down arrow button in the center of the dialog. Next, double-click the first-level entry from the list at the bottom to enter it in the first Topic Level field. Similarly, you can continue clicking the Down arrow button to create third- and fourth-level entries.

18.6 Building an Index *(continued)*

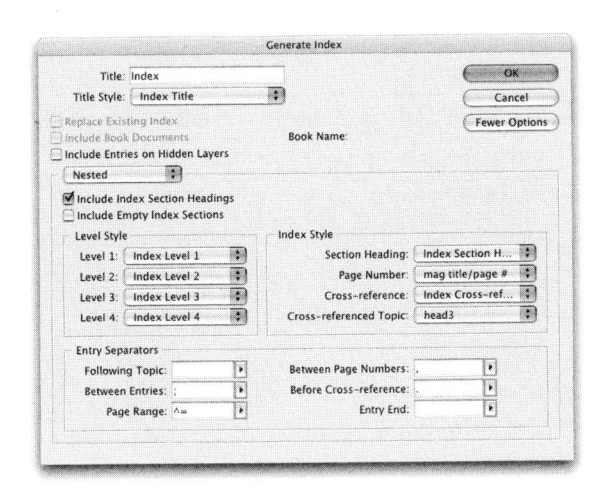

When you're ready to generate the index, choose Generate Index from the Index palette menu or click the Generate Index button. InDesign displays the Generate Index dialog. To display all available options in the dialog, click More Options. Enter a name for the index in the Title field, and choose a paragraph style to apply to it from the Title Style menu underneath. The title that you enter is placed at the beginning of the Index. Note that you can also choose the "Index Title" paragraph style that InDesign adds to the Title Style menu.

You can choose to include index entries for all documents in a book by enabling Include Book Documents. You can also choose to replace an existing index and include entries on hidden layers by enabling either option.

From the menu in the center of the dialog, choose to generate an index with nested entries or run-in entries. To place all of the entries (first- and second-level) in separate paragraphs, choose Nested. To place all the entries (first- and second-level) in one paragraph, choose Run-in.

Enable the Include Index Section Headings option to generate section heads (e.g., "A," "B," "C," etc). Enable the Include Empty Index Sections option to generate section heads for any empty sections; otherwise they are left out.

From the Level 1-4 Style menus, choose a paragraph style to apply to each level entry in the index. Note that you can also choose the "Index Level 1-4" paragraph styles that InDesign adds to the Level 1-4 Style menus. From the Index Style menus, choose paragraph styles to apply to section heading and cross-reference items. You can also choose character styles to apply to page numbers and cross-referenced topics.

At the bottom of the dialog, choose which punctuation marks to apply to the index by entering characters into the Entry Separators fields.

Related Tasks

18.2 Synchronizing Book Chapters

18.3 Page Numbering across Book Documents

18.4 Building a Table of Contents

Tip

To apply default New Page Reference dialog settings to a selected index reference, click and drag the index entry in the Index palette over the Create A New Index Entry button at the bottom of the palette.

18.7 Preflighting, Printing, and Exporting Books

Related Tasks

2.3	File Menu
4.22	Book and Library Palettes
15.1	Preflighting Fonts
15.2	Preflighting Links and Images
15.3	Preflighting Colors and Inks
15.4	Preflighting Print Settings
16.1	Printing a Document
17.1	Exporting as Adobe PDF
18.1	Creating a New Book File

Shortcuts

Open
Mac: Cmd+O
Win: Ctrl+O

Preflight
Mac: Opt+Shift+Cmd+F
Win: Alt+Shift+Ctrl+F

Print
Mac: Cmd+P
Win: Ctrl+P

Export
Mac: Cmd+E
Win: Ctrl+E

Tip

You can also package all the documents in a book for GoLive or for Print by choosing Package > Book For GoLive or Book For Print from the Book palette menu.

InDesign allows you to preflight, print, and export one or more documents from the Book palette without having to open each one individually.

To preflight all of the documents in a book, select all the documents in the palette (or select no documents) and choose Preflight Book from the Book palette menu. InDesign runs a preflight check on all documents selected in the palette.

To print all the documents in a book, select them in the palette (or select no documents) and choose Print Book from the Book palette menu. InDesign displays the Print dialog. Enter your preferred settings and click Print to send all the documents selected in the Book palette to the chosen printer.

To export all the book documents to PDF, select them in the palette (or select no documents) and choose Export Book To PDF from the Book palette menu. InDesign displays the Export dialog. Enter a name for the PDF and choose a file location on your system. Click Save to display the Export Adobe PDF dialog. Enter your preferred settings and click Export to create a PDF of all the selected documents in the Book palette.

Click the Print button at the bottom of the Book palette to print selected documents, Option-click (Mac) or Alt-click (Windows) to export.

Index

Note to the Reader: Throughout this index **boldfaced** page numbers indicate primary discussions of a topic.

A

action buttons, 9
Add Anchor Point tool, 34, 155
Add Documents dialog, 380
Adobe Illustrator
    copying images to, 286–287
    swatches from, 331
Adobe PDF
    Advanced panel, 367
    Compression panel, 364
    embedding in
        hyperlinks, 370–371
        movies and sound, 372–373
    General panel, 362–363
    Marks and Bleed panel, 365
    Output panel, 366
    presets, 116
    Security panel, 368
    Summary panel, 369
Advanced panel
    Adobe PDF, 367
    for printing, 357
Advanced Type Preferences panel, 101
Align palette, 71
Align To Baseline Grid option, 141
aligning
    baseline grids, 141
    cell data, 315
    objects, 196
    paragraphs, 241–242
    strokes, 167–168
    tab stops, 258
    text on paths, 305
Allow Object-Level Display Settings option, 292
anchor points, 34
anchored objects, 158–159
anti-aliasing options, 110
Appearance of Black Preferences panel, 112
Apply buttons, 54

applying
    blend modes, 335
    corner effects, 174
    custom strokes, 171
    gradients, 48
    hyphenation, 251–252
    justification, 253–254
    keep options, 246–247
    master pages, 134, 136
    paths
        compound, 175
        Photoshop clipping, 293–294
    styles
        character, 265
        gap color to open strokes, 172–173
        nested, 269
        object, 271–272
        paragraph, 266–267
        parent-child, 268
        stroked path start and end, 169–170
arranging
    objects, 192
    pages, 128–129
ASCII text, 216–217
Assignments palette, 127
attributes, undefined, 263
Attributes palette, 60
auto-kerning, 232
Auto Leading feature, 236
Auto Page Number character, 138
Autocorrect feature, 109, 224
Automatic Text Flow, 219
Automation palettes, 61–62

B

backward saving, 126
baselines
    grids for
        aligning, 141
        options for, 104

shift in, 237
  for text frames, 210–211
Basic Graphics Frames, 272
Basic Text Frames, 145, 272
behaviors for buttons, 49
Bevel corner effects, 174
black preferences, 112
Bleed mode, 54
blend modes
  applying, 335
  in printing, 75
Book Page Numbering Options dialog, 382
Book palette, 95
Bookmarks palette, 66
books, 379
  exporting, 388
  files for, 380
  indexes, 385–387
  page numbering, 382
  preflighting and printing, 388
  synchronizing chapters, 381
  tables of contents, 383–384
borders for tables, 319–320
Bridge application, 116, 123
Bring Forward option, 192
Bring To Front option, 192
bullets, 255–256
buttons, 9–10
  formatting, 54
  Reset, 108
Buttons tool, 49

C

case, changing, 222
cells in tables
  merging, 313
  overset text in, 308
  spacing and alignment in, 315
  splitting, 314
Centered tab stops, 257
chapters, synchronizing, 381
Character palette, 88
Character Style Options dialog, 264–265
Character Styles palette, 88–89
characters
  hidden, 224
  scaling, 234
  space between, 233, 236–237
  special, 259–260
  styles for, 88–89, 264–265
check boxes, 8

check spelling
  Autocorrect feature, 109
  text, 223–224
child pages
  creating and applying, 136
  styles for, 268
circles, 41
clipping paths
  InDesign, 295–296
  Photoshop, 293–294
closing paths, 155–156
CMYK options for soft proofing, 328
collapsing palette windows, 57–58
color, 325
  blend modes, 335
  Color Picture, 53
  converting spot to process, 332
  drop shadows, 336–337
  feathering, 338
  filling with, 160
  gap, 172–173
  grids, 142
  for imported graphics, 327
  importing, 333
  in libraries, 331
  mixed-ink swatches and groups, 329–330
  opacity level, 334
  preflighting, 344
  sampling, 46
  settings for, 326
  soft proofing, 328
  Story Editor Display Preferences for, 110
  in styles, 270
  Swatches palette for, 83–84
  text, 162–163, 166
  transparent TIFFs, 339
Color Burn blend mode, 335
Color Dodge blend mode, 335
Color Management panel, 356
Color Palette, 63
Color Picture, 53
Color Settings dialog, 326
column guides
  adjusting, 140
  preferences for, 105
columns
  layout for, 204
  in tables
    adding, 310–311
    deleting, 312
    resizing, 316–318

combining text with images. *See* images
commands, menu, 12
Composition Preferences panel, 102
compound paths, 175
Compression panel, 364
configuring plug-ins, 117
constraining
    frames, 32
    gradients, 48
    images, 149
contextual menus, 6–7
Control bar
    controls on, 29–31
    for tables, 311–312
control handles for curves, 153
Convert Direction Point tool, 34, 155
converting
    clipping paths to frames, 294
    document pages to master pages, 133
    point direction, 155
    rows into headers and footers, 323
    spot colors to process, 332
    text
        to outlines, 302
        to tables, 307–308
Copy PDF To Clipboard option, 287
copying/pasting
    drop shadows, 337
    images to Adobe Illustrator, 286–287
    master pages, 132
    objects, 194–195
    text, 214
    text formatting, 240
corner effects, 174
Create New Page control, 128
Create Packer Folder dialog, 346
cropping images, 33, 282
CS documents, 123
cursor preferences, 110
curves, 153
custom shapes
    drawing, 153
    Pathfinder for, 176
custom soft proofing, 328
custom strokes, 171
Customize Proof Condition dialog, 328
customizing workspace, 59
cutting paths, 50, 155–156

D

Darken blend mode, 335
Dash stroke style, 171

data fields, 5, 8–9
Data Merge palette, 61
Decimal tab stops, 257
default formatting, 263
default object styles, 272
default stroke settings, 39
default workspaces, restoring, 59
Delete Anchor Point tool, 34, 155
deleting
    bookmarks, 66
    master pages, 135, 201
    objects, 201
    pages, 129
    points for paths and frames, 155
    rows and columns, 312
    styles, 275
    tab stops, 257
    text on paths, 305
    workspaces, 59
deselecting
    with Direction Selection tool, 33
    with Selection tool, 32
diagonal lines in cells, 321
dialogs in menus, 12
dictionaries
    editing, 225
    with foreign languages, 226
    preferences for, 106–107
Dictionary Preferences panel, 106–107
Difference blend mode, 335
Diffused feathering option, 338
Direct Selection tool
    vs. Selection tool, 148–149
    working with, 33
discretionary hyphens, 252
Discretionary Ligatures glyph subset, 259
Display Performance option, 24
Display Performance Preferences panel, 111
display settings
    object-level, 292
    parameters for, 111
distributing objects, 197–198
docking palettes, 57–58
Document CMYK option, 328
Document Page Numbering Options dialog, 382
Document Presets dialog, 114, 121
document windows, 4
documents, 119
    baseline grid alignment, 141
    grids, snapping to, 142
    margin and column guides in, 140
    multipage spreads in, 130

Dotted stroke style • feathering

    opening
        InDesign, 122–123
        PageMaker and QuarkXPress, 124
    page numbers in sections, 138
    pages
        adding, 128
        arranging, 128–129
        deleting, 129
        master. *See* master pages
        targeting vs. selecting pages, 131
    presets for, 114, 121
    printing. *See* printing
    ruler guides in, 139
    saving, 125–127
    starting, 120
Dotted stroke style, 171
drag-and-drop text editing, 239
dragging for tables, 311
drawing
    custom shapes, 153
    freeform shapes, 154
    rectangles, ellipses, and polygons, 152
drop caps, 245
drop-down menus, 7
drop-down sliders, 9
drop shadows
    adding, 336–337
    in styles, 270
duplicating
    drop shadows, 337
    master pages, 132
    objects, 194–195
Dynamic Spelling feature, 223

E

edges, frame, 40
Edit Glyph Set dialog, 260
Edit menu, 16–17
editing
    dictionaries, 225
    drag-and-drop, 239
    frames, 155–156
    headers and footers, 323
    links, 290
    paths, 155–156
        clipping, 293–296
        compound, 175
        type on, 303–305
    presets, 114
    shortcuts, 118
    with Story Editor, 221

    styles, 273–274
    text wraps, 298–301
effects
    corner, 174
    glow, 168
    text on paths, 304–305
Ellipse frames, 40, 144
ellipses, drawing, 152
embedding
    images, 291
    in PDFs
        hyperlinks, 370–371
        movies and sound, 372–373
end marks, libraries for, 199
end stroked path styles, 169–170
EPS
    exporting to, 374–375
    importing from, 281
EPS Import Options dialog, 281
Erase tool, 38
Excel tables, 324
Exclusion blend mode, 335
Export dialog, 126
Export EPS dialog, 374
Export XML dialog, 377
exporting, 361
    as Adobe PDF
        Advanced panel, 367
        Compression panel, 364
        General panel, 362–363
        Marks and Bleed panel, 365
        Output panel, 366
        Security panel, 368
        Summary panel, 369
    blacks, 112
    books, 388
    as EPS, 374–375
    as JPEG, 376
    PDFS
        hyperlinks, 370–371
        movies and sound in, 372–373
    as XML, 377–378
external plug-ins
    configuring, 117
    preflighting, 345
Eyedropper tool, 46

F

Fancy corner effects, 174
Fast Display setting, 292
feathering, 338

fields, data, 5, 8–9
File Handling Preferences panel, 113
File menu, 14–15
files
    for books, 380
    merging, 61
Fill control with Color Palette, 63
Fill Frame Proportionally option, 279
Fill swatch, 53
fills
    gradients for, 161
    placeholder text for, 220
    solid and transparent colors for, 160
    in styles, 270
    for tables, 320–321
    for text, 162–163
Find Font dialog, 228
finding
    library items, 200
    missing fonts, 228
    text, 229–230
first line indents, 243–244
flattener, transparency, 75, 359
Flattener Preview palette, 75
flexibility, line, 39
flipping objects, 184–185
flowing text, 219
fonts
    Glyphs palette, 89
    missing, 228
    Open Type, 227, 260
    overview, 227
    preflighting, 342
    Story Editor Display Preferences for, 110
Fonts folder, 227
Footer menu, 6
footers, 322–323
footnotes, 261–262
foreign language dictionaries, 226
formatting, 231
    baseline shift, 237
    bullets and numbering, 255–256
    buttons for, 54
    copy/paste, 240
    drop caps, 245
    footnotes, 261–262
    hyphenation, 251–252
    in imported text, 215–216
    justification, 253–254
    keep options, 246–247
    kerning, 232–233
    leading, 236–237
    paragraphs, 241–244
    punctuation and indents, 248–249
    special characters, 259–260
    strikethrough, 239
    styles. *See* styles
    tabs, 257–258
    tracking, 233
    underlining, 238–239
frames, 143
    converting clipping paths to, 294
    in libraries, 96, 200
    modifying, 155–156
    for movies and sound, 372
    overview, 144–146
    rotating, 42
    scaling, 43
    with Selection tool, 32
    shapes as, 41
    shearing, 44
    stroking, 164–165
    for text
        Free Transforming, 45
        options for, 208–211
        threading and unthreading, 212–213
    tools for, 40
free-floating toolbox, 28
Free Transform tool, 45
freeform shapes, 154

G

Gallery mode in InCopy, 217
gap color for open stroke styles, 172–173
General panel
    Adobe PDF, 362–363
    for printing, 351
General Preferences panel, 98
Generate Index dialog, 387
global formatting, 263
glow effect, 168
Glyphs palette
    controls on, 89
    for special characters, 259–260
GoLive packaging, 347–348
Gradient palette, 64
Gradient tool, 48
gradients
    applying, 48
    filling with, 161
    for text, 162–163, 166
    working with, 64
graphics. *See* images
Graphics panel, 355

Gravity effect, 304–305
grids
    baseline, 141
    controls for, 104
    snapping to, 104, 142
Grids Preferences panel, 104
grouping objects, 188
groups
    mixed-ink, 329–330
    nesting in, 191
    selections within, 189–190
guides
    column and margin
        adjusting, 140
        settings for, 105
    layout for, 204
    ruler
        adjusting, 139
        units for, 103
Guides & Pasteboard Preferences panel, 105

H

Hand tool, 51
hanging indents, 248–250
Hard Light blend mode, 335
headers and footers, 322–323
Help menu, 26
hidden characters, 224
High Quality Display setting, 292
horizontal alignment, 241–242
horizontal rulers, 139
Hue blend mode, 335
hyperlinks
    creating, 66–67
    embedding, 370–371
Hyperlinks palette, 66–67
hyphenation, 251–252

I

icons
    label, 5
    libraries for, 199
    for tools, 28
Ignored Words option, 225
Image Import Options dialog, 280
images, 277
    in cells, 314
    color for, 327
    constraining, 149
    copying to Adobe Illustrator, 286–287
    cropping, 33, 282

embedding, 291
frames for. *See* frames
importing
    options for, 280–282
    process, 278–279
layer options and placed PSDs for, 283–285
in libraries, 96, 200
links for, 290
object-level display settings for, 292
preflighting, 343
resizing, 288–289
with text, 297
    converting text to outlines, 302
    editing type on paths, 303–305
    paragraph rules, 306
    tables. *See* tables
    wrapping in, 298–301
imported images, color for, 327
importing
    color, 333
    images
        options for, 280–282
        process, 278–279
    styles, 276
    tables, 324
    text, 214–217
    transparent TIFFs, 339
    XML, 218
InCopy, 127, 217
Indent To Here character, 249
indents
    hanging, 248–250
    paragraphs, 242–244
    Tabs palette for, 94
InDesign menus, 13
Index palette, 90
indexes, 385–387
Info palette, 65
Ink Manager, 332
inks, preflighting, 344
Insert Pages dialog, 128
Insert Row/Column dialog, 310
Insert Table dialog, 307
Inset corner effects, 174
interactive palettes, 66–68
interfaces, 1
    document windows, 4
    Macintosh, 2
    objects in, 5–10
    Windows, 3
Inverse Rounded corner effects, 174

invisible characters, 224
INX export, 126

J

joining paths, 155–156
JPEG, exporting as, 376
jump lines, 256
Jump Object option, 298–299
Jump To Next Column option, 298–299
justification, 253–254

K

keep options, 246–247
Keep Spread Together option, 130
kerning, 232–233
keyboard shortcuts
    setting, 118
    units for, 103

L

label icons, 5
large documents. *See* books
last line indents, 243–244
Layer Options dialog, 202
layers
    creating and naming, 202
    for images, 283–285
    objects on, 203
Layers palette, 69
layout
    adjustments for, 204–206
    for footnotes, 262
Layout menu, 18
Layout mode in InCopy, 217
leaders, tab, 258
leading, 236–237
left indents, 242–243
Left tab stops, 257
libraries
    color in, 331
    controls for, 96
    saving objects to, 199–200
Library palette, 96
Lighten blend mode, 335
Line tool, 39
lines
    in cells, 321
    drawing, 39
    jump, 256
    keeping together, 246
    on paths, cutting, 50
    selecting, 151

links
    for images, 290
    preflighting, 343
    for text boxes, 212–213
Links palette, 70
Load Styles dialog, 276
loading
    presets, 114, 116
    styles, 276
local formatting, 263
locking objects, 193
logos, libraries for, 199
Lowercase option, 222
Luminosity blend mode, 335

M

Macintosh interface, 2
manual text flow, 219
Map Tags To Style option, 218
margin guides, 140
    layout for, 204
    settings for, 105
Marks and Bleed panel
    Adobe PDF, 365
    for printing, 353
master pages
    applying, 134, 136
    converting document pages to, 133
    creating, 130, 132, 136
    deleting, 135, 201
    overriding items on, 137
    Pages palette for, 80–81
Measure tool, 47
measurement units, 103
menus, 11
    Edit, 16–17
    File, 14–15
    Help, 26
    InDesign, 13
    interface, 5–7
    Layout, 18
    Object, 20–21
    overview, 12
    Table, 22
    Type, 19
    View, 23–24
    Window, 25
merging
    cells, 313
    files, 61
Metrics kerning, 232
Microsoft Word Import Options dialog, 215

missing fonts, 228
mixed-ink swatches and groups, 329–330
modifying. *See* editing
Movie Options dialog, 372
Movie/Sound Options dialog, 372
movies, embedding, 372–373
moving
    objects, 178–179
    pages, 128–129
    with selection tools, 148
multipage spreads and master pages, 130
multiple objects, selecting, 150
Multiply blend mode, 335

N

names
    bookmarks, 66
    layers, 202
    master pages, 132
Navigator palette, 72
nesting
    bookmarks, 66
    group objects, 191
    objects, 157–159
    styles, 269
    tables, 22
    text frames, 146
New Book dialog, 380
New Character Style dialog, 264
New Color Swatch dialog, 331
New Document dialog, 114, 120
New Document Preset dialog, 120
New Glyph Set option, 260
New Hyperlink dialog, 370
New Hyperlink Destination dialog, 370
New Mixed Ink Group dialog, 330
New Mixed Ink Swatch dialog, 329
New Page Reference dialog, 385–386
New Paragraph Style dialog, 266, 269
New Stroke Style dialog, 171
New Tint Swatch dialog, 337
Next Page Number character, 256
No Text Wrap option, 298
Non-Latin text setting, 101
Non-Uniform scaling option, 289
Normal blend mode, 335
Notes palette, 127
numbering
    pages, 382
    paragraphs, 255–256
    in sections, 138

O

Object and Layout palettes, 71–73
object-level display settings, 292
Object menu, 20–21
Object Style Options dialog, 271
Object Styles palette, 74
objects, 177
    aligning, 196
    deleting, 201
    distributing, 197–198
    duplicating, 194–195
    flipping, 184–185
    grouping and ungrouping, 188
    in interfaces, 5–10
    on layers, 203
    locking, 193
    moving, 178–179
    nesting, 157–159, 191
    opacity level of, 334
    resizing, 180–181
    rotating, 182–183
    saving to libraries, 199–200
    selecting within groups, 189–190
    shearing, 186–187
    stacking and arranging, 192
    styles for, 270–272
on-off controls, 8
on/off menu items, 12
online tools, 53
opacity level of objects, 334
Open A File dialog, 122, 276, 333
Open command, 122
Open As command, 122
open stroke styles, 172–173
Open Type fonts, 227, 260
opening documents
    InDesign, 122–123
    PageMaker and QuarkXPress, 124
Optical kerning, 232–233
Optical Margin Alignment option, 93
Option/Alt dragging for tables, 311
orphans, 246
outlines, converting text to, 302
output palettes, 75–77
Output panel
    Adobe PDF, 366
    for printing, 354
Overlay blend mode, 335
Override All Master Pages option, 137

overriding
    formatting, 263
    master page items, 137
    styles, 274
overset text, 308

P

packaging
    for GoLive, 347–348
    process, 341, 346
page numbering
    across book documents, 382
    in sections, 138
PageMaker documents, 124
PageMaker toolbar, 78–79
pages
    adding, 128
    arranging, 128–129
    deleting, 129
    importing, 282
    master. *See* master pages
    multipage spreads, 130
    numbering, 382
    targeting vs. selecting, 131
    working with, 80–81
Pages palette, 80–81
Palette menu, 6
palettes, 55
    Attributes, 60
    Automation, 61–62
    Book, 95
    Color, 63
    Gradient, 64
    Info, 65
    interactive, 66–68
    Layers, 69
    Library, 96
    Links, 70
    Object and Layout, 71–73
    object styles, 74
    organizing, 56–58
    output, 75–77
    Pages, 80–81
    Stroke, 82
    Swatches, 83–84
    Tags, 85
    Text Wrap, 86
    Transparency, 87
    Types and Tables, 88–94
Paragraph palette, 91

Paragraph Style Options dialog, 266, 269
Paragraph Styles palette, 92
paragraphs
    controls for, 91
    formatting, 241–244
    rules for, 306
    selecting, 151
    styles for, 92, 266–267
parent-child styles, 268
Paste In Place option, 194
Pathfinder for custom shapes, 176
Pathfinder palette, 72–73, 146
paths
    clipping
        InDesign, 295–296
        Photoshop, 293–294
    compound, 175
    cutting, 50, 155–156
    editing type on, 303–305
    modifying, 155–156
    selecting points on, 33
    stroked start and end styles, 169–170
    stroking, 164–165
PDF. *See* Adobe PDF
Pen tools, 34, 153
Pencil tools, 38, 154
photographs. *See* images
Photoshop clipping paths, 293–294
Picture Usage feature, 290
pictures. *See* images
Place command, 148
Place dialog, 279
Place PDF dialog, 282
placed images. *See* images
placed PSDs, 283–285
placeholder text, 220
plug-ins
    configuring, 117
    preflighting, 345
points
    on frames, 155
    on paths
        adding and deleting, 155
        cutting, 50
        selecting, 33
Polygon frames, 40, 144
Polygon Settings dialog, 40–41
polygons
    drawing, 152
    settings for, 40–41
Position tool, 33

397

PostScript files, 358
preferences panels, 97
    Advanced Type, 101
    Appearance of Black, 112
    Autocorrect feature, 109
    Composition, 102
    Dictionary, 106–107
    Display Performance, 111
    File Handling, 113
    General, 98
    Grids, 104
    Guides & Pasteboard, 105
    Spelling, 108
    Story Editor Display, 110
    Type, 99–100
    Units & Increments, 103
preflighting, 341
    books, 388
    colors and inks, 344
    fonts, 342
    links and images, 343
    print settings, 345
presets, 97
    Adobe PDF, 116
    for documents, 114, 121
    for printing, 115
    transparency flattener, 359
    trap, 77, 360
Preview mode, 54
Previous Page Number character, 256
Print Presets dialog, 115
printing, 349–350
    Advanced panel, 357
    blacks, 112
    books, 388
    Color Management panel, 356
    General panel, 351
    Graphics panel, 355
    Marks and Bleed panel, 353
    Output panel, 354
    preflighting settings, 345
    presets for, 115
        transparency flattener, 359
        trap, 360
    Setup panel, 352
    Summary panel, 358
Printing Instructions dialog, 346
process, converting spot colors to, 332
proof set up, 328
PSDs, placed, 283–285
punctuation, 248–249

Q

QuarkXPress documents, 124
Quick Apply option, 275

R

radio buttons, 8
Rainbow effect, 304
raster images, 111
readability, 246
recovery locations, 113
Rectangle frames, 40, 144–145
rectangles, drawing, 152
Reference mode for indexes, 90
Remember Font with Bullet option, 255
Remove All Local Overrides option, 137
Remove Pages control, 129
Removed Words option, 225
repeating tab stops, 258
Reset button, 108
resizing
    objects, 180–181
    placed images, 288–289
    with selection tools, 149
    tables, 316–318
restoring workspaces, 59
reverting compound paths, 175
right indents, 242–243
Right tab stops, 257
Rotate tool, 42
rotating objects, 182–183
Rounded corner effects, 174
Rounded feathering option, 338
rows
    adding, 310–311
    converting into headers and footers, 323
    deleting, 312
    resizing, 316–318
RTF Import Options dialog, 215
RTF text, importing, 214–215
ruler guides, 139
    layout for, 204
    units for, 103
rules for paragraphs, 306

S

sampling colors and styles, 46
Saturation blend mode, 335
Save command, 125
Save As command, 125
Save Color Settings dialog, 326
Save Style dialog, 384

saved libraries, 96
saving
    documents, 125–127
    glyph characters, 260
    library color, 331
    mixed-ink swatches and groups, 329–330
    objects to libraries, 199–200
    presets
        document, 121
        PDF, 116
    strokes, 171
    table of contents styles, 384
    workspaces, 59
Scale tool, 43
scaling
    images, 289
    objects, 181
    text, 150
    type, 234
Scissors tool, 50
Screen blend mode, 335
screen modes, 54
Script Label palette, 62
Scripts palette, 62
searching
    in libraries, 200
    for missing fonts, 228
    for text, 229–230
section page numbers, 138
Security panel, 368
select buttons, 10
Select menu, 7
selecting
    objects
        within groups, 189–190
        multiple, 150
    pages, 131
    in tables, 309
    type, 151
Selection tool
    vs. Direct Selection tool, 148–149
    working with, 32
Semi-Automatic Text Flow, 219
Send Backward option, 192
Send To Back option, 192
Sentence Case option, 222
Separations Preview palette, 76
Setup panel, 352
shadows, drop
    adding, 336–337
    in styles, 270

Shape tools, 41
shapes, 143
    drawing, 153–154
    in libraries, 96, 200
    overview, 146–147
    Pathfinder for, 176
    stroking, 164–165
Sharp feathering option, 338
Shear tool, 44
shearing
    frames, 44
    objects, 186–187
shortcuts, keyboard
    setting, 118
    units for, 103
Show Baseline Grid option, 141
Show Hidden Characters option, 224
show/hide options, 12
Show Import Options dialog, 61, 216, 279, 327
Show Problems Only option, 343
Show Single Plates In Black option, 76
Show XML Import Options option, 218
side tabs, docking palettes to, 58
size
    corner effects, 174
    objects, 180–181
    placed images, 288–289
    with selection tools, 149
    tables, 316–318
skewing
    text on paths, 304
    type, 235
Slashed Zeros glyph subset, 259
sliders, 9
Slug mode, 54
Small Capitals glyph subset, 259
Small Caps setting, 101
Smooth tool, 38
snapping to grids, 104, 142
snippets, 378
Soft Light blend mode, 335
soft proofing, 328
solid fill colors, 160
Sort By Status option, 290
sorting bookmarks, 66
sound in PDFs, 372–373
Sound Options dialog, 372–373
spacing
    in cells, 315
    character, 233, 236–237
    paragraph, 244

special characters • tables

special characters, 259–260
spell checking
    Autocorrect feature, 109
    text, 223–224
Spelling Preferences panel, 108
splitting cells, 314
spot colors, converting to process, 332
squares, 41
stacking objects, 192
Stair Step effect, 304
Start Page Numbering At setting, 138
Start Paragraph menu, 247
start stroked path styles, 169–170
starting documents, 120
States palette, 67–68
Step And Repeat dialog, 194
Story Editor
    settings for, 110
    working with, 221
Story Editor Display Preferences panel, 110
Story mode in InCopy, 217
Story palette, 88, 93
strikethrough effect, 239
Stripe stroke style, 171
Stroke control, 63
Stroke palette, 82
Stroke swatch, 53
stroked path start and end styles, 169–170
strokes
    aligning, 167–168
    default settings, 39
    frames, shapes, and paths, 164–165
    gap color for, 172–173
    saving and applying, 171
    in styles, 270
    for tables, 320–321
    text, 166
Style Options dialog, 273
styles, 263
    for characters, 88–89, 264–265
    deleting, 275
    editing, 273–274
    in imported text, 215
    importing, 276
    libraries for, 199
    nested, 269
    for objects, 270–272
    for paragraphs, 92, 266–267
    parent-child, 268
    path start and end, 169–170

sampling, 46
stroke, 172–173
for tables of contents, 384
submenus, 12
Subscript setting, 101
subscripts, 101, 247
Summary panel
    Adobe PDF, 369
    for printing, 358
Super Autoflow text flow, 219
Superscript setting, 101
superscripts, 101, 247
SVG format, exporting as, 376
Swatch Options dialog, 332
swatches
    from Adobe Illustrator files, 331
    controls for, 83–84
    mixed-ink, 329–330
    for spot color, 332
    tint, 337
Swatches palette, 83–84
Synchronize Options dialog, 381
synchronizing chapters, 381
system requirements
    Macintosh, 2
    Windows, 3

T

Table menu, 22
Table palette, 93, 311–312
tables
    borders for, 319–320
    cells in
        merging, 313
        overset text in, 308
        spacing and alignment in, 315
        splitting, 314
    creating, 307–308
    headers and footers in, 322–323
    importing, 324
    libraries for, 199
    nesting, 22
    resizing, 316–318
    rows and columns in
        adding, 310–311
        deleting, 312
        resizing, 316–318
    selections in, 309
    strokes and fills for, 320–321
    vs. tabs, 13

tables of contents
　building, 383
　styles for, 384
tabs
　in cells, 323
　setting, 94, 257–258
　vs. tables, 13
Tabs palette
　for hanging indents, 249
　for tabs, 94
tagged text, 216–217
tags
　managing, 85
　viewing, 87
Tags palette, 85
targeting pages, 131
templates, saving documents as, 125
text, 207
　buttons for, 10
　case, 222
　check spelling, 223–224
　converting
　　to outlines, 302
　　to tables, 307–308
　dictionaries
　　editing, 225
　　with foreign languages, 226
　filling, 162–163
　find and replace for, 229–230
　flowing, 219
　fonts
　　missing, 228
　　overview, 227
　formatting. *See* formatting
　frames for
　　Free Transforming, 45
　　options for, 208–211
　　threading and unthreading, 212–213
　glow effect, 168
　with images. *See* images
　importing, 214–217
　in libraries, 96, 200
　placeholder, 220
　scaling, 150
　Story Editor for, 110, 221
　stroking, 166
　tagged and ASCII, 216–217
　wrapping, 86, 270, 298–301
Text Import Options dialog, 216
Text Wrap palette, 86

threading text frames, 212–213
3D Ribbon effect, 304
Threshold value for clipping paths, 295
TIFFs, transparent, 339
tint swatches, 337
tint vs. transparency, 163
Title Case option, 222
toggle buttons, 8
toggle controls, 10
Tolerance value for clipping paths, 295
toolbars, PageMaker, 78–79
Toolbox, 28
tools, 27
　Button, 49
　Control bar, 29–31
　Direction Selection, 33
　Eyedropper, 46
　frame, 40
　Free Transform, 45
　Gradient, 48
　Hand, 51
　Line, 39
　Measure, 47
　miscellaneous functions, 53–54
　Pen, 34
　Pencil, 38
　Position, 33
　Rotate, 42
　Scale, 43
　Scissors, 50
　Selection, 32
　Shape, 41
　Shear, 44
　Toolbox, 28
　Type, 35–37
　Zoom, 52
tooltips, 5
Topic mode for indexes, 90
tracking, 233
Transform palette, 73
transforming objects, 195
transparencies, 111
transparency and transparent colors, 325
　filling with, 160
　flattener presets for, 359
　in styles, 270
　TIFFs, 339
　vs. tint, 163
Transparency palette, 87
Transparent Background option, 282

401

trap presets
    managing, 77
    in printing, 360
Trap Presets palette, 77
type. *See also* text
    options for, 99–100
    on paths, 303–305
    scaling, 234
    selecting, 151
    skewing, 235
Type menu, 19
Type On A Path tool, 37, 303–304
Type Preferences panel, 99–100
Type tools
    Control bar for, 29
    with Story Editor, 221
    for tables, 307
    working with, 35–37
Types and Tables palettes, 88–94
Typical Display setting, 292

U

undefined attributes, 263
underlining, 238
ungrouping objects, 188
Units & Increments Preference panel, 103
unthreading text frames, 212–213
updating links, 290
Uppercase option, 222
Use Spacing option, 198

V

vector graphics, 111
vertical rulers, 139
View menu, 23–24
viewing tags, 87
visible sliders, 9

W

Web links menu items, 12
widows, 246
Window menu, 25
windows, document, 4
Windows interface, 3
Word
    tables from, 324
    text from, 214–215
words, selecting, 151
Working CMYK option, 328
workspace, customizing, 59
Wrap Around Bounding Box option, 298–299
Wrap Around Object Shape option, 298–299
wrapping text, 86, 270, 298–301

X

XML
    exporting, 377–378
    importing, 218

Z

Zoom tool, 52

After Effects® and Photoshop®:
Animation and Production Effects for DV and Film

By Jeff Foster
ISBN: 0-7821-4317-2
US $49.99

If you're in the business of motion graphics or desktop digital video production, you know that Adobe's After Effects and Photoshop are two of the most indispensable content creation tools. More integrated than ever before, the world's number-one compositing and image-editing programs can be used in tandem to create quality work at a relatively low cost. But it takes years of experience to figure out how to get the most out of this remarkable duo.

With *After Effects and Photoshop: Animation and Production Effects for DV and Film*, graphics guru Jeff Foster has created the first book devoted to showing how you can use these two programs together to produce animations and effects on the desktop. This practical guide focuses exclusively on techniques commonly used in the field as well as cutting-edge production tricks. These hands-on projects will demystify cool Hollywood effects and help you solve your daily challenges. And they'll inspire you to think more artistically when approaching your creations.

Inside, you'll discover pro techniques for motion graphics and video production, including how to:

- *Add depth and realism to your animations by mimicking real motion*
- *Use exaggerated movements to enhance characterization*
- *Apply 3-D animation to 2-D images*
- *Remove background fodder with blue-screen garbage mattes*
- *Employ rotoscoping techniques for frame-by-frame retouching*
- *Construct realistic composites and scene locations using matte painting techniques*
- *Make movies from stills by simulating 3-D camera motion*
- *Utilize perspective, speed, and scale to create believable moving objects*
- *Produce realistic special effects such as noise, clouds, and smoke*
- *Practice imaginative motion titling effects that grab people's attention*
- *Develop professional scene transitions using 3-D layer animations*
- *And much more!*

Transform the Ordinary into the Extraordinary!

With Adobe® Photoshop® Elements 3, Adobe has introduced substantial new features for digital photographers—including RAW support, organizing tools, a Healing Brush, and much more. As the software has become easier for digital photography enthusiasts to use and more compelling for serious digital photographers who seek the finest results, so has this acclaimed classic.

In *Photoshop Elements 3 Solutions* award-winning photographer and author Mikkel Aaland has extensively revised his best-seller to include all of version 3's smart new features plus many fresh techniques and examples. Whether working with digital images is a hobby or part of your livelihood, Aaland's practical solutions, stunning color images, and reader-friendly approach will guide you to a higher level of expertise.

PRAISE FOR THE PREVIOUS EDITION

"...covers everything you'll need to know to make your images appear professional, and look the way you prefer — with no red-eye, no leaning buildings, and of course, no wrinkles." —**Popular Photography**

"The engaging work of the author and his many talented colleagues will inspire you to bring out the best in your digital images. With Mikkel as your guide, you will also have fun doing so."
—Kevin Connor, Director, Product Management, Adobe

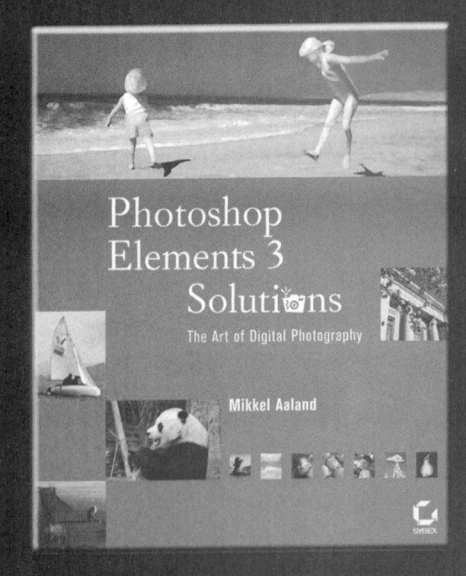

Photoshop® Elements 3 Solutions
The Art of Digital Photography
By Mikkel Aaland
ISBN: 0-7821-4363-6 · US $39.99

Inside, Aaland shows you the ins and outs of Photoshop Elements 3 for Windows and the Macintosh, including:

◆ Organizing and managing your digital images
◆ Touching up faces to make people glow
◆ Enhancing product images so they stand out
◆ Transforming outdoor and real-estate shots
◆ Fusing photos into priceless panoramics
◆ Combining images into realistic composites
◆ Working with the Camera RAW format and advanced digital photo techniques
◆ Optimizing photos for the web, screen, and e-mail transmission
◆ Creating PDF slide shows and professional-looking picture packages

...CD comes with more than 100 practice images and tryouts of fun and useful plug-ins.

...award-winning photographer and author of eight books, including *Shooting Digital*, *Digital ... for the Web*, and *Photoshop Elements 2 Solutions*. His photography has been published in *Wired*, ...European periodicals. He is a regular contributor on digital photography to *Popular Science* ...nist for *Practical Photography* magazine. Aaland served as a nonpaid advisor to Adobe's Photoshop ...velopment group.

www.sybex.com

After Effects® and Photoshop®:
Animation and Production Effects for DV and Film

By Jeff Foster
ISBN: 0-7821-4317-2
US $49.99

If you're in the business of motion graphics or desktop digital video production, you know that Adobe's After Effects and Photoshop are two of the most indispensable content creation tools. More integrated than ever before, the world's number-one compositing and image-editing programs can be used in tandem to create quality work at a relatively low cost. But it takes years of experience to figure out how to get the most out of this remarkable duo.

With *After Effects and Photoshop: Animation and Production Effects for DV and Film*, graphics guru Jeff Foster has created the first book devoted to showing how you can use these two programs together to produce animations and effects on the desktop. This practical guide focuses exclusively on techniques commonly used in the field as well as cutting-edge production tricks. These hands-on projects will demystify cool Hollywood effects and help you solve your daily challenges. And they'll inspire you to think more artistically when approaching your creations.

Inside, you'll discover pro techniques for motion graphics and video production, including how to:

- *Add depth and realism to your animations by mimicking real motion*
- *Use exaggerated movements to enhance characterization*
- *Apply 3-D animation to 2-D images*
- *Remove background fodder with blue-screen garbage mattes*
- *Employ rotoscoping techniques for frame-by-frame retouching*
- *Construct realistic composites and scene locations using matte painting techniques*
- *Make movies from stills by simulating 3-D camera motion*
- *Utilize perspective, speed, and scale to create believable moving objects*
- *Produce realistic special effects such as noise, clouds, and smoke*
- *Practice imaginative motion titling effects that grab people's attention*
- *Develop professional scene transitions using 3-D layer animations*
- *And much more!*

SYBEX®
www.sybex.com

Transform the Ordinary into the Extraordinary!

With Adobe® Photoshop® Elements 3, Adobe has introduced substantial new features for digital photographers—including RAW support, organizing tools, a Healing Brush, and much more. As the software has become easier for digital photography enthusiasts to use and more compelling for serious digital photographers who seek the finest results, so has this acclaimed classic.

In *Photoshop Elements 3 Solutions* award-winning photographer and author Mikkel Aaland has extensively revised his best-seller to include all of version 3's smart new features plus many fresh techniques and examples. Whether working with digital images is a hobby or part of your livelihood, Aaland's practical solutions, stunning color images, and reader-friendly approach will guide you to a higher level of expertise.

PRAISE FOR THE PREVIOUS EDITION

"...covers everything you'll need to know to make your images appear professional, and look the way you prefer — with no red-eye, no leaning buildings, and of course, no wrinkles." —**Popular Photography**

"The engaging work of the author and his many talented colleagues will inspire you to bring out the best in your digital images. With Mikkel as your guide, you will also have fun doing so."
—Kevin Connor, Director, Product Management, Adobe

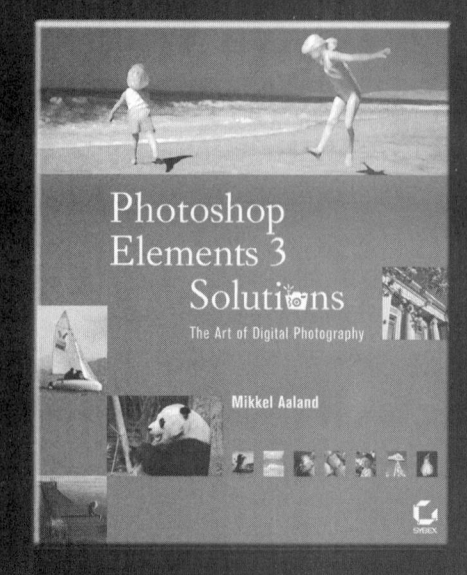

Photoshop® Elements 3 Solutions
The Art of Digital Photography
By Mikkel Aaland
ISBN: 0-7821-4363-6 · US $39.99

Inside, Aaland shows you the ins and outs of Photoshop Elements 3 for Windows and the Macintosh, including:

- Organizing and managing your digital images
- Touching up faces to make people glow
- Enhancing product images so they stand out
- Transforming outdoor and real-estate shots
- Fusing photos into priceless panoramics
- Combining images into realistic composites
- Working with the Camera RAW format and advanced digital photo techniques
- Optimizing photos for the web, screen, and e-mail transmission
- Creating PDF slide shows and professional-looking picture packages

And more...

The included CD comes with more than 100 practice images and tryouts of fun and useful plug-ins.

www.sybex.com

Mikkel Aaland is an award-winning photographer and author of eight books, including *Shooting Digital, Digital Photography, Photoshop for the Web,* and *Photoshop Elements 2 Solutions*. His photography has been published in *Wired, Newsweek,* and several European periodicals. He is a regular contributor on digital photography to *Popular Science* magazine and a columnist for *Practical Photography* magazine. Aaland served as a nonpaid advisor to Adobe's Photoshop Elements product development group.

SYBEX